ANTIQUITY

Origins, Classicism and the New Rome

ARCHITECTURE IN CONTEXT is dedicated to my wife Juliet, without whose support – spiritual and material – it would never have been realized.
CT

ANTIQUITY

Origins, Classicism and the New Rome

Christopher Tadgell

Routledge
Taylor & Francis Group

ARCHITECTURE IN CONTEXT I

First published 2007 by Routledge
2 Park Square, Milton Park, Abingdon, Oxon, OX14 4RN

Simultaneously published in the USA and Canada by Routledge
270 Madison Avenue, New York, NY10016

Routledge is an imprint of the Taylor & Francis Group, an informa business

Series design by Claudia Schenk
Image processing and drawings by Mark Wilson
Produced by Categorical Books
Printed and bound in China by Everbest Printing Co. Ltd

British Library Cataloguing in Publication Data
A catalogue record for this book is available from the British Library
Library of Congress Cataloging-in-Publication Data
A catalogue record for this book has been requested

ISBN10 0–415–40750–8
ISBN13 978–0–415–40750–2

CONTENTS

PROLOGUE: ORIGINS

The history of architecture is the history of the human quest for habitation: as complex as humanity was to become, it began before we had found ourselves in sapience, when woman, unable any longer to bear clinging offspring on extensive foraging expeditions, sat down at base and sent her man out alone – or, better, in co-operation with other males. That was perhaps two million years ago when our homanid ancestors already walked upright and could wield tools of their own making and carry things in hands and arms to bring back to their dependents. There is slight evidence of structure even in that prehuman phase but, of course, the base was usually first found, like the lairs and nests of other transitory creatures.

After perhaps a million more years the species *Homo erectus* could manage the production of heat and light through fanning fire to introduce some comfort in the enduring cave as home.[1.1] Fire also tempered tools for increased efficiency in vegetable gathering or game hunting, and cooking expanded the diet to include otherwise indigestible or unpalatable grains and meats, high in protein. With a steadily improving diet – and the challenge of expanding horizons in the hunt – body and mind grew in size and capacity, progeny needed longer to develop before and after birth, dependence was prolonged – of child on mother and of mother and child on father. And *Homo erectus* – capable of co-operation, increasingly communicative – ultimately developed the potency to mate at will, beyond the limited periods of female receptivity which constrained other mammals – that is, typically, free from subjection to the cyclical rhythms of nature – but did so in increasing personal predilection.

As an enduring unit, distinguishing social man from other animals, the family was in the future but this was its beginning and the hearth-centred cave was its preferred home until it could devise and build an alternative. That,

›1.1 (PAGES 2–3) CAPPADOCIA: limestone landscape with caves.

in the form of the primitive hut of skins on wattle or
branches leaning together over posts and beams, took at
least three-quarters of a million more years and probably
waited for *Homo erectus* to achieve sapience. For it was the
consciousness of freedom to choose and the will to change
that would distinguish man from all other creatures and
propel him to the civilization that began with his settled
family home in a place where he could control his production of food by exploiting nature.

SENTIENT MAN AT HOME

Over the aeons of terrestrial evolution – beyond our comprehension here, as is the history of the evolution of the
species *Homo sapiens sapiens* to which we belong – there
were successive extended glacial and interglacial eras:
after about three million years in which the cycle turned
perhaps twenty times, the most recent 'Ice Age' ended
some ten thousand years ago. With changes in climate,
changes in environment offered changes in evolutionary

1.2b

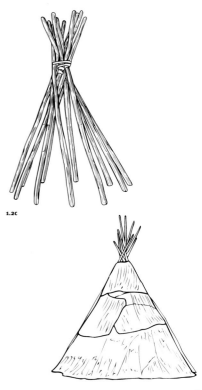

1.2c

1.2d

opportunities which are recognized to have favoured man particularly in Africa, far from the ice fields. Fully sentient man is widely apparent from secure fossilized remains some thirty thousand years old but probably emerged from Africa into west Asia at least seventy thousand years before that and he had penetrated south-eastern Europe long before the last Ice Age descended to its fullest extent. That gave him bridges from Asia to Australia and, ultimately, America – and time for diversified environments to prompt differentiated racial and linguistic development. His first age, roughly contemporary with that last Ice Age, is known as Palaeolithic because most of its fabricated remains are of chipped stone.

Throughout his 'Stone Age' man continued as a nomadic hunter and gatherer: at its beginning he and his fellows were doubtless already camping in tents[1.2] – though traces of numerous clustered tents, implying tribal organization, have been recovered only from the end of the Palaeolithic era. When he and his relatives were not on the move, following game, expanding their horizons, he still looked for

>1.2 NOMADIC TENTS: (a) traditional Iranian; (b–d) Native American *tipee*; (e, f) Mongolian *yurt*.

In the beginning, hides would doubtless have provided the tent's 'skin' over light timber 'bones' – the zoomorphic analogy is hardly irrelevant. As the earliest traces (found in France) included no post holes, a conical arrangement of poles – like a Native American *tipee* – is assumed. The more sophisticated *yurt* (or *ger*), quickly erected or struck, consists of a ring of lattice in contractable sections lashed to slender purlins radiating like the deflected spokes of a wheel from a hub, all covered in felt-backed canvas (except the hub, which is left open for light, air and the evacuation of smoke).

The modern Iranian example, of woven fabric on a grid of timber poles in accordance with ancient tradition, has the great advantage of flexibility, allowing expansion by the accretion of bays.

1.2e

1.2f

a cave as home base for his putative family and he began to embellish it at least thirty thousand years ago. Palaeolithic cave paintings have been found as far afield as western Europe, Africa, India and Australia: the subjects are invariably the animals of the chase – most notably bison, deer, horses and men. A religious motive is sometimes assumed as their context – in Europe at least – often also yielded female figurines with exaggerated abdomen and buttocks: with the bull, these anticipate the commonest cult icons of early settled farming communities. If the greatest achievement of our pre-Palaeolithic ancestors is seen as the assertion of some freedom from the rhythms of nature and of conscious adaptation against the selectivity of nature, it is not entirely implausible that their heirs willed themselves further to the conception of the possibility of influencing the forces of nature.**1.3**

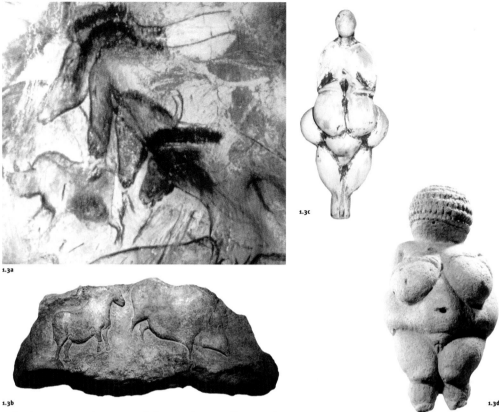

1.3a

1.3c

1.3b

1.3d

In the protracted process of climate change affecting the distribution of food resources that followed the retreat of the last Ice Age, settlers unready to forsake the comfort of the cave – and a degree of society doubtless most attractive to mothers – learned to cultivate plants and breed animals. Kinsmen freed themselves from constant foraging and ultimately increased the quality and quantity of food surplus to subsistence: this was the greatest achievement of the so-called Neolithic Age – but, of course, the period of germination had been long in an extended process. Cultivation, settlement – and the burial of dead settlers – appeared with ceramics and the polished-stone tools in many places at widely disparate times: it is, thus,

›**1.3 PALAEOLITHIC CAVE ART IN EUROPE:** (a) wall painting from the Chauvet Cave in the Ardeche (c. 30,000 BCE); (b) sculpted frieze from the Roc de Sers, Charente; (c) female figurine from Laspugue; (d) Venus of Willendorf, Austria (Paris, Museum of Man).

The tradition was mature by c. 20,000 BCE, prolific five millennia later, and there appears to have been no decline into decadence over the next five millennia before it disappeared at the end of the Palaeolithic era.

misleading to see this as defining a new era but the general prevalence of these factors in various localities may well be taken as definitive of the Neolithic Age.

Those areas are widely distributed in time and place on all the continents of the world. The claims of east Asian sites to pre-eminence among these will be considered in their own context. Westerly, our focus here is primarily on various sites in the so-called 'Fertile Crescent' between the Mediterranean coast of the Levant and the Zagros highlands of Iran.

THE FERTILE CRESCENT AND THE NEIGHBOURING NILE VALLEY

The land between the Tigris and Euphrates rivers (Mesopotamia) is girt by high and rugged mountain ranges: the Zagros in which the Tigris rises and beyond which lies the Iranian plateau to the east; the Taurus in which the Euphrates rises and beyond which lies the Turkish plateau to the north-west; and the Anti-Lebanon through which runs the Jordan river and beyond which to the west is the Mediterranean. The great Mesopotamian plain, formed by the twin rivers and their spring flood but truncated by the rising sea, gains little more than 400 metres in height over 1200 kilometres from exceptionally rich alluvial land at their confluence. This is now some 200 kilometres from the Gulf of Iran but was considerably further before the retreat of the last Ice Age left the sea approximating its definitive level c. 4000 BCE.

As the climate warmed with the retreat of the ice, forests flourished on the slopes of the framing mountains, grasses ancestral to wheat, barley, emmer and other early staple cereals grew in the milder, drier foothills and the steppes which extended from them to the rivers: wild cattle, asses and deer grazed on the steppes, the mountains supported wild sheep and goats, there were wild boar in the marshlands and canine or feline predators throughout. Dessication had produced the Iranian and Arabian deserts, where plant life and human habitation were insupportable, by c. 10,000. And by then too, dessication had produced the great Sahara desert which extended through north Africa to Egypt. There it is cut dramatically by the Nile which rises in the Ethiopian highlands and floods in summer to replenish an alluvial plain about 1000 kilometres long but rarely more than 10 kilometres wide except in the splayed lands of the marshy Delta. The main plants accommodated there by the time man turned to cultivating them included papyrus – on marshy land, especially in the Delta – emmer, barley, pulses, flax, grapes and dates. Cattle, sheep, goats and pigs were being raised to supplement game well within a millennium after settlement and there were plentiful fish and fowl – again especially in the Delta.

The regular seasonal abandonment of cave or camp for farming villages on well-watered land was initiated by kinship groups in numerous places. Evidence for the harvesting of wild grains is first found in the Jordan valley before 15,000 and the grindstones for treating them would have inhibited much movement, but signs of the selective cultivation of wheat, barley and lentils on set sites and the domestication of sheep and dogs appear across the Fertile Crescent only after 11,000. The 10th millennium provides the first evidence of the permanent settlement which established the sites of later Mesopotamian towns. And the first settlers, soon to be clothed in wool as well as hide, naturally reproduced the familiar forms of tent – mostly circular and conical – in timber and pressed mud, plastered reeds or dry stone with thatch, usually below ground level to limit construction and gain insulation: burial was sometimes under the huts, sometimes in special cemeteries.**1.4** The seeds of civilization, sown in the first ploughed land,

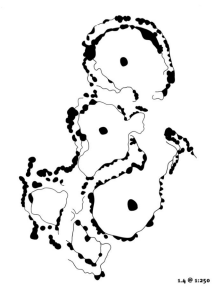

1.4 @ 1:250

›1.4 BEIDHA (JORDAN VALLEY), NEOLITHIC HOUSE: plan.

The site was occupied for about five hundred years from the late 8th millennium by farmers of emmer and barley who supplemented their diet by herding goats, hunting and gathering. Surviving pole holes reveal that the earliest settlement was a transitory one of tent-like structures. On the next level up are the remains of more permanent dwellings: roughly circular with central hearths, partially sunken, walled above the embankment with dry stone and roofed over a timber frame, these were clustered organically with work and store cells in distinct compounds. In this phase the occupants made tools and beads of stone and bone and traded. The common presence of a stone pillar near the hearth, perhaps representing a sacred tree-trunk, is seen as indicating that dwellings also served some religious purpose.

had taken root in the Fertile Crescent and they were to be transplanted to the Nile valley at some time over the next two millennia.

SETTLEMENT TO TOWN

The culture of urban man emerged with agriculture, when people realized that life in the wild was not the only way, that by working in settled society they could more easily grow their food on adjacent fields and that grain, which could be stored for future use, was a capital asset for trade – the foundation of wealth. Food abounded in good years: population grew. Developing along with agriculture, villages were most resilient in areas of high rainfall, though special challenges were offered by river valleys such as the Jordan, Tigris, Euphrates or Nile where the river might bring replenishment but the flood needed control and direction through embanking and channelling.

The earliest signs of civilization have been found in the upper Euphrates and Jordan valleys. The oldest inhabited site is probably Jericho, where round huts were built of bricks early in the 9th millennium: though the bricks were sun-dried mud loaves rather than regular rectangular blocks, it would be hard to overestimate the importance of this innovation for the advance of building technology. However, sun-dried brick is naturally ephemeral: well before its disruption c. 7000, the Jericho site was ringed with a durable wall of undressed stone connected to a round tower. This is the earliest-known fortification – whether against man or nature is not clear – but it is hardly likely that Jericho alone then had the organizational skill and resources for monumental public works.[1.5]

In the lower Jordan valley early in the 7th millennium, earlier still on the Euphrates and in southern Anatolia, circular huts were supplemented with rectangular ones, sometimes of several rooms, built of compacted mud

1.5

›1.5 JERICHO: remains of masonry defence works (early Neolithic).

The tower, 10 metres in diameter, had a stone staircase with a door at its base. The associated defence walls were ringed with a ditch.

(tauf). In addition to pedestals, which appeared in some of the earliest rooms of Jericho, animal and human skulls, human masks and even anthropomorphic images are associated with shrines in many 7th-millennium sites. Some of the images were made of clay. Neolithic man had pottery but firing did not produce efficient containers for liquids until c. 6500. Copper beads and tools, produced by specialized craftsmen, appear in eastern Anatolia and deposits of Anatolian obsidian, used for the sharpest implements instead of flint throughout the Fertile Crescent, indicate long-distance trade – though how it was furthered is unknown. Some of the settlements had more than a thousand inhabitants.

At Bouqras on the Euphrates, multi-roomed houses were separated by alleys c. 7000 and one interior was decorated with a frieze of painted birds. A millennium later, at Jarmo, the courtyard appears as an essential element of the house and, anticipating a tradition still alive in the region, it was the nuclear domestic space by the end of the 6th millennium at sites like Tell Hassuna

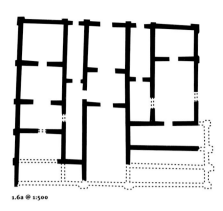

1.6a @ 1:500

›1.6 HOUSE TYPES, LATE 6TH MILLENNIUM:
(a) with rooms in three parallel rows at Tell es Sawwan, plan; (b) with rooms ranged around a court at Tell Hassuna, reconstruction.

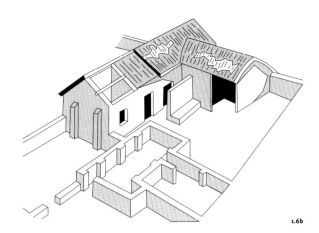

1.6b

south-west of Mosul.**1.6b** In the next millennium circular houses persisted, notably at sites associated with Tell Halaf in north-east Syria where they are domed and some have been identified as shrines or tombs. However, rectangular multi-roomed houses with hearths were common in villages throughout upland or riverine Mesopotamia and Anatolia where the natural water supply was sufficient for agriculture. Some of the later examples, from around Samarra in the central Tigris region where primitive irrigation appears, were large, regularly planned, buttressed buildings of handmade bricks: the scale, the buttressing and the regularity of plan, especially the arrangement of rooms in three parallel rows, recur further south in the early Ubaid period and anticipate the temples of Sumer.**1.6a**

Catal Huyuk, in southern Anatolia, is unparalleled in our knowledge of early urban settlement: it dates from the late 7th millennium. Accommodating a population of some five thousand at its height, about a thousand timber and mud-brick houses, each with a similar rectangular living room, were contiguous in an extended hive-like complex without courts or even lanes: while standardization asserts centralized authority, the organic approach typical of early agricultural settlements suggests the

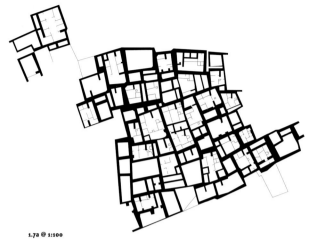

1.7a @ 1:100

1.7b

Extending over 12 hectares, the sprawling site seems to have been settled from the late 8th millennium for some fifteen hundred years but the fourteen excavated middle levels span most of the 7th millennium. Precocious in the diversity of its economy, the community derived as much from control of nearby quarries of obsidian (coveted for tools) as from agriculture. The inhabitants worked deposits of copper, too, and after nearly a thousand years of hammering it cold had learned how to smelt it before the end of the 7th millennium. Pottery was primitive. Domesticated cattle seem to have been the main source of meat but deer and boar were among the wild animals hunted (with dogs). Sheep (probably undomesticated) provided clothing as well as meat. Wheat and barley were the main cultivated cereals.

Ad-hoc development is the norm for the primitive town: growth is naturally organic before the appearfance of any organizing authority. A measure of protection was provided to the cellular organism by the unfenestrated external walls. Many of the rooms had plaster walls and floors and they must have had openings in the upper walls (clerestory) for light penetration and access over the adjacent flat roofs. The number of rooms identified by their embellishment as shrines is relatively high: several had burial pits, as did many living rooms, and the corpse was sometimes accompanied by equipment. The walls were embellished both with relief sculpture and paintings: the surviving reliefs are of animals and humans; some seem to be females giving birth, all were mutilated to the head and feet. The paintings are sometimes geometric but figural at their best – animals, especially bulls, and hunting scenes dominate. The juxtaposition of the bulls' heads and the mother-goddess figure in the reconstructed shrine has been taken to represent the former issuing from the latter.

extended family of a matrilinear society. Several of the rooms are marked as dedicated to a fertility cult by wall paintings and figures identified as the mother-goddess, but also by bulls' heads. The bull or ram and the erect stone or tree trunk (later dressed as a pillar) are ubiquitous symbols of male fertility and assertiveness. The figure of a seated woman found in one of the shrines, typical of the mother-goddess images recovered from the sites of settlement, recalls the fat female figurine from the Palaeolithic cave: passive but pregnant with new life. There

1.7c

are also stylized vultures apparently devouring human corpses though their somewhat human legs suggest that they may have been priests in ritual disguise or transformation.[1.7]

RELIGION: EARTH-MOTHER AND SKY-GOD

Fundamentally different attitudes were promoted, naturally, by the contrasting lifestyles of the farmer and the pastoralist. The latter was primarily concerned with appeasing the forces of the sky, manifest most cogently in the life-threatening storm, which was seen as male and often symbolized as a bird of prey – such as the Catul Huyuk vultures. On the other hand, devoted to the spirits of terrestrial phenomena – rocks and trees, caves and water holes in particular – the farmer was mesmerized by the mysteries of fertility and growth, the response of the earth to sun and water: the emergence of life from seeds planted in little holes in the first, penetrated by the two last, he associated with the earth-mother. Usually coupled with a vegetation-god, who died in the winter of his impotence each year, she ruled through her priestess, whose annual consort was a fainéant king. The fading sun was his; hers was the enigmatic moon, given to phases but constant in brightness, mistress of the waters and the potency of animals. And in some primitive animist societies that potency was assumed by priest-magicians (*shaman*s): transformed – often with the aid of hallucinatory drugs – into the alter ego of an animal deemed to embody the epitome of natural force, the shaman expected to turn the course of nature to his flock's advantage.

Faith in the mother-goddess, mystical but secure, tended to promote resignation and gratitude, sensuality and emotionalism in the sedentary agricultural animist. Concern with the terrible and unpredictable sky-gods, demanding constant alertness in the search for the key to placating them, tended to promote questioning and rationalism in the roving pastoralist. The efficiency of the tribe depended on the physical and mental agility of the men at the head of mobile family units, and the hazards of their existence encouraged polygamy. Primitive agricultural society, on the other hand, luxuriated in the organic growth of extended families from matriarchs, and the need for drones encouraged polyandry. From India to Greece, rich mythologies related the rape or marriage of the agrarians by the pastoralists – particularly the so-called Indo-European Aryans from the steppes of central Asia, who moved south through the Caucasus and west into Europe. In combination or confrontation, they will be of fundamental importance in our history of architecture.

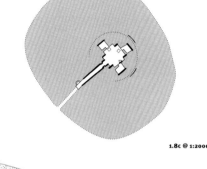

1.8c @ 1:2000

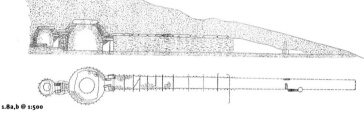

1.8a,b @ 1:500

NEOLITHIC EUROPE

The Aryans were to develop an important early culture in Europe but not until the second half of the second millennium BCE. The river valleys of continental Europe were not cradles of civilization like those of the warmer lands of north-east Africa or western Asia, to its south-east. Partly as a result of arrested development, however, its peripheries preserve the most substantial remains of the Neolithic organic hive-like complex – not unrelated to sites like Beidha but dating from towards the end of the era.

As man gradually penetrated Europe from the Balkans and elsewhere along the Mediterranean coast with the

›**1.8 NEOLITHIC EUROPEAN SETTLEMENT AND PASSAGE TOMBS:** (a, b) Los Millares, Almeria, Spain (c. 3000), plan and section; (c, d) Maes Howe, Orkney, c. 2000, plan and reconstructed view; (e) Skara Brae, settlement (c. 3100–2600), plan .

Eclipsing the simplest megalithic arrangement of orthostats and lintels over a grave (dolmen), the tomb type represented at Los Millares (with its semi-spherical chamber c. 4 metres in diameter at the end of a passage 34 metres long) is derived from the complete burial of the partially sunken, typically circular, early Neolithic house and it had reached the far north with traders from the south well before the advent of the Aryans in Greece. The Orkney example (with

1.8d

1.8e @ 1:500

burial chamber 4.5 metres square and now rising to
4 metres – about 50 cm less than the original height of
its corbel vault – at the end of a passage 12 metres
long in a mound currently 35 metres in diameter and
about 7 metres high) is of superior dry-stone construction (encased in the mound on completion) but dis-
plays limited decoration in chevron patterns.

warming of the environment, bringing animal and plant
husbandry, no uniform cultural development in the
Neolithic period is to be expected. Though commonly
protected with ditches, mounds and palisades, European
houses of that era were naturally as various as climatic conditions and local materials. However, the tradition of communal burial in trenches or pits, clustered like huts but
marked with mounds, was ubiquitous (if certainly not
invariable) and so too, once society had developed its usual
hierarchy, was the chamber tomb of the leader – the prime
closed form of megalithic structure.

In rocky areas, such as the coasts of Britain and Brittany
or the Mediterranean, the burial mound was naturally of
piled stones and the trench or chamber was hacked from,
or actually built of stone. And in these areas there were
isolated pockets of extraordinary masonry achievement –
defence apart – in cult and funerary architecture. Some
were apparently idiosyncratic, some seem to belong to a
chain of sequential development promoted along the
Atlantic seaboard by the followers of intrepid sailors whose
forebears had plied the main route from the Levant
through Cyprus, Crete and Sicily.

The passage tombs of colonists from the east at sites identified with Los Millares in Almeria represent an early link
in the western chain, and the origins of the form in the east
are not hard to fathom: from the 4th millennium, at least,
there were circular communal tombs of the Mesara type in
Crete and circular chambers at the end of passages in
Cyprus where the idea may have landed much earlier with
traders from the Tell Halaf region of north-east Syria.

The passage tombs at Ile Longue in Morbihan (Brittany), New Grange (Ireland) and Maes Howe (Orkney),
the last a square variant, mark main stages in the northern
progression of the Almerian vaulted-tomb type from the
mid-4th to the late-3rd millennium.**1.8**

On an entirely different scale, the idiosyncratic series of temples and tombs built in Malta between c. 3500 and 2500 are unexcelled.[1.9] Outstanding on any scale, if hardly idiosyncratic and somewhat later, is Stonehenge on Salisbury Plain in southern England – the supreme representative of the open type of megalithic structure.[1. 10]

Malta

Settled from Sicily – but ultimately from further east – from the late 6th millennium and the end of the 4th millennium, Malta was well to the south of the main east–west routes and, despite intermittently sustained contact with Sicily, developed idiosyncratically. Thus the cellular, hive-like form of the typical Neolithic Levantine settlement[1.4] persists long after mastery of megalithic construction techniques. The sites at Tarxian (possibly the island's religious centre) and nearby Hal Saflieni were active over the main period of Megalithic construction c. 3500–2500; the works at Mnajdra and Hagar Qim represent the main stages of development in the first half of the 3rd millennium.

Roughly circular cells appear at the start. Relatively ordered organic growth produced trilobed forms, with the sanctuary in the centre and limited assembly space in the side lobes, then multi-lobed complexes of linked temples, often with ovoid or kidney-shaped spaces, paved forecourts, and sealed subsidiary chambers for the delivery of oracles. As in the typical Neolithic house/shrine, there were freestanding internal stone pillars as well as sacrificial altars and peripheral benches. Each

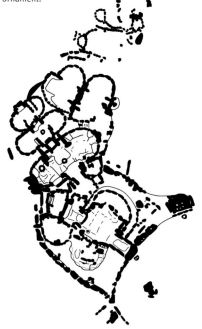

>**1.9 MALTA, MEGALITHIC TEMPLES**, c. 3500–2500: (a) Hal Saflieni hypogeum interior; (b) Hagar Qim, altar with stylized plant decoration; (c) Mnajdra, complex of three contiguous but unconnected temples developed in the same direction as Tarxian, overview from north; (d–e) Tarxian, triple temple complex developed from east to west to centre, plan, main shrine and remains of subsidiary shrine with spiral ornament.

1.9b

1.9a

1.9d @ approximately 1:1000

1.9c

1.9d

1.9e

organism was protected by a compound wall of orthostats bearing horizontal slabs which roughly followed its perimeter.

Dressed masonry appears c. 3500, with exceptionally large blocks framing doors. Wattle and daub roofs, carried on the walls and intermediate timber posts, were supplemented c. 3000 by corbel vaults over the smaller spaces. Floral spirals and some zoomorphic motifs appear on late façades. Numerous 'fat-lady' figurines were recovered from the sites and Tarxien had the base of one super-life-size image: the shrines were dedicated principally to the cult of the mother-goddess.

At the foot of the ubiquitous shaft, the earliest burial chambers were kidney-shaped but semi-circular accretions proliferated. Cut from subterranean rock – also a common practice exported throughout the Mediterranean from the earliest centres of settlement – the Hal Saflieni hypogeum is a necropolis on three levels in which structural form is faithfully reproduced. Work began on the irregular upper level and progressed to the better-dressed, more clearly distinguished near-circular or oval rooms of the second (principal) and third levels. It is estimated that the complex accommodated some thirty thousand burials over the millennium of its use but, as only one male skeleton has been identifed, it may have been the preserve of the priestesses of the mother-goddess: there was a sanctuary on the middle level.

The commonest megalithic monument in western Europe is the standing stone (menhir). Often individual, such stones may be related to others in alignment or arranged in circles which, ringed by protective ditch and dyke, are distinguished as henges. The tradition of ringing sacred sites with wooden posts or stone orthostats reached its culmination in the last phase of work at Stonehenge from early in the 2nd millennium, which marks the transition from fencing to truly monumental architecture.

Stonehenge

The site, centred on a timber structure that may have been a mortuary house, had been ringed with an embanked ditch and a fence of timber posts and beams from the middle of the 4th millennium. The sole entrance to the compound was orientated to the north-east in alignment with the most northerly position of the midwinter full moon (associated with interment rituals). After a period of abandonment and periodic sinking of holes in concentric circles, renewed work on the site c. 2200 served a cult of the sun in place of the original cult of the moon on behalf of the dead. An avenue was constructed from the north-east entrance to the River Avon and bluestone orthostats (some 4 tonnes each) were shipped from south Wales to be erected in place of the mortuary hut in two concentric circles – as at Avebury and other British Neolithic sites. The entrance was widened to frame the outlying Heel Stone, which was moved from its original position relating to the moon into alignment with the rising of the midsummer sun. Early in the 2nd millennium the bluestone circle was removed and replaced by another with orthostats (about 4 metres high) and lintels of finely dressed local Wiltshire sarsen. Within this was built a vast horseshoe of five massive dressed sarson trilothons (7.3 metres high), open to the rising of the midsummer sun. The dismounted bluestones were reused c. 1600 to form an inner ring and an inner horseshoe, open to the midwinter sunset and centred on a standing altar stone (now fallen, as is much else).

Stonehenge stands out from the many other prehistoric monuments of its type – generally called 'stone circles' – because of the complexity of

1.10a

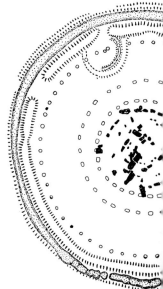

1.10b @ 1:1500

its plan, the precision with which its major stone members were dressed, and the incorporation of lintels. The joinery with mortice and tenon imitates timber, of course, but the scale and the quality of the dressing of both types of stone were unrivalled in western Europe and there was marked sophistication in the adoption of optical correction devices – tapering and slight curvature of the verticals to counter waisting and enhance apparent sturdiness. In general, moreover, the logistics of the later phases of the exercise imply that the chiefs of Wessex at the end of the 3rd millennium possessed organizational abilities hardly inferior to those of pre-Akkadian Sumer – if not Old Kingdom Egypt.

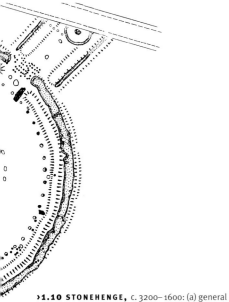

>**1.10 STONEHENGE,** c. 3200– 1600: (a) general view, (b) plan .

PART 1 WEST ASIA AND THE EASTERN MEDITERRANEAN

1.1 THE FERTILE CRESCENT AND THE NILE VALLEY

1.12

INTRODUCTION: CIVILIZATION AND ARCHITECTURE

Civilization first developed on the rich alluvial plain of lower Mesopotamia, where the flood came inopportunely in spring – to the disadvantage of sowing rather than to the advantage of growing – but water-borne transport facilitated communication, trade and the accumulation of wealth. It was marked by the organization of society on territorial rather than kinship lines and the emergence of an elite capable of promoting territorial, rather than local, public works. It depended on the progressively adroit exploitation of nature, the ordered deployment of resources and the escalation of population growth as agriculture spread with channelled water from restricted riverbank to expansive plain. As the harnessing of wind and water – no less than animals – propelled diverse people to migration and commerce, it was enriched through cross-fertilization issuing from emulation and impoverished in war born of envy.

City was ever to fight city but even more fundamental was the clash between citizen and nomad. Indeed, it must have been the primal need to order the defence of the village from marauders and their chief that prompted the emergence of the civic potentate. Essentially urban, under that potentate civilization entailed social differentation, the fostering of crafts among the increasing numbers freed from involvement in growing food, the invention of writing, mathematics and time-keeping, the standardization of language, beliefs and law, the efflorescence of religion and the construction of great buildings to enshrine the gods.

A starting point for architecture is naturally elusive in the slow process of evolution after the mud loaf had become the rectangular brick, the tent-like hut was superseded by the house of rectangular rooms and the shrine

1.13

>1.11 (PAGES 22–27) THE EUPHRATES VAL-
LEY AT HALABIYA.

>1.12 THE NILE VALLEY WITH SAQQARA IN
THE DISTANCE.

>1.13 MARI: brick tombs with walls and corbelled
arches, early 2nd millennium.

1.14

>1.14 KARNAK, GREAT TEMPLE OF AMUN: pil-
lars in the Hall of Annals of Thutmosis III (1479–1425).
The stylized lotus and papyrus represent Upper and
Lower Egypt respectively.

achieved special identity. But it was in the conception of the shrine, at the service of religion, at the instigation of the priest – society's first specialized practitioner to claim independence from the food production chain and sustenance from others – that building first flourishes as architecture. Moreover, in the art of building – religious or secular – similar conceptions were dictated by local conditions independently in several parts of the world at various times. These reveal a fundamental dichotomy: the contrasting principles are articulated primarily in the traditions of Egypt and Mesopotamia as they developed in the first half of the 3rd millennium BCE to accommodate their different ideals in enduring monuments.

The differing climatic, geological and topographical conditions of these two areas gave dominance in each to one of two basic building materials: mud brick (in Mesopotamia), and timber or reeds (in Egypt).[1.11, 1.12] These, in turn, dictated the basic structural systems: wall and arch (arcuated), and post and beam (trabeated).[1.13, 1.14] And these alternative types of structure naturally promoted two basic approaches to design, to the conception of the ordering of space: the informal or organic and the formal or rational with symmetry about a central axis. These two seminal traditions also assert the significance of form: pragmatic on the one hand, symbolic or representational on the other – that is, governed by the practical requirements of function, structure and situation or going beyond these to convey some special idea. Finally, they demonstrate the operation of patronage and ideology – the way a patron's idea of his or her role in the established order informs the meaning of a building.

MATERIALS AND STRUCTURE

The land of the Tigris and Euphrates seems to have been treeless well before history. The spring flood was generally not constrained by cliffs that would have limited the extent of inundation and maximized its impact. Thus the main impression is not of a rich green strip but of mud baked hard in the sun. From these conditions came the most elemental of building materials: mud, compacted with straw or dung for binding, and sun-dried to form bricks which, piled one upon the other, form walls.[1.13] It was soon seen that these needed protection from the weather. Baking in a kiln was developed for durability – not always for all the bricks needed for a vast walled complex, but at least for an outer skin in lieu of stone. And a malleable material like mud or clay invites moulding or the incision of a pattern – inevitably, in agrarian communities, a free-ranging, fantastic, even symbolic elaboration of motifs drawn from nature. Hence the revetment would be protective but also decorative and often didactic.[1.17]

In the Nile valley, on the other hand, the narrow floodplain, bordered not far from the river by sandstone cliffs, produced plenty of reeds which could be bound together to form posts, or woven into screens. It also supported groves of palms, producing softwood and fronds, easily worked or bound together for use in light structures. The palm and the reed bundle were alternative models: in each, the contact of load and support was celebrated with a frond-, flower- or bud-shaped capital. Groves of trees were cultivated for the food they gave and, as a source of bounty, were associated with the abode of god: they were seen as sacred. They were as important for the inspiration of form as for the provision of materials: in form as well as substance, as the tree became the column so the grove became the hall.[1.14, 1.15]

The Egyptians tell us – for instance, on the walls of the

1.15a

1.15b

›1.15 EDFU, TEMPLE OF HORUS, c. 250–116:
(a) view along the main axis from the hypostyle hall,
through the forecourt to the entrance between the
twin pylons, (b) detail of columns and beams in the
hypostyle hall at the head of the inner court.

In this typical Ptolemaic Egyptian cult temple, the
six columns of the hall façade, screened to half-
height, and the twelve larger interior columns have a
variety of capitals ranging from the traditional palm-
frond bundle (background) to variations on the lotus
theme (foreground).

Temple of Horus at Edfu – that the temple is the island of
the creator: if the plants of the Nile mudflats are recalled
in its structure, in the sacred grove is to be found the origin of its hall of many columns. Hardwood, imported by
sea from Lebanon in particular, supplanted the inadequate
local product in major buildings when transportation and
trade were sufficiently developed, and masonry had been
introduced by the end of the 4th millennium. Of course,
the Egyptians had plenty of mud for bricks too, and – unlike
the Lower Mesopotamians – plenty of stone to complement it in constructing walls and entrance pylons to protect their sacred groves. And the floriate capital of the lotus
type was extended across the top of walls as the concave
coved cornice, one of the most characteristic features of
Egyptian architecture.[1.15, 1.16]

Columns present no impediment to the flow of space,
but walls must be breached. Masonry is durable under
compression, vulnerable in tension – hence a flat lintel is
weaker in the centre and must be massive to last.[1.15] An
opening in a wall may be corbelled: the masonry is laid in
horizontal courses, each projecting beyond the one below
from a certain level until they bridge the gap.[1.13] However,

the soundest way of supporting the masonry above a hole in a wall is to bridge it with a semi-circle of bricks (or stones) in the shape of a fan: the voussoir arch.**1.17** The weight bearing down from above wedges the voussoirs tightly together, reinforcing the strength of the bridge.

ORNAMENTATION AND DESIGN

In both Mesopotamia and Egypt the properties of the local materials dictated the approach to embellishment. And the differences between the two dictated that these approaches would be radically disparate. Disposing ornament to elucidate structure (as in the capitals of columns), the Egyptian approach was essentially architectonic. It was as essentially non-architectonic to mask the wall with free-ranging fantasy in brick or tilework in the Mesopotamian manner. The difference is nowhere better illustrated than in the comparison of the hypostyle hall of the Temple of Horus at Edfu with the Ishtar Gate at Babylon.**1.16, 1.17**

Just as the basic approaches to structure and ornamentation originated in the materials to hand, so did the basic approaches to design: comprehensively ordered on the one hand, essentially organic on the other. In a forest of trees the relationship between the trunks is obvious and in a sacred grove the planting is likely to have been regular: in building, as in planting groves, people have usually been disposed to apparent order in the belief that the gods of creation are ordering agents. Appearances apart, a random set of posts is not practical: they must bear their load evenly and define clear axes.**1.15** On the other hand, there is no general incentive to align spaces when they are screened from one another by walls.**1.16**

›**1.16** (PAGES 30–31) PHILAE, TEMPLE OF ISIS: begun mid-3rd century and representing a late contracted example.

›**1.17** (PAGES 32–37) BABYLON, ISHTAR GATE: reconstructed façade, c. 600 (Berlin, Museum of the Near East).

This was the north gate of Babylon, rebuilt under Nebuchadnezzar II following the destruction of the city by the Assyrians in 689. Next to the palace, it guarded the opening of the main axis of the town. Named after the goddess of war, Ishtar, the gate was embellished with animals sacred to her and to the city's principal deity, Marduk. The circular flower (rosette) in the dado is ubiquitous.

›1.18 SUMERIAN CYLINDER SEAL, c. 2600,
impressed with one of the earliest images of a wheeled
vehicle (Boston, Museum of Fine Arts).

1 SUMER

The story of Mesopotamia is complicated – like the capriciousness of its two rivers in contrast with the singular
determination of the Nile. There were numerous
Neolithic farming villages of kinsmen along the banks
of the Tigris or Euphrates rivers but the expansion of the
population depended on the development of new land,
beyond the watercourses or oases, on the plain where rainfall was too light to support agriculture: introduced on a
small, essentially parochial scale early in the 6th millennium, irrigation had transformed the settlement pattern
by the end of the Ubaid period but most sites were still
small. That was to change from late in the 5th millennium
in Sumer where life without water control was particularly
precarious.

Since the irrigated areas that supported the cities were
separated by grazing land of variable quality, the settled
agriculturalists were in constant contact and potential
conflict with one another and with the nomadic hunting
or herding tribes drawn from the periphery of Arabia or
the mountains of Iran. As their populations grew the villages had to choose between fighting one another for the
territory between them, or co-operating to keep the
nomads at bay, master the flood and expand arable land.

Co-operation prevailed, kinship ties loosened, villages coalesced doubtless around a shrine of supra-local prestige. Lacking natural resources, moreover, the Sumerians had to embark on long-distance trade to meet many needs, not least flint or obsidian for tools, timber and metal: trade rivalry would be a future problem but in the beginning supra-local co-operation was essential. The intrusion of Arabian Semites from the 4th millennium naturally reinforced a sense of Sumerian identity – though that was not proof against territorial rivalry as the individual states prospered and proliferated.

The prerequisite skill at territorial government, the organization of trade and public works – doubtless priestly at first – and the consequent surplus production, varied land values and wealth, growth and stratification of the population at the expense of kinship ties, and commercial and industrial specialization all mark civilization, as we have seen. Primacy among its centres, accorded in ancient records to Eridu, is evident to modern archaeology first at Uruk. Well before the former was eclipsed by the latter c. 4300, the tripartite plan with the main space flanked by recesses was regular both for shrines and the more substantial houses, and standardized bricks were being mass-produced in rectangular frames. Soon after, pottery was

›1.19 RECTILINEAR ORDER: (a) brickmaker working with a square mould (Bam, modern Iran); (b) Habuba, founded towards the middle of the 4th millennium, primitive town planning and the tripartite building.

The disposition of the main recovered north–south artery in parallel to the straight line of the walls and the near-perpendicular intersection of cross streets are clear signs of determined organization. Most of the houses – and temples? – have a rectangular central hall flanked by smaller rectangular chambers.

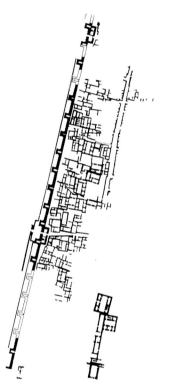

1.19b @ approximately 1:2000

1.19a

being mass-produced to standard forms on a wheel – and with its export, the dissemination of civil-ization may be traced through southern colonies established on the northern reaches of the Euphrates. It was for these colonies, moreover, that regular town planning is first known to have countered ad-hoc development: Habuba is a prime example.[1.19]

The wheel was applied to transport before the end of Uruk, c. 3300. The Bronze Age was some three or four cen-turies in the future but advances in metallurgy, particularly the smelting of copper and its hardening with arsenical alloys, led to the first Mesopotamian appearance of the plough in the domain of Uruk – though it may have been invented as much as two millennia earlier. It was late in the middle phase of Uruk – and its fortified colonies – that the cylinder seal first appears as a means of identifying the ownership of property and with its incised devices, emerg-ing in fine relief when rolled out on clay, art embarks on a perpetual career of didactic representation at the service of authority. And it was at Uruk that the first traces of writ-ing were found: with writing to supplement archaeology history begins, though it was to be a thousand years before sound history was written.[1.20]

The development of writing

Apart from images stamped on small tablets of clay – stamp seals proba-bly invented in the 6th millennium – and tokens sealed in or impressed on clay balls, the first form of record was the pictorial relief produced by rolling an incised cylinder over wet clay: elaborating on the proprietor's device, standard or devotion to a patron deity, the images of gods, humans and/or animals were sometimes isolated or episodic but the rolling medium's very nature recommended dynamic development of basic narra-tive relationships – unlike any known earlier art.

A natural progression from carving images into the surfaces of seals, flat or cylindrical, was the incision directly into clay tablets first of numbers and then of numbers accompanied by sketch pictures of objects, using the sharpened point of a reed stylus: the former is found at several 4th-millennium Mesopotamian sites as well as Susa in the south-eastern extension of the Sumerian plain in what is now Iran, and the sketched picture is unlikely to have appeared suddenly at any one place or time. Instead of drawing sketches each time, scribes naturally soon found it easier to represent typical objects summarily in stylized forms abstracted from their familiar pictograms by impressing the clay with the wedge-shaped cut end of the stylus: the process of standardizing such abstractions (and the order in which they were inscribed on the tablet) was doubtless protracted.

1.20a

Ultimately elaborated beyond the mere representation of objects to the phonetic notation of syllables corresponding to the monosyllabic names of objects (the earliest-known examples, c. 2800, were found at Ur), the Sumerian form of writing with reeds in wedge-shaped marks is known as *cuneiform* (from the Latin for wedge). Whereas the earliest tablets are roughly square and inscribed at random, usually from right to left despite the likelihood of smudging, by the end of the 3rd millennium it was normal to write on rectangular tablets in rows from left to right: by then, too, pictographic abstraction had long been uniformly horizontal in disposition though the original had naturally been vertical.

1.20b

Most of the cuneiform tablets recovered from early Sumerian sites record temple dues or business transactions enumerating goods despatched or received, but once phoneticism replaced symbolic or pictorial imagery, abstract ideas could be conveyed, procedures formulated, law codified, tradition recorded, literature invented, etc. The Babylonians took the crucial step by liberating phonetics from objective reference in the first half of the 2nd millennium. Representing abstract sound rather than substance, the cuneiform script spread widely but the multiple signs developed to represent the myriad syllables of the various Meso-potamian languages were difficult to master: it was a natural step, if not an obvious one, to reduce the burden of learning by limiting the signs to the number necessary to represent the initial letter of the first syllable of a word. The first people to attempt this, c. 1600, were Caananite: their thirty letters, initials to the words for the most common objects, were

1.20a

>**1.20 SUMERIAN WRITING:** (a) pictographic tablet; (b) tablet with early cuneiform abstraction from pictographs; (c) advanced cuneiform tablet (London, British Museum).

drawn as pictograms representing those objects. Abstract cuneiform signs were substituted for the relatively cumbersome pictographic letters in Ugarit and other Phoenician cities of the Levant well before the end of the 2nd millennium.

1.21a

1.21b

>**1.21 SUMERIAN GODS:** (a) the Uruk (Warka) vase, late 4th millennium, detail of relief ornament from the upper register showing Innana, represented by her reed-bundle pictograph behind her priestess agent, receiving offerings (Baghdad, Iraq National Museum); (b) cylinder seal of c. 2200 with Enki (with flowing water and attended by his all-seeing vizier Usmu), Shamash (rising over hills with rays above wings) and Innana (with the bow and arrow of love and war) – the horned helmet was an attribute of deity.

Before anthropomorphic imagery, the gods went undepicted or were represented by symbols: among the most persistent of these are the thunderbolt of Adad, the eight-pointed star of Ishtar, the crescent of Sin and the winged rays of Shamash, which were readily transmogrified into the winged disk borrowed from Egypt early in the 2nd millennium.

RELIGION

Before history was mythology and beyond history the mythology of the gods and their creation was always central to the ethos of a putative nation. It is impossible now to identify the primitive Sumerian religion, which presumably emerged from the animistic cults common to prehistoric farmers – and which long survived in the popular cults of demons. Personifying elemental nature, the patron deity with which each Sumerian city had emerged from its agrarian antecedents was recognized by others. Commerce led to assimilation and by historical times the intercourse of natives and nomads had fathered a composite culture with a hierarchy of gods representing all the facets of being, terrestrial and celestial, all with consorts and all conceived in ideal human terms.

The primordial ocean (the goddess Nammu) gave birth to the female earth and male sky, who produced the gods of sweet water and air, Enki and Enlil (patrons of Eridu and Nippur respectively). Enlil, separating his parents and relegating his father (Sumerian An or Anu, Semitic Anum, patron of Uruk) to outer space, established earth's atmosphere, where he unleashed wind and storm (Semitic Adad) but regulated the course of the sun (Sumerian Utu, Semitic Shamash, patron of Sippar and Akkad) and moon (Nanna or Sin, patron of Ur) to dispel darkness and set life in motion. Responsible for terrestrial matters, Enlil instituted kingship on earth and fathered the storm/warrior-god later known as Ninurta who was identified with Ningirsu (patron of Lagash and Girsu). Yet the domain of the earth-mother, impregnated by Enki but impervious to the clarity of Enlil's empyrean or the will of his terrestrial vicar, remained one of dark mystery cohabited by Ninhursag, goddess of fertility/childbirth, Ereshkigal, goddess of death, and the Venus deity Inanna (Semitic Ishtar, patroness of Uruk, Nippur and Assur), goddess of love and war. The Sumerians retained their pictographs as symbols for their deities but the Semitic intruders developed an anthropomorphic iconography: thus, for example, Sumerian Innana is usually depicted as a pair of reed bundles but Semitic Ishtar, who absorbed her, is a woman with a bow and a lion.[1.21]

Through their elaborate ritual of divine propitiation centred on sacrifice, the Sumerians sought to alter the course of nature – far though their precocious anthropomorphic idealism may have removed their gods from their animistic origins. However, connecting natural forces with the movement of heavenly bodies and seeking thus to comprehend the operations of the gods, their priests invented astrology well before the fall of Ur at the end of the 3rd millennium. Trade, of course, had required calculation from time immemorial – the sexagesimal system, which survives today in the calculation of time, was ultimately the most popular in Mesopotamia – but

>**1.22 UBAID HOUSE FROM TELL ABADA**, phase 3, early mid-5th millennium: plan.

The central core has no distinct vestibule or inner sanctum but transepts project into the range of flanking rooms: it has beeen suggested that these provide suites for the master and mistress of an affluent household. There were similar houses at Tepe Gawa and other sites in both northern and central Mesopotamia.

1.23 @ 1:500

>**1.23 ERIDU, TEMPLE FROM LATE UBAID LEVEL VII,** second half of the 5th millennium: plan.

One of the earliest examples so far recovered of the standard tripartite Mesopotamian platform temple, the building is divided into three tranches of space longitudinally and the core space is divided into three laterally – unlike even the most elaborate houses from the late Ubaid period, in which the core space was undivided. One of the side rooms generally contains a staircase to the roof. Steps to the podium (about a metre high) led to the main entrance at the end opposite the sanctuary and subsidiary openings in the sides. The rhythm of the projecting buttresses, perhaps recalling reed-bundle construction, was also to be typical.

the analyses of observations for prediction and the construction of a ritual calendar prompted the theoretical mathematics which the Babylonians advanced in the 2nd millennium.

THE TRIPARTITE PLAN AND THE TEMPLE

The earliest Sumerian Ubaid remains are at Eridu, then in the delta of the Euphrates and centre of the worship of Enki: dating from the mid-6th millennium, they include a sequence of superimposed rectangular cells similar to houses but identified as shrines because of a recess with a podium and a central platform marked by the burning of presumed offerings. A millennium later, the most substantial late-Ubaid houses had a rectangular central space flanked by smaller rectangular cells in a tripartite plan.[1.22] A similar arrangement then appears as typical of the temple too at Eridu. The many-layered mound there was surmounted by a podium bearing a buttressed building in which the main elongated space, flanked by smaller rooms, had an offering platform beyond a vestibule at the entrance end opposite an altar in the sanctuary recess. The walls were built of standardized rectangular bricks, probably made in a mould, and the buttresses were disposed in a regular rhythm like the reed columns of the people who live in the delta marshes – evidently then as now.[1.23] There were similar late-Ubaid temples at Uruk and in a triple complex at the northern Mesopotamian site of Tepe Gawra.

The Ubaid work at Uruk was overbuilt many times in the subsequent period named after the site: two distinct types, 'low' and 'high', emerged there in the process. The tripartite block was to be the principal element in religious complexes for much of the history of ancient Mesopotamia – with the entrance usually in the end wall opposite the sanctum – but the height of the temple's base varied. This is not simply to be explained by protection from flood or constant rebuilding over earlier work on the same site: that was common and perhaps initial but the high temple was sometimes raised on levelled ground. Indeed, many sacred complexes had both a 'high' and a 'low' temple dedicated to sky and earth deities respectively, the latter at the base of the former and built on a lesser platform to give it dignity. This is first known at Uruk. The carved-stone commemorative slab, the stele, first appears there too in the service of a timeless royal ideal: the lion hunt depicted on it remained the most potent symbol of royal responsibility for the defence of the flock throughout Mesopotamian history.[1.24]

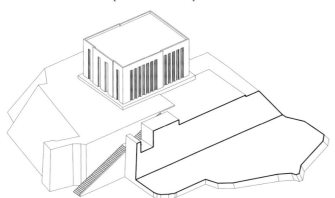

1.24a

1.24b @ 1:1000

Uruk (Warka)

At a site dedicated to the worship of the sky-god Anu, the 'high' temple – the so-called 'White Temple' – aspiring to the realm of the deity, is raised some 13 metres above ground on a battered platform incorporating the impacted remains of earlier work – the earliest dating from the Ubaid period. Access to the definitive summit temple was gained by an elongated staircase to a subsidiary terrace to the north. The tradition of the tripartite plan is sustained in the shrine itself (which, at c. 22 by 17.5 metres, roughly equalled the latest Ubaid temple at Eridu in size): entry was from the sides as well as from both ends of the nave, obviating termination in a

1.24e

›1.24 URUK (WARKA): (a, b) the high temple of Anu, 'White Temple', mid-4th millennium, axonometric and plan; (c) temple from level IVa of the Eanna site, late 4th millennium, plan with (1) arena, (2) hall, (3) Temple C, (4) Temple D, (5) so-called Temple E, (6) cone mosaic building; (d) Lion Hunt Stele (Baghdad, Iraq National Museum) bears the earliest image (carved in relief) identified as a display of the physical prowess of those whose authority was god-given: several of the statues found at the site represent a figure of authority comparable to the man on the stele but some are of bound prisoners; (e) stairs; (f) inlay.

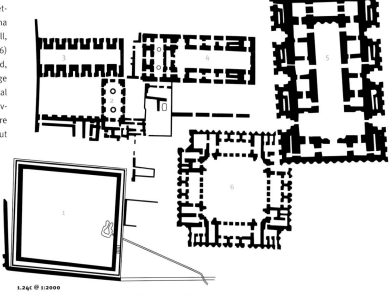

1.24c @ 1:2000

1.24d

1.24f

sanctum: there was a podium towards one end and a stepped altar towards the centre of the hall. The buttressed and niched external brickwork seems to have been whitewashed.

At the lower Eanna site, dedicated to the worship of the great earth-mother and her agents, above all Inanna, there is evidence of building in several phases – but no indication that the structures were all religious. The first phase (level V) produced a large limestone building, tripartite in plan and buttressed. The second main phase (level IVb), roughly contemporary with the White Temple, produced two walled complexes. The larger one was entered by a colonnaded staircase and through a columned portico and court in which all the surfaces were inset with small cones of red, white and black clay, their circular bases forming regular patterns; beyond was a tripartite 'temple' building and accommodation for the temple establishment; to the side was a large rectangular building, unique to the area, in which the central court, nearly square with canted corners, was addressed by an open hall on each side. The smaller compound preserved traces of a series of small buildings, the most substantial one embellished with cones. About the time the White Temple was finished, the columned court and 'temple' in the main sanctuary were superseded (phase IVa) by two larger tripartite buildings (the largest 80 by 50 metres): the main space was entered through transept arms before the inner 'sanctum' in both buildings and the smaller one incorporated a secondary tripartite element parallel to the transepts; beyond the latter was a detached pillared hall with cone decoration; to the east of the former, the so-called Red Temple (largely unexcavated) was probably administrative.

The influence of Uruk was extensive in all directions: through trading posts from Anatolia to Egypt, where Uruk-style pottery and cylinder seals – if not tripartite temples – appear in the last half of the 4th millennium, and colonies from the Levant to Susa, where there are traces of a late-Ubaid religious foundation. Susa and its trade network were annexed c. 3000 by the Elamites, from Anshan further east, and the Sumerian connection was crucial in the cultural development of their region: within two centuries Elamite power had collapsed and Susa gravitated to Early Dynastic Sumer.

1.25a

SECULAR POWER AND KINGSHIP

Some thirteen city-states had emerged in Sumer by the end of the 4th millennium: they grew from co-operation between villagers, as we have seen, but there was no co-operation between them for the formation of a nation-state. Enviable prosperity and population growth provoked war for territory between the cities and with the nomads. Development of armies – formed, doubtless, like the levies for public works – promoted military leaders to supplement the priestly ruler: authority was bifurcated.

At first the power of the secular ruler (*lugal*, 'general' or *ensi*, 'governor') was secondary to that of the chief priest and further constrained by an assembly of citizens but the secular power waxed. Inter-city rivalry apart, the cause of trouble serious enough to warrant such a shift in the structure of power in Sumer at the dawn of history in the late 4th millennium seems likely to have been the intervention of the Semites from Arabia: certainly their impact was profound. Soon after, moreover, Sumer was in its 'Bronze Age': the manufacture of tools was revolutionized but the increased efficiency of weapons was equally crucial in an increasingly contentious period. And in contention the power of the military leader grew into kingship and opened the 'Early Dynastic period' of Sumer's history, c. 2900.

The passage through contention to kingship is reflected in the most ancient Sumerian royal records, the semi-legendary 'king lists': Eridu, the cult centre of Enki, was displaced as the centre of the Sumerian world by Kish, the cult centre of the warrior-god Zababa, and Kish in turn was displaced by Nippur, the cult centre of Enlil who had displaced Anu at the centre of the empyrean after the demise of Uruk; Enlil sent kingship down to Sumer as the instrument of heaven. The king's obedience to the gods, the fount of justice, was rewarded by their favourable disposition manifest in adequate flood, and he was reconsecrated at each spring festival when fertility was reinvoked with the deity's remarriage. Thus the Sumerian king was first shown in homage to the deity, offering the bounty of his land; by the middle of the 3rd millennium this pious ideal was countered with a rather more virile one developed from the image of the *lugal*.[1.25]

›**1.26 TREASURE OF UR:** (a) Standard of Ur: war chariots (London, British Museum); (b) lion-headed eagle, Aznu, of gold and lapis-lazuli from Ur found at Mari (Damascus, Syrian National Museum).

The tombs at Ur – which contained objects inscribed with the names of King Meskalamdug and Queen Ninbanda who are elsewhere identified as the father and wife of King Mes-Anepada whose son A-Anepada built the temple of Ninhursag at Tell Ubaid – were discovered by Sir Leonard Woolley, who dated their rich contents to the mid-3rd millennium. The so-called Treasury of Ur found in the palace at Mari was identified from an inscription on a bead in the hoard which referred to Mes-Anepada, king of Ur. The appearance of the Aznu at both Mari and Tell Ubaid in contexts associated with the husband and son of Queen Ninbanda can hardly be coincidental.

The chariots of this time were drawn by onegars. The horse was not common in the Fertile Crescent until the early 2nd millennium, though it appears earlier in Anatolia.

1.25b

1.26a

1.26b

In all, there were more than twenty city-states at the culmination of the Early Dynastic period c. 2500 and the ostensible objective of their rivalry was control of Nippur. Apart from prestige and territory, however, the cities vied for dominance over an extensive network of trade routes linking Sumer to the Levant in the west and down the Gulf to the Arabian Sea coasts and even across to India. Trade stations developed into towns, especially along the Euphrates, and Akkad emerged as a region distinct from Sumer following Semite settlement and urban development in central Mesopotamia. Nippur's cultural prestige notwithstanding, after Uruk, the 'king list' accords supremacy to Ur. The latter's first dynasty, commemorated in the most splendid relics of their age, controlled the Gulf trade and is known to have been allied in marriage with the far-off kingdom of Mari which controlled movement along the upper Euphrates.[1.26]

THE PALACE

Earliest Ur has largely disappeared before later, more magnificent development but traces have been recovered of the earliest palace at Kish: descended from the most common form of prehistoric courtyard house in the region but rejecting primitive informality, the arrangement of rooms is generally symmetrical within a monumental rectangular enclosure but access to the main spaces was bent through many rectangles. The remains of the entrance are fragmentary: it seems to have been tripartite like a twin-towered portal but there is hardly enough to indicate whether the place of appearance of the vicar of god was yet related to the portal of the divine image in the palace of the god as it had materialized in the contemporary temple.[1.27, 1.28]

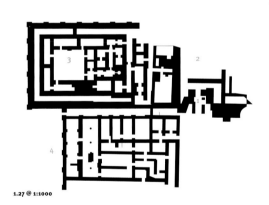

1.27 @ 1:1000

›1.27 KISH, 'PALACE A', first half of 3rd millennium: plan with (1, 2) remains of main ceremonial portal and outer court?; (3) square nuclear court, which presumably provided for private audience as it is entered by a particularly circuitous route. Even the detached fragment to the south (4), perhaps the royal family's accommodation, is regularly planned.

1.28a

THE EARLY DYNASTIC TEMPLE

In the Early Dynastic period the forecourt, already present in both main phases of construction on the Eanna site at Uruk, had become a major element integrated with the temple. It was usually disposed in parallel to the longitudinal axis of the main interior space, which culminated at the altar, and access from the one to the other was towards the end of the wall between them so that approach to the altar would be broken – as in the early 3rd millennium Innana temple at Nippur.

Later in the 3rd millennium the court was often the nucleus of a group of shrines and administrative buildings, as in the grander houses of the period: mud brick was the common material and the voussoir arch had probably been invented but the column also made an occasional appearance in elaborate external revetment.[1.28] The distinction of the high temple was usually achieved by a platform, often incorporating an earlier shrine, at the head of an elevated inner enclosure and an outer courtyard was developed within stoutly buttressed walls. In the most prominent surviving example of the period, the 'Oval Temple' of Khafaje, which takes its name from its precinct, access from zone to zone was off axis and the top shrine is presumed to have been a rectangular block with a twin-towered, arched portal towards the end of the long façade.[1.29]

1.28b

>**1.28** TELL AL-UBAID, TEMPLE OF NINHUR-SAG, c. 2500: (a) lintel, (b) column.

The temple was founded by A-Anepada, 1st Dynasty king of Ur, in a satellite settlement: only fragments survive. The portal columns were palm trunks sheathed in bitumen inset with mother of pearl and small red and black limestone tiles. The copper lintel with its lion-headed eagle (Aznu) between stags is a prime manifestation of the apotropaic tradition of representing benign spirits as syncretic guardian figures which was of perennial significance. As Aznu was the symbol of the sky-god Ningirsu, patron of Girsu and Lagash, it is not clear why it appears over the door to a temple of the goddess of childbirth in the domain of Ur: one possibility is that the foundation was instigated by the king's mother, Ninbanda, who may have come from Girsu; in any case Aznu could hardly be rivalled as a protector.

›1.29 KHAFAJE, 'OVAL TEMPLE': second half of 3rd millennium, reconstructed view.

Within a roughly oval raised compound, similarly curved walls framed a rectangular court higher again than the preceding level and dominated by the shrine on its terrace. Access from compound to court and shrine involved double turns – the final one, at least, through a twin-towered portal. The temple officials were accommodated in a courtyard complex to the left of the outer court. Magazines for storing produce offered to the deity filled the space between the curved and rectangular walls of the second court. Towards the centre was an ablution tank and before the temple platform was a sacrificial altar. The corners of the shrine were oriented to the cardinal directions.

The original Sumerian cult centres, walled against the uninitiated, were at first residential only for the priestly establishment: around them were densely populated suburbs and beyond their walls were farming villages, fields and groves. Each agglomeration belonged to a particular deity whose earthly residence was the temple central to the cult compound. The god's household proliferated: its head ruled not only by virtue of his status as high priest but also as controller of the economy. Crucial to the life of the urban community, obviously, was the collection and ordered distribution of resources, and this was bound to be controlled by the administrator of the god's estate, who must also have dominated trade.

1.30a

2 THE OLD KINGDOM OF EGYPT

Attractive to the North African Hamitic nomads following the desiccation of the Sahara after the last Ice Age, the
Nile seems not to have seen settled agriculture until the 5th
millennium BCE. The idea may have come from Palestine
to the Delta and percolated up-river with the facility of a
reed boat – though hard evidence of foreign influence first
appears a millennium later in the era of the site at Naqada.
That was framed by the loop of the Nile north of Luxor,
crossed by a route from the Red Sea to the western oases,
but its culture spread rapidly north and south.

Pictographic writing and the brick appeared in Egypt in
the middle Naqadian phase but the potter's wheel is not
known to have followed before its end. Well before that
villages had replaced tribal camps, some growing into market centres. Pit burials were covered with tumuli. Pictographic representations of the house distinguish two basic
vernacular types: the bow-roofed structure of reed-bundle
columns and matted reed walling, initially circular, of the
waterlogged Delta; and the light timber-framed structure
with wattle-and-daub walls and flat roof derived from the
tent of the southern nomads.

The earliest settlements appear not to have been stratified but venerable Hamitic clan authority was asserted along sections of the river large enough for the organization of efficient irrigation. Those who were adroit enough to levy and direct the labour for public works established themselves at the head of a social hierarchy, already implicit in the clan organization but foreign to the bifurcation of religious and secular power characteristic of contemporary Sumer, and their domains anticipated provinces by the opening of the 4th millennium.

Late-Naqadian culture, c. 3500–3000, was centred in the south at Nekhen (Hierakonpolis), the town of the falcon-god, but a secondary centre in the north is traditionally identified as Per-Wadjit (Buto), the town of the cobra-goddess. Little is left at the site of the latter (Tell el-Fara'in) but at the former (Kom el-Ahmar) remains of defence walls, a palace and temples anticipate Early Dynastic forms: the temple and palace derived from the timber-framed house with portico and enclosed forecourt which superseded the tent; contemporary pictographs show that the entrance to the temple court was flanked by flagstaffs and a staff within bore the standard of the dedicatee.

Few market centres were to develop into towns and there were no city-states of the Sumerian type. However, tradition maintains that the provincial clan territories of the Delta around Per-Wadjit and those strung out along the river north and south of Nekhen were welded into states, the kingdoms of Lower and Upper Egypt respectively. There is inevitable – and so-far indeterminable – debate about the timing of this as little is known of the process and nothing about the leading players until written records begin, c. 3200. Thereafter inscriptions in stone commemorate history and relate a great deal about the attitudes that informed it.

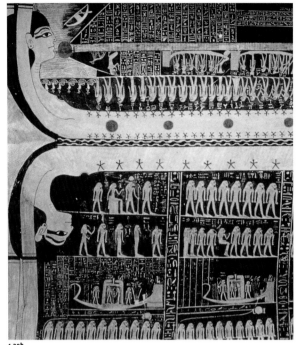

1.30b

›**1.30 THE HELIOPOLITAN GODS:** (a) the sky-goddess Nut and the cosmic passage of the sun-god Re in his celestial boat: the cosmic barque (from the Book of the Dead of Nebged, early 14th century; Paris, Louvre); (b) detail of Nut from the ceiling fresco of the tomb of Ramesses VI (1151–1143); (c) Horus embracing pharaoh (stele of King Qahedjet, 3rd Dynasty; Paris, Louvre); (d) Osiris as king of the departed attended by Isis and Nephthys (from the Book of the Dead of Hunefer, 13th century; London, British Museum).

1.30c

EGYPTIAN COSMOLOGY

The two kingdoms of the Nile had many gods descended from primitive animistic and fertility cults, above all those of the earth-mother and her seasonal partner, source of fertility, donor of the flood, dying to live again. Each god belonged to a particular locality – though their powers often overlapped – and would have been honoured in a cult temple developed, as the specific ritual required, from the primitive Naqadian court-and-cell form in the local vernacular style.

As a locality rose in importance – from village to market town to provincial centre, for instance – so too did its gods. And as one locality eclipsed another their gods were combined – hence the appearance of syncretic icons with human bodies and animal heads. Ultimately the coalescence of the two kingdoms superimposed a state pantheon of grouped syncretic deities over the local ones – all tolerant of one another. Thus the main god of Heliopolis, a Lower Egyptian seat of power, achieved supremacy as the sun-god Re and was assimilated with the primal creator Atum who then assumed the character of the sun-god as patriarch. Re also accommodated the creator-god Ptah of Memphis, another important Lower Egyptian city, in his pantheon as patron of craftsmen – though Ptah was still associated with the progenitorial bull Apis.

Creation was essentially the imposition of order (*ma'at*) on chaos: it was hard-won and tenuous. On emerging from the primordial deep with reed and palm on an island – the sacred mound of Heliopolis appearing like the first soil of the retreating flood – the creator, Re-Atum, produced the progenitors of earth and sky, the god Seb and goddess Nut respectively. Yet Nut regularly swallows and gives rebirth to Re's sun: in that capacity she is the mother-goddess Hathor. The ambiguity here, if not testimony to the sun's relatively late rise to religious pre-eminence, is indicative

1.30d

of the conservative belief in an immutable cyclical order: in the Nile valley, with its annual inundations of soil-bearing water but little rain, agriculturalists were impressed by the sky more as the realm of the life-giving sun than of the life-threatening storm. Dependent on water-borne transport, they saw the sun-god Re travelling across the sky in a boat and changing boats to travel – perilously – back through the underworld at night. And in their relatively stable sun-blessed world they were the first correctly to enumerate the days of the solar year which they divided into a calendar of twelve months of thirty days and five extra days for the new-year festival.

Seb and Nut produced Isis and Nephthys (twin goddesses of love, procreativity and protection, regenerations of the timeless earth-mother), Osiris (divine king of life on earth), and Seth (god of evil, including confusion, storms and war). Seth killed and dismembered Osiris to usurp his throne, but Isis found the parts (except the genitals), reconstituted him and together they produced the falcon-like Horus – miraculously, for her virginity was maintained. Transfigured as a star, Osiris became king of the departed, arbiter of eternity, as the resurrected god of the ever-recurring flood and of vegetation which dies in winter but is reborn in spring. Horus won back his living throne. Isis and Osiris (and Seth) acknowledged the paternity of the northern god Re, while Horus was claimed as ancestor by the kings of the south – and doubtless was in origin an ancestral Hamitic tribal deity. Assuming responsibility for the successful propagation and seasonal resurrection of agriculture as agents of Ma'at, goddess of cosmic order, the pharaohs were thus divine in their eternal essence (*ka*) and the unity and prosperity of Egypt were maintained as each in turn became Horus, son of Osiris, with whom his predecessor had been re-identified in the eternal cycle.[1.30]

>**1.31 NARMER'S PALETTE:** (a) wearing the white crown of the south, the king smites his enemies under the eye of Horus who is perched on the splayed lotus symbol of the subjected Delta kingdom; (b) wearing the red crown of the north and preceded by his stand-ards, the king inspects the enemy dead and, as a bull, batters down the towered ramparts of the enemy's seat in perhaps the earliest image of antique fortification (Cairo, Egyptian Museum).

PHARAONIC EGYPT

According to a history written for the Ptolemaic rulers c. 280, Upper and Lower Egypt were united thirty pharaonic dynasties earlier under the figure they called Menes – possibly the king 'Aha who is associated with the earliest tomb at Saqqarah. In the late-4th-millennium record, a precociously refined palette, the achievement is actually commemorated by the southern king Narmer – though a large measure of unity had probably been forged already.[1.31] The unifier (or his progeny) established him-self under the protection of his father, Horus – and tow-ered ramparts – at Memphis at the southern limit of the lower kingdom but developed Hierakonpolis as a similar seat in the south: a stele of one of Narmer's early succes-sors bears the image of the falcon-god over the twin-tow-ered gate to the capital emblazoned with the king's own sign. The recording of the royal name coincides with the proliferation of hieroglyphic notation for dating through the identification of years with significant events.[1.32]

Secure in their valley, isolated by deserts, for nearly three thousand years from the opening of the Early Dynastic period (c. 2920) the pharaohs wore the combined crowns of the two realms and the vulture and cobra of the protective deities of south and north. The dynasties are often distinguished by place of origin or burial – not necessarily lineage – but most of them ruled from Memphis or maintained a seat commanding the north there while resi-dent at Abydos or Thebes in the south. There were periods when this unity in duality dissolved under the impact of factionalism or invasion, especially the intermediate periods between the generally accepted divisions of dynastic succession into the Old, Middle and New Kingdoms (c. 2650–2130, c. 2040–1640 and c. 1540–1070), but it is the longevity of pharaonic Egypt's conservative tradition that has never failed to astonish.

THE OLD KINGDOM SUCCESSION

Little is known of the 1st Dynasty though it lasted for 150 years (c. 2920–2770) and left a series of royal tombs at Abydos around a brick temple dedicated to Osiris, the earliest-known monumental elaboration of the typical Naqadian form with a succession of enclosed spaces between the forecourt and the tripartite sanctum. As a late-Naqadian capital, possibly the first centre of a near-united kingdom, Abydos was the natural royal choice but the most important administrators of the era were buried at Saqqarah, near Memphis, and the royal necropolis was established there too by the 2nd Dynasty kings – who were hardly less obscure than their predecessors except for some evidence from the last reign of the triumph of affiliation with Horus over a challenge from Seth. The 3rd Dynasty rulers (c. 2650–2575), sometimes considered the first of the Old Kingdom, also preferred Saqqarah and it was there that the second king of the line, Djoser (c. 2630–2611), opened the main line of Egyptian cultural development with the inauguration of monumental stone building and sculpture.**1.33a**

>**1.32 ABYDOS: GRANITE TOMB STELE OF HORUS NAME OF ZET (WADJIT),** king of Egypt, 1st Dynasty, c. 2900 (Paris, Louvre). The snake adopted here is presumably the cobra of Wadjit, protective goddess of the north.

The king had three types of name: the Horus name establishing divine paternity in Horus; the throne name including the words for king and asserting divine paternity in Re (later Amun-Re); and the birth name preceded by 'son of Re'. From the 4th Dynasty each of the last two was framed by a cartouche (an oval fillet over a short line representing a knotted rope and symbolizing the eternal cycle).

The Egyptian hieroglyphs – of which the earliest examples so far recovered date from the late-4th millennium – seem to have developed from the pre-cuneiform pictographic writing of Sumeria: apart from the essential symbolism of the component elements of divine, royal and territorial titles, they represented sounds, as cuneiform writing did, but kept the imagery of the attribute rather than resorting to abstraction.

1.33a

In the remains of the palatial compound built for his *ka*'s eternal abode, his step pyramid still stands witness not only to the power of the central authority but also to the prosperity of the double kingdom. Yet we know little about the structure of that prosperity above the base of flourishing subsistence agriculture evidently augmented by trade with the Levant and Nubia.

After Djoser's successor achieved little more than the foundation of an even grander pyramid, the later reigns of the era are obscure. Royal authority doubtless proved no stronger than the pharaoh's personality yet provincial burial sites, characteristic of a weak centre, are rare. Indeed, the founder of the 4th Dynasty seems to have inherited a well-defined realm with a defensible southern frontier at the Nile's first cataract, considerable prosperity drawn from the natural order of the Nile's cyclical flood and a highly stratified society supporting a sound centralized administrative system ready for redirection by the pharaoh at its apex. Certainly the resources – human and material, administrative and executive – were to hand for the first king of the new line, Snofru (c. 2575–2551), to undertake three major pyramid-building projects as well as military activity aimed at extending the realm into Nubia, Sinai and Libya.

It was in Snofru's reign that the sun-god Re rose to pre-eminence and the pyramid began to acquire the solar symbolism perfected in the great pyramids of Khufu (c. 2551–2528) and Khafre (c. 2520–2494) – the first wonder of the ancient world, still the most astonishing mani-festation of centralized power. Excepting the quest for semi-precious stone and copper in Sinai and timber in Lebanon, little is known of these reigns beyond their pyramids and the associated palatial temple dedicated to the cult of the pharaoh's eternal *ka*. Ironically, the image of the builder of the most monumental tomb the world has ever seen is known to survive only in an ivory miniature though unquestioned omnipotence has never been better conveyed than in the life-size diorite statues of the son who ultimately followed him.**1.33b,c**

After Khafre's effort, Menkaure (c. 2490–2472) built his pyramid on a much smaller scale and was represented with his wife in more human guise but still with the strength of form drawn from stark simplicity, untrammelled by expressive or decorative detail, which is also typical of the architecture of the Old Kingdom at its most virile.**1.33d** Beyond its funerary culture his reign, like that of his father, is elusive. The last king of the dynasty built no pyramid at all. Perhaps some sense of humanity had prevailed, perhaps the kingdom's rich resources had been exhausted.

Most of the 5th Dynasty kings resorted to relatively modest pyramids – at Abu Sir, with which they are iden-

›1.33 OLD KINGDOM PHARAOHS: (a) Djoser (2630–2611); (b) Khufu (2551–2528); (c) Khafre (2520–2494); (d) Menkaure and his queen (2490–2472) (a–c, Cairo, Egyptian Museum; d, Boston, Museum of Fine Art).

Images of divine monarchy, made for the eternal repose of the royal *ka* upon which the sustenance of cosmic *ma'at* depended, inhabiting temples sometimes as the focus of Osiran cult ritual but never for exposure as monuments, these were purely functional objects – despite the supreme aesthetic accomplishment of their sculptors and their ability to soften form in the latest, more human, example.

1.33c

1.33b

1.33d

fied despite direct descent from Menkaure – and though they invented the sun temple, all their work comes nowhere near to matching the extraordinary activity of the 4th Dynasty. Yet Snofru's external adventures were long-sustained: for instance, Sahure (2458–2446) commemorated victories in Libya and Sinai and an expedition to 'Punt' (probably Eritrea or Somalia), Niuserre (2416–2392) was active in the Levant as well as Sinai, Libya and Nubia and so too in their long reigns were the last two kings of the dynasty, Izezi and Unis (2388–2356–2323).

The extent of Old Kingdom contacts with contemporary civilizations in western Asia remains elusive. Goldsmiths' work of the 4th Dynasty reached Anatolia, probably through some north Levantine port, and bronze made the return voyage but the smelting technology failed to follow until towards the end of the 3rd millennium. Yet grave goods show the Egyptians as accomplished at working copper and great riches are displayed by the increasingly lavish embellishment of private tombs.**1.34, 1.43, 1.66**

Initial success is claimed for the military expeditions of the early 6th Dynasty kings, the last of the Old Kingdom, especially the vigorous Pepi I (2289–2255 or later), but losses followed everywhere in the declining years of the exceptionally long reign of Pepi II (from 2246 to 2152, the longest ever recorded if the not-uncontroversial record is accurate). Trade with Nubia and the Levant persisted but agricultural depression seems to have resulted from inadequate floods – or ineffective water management – and the failure of the central royal authority is marked by a short succession of ephemeral reigns and the renewed proliferation of provincial burials around the tombs of autonomous governors. The kingdom reverted to division in the 'First Intermediate Period': between 2130 and 2040 the kings of several northern and southern dynasties ruled concurrently.

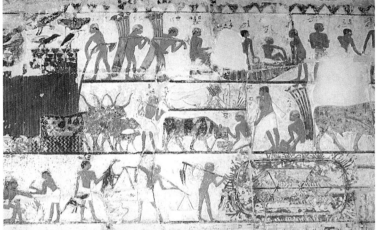

1.34a

1.34b

(a) reaping the grain harvest; (b) hunting in the marshes; (c) metal smelting with fire fanners and foreman (reliefs respectively from the tombs of Nufer, the director of singers, Ti, overseer of the royal works of Sahure and his successors, and Niankhkhnum, the royal manicurist, c. 2450, Saqqarah); (d) early 2nd millennium river craft (London, British Museum).

Religious and secular themes abound in equal profusion in Ancient Egyptian art – indeed it is difficult to separate them into those familiar categories because all were part of the fabric of the life of the god's son – and later the lives of his subjects – which the whole intent of artistic effort was directed to preserving for eternity. The naturalism with which scenes of everyday life are represented complements the convention, from which the Egyptian artist was never to waver, of the characteristic view: all the essentials of a human figure, say, are conveyed if the face is represented in personal profile but the body is given part frontally to demonstrate its essential symmetry in duality. The information on all aspects of Egyptian life provided by tomb embellishment and furniture is unequalled in any other ancient culture.

A trapezoidal sail hoisted on a bifurcated mast supplemented oarsmen on timber-hulled rivercraft at least as early as the 3rd Dynasty; larger oars were mounted at the stern quarter for steering. By the 5th Dynasty developments in ship design promoted by bulk river-borne commerce were applied to seagoing craft: as the keel plate had yet to be invented, rigidity was secured by a rope truss binding bow to stern over a series of forked posts. By the end of the millennium riverboats had a stern-mounted rudder oar and a mast fixed amidships with a rectangular sail fastened to a boom below and yard above. Applied with lateral extension to seagoing ships, this rig, and improved steerage, allowed closer hauling to the wind on voyages of variable courses.

1.34c

1.34d

PHARAONIC CONTINUUM

Sole lord of the land whose power ultimately descended from control of irrigation and reclamation, the Old Kingdom pharaoh was high priest of all temples and chief administrator. He ruled through a formidable bureaucracy of noble officials and numerous lesser scribes[1.35] – all doubled for the two kingdoms – sustained doubtless by trade, certainly by the productivity of the peasants in the incredibly rich fields. The manifestation, still astonishing, is the building undertaken for his perpetuation which depended on a facility for the organization and exploitation of mass labour, developed with flood control from peasant levies and institutionalized, rather than technological innovation.

As Ancient Egyptians were obsessed by the Nile's flood, which destroyed as the precondition of renewal in a continuous cycle, so their religion comprehended the continuum of life after death, prepared for it, and sought to ensure survival through it. As the night journey of Re was perilous, so too was the passing of pharaoh from this material world. The agent of cosmic order on earth, he could not be allowed to perish in essence or substance: the one depended on the other as, unlike soul, the *ka* – the individual essence of being – was tied to earth. Hence, in eternal re-enactment of Re's cosmic cycle and the divine drama of Horus and Osiris, the prime objective of pharaonic civilization was the preservation of the king's body which provided a home for his individual *ka* – in particular through the celebrated mummification process and the construction of the timeless vault. Ironically, however, that vault was not always well founded on solid stone: the quest for eternity prompted the perfection of mummification but not of building technology.

In Osirid principle, only the pharaoh had an eternal *ka* at least until near the end of the Old Kingdom when the

›1.35 OLD KINGDOM BUREAUCRACY: scribe (from Saqqarah; Paris, Louvre).

This 5th Dynasty study in unquestioning readiness for dictation, respect for authority manifest in the uplifted eyes, was hardly to be surpassed in its naturalism. Conveying exactly what the king's servant was like was essential, for he was to serve his master in eternity exactly as he did in terrestrial actuality and it was probable that he would be his image in that afterlife – as name or image and object were not distinguished. The vital naturalism of such images complements the early idealism of pharaoh's portraits and the stylized observation of the anthropomorphic and zoomorphic components of the largely syncretic deities.

grip of the near-centenarian king Pepi II loosened, the bureaucracy ran under its own momentum and the highest officials challenged the received dogma. However, as his *ka* needed for eternity all that the king himself had needed on earth, it was seen first that his servants had to be preserved too. But they did not have to accompany him in death: as object and name had similar validity, even identity, word and image preserved the *ka* in lieu of substance. From this derived the importance to later Old Kingdom Egyptians and their successors of tomb embellishment.

FROM MASTABA TO PYRAMID

As high temples were rising in Mesopotamia to lift man to the plane of the gods, the Egyptians were evolving the step pyramid as a tomb to accommodate their king for eternity. The greatest example was built c. 2620 to cover the pit grave in which – like most subjects of the dual monarchy – King Djoser was to be buried at Saqqarah.**1.12** His workers – mainly agricultural labourers idle during the period of inundation – may have been equipped with copper tools, but no pulleys or winches. Their job was eased only by levers, sleds, ramps, the proximity of fine limestone quarries and the relative ease of transporting harder stone from distant sites – like Aswan – during the flood. This was not to change throughout the era of Egypt's greatness.

The stepped pyramidal form was achieved pragmatically, though it may have been seen, ultimately, as a superhuman stairway to heaven. It evolved from the type of regularized pit-grave tumulus called mastaba which had appeared in place of the age-old tumulus by the beginning of the 1st Dynasty: the Arabic name is borrowed from a form of domestic bench of similar battered shape; the type derives from the primitive house of impacted mud. Built

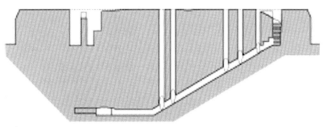

1.36a

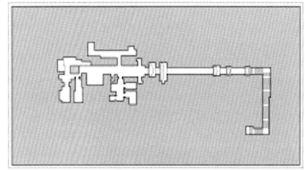

1.36b @ 1:1000

1.36c

THE MASTABA AND FALSE DOOR: (a, b) 3rd Dynasty mastaba at Beit Khallaf, section and plan; (c) false door of a red granite sarcophagus from an unknown Old Kingdom tomb, Gizeh (London, British Museum).

The primitive form was unrelieved but in some examples an unroofed brick enclosure was built against the east wall for offerings to the interred. Some of the royal tombs of the period at Abydos had storerooms within the mass of the superstructure and multiple subterranean chambers reached by inclined ramps. Palace façade imagery was comprehensive and a stele in the form of a 'false door' appeared on the inner wall of the offering chamber for the passage of the *ka*: this was later reproduced as the false door of the sealed tomb and often echoed on the sarcophagus. The *ka* was represented by disembodied upraised arms, bent at the elbow.

Within the unadorned mass of the 3rd Dynasty mastaba at Beit Khallaf, some 10 metres high, a staircase descends from the top to ground level near the northern end and an inclined ramp continues below ground to a depth of 20 metres. At the base level, several tomb chambers are fed from a central corridor. Offerings were sent down vertical shafts and five other vertical shafts, punctuating the ramp, allowed access to be blocked by rubble filling and inserted slabs of stone: tomb robbery was obviously already rife and another device commonly adopted to counter it was the substitution of vertical shafts for sloping access ramps.

of stone with a rubble core, it was to be elaborated after the example of the grandest of earthly residences and endowed with a simulated palace façade incorporating a false door for the passage of the deceased's *ka*.[1.36]

Beyond humanity, Djoser called for an experiment in which several mastabas were superimposed then extended to produce a more memorable and impressive, more monumental form – one that relies on powerful simplicity for telling impact. The result, the earliest surviving monumental stone structure, Djoser's pyramid is also the earliest building attributable to a specific architect: Imhotep, the king's vizier who may have conceived it, was certainly primarily responsible for the unprecedented organization of labour and resources to realize it and was later deified for his efforts.[1.37]

Djoser's mortuary and cult complex

The pyramid was the nucleus of a palatial complex dedicated to the deification of the king and his immortal cult but it has no space inside it: the tomb chamber is excavated from the bedrock, not encapsulated within the structure. Below ground the tomb was the eternal repository of the king's body, ultimate home of his immortal *ka*; above ground the ephemeral structures of this world, which had accommodated his corporeal reality – or so it is traditionally assumed – were made eternal to serve the immortal *ka*. Adjoining the main mass, an essential element in the conception was an offering chapel with a false door in its blind inner wall through which the *ka* could pass between the real and ideal spaces of this world and the stars: for the immortality of the *ka* depended not only on timeless security for its physical repository but on inexhaustible ministering of sustenance and ritual. As the king was twice buried, this combination may reflect pre-Dynastic burial practice in each kingdom: under the houses of the living in the agrarian north; in the sand of the desert beneath a tumulus in the recently nomadic south. This is asserted by the inclusion of two tombs – one below the step pyramid to the north, the other covered by a mastaba to the south of the main court.

The rectangular compound – 547 by 278 metres – is enclosed by a stone wall. Buttressed in the regular way that early bricklayers probably derived from reed-bundle construction and elevated to monumentality in the walls of Memphis, this was punctuated by bastions, all but one of which had false doors. The sole entrance, in the south-east corner, led to a hall with stone reed-bundle-type columns attached to its walls by stone spurs and roofed in imitation of parallel logs. Beyond this is a large altar court flanked by a mastaba to the south.

To the north of the court, towards the centre of the complex, is the pyramid (140 by 118 by 60 metres): its sides are aligned with the cardinal directions, as with most of its descendants. Attached to its north side is a room (serdab) for the pharaoh's statue adjacent to the offering chapel, with false door, and the royal cult temple before the opening of the passage down to the tomb chamber. This arrangement follows that of the more elaborate mastabas, though their entrance courts and royal cult chapels were usually on the east side.

To the east of the court and the pyramid is a succession of smaller courts. The second from the south, identified as the *heb-sed* court which catered for the perpetual repetition of the festival of regeneration marking the king's thirty-year jubilee, was addressed by replicas of chapels in the northern and southern style on the west side, the northern ones at the ends and in the centre of two groups of the southern type: the precedent for this synthetic approach has been detected in the mud-brick remains of Naqadian Hierakonpolis. The courts further north were addressed by palace halls representing Upper and Lower Egypt – the attached columns of the North House's precinct still retain capitals reproducing the papyrus of the Delta.

In the palatial compound, the buildings associated with the government of Upper and Lower Egypt may be related to primitive prototypes: the tent of the south or the light acacia structure derived from it; the reed-bundle hut of the Delta or the brick structure that replaced it. The poles and canopy of the former are reproduced literally; the frame and stretched matting of the latter, fringed with fronds at the top, have been stylized as the torus-framed flat and cove cornices which were to be as typical of Egyptian architecture as reed-bundle columns. And the rhythm

›1.37 SAQQARAH, MORTUARY COMPLEX OF DJOSER, early 3rd Dynasty: (a, pages 66–67) general view with a chapel in the northern style in the foreground and southern-style chapels centre and right, (b) plan with entrance hall (1), altar court (2), mastaba (3), pyramid (4), *heb-sed* court (5), chapels in the northern and southern styles (6, 7), northern court with palace halls representing Upper and Lower Egypt (8, 9), serdab and offering chapel (10, 11), royal cult temple (12), passage down to the tomb chamber (13), (c) section, (d) compound wall detail, (e) entrance hall (restored), (f) court of the North House, detail of engaged columns representing the papyrus emblem of the north, (g) Djoser performing the *heb-sed* festival race, limestone relief from the south tomb.

The section shows five stages in the development

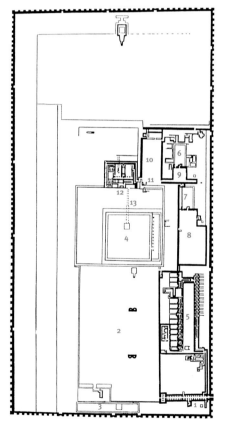

1.37b @ 1:5000

of its principal feature, the first pyramid: a conventional mastaba and its two enlargements and the stepped superstructure and its enlargement, both of which consist of a core clad with several layers of inclined masonry to an ultimate length of 125 metres, breadth of 109 metres and height of 60 metres. The underground tomb chamber was enlarged and its entrance ramps changed several times as the project developed. Subsidiary chambers were provided for other members of the royal family.

of the buttresses that reinforce the brickwork in extended works like palace or city walls echoes the incidence of reed-bundle piers separated by matting, as in Sumer. As we have seen, the hieroglyphs for the pharaoh's name include a palace façade: the place of appearance of the god-king among men, like its Sumerian equivalent, this is usually matched by the false door.

That the superstructure of Djoser's cult complex is modelled on his palace is assumed despite any knowledge of the latter not extrapolated (circularly) from the former – or gleaned from the sparse remains of the Naqadian 'palace' compound at Nekhen (Hierakonpolis). The extent of wall surface in this first great stone monument provided unprecedented opportunity for the carving of relief sculpture and the most celebrated surviving relief shows Djoser running the ritual race which, asserting sustained virility, was central to the *heb-sed* festival conducted in a special palace court.

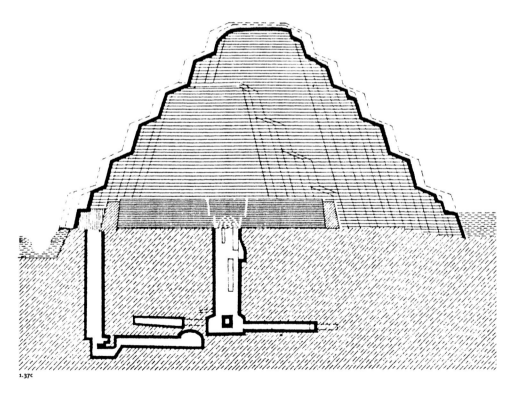

1.37c

1.37d

›ARCHITECTURE IN CONTEXT »WEST ASIA AND THE EASTERN MEDITERRANEAN

1.37e

1.37f

1.37g

In the dynasties of the sun-god Re's ascendancy, the pyramid rose no longer from a palace, fully elaborated, but was associated with a temple retaining the essential elements of the palace – the aisled hall of approach, the court of audience and the king's chamber – at the end of a causeway linking it to smaller temple at the river-bank landing stage. As far as the accidents of survival testify, these seem not to have differed essentially from the temples dedicated to the various cults of local and state deities – which varied in detailed distribution to meet specific cult requirements, as we have noted. However, the court was elaborated and extra accommodation was included for the rites of the king's transformation into Osiris, with which his responsibility for governing this world passed to his son, the new Horus. Above all, the combination of northern and southern types in the royal tomb complex was transformed. The southern tumulus was assimilated to the sacred mound of the northern centre of Heliopolis – the island on which Re alighted at the moment of creation – as a true prism.

›1.38 DASHUR, 'BENT' AND TRUE PYRAMIDS OF SNOFRU.

The achievement of the true pyramid under Snofru seems to have begun with the encasing of a step pyramid at Meidum (147 square metres, 93.5 metres high) – which may have belonged to Huni, last king of the 3rd Dynasty. At Dashur, the earlier of the two 4th Dynasty pyramids seems to have been conceived to rise at 54 degrees from a base c. 183 metres square to an apex at 138 metres but subsidence when the project was less than half complete prompted the lowering of the angle of inclination by 11 degrees to achieve a height of only 105 metres. As subsidence affected the arrangement of corridors and tomb chambers, a fresh start was made on a more stable site nearby. This work, the so-called Red Pyramid, was to rise from a base c. 220 metres square through 45 degrees to 104 metres: the funerary apartment consists of two antechambers and an interment chamber more than 8 metres long with a corbel vault nearly 15 metres high.

None of Snofru's pyramids rose from simulated palaces though there were cult facilities on their east sides and a causeway to a valley temple for the reception of the royal funerary barque and the barques of visiting deities. A temple with a statue court about half-way between the Bent Pyramid and the cultivated

1.39

floodplain was embellished with reliefs of maidens impersonating the royal estates and the king engaged in the ritual of the *heb-sed* festival. Perhaps respecting the tradition of double-burial, the Bent Pyramid was accompanied by a subsidiary pyramid for the royal entrails and most subsequent royal pyramid builders followed the example.

›1.39 SUNBURST OVER THE NORTH AFRICAN STEPPE.

Symbolism rather than mere pragmatism is apparent as the generator of pyramidal form for the 4th Dynasty pharaohs, beginning with the works of Snofru at Meidum and Dashur.[1.38] Dramatic manifestations of the sun's rays as a prism are common[1.39] and it is not hard to see a stone prism as the petrification of the rays of the sun as well as an idealized island. Symbolism apart, however, pure geometric form unrelieved by surface embellishment informed the aesthetic of all the monumental works in the extraordinary era of Khufu and Khafre: the pyramid, above all, was designed to defeat time for its incumbent and, despite the loss of the treasure of the body at its heart, it has resoundingly achieved his immortality in the spirit of memory.

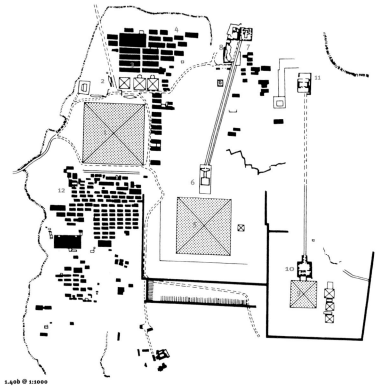

1.40b @ 1:1000

>1.40 GIZEH, PYRAMID COMPLEXES OF
KHUFU, KHAFRE AND MENKAURE, 4th Dynasty:
(a; pages 74–75) general view, (b) site plan with the
Great Pyramid of Khufu (1) with the pits to the south
and east in which the royal barques were buried;
the site of the royal cult temple (2) and the end of
the causeway from the valley temple; the pyramids of
the queens and mastabas of members of the royal family (3), mastabas of dignitaries (4), the pyramid
of Khafre (5) and its royal cult temple (6), causeway and
valley temple (7); the sphinx (8), the pyramids of
Menkaure and his queens (9), royal cult temple (10),
causeway and valley temple (11) construction workers'
village (12).

Most pyramid building sites would have had
accommodation for the king on his tours of inspection,
in planned settlements for the officials directing operations, for the labourers and, ultimately, for the priests
and bureaucrats responsible for servicing the finished
complex: the remains of Menkaure's settlement reveal
the ordered planning to be expected of such an exercise. The accommodation of the king's departed servants was rarely so ordered but the regimented
distribution of the simple and austere mastabas in the
royal cemetery at Gizeh, following the precedent set at
Dashur, reflects the authoritarian rule of the Old Kingdom's regime at its height.

The great pyramids of Gizeh

Khufu's pyramid, the largest, was 230.5 metres square and rose through
51.5 degrees to a height of 146.5 metres before it lost its outer layer of
dressed limestone. Khafre's work is slightly smaller (214.5 metres
square, rising through c. 54 degrees to 143.5 metres), but is based on
higher ground and retains the upper part of its revetment. Menkaure's
work is the smallest (105 metres square, rising through c. 51 degrees to
65.5 metres) but instead of polished limestone it was clad in granite and
has three subsidiary pyramids.

The equilateral sides of Khufu's pyramid – like the others – face the
cardinal directions. The mass is of limestone blocks (weighing an average of 2.5 tonnes) in slender vertical sections laid against a lightly battered core. First excavated below the pyramid, the tomb chamber was
ultimately built into the main mass. The corridor to the original chamber,
entered from the north above ground level, was deflected upwards and

(a) section; (b) king's gallery; (c) king's barque (43.5 metres long), recovered from southern pit without the rope binding of the timbers but with the slender canopy structure on the foredeck and around the main cabin incorporating poles with characteristically bell-shaped cap.

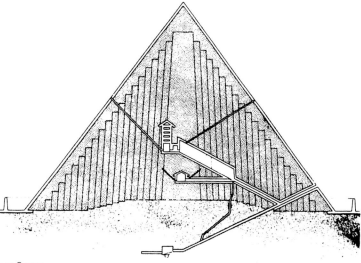

1.41a @ 1:2000

then ran parallel to the ground to a second chamber – the so-called Queen's Chamber, though it was also probably originally destined for the king. From the point where the horizontal corridor diverges from the inclined passage, the latter continues in a great corbelled gallery 2 metres wide and 28 metres high, to the chamber in which Khufu was actually interred. Clad in granite and sealed with three granite portcullises in an antechamber, the King's Chamber is vaulted to with-stand the pressure of the mass above with superimposed tiers of stone beams, the top one protected by a protean triangle or chevron, a much more efficient masonry load-bearing device than the lintel. At least from the reign of Khufu's successor, Djedefre, the tomb chamber and its antechamber, aligned east–west, and the access corridor perpendicular to them on the north, were excavated from the rock ledge site, the sar-cophagus installed, the ashlar walls built and the whole covered with chevron vaults before the mass of the pyramid was begun.

It has been detected that the tiny shaft connecting Khufu's burial chamber to the outside is aligned with the constellation of Orion in sea-son. For visionary commentators, the distribution of the three pyramids at Gizeh reflects the configuration of the main stars in that constellation: Orion is identified with Osiris and with Osiris the departed pharaoh is

1.41b

1.41C

identified. In this view the pyramid, whose form reflected the pharaoh's god-head in the sun, provided a base for his *ka* to ascend to commune with the progenitor in the realm of the immortals, manifest in the stars – and, inevitably, the great barque buried beside Khufu's pyramid is thought to have stood for the divine vessel that carried the king across the heavens, though it is certainly large and solid enough to have carried the king along the Nile to his obsequies.

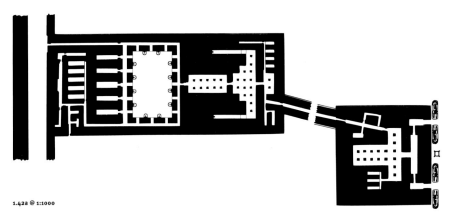

1.42a @ 1:1000

The associated temple

Little survives of Khufu's valley or mortuary cult temples but Khafre's complex has fared better. The valley temple, as it were hewn from a square mass of limestone, is notable for its extreme austerity. Twin entrances lead to a transverse vestibule before the central T-shaped columned hall, the main part divided by monolithic piers (4.1 metres high) into nave and aisles in elaboration of the main reception hall of the terrestrial palace: against the outer walls of the latter were numerous royal statues (doubtless including **1.33ᶜ**). To the south are store rooms; to the north is a passage leading to the causeway along which the barque travelled to the cult temple where the rites of the king's transition to eternity as Osiris were enacted. Now ruined, this structure too was doubtless austere: the transverse hall has three rows of square granite piers, the longitudinal one beyond matches the one in the valley temple but beyond that similarity ceases as more rooms were needed for the funerary rites. Following the

1.42b

›1.42 GIZEH, VALLEY AND CULT TEMPLE OF
KHAFRE: (a) plan, (b) view of valley temple hall,
(c) plan of the Harmakhis Temple, (d) the Great Sphinx
(usually attributed to Khafre but possibly earlier) with
the Great Pyramid of Khufu in the background.

The sphinx invariably has the body of a lion and
the head of the god whose sanctuary it guards: in lieu
of the pharaoh, divine in his interment, this may be
an animal or mythic beast but never has the apotropaic
image been more persuasive nor would any other
anthropomorphic-zoomorphic synthesis prove so
persistent.

precedent established by Snofru in the context of his Bent Pyramid at
Dashur, the central element was a transverse statue court: to its west
were five chapels which probably held cult statues of the king representing different aspects of his office and the barques on which they were carried; further west was the inner sanctum to which only the priests were
admitted. That the mummification ceremony took place in either of these
temples is the subject of some dispute.

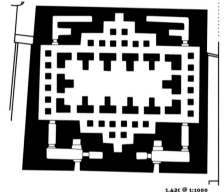
1.42c @ 1:1000

Beside Khafre's valley temple are the ruins of an enclosure with twin entrances from the east and a rectangular
central court. Known as Harmakhis and identified as an
early form of solar temple, the progressive development
of depth in the eastern and western porticoes with
niches framing paired columns has suggested dedication
to Re's passage across and back through the body of the
sky-goddess Nut. Overlooking this work, guarding the
passage from the valley to the cult temple, is the celebrated colossal image of pharaoh with the body of a lion:
this syncretic human-leonine form is known as sphinx
and we shall find no more arresting image of the king as
divine protector than the Great Sphinx of Gizeh.**1.42**

1.42d

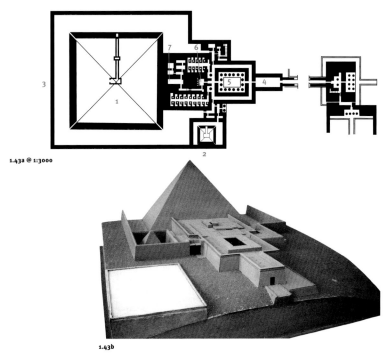

1.43a @ 1:3000

1.43b

(a)
plan, (b) model, (c) detail of court column capital, (d)
detail of court corridor relief with seagoing ships.

Following the example set at the height of the 4th
Dynasty, 5th and 6th Dynasty royal funerary complexes
consisted of the king's tomb pyramid (78.5 square
metres rising through c. 50 degrees to 47 metres) (1)
with a subsidiary pyramid (2) and the royal cult temple
to its east linked to a valley temple by a causeway. The
cult temple was now bifurcated: before a wall enclosing the pyramid compound (3), the outer part contained an entrance hall (4) and columned court (5);
beyond the wall were the inner sanctum (6) and offering hall (7). Unlike the hall preceding the court in
Khafre's temples, but like the one in Snofru's statue
temple, the hall (4) before the royal cult temple's central court was not usually divided into nave and aisles.
Entirely surrounded by a corridor, the court had a
colonnade on all four sides (5). Beyond this court, on
the higher level of the inner temple to the west, was the
sanctum with five statue cells (6), as in Khafre's complex but much smaller, and beyond that a bifurcated
corridor led between rows of storerooms (for ritual
paraphernalia) to the offering hall with a false door
immediately in front of the pyramid (7). The latter was
not a feature of Khafre's complex.

The iconographic programme – the most extensive
of the Old Kingdom – clearly related to the purpose
and, beyond that, the symbolic significance of the
major spaces. Gods and goddesses succoured or
accompanied the king in the cult chambers, of course,
and the walls of the inner sanctuary were redolent with
the images of lavish offerings. Most particularly, it is
recognized that the nucleus of the temple represented
the order won from primordial chaos which pharaoh
was divinely ordained to protect: on the corridor walls
to either side of the eastern and western entrances to
the central court were reliefs of the sea and ships
which, though representing an expedition sent by
Sahure to the Levant, serve to identify that court as the
sacred island; elsewhere on the surrounding walls
were reliefs representing the pharaonic rituals associated with the preservation of *ma' at*, the king's physical
prowess at the hunt and in battle with the forces of
chaos that threatened *ma' at* and the *heb-sed* renewal

FROM PYRAMID TO OBELISK

The endowment of a protective device with divine symbolism was doomed to fail: it was effective only so long as
the pharaoh's sword was effective, but when authority
broke down, tombs were broken into and robbed. The 5th
and 6th Dynasty kings persevered with lesser pyramids
associated with increasingly complex mortuary temples.
In these the iconographic programme in fine relief carving and the introduction of palm or lotiform columns
have been interpreted as establishing the nuclear court as
the manifestation of the sacred grove in the island of primal creation.**1.43**

Meanwhile, the increasingly powerful officials who ran
the bureaucracy that ran Egypt enlarged and embellished
their mastabas in emulation of those same temples but
with more mundane imagery.**1.44**

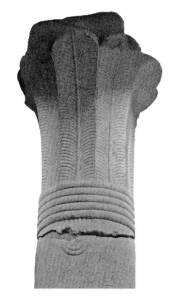

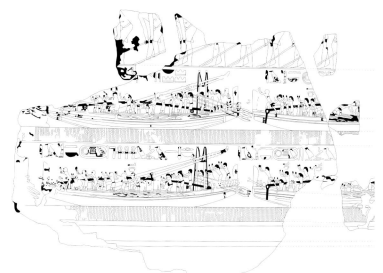

1.43d

1.43c

festival symbolizing the sustenance of *ma' at*; reliefs on the altar in the centre of the court represented the key event in the establishment of order on the terrestrial island, the unification of Egypt.

The mature mastaba

By the end of the 3rd Dynasty the offering chapel was being hollowed from the mastaba's superstructural mass together with ancilliary spaces: statues for the habitation of the deceased's *ka* were evidently introduced to the offering chapel towards the end of the period. The great pharaohs of the 4th Dynasty seem to have proscribed external relief, internal chambers, false doors and sculpture in the formally disposed, rigorously rectangular mastabas allotted to subjects: their families might have imagery but officials were allowed only an external stele and its shelter towards the southern end of the east front. Plain limestone (sometimes encasing rubble) had replaced mud-brick for the superstructure. By the end of the dynasty an offering chapel and false door and even statuary had reappeared.

In the 5th and 6th Dynasties the offering chapel and an associated image chamber (the serdab, in which the statue was sealed for its eternal protection) were within the mass again at ground level and around them developed a complex of rooms, inspired by those of the royal funerary complexes, including pillared courts or halls and altar chambers inhabited by accessible cult statues. Members of the deceased's family were catered for too in a manner befitting their rank. Naturally, the number of false doors and sculptures multiplied in these chambers and many walls were embellished with reliefs representing all the facets of the life. No longer merely the *ka*'s house, the mastaba did provide a well-provisioned eternal abode in the bowels of the earth but at ground level it had become a temple for the veneration of the departed.

Insecurity at the end of the Old Kingdom prompted the reversal of this tendency and major effort was once again concentrated on the subterranean sphere.

1.44b @ 1:1000

1.44a

1.44c

Novel in the royal repertory, however, was the setting of a prismatic form on a massive tower and podium with battered sides beyond the court of a sun temple.[1.45a] Elongated and refined, this was the prototype of the obelisk symbol of solar worship derived from the primeval mound upon which Re rested at the moment of creation. One of the largest marks the site of the sanctuary of Re at Heliopolis, but the form was also appropriated for the temples of Amun at Luxor and Karnak after Re had been absorbed by the Theban god in the later ages of Egypt's greatness.[1.45b]

›**1.44 SAQQARAH**: (a) mastaba of Perneb, model with serdab left, offering chamber right, 5th Dynasty; (b, c) mastaba of Mereruka, vizier to the 6th Dynasty King Teti (c. 2323–2291), plan and false door with emerging image of Mereruka.

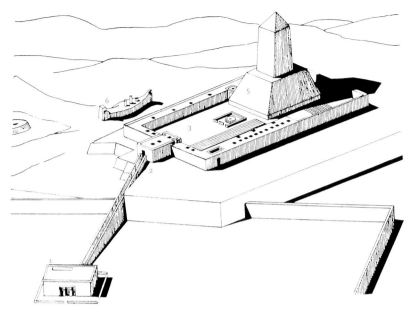

1.45a

›1.45 SANCTUARIES OF RE: (a) Abu Ghurab, Sun Temple of Neuserre, 5th Dynasty, c. 2390: reconstructed view from the north; (b) Heliopolis, obelisk inscribed by 12th and 19th Dynasty pharaohs.

The form doubtless followed the sanctuary of Re at Heliopolis, now lost; unlike the Hemakhis at Gizeh, the court is centred on an open-air altar. As in the typical pyramid complex, however, the valley temple (1) is linked by a causeway to the entrance to the main temple, facing east (2). The large open court, surrounded by corridors and magazines (3), contained an uncovered altar (4) before the obelisk built of limestone blocks on its battered base (5). A chapel to the south was decorated with *heb-sed* festival images. A room beside the chapel, dedicated to Re's bounty and unique to this type of complex, takes its name from reliefs depicting the life of the countryside in the two main seasons of the agricultural year – *akhet*, when the flood came, and *shemu*, the harvest. To the south of the compound was a representation of the solar barque in which Re daily crossed the heavens (6).

1.45b

1.46a   1.46b

›1.46 **AKKADIAN ROYAL PORTRAITURE:**
(a) copper portrait head, possibly of Sargon (Shar-rum-kin) of Agade or his grandson Naram-sin (second half of the 3rd millennium; Baghdad, National Museum of Iraq); (b) stele representing the victory of Naramsin over the Elamites, from Susa c. 2250 (Paris, Louvre).

Important as an historical document showing Naram-sin wearing the horned helmet of deity, the victory stele marks a new stage of development in representational art: advanced in his naturalism, Naram-sin's artist is the first known to have unified the compostion across the whole surface, developing dramatic momentum from the bottom to the ruler's triumph at the top of the hill which dominates the integrated landscape setting.

3 MESOPOTAMIAN EMPIRES

By 2400 BCE Ur seems to have fallen to Lagash but within fifty years all the Sumerian cities were in the grip of the Akkadian Semites led by Sargon of Agade – the first ruler of all Mesopotamia, the first emperor, with whom the earliest-known royal portrait is identified. Sargon's regime fostered trade on the basis of the routes developed east and west by the rival Sumerian cities, penetrating up the Euphrates and down the Gulf coast. His sons extended the empire in the east, conquering Elam. His grandson Naram-sin (2254–18), who seems to have claimed divinity well before the end of his long reign of extroverted ambition, extended his rule to the Levant. There the great trading city of Ebla was in the first phase of its protracted ascendancy. The site of Agade having proved elusive, the remains of the palace of Ebla's rulers are the most substantial of the Akkadian era.**1.46, 1.47**

The Akkadians established the goal of the military superstate – and the model of the warrior king – to be

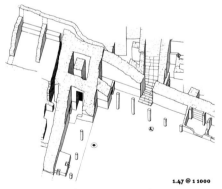

1.47 @ 1 1000

›1.47 **EBLA (TELL MARDIKH), PALACE G**
(c. 2300): survey of remains of entrance court and stairs.

The rectangular court is ubiquitous but the colonnaded portico was to be a characteristic feature of the palaces of the area throughout its ancient tradition.

›1.48 GUDEA, RULER (ENSI) OF LAGASH, c. 2120 (juxtaposed diorite head and seated figure, Paris, Louvre) and detail of temple plan.

On his skirt and seat is an inscribed dedication to the goddess Ningirsu, patron deity of Lagash, and a description of the construction of the temple of the goddess, which is known from other surviving texts to have been the major element in an extensive walled complex. Probably the earliest surviving architectural drawing in the world, it conforms in general to a long, conservative tradition.

emulated by many but Naram-sin's overextended followers were overwhelmed by a coalition of their many adversaries. The Sumerian city-states reasserted themselves in the last two centuries of the 2nd millennium. Lagash was first back to prominence, under its extraordinary priest-king Gudea who seems to have defeated Elam, freed from the late Akkadians by a local dynasty. In an assertion of wide dominion doubtless financed by profits from trade at least as much as war, Gudea claims the rebuilding of fifteen temples. Contrary to the Akkadians, his ideal of kingship is one of piety as the architect of the temple: on his lap in one of his most celebrated images is a tablet inscribed with the plan of a temple.**1.48**

Gudea's dates are unknown but he was probably an older contemporary of Uruk's king Utuhegal (c. 2119–2113), who was powerful enough to delegate authority over Ur to Ur-Nammu, perhaps his son. Ur-Nammu (c. 2112–2095) united Ur and Uruk and won hegemony in Sumer. Ruling through a highly sophisticated bureaucracy from Mesopotamia's principal port, he was the chief beneficiary of the expansion of sea trade in the Akkadian era and may have been responsible for the introduction of money to supplement barter. His resources extended to the inauguration of massive campaigns of temple building at Ur, Uruk, Nippur and Eridu based on the earliest known examples of the stepped-pyramidal ziggurat type of platform: he too chose to be commemorated as pious rather than virile, despite considerable military prowess.

Ur-Nammu's successors claimed title to both Sumer and Akkad, extended their sway into northern Mesopotamia, were probably allies rather than overlords of Mari but received tribute from as far afield as Elam and the Levant. They revived Naram-sin's pretensions to the divine, sustained the Akkadian tradition of royal portraiture and built on an imperial scale.

1.49a

1.49b

>1.49 UR AND UR-NAMMU: (a) reconstruction of Ur at its height in the late-3rd millennium (diorama, New York, American Museum of Natural History); (b) the ruler venerating Nanna, moon-god patron of Ur (stele of Ur-Nammu); (c) reconstruction of ziggurat as built by Ur-Nammu (2112–2095); (d) precinct of Nanna, plan at ground level with (1) the court ofNanna, (2) the temenos and ziggurat, (3) E-nun-mah, probably the treasury of Nanna, (4) E-hursag of Ur-Nammu's son Shulgi (2094–2047), (5) the outer temenos of the 6th-century king Nebuchadnezzar II, (6) Giparu of Shulgi's son Amar-sin (2046–2038); (e) aerial view of model of remains with ziggurat to the right, residential area to the left.

UR: SACRED COMPOUND

As we have seen, Sumerian civilization evolved on an arid plain. Beyond the plain, way off in the distance, were the mountains from which came the bounty of rain but also the havoc of storm. The forces of good and evil – and so the dwelling place of the gods – were therefore associated with high ground, and in his attempt to placate those forces man found it prudent to build mountains for the gods within the orbit of the town. Hence the ziggurat – the most monumental of all Mesopotamian building types. It was preceded by a long line of high temples, rebuilt one above the other to ever greater height. However, doubtless inspired by the early step pyramid of the Egyptian king Djoser;[1.37] there is obvious symbolic purpose in a graded series of superimposed terraces elevating the priest to a point where he could communicate with the all-high. The great ziggurat of Ur-Nammu at Ur is the earliest and supreme example.[1.49]

The ceremonial entrance to the main precinct was through monumental gates in the buttressed walls of the court of Nanna: dating initially from the 3rd Dynasty, this was enlarged in the period of Isin's dominance (early 2nd millennium) and replaced by Nebuchadnezzar.

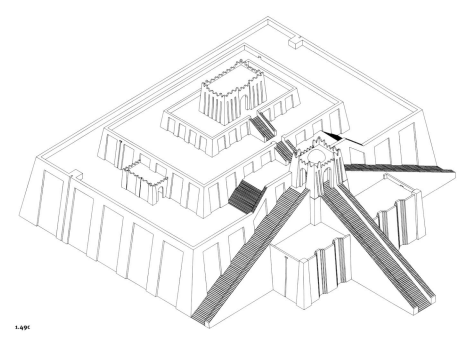

1.49C

The ziggurat of Ur-Nammu

In a compound surrounded by cells and preceded by an entrance court, the massive artificial mountain – 62 by 43 metres at its base, about 21 metres high – rose probably in three stages to the shrine of Ur's patron deity, the moon-god Nanna. It was built of mud-brick interleaved with matting for binding, and its battered and buttressed sides were protected from erosion by a skin of baked bricks. Considerable sophistication is apparent in the lowest level, which was not only battered for greater real and apparent strength but bowed to obviate the optical illusion of sagging that would have resulted had it been straight. Three flights of stairs led to the domed vestibule before the first terrace, two parallel to the south-east side of the structure, the central one perpendicular to it. The other two terraces were served by single flights of stairs continuing the line of the central one. The structure enclosed no space, though there was a domed vestibule – the prototype of the ciborium – and probably a temple on top: long lost, the idea of the latter derives from the description of Babylon and its ziggurat by the 5th century Greek historian Herodotus.

1.49d @ 1:5000

1.49e

Ancillary structure

By Ur-Nammu's time the Sumerian 'low temple' was usually a complex of cells around interlinked courts in which the major elements were formally related. The main buildings in the compound to the south of Ur-Nammu's ziggurat are of the type: that to the south-east, known as E-hursag, may have been the palace; that to the west, known as Giparu, may have accommodated both the high priestess and the consort of Nanna, Ningal. In the latter there were two parallel sets of aligned courts and longitudinal halls: as in the E-hursag – indeed as usual – access from court to hall was deflected to the sides in the northern one but in the southern one it conformed to the central axis so that the shrine-like niche at its head was visible from the entrance vestibule.

In so far as the accidents of survival testify, the axial line of access was to be common in southern Mesopotamia after the prestigious example of Nanna's Giparu. The north normally retained the traditional deflected approach.

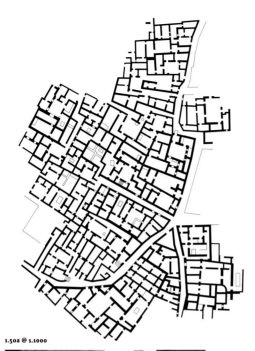

1.50a @ 1.1000

1.50b

>**1.50 ORGANIC URBAN DEVELOPMENT:** (a) Ur c. 2100, plan of residential district to the south-east of the citadel; (b) Mosul (northern Iraq), contemporary street scene.

UR: TOWN AND HOUSE

The regularity of the structure of god was not entirely foreign to the habitation of man, at least in the upper echelons of Sumer's increasingly diversified society: as we have noted, the tripartite plan appears in both shrine and house well before the end of the Ubaid period.[1.22, 1.23] By the end of the Uruk period, the central space of the town house had became a courtyard with a reception room to one side and smaller, more private spaces, which sometimes included a bathroom, to the other. Thereafter, urban development promoted cramped irregularity in variations on this theme in blocks of houses, sometimes two-storeyed and always presenting blind outer walls to narrow wayward lanes.[1.50a]

Rooms may be roughly rectangular but primitive streets are not normally straight. Before planning guidelines can be imposed, as in colonies laid out on fresh sites by pre-ordained authority, the development of towns is organic: it follows the tracks made by feet taking the lines of least resistance in the contours of the site – as at Catal Huyuk.[1.7] And as we have seen, when building with walls there is no incentive to impose an overall formality on the distribution of spaces because it can never be seen: ancient Ur is archetypical but the type is ubiquitous.[1.50b]

UR'S SUMERIAN SUCCESSORS AND THE PALACE

Ur-Nammu's dynasty was undermined by internal rebellion and tribal incursion and destroyed c. 2000 by the resurgent Elamites of Anshan and Susa. They occupied Ur but left the way open to other intruders elsewhere, the Caucasian Hurrians in the north and the Semitic Amorites from Arabia. Meanwhile, several of Ur's provincial governors declared their independence, notably at Eshnunna in northern Akkad, Larsa in southern Sumer and

Isin in the centre: the last ultimately drove the Elamites from Ur and assumed the supreme titles of its late kings. By now power was essentially secular, deriving no longer from the position of chief priest – though several of the new kings sought legitimacy for their regimes by assuming that position.

Little remains of the seats of these powers except at Eshnunna where the newly independent governor built his palace as an adjunct to the temple of the divine king of Ur – though it was really the temple that was the adjunct. Like the E-hursag and Giparu at Ur, the central complex consisted of rooms ranged around linked courtyards from which they drew their light and gained access. As at Ur, too, a measure of formality was imposed on the plan. The square palace court, throne room and private court are aligned on a longitudinal axis unrelated to the square temple but, contrary to the innovative planning of the Giparu, access between them is deflected in the trad-itional way – as at Kish. On the other hand, the strict axiality of the original temple – a variant of the ancient tripartite type with a square central space and rigorously aligned doors – is echoed by the new palatine chapel on the far side of the main court.**1.51**

THE TEMPLE IN THE EARLY 2ND MILLENNIUM BCE

The Ishtar-Kititum temple complex at Ischali, near Khafajeh in Eshnunna's domain, is perhaps the era's most spectacular example of axial planning, at least in part, and the symbolic implications of its dominant elements were profound. The highest platform of the inner court was reserved for the main sanctuary of Ishtar. The cult object was in the centre of the inner wall of the long hall, opposite the entrance from an equally long antechamber and rectangular court. Each court and each temple building

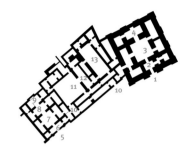

1.51 @ 1:2000

›**1.51 ESHNUNNA (TELL ASMAR),** palace and temple, beginning of 2nd millennium: plan.

The temple of Shu-shin, king of Ur, with entrance, vestibule, square central court and sanctuary (1–4) aligned on axis in a square enclosure; the similar elements of the palatine chapel (5–9); the square palace court and aligned throne room (11, 12). In accordance with a basic principle of defence, entrance to the palace (10) involves several right-angle turns through an extended series of narrow halls, and procedure beyond the throne room to the inner zone of restricted audience (13) is also off axis.

›**1.52 ISCHALI,** temple dedicated to aspects of the great goddess with Ishtar predominant, early 2nd millennium: reconstructed view.

The complex of three temples was raised on the conventional platform, its corners orientated to the cardinal directions. The main twin-towered entrance led through magazines to the southern corner of the generous court that served two of the three sanctuaries – the third had its own entrance towards the eastern corner of the complex. The dominant axis (south-east–north-west) extended up a flight of steps through another central twin-towered gate to the main sanctuary of Ishtar on the highest level. This too had its own twin-towered entrance from the street, at right angles to the entrance from the first court near the western corner. The halls of the subsidiary shrines were entered on the longitudinal axis opposite the altar at the far end.

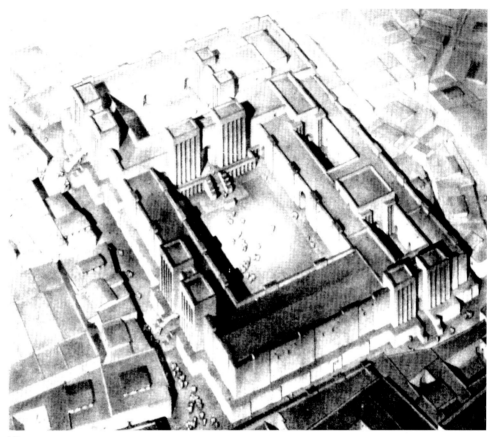

1.52

had a twin-towered portal, centrally placed in the upper zone. Presented with such assertive multiplicity in such a hallowed context, it is not hard to imagine how the arch flanked by towers became the symbol of epiphany: the place of appearance of the god among men in the divine image presented by the ruler as high priest.**1.52** And if the king of Kish had not already appropriated the twin-towered portal as the symbol of quasi-divine royal authority, the ruler of Eshnunna certainly did in annexing the temple to which it belonged.**1.27, 1.51**

AMORITES, TRADE AND THE EAST

In their advance from the south, the Amorites, having taken Uruk, Kish and Larsa, went on to dispossess Isin of Ur in the last quarter of the 20th century. With this came dominance over the lucrative maritime trade with the east which had been a state monopoly controlled by Ur-Nammu's bureaucracy. Early records list cloth and resin among the main exports, gold, lapis-lazuli, copper and tin as the main imports. The main entrepôts in the Gulf were in the states of Dilmun (including modern Bahrain) and Margan (modern Oman). The most valuable commodities came through these intermediaries from a port in the lower Indus Valley which the Mesopotamians called Meluhha. These products – and timber and stone – also came from or through Elam, at least until a dark age descended there with the collapse of the revived kingdom of Anshan and Susa in the 18th century BCE. Stamp seals from the Gulf entrepôts have been found on many sites between the Indus and southern Mesopotamia; Mesopotamian seals appear in the Indus Valley and pottery from there is not uncommon in Gulf and Sumerian sites.

THE INDUS VALLEY CIVILIZATION

The history of the Indian sub-continent opens about the middle of the 3rd millennium BCE with one of the seminal civilizations of the world centred on several settlements in the valley of the Indus and its tributaries. A wide range of objects recovered from the sites resemble those from Sumeria. Most characteristic are finely worked seals: their inscriptions remain uninterpreted but their devices have been accepted as evidence for image worship involving the mother-goddess, a horned deity, the bull, trees and the genii of sacred spots.[1.53a]

In an environment not unlike the mud-flats of lower

1.53a

1.53b

›1.53 INDUS VALLEY: (a) seal with bull device; (b) Mohenjo-daro, part plan of residential area.

Like Harappa and other cities of the Indus Valley civilization – and most of its Sumerian contemporaries – Mohenjo-daro was walled and dominated by a citadel. The main buildings excavated were the great ceremonial tank, a hall and a granary – the last related to a building traced at Susa.

Indus Valley seals have been recovered from the stratum of Sumerian sites dated to the second half of the 3rd millennium, providing proof of contact between the two civilizations and the earliest guide to dating the cities of the Indus.

Mesopotamia, brick was the standard building material and its production had been standardized for most of the building in the two greatest sites: Harappa and Mohenjo-daro. Planned with a roughly rectilinear grid, they seem to have offered a high standard of living for much of the population in substantial, well-drained courtyard houses: with the significant exception of the urban planning, much of this recalls Sumeria and even Susa.**1.53b** And as in Mesopotamia – as we shall see – this urban civilization was overwhelmed about the middle of the 2nd millennium by the tribes of fair-skinned Aryan peoples originating from the steppes of central Asia in one of the major upheavals of the ancient world.

ASSUR, MARI AND BABYLON

Trade along the main arteries of the Fertile Crescent to the west was dominated by Mari on the middle reaches of the Euphrates and Assur on the Tigris. Mari, a Semitic city, traded with the Semitic towns of the Levant, notably the ports of Byblos and Ugarit which traded with Egypt. Assur, the prime entrepôt between Mesopotamia,

1.54a @ 1:10,000

1.54b

>**1.54 ASSUR:** (a) plan of site in early 2nd millennium with (1) Temple of Assur, founded in the mid-3rd millennium, rebuilt by Shamshi-adad I and later altered, (2) ziggurat, (3) Old Palace, founded towards the end of the 3rd millennium, rebuilt by Shamshi-adad I in part and later much overbuilt, (4) the double Temple of Adad and Anu, founded c. 1900, rebuilt by Shamshi-adad I and several more times, (5) Temple of Ishtar; (b) image of the god (Berlin, West Asiatic Museum).

Anatolia and Iran, was an Akkadian provincial centre which seems to have fallen to native rulers in the centuries of Sumerian resurgence before succumbing to the Amorites some time in the 19th century.

From the confused situation c. 1810 emerged Shamshi-adad, a western Semite of obscure origins who was to be the first great Assyrian ruler – drawing his strength from the profits of trade and legitimizing his power by assuming the high priesthood of Assur. He rebuilt the venerable dynastic seat.**1.54** He also established a new capital at Shubat Enlil in the north-western quarter of his domain. His first victims were the Amorites who had taken Mari from its ancient Semitic rulers and he went on to conquer as far as the Levant and the borders of Elam. He divided

Occupied from the middle of the 3rd millennium, the site was first developed on a grand scale by Shamshi-adad I (c. 1813–1781): his work was much overbuilt, particularly on the revival of Assyrian fortunes in the mid-15th century, but with considerable respect for the original conception. His palace was based on 3rd-millennium foundations: square, it had 172 rooms about a central core of ceremonial spaces, aligned north–south but not entered on axis. The temples of Ishtar and Assur were the earliest on the site. The former went through at least five stages of rebuilding over essentially the same plan, with a courtyard entered from the west and a cult hall to the east terminating in a shrine recession at the northern end, before being rebuilt on a new site further north at the end of the 13th century. The Assur temple was also rebuilt at least five times over a plan that early included two courts aligned north-east–south-west in a rectangular compound with the cult hall disposed laterally at the northern end and entered off-centre in the court front. Shamshi-adad seems to have retained this arrangement, adding a roughly triangular outer court to the south-east and building a new cella beyond the original one to which access from the court was central but from which access to the sanctum was directed through a vestibule at the east end; another court was added to the south-west of the main sequence in the mid-13th century. Contrary to normal Assyrian practice as it developed later, the ziggurat was freestanding: the norm is represented by the complex dedicated to Adad and Anu.

his empire between his two sons – one based near Assur, the other at Mari – but after his death c. 1781 they were overcome by Elam in league with Eshnunna and by the scion of the old Mari dynasty, Zimri-lim.

The principal beneficiary of the termination of Assyria's first imperial adventure was Hammurabi of Babylon whose advent is dated to c. 1792 (or, by the main alternative reckoning, to c. 1848). He had overcome Uruk and Isin within five years but took another twenty to come to terms with the Elamites and Eshnunna. In league with the latter and with Zimri-lim, he conquered Larsa but then turned on his allies, destroying Mari c. 1757 and Eshnunna two years later: he was then master of the whole of the Mesopotamian world.

Justifying his assumption of power, and consolidating his hold on it by annexing the tradition of his most ancient subjects, Hammurabi declared that the Sumerian great god Enlil had ceded supremacy to Babylon's god Marduk (Enki's son, also called Bel or Baal: 'the Lord') with whose authority he ruled. This was the premise of his most enduring monument, the code of laws which he issued to proscribe anomalies and establish precedent for a new 'world empire'.**1.55**

Hammurabi's empire soon waned but his line continued to rule its rump from his capital until overwhelmed c. 1600 by invaders from Anatolia known to history as the Hittites. The law-giver had won such prestige for Marduk, however, that the cultural pre-eminence of Babylon was recognized throughout Mesopotamian antiquity. For that very reason it was destroyed and rebuilt many times. Traces of Shamshi-adad's palace have been uncovered at Assur but, as much rebuilding has left its mark there too, the most impressive early 2nd-millennium remains are those of Zimri-lim's Mari, which never recovered from Hammurabi's onslaught.**1.56**

›1.55 HAMMURABI RECEIVING INSTRUCTION FROM THE ENTHRONED SHAMASH, GOD OF LAW, at the top of one of the numerous stelae on which his code of laws was inscribed (Paris, Louvre).

1.56 @ 1:2000

›1.56 MARI, PALACE OF ZIMRI-LIM, early 2nd millennium: (a) plan with entrance from the north (1), the main court of audience with recess for the king (2), court of restricted assembly (3), vestibule (4), throne room (5), palatine chapel (6), king's private court (7), harem (8), (b) model of ceremonial core, (c) view from the inner court to the vestibule before the throne room, (d) apotropaic lion guardian of the temple entrance, (e) fragment of fresco decoration from the court of private audience.

Few of the roofs that survived the depredations of Hammurabi can have lasted long and few other 2nd-millennium Mesopotamian buildings survive to roof height, but there are numerous ancient records of timber beams (the best imported from the Levant) and contemporary remains (at Tell el-Rimah, for instance) include the springing of brick voussoir vaulting.

The Mari palace

It is futile to impose a formal order on the plan of a walled complex in general because all that may readily be appreciated in it is the form of each individual space and the transition to its neighbours. At the ceremonial centre, however, that transition is to be seen as all-important: as at Kish and Eshnunna, within the warren of enclosed cells at Mari regular courts of assembly are aligned with public and private audience rooms but discretion and security demanded that passage between them was deflected from the central axis – in the traditional way, as in the palatine temple. And as usual wherever there was a large contingent of royal women, the palace was divided into three zones: an informal harem, a semi-formal one for the king himself, and a formal one for public reception with ancilliary zones for administration, storage and the guard.

Roughly rectangular, the main court of audience was addressed from an off-centre recess for the king which anticipates the iwan of the later

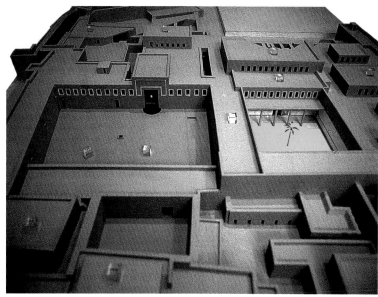

1.56b

Mesopotamian palace tradition. Doors in the four corners led indirectly to the more private parts of the palace, that to the south-west to a vestibule between a court of restricted assembly and the throne room. These regular spaces were aligned on a north–south axis but entry to the throne room was from either side of the vestibule. A similar arrangement distinguishes the palatine chapel in the north-west corner. Beyond the cere-

1.56d

1.56c

monial core, the private apartments and service quarters were knit together by a warren of corridors, and suggest organic growth, though south of the king's most private court the cells of the harem are regularly disposed.

Shamshi-adad's palace at Assur seems to have been similar in distribution but smaller and much more ordered in overall design: if order in either palace goes further than the eye can see, it is as though the once-nomadic Semites had imposed some discipline on the prolix organicism of the natives.

1.56e

Fragments of figurative fresco from Mari provide tantalizing testimony to early 2nd millennium decoration. The portal of a temple at the site was guarded by terracotta lions and there is fragmentary evidence for the device at Isin. The portal of a temple at Tell el-Rimah, a provincial centre established by Shamshi-adad north of Assur, was guarded by deities and the same site provides evidence of an architectonic approach to the relief of walls: exterior and court elevations had engaged columns of varied spiral and quatrefoil designs which represented structure despite their essentially decorative purpose. Spiral

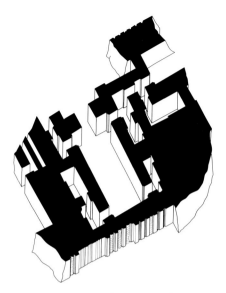

›1.57 SHUBAT ENLIL (TELL LEILAN): isometric plan of acropolis building.

The main building excavated on Tell Leilan, now generally believed to be the site of Shubat Enlil, was a temple with a long central cella apparently entered on axis from a vestibule to its south and flanked by narrow chambers east and west: recalling the ancient tripartite plan established in the north at Tepe Gawra, this seems to anticipate the classic Assyrian axial arrangement of the cella with the entrance in the short end oposite the altar. The surviving façade with the engaged columns is to the north.

columns were also engaged to the outer façade of the temple at Shamshi-adad's main seat, Shubat Enlil: embellishment with engaged columns may follow southern precedents but the plan seems to have been prophetic of classic practice in the north.[1.57, 1.49]

The world of the Fertile Crescent was disrupted in several phases throughout the 2nd millennium BCE by related migrant peoples, horse-borne and equipped with highly manoeuvrable two-wheeled chariots. The main thrust probably came from the Aryans who had descended south through the Caucasus, won dominance in a long contest for Anatolia with the kingdom of the obscure Hattians – non-Indo-European speakers who may have followed trading colonists from Assur – and descended on Mesopotamia from there: these were the Hittites who terminated Hammurabi's line c. 1600.

Carried on fleet chariots in the second half of the 17th century, the first great Hittite kings extended their sway from Hatti over their western neighbours, south-east into northern Syria and on to the capture of Babylon. Faced with troubles in Hatti, they failed to consolidate their hold on Mesopotamia and left the field in the obscurity that still veils the advent of their distant relatives, the Kassites, to power in Hammurabi's seat perhaps as much as two hundred years later.

1.58a

4 THEBAN KINGDOMS OF THE NILE

Constant conflict between the dynasties which ruled in northern and southern Egypt in the First Intermediate Period ultimately resulted in victory for the Theban king Nebhepetre' Mentuhotep of the 11th Dynasty:**1.58a** after at least a decade of effort, beginning c. 2060 (or c. 2010, by the main alternative reckoning, not followed here), he reunited the two lands. Reclaiming divinity for his immortal *ka*, he re-inaugurated the tradition of monumental building – in abeyance since the reign of Pepi II – with a great mortuary complex on a spectacular site at Deir el-Bahri opposite Thebes, which he retained as his capital.

Nebhepetre' Mentuhotep and his line had at least half a century in which to consolidate their position as kings of all Egypt and reassert themselves in Nubia: the ancient list names two more Mentuhoteps, but there is some confusion over the number and dates of the 11th Dynasty kings. However, power passed c. 1990 to the vizier Amenemhet in obscure circumstances and the 12th Dynasty was launched on its splendid career.

Amenemhet I (died c. 1962) established a new capital near Memphis, the better to control the potentially unstable north while directing his efforts to extending his dominion in Nubia – though Thebes remained the seat of power in the south. In this, and in subsequent campaigns in Libya, his principal agent was his heir, Senwosret, who was elevated to co-regency in 1971: the appointment of a co-regent was to be the regular pharaonic method of obviating disputed succession.**1.58b** Fortification and monu-

1.58b

mental building went hand in hand with empire building.**1.59** The tombs of the era were usually relatively modest pyramids but the temple assumed greater importance and set a standard to be emulated as classical in the great age of the New Kingdom after 1500.

Protection of Egypt's boundaries by conquering the neighbours continued in the following reigns. Senwosret III completed the subjugation of Nubia and extended his activity into Palestine, bringing an Asian region under Egyptian control for the first time.**1.58c** And at home the preservation of the integrity of his kingdom prompted the king to reorganize his two lands into four regions to prevent the reconstruction of rival power bases and to augment the authority of the central bureaucracy at the expense of the regional governors – many of whose predecessors had provided for their afterlives in considerable state which doubtless reflected their terrestrial circumstances. One intriguing manifestation of bureaucratic purpose is recorded by the Greek historian Herodotus: he noted that a pharaoh called Sesostris (Senwosret) divided the whole country into square plots for purposes of taxation. Regular division certainly dates from the Egyptian Old Kingdom, though not necessarily using square plots.

The legacy of peace and prosperity was marked in the reigns of Amenemhet III and IV (1844–1799–1787). They were briefly succeeded by a queen before the accession of the 13th Dynasty in 1783. The many kings of that line are undistinguished and the stability and prosperity of the realm seem to have depended on Senwosret III's bureaucracy. As in the late dynasties of the Old Kingdom, royal monuments are sparse, those of officials lavish, but the Middle Kingdom succumbed to traumatic invasion rather than internal division at the hands of autonomous governors. Known as Hyksos, the enigmatic invaders arrived c. 1640 and were not expelled for nearly a century: they pro-

1.58c

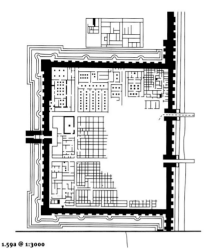

1.59a @ 1:3000

›**1.59 MIDDLE KINGDOM FORTIFICATION — BUHEN, GARRISON TOWN:** (a) plan, (b) walls and west barbican (reconstruction after Emery, 1960).

A string of forts protected communications with the garrisons and traders in Egyptian-occupied Nubia: sites dominating cataracts were of prime strategic importance and one of the main installations was the one at Buhen above the Second Cataract. Defence in depth embraced broad sloping glacis with outer wall and inner ditch, moats, walls doubled (where exposure was marked and to give the defending marksmen varied range), battered (sloping outwards at base to inhibit would-be sappers), crenellated (fringed with masonry shields separated by gaps for marksmen), even machicolated (surmounted with projecting wall walks with holes in their outer edges for dropping missiles on would-be scalers), stoutly buttressed and punctuated with regularly spaced square towers. The main entrance from the desert, elongated and restricted, was through a massive rectangular barbican. The garrison settlement within, also walled, was strictly rectangular and rational in its plan – the prime characteristic of the forts of most advanced powers.

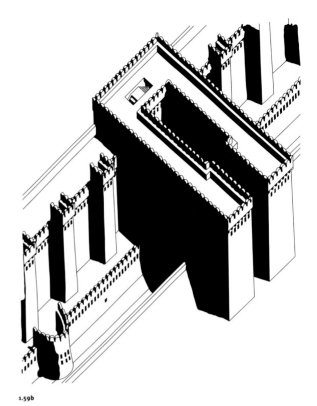

1.59b

duced the 15th Dynasty but its sway was far from complete and rival native powers had emerged in both the Delta and the Theban region well before the end of the 17th century.

Direct involvement with Asia under Senwosret III and his successors, which was certainly not lessened under the Hyksos, prompted important technological developments in Egypt. Hitherto bronze had been imported; now it was smelted at home for the domestic production of utensils and improved weapons. There were improvements to the potter's wheel and to wheeled vehicles: the horse-drawn chariot was introduced by the Hyksos. And to further trade there were important – if limited – advances in fore-and-aft rigging and steerage, enabling ships to sail closer to the wind.[1.34]

GODS AND KING

After the disintegration of the 6th Dynasty and foreign invasion, certainty about the king's relationship to the gods diminished – understandably. Not surprisingly, too, the state cult of the sun had succumbed to the darkness of the intermediate period. When the south reasserted itself against the usurpers and Thebes eclipsed Memphis, the Theban creator-god Amun emerged supreme: in alliance with the local war-god Monthu, his dominance in Upper Egypt was achieved on his association as principal in a triad embracing the war-goddess Mut and the moon-god Khons. His state pre-eminence was then asserted in his association with the local fertility deity Min and above all on his assimilation with northern Re.

In this new dawn, the royal cult of Re was eclipsed by that of his son Osiris as the once-living king, descended from heaven and resurrected from the dead to triumph as lord of the afterlife: hence the king usually had a cenotaph at Abydos, the sacred site of Osiris. Conferred with divine office in his coronation, the Middle Kingdom pharaoh was still the incarnation of Horus, mediator between the gods and man, agent of the creator, but – heir, as it were, to a vanquished god – not quite a god himself until assimilated on his death with Osiris. Responsible for sustaining *ma'at* on earth, protector of the commonweal under the auspices of Amun, he was often shown in touchingly realistic portraits as intelligently careworn in old age or apprehensively committed even in youth, rather than sublimely confident as in the past. **1.58c, 1.33**

HOUSES FOR THE LIVING AND THE DEAD

With the revival of the state under the 11th Dynasty, the symbolic pyramid of the royal tomb was eclipsed by the temples built for the ceremonies involved in the interment

›1.60 DEIR EL-BAHRI, MORTUARY AND CULT COMPLEX OF NEBHEPETRE-MENTUHOTEP, c. 2050: (a) plan, (b) reconstruction.

Preceded by a sacred grove and flanked by cliffs with the rock-cut tombs of his courtiers, Mentuhotep's complex was laid out on two terraces. The first (1), reached by a ramp and projecting forward over a portico of square piers, carried the platform of the second on a solid central core surrounded by colonnades and a thick battered wall which, in turn, was flanked by galleries of more square piers on its outer sides (2). It is traditionally thought that the second terrace was crowned by a small symbolic pyramid but some modern scholars dispute this in favour of a semi-spherical mound or even a flat terrace (3): the massive structure was dedicated to Monthu and its ambulatory was embellished with reliefs depicting life on the Nile, hunting and warfare. On the inner side, the first terrace was extended back into the cliff on axis to the north-west, where it supported a court and offering hall of ten or eleven rows of eight octagonal columns before the inner sanctum (5): the remains of the sanctum reliefs show the king in the company of Amun and receiving symbols of longevity from the gods. From the centre of the court (4), a ramp led down to the tomb chamber excavated from the solid rock under the cliff.

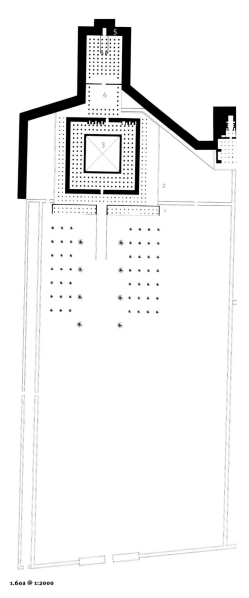

1.60a @ 1:2000

of the king and for the cult of other gods, especially Amun. Due to neglect of the former and much rebuilding of the latter in the New Kingdom and later, their remains are scanty except for the mortuary complex of Nebhepetre' Mentuhotep at Deir el-Bahri.

Like his dynastic progenitors, Nebhepetre was buried in the western rock cliffs opposite Thebes beyond expansive courts and porticoes. Amplifying the local tradition to a much greater extent than his predecessors, his temple differed essentially from the Old Kingdom royal cult complex not only in its position relative to the pyramid – if in fact there was one at all – but also in its form: beyond a square colonnaded court, from which the passage to the tomb descended, was a hypostyle hall enclosing a sanctuary in which the deceased king was associated with Amun. That association, sealed in an annual visit of the god to his son's temple in assertion of Theban dynastic legitimacy, was to be of great importance in the New Kingdom and Nebhepetre's many-columned hall was the first mature example of a major building type.[1.60]

Little survives above the foundations of the 12th Dynasty

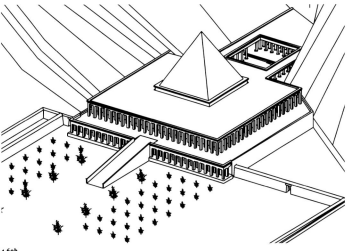

1.60b

– except for the reconstruction of a kiosk built for Senwosret 1's *heb-sed* festival.[1.61] However, based back at Memphis, the early kings of the line revived the fully developed 6th Dynasty formula both for the plan of the king's cult temple and its position east of a pyramid. Archaizing prompted plunder. Stone was quarried from Old Kingdom monuments but the structure of the pyramids was radically different: instead of solid masonry, as in their greatest predecessors, radiating and cross-walls of rough masonry formed compartments for rubble and only the outer casing and the subterranean tomb chamber were of dressed stone. Moreover, the pyramid was set on a podium and the cult temple adjoined the vertical east face of the latter rather than the sloping side of the former, as in the Old Kingdom exemplar.[1.62]

>**1.61 KARNAK: REASSEMBLED KIOSK OF SENWOSRET I**, c. 1930. The elements were recovered from the infill of 18th Dynasty pylons in the Karnak compound.

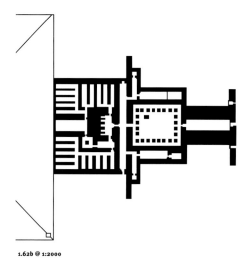

1.62b @ 1:2000

1.62a   1.62c

>**1.62 EL-LISHT: MORTUARY AND CULT COMPLEX OF SENWOSRET I**, c. 1950: (a) Osirian figure of the king (Cairo, Egyptian Museum), (b) plan, (c) the king's Horus emblem (*serekh*) applied in series to the compound walls (New York, Metropolitan Museum).

In so far as the limited traces of superseded foundations testify, the temple, usually dedicated to the state or local deity in each important settlement – constructed or rock-cut – was similar in essence to the king's cult temple. Sometimes it had a forecourt with pylons framing the entrance

Senwosret I's pyramid (105 square metres rising through c. 49 degrees to 61 metres) had a subterranean tomb chamber reached by a ramped corridor from the north. From the river, the cult temple was reached by a causeway lined with Osirian figures: the temple's central court was embellished with reliefs of the king embraced by gods and multiple royal name cartouches surmounted by Horus; beyond a square antechamber (which first appeared in the 6th Dynasty complex and housed at least one image of the king) the offering chamber had the traditional royal banquet scene and the shrine between court and hall had the traditional five barque statue chapels. After El-Lisht, Dahshur was favoured as the site of burial by the later kings of the dynasty, including Senwosret III and Amenemhet III, who augmented their complex with huge temples (now completely dilapidated).

›**1.63** EL-LAHUN: plan of part of Senwosret II's mortuary complex construction and maintenance village, c. 1850, with (1) acropolis with ruins of the governor's establishment, perhaps occupied by the king on site visits, (2) western quarter with the grand houses of the administrators, (3) cellular eastern quarter with back-to-back houses for the workers.

and a portico instead of a full colonnaded court before the entrance to the inner chambers. These typically included a transverse hall before several shrines and a long hall for offerings, as in the Old Kingdom royal cult temple, and as there the number of compartments varied.

In its forecourt and portico, at least, the temple was like the typical house of a man of means and that model was also followed for the rock-cut tombs of many noblemen. The most significant variation on the theme has been traced in the remains of the new town built for the officials and workers engaged on the construction of Senwosret II's tomb at El-Lahun.[1.63]

1.63@ 1:3000

El-Lahun

Rational in the geometry of its layout like its Old Kingdom predecessors,[1.40] El-Lahun was divided into walled zones with standardized housing for the different classes of society. The officials' houses incorporated pillared halls and porticoed courts – the latter beyond the former in the depth of the plot – but the workers were confined to cells grouped back-to-back. Beyond the off-centre entrance, the largest ones on the highest ground (including presumably the palace of the king and/or governor) are clearly ordered with private apartments (for the wife to the left) and service rooms served by corridors about the near-central spine of columned main spaces (for the patron). Otherwise the plans are generally asymmetrical and so too is the arrangement of the doors within the portico of Meket-ra's house – surely implying that the largest one, slightly off centre, leads to the main hall but the side ones lead to various smaller rooms. The model stops short of reproducing them.[1.64a] The domestic distinction of halls and columned courts flanked by smaller rooms is reflected in the design of the typical cult temple but with over-riding concern for axiality.

As an alternative to the perennial mastaba, the rock-cut tomb was favoured by provincial magnates – used to a measure of independent grandeur by the end of the Old Kingdom, throughout the intermediate period and into the Middle Kingdom. Of several sites, Beni Hasan in Middle Egypt is celebrated for its fine porticoes and columned cellas addressed by an image in a chapel above the subterranean burial chamber.[1.64b,c] Naturally there were variations of scale and decorative elaboration, especially in the number of columns, but the reproduction of the domestic formula for representational space – an enclosure with a portico before a hall – is the essence of the exercise. At its simplest, the Middle Kingdom temple (or 'chapel') consisted of a forecourt and portico preceding a cave-like cell excavated from the rock, as in the Beni Hasan tombs.

>1.64 THE MIDDLE KINGDOM HOUSE FOR THE LIVING AND THE DEAD: (a) 11th Dynasty Theban house of Meket-ra, chancellor of Sankhare' Mentuhotep, model from the owner's rock-cut tomb, c. 2000 (New York, Metropolitan Museum of Art); (b, c) Beni Hasan, rock-cut tomb No. 3, section and plan.

1.64a

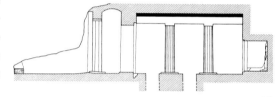

1.64b

In all these types the design of the column and its capital was usually inspired by the papyrus or the lotus – the familiar symbols of Lower and Upper Egypt given structural form at least as early as the 3rd Dynasty. And the repertoire included an abstract, faceted shaft – of eight or sixteen sides – bearing a thin rectangular block to receive the beam, which recalls the type used by Djoser in the north court of his funerary complex at Saqqarah. The simple cylindrical column persisted and so too did the square pier: joined by Osirian images in full relief in mortuary complexes, the pier was now embellished with cult images in fine relief, as in Senwosret I's *heb-sed* kiosk.[1.61]

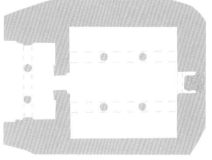

1.64c @ 1:500

1.65a

THE NEW KINGDOM AND EMPIRE

Towards the middle of the 16th century the heir to Upper Egypt at last overcame the Hyksos regime in the Delta, assumed the two crowns and inaugurated the 18th Dynasty of pharaohs as Ahmose (c. 1550–1525). His reign was spent expelling the invaders, regaining the ancient boundaries and consolidating his hold on the reunited land. Rejecting isolation in their quest for security, his heirs penetrated south into Nubia and pursued their enemy into Asia. Thutmosis I (1504–1492) reached the Euphrates. Thutmosis II (1492–1479) was in the process of securing Palestine when he died: his widow took the throne as regent for his young heir, Thutmosis III (1479–1425) but ruled herself as the pharaoh Hatshepsut (1473–1458) and found it prudent to abstain from foreign adventure.**1.65a,b**

On gaining the crown Thutmosis reversed this policy – indeed he attempted to obliterate his step-mother's memory – and took Egyptian arms to their greatest triumph, extended his rule over most of the Levant, crossed the Euphrates, received tribute from Assur and confronted the kingdom of Mittani which had emerged late in the 17th century with the coalescence of the Hurrian holdings to the north of Mesopotamia after the lapse of Hittite suzereinty. The pharaoh had the better of the conflict. Thereafter the Hurrians found it prudent to ally themselves with the Egyptians and cement the alliance with marriage to present a united front to the new Hittite power emerging from Anatolian Hatti.

Amenhotep III (1391–1353?) – who was married to a princess from Mittani, among many other women – was the grand monarch of the golden age of imperial Egypt. However, if the Theban writ ran in Asia, pharaoh's writ was not unchallenged in Thebes. Preoccupied by war, the early 18th Dynasty pharaohs bestowed enormous estates on Amun's Karnak temple in gratitude for success. The inflated priesthood – a bureaucracy in itself – rivalled the civil administration. Amenhotep III attempted containment: his son, Amenhotep IV (1353?–1335), opted for confrontation.

In the New Kingdom the king was still the supreme provider, divine in office and in essence as the manifestation of the eternal Osirian *ka*, but as Amun's warrior in his terrestrial life he was also the hero with all the physical attributes of the perfect athlete – like his foreign opponents.**1.65a** After triumph abroad and the example of Amenhotep III, the pharaoh's pretensions to divinity in this life as the son of Amun-Re were revived in colossal images**1.65b** but his son preferred extremely human realism before mannerist distortion.**1.65c,e** Orthodoxy promoted the 18th Dynasty king as Osiris mummified in full

1.65b

›1.65 PHARAOH AND THE SUPREME GODS OF THE NEW KINGDOM: (a) the virile, heroic Tuhtmose III, 1479–1425 (Karnak, Great Temple); (b) the pacific Queen Hatshepsut, 1473–58 (New York, Metropolitan Museum); (c, d) the immensely grand Amenhotep III, 1391–1353 (fragmentary head, and the Colossi of Memnon, once associated with the ruler's funerary temple; London, British Museum); (e) the ascetic Akhenaten, 1353–1335 (congenital deformity, perhaps, elaborated into a new super-natural ideal in the outer court of the Aten temple, Thebes) (Cairo, Egyptian Museum); (f) Aten worshipped by Akhenaten and his family (Cairo, Egyptian Museum); (g) Queen Tiy as Hathor; (h) Amun protecting Tutankhamun (c. 1330, Paris, Louvre).

1.65c

1.65d

1.65e

regalia in the mortuary context[1.69] and the kings of succeeding dynasties perpetuated that tradition while reasserting supreme virility.[1.73]

Countering the pretensions of the priesthood with pretensions of his own, Amenhotep III reasserted the divinity of the living pharaoh as the son of Amun-Re, with his queen as Hathor. And although he poured unprecedented imperial resources into the amplification of the state cult temple, he celebrated his own divine birth in rebuilding the temple of royal regeneration at Luxor – as Hatshepsut had done in her funerary complex at Deir el-Bahri.[1.66a,b] His son, as Akhenaten, went much further: he denied Amun and the traditional pantheon and presented himself as intermediary for devotion solely to the sun, the source of all life manifest in its disc, Aten.[1.65f] His removal of his seat from Thebes to his new town called Akhetaten – the city of Aten – and his intolerance there for all that concerned Thebes, alienated almost everyone: after his death his young heir was constrained to disclaim Aten and re-embrace Amun as Tutankhamun (1333–1323).[1.65h]

1.65f

1.65g

Akhenaten and his youthful successor were too preoccupied with internal affairs to sustain Egypt's power
abroad in contention with the aggressive Hittites. The
first kings of the 19th Dynasty attempted to regain the initiative. Seti I (1306–1290) won back much of the Levant.
His son, Ramesses II (1290–1224), claimed victory over the
Hittites in the crucial battle of Qadesh on the Orontes but
his great army was probably worsted. However, he
retained his father's gains and built – or reinforced – an
impressive chain of forts in his Levantine domains, as well
as in Nubia and the Western Desert.

The process of royal apotheosis, begun by Amenhotep
III, culminated in the great works of Ramesses II at Thebes
but he established himself back in the Delta and placed
renewed emphasis on Ptah, Re and Osiris. His successors
also favoured the north, partly to escape the thrall of
Amun's establishment, partly to meet the challenge of the
enigmatic Sea Peoples. However, Egypt's fortunes
declined erratically after the impressive Ramesses III
(1194–1163): the initial cause was palatine rivalry but the
invaders proved irresistible and for most of the first millennium Egypt was run by foreigners – or the high priests
of Amun.

1.65h

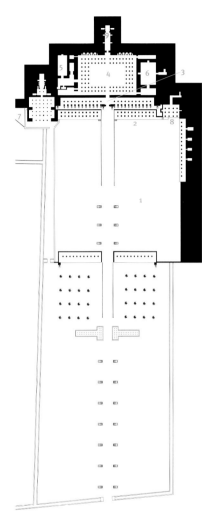

HIDING THE TOMB

Consciously emulating the work of Nebhepetre' Mentuhotep on an even grander scale at the same site, Queen Hatshepsut built a royal cult complex for her father, her husband and herself – not the first funerary work of her dynasty, but certainly the greatest. On the precedent set by her father, the tomb was concealed in the valley beyond the great spur to the north.**1.66**

Hatshepsut at Deir el-Bahri

Dedicated to Amun, Hatshepsut's royal cult complex is approached from a valley temple along an avenue of sphinxes and through a vast forecourt planted with a sacred grove – like Nebhepetre's earlier work. There were three terraces, the lower two with porticoes of square or faceted columns, the upper one supported by double and triple colonnades around the

1.66b @ 1:2000

›1.66 DEIR EL-BAHRI, MORTUARY COMPLEX OF QUEEN HATSHEPSUT: (a, b) reconstruction and plan with forecourt (1), terraces with porticoes of square or faceted columns (2, 3), upper terrace (4), with cult chapels of the queen, her father and her husband (5), the sanctuaries of Re (6), Hathor (7), Anubis (8) and Amun (9), (c,

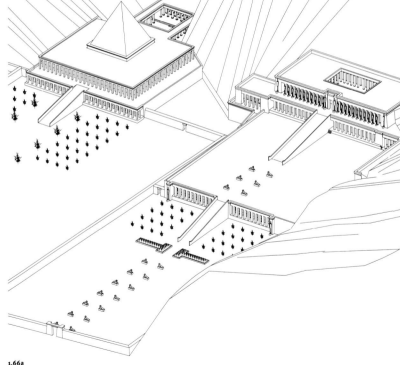

1.66a

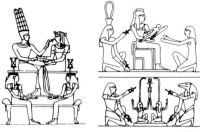

1.66d, e

Mentuhotep's complex, (d, e) drawings after reliefs of the queen's divine birth and Hathor capital from the sanctuary of the mother-goddess, (f) the queen as Osiris, (g) ships on the excursion to Punt and the royal birth record, (drawings of the reliefs in the second terrace colonnade after A. Mariette), (h) Hathor chapel from the neighbouring complex of Thutmosis III.

1.66f

forecourt of the main sanctuary of Amun and his barque – the innermost triple one, before the shrine, approximating the hypostyle hall which some modern scholars believe actually covered the whole upper terace. The lower portico terminates in colossal statues of the queen as Osiris, and similar statues stand before the piers of the higher portico. On that level, cult chapels of the queen, her father and her husband (Thutmosis I and II) were arranged to the left of the court and to the right was the hypethral sanctuary with the altar dedicated to Re. The innermost sanctum on the main axis had a false door.

On either side of the second terrace the scheme was later augmented with the major and minor hypostyle sanctuaries of the mother-goddess

1.66g

1.66h

Hathor and Anubis, guardian deity of burial places and patron of the mummification process. The most celebrated reliefs of the complex are at this level: on the one hand is the essentially terrestrial illustration of the expedition sent by the queen to the elusive land of Punt – with sleek (but still rope-hogged) broad-rigged ships in the quest for ivory, ebony, gold, frankincense and myrrh; on the other is the mystical record of her divine origin as the child of Amun united with her mother, Ahmose, in the guise of her father, Thutmosis I. The latter provided a precedent – or itself amplified one – which was to be of great importance to the royal revival movement several generations later. Images of the queen among the splendid reliefs – whose subjects ascend from the world of man to that of the gods with the ascent of the terraces, naturally – were erased by Thutmosis III. The latter reproduced the scheme of his step-mother's Hathor chapel in miniature: the back wall shows him offering to Amun, to the right he is with his queen, to the left he is nurtured by Hathor.

1.67a

1.67b

›**1.67** THEBES: (a) site plan covering both banks of the Nile showing the relationship of the Valley of the Kings (Biban el-Muluk) to the royal cult temples on the edge of the floodplain on the western bank and to the Karnak and Luxor temples; (b) Valley of the Kings.

1.68a

1.68b

›**1.68 DEIR EL-MEDINA:** (a) tomb of Sennedjem, 'Servant in the Place of Truth', fresco of the patron and his wife in fields and worshipping the Heliopolitan gods under the barque of Re-Harakhte (19th Dynasty); (b) 19th Dynasty pyramid tomb of the Sennedjem type, section.

    The tomb of Sennedjem, an overseer of the workers on the royal necropolis at Deir el-Medina, had a pyramid chapel above ground from which the vertical shaft descends some 4 metres to a corridor leading to several splendidly preserved chambers: the frescoes of life in a sun-blessed land are unexcelled.

Men of means in the New Kingdom built – or excavated – tomb chapels, containing an offering chamber beyond a court from which a shaft descends to the subterranean burial vault: sometimes the chapel was above ground, sometimes in a small pyramid. The royal tombs, of course, were vastly more elaborate. The separation of temple and tomb was henceforth the royal norm. From the reign of Thutmosis III – who built a colonnaded court and sanctuary above the two great terraced complexes at Deir el-Bahri to eclipse his step-mother's work – the former remained in the cliffs beyond the western flood plain opposite Thebes and interment was increasingly distanced from it. Unmarked by any monumental form in the attempt to ensure anonymity, the royal tomb was typically composed of a series of magnificently decorated chambers representing the stages of the king's transition to immortality, as Osiris, along the nocturnal trajectory of the barque of his father, Re. But the ruse of anonymity is known to have worked in only one case: the tomb of Tutankhamun (c. 1333–1323), whose very insignificance was an important factor in ensuring his survival. At the end of a single tunnel, the vestibule, annex and small burial chamber originally destined for the priest Ay (who succeeded the young king on his premature death) stored the royal effects. Box in box contained three sarcophagi in the royal image: the outer two were of timber and gold, the solid-gold innermost one contained his mummified body, and that, finally, was protected by the celebrated gold deathmask.**1.68, 1.69**

AMPLIFYING THE TEMPLE

If there had ever been a valid distinction between the cult temple of the royal mortuary complex and the temples dedicated to other manifestations of divinity, it had been lost by the advent of Nebhepetre' Mentuhotep whose complex at Deir el-Bahri was designed as much to receive

1.69b

The plan is not normally axial, the corridor descending to the tomb chamber departing from the inclined access way at a pronounced angle: there is usually a vestibule at the junction and the other chambers are informally disposed, sometimes between flights of stairs. In the greatest royal tombs the iconographic programme was executed in relief; fresco was more common later and in the tombs of commoners.

1.69a @ 1:1000

1.69c

1.69d

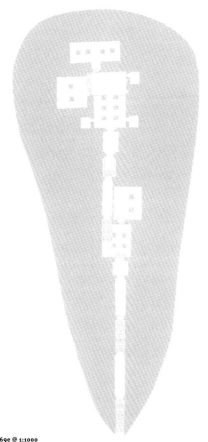

1.69e @ 1:1000

1.69f

1.69h

1.69g

›ARCHITECTURE IN CONTEXT »WEST ASIA AND THE EASTERN MEDITERRANEAN

1.70a

Amun on his pastoral visit to the west as to provide for
royal obsequies. Orientation was usually east–west and
the processional route, essential to the progressive exclu-
siveness of cult ritual, typically embraced a succession of
spaces – lateral and longitudinal entrance halls, colonnaded court, offering hall and chapel for the barque on
which the god was transported in his peregrination –
aligned axially on rising ground before its climax in the
mysterious darkness of the inner sanctum. The number
of shrines and ancilliary chambers might vary, as did the
iconography of individual kings, but from Nebhepetre's
time, at least, the king's *ka* shared the inner sanctum with
Amun.

Inspired by her neighbour at Deir el-Bahri[1.60] – indeed
intent on superseding his temple as the main base of
Amun in the west – Hatshepsut inspired her greatest successors in the amplification of the traditional shrine elements on a vast scale. Within the forbidding enclosure
wall and its entrance at the western end of the processional
axis, marked by masts since time immemorial and by
pylons at least since the early 12th Dynasty, and beyond
the colonnaded court, whose origins are represented in the
works of the Old Kingdom at Saqqarah and Gizeh,[1.41,]
[1.42] the hall of many columns is the main new element in

1.70b

›**1.70 KARNAK AND LUXOR:** (a) reconstructed bird's-eye view showing the relationship between the Great Temples of Amun (Jean-Claude Golvin, Paris, National Centre for Science Research); (b) Great Temple of Karnak: view from the east.

›**1.71 KARNAK, GREAT TEMPLE OF AMUN:** (a) main axis opened by the avenue of sphinxes guarding the king's way from the river to the first pylon, (b) obelisk of Hatshepsut, (c) *heb-sed* festival hall of Thutmosis III, nave to aisles, (d) plan of the precinct with inner sanctum (1), pylons of Thutmosis I (1504–1492) with obelisks of Hatshepsut (1473–1458) between them (2, 3), pylon of Thutmosis III (4), *heb-sed* festival hall of Thutmosis III (1479–1425) (5), southern axial courts and pylons of Thutmosis III or Hatshepsut (6, 7), and Horemheb (1319–1307) (8, 9), main axial pylons of Amenhotep III (1391–1353) (10), and Horemheb (11), great hypostyle hall of Seti I and

this definitive elaboration of the temple complex. The greatest examples are the linked temples of Amun at Karnak and Luxor.**1.70** The latter's definitive form was achieved between the reigns of Amunhotep III and Ramesses II. The great Karnak complex, with its subsidiary temples, ablution tank, offices, accommodation for priests and pilgrims, stores, etc., was built and rebuilt over more than fifteen hundred years.**1.71**

The Temple of Amun at Karnak

First built on a grand scale by Senwosret I, the complex at Karnak was renovated in the reign of Thutmosis I and immeasurably enriched by successive pharaohs with votive offerings to their supreme patron. An important axis leads south to the Temple of Mut and on to Luxor in south-

ern Thebes but the main axis runs east–west from the river in accordance with traditional practice. Nowhere better illustrates exclusive cult progression straight through varied spaces, diminishing in scale and light, to the intimacy of the inner sanctum.

Thutmosis I was responsible for the earliest surviving pylons c. 1500, four obelisks before the outer one (of which one remains standing) and the hall between them. In front of the inner pylon Queen Hatshepsut inserted two more obelisks (of which one remains standing).[1.45] Thutmosis III built the innermost pylon, the court before it and the vestibule and chapel before the inner sanctum for the solar barque on which the statue of Amun was carried in processions. Beyond a court behind the sanctum, he erected a separate temple probably for his *heb-sed* festival: the principal element is a hypostyle hall with its nave of twenty-four columns perpendicular to the main axis of the complex and rising above square piers on all four sides.

Thutmosis III (or Hatshepsut) opened the southern axis with two courts and pylons, aligned with the outer entrance obelisks of Thutmosis I. The southern axis was continued with two further courts and pylons by Horemheb. Meanwhile, Amenhotep III had added another massive pylon to the west of the obelisks of Thutmosis I, and Horemheb added yet

Ramesses II (1306–1290–1224) (12), barque temple of Ramesses III (1194–1163) (13), Temple of Khons, 18th and 20th Dynasties (14), Temple of Ptah, 18th and 30th Dynasties (15), western pylons, 21st–30th Dynasties (16), (e, f) great hypostyle hall of Seti I, nave to aisles showing papyrus columns with open-flower and closed-bud capitals, and detail of clerestory; (g) section through the Temple of Khons; (h) imaginative reconstruction of a temple of the Khons type, viewed from the outer court (F.A. Stuler, c. 1850, Berlin, New Museum).

another further west in front of which Ramesses II installed his colossal statues. Between these pylons, Seti I and Ramesses II installed the stupendous hypostyle hall of 134 papyrus columns. The central twelve, with open-flower capitals, rise to 21 metres to lift the nave roof above the level of the side aisles over a clerestory. The columns of the sixteen aisles, with closed-bud capitals, rise to 13 metres. The reliefs on the surrounding walls include scenes of the military triumphs of Ramesses II in the Levant – real or imagined – including the battle of Qadesh.

The avenue of sphinxes leading from the river is mainly attributable to the 21st Dynasty: the image of the king usually borne by the sphinx is

1.71c

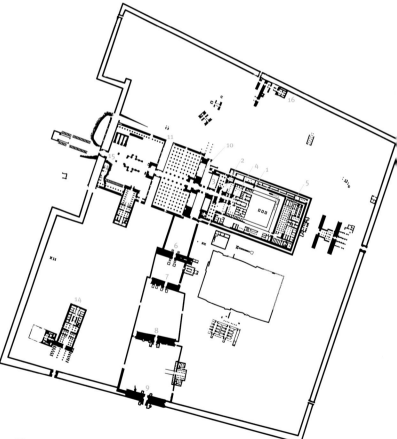

1.71d @ 1:5000

1.71e

1.71f

1.71h

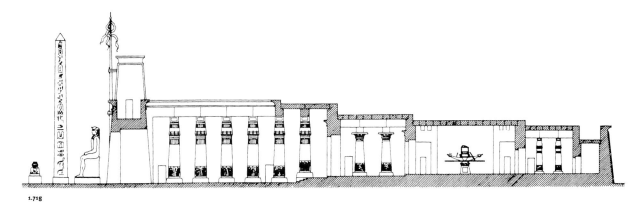

1.71g

here replaced by the head of Amun's sacred ram. Never completed, the outermost pylon was probably also conceived under the 21st Dynasty, though much of the structure seems to date from the 30th Dynasty. In the north-west corner of the first court – substantial elements of which date from the 35th Dynasty – is the barque shrine of Seti I. Breaching the southern wall is a complete miniature temple for the barque built by Ramesses III. Elsewhere in the precinct of Amun are numerous other chapels and shrines, of which the most important is the Temple of Khons to the south.

The origin of the hypostyle hall type in the many-poled marquee – and, beyond that, of the palace in the camp of many tents – is explicit in the *heb-sed* festival hall built by Thutmosis III for the royal regeneration ceremony beyond the sanctuary of Amun at Karnak: the tent-pole columns of this putative basilica reproduce the slender wooden poles of the traditional Egyptian canopy[1.41] in monumental masonry but the great work of Seti I substitutes the traditional closed and open papyrus columns, the latter rising above the former to admit light through and support a deep-blue ceiling spangled with stars. If the temple stands for the sacred island, its sanctuary raised on the primeval mound, the hypostyle hall transcends its origins as a tent and stands for the sacred grove of primeval vegetation.

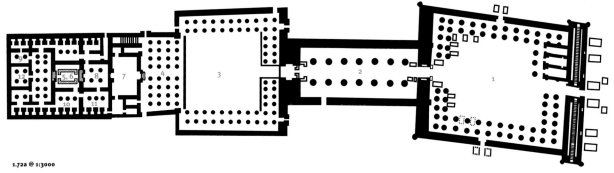

1.72a @ 1:3000

THE ROYAL CULT TEMPLE

By the accession of Amenhotep III at the height of the New Kingdom, Amun-Re was embarking annually in great splendour on two festival processions of seminal importance to his terrestrial agent. Probably initiated by Nebhepetre' Mentuhotep and revived by Hatshepsut, as we have noted, one was across the river to the west where the god was installed in his chapel at Deir el-Bahri and visited successive pharaohs in the realm of eternal repose. The other was south to Luxor where the cyclical regeneration of *ma'at*, instituted in the divine monarchy, had been celebrated at least since the reign of Hatshepsut. The most significant temples of the New Kingdom were built for these events.

The temple at Luxor, founded in the Middle Kingdom, rebuilt on a colossal scale by Amenhotep III and extended by Ramesses II, was the destination of Amun-Re on the annual festival procession from his principal seat at Karnak held early in the season of the Nile's flood. In principle (but not invariably) the god went on land and, rejuvenated, returned in triumph on the flood. The culmination of the land route of progression from the great temple's successive southern courts and pylons, along a sphinx-lined avenue parallel to the river, Amenhotep's work established the axial canon for the great imperial sanctuary.**1.72**

Assertive in its symmetry, the complex evolved over an extended campaign beginning under Amenhotep III with the sanctuary and terminating under Ramesses II with the forecourt on its divergent axis. To the south of the exceptional clerestory-lit hall, with open papyrus-bud capitals and images of the barque procession, the Court of the Sun, with its exemplary closed papyrus-bundle columns was the first element in the amplification of the original programme under Amenhotep III but was embellished under Tutankhamun with images of the culmination of the barque procession.

The reliefs embellishing the various chambers give some clues to the procedure within. First, in the Chamber of the Divine King, pharaoh resubmitted himself to the purification rites that fitted him for the endowment of divinity. In the sanctuary, the lodge of the divine visitor from Karnak (partially rebuilt c. 325), the king made key regenerative offerings (new flood-water and new plant life were among them) to Amun as Re and Min who, regenerated, witnessed the re-enactment of the coronation as the renewed transmission of his divine power to his terrestrial agent. This was recorded in the Coronation Chamber beside the sanctuary to the east and beyond that the Birth Chamber displayed the regeneration of the divine *ka* in the person of Amenhotep III: following the example set at Deir el-Bahri for Queen Hatshepsut, Amun is shown embracing the king's mother Queen Mutemwia in the guise of the king's father Thutmosis IV. The raised reliefs of Amenhotep's period, immaculate in their precision yet infused with vitality, mark the apogee of the technique. The court of Ramesses II, with statues of the king in the southern quarters, is entered past a pair of obelisks, six colossal statues and pylons bearing reliefs of the king victorious at Qadesh.

1.72b

1.72d

1.72c

Certainly no less axial but essentially uncanonical, of course, was the temple of Aten built by Amenhotep's heretical heir at his new capital, Akhetaten – and his several Aten shrines there and earlier in Thebes. In the elongated succession of courts in the great compound at Akhetaten, open to the sun's rays, a multitude of altars provided for sacrificial offerings to the ineluctable deity and the normal sanctuary in the innermost zone was replaced by high altars for the royal family's offerings.**1.65g** It soon disappeared in the religious counter-revolution that prompted Tutankhamun's recantation**1.65h** and has left little trace either in the sand or in Egypt's subsequent architectural history.

Exceptional too, in scale and iconography if not type, is the Great Temple of Ramesses II carved from the rock at Abu Simbel. There is no inner court, the hall is reduced to a minimum and the most powerful impression is made by the restricted passage to the sanctum, where colossal statues of the king as Osiris stand in sinister sentinel.**1.73** The prominence given to the Memphite and Heliopolitan gods Ptah and Re beside Amun, the inclusion of the king among them and his repeated representation on the façade as superhuman mark the culmination of the king's reassertion of divinity in challenge to the power of the priests of Karnak: nothing in the history of architecture asserts exclusivity more persuasively, or the pretensions of the patron more potently, than these giant images – except perhaps the Great Sphinx.**1.42d**

The ground for the reassertion of the king's divine prerogative was assiduously cultivated by Amenhotep III, as we have noted, and it was he who set the pattern for the colossal royal cult temple – and the colossal royal cult image – on the west bank.**1.66** After the example of Hatshepsut, he developed the traditional plan on the edge of the floodplain at Memnon, distant from his tomb: beside

›**1.73 ABU SIMBEL, GREAT TEMPLE OF RAMESSES II,** dedicated to Amun-Re and, possibly, also to the king himself as Re, c. 1290: (a) plan, (b) general view on original site, (c, d) interior of main hall and inner sanctum; (e) associated temple of Queen Nefertari; (f, pages 134–135) exterior after relocation during the construction of the Aswan High Dam.

The tradition of rock-cut temples was strong in Nubia and by the 19th Dynasty, when Ramesses II commissioned a string of them, its elaboration was advanced. As in this stupendous work, there was usually a forecourt, partially excavated, leading to the first great excavated chamber, a galleried hall, and on through an offering chamber to the shrine. Instead of pylons, colossal statues of the founder are accompanied by smaller ones of members of the royal family on the rock-face façade – 35 metres wide by 32 metres high. The relatively low door beneath the relief of Re in the centre leads to the hall of piers with attached colossal statues of the king as Osiris and reliefs commemorating the king's divine endowment, his victories as a warrior and the dedication of his conquests to the gods. The main sanctuary, flanked by unadorned chapels, contains statues of Ptah, Amun, the king himself and Re, which are lit by the rising sun twice a year. A smaller temple nearby, dedicated to Hathor, likewise exalted Ramesses II's queen, Nefertari.

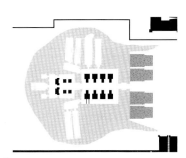

1.73a @ 1:2000

1.73c

1.73d

1.73b

1.73e

the king himself, several gods were honoured there but the principal objective is proclaimed in the foundation inscription as 'a resting place for the Lord of the Gods at his Festival of the Valley in Amun's procession to visit the Gods of the West when he will reward His Majesty with life and dominion'.

1.74a

>1.74 EARLY RAMASSID HELIOPOLITAN AND OSIRIAN WORKS: (a, b) detail of relief from chapel of Ramesses I, c. 1310 (New York, Metropolitan Museum of Art) and plan of Seti I's cenotaph temple at Abydos; (c) model of entrance obelisks, sphinxes and pylons of a temple to the sun in its various aspects projected by Seti I and/or his son (New York, Brooklyn Museum of Fine Arts); (d) relief portrait of Ramesses II probably from his cenotaph temple at Abydos.

Dedicated to the cult of the king as Osiris, to the divine triad, Osiris, Isis and Horus, to the paternal Heliopolitan creator-god, Re-Harakte, to his Theban identity as Amun-Re, to the Memphite creator Ptah, Seti I's cenotaph temple is exceptional in its lateral sequence of seven inner-sanctum shrines spanning the whole width of the main block, preceded by two transverse hypostyle halls, and in its extension into a north-western wing for the accommodation of the Memphite triad of Ptah-Sakhmet-Nefertem and Sokar (the necropolis-god) and of the holy barque: the meticulous reliefs are among the last in the raised, rather than incised, technique. Seti's son Ramesses II revised and reduced the formula for his cenotaph temple at the same site, distributing triads of shrines to the sides of two octastyle halls and surrounding the main court with colonnades.

Other than the mutilated colossi of the king, which once guarded the front, little remains of the huge scheme at Memnon. The theme was restated by the two greatest Ramessid kings for their mortuary complexes nearby on the Theban west bank. Meanwhile, Seti I had prepared the way in west Thebes and met the special requirements of his cenotaph temple at Abydos – reassertion of the Heliopolitan and Memphite gods *vis-à-vis* Theban Amun – with a unique scheme, celebrated for its transverse hypostyle halls and its superb reliefs.**1.74, 1.75**

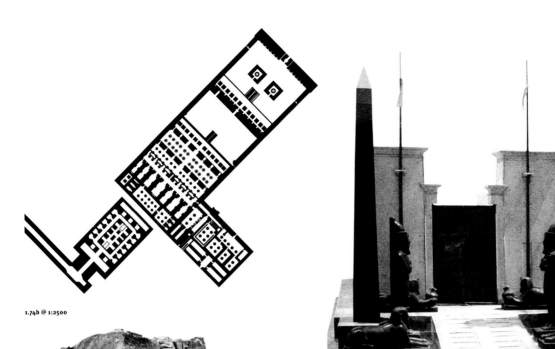

1.74b @ 1:2500

1.74c

1.74d

The royal cult temple

The Ramessid temples in west Thebes – the earlier one strangely distorted into a parallelogram, the later one strictly regular but somewhat
less ample – each has two courts with pylons, the first with Osirian statues attached to the eastern range of piers, the second with similar figures
on the north front of a double colonnade before the 'basilican' hypostyle
hall – introduced by Seti I not only at Karnak but also in his west-bank cult
temple. Beyond that were two smaller colonnaded halls, the inner one a
chapel for the holy barque, before the sanctuary. This main spine is
flanked by shrines to Re (north) and Monthu (south) and the whole is surrounded by courts for ritual sacrifices, stores and accommodation.

After the reassertion of his divinity, the living pharaoh needed accommodation when taking part in ceremonies associated with his cult:

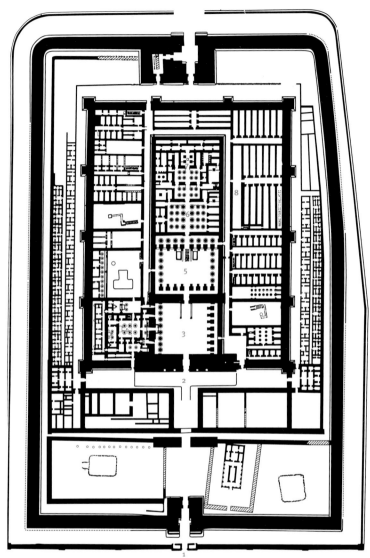

›1.75 MADINET HABU: MORTUARY AND CULT COMPLEX OF RAMESSES III: (a) plan with outer defence wall and gate (1), inner compound wall and pylon (2), outer court (3) with palace (4), inner court (5), hypostyle hall (6), inner sanctum (7), magazines, etc. (8), (b) great gate of outer enclosure, (c) inner enclosure, (d) first court of main compound, (e) pylon relief of the king in his chariot.

Ramesses III's complex was heavily defended in depth with a ditch preceding massive ramparts (10.5 metres thick at the base, 16 metres high) punctuated with towering gates to the east and west built in a style identified as Syrian: large enough for limited habitation, the eastern one had a window of appearances and reliefs showing the king with his women; this has led to its improbable identification as the harem.

hence the outer court is also the forecourt to a small palace in the Ramessid complexes – as presumably at Memnon. Relief fragments suggest that the Ramesseum, at least, also had a 'royal birth chapel' like Amenhotep III's Luxor temple.

1.75c

1.75d

1.75e

Beyond the canonical pylons, colonnaded court, outer and inner hypostyle halls, offering chamber and sanctuary, the 'royal birth chapel' (Mammisi Temple, dedicated to the birth of the pharaoh from Horus and a mortal mother under the auspices of Isis/Hathor) is a feature of the splendidly preserved temples with which – after well over five hundred years of hiatus in monumental building – the Ptolemaic rulers emulated their greatest imperial predecesors.**1.15, 1.16**

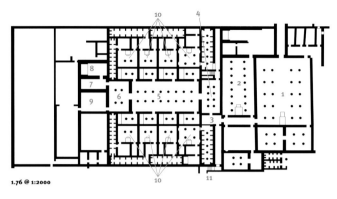

1.76 @ 1:2000

THE PALACE

The 'basilican' columned hall, like the great hypostyle hall of Seti I at Karnak, was the major element of the palace, too. The remains of the residence of Amenhotep III at El-Malqata (west Thebes), supplemented by those of the palace of his successor Akhenaten at Akhetaten, provide a rare image of how the pharaoh lived at the height of Ancient Egyptian civilization.**1.76, 1.77**

Malqata and Amarna

The palace at El-Malqata is thought to have been the principal residence of the most opulent of the Egyptian kings. The complex consisted of several autonomous units with courts, halls and pavilions disposed to the north, east and south of a great court entered from the west. The arrangement was somewhat organic, with ceremonial halls and the palatine temple to the north, private apartments to the south and the servants in between, but the main units were formal in themselves – and that at least is reproduced in miniature in the palaces of the Ramessid cult complexes. The main halls were all aisled basilicas. In the outer two, for public and restricted audience, the nave was dominated by a throne opposite the entrance; the innermost hall, flanked by the apartments of queens and princesses, led to a throne room before the king's own antechamber, bedroom and bathroom.

Akhenaten's ceremonial palace at Amarna had a double-aisled basilica to the south of the main court and a vast hypostyle hall – possibly built for the coronation of his co-regent Smenkaure – in a separate compound.

›1.76 EL-MALQATA (WEST THEBES), PALACE OF AMENHOTEP III: plan of the king's quarters.

Entrance to the first hall of the king's personal quarters (1) was from the west through a corridor linked to a neighbouring range of buildings south of the main court. This hall was probably divided into a nave and aisles by four rows of columns. A throne dominated the nave from its eastern end, opposite the entrance. Another corridor led from the southern corner of the hall, along the end of another columned basilican throne room (2), to a vestibule (3) at the eastern end of a third columned hall (4), parallel to the others. After a third right-angle turn in the centre of this third hall, the main axis culminated in a grand central hall (5) and throne room (6). Beyond this was the king's own apartment, which consisted of antechamber, bathroom and bedroom (7–9). To either side of the higher central hall were the apartments (10) of the principal women of the court, the king's sisters and daughters, but apparently not the quarters of his principal wife, Queen Tiy. Her palace (11) was to the east of the king's quarters. The two were joined at the vestibule, which opened on to the central axis via a passage at right angles to it, and to the corridor from the entrance hall. Column bases and door cills were of stone, but otherwise the structure was of timber and mud-brick.

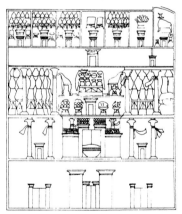

1.77a

›1.77 AKHETATEN (TELL EL-AMARNA), mid-14th century, central ceremonial area: (a) representation of the residential palace of Akhenaten with its

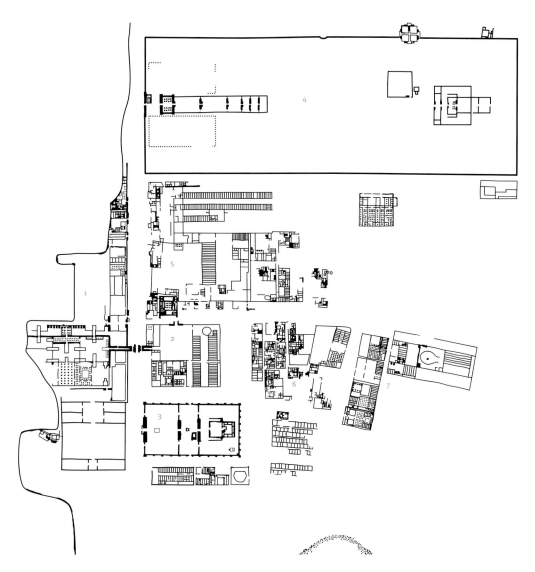

1.77b @ 1:7500

outer to inner zones layered from bottom to top (from the tomb of Meryre at Amarna), (b) plan with (1) ceremonial palace with great court to the north, flanked by the so-called harem buildings on the east and the audience hall and ancillary spaces (centre), with the great festival hall to the south, (2) the king's private quarters, (3) palatine Temple of Aten, (4) Great Temple of Aten, (5) storehouses, (6) offices, (7) barracks.

The royal family's quarters were set in a garden compound, linked to the ceremonial court by a bridge over the main road. The main spaces were embellished with images representing their use. Less formal rooms were elegantly decorated with motifs drawn from nature, especially the flora and fauna of the river. Even floors were plastered and painted, often with a pool surrounded by reeds with birds and animals, as in a garden.**1.78**

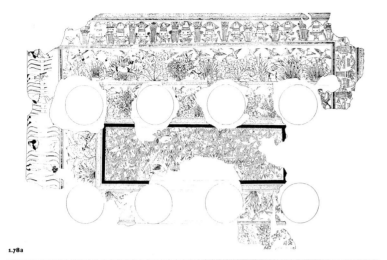

1.78a

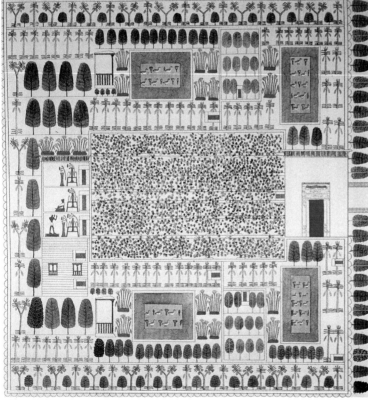

1.78b

›1.78 GARDEN IMAGERY IN 18TH-DYNASTY
DECORATION: (a) Akhetaten, palace of Akhenaten,
drawing of polished plaster floor; (b) West Thebes,
tomb of Sennefer, mayor of Thebes and overseer of
gardens under Amenhotep II, drawing of vault fresco
(c. 1410).

›1.79 THE NOBLE HOUSE: (a) The vizier Nakht's
Amarna residence, reconstructed plan with entrance
through two vestibules and three right-angle turns to
the main reception hall (1); at right angles to this hall
and aligned with the central bay of its colonnade is the
central living/dining room (2) with its large divan platform and smaller washstand; flanking and insulating
this central space, in addition to service rooms and
storehouses, was a second hall to the west (3) and a
withdrawing room to the south (4) between two apartments – as in the palace, these consisted of antechambers, bathrooms and bedrooms (5–7). The staircase
obviously implies a second storey, presumably of
rooms for other members of the family; (b) Thutnefer's
Theban residence.

Compared with Nakht's Amarna residence, the
typical Theban residence, even of a grand official,
had less room to expand like a villa in a garden. In
Thutnefer's main central space is a hall, presumably
with four columns, surmounted by a less-elevated
room, also with columns. Beyond these are more private reception rooms surmounted by withdrawing
rooms. The basement was apparently given over to
service and crafts.

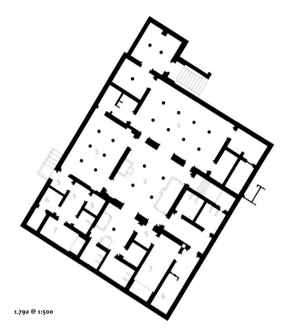

1.79a @ 1:500

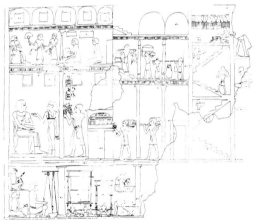

1.79b

The house of Akhenaten's vizier Nakht at Akhetaten was a villa in its own garden: a square, court-like room was preceded by a great hall and surrounded by private suites on its other sides.[1.79] Columns raised the central room's roof above the level of the others to admit light through windows in the superstructure. With less ground, especially on older-established sites, the better houses would usually have a vestibule, columned hall and reception room with clerestory, backed or flanked by bedrooms and bathrooms and aligned to the south of a portico and entrance court.

The Egyptian villa garden introduces all the features of formal landscaping to be developed over the following three millennia: regular enclosure; plants, useful as well as beautiful, set in ordered rows and clipped to regular forms (topiary); a central axis with symmetrical paths; pools for irrigation and fish; a framework for climbing plants to provide shade (pergola); and statues representing the gods presiding over a special place descended from the sacred grove, the scene of the mystery of growth, of the provision of food and medicine, where people confronted the forces of nature over which they had little control but upon which they depended for their existence.[1.79]

THE TOWN: GRIDS AND ZONING

Old Memphis and Thebes were doubtless as organic in their growth as the cities of Sumer – or any other natural settlement. The new capital built by royal decree on a fresh site, Akhetaten seems to have been planned with three dominant arteries parallel to the river between affluent residential suburbs north and south and something of a grid in its centre, though its development along the river seems to have obviated further order. No doubt the grid took the great hypethral temple of Aten and the royal palace as its points of departure[1.77] – though it is obviously efficient to provide regular blocks for houses without awkward junc-

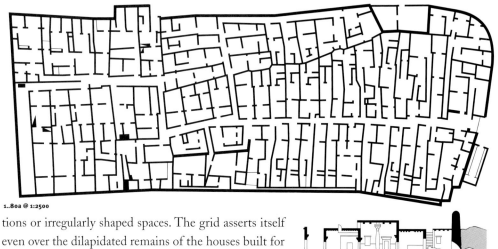

1..80a @ 1:2500

tions or irregularly shaped spaces. The grid asserts itself even over the dilapidated remains of the houses built for the workers of Ramesses III at Madinet Habu as it had done at the height of the Old Kingdom at Gizeh, in Middle Kingdom El-Lahun and at Deir el-Medineh at the outset of the New Kingdom.**1.80, 1.40, 1.63**

1.80b

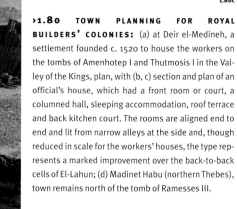

1.80c

>**1.80 TOWN PLANNING FOR ROYAL BUILDERS' COLONIES:** (a) at Deir el-Medineh, a settlement founded c. 1520 to house the workers on the tombs of Amenhotep I and Thutmosis I in the Valley of the Kings, plan, with (b, c) section and plan of an official's house, which had a front room or court, a columned hall, sleeping accommodation, roof terrace and back kitchen court. The rooms are aligned end to end and lit from narrow alleys at the side and, though reduced in scale for the workers' houses, the type represents a marked improvement over the back-to-back cells of El-Lahun; (d) Madinet Habu (northern Thebes), town remains north of the tomb of Ramesses III.

1.80d

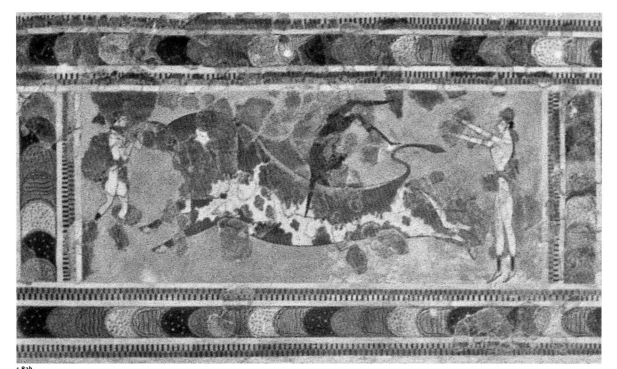

1.82b

1.2 THE AEGEAN, ANATOLIA AND THE ARYANS

5 MINOANS AND ACHAEANS

CRETE

About the time that the greatest phase of development at Stonehenge was approaching its apogee, Old Kingdom Egypt had disintegrated, Ur had been reduced to confusion by the Amorites, and the first true civilization in the orbit of Europe was emerging in Neolithic Crete. The earliest inhabitants of the island, which straddles the southern Aegean, possibly crossed from Asia Minor in the Ice Age, when the Mediterranean was low, but similarities between early Cretan and Anatolian Neolithic culture suggest that an important contingent, at least, may have come much later – at about the time of Catal Huyuk.

The island prospered on settled agriculture, in particular on olives and grapes, which its rocky terrain was always to excel at producing, and on wool. The settlers proliferated and the agglomeration of their irregular, flat-roofed houses had become towns by the middle of the 3rd millennium. Further immigration from Anatolia followed Aryan invasion there and cultural assimilation was advanced by maritime contact, particularly in ways of regulating and organizing rural and urban society, writing and recording, which were derived through the

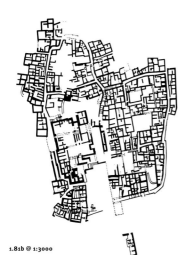

1.81b @ 1:3000

1.81c

>**1.81** THE UNDEFENDED ORGANIC MINOAN TOWN AND ITS HOUSE: (a) Thera (Santorini), fresco with ships off a Cretan palace-city (before 1500, when the volcanic island exploded; Athens, National Museum); (b, c) Gournia, plan and overview; (d) faience plaques of fenestrated house façades (Knossos, early 18th century).

1.81d

Levant from the Fertile Crescent or directly from Egypt.

About the beginning of the 2nd millennium, the appearance of great extroverted palaces on the edges of the hive-like urban organisms marked the advent of a new civilization, specifically Cretan if not uninfluenced by Mesopotamia. Its wealth was based on trade between Egyptians and Phoenicians, Anatolians and Europeans and through its intermediacy the west gained much from the civilizations of the east. Its power was maritime, advanced by the great improvements in sea-going shipping following the Egyptian introduction of the rectangular sail to supplement man and his oar in the late 3rd millennium and subsequent improvements in rigging and steerage.**1.34d** As the main maritime powers were its trading partners and large aggressive navies had yet to be launched, it felt secure enough for its seaside centres to be undefended.**1.81**

MINOS AND THE BULL

Long before the import of wealth, Cretan attitudes were moulded by the combination of agriculture and pastoralism. Their towns grew naturally in accordance with the contours of the site, as in ancient Anatolia.**1.7** Seeking harmony

1.82a

›1.82 THE CRETAN BULL: (a) Knossos, Palace of Minos, fresco from the north portico c. 1600, bull with leaping youths; (b, page 145) Hagia Triada, fresco from a sarcophagus, 14th-century bull sacrifice (Herakleion, Archaeological Museum).

Minoans slaughtered bulls in sacrifice, and bull leaping was probably part of the preparatory rites that took place in the great court of Minos's palace at Knossos. The most sacred ceremony of the Cretan calendar, central to the New Year festival as in Mesopotamia, was the remarriage of the priest-king to the mother-goddess (the queen as priestess), which stood for the annual death and rebirth of the vegetation-god. Minos was descended from the union of the mother-goddess and her consort, whom he impersonated in the remarriage ceremony, but he was also the son of Zeus disguised as a bull, and the bull was his natural surrogate when his death and replacement ceded to remarriage each year.

with cyclical nature, like their Anatolian antecedents, the islanders were originally devoted primarily to the mother-goddess – especially in her manifestation as the moon, mistress of animals. At each New Year regeneration festival she married a sacrificial consort. Excited to resurrection in phallic cults, focused on pillars – natural like a stalactite in the womb of a cave or fashioned by man – the consort survived sacrifice as priest-king and found a surrogate in the bull, icon of male potency, whose horns appear on palace terraces. The king's symbol was the sacrificial axe with its double moon-shaped heads, the *labrys*. His ascendancy informed the legend of Minos, after whom the civilization is called Minoan.**1.82**

Minos was the son of the great sky-god whom the later Greeks called Zeus. Zeus was the Cretan-born son of Kronos and Rhea – themselves the offspring of Uranus, king of the heavens, and the earth-mother Gaia. Having gained supremacy, Zeus disguised himself as a bull to abduct the Phoenician princess Europa: Minos was the product of their union. Minos's wife, Queen Pasaphae, also coupled with a bull: the issue was the man-bull Minotaur. The Greek legend of Theseus concerns Crete's rule in the Aegean world, the future Hellas, and exaction as tribute of the flower of its youth to be devoured by the Minotaur in his incomprehensible labyrinth: that may have been the characteristic Cretan necropolis of rock-cut room-like tombs or Minos's palace at Knossos.**1.83**

Knossos

There were several autonomous palatine cities on Crete, but Knossos, first built c. 2000 and rebuilt after a catastrophe c. 1700, seems to have been the seat of a pre-eminent religious, secular and economic authority: the palace was in fact a temple, royal residence and centre for the collection and redistribution of supplies. Organic in its growth about a court, like its lesser contemporaries, yet outward-looking to the landscape through loggias and terraced to the contours of the site, the flat-roofed agglomeration of rooms was served by circuitous corridors, which must indeed have seemed labyrinthine.

More completely organic than any in Mesopotamia and always growing, the complex had three once-independent, well-drained, multi-storey zones about the great court. The western wing accommodated royal ceremonial and cult ritual, notably pillar worship, beside and above stores for produce and archives hardly less extensive than those of the most assiduous Mesopotamian bureaucratic record keepers; the eastern one housed the king and his family; the north was divided between guests and servants.

Excavated and partially restored from 1900 by Sir Arthur Evans, who named its spaces, the palace is approached from the south over a viaduct and from the west up the 'Royal Road' or 'Sacred Way'. At the top of this

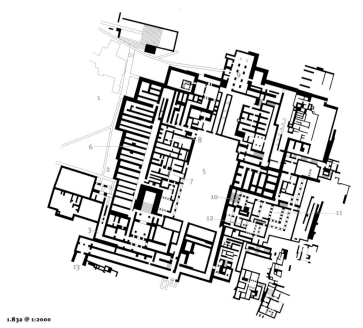

1.83a @ 1:2000

›1.83 KNOSSOS, PALACE OF MINOS, largely rebuilt c. 1700 after incorporating parts of the palace begun three centuries earlier: (a) view through colonnade and over terrace to the countryside, (b) plan with (1) 'West Court', (2) western entrance, (3) 'Corridor of the Processions', (4) portico and grand staircase to ceremonial rooms on the first floor, (5) great central court, (6) magazines, (7) pillared crypt below the ceremonial rooms, (8) 'Throne Room', (9) northern entrance and portico, (10) royal apartments, main staircase, (11) 'Hall of the Double Axes' in the king's quarters, (12) 'Queen's Suite', (13) southern entrance, (c) main staircase to royal apartments, (d) so-called bull portico and its context south of main court, (e) 'Queen's Suite' and adjoining colonnaded court, (f) 'Throne Room', detail showing restored frescoes with heraldic beasts; (g) Amnisos villa, lily panel.

1.83c

route is a stepped platform for ceremonial performances (called the 'theatral area'), beyond which is the northern entrance. This leads through a grand pillared hall and corridor directly to the central court. Separating the public and private ranges, the latter was overlooked from loggias and served as an arena for ritual contests such as bull leaping. Though the concept of the court was probably borrowed from Mesopotamia, it was not a place of assembly orientated to the rooms of state with preconceived formality, but residual space encroached upon by service rooms.

The principal entrance to the state apartments in the west wing, known as the 'West Court', opens from the south-west corner of the piazza south of the 'theatral area' and west of the palace. This leads from a portico, with one column in antis, to the processional corridor – with its vivacious fresco of processing tribute-bearers – which turns through a right-angle towards a grand inner propylon. To the north of this was the ceremonial staircase to the main audience halls on the first floor. The stout walls supporting them, not necessarily related to the superstructure, enclosed the storage magazines and crypts. Two of the latter contain stone pillars inscribed with the sacred *labrys* and flanked by shallow troughs to receive the liba-

1.83d

The 'Royal Villa' to the west of the palace was built to a small scale in the late Minoan period: not the product of organic growth, it was asymmetrical by design if more formal than the Minoan norm. The 'Royal Villa' (c. 1600) at Amnisos near the harbour yielded the celebrated wall decoration with a lily motif.

tions of a fertility cult, doubtless involving the dedication of agricultural produce from the neighbouring stores at a harvest festival. To the north is the so-called 'Throne Room'. A splendid throne, flanked by benches, was found here: addressing a sunken tank in an open court (one of several in the palace) and with adjoining facilities for ritual libation, it was possibly the scene of the king's annual remarriage to the mother-goddess.

The royal apartments in the east wing are ranged on five levels connected by the magnificent staircase restored by Evans. At its foot, the 'Hall of the Colonnades' is joined by a corridor to the king's main living room – called the 'Hall of the Double Axes' by Evans because of the many *labrys* carved into its walls. Subdivided by piers, lit from a court to the west and connected with another suite to the south (called the 'Queen's Suite' without evidence), it opened through a colonnade on the east and south to a garden terrace and magnificent view of the valley below. There were similar suites upstairs. The interiors were renovated in the late-Minoan period and restored after Evans: though based on fragmentary evidence, the restoration conveys something of the palace's late style.

1.83e

1.83f

1.83g

At Knossos as elsewhere, the Cretans built with brick or rubble and used a considerable amount of stone, at least on the ground floors of their palaces. The flat roofs of large buildings were supported on a timber frame with rubble or brick infill where stone was impractical. Columns were usually of wood, the tree trunk dressed and inverted to taper down to the slot in a stone base. Thus the column presented its greater diameter to the load transmitted through the slab (abacus) and cushion (echinus) of its capital, also of wood. Abacus and echinus are separated by shallow grooves and the capital from the column by a ring moulding (astragal). Columns often alternate with rectangular piers. Walls were diversified in plane to avoid monotony. The colourful decoration ignored integrity of form, with frescoes ramping freely around corners: fish, birds, animals (real or heraldic) and elegantly stylized plant motifs abounded, as they always did in communities dedicated to the worship of the female principle. The most common decorative motifs were waves of interlaced spirals, rosettes, and rosettes split by spirals in vertical bands.

CRETAN CATACLYSM

Knossos and the other Minoan cities were destroyed around 1450, perhaps by invaders but most probably by natural cataclysm. Native Minoan civilization failed to recover, though the palaces were rebuilt in part and occupied for another century by intruders from Greece. These Bronze Age warriors were called 'Mycenaean' after the stoutly fortified, lion-guarded seat of a ruler identified as Homer's Agamemnon, the king who seems to have asserted suzerainty over several petty rulers.[1.84] Their ancestors were the Aryan speakers of an Indo-European language, later to develop as Greek, who originated in central Asia, moved south to infiltrate India and overrun Iran

but also south-west through the Caucasus and west into Europe or, possibly, crossed the Hellespont from north-east Anatolia after establishing themselves in the citadel at Troy (Hissarlik).

The invaders had subjugated the inhabitants of the Aegean hinterland of modern Greece – Minoan by persuasion if not origin – from castles on sites such as Mycenae by the 18th century, but were themselves overwhelmed in about 1500 by further waves of Aryans, generally called 'Achaeans'. They had mastered the sea, however, and it may have been the consequent turmoil that destroyed the Cretans. Patriarchal warriors and sky-god worshippers, the Aryans could hardly have been more different from the luxurious and genial earth-mother-worshipping Aegeans, whose Cretan ways must both have attracted and repelled them. The impact is a main concern of Greek mythology, especially the rape or marriage of the local queen, priestess and goddess by the tribal chief and his patron.

A measure of cultural integrity, drawing on but supplanting the Minoan, is identified as Mycenaean despite considerable linguistic diversity but internecine rivalry began to sap the Achaeans' strength in the 13th century. Though an Achaean contingent seems to have overcome Troy towards the middle of that century, they fell to invaders from the north soon after. The newcomers were Aryans too, but armed with iron rather than bronze and destructive of the elements of civilization that had enriched the Aegean region for so long.

ACHAEANS AND TROJANS

Ideologically relevant as Minoan ornament may have been, it masks rather than elucidates the realities of building. The Achaeans employed Cretan artists, but their obsession with logic, which they brought to the comprehension of

1.84b

›1.84 MYCENAE: (a, pages 154–155) view from the south with the citadel (top) and outer defences of the surrounding settlement, (b) entrance (Lion Gate), (c) plan with (1) Lion Gate, (2) main hall (megaron).

The citadel may have been founded as early as c. 1750, but in the main dates from the 14th century. Sacked c. 1200 and partially rebuilt, it was destroyed again c. 1100. The massive stone lintel and corbelled tympanum with inset heraldic lion device are typical of Achaean work; the sacred pillar between the lions reproduces the Cretan type of column.

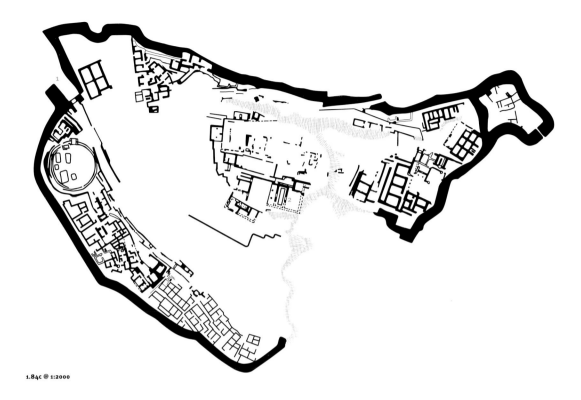

1.84c @ 1:2000

the order of creation, determined their own approach to decoration and planning: to the organization of space and the articulation of mass in terms of structure.

On the portal of the fortress at Mycenae, the dominant element is obviously heraldic: the lion is a ubiquitous symbol of royal power and the pillar is the age-old male fertility-cult object that we found specially accommodated in the crypts of Knossos. However significant, ornament does not conceal structure. The great stone walls are seen to support a massive lintel over the entrance and, limiting the pressure on the lintel, the courses of masonry above are corbelled. A symbolic device is slotted into the cavity left by the structure: ornament is disciplined by building.**1.84b**

In planning, it was characteristic of the Achaeans and

1.85a

their Trojan cousins not to leave things to whim but to impose order in terms of planar geometry and axial alignment, at least of the main units. Their citadel palaces were dominated by one big hall, the standard unit of pre-Hellenic residential accommodation: Homer's megaron. In its grandest form it was preceded on axis by a vestibule and/or portico and had a central hearth flanked by four columns, as at Hissarlik.[1.85] The royal megaron at Pylos is among the best-preserved of its type but, Mycenae apart, the outstanding Achaean legacy is the citadel at Tiryns.[1.86, 1.87]

›1.85 HISSARLIK (ANCIENT TROY): (a) walls, (b) plan of excavations of the citadel by Schlieman (1870–90), Dörpfeld (1893–94) and Blegen (1932–38) superimposing the phases of development as levels I, II, VI (early 3rd millennium to late-2nd millennium) and later (the site was occupied for nearly 2500 years), (c) overview of megarons, which probably formed the nucleus of the second citadel palace.

Troy was a citadel rather than a city for most of its history. Its battered walls were based on dressed stone from the mid-3rd millennium. Though contained by the earliest walls, the four parallel buildings at the top, opposite the main gate with back-to-back porches, probably formed the nucleus of the second citadel palace, destroyed towards the end of the 3rd millennium. The integrity of each unit is noteworthy: the megarons all have a hall with a porch, some have a false porch behind the hall, and one has a vestibule between its porch and hall. With greater width came the need for internal columns (two side by side in the porches, several in a row in the largest of the early palace buildings, as in the central structure to the south of level VI). The earliest house excavated at the site has a hall and porch, but little remains of any town around the citadel.

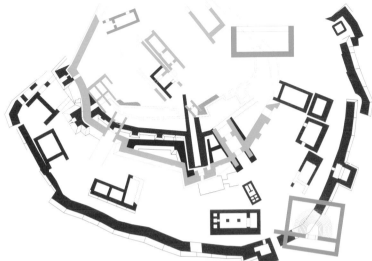

I	
IIA	
IIB	
IIC–G	
VI	
IX	

1.85b @ 1:2000

1.85c

At the centre of an extensive complex, the megaron had a porch and a circular central hearth flanked by the bases of four columns. Columns flank the grandest hearths, as here, from the late-3rd millennium. According to the Iliad, King Nestor of Messenian Pylos provided the second-largest contingent of Greek ships in the war against Troy.

Tiryns

Entrance is via a ruggedly corbelled passage skirting cyclopean walls, via a right-angle turn into the rectangular outer court and then, after another sharp turn, through the off-centre gate into the square inner court: involving the exposure of the unprotected right flank of an approaching enemy in time-honoured fashion, this has early Anatolian precedents (for instance, at Alisar). The massive blocks of undressed masonry, with courses corbelled and inclined to form a triangular vault, are typical of the early Achaeans and their Aryan cousins in Anatolia but were attributed by later ages to the giant race of Cyclops, hence the name 'cyclopean' for such megalithic masonry. The propylaea, at the head of the entrance passage, are regularly planned structures consisting of similar colonnaded porticoes set back to back: the type clearly recalls the portal at the foot of the ceremonial staircase at Knossos and is also related to the gates of the Trojans and Hittites.

Dominating the court from the centre of the north side, opposite an open-air altar, is the main element of the complex: the porticoed megaron (9.8 by 11.8 metres) with its four columns surrounding the king's hearth. The formula is repeated on a smaller scale in parallel, as at Hissarlik. To its west was the royal bath and service rooms. In parallel to the east was a private court. An earlier ante-court and porchless megaron are entered through separate corridors from both propylaea.

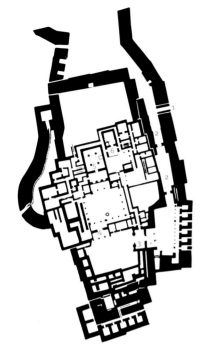

1.87a @ 1:400

1.87b

1.87c

>**1.87 TIRYNS, CITADEL,** c. 1400–1200: (a) plan with (1) entrance ramp, c. 1280, (2) passage crossed by gates, (3) first portico (propylaeum), entrance to forecourt, (4) second propylaeum, entrance to main court, (5) ruler's main reception room (megaron) with central hearth, vestibule and portico, (6) private court and megaron, (b) reconstruction of the portico of main megaron, (c) entrance passage and inner gate.

Like the rest of the palace but in contrast to the defence works, in the late 13th century the main megaron was built or rebuilt of adobe and timber in the Cretan manner (the reconstruction assumes the pitched roof and gable, almost certainly wrongly). The decorative motifs were Cretan too. The frieze with half roundels separated by verticals in triads (a common Cretan motif), reconstructed from surviving fragments of alabaster and glass, was probably a dado rather than a cornice moulding. In the main court is an open altar, suggesting that the Achaean palace was a sacred complex, like its Cretan predecessors.

Outside the citadels, as within them, most Achaeans lived in a form of megaron. In Thessaly, for example, there are 4th millennium houses with colonnaded porch, hall and storeroom between parallel walls, though the internal partition was not necessarily rectilinear and the back wall was sometimes curved. Many early Greek houses were horseshoe-shaped – like caves, but perhaps derived from the circular hut with annex. The side walls were straightened, the apsidal end screened off and then made rectangular, as at Hissarlik: the porch was optional and an anteroom appears only in the middle of the 2nd millennium.

There is no specifically religious architecture of any importance dating from the Achaean age apart from palaces and tombs. The monumental descendant of the ubiquitous primitive circular hut, long since sunk into a mound at the end of an access corridor for the interment of the important, the Mycenean tholos tomb of the

>1.88 MYCENAE, 'TOMB OF AGAMEMNON' OR 'TREASURY OF ATREUS', possibly c. 1250: (a, b) section and plan with (1) entrance passage (dromos), 6 by 37 metres, (2) the main offering chamber (tholos) with its corbel vault, 14.5 metres in diameter and 13.2 metres high, was once decorated with rows of metal rosettes, (3) burial chamber, (c) view of entrance, (d) reconstructed view of portal.

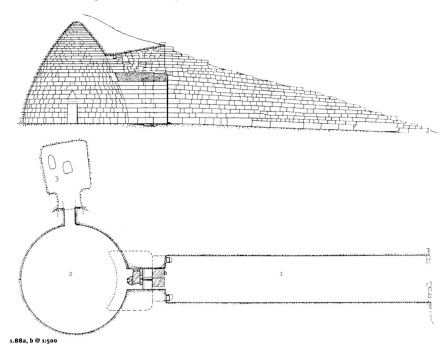

1.88a, b @ 1:500

1.88c

1.88d

Achaean warlord is the grandest of several Aegean mortuary types, including rectangular pits lined and sealed with stone and rock-cut chambers. The earliest examples, built largely of rubble, date from the late-16th century. Three hundred years later, dressed stone was used for a circular chamber with a corbelled dome on axis with a long passage. At the end of the passage was a polychrome portal with attached columns of the Cretan type supporting a lintel from which the pressure of the upper masonry was deflected by a corbelled triangular tympanum in the Mycenaean manner: much play is made with Minoan spiral motifs but ramping is prevented by the triangular geometry of the zig-zag bands on the columns and the firm horizontals of the tympanum courses.**1.88d** And across the centuries of the dark age that obscured Hellas after the passing of the Achaeans, it was the rational, not the vegetal, that would triumph when the decorative arts revived – even in Crete.**1.89**

THE TRIUMPH OF REASON

The formal planning and. heroic fortifications of the Mycenaeans are a stark contrast to the organic growth and openness of the rampartless Cretan seats of power,**1.83, 1.87** though in both cases the irregular line of approach follows a universal principle of defensive planning – security depends on a tortuous approach. Guided by pragmatism for security and by reason for hierarchy, the Mycenaeans overlaid the defensive on to the ceremonial, the baffling on to the ordered. For the Cretans, prestige was won in the service of security by mystifying design. The labyrinth is essential to the myth of the Minotaur who lurked at the heart of Minos's palace. But among the youths sent annually as tribute to Knossos, the Athenian prince Theseus was able to kill the monster and unravel the labyrinth with a string of twine given him by the Cretan king's daughter: reason triumphed over mysticism.

The disparate styles of Knossos and Tiryns – one arousing emotion, the other appealing to reason – are characteristic respectively of earth-mother-worshipping people, baffled by the mystery of fecundity, and of sky-god worshippers, alert to the terror of divine wrath and striving to understand its purpose in the analysis of cosmic order. Given the complexity of early Aegean history, this may be seen as simplistic, but it is inescapable that the male and female principles representing the attitudes of mind of pastoralists and agriculturalists respectively lie behind these basic approaches to architecture.

THE HITTITE ANATOLIAN ORDER

The Hittites, whose fortunes had revived to meet the challenge of imperial Egypt in the 14th century, developed a syncretic pantheon – like their affiliates elsewhere. In addition to their own Aryan sources, primarily the angry skies, there was the inheritance of the Hattians and the

›1.89 VASE WITH GEOMETRIC ORNAMENT, recovered from north-western Crete: 8th century (Khania, Archaeological Museum).

The earliest tumulus tomb so far identified in the Aegean (on the island of Leukas) dates from the 3rd millennium and contemporary burials in Crete were in round stone buildings, sometimes with passages, but the precise precedent for the Mycenaean tholoi remains elusive.

The king is presumed to be the last great Hittite
king, Tudhaliyas IV (c. 1250–1220), who is known to
have reigned under the patronage of Sharruma. Hittite
gods wear horned helmets.

contribution of the Hurrians. An Aryan storm-god seems
to have been assimilated with a local water-god, consort
of a goddess of the nether-region who probably produced
the sun. Then known as the weather-god of Hatti and the
sun-goddess of Arinna, these were identified with the
Hurrian storm-god Teshub and sun-goddess Hebat – the
former still subordinate to his wife – who produced the
great Hittite sky-god Sharruma.[1.90]

Developments in Hatti are far from clear before the
Hittites had reconsolidated their hold in the early 14th
century. Under Sharruma's banner, Suppiluliumas I (c.
1380–1334) led them into northern Mesopotamia: they
had weapons of iron which must have given them some
advantage but the metal was expensive and its smelting
was yet to be mastered. Egypt, in internal turmoil as a
consequence of Akhenaten's Armana revolution, was in
no position to aid its Hurrian allies: the Hittites overcame
Mittani, absorbed much of Syria, and their king married
the king of Babylon's daughter. The inevitable clash with
Egypt for ascendancy in the Levant was led by Suppiluliumas's son, Muwatallis II (c. 1308–1285), who probably had
the better of the encounter with Ramesses II at Qadesh
c. 1286. The southern Levant remained in the Egyptian
sphere but the important northern port-city state of
Ugarit, which had prospered on trade in local timber and
copper from Cyprus under a dynasty of kings protected
by Egypt, transferred its allegiance to Hatti.

Dynastic rivalry soon began to weaken the Hittites at
home in Hatti in the face of new waves of aggressive Indo-
Aryans from the west who were also armed with iron.
Hatti actually fell to a horde from Phrygia at the end of
the 13th century but much of its former empire – like Egypt
in its turn – was devastated by the enigmatic 'Sea Peoples'
who may have been led by refugees from fallen Mycenaean
kingdoms and their Aegean dependencies.

1.91a

›1.91 HATTUSAS (BOGHAZKOY): (a, b) Lion Gate and access gallery through the Yerkapu hill below the southern gate; (c) related sphinx gate at Alaca Huyuk with double-headed eagle near base of the jambs (14th century); (d) 'Temple 1', c. 1350: plan with (1) circuit of magazines, (2) double portico with square piers facing out and into main court, (3) 'king's chamber', probably for ritual washing and/or dining, (4) twin shrines.

The site of the Hittite capital was occupied from late in the 3rd millennium. Within two hundred years it harboured a colony of traders from Assur. The Hittites adopted it as their capital c. 1650. The walls were repaired and extended to some 6 kilometres with the revival of Hittite power in the mid-14th century. Built of stone, doubled and punctuated regularly by towers, these were based on earth mounds (glacis) faced with stone and pierced with corbelled tunnels. The Yerkapu hill had a gate with winged sphinxes, represented from the side as well as the front. The sphinx was probably imported into Anatolia from Syria, where it had been taken by Middle-Kingdom Egyptians. 13th century Hittite rulers borrowed sculptors from Babylon.

The king officiated at certain religious ceremonies at the dual sanctuary of the great god of Hatti and his consort Arinna in the northern sector of the walled area of the town: he processed through the royal gate, and, enthroned, shared a ritual meal with the gods. With windows in the walls of the main shrines, the sanctuary was defended by the closed circuit of magazines. Above a rough stone base and dressed vertical slabs (orthostats), the structure of most Hittite buildings was of sun-dried brick reinforced with timber.

CITADELS AND SANCTUARIES IN ANCIENT ANATOLIA

Like Hissarlik (ancient Troy), the Hittite capital at Hattusas was dominated by a citadel from the outset and like the walls of Tyrins, its defences were built of cyclopaean masonry. After their military career took Sharruma's followers to familiarity with their more sophisticated Mesopotamian and Egyptian adversaries, the gates in these walls were guarded by apotropaeic lions and sphinxes – visible sometimes from side and front – and these were their most imposing architectural legacy.**1.91a–c, 1.87c**

Within the defences, the buildings were generally unrefined, but their distribution reveals an order foreign to the organic development of their predecessors in Anatolia – or to their Mesopotamian neighbours – but comparable to that of the Trojans. Of the citadel palace, nothing

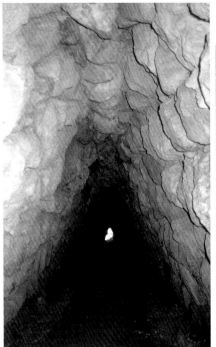

1.91b

1.91c

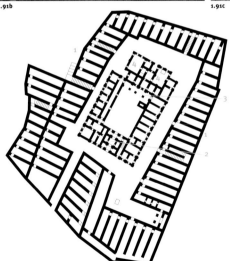

1.91d @ 1:2000

remains above foundation level. Of several temples built below it in the 14th century and later, the bases of walls reveal at least the plan. The main compound of 'Temple 1' is assertively rectilinear, in contrast with the ranges of magazines surrounding it, and is entered from a central portal. With a tripartite vestibule between twin columned porticoes facing out and in, the portal conforms to a recurrent type found in the lower levels of Hissarlik and characteristic of early Bronze Age houses in Anatolia: indeed, like the shrines at the head of the court, this is a variant of the megaron that was home to the Trojans.**1.91c, 1.85, 1.86**

1.3 ISSUES FROM A DARK AGE

1.104a

›ARCHITECTURE IN CONTEXT »WEST ASIA AND THE EASTERN MEDITERRANEAN

6 LEVANT

A major beneficiary of the Hittite assault on Mittani was the king of Assur: with his Hurrian overlords losing their grip, Assur-uballit I (1363–1328) asserted Assyrian independence and proceeded to reclaim the rich hinterland of his ancient seat in northern Mesopotamia, the heartland of future empire. That empire was to be long in building and there were to be serious reverses: its final achievement lay beyond a dark age of world fragmentation.

Assur-uballit was powerful enough within thirty years of his independence to thwart a rebellion in Babylon on behalf of the Kassites who still ruled in obscurity there. However, the latter turned on Assur-uballit's successors and claimed to have defeated them: indeed, the inscriptions of the Kassite king who owed his throne to the Assyrians, Kurigalzu II (1338–1308), claim victories over his Elamite and Sumerian neighbours as well and Kassite rule persisted in Mesopotamia until destroyed by avenging Elamites in the middle of the 12th century.

Apart from new work at Uruk,[1.92] among the few important traces of it remaining are the ziggurat and palace at Kurigalzu's new capital north of Babylon. It stood on a platform large enough to accommodate a temple before the central stairs: the remains of the structure itself reveal the reed matting laid at regular intervals in the brickwork as a binding agent. The palace was a complex of several courtyards covering some 300 square metres: the remains are obscure but, unusually, the main ceremonial rooms had multiple entrances.

A similar complex was built near Susa in the new capital laid out in the middle of the 13th century by Untash-Napirisha, the fourth king of the line of rulers who restored Elamite power after the Kassite invasion: the remains of the palaces are sparse but those of the sacred compound and its ziggurat are more substantial.[1.93]

1.92

The ruler of the rump of the Mittani empire and his capital fell to the Assyrians under Adad-nirai I (1305–1274), who had rebuilt Assur.**1.54** He took his dominion south to the Euphrates and his heir, Shalmaneser I (1273–1244), bent himself to consolidating his position north and south. As a consequence the Egyptians, Babylonians and Hittites entered into a defensive alliance. Before the century was out, however, the Hittites had succumbed to the 'Sea Peoples' who were also preoccupying Egypt – as we have seen. The Kassites in Babylon found themselves unsupported and fell to the next Assyrian king, Tukulti-Ninurta I (1243–1207), but the puppet regime installed in their stead succumbed to the Elamites. Tukulti-Ninurta was deposed but his successors proved ineffective for several generations.

Elam seized the initiative, captured Babylonia, and took the principal statue of Marduk, as well as Inanna of Uruk, back to Susa. However, the Elamites soon gave

>**1.92 KASSITE BUILDING:** Uruk, Temple of Karaindash, detail of baked-brick revetment with deities in niches, 14th century (Berlin, West Asian Museum).

>**1.93 ELAMITE BUILDING:** (a) Susa, Temple of Inshushinak, mid-12th century, detail of revetment; (b) Dur-Untash-Napirisha (Choga Zanbil), reconstruction of ziggurat (mid-13th century); (c) Sit-Shamshi, 12th-century model of ziggurat temple compound (Paris, Louvre).

The initial work at Dur-Untash-Napirisha was a courtyard temple developed from the type imported into Elam from Sumeria earlier in the millennium (in the period of Anshan's revival after subjection to the Akkadians and Ur): an outer court was surrounded on three sides by storerooms – suggesting that the complex and its priesthood were involved in commerce – and on the fourth by a shrine that communicated with an inner court. The outer court was subsequently filled in to provide a base for the towered structure of four stepped stages (c. 54 metres high), each emerging from the one below in a telescopic manner. A temple on the top terrace, reached up an internal vaulted staircase from the southeast, was dedicated to Napirisha, the patron deity of Anshan. An irregular circuit wall enclosed the ziggurat and the temple of Inshushinak.

The Inshushinak temple of Susa, with its figural revetment of moulded and glazed faience, was built by King Shutruk-Nahhunte and his sons Kutir and Shilhak-Inshushinak, in whose time Babylon was conquered and many of its treasures (including the stelae of Naram-sin and Hammurabi)**1.46b, 1.55** were brought to Susa: the influence of the Kassites is clearly apparant. The Sir-Shamshi ('Rising Sun') bronze model was a votive offering of Shilhak-Inshushinak reproducing the cult centre of Susa.

1.93a

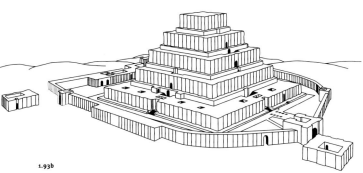

1.93b

way to the scion of a new dynasty in old Isin: Nebuchadnezzar I (1125–1104) took the conflict back to Elam, was ultimately victorious and restored Marduk to Babylon. In the north he was confronted by the brief revival of the Assyrians under Tiglath-pileser I (1114–1076) who had successfully defended his realm from waves of the same Phrygian marauders who had caused

1.93d

desolation to the Hittites. He campaigned as far as the Levant and though his conquests were short-lived, he had ensured Assyria's survival to fight for empire another day. That day was two hundred years off, beyond the dark age drawn down upon the whole civilized world by the marauders who invaded it from their many directions and, beyond them, perhaps by some reverse of nature.

THE DARK AGE AT THE TURN OF THE SECOND MILLENNIUM

The extinction of the Hittites and the withdrawal of the Egyptians at the onset of the 'Sea Peoples' left a power vacuum in west Asia for several centuries. Ugarit (Ras Shamra) and the Phoenician Levantine ports shared the fate of their Hittite overlords at the hands of a wave of the 'Sea Peoples' known as Philistines: seeing off the Egyptians by the end of the 12th century, they gave their name to Palestine. They, in turn, were overrun by mauraders from the north known as Aramaeans who penetrated deep into the Fertile Crescent and cast an unexpected ray of light beyond the dark age: Aramaic, and the alphabet developed for it in great cosmopolitan trading centres like Ugarit, prevailed not only in the Levant but ultimately throughout all Mesopotamia.

The 'Sea Peoples' and Aramaeans were not the only marauders of western Asia's dark age: in southern Babylonia the Chaldaeans followed in the Aramaean wake; to the north-east Aryan nomads – of the so-called Indo-European group – had crossed the Elburz mountains and penetrated the foothills of the Zagros in the west of the country to which they would give their name, Iran. In south-eastern Anatolia and northern Syria meanwhile, the numerous so-called neo-Hittite states, many incorporating the hinterland of cities once subject to the Hittites, emerged from the dark age to independence and flour-

›**1.94 ALALAKH (TELL ATCHANA), PALACE OF NIQMEPA,** c. 1500, plan with (1) entrance to the outer court, (2) vestibule with colonnaded portico and side chambers (3) anticipating the bit-hilani, (4) small apartment with bedroom and bathroom, (5) large apartment with antechamber, bedrooms and bathroom, (6) annexe with megarons.

Niqmepa of Alalakh was a vassal of Mittani: the main rooms of his palace had a dado of orthostats rising to about a metre, like those of the nearby Palace of Yarimlim where the plan form is also anticipated. The latter was occupied – and developed – for about a century from c. 1725.

›**1.95 UGARIT (RAS SHAMRA), PALACE,** 13th century: (a) plan of first six stages of construction with stage 5 entrance portico top left, (b) overview of the remains with entrance portico in the foreground.

Formality is appreciable only in the entrance sequence and passage to the main audience court. The walls were of masonry and many of the rooms small enough to be corbel-vaulted like the main chambers in the necropolis.

ished from the 9th century behind formidable fortifications: among the most notable were Carchemish, which had developed over several millennia before submitting to Mittanians and Hittites, and Zincirli. In eastern Anatolia Urartu, fragmented after the withdrawal of the Hittites from the area around Lake Van, united in the 9th century against resurgent Assyria, which was soon to overcome almost all.

THE BIT-HILANI

The Hittite type of architectural order had reached the outposts of Mittani – whose capital has yet to be located – and, across the dark age which descended with the 'Sea Peoples', was sustained in the citadels of the neo-Hittites and their neighbours. Following a formula first encountered c. 2300 at Ebla, the portico of the palace at Alalakh was screened like those of contemporary Hattusas – though with columns rather than piers on one side only – and flanked by two square chambers. The plan is notably regular but not axial: access to the central court and the apparently private apartments around it is turned through the western chamber of the portico and the eastern chamber leads sideways into the court before the megaron annex, where the king presumably gave audience.**1.94** Two centuries later at Ugarit a similarly columned portico leads straight to the hall and the main court is beyond, to the right, in an otherwise organic masonry complex.**1.95** The

1.96

>**1.96 AIN DARA:** unidentified temple remains including podium orthostats, embellished with syncretic beasts and lions (early 10th century). The heavy sculptural style is characteristic of the early Neo-Hittites but the developers of the site at Ain Dara have yet to be identified.

>**1.97 CARCHEMISH:** (a, b) plan and reconstruction of bit-hilani portico, (c) apotropaic lion head.

columned portico, flanked by square chambers and leading to a rectangular reception room, is the so-called bit-hilani: at Carchemish, Zincirli and related neo-Hittite sites such as Ain Dara, the Syrian form incorporates square towers like the Hittite city gate and formidable apotropaic defenders also recall the Hittite example.**1.96–1.98**

Hittite influence also echoes through the remains of the fortified citadels of the early 1st millennium Urartians: the palace at Altintepe, for example, is entered through a rectangular vestibule flanked by square chambers though the

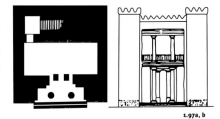

1.97a, b

1.97c

>**1.98 ZINCIRLI:** (a) site plan with twin-towered portals (1, 2), lower palace (3) with bit-hilani portico, upper palace (4) with (5) bit-hilani entrance to main apartment reception room, bedroom, bathroom and cubicles, and (6) bit-hilani entrance to self-contained apartment's bedroom and bathroom, (b) column base.

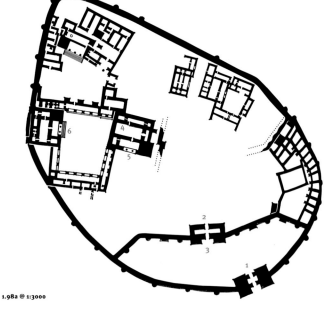

1.98a @ 1:3000

1.98b

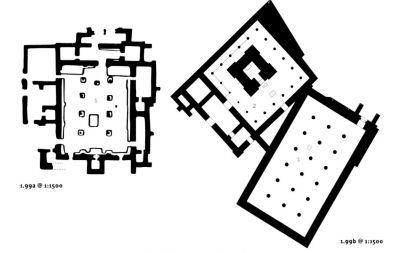

›1.99 URATIAN TYPES: (a) Hasanlu, columned hall, 9th-century plan; (b) Altintepe, palace and/or temple, 7th century, plan with (1) colonnaded hall entered from the east, (2) square shrine with bit-hilani entrance to the west; (c) Adilcevaz, Urartian relief, 7th century (Ankara, National Museum); (d) winged human-headed bull from Rusahinili (near Lake Van in the centre of former Urartian domains), perhaps from a throne (London, British Museum).

The relief shows the winged storm-god Teiseba against defence walls typical of fortresses from time immemorial. Beyond the literal, the Urartian artist's extreme elongation of the tower buttresses suggests the representation of a great columned hall in elevation and section simultaneously – as three-dimensional objects are viewed through them. A regular succession of towers, providing cover for the recessed main face of the wall, is known from the mid-6th millennium settlement at Hacilar in south-west Anatolia. Battering was fully developed in the mid-3rd millennium walls of Troy. Wall walks, high above the enemy, are rare survivals, but mid-2nd millennium Hittite clay models show them projecting with crenellations for the protection of marksmen. It is unclear whether the corbelled projection incorporated machicolation – as is postulated for Middle Kingdom Egyptian forts:1.59 the technique developed from the practice of ringing the tops of towers with timber hoardings and that was apparently widespread by the mid-2nd millennium.

1.99a @ 1:1500

1.99b @ 1:1500

typical bit-hilani colonnaded entrance screen was replaced by an arch. In so far as the sparse remains indicate, the principal Urartian shrine type was a thick-walled tower built over a square plan. The most distinctive building type in the orbit of Urartu, best known from the domain of Hasanlu which the Urartians may have devastated in conquest, seems to have been an indigenous invention with the fine timber available: a portico and vestibule, sometimes columned and flanked by square towers in remote echo of the bit-hilani, precede a rectangular hall with a flat roof supported on two rows of columns.**1.99**

1.99d

1.99c

Sustaining a long tradition, the bit-hilani portico is related to the portals of Troy and Tiryns, the earliest built no later than the end of the 3rd millennium. On the other hand, syncretic works like the complex at Altintepe, where numerous columns were used to support the roof of the inner shrine-chamber and adjacent audience hall, also perpetuate the many-poled marquee in which the many-columned great halls of all eastern potentates find their origin.

THE HEBREWS

The Dark Age obscured much, not least the advent of the peripatetic people who developed their idiosyncratic religion in the land of Canaan, the hilly region to the west of the River Jordan. The Jewish chronicles, later enshrined in the Bible, locate the tribes that ultimately constituted the nation of Israel in Chaldaea. Early in the 2nd millennium, the patriarch Abraham led them from fallen Ur to Canaan. The infertility of the land ensured the survival of their pastoralism there and sent some looking for better conditions elsewhere, notably in Lower Egypt where they were called 'Hebrews' – wanderers.

Having prospered in Egypt, the Hebrews were reputedly enslaved under the resurgent New Kingdom and their exodus is not implausibly dated to the reign of Akhenaten (c. 1353–1335), whose monotheism may not be coincidental with the cataclysmic revelations of Jehovah (Yahweh) to their leader, Moses, on Mount Sinai: both were revolutionary in the abstract concept of a transcendent god not to be represented in human terms or endowed with human needs and, confronting ubiquitous pantheism, in their uncompromising intolerance.

While Akhenaten's faith was soon extinguished by the old priesthood of Amun, the commitment of Moses and his followers to their covenant with the one true god ensured the survival of Hebrew monotheism: they would dedicate themselves to worshipping him alone and keeping his commandments, the ineluctable moral basis for their unique religious and social order, and he would protect them in the land he had promised them. And their decades of wandering through the wilderness, drawn on by that promise, forged their sense of national identity.

Canaan was regained after protracted Dark-Age dispute. The nation of Israel was constituted as a federation of twelve tribes, but the tribe of Judah – the largest – was always distinct from the rest. At first disputes were settled by judges but the tribes had no real political cohesion, let alone organized government. In the struggle for Canaan, their moral integrity sometimes failed them. They appropriated existing sanctuaries – usually 'high places', as in Mesopotamia – for Jehovah, but the old associations persisted and at times inspired syncretism, contrary to the Covenant. The consequences were articu-lated by prophets – teachers and communicators, as well as tellers of the future – who promoted the centralization of the cult about the Ark enshrining the Covenant.

Towards the end of the 1st millennium BCE, kingship was instituted to further the political unity of Israel – probably in the wake of invasion by 'Sea Peoples' like the Philistines. Success was limited to the generations of David and Solomon (c. 1000–930). The former despatched the Philistine threat, purloined their iron equipment and extended his rule throughout the Phoenician Levant, his son Solomon consolidated the kingdom and built the cult centre at the new-found royal seat, Jerusalem in Judah, to hold the Ark of the Covenant. Ambiguously described in the Bible, little of Solomon's temple remains beyond the platform providing its high place but it may well have incorporated a bit-hilani.**1.100**

›1.100 JERUSALEM, TEMPLE OF SOLOMON:
reconstruction.

Though detailed, the biblical account (1 Kings 6 and 2 Chronicles 3, with some inconsistency) of the temple built by Solomon c. 950 has proved elusive as the basis for a generally accepted reconstruction: its rectangular volume is defined as 60 by 20 by 30 cubits (about 33.5 by 11.2 metres and 16.8 metres high); the main space of the sanctuary (20 by 40 cubits) was divided by a curtain into two cubes, the inner one for the seclusion of the Ark; on the north, south and western sides there were three storeys of cells; the eastern entrance porch is described as having two columns but it is not clear whether they were framed or free-standing.

The temple was destroyed in 586 by the Babylonian forces and rebuilt late in the 6th century after the repatriation of the Jews from captivity in Babylon on the triumph of Persia.

After Solomon, Judah was divided from Israel as a separate kingdom. The fallibilities of mighty kings and cosmopolitan courts in both realms were countered by the prophets as the guardians of the moral order which distinguished Judaism. And when they were ignored they could lament the consequence: first Israel, then Judah fell to the Mesopotamian powers whose pretensions to world dominion succeeded one another between the 8th and the 6th centuries and the Great Temple was destroyed.

1.101b

7 SABEA

1.101a

According to one tradition the queen who made her celebrated pilgimage to – and union with – the Hebrew king Solomon in the 10th century BCE was Bilkis of Sabea (Sheba) in southern Yemen. According to the alternative version, she was Makeda of Sabea in the region of northern Ethiopia subsequently known as Tigrai, the descendant of the great-grandson of Noah named Ethiopic. The fruit of the union between the king in Jerusalem and the queen from Africa is traditionally identified as Menelik who succeeded his mother on returning from a visit to his father in his early twenties – founding the Solomonic dynasty which asserted its legitimacy in power until 1974 CE. The legend adds that on setting out for home he purloined the Ark of the Covenant – the vessel made to God's prescription for the tablets of the Law confided to Moses on Sinai.

1.101d

>1.101 SABEA, TERRACING AND THE VER-
NACULAR: (a) queenly figure from the Melazo area
of Tigrai (5th/4th century BCE; Addis Abbaba, National
Museum); (b) the highlands of Tigrai with its agglommerations of circular houses; (c, pages 180–181) the
highlands of central Yemen with its agglommerations
of multi-storey houses; (d) high-rise houses in Yemen.

Yemen's high-rise houses may extend to as many
as nine storeys to accommodate an extended family:
few are older than the 17th century in their present
form, but the type is of undetermined antiquity. The
Ethiopian vernacular house is universally circular:
undressed stone supersedes wattle and daub in the
north and in the Axum region two storeys are common.

Makeda reputedly ruled over both Ethiopia and Yemen
– both Sabeas, if there was such a distinction. History
knows that southern Yemen and the northern part of the
Ethiopian realm were united at various times – though the
first inscriptional record of assimilation is the boast of an
Ethiopian ruler of a realm called Sabea in the 6th century
BCE. By then, Semitic merchants had doubtless led emi-
grants from south-west Arabia across the narrows of the
Red Sea to the Horn of Africa and its hinterland: similar
stone terracing supports agriculture in the rugged – geo-
logically related – terrain of both these areas and similar
technology was used for water control.[1.101]

Archaeology, far from comprehensive as yet in Ethiopia,
has traced an agriculture-based civilization back at least to

the early 1st millennium BCE – that is to the era of Solomon – and recovered artefacts indicate trade contacts with Egypt and the Levant as well as southern Arabia. The Egyptians record trade with Punt – as we have noted, probably Eritrea – but their interest was confined to the commodities obtained there – especially black slaves, aromatics and precious minerals. The biblical Old Testament refers to the lands of the Africans south of Egypt as 'Cush' – without distinguishing any specific realm. The indigenous language of northern Ethiopia is consequently called Cushitic – at least by Western anthropologists – but the early immigrants from southern Arabia contributed the Semitic basis for the Ge'ez vernacular of ancient Axum and its progenitive script.

The Bible records even deeper Semitic penetration than that of the southern Arabian merchants: in the 7th century Zaphaniah refers to the dispersal of the Lord's Chosen People beyond the rivers of Cush. Settled beyond the source of the Blue Nile in Lake Tana, these ancient Jewish emigrés were the ancestors of the Falashas who sustained Ark-centred rites, superceded in the Holy Land after Solomon's Holy of Holies was supposedly desecrated in the 7th century BCE, until the final return of their depleted community to Israel in 1991: far from their Hebrew homeland and distancing themselves from its reformed practice, those ancestors adopted Ge'ez.

SABEA AND AXUM

The most tangible evidence of civilization in the Sabea of Makeda and her son's successors is provided by the temples of Yeha and several related sites in the vicinity of Axum. They were pagan. Dated to c. 500 BCE, they were built of fine ashlar unprecedented in Ethiopia but familiar on a massive scale in the great dam of Ma'rib, the capital of Sabea across the straits in south-west Arabia. The

1.102a

1.102b

1.102c

1.102d

›1.102 SABEAN BUILDING AND THE IBEX:
(a, b) Ma'rib dam and Moon Temple (c. 500 BCE); (c, d) Yeha Temple, Tigrai (c. 400 BCE), remains from the west, and detail of stylized ibex frieze inserted in the wall of the modern church; (e) ibex lamp.

Like the 8th-century temples of the moon-god Almaqah at Masajid and Siwah and the 5th-century temple of 'Athtar (god of the morning star) at Ma-in (all in the Ma'rib region), the rectangular cella of the Yaha Temple (18.5 by 15 metres) is built of well-dressed limestone, laid immaculately without mortar on a slightly stepped podium. part of the walls framing the entrance and most of the double skin of masonry on the other three sides remain (to a height of 13 metres). Within, a rectangular trough is sunk opposite the western entrance, beside the eastern wall. In addition to the crescent, which appears on Axumite coinage, the ibex was an attribute of Almaqah.

temple at Yeha yielded inscriptions in southern Arabian characters – among the first recovered from pre-Axumite Ethiopia – and a frieze of ibex also closely related to Ma'rib work. Nearby, moreover, the stumps of a series of aligned piers recall – for some – the rows of piers which defined the Moon Temple at Ma'rib.**1.102**

Yaha and its relatives emerge from total obscurity at about the same time as the unvocalized Semitic script which was adopted as the basis of Axumite Ge'ez: they seem to have belonged to a polity called D'MT (Damat?) whose relationship with the future imperial city of Axum is unclear. There is scant evidence of urbanization at the site of the latter before the end of the last millennium BCE but by the 2nd century CE it had emerged as the seat of a centralizing power built on the profits of agriculture and of trade through its Red Sea port of Adulis. Probably far-flung and certainly crucial, the network of the latter remains incompletely defined as, too, is the pattern of imperial politics. Evidently confident of homeland secu-

1.102e

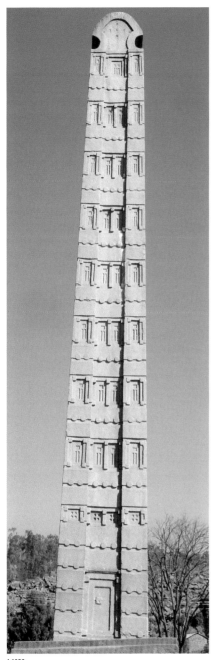
1.103a

rity – its central cities were unwalled – its importance lasted for half a millennium thereafter.

By the end of the 3rd century, the Axumite kings were issuing splendid coins: in gold, silver and bronze, these bore the device of the crescent and disk which provides the main evidence for their astral polytheism. However, the magnificence built on their wealth is represented not by identifiable temples – though imposing female figures have been recovered from ill-documented sites – but by royal monuments, suggesting that the king was at least quasi-divine. There are the smashed stepped stone bases of their canopied thrones, numerous enough to be specific to each reign. There are fine ashlar tombs in the royal necropolis commodious enough for burial goods whose reputed richness attracted robbers as soon as royal authority flagged. Above all, there are the astonishing commemorative stelae associated with the tombs but apparently representing palaces: the greatest of these works are generally dated to the 4th century when the monarchy clearly had reached the height of its affluence and its power to recruit and organize labour.[1.103]

Axumite achievement: accommodation of the living and the dead

The ashlar masonry of the subterranean tombs is generally as fine as it had been nearly a millennium earlier at Ma'rib and Yaha – though there is one wayward example in which great blocks are cut precisely to match along irregular lines. Typically consisting of a rectangular burial chamber framed by a corridor on three sides, several of the tombs were associated with the commemorative stelae for which Axum is most celebrated.

Tipped into masonry-lined pits, which were finally sealed with twin capstones cut to frame them, the tapering shafts of the most impressive stelae were modelled on multistorey palace buildings and increasingly exaggerated in height to match the waxing pretensions of their royal dedicatees. With projecting bays to each side of the central bay, in which the

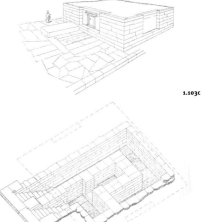

1.103c

1.103d

1.103b

›1.103 AXUM: (a) Stele 3 from the south; (b, c, d)
Tomb of the False Door, entrance and plan; (e) reconstruction of structural system (after Buxton and Mathews 1974); (f, g) Dungur mansion (3rd/5th century?)
overviews of remains from north and west, reconstruction (after Kreccker, 1913).

Of some seventy-five stelae in the main necropolis, various in type and degree of embellishment, six
represent multi-storey buildings. Number 3, the
largest stele still standing, is traditionally attributed
to the early 4th-century King Ezana (without substan-
tiation but not implausibly): it rises through eleven
storeys (and 20.5 metres) to a waisted finial – the characteristically Axumite keyhole form. The unknown system of erection was tested to destruction with the last
and largest (33 metres high, 520 tonnes) which fell in
the process.

The Nafas Mawcha tomb, on to which the latest
stele fell, represents the single-chamber norm but,
exceptionally, the chamber was covered with a single
colossal stone (nearly 17.5 by 6.5 metres). The so-
called mausoleum nearby is atypical: twin ranges of
five chambers flank a central corridor entered from
each end through portals like the ones represented on
the 'palace' stelae. The same motif gives its name to
the Tomb of the False Door: that provided the false
façade erected over twin excavated staircases, one
serving the subterranean vestibule and inner chamber, the other a passage surrounding the chamber on
three sides but not connected with it.

door at ground level is usually equipped with the representation of lock
and handle, they are wholly trabeated in simulated structure.
Idiosyncratic are the square blocks and circular disks which represent
the projecting ends of timber beams and joists inserted to join the
recessed horizontal courses of timber as bracing for rubble walls: the
square ones are invariably associated with the frames of doors and
grilled windows; the circular ones (colloquially known as 'monkey
heads') may denote support for internal floors. The precision of the carving is hardly less impressive than the technical expertise manifest in the
raising of monol-iths which ultimately exceeded the height and weight of
the obelisks of 18th Dynasty Egypt

The structural type is deduced from the earliest surviving works of any
substance – in the monastery of Debra Damo (see below) – but the near-
est known parallel to the prototype of the Axumite stelae are the tower
blocks of Yemen – timeless, except perhaps for their arcading. The traces
of ancient Axum are too sparse to reveal whether any of its inhabitants

1.103f

Like the larger complex at Ta'skha Maryam (180 by 260 metres) – which had double outer ranges to the north and south – the Dungar compound is a regular rectangle (55 by 52 metres) with a central court defined by store, service and subsidiary accommodation ranges. A grand staircase on the main longitudinal axis serves the main pavilion (18 metres square) raised on a central podium. The recession of the central bay in a tripartite scheme, horizontal banding of rubble and stone courses over a slightly stepped base and the reinforcing of the corners with granite coins are typical of classic Axumite remains except that timber was less extensively employed for bracing.

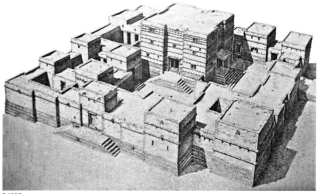
3.103g

lived high above the ground in towers – like those of Sa'ana, say: in actuality, internal staircases indicate that the central blocks of Axum's mansions (called 'elite residences' by the excavators) rose to more than one storey but it is assumed that the maximum was three. The grandest, called Ta'aka Maryam, has been dated to the 3rd century CE: the remains of its structure, undressed masonry with timber bracing within dressed stone quoins, verify the interpretation of the stelae imagery. The recovery of smaller complexes, like the one at Dungar, has made it clear that the buildings of the type were not exclusively royal.

1.103e

1.104b

8 WORLD EMPIRE

ASSYRIA AND BABYLON

A long line of undistinguished Assyrian kings had
sustained their control over the heartland of Assur
throughout the dark age which followed the incursion of
the 'Sea Peoples', despite constant pressure from the
Aramaeans. The resurgence that was to lead them finally
to world empire began with incursions into former
Mittanian domains and an assault on Babylon led by
Adad-nirari II (911–889). Respecting the resultant border
agreement with the Babylonians, Tukulti-Ninurta II
(889–884) consolidated his father's considerable gains.
His greater son, Assurnasirpal II (883–859), instituted
wide-ranging annual campaigns, exacted tribute from the
petty states into which much of Mesopotamia had fragmented under the impact of the Aramaeans, turning his
attention to Syria, Israel and the Levant.[1.104]

The prime objective at the outset of Assyrian resurgence was the assurance of trade dominance rather than
imperial dominion. This, of course, was not inconsistent
with the revival of the fortunes of Phoenicia, despite

1.104c

(a, pages 168–169) Assurbanipal as the virile protector of his flock hunting lions in keeping with the most ancient Sumerian royal iconographical tradition; (b) Assurnasirpal encamped and assaulting a town on campaign (Kalhu throne-room orthostats, London, British Museum); (c) stele of Assurnasirpal II, of the type set up to mark the extension of his power and at his seat, shows him as chief priest of Assur ringed by the symbols of the principal Mesopotamian gods honoured throughout his domains (from right to left, the horned helmet of divinity, doubtless representing Assur, the sun disk of Shamash, the crescent moon of Sîn, the thunderbolt of the storm-god Adad, the star of Ishtar, goddess of love and war); (d) relief panel showing the seige of Larchish.

Aramaean infiltration in the Levant: in the 9th century, from their major ports of Tyre, Sidon and Biblos, they re-established their pan-Mediterranean maritime trade dominance with imports of copper from Cyprus and exports of Levantine timber, and they planted colonies widely. These flourished as trading stations and gained enhanced importance in the Phoenician world after the home ports were absorbed by Israel and threatened by Assyria with changed objectives in the 7th century.

Sustained annual campaigns to reassert overlordship and reassure trade dominance reduced the Levantine, Hebrew and neo-Hittite states to suzereinty under Assurnasirpal's heir, Shalmaneser III (858–824), who then turned his attention to the former Hittite domain in Anatolia. Respecting the accord with Babylon, he supported the legitimate king against the Chaldaeans who had begun their incursions into lower Mesopotamia in the wake of the Aramaeans. He also campaigned east and encountered the Medes who had entered Iran in the dark age of widespread marauding but seem not yet to have forged the kingom that was to be of great importance in the final chapter of Assyria's history.

After sixty years of rebellion and reverse, Tiglath-pileser III (744–727) reasserted royal authority in northern Mesopotamia and inaugurated the final thrust towards universal dominion. Commanding a reformed standing army of mercenary foot soldiers and mounted Assyrians, armed with iron and backed by advanced siege machinery, he defeated a challenge from the north led by the Uratian king, but failed to take the kingdom. In the south he overcame the Chaldaeans, whose leader had taken advantage of Assur's recent impotence to seize the throne of Babylon, and assumed Marduk's mantle in 729.

No longer content with controlling trade routes through overlordship of tributary states reasserted in annual campaigns, Tiglath-pileser annexed widely and displaced peoples *en masse* to sap their national identities. He imposed a standard system of law and, in place of local rulers, he appointed eunuchs as governors to slight the hereditary nobility who had purloined power under his weak predecessors. To ensure that distance did not mean delay in receipt of imperial commands, he ordained a network of arterial roads with regular staging posts for a rapid-relay imperial messenger service.

Most of Syria and the Levant were resubjected to Assur under Tiglath-pileser: Israel followed in the next reign, that of Shalmaneser v, which ended in some turmoil in 722. This was perhaps instigated by the successor, Sargon ii (721–705), who then had to reconsolidate

1.104d

Assyrian power, taking it to the borders of Egypt in the process and reaching out to Cilicia through the annexation of Carchemish and its rival neo-Hittite domains. Of the major powers, only the Phrygians of Anatolia, Uratu and Egypt remained beyond the Assyrian pale. The Phrygians were momentary allies against common enemies like the Cilicians and the Uratians. Uratu was defeated once again but again eluded annexation. Egypt came to the aid of Levantine rebels in the reign of Sargon's heir, Sennacherib (704–681), and the outcome was inconclusive after a protracted campaign which included a failed attack on Jerusalem. Inconclusive at first, too, was Sennacherib's response to rebellious Babylonians and Chaldaeans, aided by the Elamites, but faced with renewed trouble to his south he finally triumphed and destroyed Babylon in 689, supplanting Marduk with Assur as the king of the gods.

After several unsuccessful campaigns, reckoning with Egypt and the apogee of Assyrian power came in 671 when Sennacherib's heir, Esarhaddon, entered Memphis in triumph. Neither Esarhaddon nor his triumph proved durable: the king was dead within two years and Egypt rebelled. The new Assyrian king, Assurbanipal (668– c. 627), pursued reconquest for much of his first decade before finally regaining Memphis and the allegiance of Egyptian factions who found advantage in his protection. He then turned on Elam, which had again supported rebellion in Babylon. Babylon was resecured in 648 and the Elamites despatched brutally. For the remaining two decades of his reign Assurbanipal retired to his celebrated library to pursue scholarship, rather than enemies, and to render immeasurable service to posterity in commissioning exhaustive copies of the records and literature of his Mesopotamian predecessors – when he was not in his garden with the queen and elaborate furniture of repose.

1.105a

SEATS OF ASSYRIAN POWER

Assurnasirpal II extended the walls of Assur and restored the Old Palace. He and his heirs were buried there but from c. 880 he built a splendid new capital at the old provincial centre of Kalhu (Tel Nimrud), near the confluence of the Tigris and Zeb rivers, with some 8 kilometres of walls protecting the temples of nine Assyrian and Sumerian gods and an exceptionally grand palace.

The temples were of the traditional courtyard type represented at Assur by Shamshi-adad's foundations: the shrine building, as broad as the court, consisted of two parallel halls with doors aligned off-centre in their long sides, the inner one distinguished by a dais for the cult image in a recess at the far end. The palace was also of the traditional courtyard type, first represented on the grand scale at Mari and Assur, with its three clearly defined zones – for public ceremonial, private council and the royal women.**1.54, 1.56** The entrances were guarded by great syncretic monsters (*lamassu*) with the fierceness of the lion, the far-sightedness of the eagle and the wisdom and intelligence of man: deriving from the ancient Mesopotamian apotropaic tradition, the human-headed leonine guardian has its

Egyptian and Hittite precedents but never has there been a more potent icon of royal prowess.**1.42, 1.91**

Assurnasirpal's heirs sustained Khalu for one hundred and fifty years: his son added the heavily defended four-court complex of Fort Shalmaneser in the south-west quarter of the city to accommodate the treasury, the armoury and the military commissariat, and several later kings built new palaces. However, perhaps because he did not spring from the main royal line of Assurnasirpal's heirs and wished to establish a new identity, Sargon II commissioned a vast new seat at Dur-Sharrukin (Khorsabad) c. 717 and inaugurated it just before his death.**1.105, 1.106**

1.105b

Kalhu

At Kalhu the king's principal residence was to the north-west of the citadel platfrom: entrance from the east was centred on the main court of public audience at right-angles to the entrace of the throne-room suite; this was centred on the south side of the court and asserted the dominant axis though access beyond it to the hall and court of private audience was staggered. The latter was flanked by private apartments and service quarters, beyond which were the tombs of the queens. Both the audience hall and council chamber, each with a dais at the end furthest from the courtyard door, were backed by a withdrawing room – the equivalent of a latter-day cabinet.

Mud-brick was the main building material, protected by stone where

1.105c

1.105e

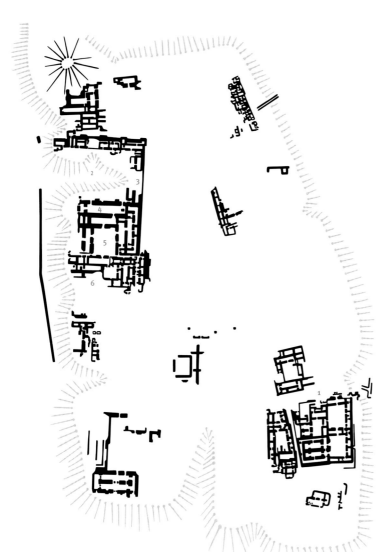

›1.105 KALHU (NIMRUD), PALACE OF ASSURNASIRPAL II, 883–859: (a) great panel from behind the throne showing the king (wearing the fez-like hat with top-knot reserved for royalty) as the devout agent of Assur ensuring the prosperity of his land with his libation of the sacred tree of life surmounted by the deity in a winged disk and supported by winged genii wearing the cap of divinity (London, British Museum), (b) reconstruction of throne room (after Layard), (c) human-headed winged lions from the throne room entrance, (d) plan of palace remains with (1) entrance from the east, (2) court of public audience, (3) possible eastern entrance forecourt, (4) throne room, (5) hall and court of private audience, (6) necropolis of the queens, (e) ivory panel from Phoenicia of the type applied to royal Assyrian furniture (Paris, Louvre), (f) detail of timber and bronze gates of Kalhu's defensive outpost, Balawar, showing the siege of Carchemish.

vulnerable to damp and supplemented by timber: the main openings were arched but only the smallest rooms were vaulted; the main spaces were spanned by great cedar trunks from Lebanon. In the outer two zones, at least, mural decoration usually consisted of frescoes and glazed-brick panels above a revetment of carved stone orthostats

1.105f

painted in black, white and primary colours: the didactic subjects of both were appropriate to the designation of the space. The portals, of stout timber bound with bronze, were guarded by the *lamassu*.

The main entrance was not recovered by A.H. Layard, who excavated the remains from 1845, but the triple entrance from the main court to the throne room was guarded by the *lamassu*: represented in deep relief, to be viewed orthogonally from the front and the sides of the portal arch, these appear to have five legs when seen obliquely from the corner. Syncretic images of the power of the king, high priest of Assur, they are invariably accompanied by sacred protective genii carrying a pot of holy water and a sprinkler or sacrificial animals and implements.

The court walls to either side of the throne-room entrance were embellished with reliefs of foreigners bearing tribute. The hall reliefs displayed the king's divine authority and super-human prowess in battle and the hunt: they include the image of a fort which cedes nothing in the authority of its centralized geometry to anything produced by later imperialists (see pages 168–169). The court of private audience was embellished with reliefs of the king in council with priests and officials and other ceremonial scenes. The orthostats were originally painted in black, white and the primary colours and were surmounted by colourful, if didactic, murals. The furniture was embellished with fine ivory panels produced by the eclectic artists of the Phoenician Levant.

Dur-Sharrukin

The complex of palace, temple and ziggurat on the vast terrace at Dur-Sharrukin brought the Mesopotamian architectural tradition to its apogee: there was little structural innovation but, in addition to the courts of public and private audience aligned on axis with the throne room between them, there was a near-square forecourt offset on the subsidiary perpendicular axis. All three gatehouses led straight through to this outer court, where those seeking or summoned to audience presumably assembled. The offset exit restricted access to the great audience court, which was dominated from the centre of its south-western side by the twin-towered portal of the throne room: the throne, if not set in the central arch to command large gatherings outside, stood before the end wall to the left.

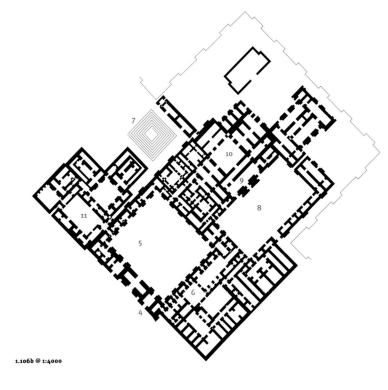

1.106b @ 1:4000

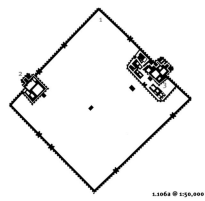

1.106a @ 1:50,000

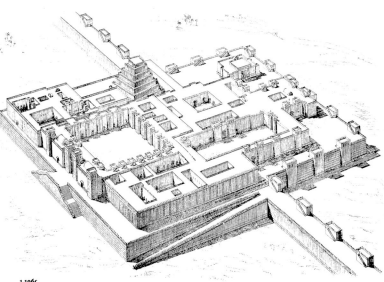

1.106c

1.106g

›**1.106   DUR-SHARRUKIN (KHORSABAD), PALACE OF SARGON II,** 722–705: (a) block plan of town, (b, c) plan and reconstruction of palace, (d, pages 196–197) human-headed winged bull *lamassu* from the throne court and tribute bearers, (e, f) the shipping of timber and rough-cut stone *lamassu* for the palace, (g) fresco of courtiers of the type that embellished the upper walls (from Tel Barsip; Paris, Louvre).

Roughly square, the area enclosed by the town walls (1) covered nearly 2.6 square kilometres; step-crenellated and buttressed, the walls were pierced by seven gates of which the main one (2), facing in the direction of Kuyunjik (Nineveh), was guarded by the fortified arsenal on a platform; the raised citadel, containing the official and cult buildings, was incorporated within the town defences towards the northern corner (3); rising out of it on a great platform (315 by 195 metres), equal to the height of the walls and projecting beyond them, was the king's palace. A ramp led from the central square of the citadel, where the

Two further right-angle turns led slightly off axis to the king's apartment, centred on the court of private audience and its three flanking suites. By now the withdrawing room of the royal audience suite communicated with a paved and drained chamber usually identified as a bathroom. The upper walls of courts and halls were largely embellished with images of the king and his courtiers, and, as well as military and religious subjects, the ortho-stat reliefs included graphic accounts of shipping timber and massive stone *lamassu* – human-headed winged bulls, rather than lions as at Kalhu.

1.106e

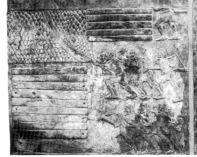

1.106f

king would appear before the masses, to the main twin-towered portal of the palace (4) and then to the outer court (5) flanked by offices (6) and the ziggurat temple complex of Shamash, Sin and Ningal (7). Exit from the northern corner of the outer court led to the southern corner of the great audience court (8), beyond which were the throne room (9), the king's apartments (10), and the adjacent rooms of his women; to the south-west of the throne court was a double temple whose dedication was probably to Nabu (god of writing) and his consort Tashmetum (11).

The temples adjacent to Sargon's palace mark a departure from the traditional arrangement: in place of parallel broad chambers, the inner sanctum is perpendicular to the antechamber and all the doors are aligned on axis. Inspired by the southern tradition, the axial approach was to be standard for the late-Assyrians who were increasingly involved with Babylon: Sargon's son Sennacherib adopted it for a new temple dedicated to the New Year festival at Assur and gave it particular authority with a new eastern forecourt and entrance to the shrine hall of the ancient temple of the city's venerable patron deity.[1.54]

Owing to his father's inauspicious death, Sennacherib abandoned Dur-Sharrukin before it was completed and moved south to the important old town of Nineveh, which controlled a major crossing of the Tigris: girded by some 12 kilometres of walls, the new town was dominated by a

1.107a

1.107b

›1.107 NINEVEH (KUYUNJIK): (a) restored walls and gate; (b) relief from Sennacherib's palace showing detail of encampment before the city walls; (c, d) reliefs from Assurbanipal's palace showing the king in his garden and in repose with the queen (London, British Museum).

The defences (12 kilometres in extent) were in depth: a moat preceded doubled walls, of stone with stepped crenellations outside, of mud brick rising to a greater height inside. There were eighteen gates. The reconstruction is based on the evidence provided by reliefs like the one of the siege of Larchish. The palace was on a terrace to the south-west: the largest of its type, it has been incompletely excavated but was doubtless conservative in distribution except for the apparent addition of a second private audience court. Neither Esarhaddon's South-West Palace nor Assurbanipal's North Palace has been extensively excavated.

The garden is notable for its ordered design: the cloistered enclosure seems to have been rectilinear, the irrigation canals seem to join at right-angles and the planting is in parallel rows.

reformed citadel on the high ground of the original settlement – as at Nimrud – and the temple-palace complex within it surpassed even his father's great work. However, as the city was destroyed by its enemies rather than abandoned by the Assyrians themselves, the excavated remains are less extensive than those of Dur-Sharrukin and, like those of the palace added by Assurbanipal in the middle of the 7th century, are most celebrated for their superb orthostats: the king is shown in the usual guises and contexts appropriate to the public or private parts of the palace, notably leading the assault on the enemy's city or enjoying peace in his formal garden, but nowhere more memorably than as the heroic protector of his flock hunting lions in the type of chariot (light and fast but strong) that had taken so many of his forebears to victory in war. **1.107**

1.107c

1.107d

THE FALL OF ASSYRIA AND THE NEO-BABYLONIANS

Over-extended and universally hated, Assurbanipal's line was eradicated in 612 by resurgent Babylon which, despite Chaldaean disruption, had seen considerable prosperity when aligned with Assyria, especially in the period of reconstruction after the devastation of 689. On the coincidental deaths c. 627 of the kings of Assyria and Babylon – which has prompted the speculation that Assurbanipal may himself have assumed the Babylonian crown – the Babylonian throne was seized by the obscure Chaldaean Nabopolassar, who claimed lowly origin and instituted a war of liberation.

By 616 Nabopolassar had consolidated his hold on Babylonia and took the offensive against Assyria. He was joined by the Medes who, settled to the north of Elam, had been preoccupied with marauding Scythians from central Asia until affronted by Assurbanipal's assault on Elam. After several reverses, the Assyrian myth of invincibility was finally shattered, and Nineveh fell to the allied enemy forces: the last king of Assyria died in the siege of his capital and the immediate collapse of the centralized administration left the fate of the empire's heartland in obscurity.

The Medes took north-eastern Mesopotamia from the Assyrians, went on to the conquest of Uratu c. 590 and found themselves confronting a new power from the west over Anatolia: this was Lydia, which had eclipsed the Phrygian regime in western Anatolia and extended to the Aegean coastal cities of the Ionic Hellenes under the fabulous king, Croesus. Meanwhile the Babylonians had reclaimed the south and had rebuffed the Egyptians, who had come to their Assyrian master's aid, by 605.

The son of Nabopolassar, Nebuchadnezzar II (605–562), asserted his rule over the Levant, crushing Judah and destroying Jerusalem in 581 after several bouts of rebellion, reprisal and deportation. He then devoted his vast resources to restoring Sumer's most venerable shrines and, above all, rebuilding Babylon as the greatest city in the world: and as the rulers of the world came there annually to kneel before the king, so the images of all the gods of the world – except Jehovah, of course – came to the temple of Marduk to submit to the great Babylonian deity whose pre-eminence was established nearly fifteen hundred years before by Hammurabi.**1.108, 1.17**

1.108a

›**1.108** BABYLON: (a, b) part model and plan (after Koldewey) of the ceremonial centre and district east of the Euphrates as rebuilt by Nebuchadnezzar II towards the end of the 7th century; (c) plan of the fortified city divided by the Euphrates; (d) detail of the revetment of Nebuchadnezzar's throne room (Berlin, West Asian Museum).

The main royal residence, adjacent to the citadel in the western outwork, is identified as the 'Southern Palace' to distinguish it from a second palatial building, in the outwork to the north of the main line of ramparts, which may have been a 'museum' housing Sumerian and Babylonian antiquities recovered from Assyria and Elam; a third palatial complex at the northern extremity of the outer defences, misnamed the 'Summer Palace', was a fortified command post.

The fortified city had five ranges of brick walls, the outermost one (extending for 8 kilometres between the northern and southern ends of a curve in the river east of the city) of baked brick, the others sun-dried, and a wide road was based on rubble infill between the outer and the inner pairs of ranges. Moats to both the outside and the inside of the circuit were connected to the Euphrates.

Nebuchadnezzar's Babylon

The largest of Mesopotamian cities – despite the best efforts of Nineveh's imperial builders – Babylon had been inhabited from time immemorial but the earliest settlements disappeared under Hammurabi's capital, which in turn disappeared under the Kassites – and all of these under the assault of

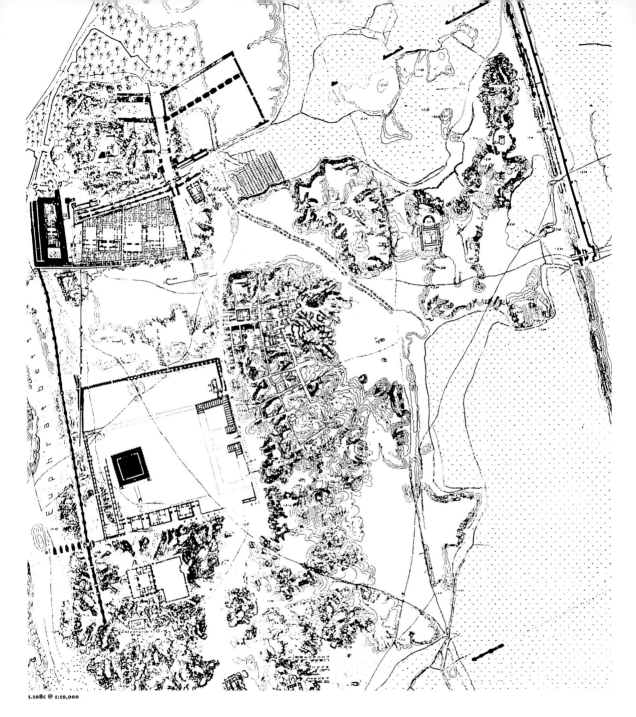

1.108c @ 1:10,000

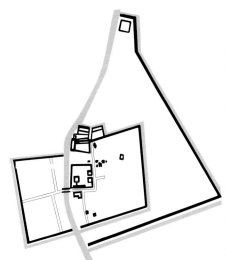

1.108c @ approximately 1:70,000

1.108d

the Assyrians and the Euphrates watertable. Within the most impressive ramparts of their time, the river intersected the city as rebuilt in the 7th century: the ceremonial sector was based on the original settlement to the east, a new suburb was laid out to the west. The Greek historian Herodotus describes the streets as straight, parallel and perpendicular to the river, and excavation in the Merkes area confirms that, over the old organic growth pattern, the main streets of Nebuchadnezzar's city were more or less parallel or perpendicular to the ceremonial axis from the Ishtar Gate in the north, past the palace to the central Esagila Temple of Marduk. Under a strong central authority, regulated rebuilding must have prevailed and the ceremonial axis was reputedly the grandest thoroughfare of pre-Roman antiquity.

Little survives of the principal temples but there is enough to indicate that their plans conformed to the ancient southern tradition with axial access from court to antecella and cella – as in the remains of the Temple of Ninmah beside the Ishtar Gate. And as of old, the Palace of Nebuchadnezzar II was a warren of rooms around regular courts but the axial alignments distinguish it from its grand Assyrian predecessors: the principal court of public audience was preceded by two forecourts and succeeded by two courts of private audience, all aligned on the east–west axis of entry; the throne room and the halls of private audience all addressed their courts from the south through central entrances on axes perpendicular to the main one. In the tiled panel from the huge throne room in the south-centre of the main palace, the lotus motif with curved petals superimposed on stems in the centre and the stylized palm-frond motif (palmette) in the border variously relate to the Assyrian sacred tree and the characteristic Egyptian lotus.

The site of the celebrated hanging gardens is conjectural: they are sometimes placed in the north-east corner of the palace, beside the Ishtar Gate, sometimes on the terraces of the great ziggurat known to much of posterity as the Tower of Babel – but little more than a denuded stump after the destruction of the city by the Persians early in the 5th century. That ziggurat, those gardens, the Ishtar Gate and the walls to which it was attatched were ranked among the foremost wonders of the ancient world – the last not least because of its spectacular revetment.

1.109a

›1.109 THE IMAGE OF THE ACHAEMENID
KING: (a) Darius I in audience: relief from the so-
called Treasury at Persepolis (Tehran, National
Museum); (b) Darius II attending sacrifice at the fire
altar (relief from his tomb at Naqsh-i-Rustam.

The ancient Sumerian image of royal attendance
on the patron deity, which must have been known in
Susa since the days of Ur-Nammu, is here appropriated by the quasi-divine monarch, receiving obei-
sance under his protective canopy.

THE ACHAEMENIDS AND THEIR WORLD EMPIRE

The neo-Babylonian dynasty lasted for hardly a generation after the death of Nebuchadnezzar before falling to a
new power from Iran. This was Cyrus of the Achaemenid
clan of the Indo-Aryan Persians, who were still in the
process of settlement east of their cousins the Medes. In
contention with the latter c. 550, perhaps for liberation
from vassalage, perhaps for control over embittered Elam,
Cyrus won and claimed the Median throne of his mother's
father.

The Lydians, seeking to benefit from the defeat of the
Medes with whom they had been in uneasy truce, moved
into eastern Anatolia where they were surprised by the
agile Cyrus who turned them back west and took Croesus
– his mother's uncle – in his seat at Sardis c. 547. He then
attacked Babylon in 539, and won the immense prestige
which went with the title of its king. He also won a reputation for magnanimity in victory in part for repatriating
captive gods and the Hebrews: after the Assyrians and
Babylonians, his yoke was found to be easy and he was tol-

erant of the religions of his disparate subjects. He established his capital on the Pasargadae land of his clan.

On his death in 530 Cyrus was succeeded without trouble by his son Cambyses, who proceeded to complete the acquisition of all the territories that had once fallen to the Assyrians, Egypt in particular. This was achieved by 525 and Cambyses reigned in Egypt for more than two years of consolidation. He died on his way back to Persia, perhaps at the hands of a rebellious brother, and was succeded by his distant cousin Darius, who had despatched the brother.[1.109a]

Darius (522–486) had to eliminate a clutch of rebels from Media and Persia to Assyria and Egypt: he did so with no less vigour than Cyrus had usually displayed and, with equal sagacity, married the daughters of their leaders as well as the sisters and daughters of Cambyses. In the east he took his frontier to the Indus in the east. In the west, with questionable sagacity, he ignored the natural boundary between Asia and Europe, crossed the Hellespont and initiated a long conflict with the mainland Hellenes which would end in his only major humiliation at celebrated Marathon.

Darius established his principal seat in the prestigious ancient Elamite capital, Susa. He proceded from there to reform the administration of his vast empire by dividing it into provincial satrapies, which were usually delegated to an Achaemenid. And Darius's line held the diversified peoples of west Asia together most effectively with their firm grasp of administration, common law, regular taxation, network of roads with relay posts extended from the Assyrian legacy and a highly effective professional army. Also indebted to the Assyrian precedent, the latter was mobilized under the special protection of the supreme god Ahura Mazda who appears over the king in a winged disk – like Assur.[1.109b]

1.109b

Though he was not originally conceived anthropomorphically, Ahura Mazda presided over a family of deities brought to Iran by the Aryans – in much the same way as Zeus dominated the Hellenic pantheon. The upholder of the good in the cosmic struggle against evil – like Indra in Vedic India – his cult was reformed before the advent of the Achaemenids by the semi-legendary Zarathustra (Zoroaster to the Greeks): aware of the god's supreme virtue, humanity is free to choose between good and evil but, at the final judgement, Ahura Mazda would preside over trial by fire in which the evil would perish.

Ahura Mazda was the ideal model for Darius I and his successors as the Great King imposing order on earth. Yet, though Zoroaster may have anticipated monotheism, imperial eclecticism prompted the Achaemenids to tolerate the religions of their subjects and to promote syncretism – hence the apparent identification of Ahura Mazda with Assur and the development of a triad in which he was associated with Mithra (a sun-god like Indian Surya, if not Hellenic Apollo) and Anahita (a female deity like Ionian Artemis).

Darius's successor was his son Xerxes by a daughter of Cyrus. His immediate problem was to quash rebellion in Babylonia and Egypt. Then he turned his attention to avenging his father's defeat in Hellas but, after long preparations and initial success, he too was forced to retreat to Asia after crushing defeats on sea and land (479). However, only the European territories eluded him: the Ionian cities gained a measure of independence until trouble within Hellas later in the 5th century left them at the mercy of the Persians.

Despite palace coups, murdered heirs, peripatetic rebellion and unprecedented vastness, the empire persisted for nearly two hundred years on the strength of the army, the effectiveness of the imperial administration, the ability

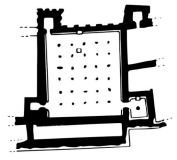

›1.110 THE EARLY IRANIAN COLUMNED HALL:
(a) Godin Tepe (Hamedan), plan of 7th-century hypostyle hall with corner towers framing porticoes; (b, c) Pasargadae (Persia), camp-palace of Cyrus the Great, hypostyle hall c. 540, remains and plan with the bit-hilani porticoes and loggia surrounding the colonnaded hall.

Overlooked by a great platform built of cyclopean masonry, the three pavilions of Cyrus's palace were informally disposed like the tents of a camp in an enclosure. All had tent-like columned halls flanking which the Uratian columned portico was transformed (doubtless by Ionic masons) into galleries like the columned sides of the temples Croesus was building in Ionia: the interior columns of the great audience hall were 11 metres high, double those of the porticoes. The enclosure was entered through a portal guarded by winged, human-headed bulls related to the Assyrian *lamassu* (see **1.106d**).

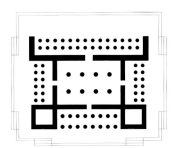

1.110c @ 1:2000

and longevity of the kings who survived their first few months – Artaxerxes I (465–425), Darius II (424–405), Artaxerxes II (404–359), Artaxerxes III (359–338) – and the fabulous resources at their disposal to buy off opposition or foment dissent among fractious rivals. The end came with a usurper, Darius III (335–330), at the hands of Hellenic avengers.

1.110b

SEATS OF ACHAEMENID POWER

At Cyrus's Pasargadae camp the Persians seem first to have translated their informally distributed tents into multi-columned timber pavilions under the inspiration of the Urartians, transmitted directly but also already domesticated in Iran in the heartland of Media around Hamedan. And like their Uratian predecessors and Median cousins, they added columned porticoes indebted to the Anatolian bit-hilani as much as to the Ionian temple.**1.97a**

With no tradition of monumental architecture, indeed still living in tents for most of the time, Cyrus and his Achaemenid successors had to devise one: with many immediate precedents to hand, their synthesis was at once pragmatic in its mobilization of available resources and symbolic of the world dominion which provided them. As his capital, Darius completed the restoration of Susa more than a century after its destruction by Assurbanipal in emulation of the great Assyrian palace platforms supporting walled courts and rooms protected by *lamassu* and, of the Babylonian dado with its glazed bricks, of the hypostyle halls and cyclopaean masonry of Media, Uratu, Egypt – and Cyrus the Great's Pasargadae. And he developed the hybrid formula on an unprecedented scale at Persepolis, the new dynastic cult centre designed primarily to cater for the rites of the spring fertility festival.**1.111, 1.112**

›1.111 SUSA: (a) Palace of Darius I, plan; (b, c) glazed brick revetment with guardsmen from the outer court and capital from apadana column (Paris, Louvre).

The palace, on its terrace (1), had the first truly imperial apadana (2). The walled range was entered from the east, like the Babylonian palace, through a freestanding propylon (3) off axis with the main portal (4): the first court, for public audience, was addressed from the south by the main throne hall preceded by three parallel vestibules (5); the second court provided ante-space for the third, the court of private audience addressed by a doubled throne hall in the south range (6); the harem apartments bordered the south side of the complex.

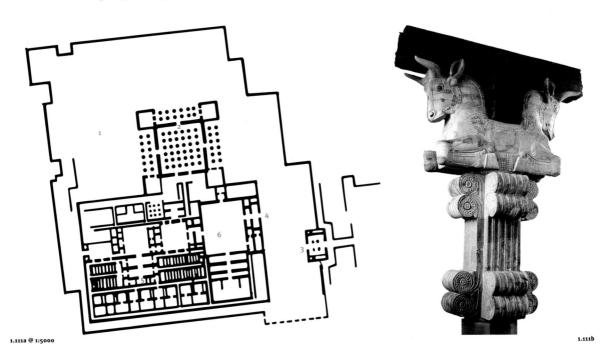

1.111a @ 1:5000

1.111b

Susa and Persepolis

Intended to supplant Babylon, Susa was the empire's enduring administrative capital, not abandoned by new monarchs with fresh pretensions:
extensively built over, much of it has been lost to unscientific excavation
but it clearly combined Pasagardae's monumental masonry translation of
the tent-camp with Babylon's brick complex of aligned courts and throne
rooms. Varying the formula evolved at Pasagardae, the great columned
hall (apadana in its Darian form) was based on the square rather than the
rectangle and there was a similar portico to all sides except the south
where it adjoined the courtyard palace: the columns and their capitals,
with addorsed animals over vertical volutes, were eclectic but the Persians certainly made the hybrid form their own. Like those of Babylon, the
walls of the courtyard complex were covered with glazed bricks in dazzling
relief.

In contrast to Susa, the remains of Persepolis are overwhelming.
Beyond the great ceremonial entrance, guarded by syncretic monsters in
the Assyrian (and Hittite) manner,[1.91, 1.105] the palace platform was
divided into three zones – as all its great Egyptian and Mesopotamian
predecessors were and as oriental palaces were generally to be. The
outer zone was dominated by the apadana in which the king held public
audience. A smaller, screened hall provided for private audience in the
central zone of the king's personal quarters (the hadith). The innermost
zone, the walled harem, alone recalls the typical Mesopotamian
approach to palace design. If parallel to one another, the main elements
are informally grouped, as at Pasagardae, but much closer together and
usually square in plan.

The propylon, built under Xerxes I after the model of one at Pasagardae, with syncretic monsters to both portals and a columned waiting hall
between, was the ceremonial entrance for official visitors, notably subject rulers: the apotropaic monsters follow the Assyrian and Hittite precedents but clearly relate to Uratian artefacts as well.[1.99] It led
ahead to the precinct of Xerxes, left to the apadana of Darius. The latter,
with thirty-six columns supporting a timber coffered ceiling, lower bit-
hilani porticoes to the three outer sides and service rooms by the hadith
to the south, is reached by two sets of broad stairs (north and east)

1.111C

1.112b

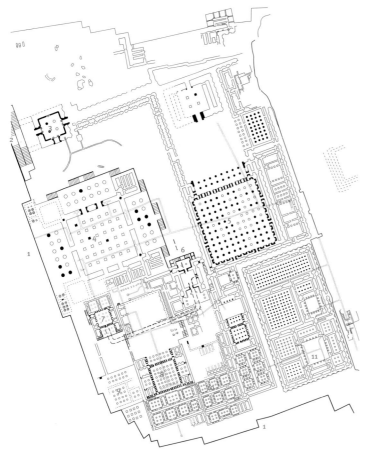

1.112c @ 1:4000

>1.112 PERSEPOLIS, GREAT PALACE, begun c. 500 by Darius I and substantially complete a century later: (a, pages 212–217) general view from the east; (b) restored perspective from north; (c) plan with platform (c. 500 by 300 metres and up to 20 metres high) (1), entrance stairs (2), propylon (3), apadanas of Darius (62 metres square on its own terrace 82 metres square with thirty-six stone columns) (4) and Xerxes (5), triple gate (tripylon) (6) leading to the private apartments (hadith – 'dwelling place') of Darius (7), Xerxes (8) and Artaxerxes III? (9), the harem (10) and offices (11); (f) propylon; (e) hadith of Darius I: general view from east with apadana of Darius I beyond, (f) Xerxes I progressing under the protection of Ahura-Mazda, (g, h) details of apadana staircase revetment.

The columns in Darius's palace had torus, perhaps from Ionia like the fluting, supplemented at the base by a foliate bell-shaped moulding that recalls Susan royal portrait statuary at the height of Elam's power c. 1250;[1.93] the tassel-like fringe of drooping sepals at the base of the capital recalls the cord bound round the top of a timber post to prevent splitting and the corola recalls the Egyptian palm-leaf motif, especially when etched with a papyrus flower; the lotiform scrolls of the block below the bracket disposed vertically as they sometimes were in the Levant and even Nebuchadnezzar's Babylon, and the bracket with addorsed animals possibly derived from Uratu.

1.112g

1.112d

1.112h

embellished with tiered reliefs of Median and Persian soldiers and tribute bearers from all over the empire. Xerxes's hall of one hundred columns, with one portico to the north and corridors to the other three sides, was enclosed by screen walls with two doors to each side, windows to the portico and niches along the corridors. The hadiths also had one portico but the central hall was flanked with living rooms. Beyond the similar first hall of the harem, a grid of corridors served the individual apartments of the royal ladies. The niches and portals in the private audience hall and elsewhere, usually carved from single blocks, were spanned by Egyptian cavetto lintels.

1.112e

The foundations, platform and structural members – columns, door and window frames – were built of limestone; brick infill for walls had a revetment of glazed tiles; all sculpted surfaces were brightly coloured.

Like the timber work, some of the columns were inlaid with precious metals and ivory. The reliefs, which represent the king and his entourage as they would actually have appeared in each particular part of the complex, recall their Assyrian equivalents in their precise detail and especial facility with animals but, executed in marble rather than tiles, have something of the elegance already evolved by Ionic Hellenes in the service of the king of Lydia. As at Susa, the evolving Ionian tradition and its sources were also drawn upon liberally (and irrationally) for the design of the columns but, highly complex in their derivation, these are also clearly indebted to Egypt and the Uratians.

The new emperor readily acknowledged his imperial eclecticism in the inscription celebrating the completion of the palace at Susa:

> I am Darius, great king, king of kings ... This is the palace I erected ... That the earth was dug down and that the rubble was packed and that the brick was moulded, all was due to the Babylonians. The cedar timber was brought from the mountains called Lebanon ... Gold was brought from Sardes and Bactria ... Lapis lazuli and car-

1.112f

nelian were brought from Soghdiana and turquoise from Khwarazm. Silver and ebony were brought from Egypt. Ivory was brought from Ethopia, India and Arachonia and wrought here. The stone, here wrought into columns, came from Abiradu in Elam. The stone-cutters and sculptors who made them were Ionians and Sardians. Those who wrought the gold were Medes and Egyptians. The wood-carvers were Sardians and Egyptians. Those who made mosaics in ivory were Babylonians and Ionians. Those who adorned the walls were Medes and Egyptians. By the grace of Ahura Mazda I constructed the magnificent palace in Susa. May Ahura Mazda protect me and my line and my country.

Cyrus was buried in a simple rectangular, gabled building on a stepped stylobate: the type was to be common in

›1.113 THE PERSIAN IMPERIAL TOMB: (a) Pasagardae, Tomb of Cyrus the Great; (b) Naqsh-i-Rustam, rock-cut tombs of Darius I (right) and Xerxes I.

Instead of Cyrus's western model, derived from his grandfather's domain, Darius revived the Median tradition of the rock-cut tomb presumably considering it more appropriate for an Achaemenid without his predecessor's connections. In his funerary inscription he proclaimed that he had been made king by Ahura Mazda, creator of the world; he promoted the good and pursued evil; he protected the weak from the strong and the strong from the weak, he was a good horseman, archer and spearsman ...

As in Vedic India, religious ritual was centred on the sacrifice of a sacred juice (haoma in Iran, soma in India) at a fire altar. Mithra seems to have been, or to have become, the specific dedicatee of haoma though fire itself, specially sanctified as the essential element of purification, belonged to Ahura Mazda. The special status accorded to fire meant that the cremation of the dead was proscribed and the body was interred or exposed for consumption by birds.

›1.114 ROYAL CAMPAIGN TENT: early 19th-century Indian miniature.

1.113a

1.113b

›ARCHITECTURE IN CONTEXT »WEST ASIA AND THE EASTERN MEDITERRANEAN

Lykia, the southern part of his mother's maternal homeland, Lydia, but it most resembles the simplest form of temple then evolving in the Hellenic towns on the Aegean coast of his grandfather's kingdom.[1.113] The temple is not a characteristic Achaemenid building type: the kings led devotion to fire as the visual manifestation of the divine Ahura Mazda and though the remains of square towers related to those of the Uratians and Medians have been identified as fire temples, the cult seems primarily to have required an open-air altar. The ceremony is depicted on the magnificent series of imperial tombs at Naqsh-i-Rustam and Persepolis: as high priest before the altar presided over by the great god Ahura Mazda, the king is carried by the peoples united under his imperium. The tomb itself below, carved into the timeless cliff for an Egyptian eternity of the royal being, is the imperial apadana portico, complete with the dentillated cornice of a heavy beamed roof. From its anticipation in durable stone at Pasagardae to its apotheosis in the living rock, the apadana ceded nothing in monumental grandeur to the festival halls of the pharaohs, and oriental potentates were never to forget it – or its origin in the tent.[1.114]

1.114

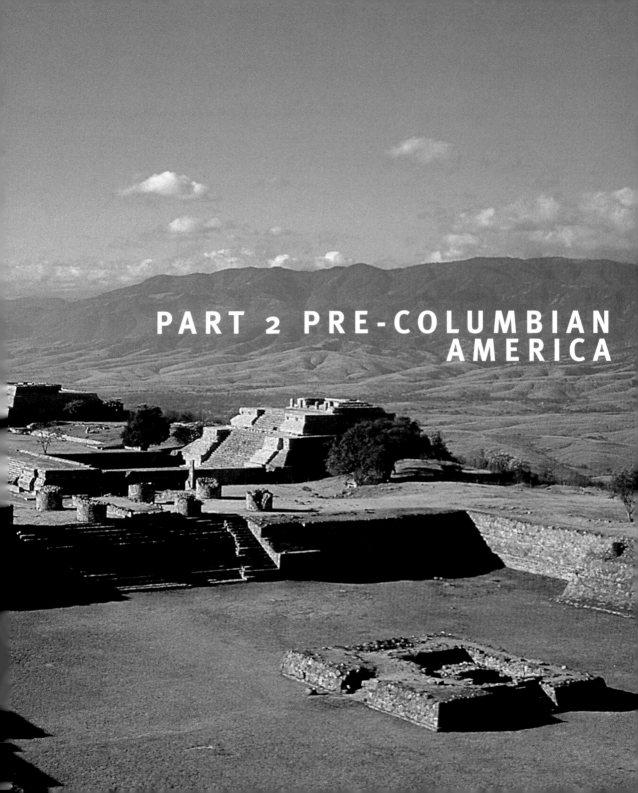

PART 2 PRE-COLUMBIAN AMERICA

2.1

›ARCHITECTURE IN CONTEXT »PRE-COLUMBIAN AMERICA

INTRODUCTION

Occupied by nomadic groups pressing southward from Alaska c. 12000 BCE, the area stretching from northern Mexico to Honduras and the region of the central Andes were the scenes of the highest form of civilization in America before the arrival of the Spanish *conquistadores* in the 1530s. Indeed, apart from China and the Indus valley, these are the greatest areas of early civilization outside western Asia, Egypt and the Aegean. Between the Mesopotamian and Mesoamerican – even South America's pre-Columbian – cultures there are similarities of evolution, of rural development, of urbanization and of monumental form. Some commentators, unready to accept coincidental solutions to universal problems, would connect them despite improbability of contact – let alone differences of time, language and ideology.

Mesoamerica, like the Andean region but unlike Mesopotamia, is marked by sharp disparity between highland and lowland zones and between dry and wet climates. Dominated by some of the highest peaks in the world, the central Andes offer well-watered but precipitous valleys and dry plains some 4000 metres above sea level: maize and other cereals may be grown on sheltered land here but on the exposed plateau only root crops – especially the potato – supplement the grazing of native animals – the llama and alpaca in particular. The central and southern highlands of Mexico, peaking at more than 5000 metres, are more generally dry but increase in aridity from south to north: maize and beans are staples here, as widely elsewhere, but supplementary water was needed for efficient highland agriculture. The Pacific coastal plain, relatively narrow in Peru, exceptionally so in most of Mexico and Guatemala, is exceptionally arid in Peru, relatively so in Mexico: seafood is the main source of protein but corn may be grown where there is fertile hinterland or riverbanks. The wide Gulf coast of Mexico ranges from dry in the north and northern Yucatan to very humid in the broader swathe of lowlands that links it to the north-east-facing foothills of the Guatemalan (Mayan) range: cereals apart, cotton and cocoa – and the feathers of exotic jungle birds – were the most important ancient lowland products.

There was seasonal settlement in camps or caves and cultivation of staples like maize or beans in much of Mexico by c. 3500 BCE. Semi-permanent settlements in alluvial valleys, as well as coastal areas dependent on fishing, appear during the next millennium: pottery appears with them from c. 2300. The Andean region was possibly a millennium behind in settlement and along the coast succesful extraction of protein-rich food from the sea delayed the general cultivation of plants until early in the 2nd millennium. South America led, however, in the production of pottery and metallurgy: the former appears in Columbia by the beginning of the 3rd millennium and the skill had worked its way down the coast into Peru by around 1800; the working of gold leaf is known in the south-central Andes c. 1500.

As in Mesopotamia, broad transition from the nomadic life of the hunter and gatherer to the sedentary life of the agriculturalist in America depended on water management, primitive and local at first, attendant on basic local society capable of co-operative public work. As usual, civilization began in the areas where the water problem was at its most acute: the Gulf coast of Mexico crossed by the rivers rising in the Mexican central highlands and subject to devastating but soil-enriching annual floods like the Nile valley; the dessicated coastal plain of Peru, cut by snow-fed rivers at 18–25-kilometre intervals, where agricultural expansion depended on irrigation. Water management on the Mexican Gulf coast can hardly have begun much later than c. 2000 and it was even earlier that the inhabitants of the Andean Santa Valley began to develop irrigation farming: archaic sites are sparse but after c. 2000 they proliferate in both regions. Irrigation was important, too, in the dry upland basin and valleys of central and southern Mexico and in the high Andes, but agriculture could only be expanded in the valleys with terracing: civilization appeared in these areas hardly much later than in the lowlands.

Tools were of stone, flint or highly prized obsidian in most of pre-Columbian American – the impact of copper preceding the Spaniards by less than half a millennium though it had long been prized for decorative objects, and bronze had appeared in South America much earlier. The potential of the wheel was unrealized and the plough unknown there; agriculture was not generally combined with cattle grazing, as in ancient Africa and Asia where the one manured the other, and there were no draft animals – except, to a limited extent, in the high Andes where llamas provided carriage, wool and food.

Settlement and the improvement of husbandry led to population growth and, ultimately, to pockets of population density not inferior to those of Mesopotamia – partly because of the easily worked nature and extent of much of the land won through irrigation and terracing.**2.1** Certainly, the infrastructure of improved husbandry implies centralized authority – 'chiefdom' – capable of mobilizing people and materials on a supra-local scale as in Mesopotamia – the waxing of individual fortunes doubtless responding to luck in landholding and/or skill in land management. Asserting the superiority of man over man, the advent of the chief and his family marked the crucial transition from the egalitarian village, where subsistence farming preoccupied all, to hierarchical urban civilization, the realm of the specialist sustained by the labour of others. Thus were laid the foundations of the state and prince or priest – or priest as prince – legitimized supreme authority in ritualistic religion.

Mesoamerican history – pieced together from records which developed in sophistication especially among the Mayas across the 1st millennium CE and chronicles transmitted orally for many generations before the arrival of the Spaniards – is conventionally seen as rising to a classic eminence with the Teotihuacanos, Zapotecs and Mayas in the 7th century CE: the pre-Classic or Formative period, prepared from c. 2000 BCE and promoted by the chiefdoms emergent within five centuries, is conventionally – if not uncontroversially – opened with the advent of the Gulf coast Olmecs and divided into early, middle and late phases (c. 1500–900, c. 900–300 and the last three hundred years BCE); a proto-Classic phase is recognized in the first three hundred years CE and the post-Classic period is usually divided between the Toltecs (c. 900–1250) and the Aztecs (c. 1250-1519).

As writing apparently eluded the early inhabitants of the South American continent, the piecing together of the strands of history is vastly more problematic there than in Mesoamerica. Archaeology has found numerous centres of civilization in the coastal plains and uplands of the Andean region, between which resources had long been exchanged and across which South America's highest cultural development was to be attained. After an 'Initial' period opening c. 2000 BCE, and thus contemporary with the preparation of the Mesoamerican Formative period, several of these dominated vast tracts of territory, especially along the coast of modern Peru. Punctuating periods of singularly regional significance, three are identified as quasi-imperial 'Horizons': the first, named for Chavin in the north-central Andes but almost certainly earlier in inception than the earliest monumental works at that site, opened perhaps as early as 1700 BCE and lasted for more than a millennium; the second is associated with the south-central Andean sacred site of Tiahuanaco and the more central metropolis of Huari, both of which were waxing c. 600 CE and declining four hundred years later; the third was forged by the Incas in the second quarter of the 15th century and taken by the Spaniards within a hundred years. In both the later cases, at least, imperial ambition was prompted by the need for resources lacking at home but available elsewhere in the ecologically diverse central Andean highlands and lowlands.

2.1 MESOAMERICA

1 THE PRE-CLASSIC ERA OF THE OLMECS

The early Mesoamericans, like other primitive peoples the world over, were animists doubtless dedicated to placating the spirits of natural phenomena most mysteriously present in the fertile earth and the healing sun, most potently represented by seismic activity, storm, rain, and inhabiting the select rock, pool, tree, etc. Naturally too, given a volcanic environment subject to rapid climatic change, they believed that existence was cyclical.

The principal medium of communication between man and the spirit world was the priest-magician (*shaman*), who could assume the character of an animal familiar, deemed to embody the epitome of natural force, through trance induced by hallucinogenic drugs and, as its alter ego, turn the course of nature to his flock's advantage – particularly in warding off evil spirits, bringing rain, effecting healing, guiding the processes of birth and death. The fount of knowledge, the shaman's power lay in his comprehension of plants and animals and the movements of the heavenly bodies that affected them.[2.2]

With the welding of agricultural settlements into chiefdoms, the spirits on which life depended – the sun, the sky and rain, the earth, and staple crops such as maize – were deified and man's main concern was with their ritual propitiation. The *shaman* survived but his power of confronting the spirits of nature through zoomorphic transformation was challenged by the chief whose assumption of divine ancestry – if not priesthood – entailed the power to intercede with gods and ancestors and win divine protection. The new elite were to accommodate their deities in monumental centres, clothe themselves in ceremony and, in perpetuation of the divine ancestral line, have themselves interred in tumuli.[2.3]

A major condition for the rise of chiefs, the coalescence

2.2

›**2.2 THE SHAMAN:** figures from the Gulf coast of Mexico representing the transformation of man into jaguar, first half of the 1st millennium BCE (Washington, DC, Dumbarton Oaks Collection).

The nocturnal predator of fearsome silence in the jungle, emulated by the hunter, prime metaphor for the supernatural, the jaguar – or the serpent deemed its natural opponent – was the most usual familiar of the *shaman*.

of villages into towns under them and, beyond, the coalescence of regions, was the development of long-distance trade: or, rather, the transition from ad-hoc to regulated contact between relatively distant peoples for reciprocal benefit implies some form of supra-village organization. The exchange of northern maize for southern root crops goes back at least to the early 3rd millennium and pottery was being traded throughout Mesoamerica a millennium later. Southern cacao and cotton from well-watered plains were staples foreign to the arid central and northern highlands but well before the middle of the 2nd millennium these and luxuries like hard greenstone – serpentine, jade and jadeite in particu-lar – were being exchanged for the obsidian from which the era's most efficient tools were made. The last was imported from the volcanic regions of both the central and southern highlands by the Olmec peoples of the Gulf coast to further their Formative culture in the last half of the 2nd millennium BCE.

Dating from perhaps a millennium after the advent of the first chief, of whom there is of course no record, the figure is central to a composition in which four cleft elements, sprouting new growth, doubtless represent the four cardinal directions of space and, therefore, the cosmos. Vegetation motifs relieve a forehead band over almond-shaped eyes, bulbous nose and open mouth. Over the cleft cranium an elaborate headdress incorporates a cruciform maize motif. Detached hands offer a tasselled bundle or scroll.

Serpentine was known to these peoples in the early Formative period but it was rare: by the mid-Formative period the coastal elite and their contemporaries in the central highlands used increasing quantities of jade and jadeite. Several types of greenstone were found on the Pacific side of the central mountains but early Mesoamerican jade seems to have come only from Guatemala.

OLMEC CENTRES

The Mexican Gulf coast inhabitants known as Olmecs – the term derives from the Spanish name for the inhabitants of that rubber-producing area – promoted the major advance represented by the institution of regional authorities in the Formative period (c. 1500–900). Their main known centres are located in the south of the region between San Lorenzo and Tres Zapotes, respectively on the Coatzacoalcos and Hueyapan Rivers in Veracruz state, and La Venta on the Tonala River in Tabasco. Maize, beans and squash appear to have been original staples. Obsidian from central Mexico and Guatemala bears witness to long-distance trade.

San Lorenzo was founded towards the middle of the early pre-Classic period and declined after 900 BCE. La Venta developed in the middle-pre-Classic period and disappeared after 600 BCE. Tres Zapotes, and several related sites, survived until the end of the 1st millennium BCE. All were once identified as purely ceremonial centres but it is now known that the great structures of the elite – spiritual and temporal, if there was such a division – formed the nucleus of numerous sub-urban villages in which kindred inhabitans lived in huts grouped around plazas.

The identification of Mesoamerica's formative culture with these sites was widely assumed as their exploration progressed to the discovery of San Lorenzo in 1945. Now that is often contradicted on the grounds that a culture as advanced as its earliest manifestation at San Lorenzo must have had antecedents, that some of its characteristic features – pottery forms and iconography in particular – appear to have developed in several chiefly centres simultaneously throughout Mesoamerica, and that some aspects – portable greenstone carving in particular – may have appeared earlier on the Pacific side of central Mexico's spinal mountain range. Of course there will have been cross-fertilization of ideas along with the exchange of goods and the process both prompted and was promoted by the emergence of other early-Formative chiefly societies not only in the Gulf coast region but also in the Mexican basin, in the Valle of Oaxaca, in Morelos, Guerrero, Chiapas and Guatemala. Yet there is still considerable reluctance to deny that San Lorenzo, the largest of Olmec centres, precocious in its hierarchical society, seminal in its production of large-scale stone monuments, played the key role in effecting a synthesis of pan-Mesoamerican beliefs and the symbols with which they were represented.

By 1000 BCE, when San Lorenzo was declining, population growth consequent on increased agricultural efficiency had produced a proliferation of villages and chiefly seats in many parts of Mesoamerica and that meant an increasingly complex network of exchange, especially as the elite developed its characteristic taste for ornaments, monuments and elaborate burial: ceramics embellished with the motifs of Olmec divinity and figurines with infantile characteristics like many recovered from Olmec sites have been found widely distributed elsewhere in graves contemporary with those of late San Lorenzo. In the mid-Formative age of La Venta these are generally supplemented, then supplanted, by less-elaborate ceramics, less-stereotyped figurines and by the proliferation of greenstone jewellery and celts engraved with motifs derived from the earlier ceramics. By San Lorenzo's demise, important centres of hierarchical civilization – 'olmec' if not Olmec – had emerged outside the Gulf coast region: at Tlapacoya or Tlatilco in the Mexican basin, Chalcatzingo in Morelos, San Jose Mogote in Oaxaca, Teopantecuanitlan in Guerrero, for example. However, no mid-Formative centre outshines La Venta.**2.4, 2.5**

2.8a

San Lorenzo and La Venta

Olmec sites were orientated to ensure harmony with the cosmos, the north–south axis dominant. San Lorenzo was less formal than its successors in the relationship of its major elements: on the highest ground in its region's floodplain, rising to about 80 metres above the water level, it was based on the monumental modification of the contours – levelling plateaux for platforms, filling ravines, constructing terraces and causeways across marshy ground – which must have absorbed huge resources of labour. The earliest signs of settlement date between 1500 and 1350 when a chieftainship, possibly a state, was based on control of the highly productive river levee lands and waterways. Not devoted solely to ceremony, but not itself the scene of agricultural activity, the site was the political and religious centre of a hierarchical system of district and local administrative units. Control over the distribution of resources, local or imported, was obviously vital to the rulers of San Lorenzo and their decline may have been furthered by tectonic activity changing river courses.

The rulers were commemorated by colossal heads, presumably originally sited on the ceremonial platforms but subsequently displaced, ritually mutilated and buried in trenches. The elite were accommodated on the highest ground and buried in central locations: among the most prominent residences, the so-called Red Palace was not atypical in incorporating stone columns and retaining walls. Craftsmen were accommodated near the palaces but in general commoners lived in clusters on lower terraces and were buried under their houses. The typical habitation of the extended family was centred on a patio with an altar.

Olmec occupation of the La Venta site, on a natural eminence in a floodplain as at San Lorenzo, is dated between 1200–400: the ceremonial centre seems to have developed from the 12th century and reached its final formal order c. 600 BCE. The earliest works were a conical mound (30 metres high, 130 metres diameter) and its smaller satellites (for houses and burials) based on levelled hills. The later parallel terraces to the north, defining a north–south axis, led to the plaza, which was also based on raised ground. Another plaza, added to the north in the last phase of the site's development, was dominated by a stepped pyramid containing

2.4 @ 1:10,000

›2.4 SAN LORENZO: site plan (after Coe) revealing terrace-framed plazas to north and south of a central mound: the monumental sculptures and main buildings, including the 'Red Palace', were located to the north of the mound.

a tomb: rising to 30 metres on a platform with central projections, this is the earliest-known Mesoamerican structure of its type.

Colossal heads were found (mutilated and displaced) at both ends of the site, thrones (once thought to be altars) and stelae (commemorating the achievements and lineage of rulers) on the platform of the pyramid and in the plazas. Many jade objects and three spectacular mosaic pavements, representing were-jaguar masks in serpentine, were uncovered. There were reservoirs connected with water channels. Several courts possibly catered for the ritual ball game that was to prove so perennially important throughout Mesoamerica. The commoners lived on subsidiary mounds beyond the main axis.

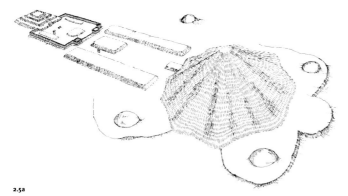

2.5a

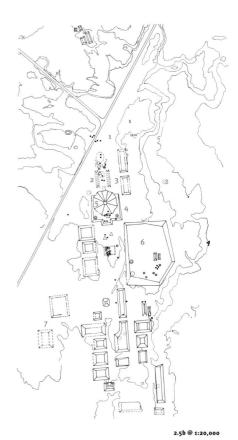

2.5b @ 1:20,000

›**2.5 LA VENTA:** (a) reconstruction of major features with conical mound, (b) site plan with (1) parallel terraces leading to raised plaza (2, 3), northern plaza and stepped pyramid (4, 5), 'Great Pyramid' complex (6), presumed administrative 'acropolis' named after its excavator, M.W. Stirling (7), unidentified platforms (8) (after Corella, etc.).

The nature of the power competent in the control of sufficient labour for such monumental architectural and sculptural exercises, let alone extensive irrigation facilities, is elusive: the forger of the state, it is hewn to its awesome human face in the portraiture of the colossal heads, it is etched on the stelae that inaugurated a major Mesoamerican tradition in the commemoration of regal achievement and lineage, it is profoundly impressed on the thrones that distinguish Olmec ceremonial platforms and related reliefs. The most characteristic throne motif is a central figure emerging from the cave: the legitimacy of authority has rarely been more forcefully – and economically – asserted than in this association of

2.6b

2.6a

›**2.6** **OLMEC THRONES:** (a) from Potrero Nuevo, early Formative period (Monument 2, Jalapa, Museum of Anthropology); (b) from La Venta, mid-Formative period (Mexico City, National Museum of Anthropology).

The motif of the paired atlases of Potrero Nuevo, united in support of the world order sustained by the enthroned king, is singularly appropriate in this context, if far less familiar: beyond the elevation of temporal power, it anticipates the Mesoamerican propensity to pair deities, most notably the later cosmological pair of creator gods who raised heaven from earth in preparation for the advent of man, and foreshadows the widespread Mesoamerican myth of the heroic twin champions of harmony in the reconciliation of the conflict implicit in duality.

›**2.7** **COLOSSAL HEAD FROM SAN LORENZO** (Monument 1, Jalapa, Museum of Anthropology).

Some ten colossal basalt heads (about 2.8 metres high) were found at San Lorenzo, four at La Venta and three at Tres Zapotes. Central authority must have been impressive to control a labour force sufficient for the transportation of blocks weighing about 44 tons from distant basalt quarries for these exercises. It is now generally thought that they were portraits of individual rulers: the discovery of a defaced head dated to c. 600 BCE in a crypt grave at Chalcatzingo (Morelos) has been taken as evidence that the mutilation and burial of the image were a ritual performed on the death of the patron. The headgear is probably military but it has led some to identify it as the helmet of a player in the type of ritual ballgame later common throughout the area.

the ruler, the intercessor with the supernatural forces controlling rain, with the creation myth of progenerative man emerging from the womb-like orifice of the great earth-mother. And, beyond the image of terrestrial power, these altar-like monoliths introduce icons of cosmic significance.**2.6, 2.7**

OLMEC GOD, MAN AND MEDIATOR

The earliest of Mesoamerican cultures, sustaining the elite in its association with the gods on the high ground of the ceremonial centres, established a vertical axis of communication between man on middle earth and the upper and lower zones of the spirit world – in addition to the horizontal ones, linking the cardinal directions, which ordered the cosmos. Beyond the anthropomorphic image of that axis as the sustaining atlas, or the equally ubiquitous arborial one with roots in the underworld and branches canopying heaven, the mountain and the cave were particularly revered as the junctures of man's zone with the realms of the deified spirits. Of those spirits much remains obscure, of course, but it seems that the Olmec priest – the community's prime specialist – forged from his animistic inheritance, rich in zoomorphic symbolism, a complex art comprehending man and the supernatural in a triad of motifs: man himself, generally represented in terms usually defined as 'baby-faced'; the gods of the sky, the earth, the underworld and the primordial ocean represented in standardized zoomorphic terms primarily derived from the eagle, the jaguar, the serpent, the cayman and the shark; and the medium for effecting commerce between them represented in the composite anthropo-zoomorphic terms – parts representing wholes – essential to the *shaman* since time immemorial.**2.8**

2.8b

›**2.8** OLMEC INFANTILE FIGURINES AND ATTRIBUTES OF ELEMENTAL DIVINITY: (a, page 232) spreadeagled, Veracruz, early Formative Period; (b) Kunz celt, mid-Formative Period (New York, American Museum of Natural History); (c) seated greenstone figure nursing an infantile were-jaguar and incised on shoulders and knees with (d) zoomorphic images, mid-Formative Period (Las Limas Monument 1, 'The Lord of Las Limas', Xalapa, Museum of Anthropology).

Olmec emblems of elemental divinity

All three realms of imagery distinguish the nursing figure recovered at Las Limas in Veracruz. The adult's features are not quite as infantile as those of the most characteristic Olmec figurines, but the physiognomy of the cradled infant and the cleft-headed zoomorphic profiles incised on the crossed legs and shoulders, attributes of the four elemental spirits paired for the maintenance of cosmic order in the balance of opposing forces, are of perennial significance. On the right shoulder the monster with banded

2.8c

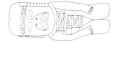

2.8d

eye, eagle-beak and fangs is a sky deity who seems to prefigure the god of spring regeneration associated with rain. On the left shoulder the celestial bird-monster, also eagle-beaked and fanged but flaming at the brows, is the progenitor of the fire-god, First Lord of Day and Night, doubtless as agent of the sun whose energy is life and whose passage is time. On the right knee is the foliage-fringed terrestrial dragon monster, with cross-faceted oblong eye and gaping maws representing the cave orifice through which potent forces emerged from the underworld, prefiguring the principal god of creation. On the left knee is the spine-toothed, crescent-eyed, blunt-nosed shark-monster of the primordial ocean or underworld, who spawned the god of death. The infantile were-jaguar, with human nose splayed over jaguar snout, squalling toothless mouth, distinctive ruffled or crinkled ear-covers suspended from a pleated headband and crossed tunic, has been identified as an offering to or representation of the agricultural fertility-god, bringer of rain, to whom the new fruit of the fertile womb may have been sacrificed: certainly, the were-jaguar is ancestral to all later rain-gods.

The concept of duality was to remain fundamental to Mesoamerican religious thought and variations on the iconic themes represented on the 'Lord of Las Limas' were rife.**2.8, 2.9** The dragon monster is perhaps the most prodigal in the assimilation of attributes borrowed from creatures as diverse – but iconographically potent – as the eagle, the serpent and the jaguar: the major permutation is the plumed – rather than foliage-fringed – serpent of Quetzalcoatl, the great creator-god with special briefs for agriculture, science and the arts.

The animal most closely identified with the force of nature, the jaguar seems to have been associated with rain and earth but also to have represented the sun in the underworld – his skin the cloak of night's star-speckled sky. Crossed with man, the were-jaguar is perhaps the most characteristic and certainly the most elusive presence in Olmec cults: one explanation of its association with

2.9a

2.9b

›2.9 WERE-JAGUARS AND PLUMED SERPENTS, mid-Formative period: (a) Kunz celt (New York, American Museum of Natural History); (b) seated figure with were-jaguar headdress from San Martin, Veracruz (Jalapa, Museum of Anthropology).

fertility – and by extension with life-giving rain – is that it resulted from a progenitive union between the primordial beast and an ancestral human.

The corn-god is clearly related to – often paired with – the were-jaguar deity but is distinguished by plants sprouting from the cleft in his head and corn cobs on his

›2.10 MASK OF LIFE AND DEATH FROM TLATILCO: early mid-Formative period (Mexico City, National Museum of Anthropology).

Essential to belief in the cyclical nature of existence, the concept of unity in duality, of the entity of opposites, was often to be restated but never more directly than in this primitive example.

›2.11 CAVE ORIFICE WITH 'EL REY' AT CHALCATZINGO, MORELOS: rock-cut relief, mid-Formative period.

Carved on a cliff adjacent to a natural watercourse and clearly related to the motif of the ruler in the cave common to several of the La Venta 'thrones', here a figure in an elaborate headdress sits holding a scroll in the cavernous mouth of the earth monster: rain issues from clouds above and, as in at least one of the La Venta thrones, a raindrop motif is incorporated in the headdress.

headband. Rulers, primarily responsible for propitiating the fertility deities, are often depicted crowned like the corn-god – assuming his attributes: the multi-headed figure, common in most Mesoamerican cultures, is indeed generally a lord spiritual or temporal wearing a zoomorphic headdress as a mark of supernatural protection. In the representation of divinity itself, moreover, the future lay with the human form, sometimes with monstrously contorted features but usually crowned with their attributes envisaged in zoomorphic terms.**2.10, 2.11**

OLMEC LEGACY

If Olmec culture developed from a San Lorentian synthesis of forms and ideas derived from disparate sources, after the millennium of its evolution and dissemination throughout Mesoamerica the differentiation of regional development produced the array of disparate cultures from which the great classic traditions of the Mexican basin, the Valle of Oaxaca and the Mayan lowlands were to emerge dominant in the early centuries CE. Writing and calendrics apart – which may have been acquired on the way in the Valle of Oaxaca – the enduring Olmec legacy was comprehensive: the recollection of shamanism, the syncretic deity; institutions of state and hierarchical society culminating in the ruler crowned in divine protection with the fountainheads of fertility, monumental masonry stelae in particular; the mound supporting a house and entombing the dead, and the formal distribution of plazas, platforms and pyramids in ceremonial centres.

The temple on its pyramid had its origin in the house on its mound.**2.12** Well before the end of the pre-Classic era – at La Venta, as we have noted – the platform was overshadowed by the temple pyramid which grew from the mound with the growth in stature of the elite. The mound took on a pyramidal form and the platform was recalled in its stages: each of these was set back from the one below and battered – that is inward sloping from a broad base – to form a talus (talud) for stability of structure in unstable materials like mud-brick, rubble, or ragstone. Within or below the mass, the burial chamber was retained for the great personage and his ancestral deity was accommodated in a summit house. The latter – usually long-gone but presumably little-changing over two millennia – was not congregational: at most its simple cella accommodated priestly rites while the assembly of devotees was accommodated in a plaza below.

The earliest example of a pyramidal temple found in the Mexican basin is the exceptional circular one at Cuicuilco. Though stone-clad, its superstructure disappeared ages ago but its grave contained a rich hoard of distinctive local ceramics, some marking a crucial stage in the evolution of the iconography of the gods.**2.13**

Long linked by trade with the Mexican basin, the Zapotec settlers in the Valle of Oaxaca seem to have emulated the Olmecs in the development of common ceremonial centres at successive sites. Well before the beginning of the mid-Formative period (c. 800 BCE) the settlement at the site of San Jose Mogote was the largest in the valley and its major chiefly centre, a key station on the spinal trade route that linked the Mexican basin and the Gulf coast to its north with the Pacific coast and Guatemala. A platform on a natural mound there, dated to c. 600 BCE and hence contemporary with La Venta, was embellished with primitive reliefs, like the stelae of La Venta but rather coarser in style than the best Olmec work: they incorporated the oldest-known Mesoamerican calendric notation. Some form of ritual calendrics and notation may have been developed by the Olmecs in the era of late-Formative Tres Zapotes but, earlier, the

>**2.12 CLAY MODEL OF A HOUSE RAISED ON A PROTECTIVE PLATFORM** (New York, Museum of American History).

The hut was the ubiquitous dwelling, raised above ground on a platform of compacted earth or rough masonry for protection as much from predatory animals as from flood, for the better circulation of air and, ultimately, for burial. For many centuries palace and temple were grander huts and well into the Classic period the temple structure on top of the stepped-pyramidal platform reproduced the primitive trabeated and thatched hut as the stepped pyramid itself reproduced the primitive base in superimposed accretions.

2.13b

>**2.13 CUICUILCO:** (a) circular pyramid (reconstruction model); (b) ceramic image of the fire-god Huehueteotl, late-Formative period (both Mexico City, National Museum of Anthropology).

The pyramid had four tiers of clay and rubble clad in volcanic stone, and stairs flanked with ramps (alfardas). The circular form was rarely to be repeated in the

ceremonial architecture of the Mexican basin – or elsewhere in Mesoamerica except the highlands around
Teuchitlan in the region of Jalisco.

Known as the 'Old God', Huehueteotl is here represented as an old man relieved of his Olmec ancestor's
zoomorphic iconography but bearing a naturalistic brazier instead: the image was to become classic in central
Mexico.

›2.14 MONTE ALBAN: (a) Plaza Central with Monticulo J (centre), Edificios G, H and I (left); (b) 'Danzante'
panel detail.

The first phase of construction has been obliterated
by the many later phases. Edificio H was built over a
natural outcrop in a second post-Olmec phase but
joined to G and I to form the central ceremonial complex
in the proto-Classic period c. 100 CE. Exceptional in its
arrow-head shape, Monticulo J is the only terraced
structure to survive from phase two. It was built of first-
phase material taken from the 'Monumento de los Dan-
zas', restored in the third phase and misnamed for its
reliefs of running warriors, ballplayers or sacrificial victims: these were accompanied by calendric notations
in bars and dots of the kind that first appeared at San
Jose Mogote and then on Monticulo J.

2.14a

2.14b

2.13a

Zapotecs in the Valle of Oaxaca are the first Mesoamericans known to have used writing – of a mixed pictographic and phonetic type, like future Mayan – and to
have mastered the computation of time.

After its emergence to pre-eminence in the Valle,
around 300 BCE, Monte Alban recalled Olmec sites in its
axis of ritual platforms crossing an extended plaza
between raised terraces, the central one with relatively
low tiered structures based in part on natural outcrops of
rock, but its tombs were subterranean. The earliest monuments were embellished with reliefs recalling in style
those of San Jose Mogote.**2.14**

In the late pre-Classic period, Olmec influence was
transmitted far to the south by people from the central-
Gulf coast known as Izapas. Bypassing the central Mexican highlands and the Oaxaca valley, they left a chain of
sites along the Gulf, across the isthmus of Tehuantepec and
thence around the Pacific rim to their eponymous capital
on the coastal plain and up to Kaminaljuyu in the highlands of modern Guatemala. Their gods were syncretic

zoomorphs – in attribute and sometimes in form. Their sculptors seem to elaborate on the Olmec approach, especially to stelae, and were to inspire the Maya.**2.15, 2.9**

No calendric records have been recovered at late-Formative Izapa itself but examples from contemporary sites in the high Guatemalan hinterland, following Gulf coast developments, long precede the earliest Mayan exercises. Rich in sculptures of rulers and in inscriptions with the oldest glyphs and numeric symbols in the southern highlands, Kaminaljuyu – like Izapa – was dominated by stone-clad pyramidal mounds but the late-Formative work disappeared under later accretions.

Beyond the Izapa domains to the north, the lowland plain stretching to Yucatan seems to have been settled only after the appearance of the Mayas c. 800 BCE. The origins of the latter are obscure but they were related to the Olmecs linguistically and some would see their forefathers as refugees from San Lorenzo. They had established several ceremonial centres by the end of the pre-Classic period: primacy was asserted by Uaxactun with a stepped pyramid of four steeply inclined tiers, four stairways set into the base and the four columns of a summit temple, foreshadowing the earliest works at Tikal.**2.16**

2.15a

›**2.15 IZAPAN SYNCRETISM IN THE LATE-FORMATIVE PERIOD:** (a) relief of the skeletal god of death (Stele 50, Mexico City, National Museum of Anthropology); (b) jaguar deity altar (New York, Metropolitan Museum of Art).

2.15b

›**2.16 UAXACTUN, THE LATE-PRE-CLASSIC STEPPED PYRAMID:** (a) model, (b) cast of part elevation (Guatemala City, National Museum of Archaeology and Ethnology).

Uaxactun, like Kaminaljuyu and many other related sites, had a thatched pavilion on the summit of its pyramid but masonry superstructures with corbel vaulting seem first to appear on the early works of Tikal. Gigantic masks – often derived from the jaguar on the lower levels, the eagle above – are characteristic of late-Formative Mayan pyramids: the one at El Mirador, north of Uaxactun, was the largest in a series of works noted for their great scale.

2.16a

2.16b

›2.17 CLASSIC TEOTIHUACAN: tectonic and architectonic incense burners – the latter a miniature of the pyramid summit-temple type.

2 CLASSIC ACHIEVEMENT

In the first centuries of the Classic era – the first two of the Christian era – there was rapid advance towards the full realization of the diversified urban civilization anticipated in the late-Formative period. As provisioning the proliferating proletariat exceeded local means, despite the expansion of agriculture, the corollary was the development of a limited number of quasi-feudal domains by the most powerful urban elites. Alliance and vassalage were the normal bonds but militarism was yet to be generally as important as economic advantage in long-distance trading co-operation. The period was characterized above all by Teotihuacan, Monte Alban and Tikal dominating the Mexican central highlands, the southern highlands and the Mayan lowlands respectively. All three reached their height in the 7th century when the population of Teotihuacan was probably in excess of 100,000, that of Monte Alban between 30–50,000 and Tikal some 70,000.

The Teotihuacanos have left a rich legacy of figural paintings and sculptures but no written records beyond calendrical hieroglyphs. The Zapotecs were also prolific in

sculpture and precocious in recording calendrics and significant events. The Mayas were Mesoamerica's supreme
intellectuals, building on Olmec foundations to attain
unsurpassed heights in calendrics, astronomy and mathematics and far surpassing the Formative Zapotecs in the
sophistication of writing: yet they were virtually unique in
developing civilization in primeval jungle and relatively
primitive in their swidden – slash-and-burn, rather than
fixed-field – farming methods.

   With the great economic advantage of controlling the
central-Mexican black obsidian mines, Teotihuacan had
eclipsed Tlatilco in the later years of the Olmec era and
emerged supreme in the Mexican basin on the destruction
of Cuicuilco by the eruption of the Xitle volcano at a disputed date about the end of the late-pre-Classic period.
The extent of Teotihuacano irrigation and monumental
works at the time implies the development of centralized
power far exceeding the achievement of the Olmecs, promoting Mesoamerica's first truly urban civilization, but in
the absence of written records its nature is obscure.

   Against some dispute, most scholars maintain that
Teotihuacan's economic base was agriculture expanded by
irrigation and perhaps by the type of swampland reclamation later known to the Aztecs as chinampa. However,
its eminence was essentially commercial rather than political, assured by its near monopoly of obsidian production,
control of the route north to the source of other highly
prized minerals and by its consequent dominant position
in the Mesoamerican trading cycle: it was unfortified and
no depictions of violent conflict have been found among
the remains but there is a rich legacy of sculpture and
fresco devoted to religious and mythological subjects,
especially concerning water, animal, vegetable and marine
life.[2.17]

   Decline seems to date from c. 650 when the city was

2.18a

2.18b

2.18c

>**2.18** **TIKAL, DYNASTIC RECORDS:** (a–c) early, mid and late stelae (Tikal, site museum and Guatemala City, National Museum of Archaeology and Ethnology).

Stelae usually bear the image of the donor and a date: the oldest (a) corresponds to 292, the latest (c) to 869. Thirty-two rulers are recorded between the 3rd and 9th centuries.

The Mayas were unique in the pre-Columbian world in developing writing to the stage where they could record anything in their spoken language: like the Formative Zapotecs they achieved this by combining ideographs and phonemes, retaining the former though they had a symbol for each syllable – unlike the Zapotecs.

ravaged by fire: over the following century the population fell by perhaps as much as three-quarters, the obsidian monopoly was lost and the trade empire collapsed. Cities in and around the central Mexican plateau and adjacent Gulf coast area, which had prospered with Teotihuacan, benefitted from its decline: in particular Cholula, which gained dominance on the old route south, El Tajin, which took the lead in the ancient Gulf coast maritime trade, and Xochicalco, whose position on the major route west from the basin gave it a dominant interest in Pacific coastal trade.

Unlike that of Teotihuacan, the eminence of Tikal seems to have been promoted by an adroit dynasty of rulers, first mentioned in the 4th century in the stelae inscriptions with which the Mayans excelled in the recording of history. They do not seem to have forged an empire but, obsessed with their genealogy, dynastic marriage alliances included an early one with Teotihuacan and doubtless recurrent ones with independent – or at least autonomous – Mayan city-states, some of which may have been reduced to vassalage to secure tribute and profits from the control of trade.**2.18** By the 5th century greater riches – and population – may have followed the introduction of some fixed-field farming, perhaps learned from Teotihuacan.

The absence of inscriptions for several generations from the mid-6th century indicates severe dynastic reverse and, indeed, in 562 the city of Caracol claimed victory over Tikal after a protracted war. The renewed proliferation of stelae in the 7th century records spectacular revival, in which military power played an enlarged part, but by the early 8th century the economy was badly affected by the disruption of the long-distance routes to Teotihuacan. There were local problems too: for several generations rapid population growth had led to over-exploitation where new clearance for agrarian expansion was no longer possible. As elsewhere the strain on food production was the greater because the development of sophisticated urban civilization had removed increasing numbers of people from subsistence farming. Meanwhile, several other Mayan powers had risen to significance. Foremost among these as patrons of art and architecture – at least insofar as the accidents of survival testify – were the kings of Palenque.**2.19**

Oaxaca benefitted from its geographical position between the Mayan and Teotihuacano great powers, and its rulers – secular or sacerdotal – seem to have sustained its prosperity in peaceful contact with both and with their satellites. That prosperity – and the position of the elite – were bound to be affected by the dislocation of the Teotihuacan-Tikal axis of trade: by the 9th century, Monte Alban had lost its pre-eminence and the Zapotec valley confederation disintegrated into independent city-states in which the once-subordinate Mixtecs assumed dominance. Ultimately they formed a loose confederation that recaptured something of the regional order once emanating from the Zapotec centre. A militaristic people, their most impressive remains – at Mitla – are secular.

COMMON BELIEFS

Teotihuacan, Monte Alban and Tikal each had its distinct artistic, religious and social characteristics – let alone different languages, but by the Classic era several basic concepts were held in common: the most notable was duality expressed generally in pairing a male god with a female consort but also in the conjunction of opposites (life/death, good/evil, day/night, etc.), most potently manifest in the daily struggle between the sun (male) and the moon (female). Following the course of sun and moon, existence was seen as cyclical – and measured by all pre-Hispanic Mesoamerican cultures in idiosyncratically

›2.19 PALENQUE: royal images.
Though vassals, the rulers of Palenque claimed divine descent like their overlords. The rich series of their inscriptions first mentions a Queen Kan-Ik c. 583 and last names a King Kuk who disappeared c. 784; their great age was initiated by Queen Zac-Kuk, regent from 612 to 627 for her son King Pacal who subsequently reigned until 683, and continued through the reigns of Pacal's sons King Chan-Bahlum (683–702) and King Hok (702–25).

Most Mesoamericans measured time in accordance with a 365-day solar cycle; however, their calendrical year consisted of 360 days (eighteen months of twenty days) plus five days of ill omen at the end. Concurrently, they recognized a ritual cycle of 260 days (of thirteen by twenty days). The months and days of both were named in fixed order and the days numbered. Concordance between the calendrical year and the ritual cycle was achieved every fifty-two years (18,980 days, the lowest common multiple of 365 and 260). Thus each fifty second year began a new cycle. The first cycle began with the creation of the first man and woman – but the location of that event in time was, of course, unstable. The Mayans, who were the only Mesoamericans to invent zero, obviated the problem by designating the foundation of their culture as date zero (convertible to 3114 BCE): that is known as the 'long count' in distinction from the later, truncated 'short count' from a designated intermediate position.

In the top register a dot represents 1 and a bar 5.

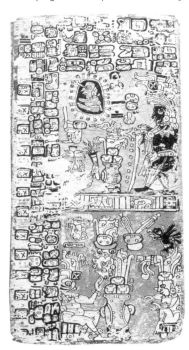

complex calendrical terms involving the conjunction of a 260-day ritual cycle with the solar year.[2.20]

Moreover, the degree of consistency that had developed in Mesoamerican beliefs across the Formative period – despite extreme linguistic diversity – was not entirely lost and trade contacts fostered cross-fertilization in arts primarily concerned with the elaboration of pantheistic iconography. Comprehension of the ceremonies and priestly rites for whose public display or secret performance the religious complexes were designed is lost to us but the Olmec ancestry of identifiable gods – especially the great gods of creation, preservation and destruction – may be traced through persistence of shamanism, reflected by the syncretic attributes of major deities, in parallel with persistent cosmological beliefs.[2.21, 2.31b,c, 2.36]

Attributes of elemental Classic gods

The cosmos was layered, as in Olmec times, but somewhat more complex: by Aztec times it had five solar cycles of which the fifth was current. The four cardinal directions of the cosmic space were joined by axial routes to the tree of abundance in the centre: the heavens had thirteen layers, the underworld nine; the horizontal directions and vertical layers had their colours and their gods which varied from region to region. The fundamental concept of the interdependence of opposites in the cycle of life was pervasive but never more persuasively articulated than in Zapotec and Teotihuacano images of microcosm and macrocosm. Life emerging from death like the seed sprouting from the decaying husk is most gruesomely represented by the central-Mexican god of propitiation, regeneration – and spring – Xipe Topec: not without phallic significance, an anthropomorphic deity is sheathed in the flayed skin of a human sacrificial victim. The Zapotec version holds the sacrificial head and sprouts new growth.

From region to region, Classic to post-Classic, too, there was a measure of consistency in the conception of the supreme deities and, through the survival of some syncretic elements over a thousand years of evolution in the iconography of the gods, but not least through analogy, it is

2.21e

2.21a

2.21c

possible to relate them to the principal figures of the Olmec pantheon represented on the body of the so-called Lord of Las Limas and other images from the Formative period.**2.8, 2.9**

The father/creator-god – archetypical in his constitutional duality – is represented as a bird/reptile or feathered serpent and known to the Teotihuacanos (and a thousand years later to the Aztecs) as Quetzalcoatl, to the Maya as Kukulkan, to the Zapotecs as Pitac: he seems prefigured by the icon on the right knee of the 'Lord of Las Limas' and the plumed serpent surmounting the priest from La Venta. Similarly the fire-god known in central Mexico as Huehueteotl, to the Mayans as Itzamna, seems to descend from the one-fanged monster fire-serpent/harpy eagle represented on the Lord's left shoulder: the Olmec attributes are still clearly discernible in the zoomorphic headdress of the Zapotec version but elsewhere in central Mexico the brazier of late-Formative Cuicuilco was common.**2.13b** Mayan Itzama is the aged king of the gods with various responsibilities, including healing: in his fiery dimension he is – or

2.21b

›2.21 ELEMENTAL CLASSIC GODS, THEIR ATTRIBUTES AND DUALISM: (a, b) the entity of life and death and the mask of the death-god, Mictlantecuhtli, in the life-giving aureole of the sun (mid-Classic ceramic mask from Soyaltepec, Oaxaca, and early Classic stone revetment medallion from the Pyramid of the Sun at Teotihuacano; (c, d) the god of regeneration Xipe Totec, Classic Teotihuacano and Zapotec terracotta figures; (e, f) frescoed wall panels from the Gran Basimento at Cacaxtla representing shamanic priests, one as a jaguar on a serpent jaguar (left), the other as an eagle on the feathered serpent of Quetzalcoatl, late-Classic; (g, h) the 'Old God' of fire, Huehueteotl, mid-Classic ceramic figures from Monte Alban, Oaxaca, and Cerro de las Mesas, Veracruz; (i, j) the Mayan gods of sun and rain, Kinich Ahau and Chac, mid-Classic brazier relief from Palenque and post-Classic terracotta figure from Mayapan; (k) the rain-god Tlaloc in the orbit of Teotihuacan, mid-Classic relief from Xochicalco, Morelos; (l) the Zapotec rain-god Cocijo with the maize-god Pitao Cozobi, mid-Classic incense burner from Monte Alban (all from Mexico City, National Museum of Anthropology).

2.21f

2.21d

2.21g   2.21h

2.21i

fathered – the sun-god Kinich Ahau, whose essentially anthropomorphic head still has a fang-like tooth and flaming eyebrows, in addition to a flame-like beard, but the Olmec syncretism is most pervasive in the head-dress drawn from the jaguar, eagle and snake.

The infant were-jaguar on the lord's lap is seen as remotely ancestral to the water- or rain-god of preservation (and destructive flood), known to the Maya as Chac, to the Zapotecs as Cocijo, and to the Teotihucanos (and Aztecs) as Tlaloc (whose consort was Chalchiuhtlicue, the water-goddess): the jaguar provides Tlaloc's most pervasive features, the goggle eyes and sharp-toothed mouth, and even when his reptilian snout is superseded by a grotesquely pendulous nose, Chac has feline fangs. And the Formative relationship between the rain- and maize-gods is perpetuated most persuasively in the iconography of Zapotec Cocijo and Pitao Cozobi, the one bearing the other as his headdress here, but Pitao Cozobi has his independent existence, like Mayan Ah Mun, as a youth sprouting corn.

There were, naturally, many permutations of these universal deities, paired in accordance with Formative principles with wives or sisters or twins, and with the development of sophisticated urban civilizations in the

2.21j

2.21k

2.21l

Classic era, the Mesoamerican pantheon grew in special-ized significance to match the specialization in the life of man. Above all, of course, the most awesome pair were the creative and destructive brothers, known to the central Mexicans as Quetzalcoatl and Mictlantecuhtli, driving the cycle of that life. Death – as end and begin-ning – was a general obsession and sacrifice ubiquitous: plants and animals, time and effort, would satisfy many divine purposes but only humans were adequate to nour-ish the sun to ensure his repeated victory over the moon.

Most specifically, perhaps, the ball-game (tlachtli) was important to all Mesoamericans – except, enigmatically, at Teotihuacan. A religious exercise whose outcome was determined by the gods doubtless for the designation of sacrificial victims, the rules are obscure but clues to the procedure are provided by statuettes of players from many sites of most periods, by illustrations in post-Classic Mexican codices and earlier graphic embellishment to several of the various masonry courts preserved in cermonial complexes throughout Mesoamerica.**2.22**

2.22a

›2.22 BALL-COURT AND GAME: (a) ballplayer from Colima; (b) model with game in progress (Oaxaca, Rufino Tamayo Museum); (c) plan with players (Codex Borbonicus, Palais Bourbon, Paris); (d) general view of north court, Oaxaca (built between 300 and 600 CE, among the earliest-known with the typical 'I'-shaped plan, vertical end walls and battered sides supporting narrow viewing galleries; (e) relief from ball-courts at Chichen Itza showing respectively the dedication of the confronted contestants to a god and the decapitation of the loser by the winner (probably 11th century CE).

The male contestants (sometimes only two) confronted one another from the ends of a court. Hitting a substantial rubber ball only with head or body – not hands or feet – and preventing it from touching the surface of the court, the object was to penetrate the

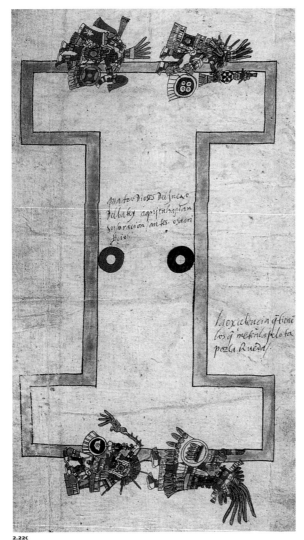

2.22c

2.22b

2.22d

opponent's ring. Players were protected with padded leather belts.

An essential element in one of the most pervasive creation myths – at least for the Maya – is the victory of hero twins, consummate ballplayers, over the lords of the underworld before their apotheosis as the sun and moon: their game was that of life, descent into the realm of death and resurrection. The solar trajectory was traced by the ball and – for late-Classic and post-Classic players at least – its fall portended the disaster of the sun's failure to rise and the end of the last solar era: the team forced into that fault was the loser and its players could be sacrificial victims.

2.22e

THE STATE

Religion permeated all aspects of life yet secular authority grew with the proliferation of the bureaucracy needed to run diversified urban civilizations, impose an efficient taxation system and oversee continuous public works, religious and secular: none of the Classic cities seems to have been theocratic although the ruling elite of Monte Alban was closely connected to the priesthood. Society was rigorously stratified, like a stepped pyramid: it is probable that the pattern discernible in the later phases of Mesoamerican civilization, for which there are clear records, was already approximated at Teotihuacan and that the other great Classic centres were not notably dissimilar.

At the top, naturally, were the patricians who filled the chief offices of state and temple, then noble descendants of subsidiary lines in subsidiary offices responsible for public works, irrigation, agriculture and trade: their only obligation was military service. In principal, the rest of society was subject to both military service and forced labour but, next after the nobles, the merchants and skilled artisans were organized in guilds strong enough to win them privileges according to the value of their work, especially exemption from taxation in labour. Agricultural workers, next down the scale, also claimed some exemption from civil-labour obligations in virtue of their economic importance. Below them, with no privileges and heavy labour obligations in the absence of draft animals, came the urban proletariat. Finally there were those reduced to slavery by debt, crime or defeat in battle.

In all ranks, groups of extended families – probably related, usually subscribing to belief in descent from a common ancestor – lived in distinct wards under a council of headmen, responsible above all for taxation, and the presidency of an elected or hereditary arbiter. Ultimate

>2.23 THE MAYAN RULER: (a) Dignitary, terracotta statuette from the late-Classic Mayan necropolis on the Jaina Island, Campeche (New York, American Museum of Natural History); (b) king enthroned, beaker embellishment (Tikal site museum).

2.23a

2.23b

authority was vested in the elective or hereditary head of state – the chief executive, chief justice, commander of the armed forces and titular head of religion who oversaw the administration from his sumptuous palace.[2.23]

SITING AND PLANNING

Urban morphology naturally responded to political structure and social stratification but distinct regional ways followed from diversity of cultural inheritance. Teotihuacan – like most Classic towns on highland plains – had a densely populated grid with two major axes aligned with the cardinal points, lined with the palaces of the nobility and crossing beside the major cult complex.[2.24]

2.24a

Teotihuacan

The original city grew around a platform, Olmec in profile, erected over a natural grotto of sacred significance. A pyramid, orientated to the course of the sun at its zenith, had been built on the platform well before the end of the pre-Classic period but was continuously augmented until c. 150 CE. Crossing to its south and orientated with it, the major axial avenues were laid out at the beginning of the Classic era: the main north–south one (c. 50 metres wide, 4 kilometres long and rising through 27 metres in stepped sections) was named for the dead by the Aztecs because they identified its ruined pyramid mounds with tombs.

The conjunction of a layered pyramid with subterranean zones and axial avenues crossing at right-angles can hardly have been devoid of cosmological significance but the Sun Pyramid was not at the junction. That place (east of the crossing) was taken by the pyramid of Quetzalcoatl in the precinct known as the Citadel because of its raised perimeter: it was established c. 100 CE and the market square opposite to the west of the intersection was probably contemporary. Terminating the Avenue of the Dead on raised ground to the north, the precinct and Pyramid of the Moon were completed some one hundred years after the Pyramid of the Sun (c. 250): echoing the profile of Cerro Gordo to the north, the new pyramid was aligned with the older one and Mount Patlachique to the south-east. The progress of construction of the major monuments at the site may be monitored by potsherds in their core.

Temple compounds, many with a triad of pyramids, lined the main axis. Associated with them were priests' quarters and the greater walled palaces – but no ball-courts. Lesser gradations of the elite lived in smaller courtyard houses or in apartments in the grid of streets orientated to the main axes in the four quarters between them. The merchants and artisans had their designated zones, with housing graded to their economic importance and corresponding affluence: there were special enclaves for foreigners too. The proletariat was confined to peripheral warrens of crowded dwellings and the agricultural workers lived somewhat less incommodiously on the outskirts for ready access to their fields.

2.24c

>**2.24 TEOTIHUACAN** ('Place of the Gods' to the Aztecs): (a, b, pages 256–257) general views north from the Pyramid of the Sun, with the Pyramid of the Moon centre, and south from the Pyramid of the Moon, with the Pyramid of the Sun left; (c) model of the city at its height in the 7th century CE (Teotihuacan site museum), (d) plan of excavated site to either side of the so-called Avenue of the Dead (1) with the Plaza and Pyramid of the Moon (2), Palace Complex of the Plumed Butterfly (Quetzalpapalotl), the Jaguars and its substructure of the Plumed Shells (*Caracoles Emplumados*) (3), Plaza and Pyramid of the Sun (4), Temple of Quetzalcoatl (so-called *Ciudadela*) (5), so-called Great Compound (6).

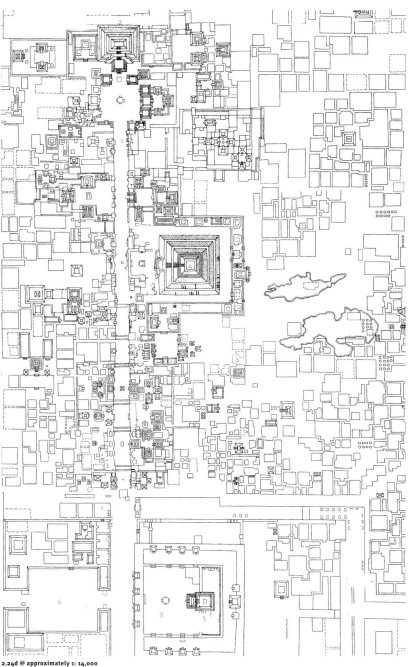

2.24d @ approximately 1: 14,000

2.25a

2.25b

›2.25 EL TAJIN: (a) model (Jalapa, Archaeology Museum); (b) view of site from El Palacio.

Probably with a population of around 13,000 at its height, the city was divided into two parts: El Tajin proper, orientated to the cardinal directions on level ground and developed informally from the 3rd century CE, and Chico, on terraced ground to the north begun some three hundred years later. The first temple pyramid was built in the later phase of the first main period of development, the 4th century, but has disappeared below later work. Most of the important monuments date from the second and early third stages, the 6th–8th centuries, during which the city emerged from subordination to Teotihuacan, and the succeeding century when it was dominant in the Gulf coast trade. Eclectic in style, they reflect the city's diverse contacts as an intermediary in trade between the Mexican basin and the Mayan Yucatan.

The main terrace of Chico has two irregular plazas once surrounded by civic and residential buildings of various dates predominantly in the later phases of the site's development; these were overlooked by the Edificio de las Columnas, called after its eastern portico of seven columns engraved with calendrical motifs.

›2.26 XOCHICALCO: plan.

The great plaza (2), a platform levelled from the summit of the main hill, was among the earliest ceremonial works begun in the 3rd century but the assertively axial avenue ascending the hill (1) and the main monuments, including the Platform of the Plumed Serpent (3), date from the city's independence between 600 and 900 when considerable terracing was undertaken to accommodate the populace. Thereafter the major effort was spent on impressive fortification against marauding northern tribesmen – unsuccessfully, as the city fell in the 10th century and was abandoned.

As at El Tajin, the works of its prime are eclectic, reflecting Xochicalco's main trading contacts – Teotihuacan, El Tajin, Monte Alban and the Mayans. It has been suggested that a conference on the coordination of the calendar was held in the town c. 650, to which delegates came from all the main centres of Mesoamerica.

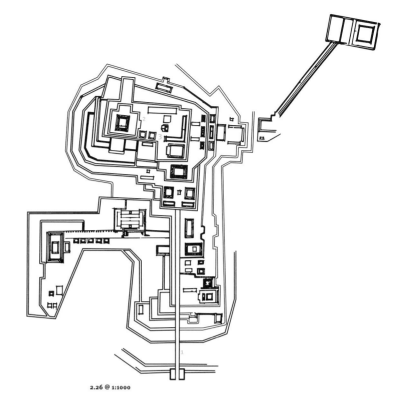

2.26 @ 1:1000

Neither entirely foreign to axiality, El Tajin and Xochicalco developed along the lines provided by the contours of their sites – the former undulating, the latter mountainous – after they had emerged from subordination to the order of Teotihuacan.[2.25, 2.26] The topography of a spectacular acropolis governed the distribution of building at the principal Zapotec centre too, permitting considerable axiality. The elite lived on terraces won from the steeply sloping ground below the ceremonial plateau of Monte Alban and were buried in rock-cut tombs. The people at large were accommodated lower down or dispersed in valley suburbs. Their Mixtec successors were similarly inclined in their several settlements further up the valley, though the main sites are less precipitous than Monte Alban.[2.27]

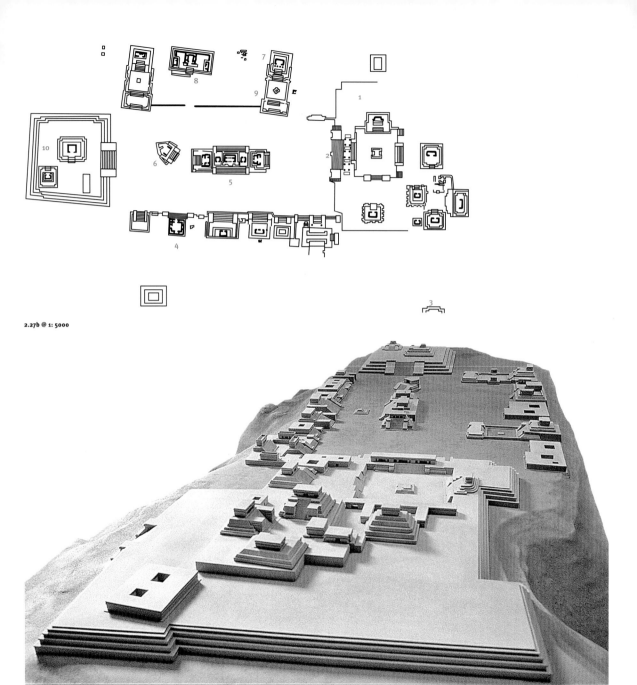

2.27b @ 1: 5000

2.27c

›2.27 MONTE ALBAN: (a, pages 220–221) general view from north, (b) plan of excavated site with 'Northern Acropolis' (1), northern platform with its sunken patio and colonnaded portico (2), ball-court (3), 'palace' (4), complex with Structures G, H and I (5), Structure J (6), Complex IV (7), Complex of the 'Dancers' (Danzantes) (8), Complex M (9), 'Southern Acropolis' (10), (c) model of the city at its height early in the 8th century (Mexico City, National Museum of Anthropology), (d) view from south.

2.27d

Monte Alban

The orientation of the main elements is not uniform. To either end of the main plaza (320 by 140 metres), the north and south temple platforms were begun towards the end of the pre-Classic period and completed in the early Classic phase: the southern one (c. 136 metres square at base), stepped in a semi-pyramidal way with a wide stairway to the north, supported two small stepped temple pyramids; the much more extensive northern one, with broad stairs to the south in a once-colonnaded portico, has a sunken patio (c. 45 metres square) once centred on an altar. In the early Classic period too, the eastern terrace was built up as a base for several temples; the ball-court was added at its northern end and the only recognizable palace (El Palacio, with subterranean tomb) to the south in the mid-Classic phase. Twin pyramid temple compounds were erected on the western side of the central plaza in the early Classic phase and the three shrines near the centre were reformed into a symmetrical complex with a double one on a terraced platform flanked on a lower level by square ones. There was accommodation for priests, presumably also for administrators, but housing was generally supported on terraces below the ceremonial plateau.

With extensive terracing of the valley walls and irrigation on the valley floor, suburban sites proliferated from some twenty to two hundred between the pre-and high-Classic eras.

In lush jungle lowlands, where agriculture organized along irrigation lines was impossible and new land was constantly being won from deforestation, organic growth was the urban norm. Tikal was archetypical in its loose, centripetal sprawl, decreasing in density outwards from the ceremonial centre, which was itself informal in its organization: it represents the antithesis to the rational order of Teotihuacan and, indeed, some scholars maintain that it was never more than a ceremonial centre for dispersed agricultural communities.[2.28] Generally more compact, the lesser centres of the Yucatan seem also to have been primarily ceremonial: monumental buildings are generally disposed with marked sensitivity to the nature of the site and there was housing only for the elite – as at Palenque.[2.29]

2.28a

›2.28 TIKAL: (a, b) overviews of ceremonial central plaza south from the Northern Acropolis, with Temple I to the left, II right, and north from the Central Acropolis, with Temple II to the left, I right, (c) plan of excavations with Temple I (1), Temple II (2), Great Plaza (3), Northern Acropolis (4), Central Acropolis (5), (d) site plan, (e) model of the site at its height in the 7th century CE.

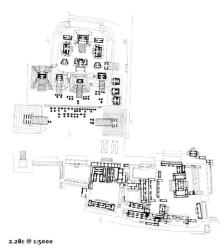

2.28c @ 1:5000

Tikal

Natural depressions contained reservoirs, natural eminences supported the main cult centre to the north of the plaza (the Northern Acropolis) and the supposed seat of secular power to the south-east (the Central Acropolis), which overlooks administrative buildings and public facilities – notably the ball-court and market – around another plaza to the east. There is a further plaza to the west and two more bordered by yet more temple pyramids and palatial buildings on the so-called Southern Acropolis. Defended by circuit walls, this ceremonial core is linked to outlying temples and residential suburbs by causeways: projected in accordance with the aspects of the site, yet doubtless of cosmological significance, these arteries provided scenographic vistas usually closed by monuments sited in accordance with the contours.

The central ceremonial plaza, bordered with stelae and sacrificial altars, is overawed by some sixteen temples. The tallest, Temples I and II, are to the east and west respectively. The Northern Acropolis – the main royal necropolis – bears a stepped platform with a group of four temple-pyramids addressing the plaza and a triad on the upper platform with subsidiary shrines in the centre and on the corners: except for the westernmost temple of the forward range and three small shrines to the

2.28b

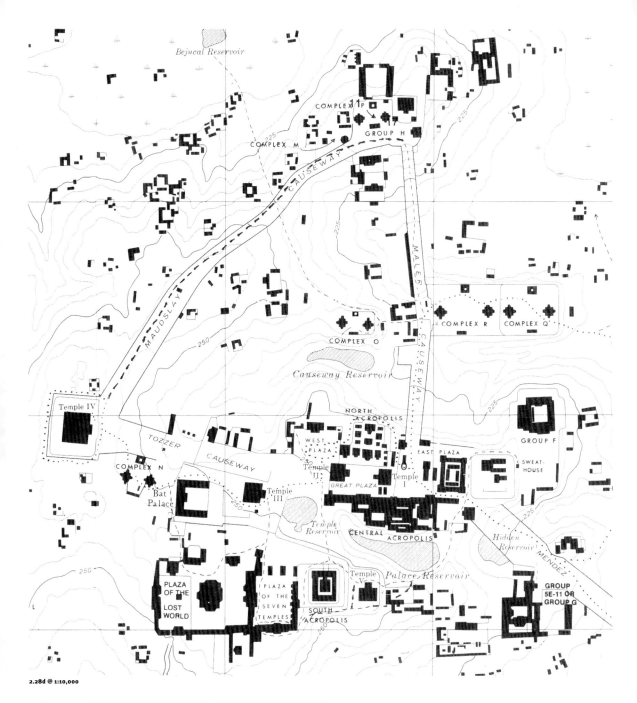

Bejucal Reservoir

COMPLEX P

COMPLEX M

GROUP H

225

COMPLEX 225

CAUSEWAY

MAUDSLAY

225

MALER

COMPLEX R   COMPLEX Q

COMPLEX O

250

Causeway Reservoir

CAUSEWAY

225

Temple IV

NORTH
ACROPOLIS

GROUP F

TOZZER

WEST
PLAZA

EAST PLAZA

SWEAT-
HOUSE

CAUSEWAY

COMPLEX N

Temple
II

GREAT PLAZA

Temple
I

250

Bat
Palace

Temple
III

CENTRAL   ACROPOLIS

Hidden
Reservoir

MENDEZ

225

Temple
Reservoir

Palace Reservoir

250

Temple V

PLAZA
OF THE

LOST WORLD

PLAZA
OF THE
SEVEN
TEMPLES

SOUTH
ACROPOLIS

GROUP
5E-11 OR
GROUP G

250

2.28d @ 1:10,000

2.28e

east, this group is unusual among the complexes of the site for its near-symmetry. The palaces of the eminent are adjacent to the core, but in the ad-hoc sprawl beyond accommodation was increasingly dispersed. The norm was the cluster of two to five houses around a patio in unplanned hamlets: these were grouped into zones around minor ceremonial centres, which were in turn grouped into districts around the major ceremonial centre.

The earliest architectural remains are of the first phase of pyramid building under the main temple of the North Acropolis: late-pre-Classic, they are related to the earliest remains of Uaxactun. As the main cult centre developed in the Classic era – like a volcanic site – this early pyramid

2.29a

was incarcerated in several later layers and ringed by a veritable mountain range of new peaks, most containing the tombs of rulers. Dating depends on stelae: the extensive ceremonial centre seems to have achieved its final form between a spectacular revival in the early 7th century and the beginning of terminal decline two hundred years later.

›2.29 **PALENQUE:** (a) overview from Temple of the Cross; (b) plan with 'palace' (1), Temple of the Inscriptions (2), Temple of the Sun (3), Temple of the Cross (4), Temple of the Foliated Cross (5), southern group remains (6), northern group remains (7), ballcourt (8), Temple X (9).

The terraced site, on fingers of low spurs, seems to have been subjected to no comprehensive urban plan

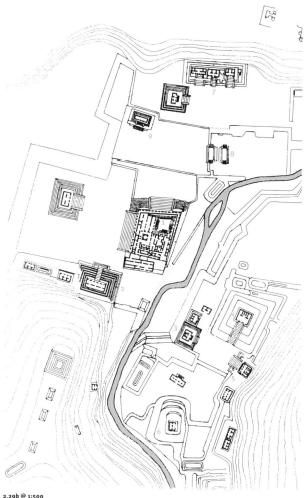

2.29b @ 1:500

but the buildings are related to their physical environment with notable sensitivity: unusually there is no ceremonial plaza, indeed no apparent centre at all – apart from the so-called palace. On the other hand, the prominence of an irregularly distributed complex of courts, galleries and chambers on a stepped platform – not uncontroversially called a palace – is typical of Mayan sites.

UBIQUITOUS FORM

Massive masonry – or rather rubble bound with mortar and faced with stone – and the lintel-bearing stone pier were ubiquitous in Classic Mesoamerica, despite failure to advance beyond neolithic technology. And the opposition of monumental mass with grand space was a common objective. There was much consistency of type too: the plaza, the ball-court, the platform and above all the temple pyramid, tiered like the cosmos and ascended by a staircase from a cardinal direction, which raised the most elite of men to a height from which he could commune with the gods – like the Mesopotamian ziggurat.

Naturally there were distinct regional styles. There were distinct regional types, too, and it is not always possible to define their purpose – even conclusively to classify them as religious or secular. The prime example is the Mayan complex with outer and inner galleries around courts and a warren of narrow corbel-vaulted halls: based on a platform, like a temple but lower in elevation, this is conventionally called 'palatial' though there is no firm evidence that the dank and restricted interiors were designed for human habitation rather than for cult ritual. Undoubtedly residential, on the other hand, were the grand courtyard houses with their colonnaded bays that flank the main arteries of Teotihuacan. Characteristic of that city, moreover, is the differentiation of residential complex types in accordance with the stratification of society.

TYPE AND STYLE IN THE ORBIT OF TEOTIHUACAN AND MONTE ALBAN

In sharp contrast to the Maya, who preferred steeply inclined verticality for their pyramidal temples, the Teotihuacanos stressed the horizontal integrity of their more broadly based tiered taluds. To that end, in the amplifica-

>2.30 TEOTIHUACAN, PYRAMID OF THE SUN: (a) the main mass, completed c. 150 CE, as restored from 1905; (b) detail of the talud/tablero motif from the projection at the base of the west staircase.

Beyond a platform plaza (c. 70 metres square) flanked by palaces and/or grand priestly quarters, the pre-Classic structure had acquired five massive battered tiers some 225 metres at base and rising to about 75 by 150 metres: it is now some 10 metres less and the differentiation of the small intermediate tier between four and five is unsubstantiated.

The largest structure in ancient Mesoamerica – except for the later pyramid of Cholula projected to surpass it – it was built primarily of brick, faced in stone and a form of cement plaster. The summit temple has disappeared and was omitted in the controversial restoration: it was doubtless a simple cell with portico but no windows, as was the norm throughout Mesoamerica, and as the Teotihuacanos themselves represented it in miniature as the lid of an incense burner.**2.17**

The staircase rises through low balustrades (alfadas) from the later triple-tiered platform with its own stairs to north and south which cut through the novel tablero: most of the surviving architectural detail comes from this area and presumably post-dates the completion of the main mass of the pyramid. The tablero motif was probably invented in the neighbouring Tlaxcala valley and adopted by the Teotihuacanos c. 200.

2.30a

2.30b

tion of their great Pyramid of the Sun with the subsidiary
triple-tiered platform to the west, they introduced the
tablero: a parapet moulding cantilevered out over the talud
at each level, elevated and divided into framed fields for
iconographical embellishment. Countering the horizontals only if viewed orthogonally, the single staircase rose on
the west front in conformity with the slope of the taluds
and its balustrades broke back with each tier.[2.30]

The form was followed on a slightly lesser scale, but on
higher ground, for the Pyramid of the Moon, which was
completed at the head of its symmetrical plaza about a
century later. Smaller still and earlier, the central cult complex of Quetzalcoatl was also in the van of tablero development but there, embellished in high relief, the tablero
tends to overwhelm the talud: the pyramid rose from a
sunken precinct centred on an altar and bordered by terraces supporting small, regularly spaced pyramids.[2.30, 2.31]

The tablero quickly reached Monte Alban. There the

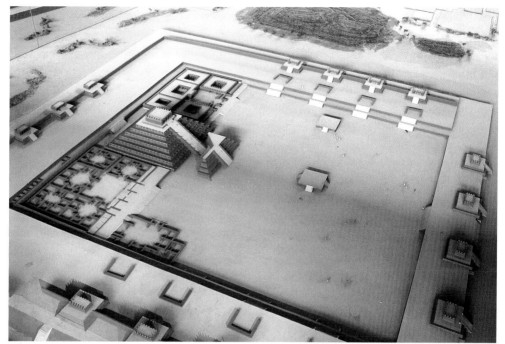

2.31b

›2.31 TEOTIHUACAN: (a) Plaza and Pyramid of the Moon, view from Calle de los Muertos (c. 250, restored); (b, c) Temple of Quetzalcoatl, c. 200: model (Teotihuacan site museum) and detail of balustrades of west frontal stairs and talud/tableros.

The symetrically disposed precinct and four-tiered Pyramid of the Moon (c. 150 by 125 metres at the base and 45 metres high) has a projecting staircase to the south. The five-tiered southern platform, with its talud and tablero, was a later addition, like its counterpart at the Pyramid of the Sun.

From the east side of the sunken court (410 metres on each side), the main pyramid of the Temple of Quet-zalcoatl probably rose through six tiers, each bordered by tablero decorated with the feathered serpents of Quetzalcoatl alternating with masks of Tlaloc (once brilliantly coloured). The subsequent juxtaposition of a tiered platform masked and preserved the western range of tablero embellishment.

2.31c

2.32

talud usually projected beyond the stairs and typically supported a vertical wall with a heavy hooded – often double-hooded – cornice but no continuous frame: the so-called Oaxacan scapulary tablero which also appears to varying scales over doors and niches.**2.32, 2.33** Other permutations of the motif – virtually ubiquitous outside Mayan domains and adopted occasionally within them – are major distinguishing marks of regional styles. So too are variations in the degree to which staircases diverge from classic conformity to the pyramid's angle of incidence, their projection or recession from the plane of the talud and in the amount of embellishment to their ramps.**2.34, 2.35**

Ubiquitous outside Mayan domains, too, is the tra-

›2.32 MONTE ALBAN: 'Complex IV' from the northern platform showing terracing with the characteristic Zapotec talud and 'scapulary tablero' to either side of the central stairs: the broadly inclined talud is raised on a vertical socle with a plain drip-course moulding; the tablero is lower in elevation than at Teotihuacan and its frame is reduced to a hood-like form in two projecting planes with no lower moulding.

›2.33 EL TAJIN, PYRAMID OF THE NICHES: probably begun over an earlier core c. 600.

The six-tiered structure (35 square metres at base and 18 metres high without the missing summit temple) has rubble core to full height and niches in each face of each level – 365 in all with obvious calendrical significance. The battered base of each level is essentially a talud but the tablero has been transformed into a trabeated gallery with stepped cornice – a distinc-

2.33

tively local approach though echoing the characteristic structural system of Teotihuacan which was presumably adopted for the summit temple. The one staircase, east, with altar platforms protruding at each level, projects beyond the cornice of the tablero galleries, well beyond the plane of the talud.

›2.34 XOCHICALCO, PLATFORM OF THE PLUMED SERPENT (Quetzalcoatl): detail of talud/ tablero reliefs.

There were several structures on the ceremonial centre's great plaza, but the most notable survivor is the platform of a shrine (restored in part) associated with Quetzalcoatl who seems to have been the patron deity. The Teotihuacano talud/tablero form is retained for the platform sides but both were embellished and the talud, with its magnificent frieze of undulating plumed serpents, eclipses the tablero in scale. The latter is crowned by an outward-sloping cornice in the manner, if not the precise form, of El Tajin and the alfadas of the projecting staircase ascend to it on the west.

2.34

2.35a

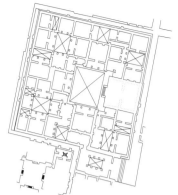

2.35b @ 1:1000

›**2.35 TEOTIHUACAN, MULTIPLE FAMILY RESIDENCES:** (a) Palace of Atetelco, nuclear court; (b, c, d, pages 228–229) Palace of Tepantitla, plan, reconstructed interior with mid-Classic period sculpture of the 'Old God' in the foreground, and detail of mural (Mexico City, National Museum of Anthropology).

A walled complex (82 by 64 metres) with several courts and numerous suites of rooms, this seems to have been the habitation of an extended family – a calpulli unit – probably of the merchant class.

2.35c

beated structure sheltering the spaces dedicated to gods or inhabited by men. Most of the former are reconstructed on surmise but the prime surviving Classic examples of the latter are the palaces and lesser residential complexes of

2.36a

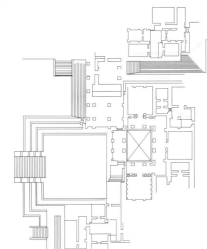

2.36b @ approximately 1:1000

Teotihuacan. The nuclear patio is generally cloistered and always surounded by rooms of various sizes in which posts carry the main load of the flat roof and partition walls are of secondary structural significance: one of the grandest, the so-called Palace of Quetzalpapalotl, is located to the south-west of the Pyramid of the Moon; off axis, the so-called Palace of Tepantitla well represents the residential complex of the extended family lower down the social scale.**2.36**

Unlike most Mayans, the peoples of Teotihuacan and their orbit tended to confine ornament to the framed recess of the tablero and other distinct areas like the sides of staircases or clearly defined panels of piers and walls. Sculpture ranged between low and high relief: the latter

2.36c

is at its boldest on the tablero of the Temple of Quetzel-coatl's pyramid, the former at its most refined on the piers of the Palace of Quetzalpapalotl's nuclear court. Plast-ered walls were usually embellished with mytho-logical images or stylized animal and vegetable motifs in brightly coloured fresco. Geometric motifs were also popular.**2.37, 2.38, 2.21e,f**

2.36d

›**2.36 TEOTIHUACAN, PALACE OF QUETZAL-PAPALOTL AND ASSOCIATED STRUCTURES:** (a, b) view of restored main court and plan; (c) fresco of parrots spouting water from the substructural remains of the Palace of the Plumed Shells (the remains of a palatial building dated to the 2nd–3rd century CE); (d) fresco from the Palace of the Jaguars of a plumed jaguar, embellished with shells, blowing on a plumed strombus shell.

On a talud, the palace is entered through a lobby with stone columns. This leads to the nuclear clois-tered court: the square piers are decorated with the plumed butterfly and other sacred motifs in low-relief, the walls and the merlons that crown the parapets with images of Tlaloc and other motifs drawn from water mythology (typical of the site, the merlons are sometimes misidentifed as crenellation though obvi-ously not defensive). The ceilings of the surrounding rooms were usually carried on beams carved from a single tree-trunk and were therefore restricted in their dimensions.

2.37a

›2.37 MONTE ALBAN, TOMB 104: (a) hooded entrance, (b) frescoed interior.

Numerous subterranean tombs consisted of a long flat-roofed or corbel-vaulted chamber, with or without cruciform adjuncts: the most sumptuous are embell-ished with divine and mythological motifs in sculpture outside, fresco within.

›2.38 LAMBITYECO: HOUSE-TOMB 2. The images over the doors are of the Zapotec rain-god Cosejo.

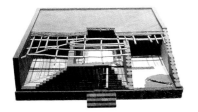

›2.39 MONTE ALBAN, 'THE PALACE': model showing its court and surrounding rooms (Monte Alban site museum).

2.37b

The best surviving examples at Teotihuacan are in the substructural remains of the Palace of Plumed Shells. Sub-terranean in origin, naturally, the tombs of Monte Alban also preserve splendid examples of Classic fresco embell-ishment. Outside, the keystone of the portal introduces the *cosejo* motif in relief in the context of the Oaxacan 'scapulary tablero'.

The one building at Monte Alban that is identified as primarily residential – the so-called palace at the south-ern end of the eastern terrace – conforms to the trabeated building type with central courtyard.**2.39** At Monte Alban, moreover, a grand colonnaded portico stood on the steps between the Central Plaza and the religious complex centred on the 'Patio Hundido' or Sunken Courtyard. Variations on the type, possibly religious, probably secular, include the Building of the Columns at Tajim Cico and the later Gallery of the Columns in the main building of the Group of Columns at Mitla. Most spectacular at Mitla, however, is the treatment of the wall to a dazzling array of geometrical motifs in the clearly framed context of the Mixtec reinterpretation of the Zapotec 'scapulary tablero'.**2.40**

2.40b

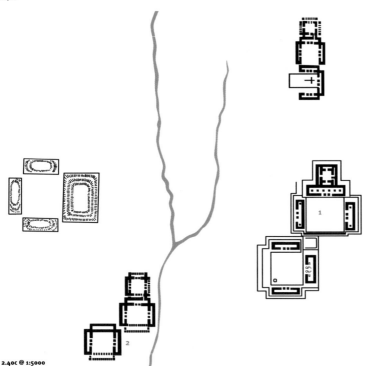

2.40c @ 1:5000

›2.40 MITLA: (a, pages 280–281, and b) Palace of the Columns, main façade and inner court, (c) site plan (9th century?) with the Palace of the Columns, main court (1), Group of the Arrroyo (2).

Of five complexes, which all seem to be primarily residential with one or more courts surrounded by platforms supporting rooms, the largest is the so-called Palace of the Columns. Unlike the earlier ones, in which the main spaces are aligned north–south, but like the smaller 'Group of the Arroyo' nearby, the two main courts are disposed diagonally but not interconnected: the courts are sunk into the platforms supporting the main chambers, the north-eastern one with a higher colonnaded gallery on its north side, beyond which is a private court surrounded by intimate rooms; below the south-western court are two cruciform tombs. The form is of the talud/tablero type: the tablero is vertical, set back from the top of the inclined talud, surmounted by a rising and falling cornice reminiscent of the Zapotec scapulary type, and embellished with three bands of horizontal relief in a variety of semi-geometric patterns not unrelated to contemporary north-Mayan work.

›2.41 EARLY CLASSIC TIKAL: (a) North Acropolis: structure 33 (centre of first range), mask from the
original early Classic work covered by the expanded
platform of the latest work (7th century); (b) Temple V
(49), in the so-called Lost World Complex.

CLASSIC MAYAN IDIOSYNCRASY

From its primitve manifestation in the earliest pyramidal
remains at Uaxactun, the Mayan style of architecture
evolved over some six centuries until it appears in its first
maturity c. 300 CE in the earliest remains of Tikal. Taken
to its apogee there in the phenomenal building campaigns
of the 7th- and 8th-century dynasts, it is still massive but
its prime characteristic is verticality.

Among the pyramids of Tikal, generally funerary, there
are exceptional works revealing overt Teotihuacaono
influence in the counterpoise of talud and tablero but, typically, the steep profile derived from the superimposition
of slightly battered tiers is relieved by relatively thin
'aprons' of projecting and recessed horizontal mouldings,
which mark the slender terrace at each level. The rectangular summit temple is usually built on a platform covering most of the top terrace. Crowning it, the uniquely
Mayan finial known as 'roof-comb' enhances aspiration:
based on the thickened back wall of the cella, this is faced
with an accumulation of decorative mouldings and backed
by a tapering spine of lightly projecting masonry rising
from the cella's base. There is also lavish ornament in a

deep frieze and on the walls or piers below: once painted in bright colours on a deep red ground, this is usually dominated by a mask of divinity and naturally a people attuned to the nature of their lush environment were naturalistic in their decorative exuberance.**2.41–2.43**

Equally characteristic is solidity: Mayan dependence on masses of masonry, usually stone-clad rubble or limestone faced with plaster, and on corbel vaulting, which was first developed to protect subterranean tombs, radically restricted internal space. In contrast to the flexible columned bay, common in the orbit of Teotihuacan, this produced halls or corridors rarely approaching 3 metres in width and readily duplicable only in parallel rows sepa-

›2.42 TIKAL, CENTRAL PLAZA: Temple II from the North Acropolis.

Temples I and II (c. 710) dominate the Central Plaza from the east and west respectively. The former, enshrining a royal tomb, rises abruptly through nine tiers (to 50 metres), with one steep staircase on the west leading to a triple-galleried summit temple. The latter, with four less steeply graded, more massive tiers, is ascended from the east. Both temples have vestiges of high and elaborate roof-combs.

2.43a

›2.43 TIKAL, TEMPLE IV: (a) section through summit temple, (b) model showing reconstruction of decorative detail, (r) detail of patron's image on wooden lintel (facsimile, New York, Museum of American History).

Built c. 750, and also enshrining a royal tomb, this pyramid was the tallest in Mesoamerica (70 metres): in addition to the base platform and four tiers, it has a superstructural platform and a podium for the summit temple with its high roof-comb.

2.43b

2.43c

rated by their heavy load-bearing walls. Spatially and formally, thus, Mayan architecture is external: the temple was a mountain for the exclusive communion of priest and god, the populace witnessing the mystery from the plaza below – as elsewhere. And secular life must also have been led primarily out of doors in broad courts shaded from the sun by canopies rather than roofs carried on posts and beams.[2.44]

Characteristic Mayan features spread through the central lowlands – from El Peten of Tikal to Usumacinta of Palenque, Rio Bec, Chenes, Puuc, and northern Yucatan.

2.44a

Verticality and solidity remain characteristic of sensitively sited pyramidal temples. The corbel vault prevails but the shifting of lighter roof-combs to the centre of roofs, over the partition wall between parallel halls, lightens the structure. Palenque, whose relatively brief efflorescence spanned little more than the 7th century, offers prime examples – religious and apparently secular.**2.45, 2.46**

Palenque: the buildings

Apart from the extraordinary complex known as the palace, the legacy of vigorous royal patronage at Palenque includes several intact temples, especially the royal funerary Temple of Inscriptions from which King Pacal's fabulous jade hoard and much information on his line were recovered. The steeply stepped temple platform, corbel-vaulted gallery, roof-comb and stucco embellishment including portraiture are typical of Mayan sites – as we have seen. Here, however, the upper wall is inclined in parallel with the slope of the internal corbel vault and the roof slightly pitched, producing a 'mansard' profile: reducing the weight bearing down on the walls, this obviously allows the latter to be thinner and pierced with wider openings than at Tikal. Niches and overdoors of varied profile further reduce the weight of structure. The inclined wall plane, treated as a deep cornice, is embellished with low-relief carving which continues up into the roof-comb. An open filigree, this surmounts the bulkhead between the parallel vaulted halls rather than an especially thick back wall, as at Tikal. External and internal piers are also embellished in carved stucco.

2.44b

›2.44 TIKAL, CENTRAL ACROPOLIS: (a, b) residential complex and hall.

The so-called Central Acropolis is a tiered platform carrying a highly irregular complex of palace buildings and patios. Entered from the plaza but orientated to the view out over the valley to south and east, the palace is an informal arrangement of long, narrow corbel-vaulted halls – dark and damp and presumably disagreeable if designed for permanent habitation – on two main levels around terraces of spacious courts all rising from a platform to an average of some 10 metres above the plaza. The ceremonial entrance from the plaza leads to the largest court, presumably for public assembly at the appearance of the ruler.

2.45a

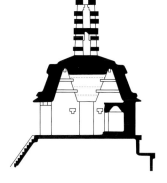

2.45c

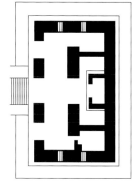

2.45d @ 1:2000

2.45b

2.45e

›2.45 PALENQUE, TEMPLES: (a, b) Temple of the
Sun, c. 640, cut-away model and general view; (c–e)
Temple of the Cross, c. 690, plan, section, and view of
ruin showing corbel-vaulting of portico; (f, g) Temple of
the Inscriptions with tomb of King Pacal, plan and longitudinal section.

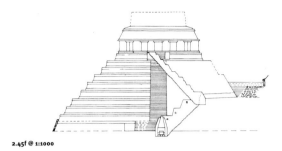

2.45f @ 1:1000

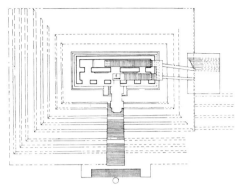

2.45g

The many temples on the site consist of a cella with three-bay portico and two small chambers flanking a central shrine, or double galleries with parallel corbel vaults, on a stepped platform with central staircase, but elongation often produces double galleries. The Temples of the Sun, the Cross and the Foliated Cross are prominent examples – the first and last on stepped bases, the other on a pyramidal mound. The Temple of the Inscriptions has a five-bay gallery for its portico and elongated central gallery-like shrine chamber: it is supported by an eight-tiered pyramid incorporating a natural mound into which a burial crypt was sunk. In all these works, characteristically, the roof-comb is supported on the central wall in which several doors open between the galleries.

The irregularly distributed complex of courts, galleries and chambers on a stepped platform (c. 70 by 55 metres) towards the centre of the site, overlooked by the Temple of the Inscriptions, is usually identifed as the palace: some commentators find the rooms too restricted for comfortable habitation but no other possible royal residence has so far been uncovered. The two northern courts, with flanking porticos or verandahs and galleries (with stucco reliefs of King Pacal), were no doubt ceremonial spaces – perhaps for public and private audience. If this was the royal residential palace, the apartments of the king and queen were doubtless composed principally of the twin suites of rooms to the south of the north-eastern court and the warren of rooms to their south was doubtless for other members of the family, retainers and servants. A vaulted watercourse seems to have acted as a sewer for lavatories. The four-storey corbel-vaulted observatory tower (with astrological decoration on a landing of its stairs) seems to have been the last addition to the palace but it completed a masterly exercise in balanced asymmetry.

The Temple of the Inscriptions takes its name from calendrical and dynastic records on the interior wall and is also notable for the life-size god-bearing stucco figures embellishing the pillars of the portico. King Pacal's burial crypt is entered down a corbel-vaulted staircase from the cella and, as in other tomb temples on the site, ducts between the burial chamber and the cella floor allow the spirit of the interred to participate in the cult rites.

›**2.46 PALENQUE, THE PALACE** ('El Palacio'), probably begun under King Pacal, remodelled and extended by King Hok: (a) plan, (b) corbel-vaulted gallery, (c) north-east court looking south-east with principal apartment to the right, (d, pages 290–291) overview.

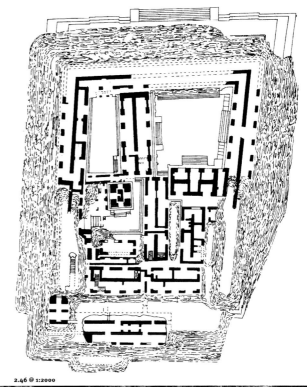

2.46b

2.46 @ 1:2000

2.46c

LATE-CLASSIC MAYANS

The last known inscriptional record at Tikal is dated to the equivalent of 889 CE: the phenomenal building campaigns had ceased earlier, maintenance had ceased too, artisans and traders were destitute, the population declined as the hungry sought sustenance back in the overworked countryside and endemic internal strife invited foreign invasion. Palenque had also dwindled into insignificance. Dissecting the domains of their former overlords, many highland and lowland Mayan communities reasserted their independence in the 8th century and by the 9th century several cities of northern Yucatan had won spectacular prosperity from the development of seaborne trade.

Tikal and Palenque both exerted their influence over the central Yukatan but the sites there had their idiosyncrasies too, of course. In the Rio Bec area, for example, towers recall the profile of the steepest Tikal form but they may support temples in the Classic manner or they may be false and frame tripartite complexes: Becan has both, Rio Bec itself provides outstanding examples of the false tower. Roof-combs are usually light and central but

>2.47 HOCHOB: the central section of a tripartite building (variously interpreted as religious or secular) with an elaborate revetment of the Chac mask theme around a spectacular monster-mouth portal – the latter recalling the orifice of the pre-Olmec dragon monster of the earth, ancestor of the creator-god.

>2.48 COMMEMORATIVE OPULENCE: (a) Copan, Stele H: c. 782; (b) Piedras Negras ruler's throne (Guatemala City, National Museum of Archaeology and Ethnology).

Apart from its prodigious stelae, the site is noted for the staircase embellished with hieroglyphs recording its conquest in 737 by the neighbouring city of Quirigua.

2.48a

2.48b

>2.49 RIO BEC, PRINCIPAL TRIPARTITE BUILDING: model (New York, American Museum of Natural History).

>2.50 BECAN: overview of site (reconstruction after Potter).

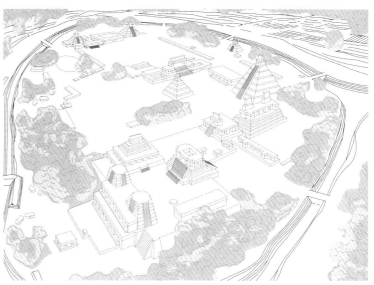

the rectilinear roof profile of Tikal persists as an entablature as well as Palenque's inclined upper wall plane. Vertical continuity of ornament from wall or cornice to roof-comb is, therefore, not always invited but the figural relief of Palenque's picrs is often abstracted and set in vertical panels of superimposed masks to relieve the plane of walls. Beyond that, sometimes a lush creeper of vine-like mouldings breaks with constraint to ramp around and over doors in the form of monster masks – notably in the Chenes region at sites like Hochob.**2.47** It was on the Pacific side of the southern highlands, in the region of Copan, that iconographical embellishment made its most overwhelming impression on architecture in high-relief sculpture which some commentators define as 'baroque' because of its convoluted complexity and lush exuberance.**2.48–2.50**

The late flowering of Classic Mayan civilization in the Puuc region of north-west Yucatan is most splendidly represented at Edzna and Uxmal and at the latter's satellites, Sayil, Labna and Kabah. For a Mayan site Edzna is

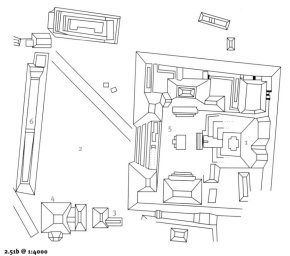

2.51b @ 1:4000

2.51c

›2.51 EDZNA: (a, pages 294–295) main pyramid from the west, (b) plan with (1) main pyramid, (2) main plaza, (3) ball-court, (4) south-west pyramid, (5) Great Acropolis, (6) western terrace, (c) view to the west.

Strategically placed on the route linking the Puuc region and the rest of northern Yucatan with Peten, Edzna offers a rare synthesis of types and styles. On the east side of the main plaza (159 by 100 metres), is the main platform with the main pyramid east of its precinct rising to 30 metres through five terraced and galleried tiers: the fourth level has colonnaded bays like those of characteristically Puuc palatial buildings and the summit temple is surmounted by an open-work roof-comb in the Peten manner. Other temples, showing Peten traits, and accommodation for priests flank the central plaza to north and south. An elongated platform, with much dilapidated superstructure that may once have been palatial, closes the composition to the west beyond a broad lower plaza.

uncharacteristically formal in distribution: a unique synthesis of pyramid and palace, its principal group recalls the acropolis at Tikal, perhaps, but the grandeur of its symmetry is now second only to the Moon Complex at Teotihuacan in all Mesoamerica.[2.51] Uxmal has its formal elements but in general its distribution follows the contours of the site in the usual sensitive Mayan manner.

Uxmal is celebrated for its rectilinear palace ranges as well as its temple pyramids; each of its satellites has one of the most notable pre-Columbian palatial complexes.**2.52, 2.53**

A measure of eclecticism – naturally derived from far-flung trading contacts to which the frescoes at Cacaxtla seem to bear witness**2.21e,f** – is most prominently displayed in the extraordinary 'Pyramid of the Magician' at Uxmal but the Puuc style is generally characterized by clarity of composition and line drawn from an essentially architectonic articulation.

The external use of the corbel arch (rare elsewhere) is characteristic: beyond support of staircases on buttress-like segments, as in the 'Magician's Pyramid', the provision of a monumental entrance like that of the Uxmal 'Nunnery', the linking of distinct elements in complexes like the palaces at Uxmal or Labna, and the spanning of a causeway with a triumphal portal, as at Labna, are prime local exercises – again insofar as the accidents of survival testify.

Columnar bays (also rare in the Mayan world but the key to the synthesis at Edzna), support rectilinear parapets delineated by strong string courses and sometimes surmounted by canted cornices: sturdy square piers are characteristic of Uxmal; at Edzna, as more extensively in the palatial buildings of Sayil and Labna, the columns in antis are bold in entasis and their capitals are invariably thick rectangular blocks.

Framing these open bays, wall panels are relieved with geometric motifs or applied colonettes: the latter, complementing the rustic order, derive from the vernacular reed post doubled with a knot motif – as at Sayil or Labna. Chac masks often alternate with panels of colonettes or geometrical motifs – as at Sayil, Labna and Uxmal. Rarely is floral or figural ornament overwhelming, as in Chenes or Copan: Kabah's palace is exceptional.**2.54–2.56**

2.52a

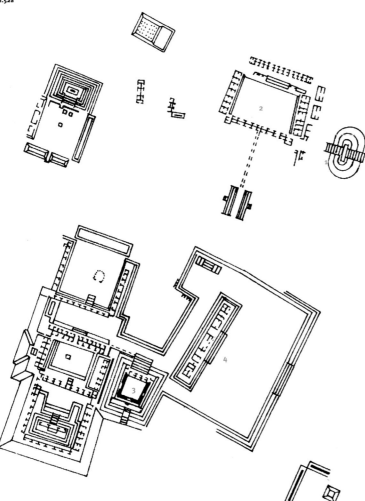

>2.52 UXMAL: (a) general view north from summit of Grand Pyramid, (b) plan with (1) 'Pyramid of the Magician' (2), 'Nunnery' (3), Grand Pyramid, and 'Governor's Palace' (4); (c) 'Pyramid of the Magician' ('del Advino') (d) 'Nunnery', (e) south entrance, (f) court to north-west and central portal of north range, (g) detail of east range.

2.52b @ 1:5000

2.52c

Uxmal

The most important site of the region (known as Puuc from its low hills extending from Campeche to Yucatan), Uxmal was inhabited in the 6th century but the main period of its development was between the 8th and 10th centuries – like its satellites. There is an impressive range of temples, palatial buildings and a ball-court. The city's style is characterized by precision-cut revetment of square limestone slabs over a core of rubble, corbel vaults and walls divided into plain and embellished registers by a string course and crowned by a plain outward-sloping cornice.

The earliest temple remains on the site are embedded in the foundations of the extraordinary elliptical 'Pyramid of the Magician': the

2.52d

2.52e

2.52f

2.52g

wooden doorframe has been dated to the late-6th century. The associated façade in the Puuc style has a decorative register above lintel level but also masks of the Teotihuacano rain-god Tlaloc as well as his Mayan counterpart. Two further enlargements were replaced in the 10th century by a fourth one facing west and built by immigrants from the Chenes region to the south. Staircases to either side of the fourth temple's façade and to the east led up to the fifth temple on the summit. The fourth temple is overlaid with revetment in the Chenes style of stacked Chac masks; the fifth one is predominantly Puuc in its tectonic sobriety and may have been arrested after the Puuc region had been infiltrated by Toltecs from the west.

West of the Pyramid of the Magician is a quadrangular compound known as the 'Nunnery': the use of the building is uncertain but it probably accommodated the principal executives, administrators and their staff. The main entrance is through a great corbelled arch in the southern range. Each range except the southern one has a platform base, steps and galleries on the upper level. The main range, on the northern side, is set on a higher platform which incorporates an earlier building: the principal suites of rooms are in parallel ranges on the upper level; serpent, bird, animal, human and architectural motifs are interspersed with lattice and chequerboard designs and superimposed Chac masks crown the generous doors – like advanced roof-combs. Chac masks, serpents, a turtle god and other symbols of the divine relieve the other ranges but the patterning of the decorative registers is primarily geometrical.

To the south of the site is a grand platform supporting another complex with pyramid temple and a long building of the same type as the east range of the Nunnery, known as the 'Governor's Palace'. The latter (100 metres long), built over an earlier structure in the late-10th century, is one of the latest works on the site. In adition to parallel ranges of halls and chambers in a central block, lit from the east, there are two side pavilions with identical five-roomed apartments beyond recessed passages with corbel vaults. The embellished register, with geometric variations and Chac masks, is centred on a seated figure in ceremonial dress.

›2.53 (PAGES 302–307) UXMAL, 'GOVERN-OR'S PALACE': east front.

2.54a

>**2.54 LABNA:** (a) three-storey palace of three courts, each with a range of rooms to its north built in several phases culminating in the early 9th century; (b) arch: west front with guard posts and niches in the form of the vernacular hut, geometrical ornament, Chac masks and engaged columns on the corners and canted cornice. To the east is the pyramid known as 'The Viewpoint' ('El Mirador').

2.54b

2.55a

›**2.55 SAYIL:** (a, b) mid-9th-century 'palace' with corbel-vaulted chambers, colonnaded bays, panels of knotted reed motifs modelled on a vernacular type of post and, at the top, Chenes-style masks with convoluted serpent mouldings separated by repeated vertical slabs.

2.55b

2.56a

2.56b

›2.56 KABAH: (a, b) palace wing known as 'Codz Po'op' ('rolled mat') with its extraordinary three-register revetment of multiple hook-nosed Chac masks in high relief.

›2.57 MIXTEC GOLD PECTORAL in the form of the mask of Mictlantecuhtli from Monte Alban, Tomb 7, 10th century? (Oaxaca Regional Museum).

The Zapotec tombs of Monte Alban were reused by the Mixtecs from late in the 9th century. The appearance of relatively accomplished copper and gold jewellery in them without evidence of local experimentation implies that the Mixtecs acquired the objects, then the skills, fully formed: the lost-wax technique was used at first for delicate votive objects in precious metals rather than large-scale, heavy tools and weapons. Bronze remained unknown – or at least unused – by the Mesoamericans despite its fabrication in the Andean region.

3 THE POST-CLASSIC WORLD OF THE TOLTECS AND AZTECS

In the turmoil entailed by the fall of Teotihuacan and Tikal, the decline in the agrarian economy led to mass movements of peoples and new settlements, and the eclipse of the old spinal land route of trade by new sea lanes changed the pattern of economic relationships. That provoked social and cultural change: its degree has been exaggerated but Olmec iconography may still be traced. There was continued expansion in the pantheon of deities and some redefinition of significance within it. There was a militant quest for empire but the Classic period was not without militarism, as we have seen. There was a new degree of bellicosity in the arts, but the Classic exemplars were certainly not overlooked in the styles which continued various and changeable among the widely disparate linguistic groups of the region.

Maritime trade with South Americans or their intermediaries brought metallurgy – first to the Mixtecs in the vale of Oaxaca – provoking the transformation of Mesoamerican technology, at least in jewellery.[2.57] And early in the period conventionally labelled post-Classic, writing was advanced among the ruling elites and truly historical records of dynastic achievements appear beyond Mayan domains for the first time.

THE NORTHERN CHICHIMECA AND THEIR PROGENY

Into the vacuum left by Teotihuacan poured waves of Chichimeca tribesmen from the north-west: these migrations are shrouded in legend and, unlike the later Aztec records, the chronicles give no clear idea of time or place of origin. Archaeological evidence supports the contention that the Toltec emerged from among them to establish themselves towards the end of the 10th century in the former Teotihuacano settlement of Tula.

Tula's founder called himself Quetzalcoatl Topiltzin but he seems to have succumbed to the most bellicose of his tribesmen, dedicated to the war-god Tezcatlipoca and to human sacrifice for his appeasement. Stoutly defended, the ceremonial centre was dominated by a four-tiered pyramid and a three-tiered temple platform dedicated to Quetzalcoatl in his manifestation as the god of the dawn or the morning star (Tlahuizcalpantecuhtli) but the latter is subjected to – and popularly named for – the rank of martial atlantes guarding its shrine.[2.58]

Recognizing the importance of controlling the obsidian quarries that had provided the basis of Teotihuacan's mercantile ascendancy – for as yet metal was too expensive to be widely used instead of stone – the Toltecs fostered a revival of trade. They developed a northerly route through the lands of the Huastecs as access to the Gulf routes was controlled by El Tajin in the adjacent coastal region. The old land route to the south was closed to them

›2.58 TULA (TOLLAN): (a, b) site overview and plan with (1) ruined main plaza, centred on an altar orientated to the cardinal points, (2) ball-court, (3) main four-tiered pyramid temple, (4) colonnaded galleries, (5) the three-tiered platform of the Temple of Quetzalcoatl; (c, d) Temple of Quetzalcoatl, detail of crennelated temple precinct wall with reliefs of Quetzelcoatl and platform with atlante; (e) Chacmool.

The remains of the Teotihuacano settlement were eclipsed by the city developed by the Toltecs in the 10th and 11th centuries around a new elevated ceremonial complex (Tula Grande). As is to be expected in a trading city, developed by various waves of immigrants, the style is eclectic but much was derived from Teotihuacan. The Temple of Quetzalcoatl is of the Teotihuacano talud/tablero type – insofar as the limited remains of the latter testify – the talud of the base was unadorned but the tablero had two registers embellished with the jaguars, coyotes and eagles emblematic of military orders. The atlante, representing armed and armoured Toltec knights facing south, were the outer members of the colonnaded summit temple, preceded by portico columns in the form of a serpent (head to ground) at the top of the boldly projecting staircase. A precinct wall, novel in the Mexican highland, was crenellated above two registers, one carved with geometric patterns, the other with the feathered serpent of Quetzalcoatl consuming skeletons.

An extended gallery of three rows of square piers linked the temple and the adjacent palatial complex of colonnaded courts: several of the enclosure walls were lined with benches embellished with reliefs of priests and warriors in procession and the courts contained altars in the form of a reclining figure supporting a receptacle on its stomach (Chacmool). The gallery also turned south on the base platform towards the main pyramidal temple. The ball-court is closely modelled on one at Xochicalco.

2.58a

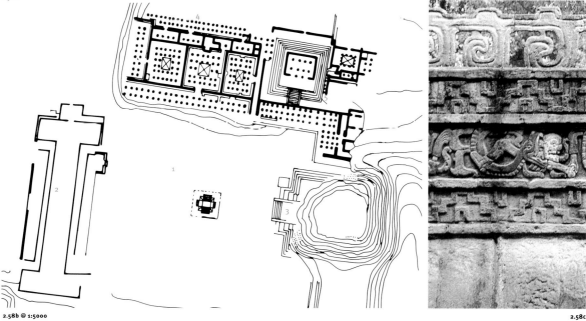

2.58b @ 1:5000

2.58c

by Cacaxtla and Cholula, to the east of the Mexican basin: revived following Teotihuacano decline by other Chichimec invaders, Cholula seem to have maintained formal contacts with the Mixtecs in the Oaxaca valley to the exclusion of the Toltecs. Instead, the Tula merchants found a route through Teotenango to the Pacific coast which they then skirted to the isthmus. Crossing the isthmus, they seem to have reached the west coast of the Yucatan by sea and forged a strong connection with the Itzas.

Largely inexplicably, post-Classic habitation in the Yucatan peninsula – relatively evenly spread throughout in the great age of the Maya – was reduced to the littoral. Chichen Itza appears as a significant power in the northern fringe at much the same time as Tula was elevated by the Toltecs. Beyond mere coincidence, an ancient legend maintains that Quetzalcoatl Topiltzin, ousted from Tula, led his faction to the Yucatan where, as Kukulkan (the Mayan equivalent of Quetzalcoatl), he established himself at the Itza centre, which *ipso facto* acquired the prefix Chichen. Some modern scholars – certainly not all – see evidence for this in representations in the reliefs found on the site of conflict between typical Toltec warriors and Mayans and the appearance of Kukulkan to supplement – if not supplant – the traditional Mayan pantheon.

Certainly, there is some similarity between important elements of the Toltec ceremonial centre at Tula and the new ceremonial centre developed to the east of the original Itza site from the late-10th century: unlike the dispersed earlier Mayan cities, but as at Tula, the population (of some twelve thousand) was confined within massive stone walls; as at Tula, but contrary to the Mayan norm beyond Edzna, there is considerable formality in the relationship between the major elements; column and beam confront the Mayan corbel vault, as Toltecs in

2.58d

2.58e

cylindrical helmets confront Mayans in feathered head-dresses and, apart from the new prominence of Quetzal-coatl, alien are the birds of prey devouring human hearts, feathered serpents consuming skeletons, serpent columns, Chacmools, and atlante warriors arrayed like Toltecs.**2.59–2.62**

Chichen Itza

To the south are the remains of the original Mayan settlement, with the earliest buildings on the site including the so-called House of the Nuns. This sector is dominated by the pyramid tomb-temple ascribed to the high

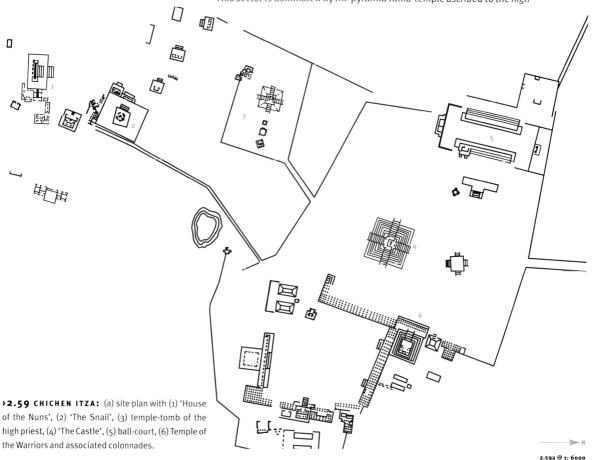

›2.59 CHICHEN ITZA: (a) site plan with (1) 'House of the Nuns', (2) 'The Snail', (3) temple-tomb of the high priest, (4) 'The Castle', (5) ball-court, (6) Temple of the Warriors and associated colonnades.

2.59a @ 1: 6000

2.60a

>2.60 CHICHEN ITZA: SOUTHERN SECTOR:
(a) 'House of the Nuns' (so named because of its supposed resemblance to a Spanish convent) with annex
left and pavilion ('Church' or 'Iglesia') right; (b) 'The
Snail' (Caracol, so named for the spiral staircase but
also called 'The Observatory' because astrological
observations might have been taken from the upper
room).

priest, rebuilt in the 10th century. Beyond it is the slightly later two-tiered
platform and tower called 'The Snail' (Caracol), with doors aligned with
the cardinal directions, Mayan Chac masks, Toltec-type warrior heads,
serpent rails and an internal spiral staircase leading to a rectangular room
at the summit: the circular form, not uncommon in the Chichimeca north,
is rare in the Mexican highlands but unique in the Mayan world. The third
main element, the so-called 'House of the Nuns' incorporates a pyramid
tomb with an annex and a detached pavilion in the Chenes and Puuc styles
respectively.

2.60b

2.61a

To the north a new ceremonial centre was developed over the century following the Toltec intervention – traditionally dated to 987 – with the so-called Castle as its nucleus, the most monumental of all surviving ball-courts to the west and to the east the 'Temple of the Warriors', associated with extensive colonnades as at Tula.

Incorporating an earlier pyramid, the nine-tiered 'Castle' (24 metres high) has been identified as the Temple of Kukulkan (Quetzalcoatl): the hooded form of the Zapotec tablero has been etched on the talud of each tier; the stairways, unusually giving access to the summit from each side

2.61b

2.61c

as in the earlier Itza pyramid, have serpent balustrades; the summit temple has serpent columns, square internal piers supporting a flat roof over the inner sanctum, corbel-vaulted ambulatory and no roof-comb.

The ball-court north-west of the Grand Plaza (146 by 37 metres with 8-metre walls), is of the usual I-shaped plan but with benches of the Tulan type along the sides. It is noted for its reliefs recording two fully equipped teams opposed to either side of death and with one team leader holding the severed head of his counterpart. An associated temple is noted for a great painting of an attack on a Mayan town (which has obviously been interpreted as the Toltecs assaulting Itza).

The eastern side of the plaza is bordered by an extended colonnade (the 'Group of a Thousand Columns'). This was later repeated at right-angles to form the northern boundary of a second plaza to the east and the scheme was completed by the colonnaded portico of the cloistered

market square to the south: unusual in Mesoamerica, plaza colonnades of this scale are unique in the Mayan world. The original section of the older colonnade, with square piers rather than the later circular columns, formed a portico to the north-eastern quarter's main monument, the four-tiered Pyramid of the Warriors. The name derives from the atlantes that support the altar table in the summit temple: the roof of this shrine was caried on square piers and the portico before it has serpent columns; the tiers have tablud and tablero registers, the latter much less elevated than the former and embellished with Toltec-type reliefs of eagles and jaguars devouring hearts; Toltec Tlahuizcalpante-cuhtli is engraved on the portico columns and serpent columns frame the entrance. The complex as a whole thus bears close comparison with the Temple of Quetzalcoatl at Tula – except for Mayan Chac masks on the exterior walls and the Chacmool figures reclining before the entrance.

2.62a

2.62b

2.62c

Prospering from its Toltec connections and maritime trade in an age of inland turmoil, Chichen Itza extended its sway over north Yucatan from early in the 11th century in alliance with Mayapan and Uxmal, exacting tribute from smaller cities. The alliance disintegrated in the mid-13th century and Chichen Itza was sacked by Mayapan. The latter in turn fell to Uxmal a century later.

›2.62 CHICHEN ITZA: EASTERN SECTOR, Temple of the Warriors and associated colonnades: (a) general view, (b) western colonnade, (c) platform revetment with masks of Quetzelcoatl and Chac.

Meanwhile pressure of tribes from the increasingly dessicated north looking for new land in the Mexican basin weakened the Toltecs and undermined their leadership. Loss of control of the main sources of obsidian precipitated the fall of Tula c. 1170. A small population lingered on at the devastated site, but Tula's enduring legacy was the legend of a golden age of military glory and the purity of the dedicated warrior. The inspiration was vital to the next great wave of invaders, the Aztecs.

2.63a

MEXICA AZTECS

Several Tolteca-Chichimeca tribes had settled in the Mexican basin and acquired the names of the cities in which they established themselves around Lake Texcoco. In the declining years of Tula, another wave (known as Aztec from their ancestral homeland, Aztlan) invaded their older cousins and occupied several of their cities. The last in the field, the Mexica (known as Tenocha after their leader, Tenoch) unleashed several generations of rape and pillage in search of a base until late in the 13th century they enlisted as mercenaries of the venerable Toltec city of Colhuacan and claimed the Toltec ancestry of their patrons through marriage. By 1325 they had switched their mercenary service to Azcapotzalco, the dominant power on the west bank of Lake Texcoco. They settled on a marshy island in the lake adjacent to that city and founded Tenochtitlan beside the probably pre-existent town of Tlatelolco. Their subsequent rise was attributed in their extensive records to the patronage of the sun-god Huitzilopochtli: they were his chosen people.

On one interpretation of Aztec lore, sovereignty was shared between a warrior king responsible for external affairs and a more shadowy lord of the palatine domain: it is assumed that the list compiled by the chroniclers of Aztec history after its termination is of the former. The first three served their suzerain, the ruler of Azcapotzalco, in his wars of expansion. The last of these died under circumstances that his followers blamed on their overlords and his successor, Itzcoatl (1426–40), renounced his vassalage and entered into alliance with the current enemy, Texcoco. In league with other vassals, they attacked Azcapotzalco and destroyed it. The alliance was sustained until near end of the reign of Moctezuma I (1440–68) but Tenochtitlan was its dominant force.

Axayacatl (1468–81) and Tizoc (1481–86) asserted their suzerainty over most of the former allies and claimed supremacy in all the central highlands. Ahuitzotl (1486–1502) pressed south-east to Oaxaca, subjecting the Mixtec cities of the valley to his suzerainty, and on to the Pacific coast of the Tehuantepec isthmus, from whose ports his servants controlled maritime trade. Moctezuma II (1502–20) failed to take Tlaxcala but skirted it and asserted suzerainty over the Gulf coast in the region of modern Veracruz – and over its seaborne trade. All this was hardly achieved when a band of five hundred Spaniards landed on the Gulf coast in 1519.

In the time-honoured manner of the Toltecs and the venerable Teotihuacanos, whose magnificence set the standard to be emulated, Aztec conquest of city-states usually meant vassalage and tribute rather than political integration. The Toltecs provided the model of ruthless militarism – especially with military orders dedicated to the eagle and the jaguar – but the Aztecs were the first to keep a majority of males ready for war and excelled their mentors in ferocity. To reinsure compliance, the most venerable idols of the conquered were held hostage in Tenochtitlan but the power and ferocity of the imperial forces encouraged little effective resistance to the enforcement of allegiance.

The Aztecs drew heavily on earlier Mesoamerican religion, especially the Teotihuacano tradition, and had evolved a vast pantheon of gods for all their subject

2.63b

peoples and their occupations but the imperial warriors were the more alien for their messianic zeal on behalf of Huitzilopochtli. They accepted the ancient Mesoamerican mythical tradition of five solar cycles of human existence of which there had already been five creative phases and four destructions. As destruction attended the death of the sun, their mission was to ward off the end of the fifth phase by ensuring the sustenance of Huitzilopochtli in his nightly struggle against the moon. That meant the sacrifice on an unprecedented scale of beating human hearts. Seen to reflect the celestial trajectory, the ballgame was dedicated to the sun and resulted in sacrifice but much more was needed. Thus the ferocious militancy of the Aztecs is to be explained in religious terms: beyond territory and tribute, it won the blood of massed prisoners to slake the thirst of Huitzilopochtli.[2.63]

Yet the Aztecs also acquired the traditional Mesoamerican arts of peace – or, rather, imitated them. Apart from painting, sculpture and architecture – which served the state, the temple and the ideology of war – these primarily sustained the economy. To feed a growing population – unprecedented in density ultimately – they furthered the efforts of their predecessors around Lake Texcoco to extend the arable area of their dry, erosion-prone hilly heartland with irrigation and swamp reclamation: they specialized in island-like plots of marshland reclaimed with soil and pond-weed deposits between canals (chinampas) and they pre-empted famine with myriad grain stores (cuezcomates). And like the Teotihuacanos and Toltecs, they traded the obsidian of their highlands for tropical necessities like rubber and luxuries like cotton, cocoa, feathers, precious stones and metals.

The tributary cities of the Teotihuacanos and Toltecs were the constituent elements of the Aztec heartland too: some sixty of them averaging 25,000 inhabitants. And the

2.63c

>**2.63 THE AZTEC GODS AND THE SUPREME CULT OF THE SUN:** (a) King Tizoc (1481–86) attending sacrificial rites in the guise of Huitzilopochtli ('hummingbird of the south', after the bird that represented warriors who had given their blood for the sun) on the cylindrical altar known as the Piedra de Tizoc; (b) Coatlicue, the earth-goddess mother of Huitzilopochtli (whose extreme complexity of form, with snakes of spilled blood, recalls Olmec zoomorphic symbolism in the spirit if not the letter); (c) the feathered serpent of Quetzalcoatl; (d) Tlaloc (double image with the Teotihuacano model over the Aztec variant); (e) the 'Old God' Huehueteotl (stone image from the great temple of Tenochtitlan, closely modelled on the Teotihuacano type but with fangs recalling Olmec syncretism); (f) the 'Stone of the Sun' (all Mexico City, National Museum of Anthropology).

Conceived by the earth-goddess Coatlicue, who had previously born the moon and stars, Huizil-opochtli was delivered despite the matricide committed by his sibling luminaries out of fear for their eclipse. In danger of their ultimate triumph while on his nightly passage through the world of the dead, he would re-emerge only if sustained by the blood of sacrificed warriors. Destined as the table for the excision of living hearts to quench this thirst in the god's main shrine at Tenochtitlan, the Stone of the Sun was probably carved under Moctezuma II (1502–20) but broken in transit from the quarry and doubtless rejected by the priests: the anthropomorphic representation of the sun, with sacrificial knife protruding from its mouth, is central to a hieroglyphic almanac in which primacy is given to the sacred record of the cycles of the four previous suns and the predicted course of the fifth and last.

2.63d   2.62e

2.63f

structure of those states was traditional: groups of extended families lived in wards under a council of headmen responsible for raising tax, military service and civil labour levies. Society was traditionally stratified into hereditary ranks determined by occupation: the administrators, the merchants – whose economic importance and guild organization retained for them the privileges won at Teotihuacan – the luxury craftsmen, the artisans, the agricultural labourers, the urban labourers and serfs.

The Aztec empire was a confederation for well over a century. As it waxed to more than four hundred conquests, however, the rulers found it politic to marry the issue of the associated rulers and, ultimately, to define thirty-eight provinces with Aztec governors and garrisons of Aztec soldiers/colonists in fortified compounds. Stability encouraging prosperity, trouble was minimized in the heartland if not among the grander tributaries with a proud legacy of independence and especially not on the periphery where the manic pursuit of conquest had left the problems of assimilation unresolved. The Spaniards had little problem penetrating the coast and readily found allies for assault on the seat of an alien emperor.

Moctezuma's seat, which Cortes called the most beautiful in the world but proceeded to obliterate, had incorporated Tlatelolco and, beyond that, had grown on chinampa reclamation and lakeside communities connected to the island by causeways. Causeways and aqueducts were certainly not new to Mesoamerica but the Aztecs conceived them on an unprecedented scale: the dissection of the island by the main arteries issuing from them took formal planning further even than the builders of Teotihuacan which the Aztecs revered.

If planning was essentially Teotihuacano – like the social structure – the style of religious architecture that reached its climax in the central sacred precinct, Teocalli, was Toltec in inspiration, but on a much grander scale than anything at Tula. Tlatelolco had its major cult centre too and there were hundreds of smaller temples in the many districts designated not only according to rank but also to occupation. Little of Aztec building above foundation level survived the ravages of the *conquistadores*. Reconstruction is generally based on surveys of the substructure and the often-vivid accounts of Spanish chroniclers or early Aztec converts to Spanish culture.**2.64, 2.65**

›**2.64 TENOCHTITLAN:** (a) mural overview by Luis Coverrubias (Mexico City, Aztec Gallery of the National Museum of Anthropology); (b) plan illustrating an edition of the letters of Cortes published in Nuremburg in 1524.

2.64a

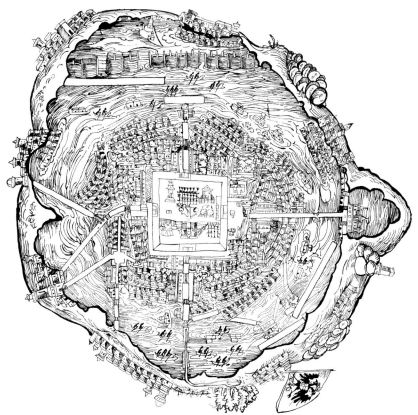

2.64b

›ARCHITECTURE IN CONTEXT »PRE-COLUMBIAN AMERICA

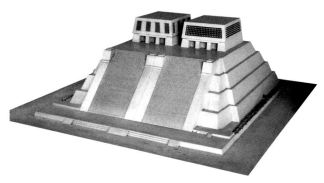

Founded in the early 12th century, the pyramid was rebuilt many times (perhaps to mark the close of calendrical cycles). The double staircase and twin shrines seem to date from the late-12th century second phase. The several Aztec campaigns culminated in the work of Moctezuma II in 1507, which closely resembled the main pyramid of the Tenochtitlan Teocalli in its final form.

Tenochtitlan and Teocalli

The largest of Mesoamerican cities, in 1519 Tenochtitlan covered 13 square kilometres and probably had a population of c. 200,000. Development was disciplined in general by a grid imposed on the flat island, as at Teotihuacan – though, inevitably, some distortion rippled through the outer zones from the unstable perimeter. The crossing of the main arteries at the ceremonial centre was rectilinear, again as at Teotihuacan, but the east–west axis was at least as assertive as the north–south one. The Great Temple (Teocalli) was on the crossing, its main axis aligned east–west: the compactness of its distribution was characteristic of the Aztecs.

To the south was a grand plaza addressed by the royal palace from the east: greater in extent even than the Teocalli compound, the three main courts and three hundred rooms of that complex accommodated the emperor, his wives, entourage, guards and the central bureaucracy. In the four quarters of the city adjacent to this ceremonial nucleus, residential buildings were graded in accordance with the rank of the occupants, as at Teotihuacan, with the houses of the workers crowded into the peripheral areas of the island and the satellite settlements.

Dominating the ceremonial centre at the crossing of the causeway arteries, the Teocalli complex was begun under the first emperor and extended, refurbished or rebuilt under all his successors till Moctezuma II. Its builders emulated the greatest works of Teotihuacan but doubled the main pyramid to support the twin shrines of Huitzilopochtli and Tlaloc, perhaps after the precedent set nearby at Tenayuca. The temple precinct (c. 300 metres square), surrounded by a serpent wall and near-symmetrical in general distribution like the earlier ceremonial precincts

›2.66 TENOCHTITLAN, TEOCALLI: (a, b) plan and model with north, south and west entrances (1), ball-court (2), Temple of Quetzalcoatl (3), Temple of Xipe Totec (4), Temple of the Sun (5), unidentified temple (6), Temple of Tezcatlipoca (7), Temple of the Great Pyramid (8) with temples of Tlaloc (9) and Huitzilopochtli (10); (c) cut-away model showing phases of construction of the double pyramid bearing the twin sanctuaries of Huitzilopochtli and Tlaloc.

at Tenayuca and Tlatelolco, was entered from the west. The first building on the main axis, immediately within the entrance, was the ball-court. To either side, in the north-west and south-west corners of the compound, were the Temples of the Sun and Spring, Tonatiuh and Xipe Totec. In the central zone, the Temple of Quetzalcoatl was flanked by two pairs of small temples. The eastern zone was covered by the main pyramid platform: to its north and south were the twin temples of an unidentified god (north) and Tezcatilpoca and in the centre the great double pyramid (100 metres at base, 30 metres high) of Tlaloc (north) and Huitzilopochtli (south) with its paired staircases (projecting beyond the tiered taluds, as at Tula). Within the southern shrine chamber was the sacrificial slab on which the victim was spreadeagled for the priest to excise his beating heart and consign it, through fire, to the god upon whom the continuation of cyclical existence depended.

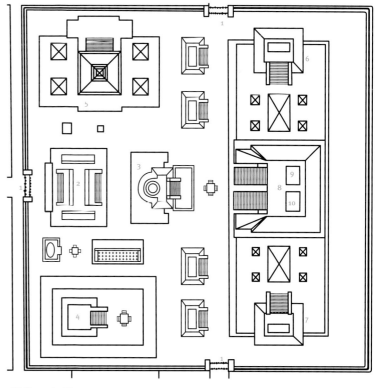

2.66a @ approximately 1:4000

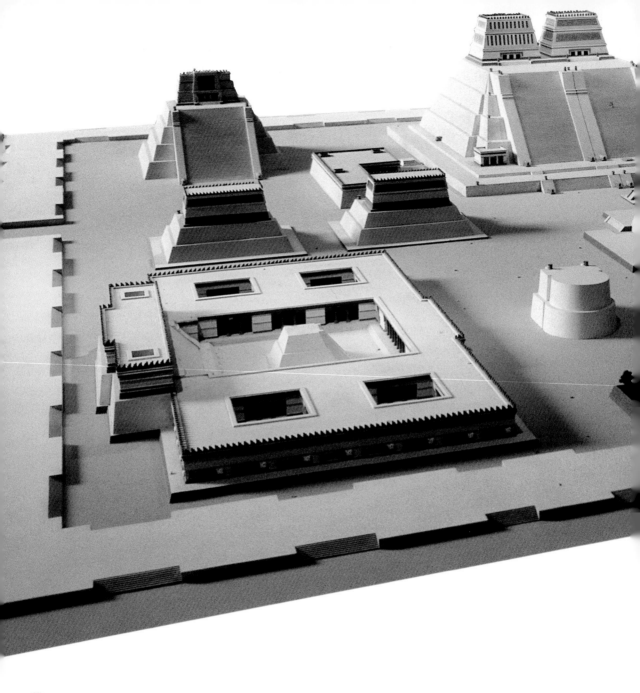

2.66b

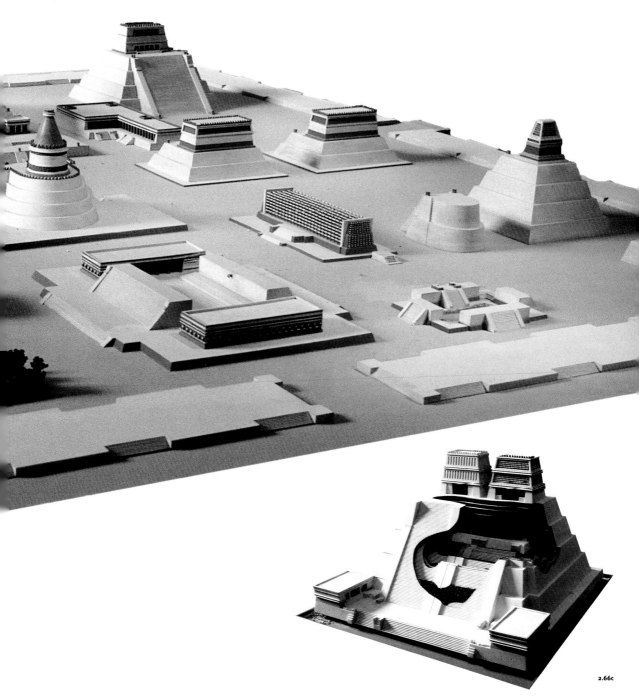

2.66c

›ARCHITECTURE IN CONTEXT »PRE-COLUMBIAN AMERICA

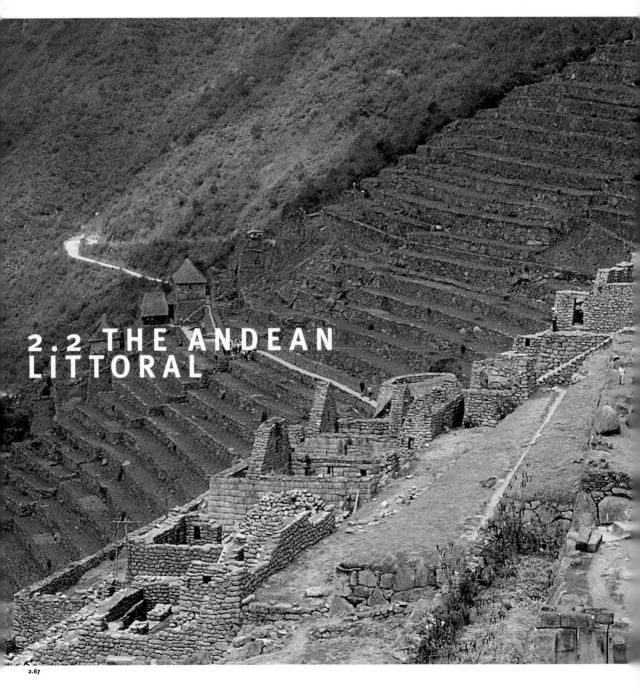

2.2 THE ANDEAN LITTORAL

INTRODUCTION

About the time pottery first appears in the Andean region (c. 1800 BCE) – simultaneously in coastal and highland areas but spreading erratically over several centuries – putative state institutions were emerging from chiefdoms constituted over large settlements of multi-kinship groups. The chief was responsible for protecting and expanding territory and furthering the supply of food and the idea that religious rites were essential to ensure his success led to the emergence of an official religion and a priesthood. When the chief was succeeded by right of birth, the lines of caste were drawn on the basis of inherited occupation – from which success at arms was the primary means of ascent. Where the chief acknowledged that only the priest could properly install him, he ceded superiority: the limited evidence available suggests that Peruvian regimes were sacerdotal until the second half of the 1st millennium CE – and then the king ruled as a god.

As in Mesoamerica – and most other early cultures – Andean religion developed from animism, venerating natural phenomena in venerable places (huacas), to the deification of nature's forces emanating from earth and sky, particularly those proffering or retaining water. In most of South America the creator-god was of the sky and the high mountains that pierce it, transmit water to man and send the sun on its daily course: the ancestor of the great horizon-god, Viracocha to the Incas and probably to their imperial predecessors, his worship involved veneration of his progeny, the tribal ancestors. As it developed, religious observance followed the cycles of nature. Sacrifice of animals and plants was endemic but human sacrifice was ever the principal propitiatory practice.

With the advent of the deity came the founding of the

primitive temple on the village huaca, particularly a rock. By the late-3rd millennium BCE, as villages were absorbed into chiefly polities, the centralizing power was asserted in the ceremonial centre focused on the huaca of ancestral burial where the elite tomb was increasingly elaborate – like elite apparel, particularly headdress and ear ornament. The frequent – if not invariable – incidence of duality in ceremonial structure suggests the bifurcation of kinship groups that was to be characteristic of the region throughout the pre-Columbian era. Ceremonial architecture is significant mainly in the central Andean region. Typically, the primitive centre associated amphitheatrical sunken courts with the stepped platforms of rough masonry plastered with adobe – or, in some coastal areas, entirely of adobe. As at Kotosh on the Higueras near the watershed, there were usually two platforms for two elite ranks, riddled with cellular rooms and ultimately surmounted by a niched chamber. Both social duality and the elite motif of the niche were long to endure in the Andes.

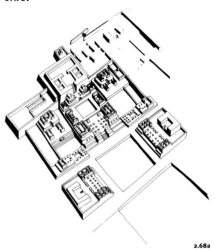

›2.67 (PAGES 328–329) ANDEAN TERRACING.

2.68a

›2.68 THE CEREMONIAL COMPLEX OF THE INITIAL PERIOD: (a) Huaca los Reyes, aerial perspective of restored site (after 2000 to c. 1400s) starting with twin court complexes and the foundation of a central platform. The twin complexes and biaxial symmetry are continued on the central spine as it descends from the huaca platform through an intermediate court complex to the sunken assembly court at base. The site is distinguished by its several colonnaded porticos incorporating monumental frieze panels; (b) Sechin Alto, aerial perspective of site developed in the second half of the 2nd millennium BCE.

The dominant element was the stone-faced platform, c. 300 metres long, 250 metres wide and 40 metres high – the largest American structure of its era – which closed the main U-shaped space. Beyond the open end, circular sunken courts were aligned with the platform along an axis closed by a low U-shaped terrace.

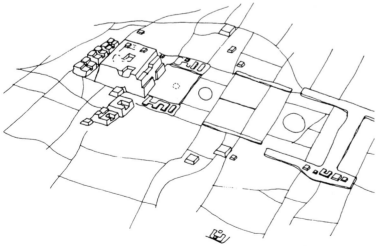

2.68b

Highland platforms supported exclusive ritual enclosures with cermonial hearths, as at La Galgarda in the Santa River uplands where the chambers were later used for interment and ultimately surmounted by a U-shaped complex. In coastal regions, as at Aspero on the Fortaleza estuary, the main ceremonial platforms were usually larger and open at the top, so that ritual was displayed to the congregation below, but there were others with summit chambers for habitation and burial. At the latest pre-ceramic coastal sites, like Huaynuna in the first quarter of the 2nd millennium, bilateral symmetry was preferred in the distribution of courts and rooms about an access hall.

By the 2nd millennium BCE the U-shaped terrace framing a plaza was dominant: the form evolved in scale and purpose but never disappeared from ceremonial building in the pre-Columbian Andean region. El Paraiso, at Chuquitanta on the Chillon estuary, is usually recognized as the prime example from the opening of the rich and highly diversified Initial period: still being developed after the introduction of pottery, it is distinguished by a complex of rooms with an axial entrance to a square hearth court at the base of the huge U-shaped plaza. The Caballo Muerto complex known as Huaca los Reyes, in the upper Moche valley, represents the elaboration of the formula ultimately to embrace three parallel and two lateral U-shaped structures about rectangular sunken plazas. And the later gigantic complex at Sechin Alto, in the highlands further north, retains circular sunken courts and a U-shaped terrace on one great axis.**2.68**

The complex at La Florida, on the Rimac estuary, represents the rationalization of the formula c. 1700 BCE. Seven centuries later, at the end of the period, the builders of Chiripa on Lake Titicaca took symmetry to an extreme with the sixteen rectangular pavilions of their platform complex disposed octagonally around a square sunken court: the inner face of each pavilion had a central entrance with a double-jamb portal of lasting significance.**2.69**

Developed before the opening of the ceramic era, several 2nd millennium sites were dominated by truncated stepped pyramids. Such complexes proliferated for centuries and some of the earlier ones ceded to greater ones nearby with advanced prosperity. El Paraiso seems to have been eclipsed when La Florida reached its apogee c. 1500, for example, and at Las Haldas, in the north-central region of Casma, there was an extensive residential district associated with the large ceremonial complex contemporary with La Florida.

The Initial stage of political, social and ceremonial development covered most of the 2nd millennium BCE. It was the prelude to the achievement of the north-central Chavin peoples (c. 900–200): uniting extensive lands, culturally at least, they fostered the so-called First Horizon.

THE FIRST HORIZON

The site from which the dominant Peruvian culture of the last millennium BCE takes its name is Chavin de Huantar in the highlands north of modern Lima. The monumental U-shaped terraces and plazas, which have been taken to define their era though anticipated at several late-2nd millennium sites, mark the culmination of Chavin architectural development c. 300. Also prefigured, perhaps, at 2nd millennium sites like Huaca los Reys, Chavin's syncretic zoomorphic-anthropomorphic deity sprouting fangs was of widespread and lasting significance.**2.70**

Chavin

The Huantar site, at an altitude of 3200 metres, is distinguished by a ceremonial centre serving a town – unlike most earlier centres except Las Haldas. In general aligned with the cardinal points, the monuments include a group of rubble platforms, some tiered and with refined stone

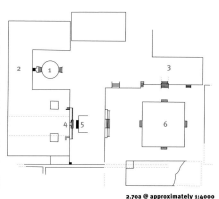

2.69 @ 1:100

›2.69 CHIRIPA, PLATFORM SUMMIT COMPLEX, after 1000 BCE.

The detached rectangular pavilion with double-jamb portal was to be characteristic of the Titicaca region in the great age of Tiahuanaco and of the complexes of its later Inca rulers.

2.70a @ approximately 1:4000

›2.70 CHAVIN DE HUANTAR: (a) diagrammatic plan with sunken circular court (1), 'U'-shaped terrace of 'Old Temple' (2), lateral extension of 'New Temple' after c. 400 (3), portal and steps of black and white stone (4, 5), sunken court from latest period of development (6); (b) representation of the 'staff-god' (after the Raimondi Stele, Lima, State Museum).

2.70b

2.71a

>**2.71 NAZCA:** (a) headdress ornament, 500/600 CE (Dallas Museum of Art); (b) 'geoglyph' of a bird engraved on the earth by the removal of the dark surface shale to reveal the lighter sub-soil. Appreciable only from the air, the purpose of such images and the means of their construction remain speculative.

revetment, galleries at different levels and sunken courts – as in other contemporary sites. The circular precinct of the oldest structure on the site, pre-5th century, is framed by a U-shaped terrace to the upper level of which it is linked by a staircase. Known as the 'Old Temple' (in distinction to a later larger U-shaped structure in part contiguous with its south wing), the terrace enshrined a cruciform chamber containing a shaft of white granite carved with the image of a 'smiling' deity with fangs, snake hair and superimposed feline faces. This syncretic icon enigmatically represents natural force in zoomorphic terms derived from creatures of the Amazonian jungle (perhaps through 2nd millennium central Andean sites like Kotosh on the eastern side of the watershed). It is related to another semi-anthropomorphic image on a stele recovered from elsewhere on the site, with superimposed fanged heads and multiple fangs forming staff-like objects in each hand.

By 500 BCE there were towns and temples, priests and nobles, craftsmen and conscript labourers, terracing to increase the amount of arable land in mountainous terrain and extensive, but uncoordinated, irrigation and communications systems. With irrigation came the mud-brick. And progress was immeasurably assisted by the development of metallurgy: first known in the primitive jewellery of the southern Peruvian highlands, it extended from the production of tools and weapons as it gradually penetrated north in the Chavin period. The new technology ensured that many kinship fiefdoms were absorbed into valley, then regional, states after the close of the Chavin era.

There were mountain domains, like those ruled from the hilltop towns of Marcahuamachuco and Pashash, with imposing masonry monuments but the most notable states were based on coastal towns like Gallinazo or Moche in the north and Nazca in the south. In between there were important pilgrimage cult centres like Pachacamac and an impressive network of roads across the desert tracts. Everywhere there were more towns than cer-

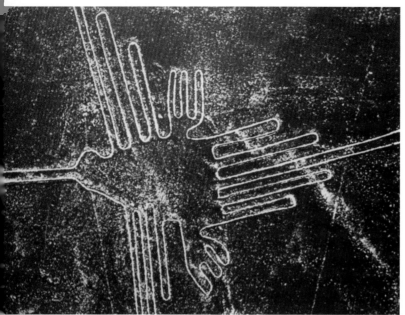

2.71b

(a) gold and turquoise ear flare (c. 400 CE); (b) 'Huaca del Sol', general view; (c) 'Huaca de la Luna', detail of terraced platform with plaster revetment and polychrome embellishment.

The site, near modern Trujillo, was active from early in the 1st century CE and reached its apogee as the dominant influence in the river valleys of northern coastal Peru towards 500: pottery of Mochica style has been found as far south as the Huarmey Valley and as far north as the Piura though Moche monuments are known only between Panamarca, in the Napena Valley, and Pacatnamu on the Jaquetepec. The stepped pyramidal complex at Moche itself is the greatest of the age. Begun in the 2nd century and reaching its final form with more than 100 million bricks by c. 500, the structure associated with the sun (c. 340 by 160 metres and more than 40 metres high) consisted of a cruciform platform ascended by a single ramp to the north and supporting a truncated pyramid on its southern half: there were burials at the main levels. The contemporary 'moon' complex consisted of patios and some six superimposed platforms with a maze of rooms: the irregular brickwork was covered by plaster painted with anthropomorphic, zoomorphic, botanical and architectural motifs notable for their realism – even as the components of syncretic monsters. The gridded pattern framing stylized crabs shown here, however, was probably the work of later occupants of Moche from the Andean highlands: underneath comparable works on the site are images of a staff-god.

The original purpose of each component of the complex remains a subject of debate though few doubt that it was primarily religious: the 'moon' huaca has yielded evidence of human sacrifice but probably embraced a palace as well as ritual chambers and it is possible that

emonial centres and power, possibly divided in accordance with the bifurcation of the dominant kinship group, seems to have been essentially secular.

The southerners had a city in most of their valleys and communal ceremonial centres with multiple platforms often based on natural mounds. Pachacamac was similar. As there was little masonry, there are few remains of Nazca buildings if rather more at Pachacamac – partly because of the revival of the site in the period of the Middle Horizon. Nazca culture, therefore, is mainly notable for the extraordinary animal, avian and geometrical figures etched on the earth at a vast scale.**2.71**

The northerners lived in scattered settlements also dependent on sanctuary centres (huacas) dominated by stepped pyramids of adobe brick, often based on natural eminences: they departed from the U-shaped lines developed by the Chavin but perpetuated several aspects of the Chavin type of syncretic deity – particularly the feline

2.72a

2.72b

the 'sun' pyramid supported accommodation – religious, secular or both; it is certain that it contained rich tombs. The combination would accord, of course, with the tradition of burial under the residence of the deceased familiar in pre Columbian America – and elsewhere.

Sophisticated metalwork was being produced by the Chavin as early as 800 BCE. A thousand years later Mochica goldsmiths took their art to heights rarely equalled in the Americas – achieving a new level of realism in the depiction of man and terrestrial nature.

2.72c

fangs. The greatest coastal power was the Mochica which lasted for most of the first six hundred years of the Christian era. At Moche, their ceremonial centre on the river of the same name, two stepped structures, suggesting duality of power but of unknown dedication despite their traditional association with the sun and moon, faced one another over a plaza and were surrounded by a richly diversified town.**2.72**

Moche was overwhelmed by flood and sand after a thirty-year drought about the middle of the 6th century but the culture subsisted elsewhere for another one hundred and fifty years: disaster had come from the sea and old Moche's tradition of terrestrial realism in decorative detail ceded to obsession with the marine.

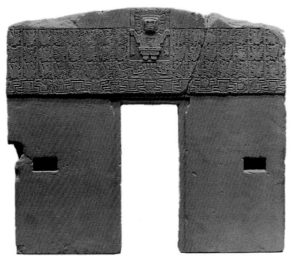

TIAHUANACO AND THE MIDDLE HORIZON

Contemporary with Moche and Nazca there were several states in the highlands, most notably the nucleus of the future kingdom of Tiahuanaco in the south-central Andes which rose to half a millennium of eminence towards the end of the 6th century. The name is attached to a formally planned ceremonial complex but controversy persists over whether it was the nucleus of a city or the centre of authority over a dispersed population. The monumental remains suggest that it was the seat of a theocracy and, as the extent of its domain has been gauged from the incidence of related cult objects, its expansion may well have been motivated by religious zeal. The site's most potent legacy, apparently not reproduced elsewhere, is the ceremonial 'Gateway of the Sun' bearing the image of a staff-god that seems to have been the main icon of an imperial cult descended from Chavin and which earns the era of Tiahuanaco the title 'Middle Horizon'.**2.73**

Tiahuanaco

The site on the Bolivian shore of Lake Titicaca, 3842 metres above sea level, first occupied c. 1500 BCE, is divided into rectangular zones perhaps by streets: cardinal axes have been detected. The largest elements – earlier than 500 CE in inception – are the so-called Akapana in the eastern sector and the Kalasasaya to its north: the former consists of a stone-faced platform (roughly 200 metres square, 15 metres high), which may have supported shrines on superimposed terraces, and a sunken plaza shrine related to the one at Chiripa; the Kalasasaya was a rectangular terraced compound, of ashlar between sandstone pilasters, protecting the principal complex of single-cell buildings flanking the central court; between the two was a sunken plaza; to the west was another complex, the Putuni, which may have been palatial.

The monolithic 'Gateway of the Sun', erected c. 500 and now located out of formal context on a corner of the Kalasasaya's upper level, is one of several found at the site. Its lintel is embellished with a stylized high-relief figure holding staves. Like several stylized monolithic columnar figures holding ritual objects found elsewhere at Tiahuanaco, the image derives from the Chavin staff- or lightning-god: always standing in a full-frontal posture wearing a kilt, sometimes with snake-like hair and often accompanied by similarly clad flying figures in profile, he probably represents the primal creative force that broke the celestial pot in which the rains were stored and hence, in association with the sun, controlled agriculture. He was ancestral to the creator/sky-god later known in the Andes as Viracocha.

While Tiahuanaco was growing in the south from c. 500, quasi-imperial power expanded over several centuries from Huari, in the central highlands, northwards along the mountains and westwards to the sea. Important cult centres like Pachacamac were absorbed; Moche held out though it was ultimately worn down by drought and Huari pressure.

As the nature of the regime at Tiahuanaco is unclear, so too are its relations with Huari. Due to particularly extensive and sophisticated systems of irrigated terraces, both seem to have weathered the drought that killed old Moche. Huari, at least, capitalized on its prosperity by extending political sway over less-adroit or well-favoured communities from implanted administrative and garrison centres. It does not seem to have been a theocracy but it does seem to have shared – or adopted – an imperial cult like that of Tiahuanaco: Tiahuanaco may have been the principal cult centre, Huari the secular capital. There are ashlar remains at both sites but the sculpture at Huari is inferior and the staff-god motifs, with other traces of divinity, are found mainly on ceramics there – suggesting that the cult iconography may have been imported.

If the remains of Tiahuanaco are ambiguous, those of Huari and its provincial capitals certainly mark the advent of an urbanism radical in the assiduity of its segregated zoning, though the dominant building type was known at earlier mountain sites like Marcahuamachuco. Great enclosures for administrative, military and civilian occupation were imposed on broad, well-drained terraces: high-walled and exclusive, usually but not invariably rectilinear, they were subdivided into rectangular compounds of multi-cellular rectangular units about nuclear patios. With these formidable bases, constructed to a formula in a defined campaign, Huari laid the foundations of an integrated imperial infrastructure – roads, canals, terraces – and is thus identified with the so-called Middle Horizon.[2.74]

After the disappearace of Huari (between 800 and 1000, for reasons unknown), Tiahuanaco seems to have developed imperial institutions – if it did not have them already – and further expanded its domain from the mountains of Bolivia to the sea beyond Lima before disintegrating in the 14th century: after dilapidation of unknown cause and date, there was a period of inexpert renovation, which indi-

›2.74 PIQUILLACTA: town plan.

A regional administrative centre in the highlands south-east of Huari, the town's layout has been reconstructed to a greater extent than that of Huari itself and is usually quoted as a prime representative of the era's sophisticated urban order. Evidently like Huari, its ceremonial centre was formed of great rectangular enclosures built of undressed masonry. However, the degree to which this particular ideal represents pre-Inca reality is sometimes questioned. A similar formality marks Viracochapampa, a Middle Horizon site remodelled – and presumably renamed – by the Incas.

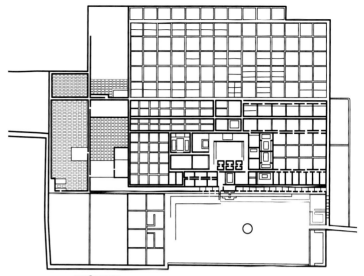

2.74 @ 1:10,000

cates enduring recognition of the spiritual significance of the site.

Other states appeared on the coast. One, based in the Lambayeque valley at the Batan Grande site of a U-shaped temple dating from c. 1500 BCE, is noted for its necropolis of exceptionally rich tombs spanning the century from c. 850. Most notably, the former Huari imperium north of Lima was assumed by the Chimu. Their origins are obscure before their semi-legendary first king invaded the old Mochica heartland, known as Chimor, at about the time that Huari's power had begun to wane. Over some five hundred years from the mid-9th century, his deified heirs extended their dominion from Tumbes, in the southwest corner of modern Ecuador, to the Chillon valley north of modern Lima.

Tiahuanaco/Huari greatly expanded arable land with superb terracing, as we have noted, and the Chimu were totally dependent on developing the irrigation systems they had inherited from their predecessors: at the height of empire it held most of the irrigated coastlands. Efficient

2.75a

2.75b

›**2.75 CHAN CHAN:** (a) platform of 'Arco Iris' citadel; (b) Chimu gold ear flare with enthroned king; (c) aerial view of 'Rivero' citadel; (d, e) part-plan and model of central audienca of the Tschudi citadel (New York, American Museum of Natural History).

administration, the key to empire, depended on the most extensive system of overland transportation in all America: it linked cities with increasingly prominent secular works. There were sacred platforms, of course, but they were primarily for royal burial. If the Creator was linked with the sun in the main cult at Tiahuanaco, Chimu's rulers were devoted primarily to the moon-goddess whose aura was enhanced by the all-important sea – from which, like the late Mochicas, the Chimu drew many of their motifs.

Some ten or twelve kings promoted the cellular development of the capital, Chan Chan, in Moche's valley: each added a palatial complex of platforms, courts and chambers within a high-walled rectangular compound, related to the Huari type but unprecedented at Moche, which became the late ruler's tomb and was usually – but not always – preserved and even developed by his successors. Stepped pyramidal platforms were relatively insignificant but numerous small elevated U-shaped buildings in inner courts, known as audiencias, recall the most ancient of sacred plan forms. The multiplicity of enclosures (so-called cuidadelas) indicates multiple royal kinship groups and there is some evidence that two were under construction simultaneously, suggesting duality of rule.**2.75**

The site at the confluence of the Mocha and Chicama rivers (opposite old Moche), near modern Trujillo in northern Peru, was developed as a quasi-imperial capital from the mid-9th century CE by kings claiming divinity: the royal centre covers some 6 square kilometres. Orientated rectangles (in principle, if not always in strict practice), with a dominant north–south axis, the compounds were built of the familiar coastal adobe, rather than the stone of Huari, and divided into sectors. A single door gave access from the north through a corrridor to the first sector, roughly square, with a large entry court as its nucleus and densely packed accommodation around smaller courts raised on a platform beyond a ramp to the south. Further south, another single door gives access to the second roughly square sector of the ruler's private quarters in which the dominant element is the royal burial platform with its many interior chambers for the ruler and his most important lineal descendants. A third sector was for servants and services, notably water tanks. In the first two sectors there are several U-shaped audiencias with interior niches and images of the ruler before his people as well as marine motifs. The adobe walls of other principal spaces are embellished mainly with marine motifs, many of which descend from late Moche.

Outside them, the nobility had lesser compounds and the populace at large lived and worked in extensive areas of organic development. Other Chimu cities were similar, their official enclosures with audiencias, but not burial platforms, as nucleii.

2.75e

2.75c

2.75d @ 1:1000

›ARCHITECTURE IN CONTEXT »PRE-COLUMBIAN AMERICA

THE LATE HORIZON OF THE INCA

After the disintegration of Tiahuancao, a loose confederation of city-states supervened in coastal Peru south of
Chimu, and in the highlands around Titicaca several
tribal nations – the Colla, Quechua, Chanca and Lupaqa
– were ruled as personal fiefs by their chiefs. The leaders
– *incas* – of a Quechua linguistic group emerged from the
upper Cuzco valley in the quest for more varied land to
provide for their tribal self-sufficiency and are reputed to
have taken the site of Cuzco from neighbouring tribes by
the end of the 13th century. There are no secure dates in
pre-Columbian South American history and the few relatively sound ones derive from the living memory of professional memorizers: those retained by the *incas* to
remember the offical line were lost with the *incas* themselves and the reconstruction of Inca history is mainly
based on later recollection.

Conquest beyond the Cuzco valley is credited first to
the fifth *inca* but expansion reputedly began in earnest
three generations later, early in the 15th century, under
Inca Viracocha. Towards the end of his reign – in the
year generally accepted as 1438 – Viracocha was confronted by the comparable power of the Chanca, expanding in the opposite direction. As they approached Cuzco
he withdrew to a strategic fort with his preferred heir but
was displaced in the capital by his younger son who
repulsed the Chanca, usurped the throne and went on to
a great career as Inca Pachacutec – the 'Earthshaker', the
bringer of true civilization.

Pachacutec overcame the other nation-states of the Titicaca basin and before his reign was out his forces had conquered Chimu. On its model, as much as that of
Tiahuanaco/Huari, he began to build an empire which
was unusual in its diversity of peoples and would be called
Tahuantinsuyu – 'Realm of the Four Quarters': Chincha-

suyu, the coastal domain of the Chimu to the north-west; Antisuyu, the region of the Andes around and beyond Huari to the north; Collasuyu, the heartland of Tiahuanaco to the south-east; and Cuntisuyu, the land of cotton on the dry coast to the south.

In a reign of thirty years Pachacutec reformed Cuzco – 'navel of the world' – as an imperial capital with four quarters of royal and ceremonial buildings defined by the four avenues leading out to these four imperial suyu – the dominant one following the course of the sun. He instituted an imperial bureaucracy and adopted the Chimu system of forced migration which exchanged parts of conquered ethnic groups for colonies of tribal loyalists. Above all, inspired by Tiahuacano, he instituted an imperial cult of the sun, Inti, declared the progenitor of the Inca, and he imbued his followers with the mission to inculcate Inti's truth – the essence of true civilization – universally. And for all this he forged a formidable army that would wage constant war against scores of peoples with distinct languages and religions.

Pachacutec's son, Inca Tupac (1471–93), furthered the development of imperial bureaucracy most notably by systematizing the levy of labour tax and military service and instituting the sisterhood of unblemished 'chosen women' as imperial temple servants charged with the weaving of the Inca's daily poncho and all priestly vestments. He also furthered expansion, consolidating control over the Tiahuanaco heartland of Bolivia, penetrating deep into Chile and reinforcing the extended imperial road network with new garrison towns and staging posts (tambos).

Tupac's son, Inca Huayna Copac, was in the process of subjugating Ecuador in 1525 when he – and many of his subjects – died of a disease introduced by the Europeans who had begun their infiltration of South America early in the decade. It is estimated that by then the Inca ruled over some 12 million people of more than a hundred ethnic groups speaking at least twenty unrelated languages.

In the absence of a designated successor to Huayna, civil war broke out. The Spaniards capitalized on the situation and on antipathy to the Inca yolk among the unassimilated peoples of the newly conquered north. In 1532 they captured and executed Huayna's son Atahualpa, who had dispatched his older brother, and betrayed their alliance with his younger brother, Manco. The last of the *incas*, Manco escaped into the mountains in 1535 and ruled an elusive rump state until 1572.[2.76a]

INCA STATE AND HIERARCHY

The heirs of both Chimu and Tiahuanaco – cultural, political and economic – the Incas built on their prosperity and experience. They had bronze tools and weapons – and were responsible for introducing bronze to areas in which it was as yet unknown – but still worked stone with stone. Deploying gangs of conscripted labourers far from their homelands, their work on the infrastructure of empire ranged from construction of new administrative centres, strategically placed for control and garrisoned but evidently not fortified, to the extension of the magnificent irrigation and terracing works of their predecessors,[2.67] and the integration of some 40,000 kilometres of coastal and highland roads into a network of arteries for the rapid transit of their communicators, administrators, soldiers, labourers and traders – despite their lack of wheels.

In achieving all this, the Incas proved themselves masters of bureaucratic regimentation: statute replaced custom to regulate every facet of life in a rigorously hierarchical society. The essential social element was the kinship group (*ayllu*), graded by virtue of occupation and divided in accordance with the topography of the ances-

2.76a

toral base into an upper (hanan) and lower (hurin) sector, each with its authoritarian head: as we have seen, social duality was age-old in the Andes.

The nature of the Inca's authority at the apex of the social pyramid is the subject of some debate: it is usually assumed that it was vested absolutely in a semi-divine monarch and passed to a son of his line chosen in accordance with special rites of augury; some modern scholars contend, however, that the hanan and hurin chiefs of the Inca *ayllu* shared power in a diarchy and that the ten generations of *incas* listed by the Spanish were actually five. Be that as it may, the descendants of defunct *incas*, 'incas by blood', constituted the ruling *ayllu* of senior administraters based in Cuzco, including the ministers responsible for the four sectors of Tahuantinsuyu. Below them were the elite of the Quechua-speaking ethnic group, 'incas by privilege', selected to supplement the ruling class overstretched by imperial responsibilities, who were sent out to lead colonists and supervise provincial administration. This was usually left to the conquered traditional leaders, who were rewarded for diligent submission by enrolment among the 'incas by privilege' and confirmed in their hereditary rights but forced to reside in Cuzco for four months each year and leave their heirs there as hostages to imperial indoctrination.

The principal responsibility of the chief provincial administrators was to oversee the levying of tax by a hierarchy of officials in charge of subdivisions of the ethnic groups and, at the base level, the *ayllus* in which property ownership was vested – and in virtue of which productivity was assessed. Tax was of two kinds: in days spent on military service or state labour and in days spent working the land to provision the *incas*, the government and the state religious establishment.

Beyond the official levy and the measure which the

ayllus were allowed to retain for their subsistence, state-controlled agriculture – dependent on central direction of irrigation and terracing works – produced considerable food surpluses in good years. Stored in state warehouses throughout the empire, these were distributed to the urban ayllus in the diversity of their occupations graded from merchants and artisans down to labourers: in accord-ance with statutory regulation, all received their allocation from the *inca* and the rest was retained for years of famine. The system naturally depended on a comprehensive census (recorded, like much else, with a *quipu* of knots in coloured cords attached to a main cord), on the stand-ardization of weights and measures and on a standard calendar (of twelve months of thirty days and five days for the ceremonies of the summer and winter solstices).**2.76b**

At its height the vast empire was ruled by no more than forty thousand scions of the *inca* lineage. Until the arrival of the *conquistadores* at a time of central strife and the incomplete assimilation of unwilling tributaries, army terrorism and bureaucratic efficiency were supported in sustaining the integrity of the empire by spies drawn from the resettled loyalists, kept ethnically distinct from the local population. Apart, too, from the forced resettlement of ethnic groups and the enforced guardianship of their leaders' sons in Cuzco, the most revered images of their deities were sent hostage with their priests to Cuzco and held there in deference to the supreme imperial god.

INCA RELIGION

The Incas claimed descent from the sun-god Inti and, therefore, ruled by divine right. Provided this was acknowledged by the conquered, however, they tolerated a polytheism embracing age-old animism, fetishism,

2.76b

>**2.76 INCA RULE AND RITUAL:** (a) Atahualpa enthroned; (b) *quipu*; (c) leading the annual festival of the sun; (d) sacrificing a llama (from the graphic account of the Inca civilization by the native chronicler of the early Colonial period, Poma de Ayala).

2.76b

2.76d

ancestor worship and cults like those of the Chavin. Among several origin myths – including the one of Inti promoted by Pachacutec for the Incas themselves – they believed that ancestral man, fashioned by Viracocha from clay, was brought into the world from watery, stoney caverns and the age-old animist devotion to sacred springs and stones was perpetuated in marking the boundaries of imperial Cuzco and directing the routes radiating out to the corners of Tahuantinsuyu in accord-ance with the incidence of huacas.

The venerable creator-god Viracocha seems to have been accorded primacy in this pantheon as Inti's progenitor until the reign of his namesake, Pachacutec's father. Forming imperial Cuzco under the inspiration of Tiahuanaco, the new *inca* preferred the sun-god: the Lord of Creation had a temple on the central square beside Inca Viracocha's palace and his veneration was promoted throughout the empire.**2.76c** However, Pachacutec's ancestral Sun Temple (Coricanda), established as the dynastic necropolis, was given the central role in the imperial cult and a venerable site commanding the road to the south-east – the quarter of the rising sun at the summer solstice. On its wall, the illuminated image of the sun with the face of the *inca*'s divine ancestor signified the god's mandate to rule: and that mandate was sustained so long as the *inca* tended his people – the god's flock – as they tended their llamas.

The sun had shone in supremacy over Tiahuanaco whose Gateway of the Sun on the shore of Lake Titicaca was of profound inspiration to its Inca conquerors. On the other hand, defiant moon-worship and a cult of the dead reinforced the Chimu peoples in cohesive resistance to the Incas – for whom the moon was of secondary, doleful, significance. The sender of rain, most potently represented as the staff-god of Tiahuanaco descended from

Chavin,[2.70] was naturally crucial to Inca agriculturalists in association with the sun and there were many manifestations of his worship among the subject peoples.

As all life was controlled by invisible powers, divination was the prerequisite for all action: this depended on magic formulae for interpreting oracular phenomena – such as the patterns of the veins of the inflated lungs of the white llama – and often required narcotic hallucination. Sacrifice of time and effort – not least in ritual games – was deemed essential to ensure the favour of the gods. Human sacrifice – of prisoners of war or the specially elect such as a 'chosen woman' – was offered to appease them when disaster supervened and on special occasions like the accession of a new emperor. Llamas stood surrogate for man at times of atonement and on important calendrical occasions; lesser animals, vegetables and fermented liquors – and the emperor's poncho – were sacrificed daily.[2.76d]

Parallels are sometimes drawn between the Incas and the Aztecs. Both worshipped the sun but so too did many other peoples, not least the Egyptians with whom we began: pharaoh found surrogates for human sacrifice much earlier but Akhenaten was hardly inferior to Inca or Aztec in messianic zeal. A strictly graded social pyramid with serfs at base and a divine emperor at the apex is common to both pre-Columbian realms – but it is virtually ubiquitous. Much of the similarity, therefore, is to be explained by the natural evolution of similar solutions to similar problems. The great difference between the two is cultural and it is particularly pronounced in building.

INCA BUILDING

Over the four hundred years of their empire, the Incas' principal building works ranged from the establishment of Cuzco as the imperial capital to the installation on the

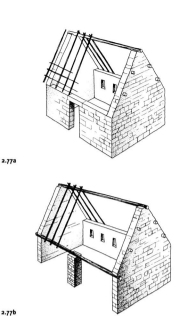

2.77a

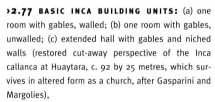

2.77b

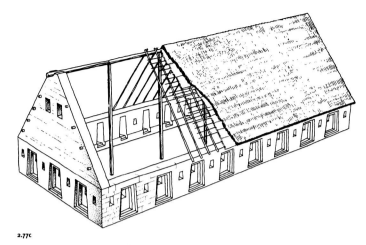

2.77c

>**2.77 BASIC INCA BUILDING UNITS:** (a) one room with gables, walled; (b) one room with gables, unwalled; (c) extended hall with gables and niched walls (restored cut-away perspective of the Inca callanca at Huaytara, c. 92 by 25 metres, which survives in altered form as a church, after Gasparini and Margolies),

The hierarchy of building began with the single-family dwelling (6–15 square metres): the poorest were hip-roofed but gables were most common. The stone or adobe walls, uniform in height, supported the roof frame of rafters, purlins and ridge pole but no cross-beams: the high pitch required in the wet highlands permitted the installation of a loft storey but this was entered from a raised external terrace, not from the main floor below. There were open-fronted units – presumably not for habitation – with timber posts or stone piers supporting the longitudinal base beam of the roof frame. Intermediate timber posts or even an internal wall were introduced when the building was elongated beyond the length of readily available timber – usually for assembly halls (callanca) rather than dwellings – but internal walling might separate dormitories for troops or labourers.

imperial arteries of a chain of administrative centres, five days' travel apart with staging posts for labour gangs, troops, traders, travellers and stores at daily intervals between them. In addition, existing centres inherited from conquered kingdoms and provinces – especially Chimu and the Tiahuanaco succession states around Titicaca – were equipped with Inca facilities. Massive resources of labour and material were also devoted to the paving of the imperial roads themselves – and to the extension of agriculture with stone terracing, drainage and irrigation. This extraordinary effort required exceptional organization which obviated the uncertainty of innovation. Regulated by the bureaucracy, like everything else in Pachacutec's state, Inca building was standardized in plan, construction and the regimentation of tributary labour: indeed, consistency has often inhibited identification of even the greatest buildings without some extra-architectural sign or reference to Cuzco where the prototypes were established.

The official types ranged from the ceremonial platform (usnu), the temple (often a U-shaped complex in a compound, called after the dedicatee with the suffix *huasi*) and palace (incahuasi), with associated convent for the 'chosen women' (acllahuasi), administrative complex and civic hall (callanca) – for audience, council, festivities – to the civic barracks, the storehouse and the hostels on the imperial roads. Housing was strictly hierarchical, of course.

Following the highland vernacular, the basic unit for all roofed types – except the occasional cylindrical store – was a simple rectangle enclosing a single oblong space. Though associated with others of various sizes in walled ayluss complexes (cancha), each unit was a discrete entity, usually completely detached and entered from one long side, but if neighbours were juxtaposed, there was no internal connection. Roof form varied in accordance with climate rather than status. In the coastal plain it was flat. In the Andean highlands it was invariably pitched in thatch on a timber frame, and small-scale dwellings occasionally had rough corbel vaulting – long common in the Andes but never refined or exposed as an aesthetic device.**2.77, 2.78**

Adobe brick was common in the lowlands, masonry in the highlands, but instances of each are not infrequent in either and brick superstructure over stone substructure is ubiquitous in Inca works. Stone was, of course, particularly important for terracing to support ceremonial buildings and housing in mountainous terrain – as for agriculture. For greater strength, real and apparent, stone base walls were usually battered: the practice doubtless derives from the dry ragstone and adobe traditions of an area of seismic activity – the former unstable unless thickened at base, the latter vulnerable to perishing damp and undermining. As in mass, so in void: the inclined profile is reflected in the trapezoidal shape of the typical Inca door, formed on the stout corbel principle under a monolithic lintel, and of the niches which – since pre-ceramic times – distinguish the rooms of the elite. Andean masons

2.78a

2.78b

›2.78 WINAY WAYNA: (a) general view, (b) detail
of the Inca settlement

had long used metal tools but – unlike the mud-brick of
Chimu – granite and basalt discouraged ornamentation.

Ragstone laid in mud mortar was a highland tradition
that persisted throughout the Inca era for housing and
public building of secondary importance. As at Tiahuanaco, the greatest prestige in building required dressed
hardstone: Tiahuanaco, indeed, had set the highest standard of Andean masonry and Tiahuanaco's Titicaca successor states of Colla and Chucuito paid their labour tax
to their Inca overlords in masons. Tiahuanaco's masonry
tradition – insofar as it was sustained across the centuries
between the close of the Middle Horizon and the opening of the late-Inca one – was regular. Most Inca masonry
was also regular: rusticated as in the Cuzco acllahuasi or
plain, as in the redoubtable curved base of the Coricancha. However, the practicality of fitting undressed blocks
together in irregular courses, with stones chosen to

2.79b

›2.79 INCA MASONRY AT CUZCO: (a, pages 352–353) acllahuasi, rusticated rectangular masonry of base wall; (b) Coricancha, unrusticated ashlar of curved wall protecting the original huaca (and supporting the colonial church of S. Domingo); (c) Sacsahuaman, polygonal masonry of zig-zag walls probably built to assert the exclusivity of a key dynastic sanctuary rather than to protect Cuzco or provide defensive refuge for the Inca. Destruction of the enclosed buildings by colonial pillagers of masonry obviates conclusive identification of their purpose. The similarly defended complex at Puma Marka is equally enigmatic.

complement the configuration of their neighbours, seems to have been taken to the impractical extreme of informing even the grandest dressed-stone works in the Inca's imperial capital. Thus, the most celebrated Inca masonry is polygonal, with large bevelled blocks dressed to fit the contours of the ones below – as in the most formidable of Inca works such as the cyclopean Sacsahuaman compound overlooking Cuzco.**2.79**

›2.80 VILCASHUAMAN: usnu as recorded in 1880 (C. Wiener, *Perou et Bolivie: Récit de voyage suivi d'études archéologiques et ethnographiques*, Paris 1880).

THE TEMPLE

Common worship focused on myriad huacas, sacred sites which might be natural or man-made: animistic veneration of pools or rocks was ubiquitous and wayside cairns were particularly popular in marking passage over arduous mountain roads. The most important huacas were enclosed in curved walls but ceremonial worship focused on temples as houses of ancestral spirits: exclusive of all except the select initiates, they were not congregational but addressed places of mass assembly. From the 2nd millennium BCE at least, in the highlands and on the coast, in stone or brick, they had incorporated terraced platforms or pyramids and the open-ended – U-shaped – rectangular court was persistent.

As we have noted, maximum size of pyramidal mass seems to have been achieved by the 1st century CE in the Huaca del Sol at Moche.[2.72] The pyramid had diminished in scale by the end of the 1st millennium CE at both Chan Chan and Tiahuanaco but its platform and compound had grown to accommodate priests and to cater for their rituals: within Chan Chan's numerous com-

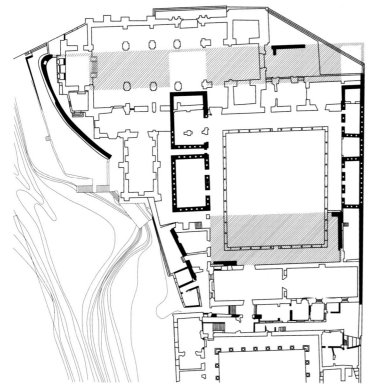

2.81a @ 1:2000

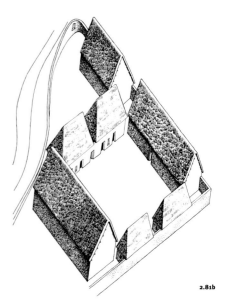

2.81b

›2.81 CUZCO, CORICANCHA COMPLEX: (a) plan, (b) reconstruction.

Colonial observers in the 16th century record six halls around a square court, the main one to the north-east, fronting the road to Cuntisuyu: facing south-east over the court, this could well have been orientated to the rising sun at the summer solstice for the illumination of the golden image reputedly emblazoned on its façade. The dedication of the other units framing the court is conjectural but the southern-eastern one, matching the main one in scale and facing it over the court, doubtless belonged to the moon. The projection of an isolated chamber to the south-west is based on early 20th-century reports of masonry remains under the floor of the colonial church, indicating the continuation of the street-front of the main block to the curved western corner enclosing the original huaca.

pounds the temple pyramids rose to less than the height of the boundary walls (c. 10 metres); the pyramid of the main Tiahuanaco temple, the Akapana, was 15 metres high. The Inca usnus at Huanuco Pampa and Vilcashua-man have pyramids rising to only 5 and 10 metres respec-tively.**2.80**

There was no pyramid in the empire's principal shrines: the Temple of Viracocha was a great hall and the Coricancha, built beside the first huaca of a sacred line stretching into the Cuntisyu division, was a U-shaped complex of rectangular cellas. The dedication of these reputedly embraced the sun and the embalmed bodies of the *incas*, the moon and the embalmed Inca queens, the morning star and the rainbow.**2.81**

COMPLEX AND TOWN

Cuzco was the model for new imperial towns, though local topography dictated variety and some building types – storehouses in particular but also mass housing for itinerants – were more important in peripheral towns than in the centre. Regional traditions were widely sustained. The capital and the new administrative seats were typically open and undefended: the Incas relied on mobility – of troops, labourers and bureaucrats – rather than fortification and won prestige from scale.

Naturally complex purpose dictated the grouping of units in walled compounds (canchas) in which the occasional nuclear space was left unroofed: the units were generally symmetrical, the complexes rarely so – even the principal residence of the *inca* at Cuzco. As the nucleus of the complex was the patio, the nuclear unit of the town was the central plaza that usually divided it into upper and lower – hanan and hurin – sectors. The plaza contained the state usnu and was addressed by at least one temple, the palace and the civic hall. The enclosed complexes, varied in size from the palace down, filled the blocks between the streets that extended a rough grid in each direction.

Imprecise grid planning was the Inca norm, perhaps as a distorted mountain echo of the order of coastal cities like Chan Chan. It is possible that the Chimu builders of Chan Chan derived their formality from the highland Huari and that the latter shared their approach with the Tiahuacano who impressed the Incas. Be that as it may, the Incas seem to have been unconcerned to impose the rational order of Piquillacta on highland topography, which naturally obviated precise axial alignment and often completely contradicted formality. Cuzco well represents this tempering of rationalism, asserting the authority of man, with pragmatism, conceding the supreme authority of nature.**2.82**

2.82

>**2.82 CUZCO:** plan with Sacsahuaman to the north-west, Pumachupan to the south-east, the central Plaza Huacaypata (c. 2500 square metres) and its vaster extension to the south-west, beyond the Huantanay River, the Cusipata marketplace. In the hanan sector Viracocha's incahuasi, to the north-east, was associated with the great hall-temple dedicated to his patron deity; Pachacutec's was north-west, beyond the Cassana assembly hall, Tupac's was east, beyond the Viracocha complex. In the hurin sector, the northern entrance to the Coricancha faces the high priest's headquarters beyond which, bordering the Huacaypata, was the acllahuasi.

>**2.83 ADMINISTRATIVE CENTRES:** (a) Huanuco Pampa, model (New York, American Museum of Natural History); (b) Ollantaytambo, plan.

At the high grassland centre of Huanco Pampa, as at Cuzco, the vast central plaza (540 by 370 metres) is crossed diagonally by the main imperial artery linking the capital to the north-western conquests. The usnu is central to town and plaza, the callanca of the imperial

2.83a

Cuzco

Dominating the valley of the Chunchillmayo, Huatanay and Tullumayo rivers, at their confluence some 3560 metres above sea level, the site of Cuzco was inhabited for nearly three millennia before the Incas settled on it: to the south the confluence of the Huatanay and Tullumayo is called Pumachupan, 'puma's tail', as the whole was likened to a puma with a northern eminence at the head – the site of Sacsahuaman. As the imperial capital from the reign of Pachacutec, replacing the vernacular settlement, it was divided into hanan and hurin sectors by the avenue that led from cult temple, the adjoining incahuasi (for the representative of the inca) and the acllahuasi address it from the east. To the north are some fifty industrial buildings or barracks, most of them identical, and to the south some five hundred similar storehouses.

At Ollantaytambo (a pre-Inca site straddling the Patacancha River at an altitude of c. 2850 metres, c. 60 kilometres north of Cuzco) the extensive building works that established the town as a provincial capital were initiated by Pachacutec and furthered by his successor Tupac, reworked by Inca Manco as his capital before he retired to Machu Pichu, and left unfinished. The hanan sector on the west bank's high ground, fortified well before the Inca conquest but rebuilt in spectacular polygonal masonry, was endowed by Pachacutec with the Sun Temple, the ceremonial plaza, palace and administration complex. The trapezoidal hurin sector on the east extended to a grid of eighteen blocks, each with the typical Inca complex of rectangular rooms and courts.

the central plaza north-east to Antisuyu and south-west to Cuntisuyu; the road linking Collasuyu and Chinchasuyu to the south-east and north-west, the backbone of the empire, zig-zagged across the town. The main feature is the central space, Huacaypata, not a dominant mass: it was the 'holy place' because it accommodated the imperial usnu, beside the Temple of Viracocha. Most of the hanan sector, around the Huacaypata, was occupied by the incahuasi of successive rulers, including assembly halls and administrative buildings, as well as accommodation for subject rulers during their enforced residency, and embassies. The hurin sector, dominated from a hillock above Pumachupan by the multi-shrined Coricanda, accommodated the priests of the principal imperial temples and the acllahuasi. The populace at large lived in satellite communities.

The imprecise grid of long straight streets but few rectangular blocks and semi-trapezoidal central plaza is far from unique to Cuzco. The many other examples include administrative centres like Huanuco Pampa and Ollantaytambo.**2.83** Topography defeats formality on several splendid sites, including those of small staging posts like Pisac.**2.84** Most celebrated is Machu Picchu, the penultimate resort of the last *inca* in retreat from the Spanish:

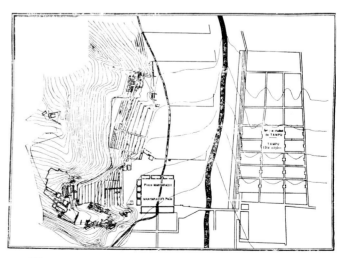

2.83b

›2.84 PISAC: overview.
Of uncertain function, the settlement well represents the scale of the staging-post on an arterial road.

›2.85 MACHU PICCHU: (a) overview, (b) plan with (1) sacred plaza, (2) Temple of the Sun, (3) Temple of the Three Windows, (4) Intihuana, (5) Intimachay enclosure; (c) at the hanan head of the stairs, which flank the palace, was the small Sacred Plaza, the nucleus of the imperial cult buildings – the Temple of the Sun, the so-called Temple of the Three Windows (perhaps the shrine of Viracocha) and the residence of the high priest; (d) the rock-cut altar of the Intihuatana ('the tying post of the sun') and the Intimachay stone, which, with windows in its semi-circular tower, probably served solar observation; (f, pages 362–363) general view.

2.84

there and then the ancient Andean tradition was lost to the night just as the new dawn of the modern world was breaking in the Europe of its conquerors.**2.85**

2.85a

Founded by Inca Pachacutec on a spectacular saddle between two peaks 600 metres above a hairpin bend in the River Urubamba and 2743 metres above sea level, the settlement was probably primarily dedicated to solar observation but was developed most notably as an impregnable ceremonial seat by Inca Manco after 1532. A relatively small complex of about two hundred buildings entered from the south, it was divided into the usual hanan and hurin sectors, linked by a stepped street lined with baths and sources of water, and separated by a roughly rectangular plaza stretched along the main north-south axis of the site (4). The principal cult buildings, open fronted and grouped around a small U-shaped plaza, dominated the plaza from the high ground to the west and the palace overlooked it from the south.

Topography prevented centralized layout and naturally encouraged asymmetry but orthogonal planning was represented among a wide variety of patterns in the distribution of standard rectangular units in the cancha complexes. Construction material – mainly granite – was quarried on site and assembled for the main buildings in accordance with the highest standards of Inca masonry, polygonal and rectangular. Some monuments were carved from the living rock. Superb terracing adapted the contours of the site for housing, graded in quality but all well-drained.

2.85b @ approximately 1:10,000

2.85d

2.85c

PART 3 THE CLASSICAL WORLD

3.1 HELLENIC ORDER

INTRODUCTION: HELLAS AND HELLENIC SOCIETY

It will be recalled that in the last quarter of the 2nd millennium BCE, tribes from the Aryan linguistic group of peoples poured down into Greece in several waves. The subjects of Homer rather than the grander Mycenaean kings – and tenacious of clan distinctions under factious warlords – they swept their Achaean predecessors down the Attic peninsula and out into the Aegean where Achaean bands had long rampaged of their own accord, cohabiting with the natives of the islands and the neighbouring coast of Aeolia and Ionia (modern Turkey). A protracted process of infiltration in an age of chaos, rather than a shock invasion, seems to have culminated in the advent of the 'Dorians': during the dark quarter-millennium from c. 1150 a primitive Greek dialect known as 'Doric' gained predominance in mainland 'Hellas', especially in the Peloponnesos, and a related dialect, later called 'Ionic', spread from Attica to the islands and the coast of Asia Minor.

Related though they were, the two main branches of the Hellenes – as they were to be called after they had settled – were to be differentiated as Ionians and Dorians. Likewise the two main strands of Classical art, woven in Ionia on the one hand, in the mainland of Greece and the Peloponnesian peninsula on the other, were to be called Ionic and Doric.

The area into which the Achaeans penetrated had long been dominated by Crete and, through the intermediacy of the trading Phoenicians with their Levantine coastal ports, influenced by ideas from Mesopotamia. Nomadic herdsmen, the invaders were primarily concerned with appeasing gods of the sky, representing the forces of nature, which they personified as male. The native agriculturalists were primarily devoted to the

3.1

›3.1 ZEUS (OR POSEIDON): bronze statue from c. 560 BCE found in a shipwreck off Cape Artemesion (Athens, National Museum).

›3.2 ARTEMIS OF EPHESOS: marble statue incorporating the fertility attributes of the Anatolian mother-goddess Kybele, 2nd century CE (Selcuk, Ephesos Museum).

earth-mother-goddess as fount of fertility and growth. We have noted the fundamentally different attitudes promoted by these contrasting orientations: mysterious but secure, awe of the earth-mother tends to promote resignation and gratitude, sensuality and emotionalism; the need for constant alertness and rigour in the quest for the key to placating the sky-gods tends to promote questioning and rationalism.**3.1, 3.2**

Not least in architecture, the way of the invaders was now to be imposed throughout the Aegean and beyond. However, longer familiar with the ways of the Great Goddess and exposed especially to her cult of the moon, the Ionian Hellenes compromised their ideals with the softer attitudes of the indigenes – doubtless often in marriage. The Dorians, on the other hand, last to come in from wandering under turbulent skies and uncompromising rulers on the mainland, stuck to an austere rationalist conception of the gods and their creation. Both saw the gods in human form – that is as anthropomorphic – and devoted themselves to the perfection of the human image to represent them: the Dorians were obsessed with the male

3.2

3.3a

3.3b

›**3.3 DEATH AND REGENERATION:** (a) Demeter (London, British Museum); (b) Hades and Persephone (terracotta plaque, Reggio, National Museum): Demeter's daughter abducted by Hades, Persephone wintered in the Underworld and brought life back to earth with her return to her mother in the spring.

body, the Ionians were devoted to representing woman in a synthesis of Achaean ideals and those long dominant in the area.

The poems attributed to Homer and Hesiod – set down in the early 7th century BCE at the earliest – relate an ancient tradition of which the humanizing of the gods is the most characteristic feature. Representing natural forces, the inhabitants of Olympos have superhuman attributes that account for the extraordinary in human experience, but conceived in human form, their manoeuvres were explained in terms representing ideals of all the traits of humanity. Hence the myths as many and various as the Hellenic communities that emerged from the dark ages following the last wave of invasion, defining man's relationship to the divine, exorcizing his phobias about the forces of nature and relating the impact of one way of life upon another.

THE OLYMPIAN GODS

The chief god of the Achaeans, lord of the sky, wielder of the thunderbolt, was identified with the Cretan-conceived Zeus.**3.1** The sea and the realm of the dead below earth belonged to his brothers Poseidon and Hades respectively. With the assertion of the invaders over the natives – of the male over the female – Zeus married the Great Mother (called Hera by the Hellenes).

Zeus bestowed Hera's responsibility for agriculture on his sister Demeter, and through various extramarital liaisons claimed paternity over other key pre-Hellenic deities, notably Apollo and Artemis, Athena, Aphrodite and Dionysos.**3.3** Apollo was the sun-god, cousin of Indo-Aryan Surya and rather more like Assyrian Shamash than Egyptian Ra. As the propagator of plants and patron of healing and art, his mystery cult invoked the great oracles of Delphi**3.4** and Delos and spanned Hellas. His twin sister Artemis was the moon-goddess, mistress of animals and patroness of the hunt, whose cult as a protectress of motherhood assimilated the Anatolian mother-goddess Cybele in Ionia. Athena, patroness of ploughing, was a war-goddess like Babylonian Ishtar but was primarily concerned with upholding order and promoting wise council in the settlement of disputes: she fought off Poseidon's challenge for Attica. Aphrodite was a goddess of procreativity, also like Ishtar, ultimately associated with love. Dionysos, originally the vegetation-god who dies in winter and is reborn in spring, like Egyptian Osiris, was associated in particular with the vine and wine, intoxication, irresponsibility, ecstasy, inspiration – and theatre.

Presiding like a great king over his family court on

3.4a

3.4b

›3.4 APOLLO: (a) marble statue from the Temple of Zeus at Olympia (Olympia, Archaeological Museum); (b) Delphi, sanctuaries (the principal cult temple of Pythian Apollo, founded in the mid-6th century BCE on earlier remains, is in the foreground).

›3.5 THE PRIMITIVE HOUSE AS HOUSE OF GOD: (a) terracotta model from the sanctuary of Hera, Argos, late-8th century BCE; (b) terracotta model from Siracusa.

These may be houses or temples but from such buildings the evolution of the temple took its departure. Remains of prehistoric temples representing various stages in the development of the house – from circular hut through horseshoe, apsidal and rectangular forms – have been found in mainland Greece and the Aegean islands. Rarely as well built as the Mycenaean megaron, their walls were not thick enough to carry substantial flat roofs: the model from Argos represents the age-old structure of wattle and daub covered with a pitched roof of mud and thatch. As structure improved, tiles were adopted instead of thatch, and the pitch was lowered to approximate the shallow triangle of the later pediment.

›3.6 DELPHI, SANCTUARY OF APOLLO, TREASURY OF THE ATHENIANS, c. 507 BCE.

Olympos, Zeus was not omnipotent. The most primitive of natural forces were beyond his control: essentially female but alienated from the earth-mother when her realm was ceded to Hades, they sprang from depths unfathomable to reason. Dominating popular religion on the impulse of passion checked by the constraints of civilization, their exorcism in the ritual breaching of taboo achieved state sponsorship in the fertility-mystery cults centred on Demeter and Dionysos but, represented most terrifyingly as the Furies pursuing Fate, they were recognized even by philosophers as irrational 'necessity'.

3.5a

3.5b

EARLY TEMPLES

Many peoples saw their gods in the image of their king, the greatest figure they knew. As super-kings, the gods would often be worshipped in accordance with formulas derived from attendance at the royal court. As the settled Hellenes evolved their concept of the deity, a house for a personification was needed to supplement the Achaean open-air altar (as in the court at Tiryns).**1.87** So the megaron of the Achaean king was adopted for the temple and for the small treasuries built by various states for their offerings to the gods.**3.5, 3.6** And the megaron continued to dominate the rare palaces of the post-Achaean Greek world.**3.7**

3.6

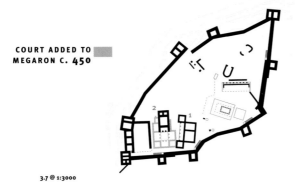

COURT ADDED TO
MEGARON C. 450

3.7 @ 1:3000

In the development of the temple, as with the Achaean megaron, greater width dictated the introduction of posts to provide intermediate support for the roof structure: the beginning of the process may be seen on the Ionian island of Samos and at Thermon in Thrace.**3.8** The columns were in an extended row rather than in pairs like those framing the secular hearth. Sometimes the walls closed both ends except for a door in the entrance front. Sometimes the central row of posts continued through the portico and a false porch (opisthodomos) added for symmetry at the other end – as in Level II houses at Troy. The outer columns of the central row are seen 'in antis' (that is, framed by the ends of the walls). Finally stone replaced timber, not only for its greater durability, but perhaps primarily to support the greater weight of roofs when terracotta tiles replaced thatch or shingle – as at Thermon. With tile too came the lowering of the roof ridge and a strictly rectilinear plan.

At Thermon and in the Heraeion at Samos we can trace the evolution of a walled structure with central columns to one surrounded by a verandah (pteron) to protect the mud-brick walls from the elements. However, before following the evolution of the classic Hellenic temple from these primitive beginnings, let us study the development of the society responsible for it.

›3.7 LARISSA, PALACE, 6th and early 5th century BCE: plan.

The original structures, built by a vassal of the Persians, included the twin-towered pavilion with portico (1), closely following the Syrian bit-hilani prototype but clearly incorporating two megarons, and the main megaron (2), which was augmented c. 450 by a court flanked by three porticoes, each with a pair of columns between projecting walls (distyle in antis). The introduction of the bit-hilani may have followed the precedent set at the palace of the Persian satrap of Sardis which, in turn, was probably modelled on the palace of Cyrus the Great at Pasargadae.

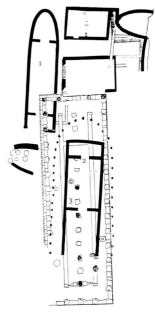

3.8 @ approximately 1:1000

›3.8 THERMON (AETOLIA): plan of site showing late-8th century BCE apsidal and rectangular megarons (1 and 2) and the mid-7th-century BCE Temple of Apollo (3).

The remains of prehistoric megarons at Thermon include several with a curved room at the end – perhaps for the image of a deity – under a primitive temple. The unique curve of posts around the megaron under the temple was possibly original. The temple, with cella and opisthodomos, had five posts to each end and fifteen to the sides on a stylobate 12 by 38 metres. The roof, originally gabled at the front end and hipped at the back, is the earliest known to have been covered with terracotta tiles. Its exposed timbers were protected with decorated panels also of terracotta.

HELLENIC SETTLEMENT

The Aegean was a cradle of civilization but, unlike the grand river systems of Egypt and Mesopotamia where irrigation made lucrative crop-farming practicable on a large scale, its agriculture was confined to narrow valleys or strips of alluvial plain, separated by rugged and often well-forested mountains. The Hellenic corps that took these valleys settled about some defensible eminence (acropolis) from which they managed the land. Each entity was to preserve such distinction as topography and geography determined, despite a general sense of linguistic affinity in the face of unintelligible 'barbarians'.

Self-sufficiency was generally a sustainable ideal among frugal people who could live much of life out of doors. Their polity was moulded accordingly. However, with open access to the sea, prosperity was furthered through combining agriculture and fishing with trade and mercenary soldiering abroad. Ideas came with cargo along the sea lanes developed by the Phoenicians, of course, but the Mediterranean was quiet in the centuries over which the Hellenic communities were evolving and no external pressure forced interdependence to eclipse individuality. On the contrary, their individual needs for more land to cope with population pressure and, later, trading posts in areas rich in grain or the minerals lacking at home, together with adventurous navigation, led to far-flung colonization from the mid-8th century until the Greek world extended from the shores of the Black Sea to the coasts of Iberia.

TOWARDS DEMOCRACY

Trade meant specialization and commerce, especially where the soil was too poor to grow enough grain for an expanding urban population – as in Attica where only the olive thrived and, apart from oil, pottery and silver paid for imported corn. The community of farmers became a market town and trade surpassed land as a source of wealth, though land conveyed status in the aristocratic societies that had emerged from the dark ages following the fall of Homer's heroic kings. The new affluence led to reform.

As more men could afford to arm themselves, disciplined co-operation in cohesive ranks of infantry outweighed the virtuoso contribution of the mounted elite in the armed conflicts provoked by rivalry between the entities. Within them, the new class promoted the ideal of collective action following communal discussion among a citizenry never too large for open-air assembly – except in ultra-conservative Sparta where the citizen minority faced the problem of enslaving the conquered majority with austere rigidity. Atypical in size and commercial enterprise, Athens led the way: early in the 6th century her law-giver, Solon, protected small farmers and encouraged specialized traders by limiting the size of land holdings and the aristocratic rule that had supplanted monarchy in the dark ages.

A sense of 'commonwealth' emerged from the 6th-century reforms, though not across the geographical boundaries that fragmented Hellas. In an era of dramatic change, the rule of the individual (tyranny) was to curtail freedom in several states for a generation or two, and the rule of the few (oligarchy) sometimes did so later, but the rule of the many (democracy) was the evolving ideal – often under the direction of responsible oligarchs or even monarchs. Athens, for example, prospered under the tyranny of Peisistratos (561–527) but rejected his somewhat less-enlightened sons in 510. Proceeding to abolish clan grouping and property qualification for the election of the principal officers of state, Athens entered the Classical age of the 5th century BCE with a political organism of unprecedented representativeness – restriction of citizenship to native kinsmen and the subsistence of slavery notwithstanding.

THE POLIS

The Classical *polis* (inadequately translated as 'city-state' since it transcended the urban and, indeed, the territorial) was dependent on the assembly of all its citizens for determination of policy and administration of justice. But it was no mere association for security or economy: it was a focus for all the aspirations of morality, sensibility and intellect, secular and religious indivisibly; it was a community of shared ideals imparted in school and gymnasium and expressed in the games or festival arena and theatre as essentially as in the legislative assembly or before the temple; it was a living organism to every aspect of whose being every citizen contributed directly through his membership of a multiplicity of social groups.

Ideally of no more than ten thousand citizens, the polis overcame individualism by binding the citizen into an intricate web of associations. But its autonomy under its patron deity (invariably one of the Olympians worshipped by all Hellenes) was never to be overcome by Hellenic community of culture. Indeed, beyond language, it was his sense of the dignity of man, his freedom, that set the Greek apart from the barbarian: he was a citizen not a subject, his government was responsible not arbitrary, and his unique democracy depended on the scale of his polis.

THE PERSIAN MENACE

The age of the Classical polis opened with the frustration of the attempts of the Persians to absorb Hellas into their empire, as they had absorbed Ionia. Disunited and always subject to eastern influences transmitted through the Anatolian hinterland, the Achaean settlements in Ionia were brought under the hegemony of Lydia c. 570 BCE by King Croesus, who ruled from Sardis until he in turn fell to Cyrus the Great in 546. The extension of Persian ambition through the invasion of European Hellas in the first two decades of the 5th century was conceived by Darius I and furthered by Xerxes I partly to secure Ionia. They were defeated largely at the hands of Sparta and Athens, primarily on land at Marathon in 490 and on the sea near Salamis in 479. The surge of pride generated by these victories over great odds propelled the cities of Hellas along the road to supreme cultural glory – and self-destruction.

The confidence with which the Athenians in particular emerged from the initial disaster of destruction by the invaders took them to unprecedented achievement. However, at the head of a league dedicated to freeing their relatives in Ionia from the Persians – and to guaranteeing the maritime commerce on which their increasingly specialized economy depended – the Athenians were overbearing: they enforced subscription, prevented secession and diverted league funds to their own purposes, especially the rebuilding of the Acropolis devastated by the Persians. Wary that an institution for countering imperialism was becoming an instrument for its furtherance, many of the confederates turned to the championship of jealous Sparta. Though rising to a high point in the history of civilization, Hellas fell to exceptionally sordid economic and political wrangling in the second half of the 5th century, and ultimately to war.

PHILOSOPHY

As morality was the concern of society, unprecedented philosophical enquiry into the rights and obligations of the individual was both cause and effect of the development of the polis. Naturally such enquiry extended to the order of the gods.

A millennium after it was woven in the dark ages, the mythology of invasion was embroidered by Greek and Roman poets into the chronicles of libidinous frivolity, which deny decorum to Zeus's court on Olympos. Morality was not the original purpose of the gods but even in Homer there is a dim recognition that, like humanity, the gods were subject to the principles of a grand design – to fate or law – and, unlike humanity, they could see the logic of the whole. Popularly credited to Zeus, Lord of Oaths, law was order and if the order of the universe was not apparent to senses attuned to the experience of this world, its logic could be grasped by reason. Most approached the divine in the traditional way, without necessarily taking the myths literally, but at the highest intellectual level myth was supplanted by philosophy, by enquiry into the nature of order without any necessary denial of divinity. As nature and human nature were not distinguished, that order was seen to be moral as well as material.

Denying the evidence of their senses – ultimately maintaining the relevance only of reason in seeking after truth – the first philosophers postulated unity beyond diversity, variously reducing all the material of creation to a single element, or the nature of reality to a single condition. This essence was first defined as water – doubtless not without reference to the creation myths of the great river valleys – and subsequently as unknowable to the senses, then as 'mind' itself (which might even be called Zeus). Two of the most influential early philosophers, Herakleitos and Parmenides, saw the nature of reality respectively as constant flux and immutable homogeneity behind apparent change. Combating diversity, the Eclectics selected and recombined all they thought best from all of this and more.

MATHEMATICS, MUSIC AND MYSTERIES

With the revelation of the inner logic of mathematics, the definitive element was seen to be 'number'. The geometry of natural phenomena was persuasive but Pythagoras of Samos was seduced by the mathematical basis of musical harmony – the realization that musical intervals may be expressed as mathematical ratios. About 530, he emigrated to southern Italy where he was strongly influenced by the reformed Dionysian mystery cult inspired by the divine musician Orpheus who had entered and left the world of the dead. Orphics believed that man has a divine soul condemned to endless reincarnation by the polluting matter of the body. Seeking the permanent release of the individual soul to union with World Soul, they substituted ascetic abstraction for the physical intoxication that gave temporary release to the Dionysiac, and detected a magic formula revealed by Orpheus as a guide to the passage.

To Pythagoras, at least, that formula was mathematical and the soul's release was the knowledge of truth: harmony, the music of the spheres that resolves itself into number, above all the 1 of eternal reality beyond this illusory world, the supreme good, God.**3.9** God's creation is all number, the linear and volumetric manifestation of which is the geometry of its molecular elements. Thus, generated by pure thought from the objective truth, Pythagorean geometry was theological and, the key to the transcendent beyond the subjective experience of observation, Pythagorean rationalism was mystical. Imbibed by Plato in the 5th century, this potent mixture was to have a profound effect on the whole development of European thought.

›3.9 THE POWER OF MUSIC: (a, pages 364–365) Orpheus and Euridyce (Poussin, Paris, Louvre); Apollo, painted kylix, early 5th century BCE (Delphi, Archaeological Museum).

>**3.10** FOUNDATIONS OF THE ANTHROPOMOR-
PHIC IDEAL: (a) kouros: possibly Boeotian marble,
c. 560 BCE (London, British Museum); (b) kore: Attic
marble, c. 510 BCE (Athens, Acropolis Museum).

3.10a   3.10b

1 THE ORDERING OF ARCHITECTURE

Awe for the forces of nature was always to sustain an irrational strain in popular Greek religion. However, the essentially social attempt to fathom the universe as a rational creation, which advanced logic, mathematics and geometry as branches of theology, moulded the production of houses and images for the Olympians as ideal personifications of those forces. The temple and the image of the deity – or the devotee – were the main subjects of Classical art. In the constant quest for perfection, the subjection of structure to an intellectual conception founded on the timeless symmetry of mathematics clearly differentiates it from all that went before, no matter how important much of that was as inspiration. At the moment of triumph, however, Aryan reason alone was found wanting: vitality was generated only in cross-fertilizing it with Aegean irrationality.

THE ANTHROPOMORPHIC IDEAL
OF ORDER

Hand-in-hand with the transition of structure from timber to stone and greater security went the evolution of the
idea of architectural order. The temple was to house the
god and the god's house had to reflect the work of the gods
in ordering creation: it had to represent the perfection of
their order. The principles underlying that order in its
totality, the macrocosm, could be deduced from the study
of man, the microcosm created by the gods after their own
image. Since divine perfection was inconceivable in the
diversity of human identities, the object of that study was
ideal: the image of man as god.**3.1**

Dedicated to the representation of an anthropomorphic
ideal, Hellenic art is called Classical precisely because it
depends on the classification of a range of observations to
determine the mean between the extremes both in part
and, through the deduction of mean ratios, in whole – a
rational process of comparison, selection and synthesis.
Take a sample of athletes, let us say, average the measurements of all the parts of their bodies to establish means,
abstract those that come closest to the mean and recom-
bine them to produce the idealized form.

The ideal evolved with increasing rigour and the substitution of marble for stone, admitting unprecedented
precision, was the key to the perfection of the process – the
motive of extreme conservatism. Structural logic is the
essence of Classical art yet the Hellenic artist came to see
that intellectual abstraction led to aridity but vitality
sprang from physical sensation.

Preceding the definition of the Classical mean, the typical Archaic kouros and kore represent the foundations on
which the anthropomorphic ideal was to be realized by the
Dorians and Ionians respectively.**3.10** Stripped to the bare
essentials, the male figure is certainly not natural: the ratio-

nalist approach to the conception of its design is governed by a mechanical sense of symmetry and exaggerated geometry in the differentiation of the parts. Even in Attica, on the other hand, the Ionian conception of female form is much less rigid. Long cohabiting with Aegean mother-goddess worshippers, as we have seen, and familiar in their adopted homeland with attitudes and motifs carried across the sea from Egypt and Mesopotamia by the Phoenicians or brought home by mercenaries from service with Assyrian kings, the earlier Achaeans tempered their native rationalism with a certain sensuality: their kore is rationalist in her proportions but she also appeals to the senses through the styling of her hair and the ephemeral beauty of her costume – tantalizingly concealing and revealing.

Seeking the ideal synthesis in the image of humanity, the Greeks were doing two things with the house in which that ideal image was to be placed: they were making its structure durable and secure by replacing timber with stone, and they were refining its proportions in line with their conception of ideal human form. The Doric and Ionic systems, evolved simultaneously from the male and female ideal respectively, are called Orders because they enshrine the principles for ordering design. Beyond the conventional arrangement of the parts, the set of mathematical proportions underlying each is the key to the coherence of building design – it orders building, it introduces a sense of integrity because those mathematical principles inform all the parts of the work.**3.11, 3.16**

The Doric Order

Presumably derived from the structure of primitive temples like those at Thermon,**3.8** the Doric Order was wholly pragmatic in origin: that is, its conventions are drawn from the practical necessities of a timber trabeated structural system. When translated into stone all the parts were at first represented but their natural slender proportions were lost to inefficiency

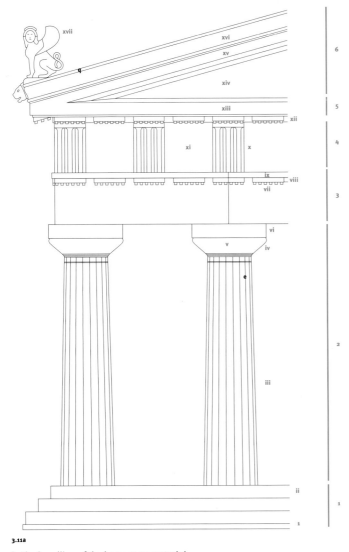

3.11a

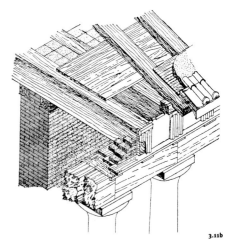

›3.11 THE DORIC ORDER: (a) the mature Order of stone with crepidoma (1) of euthynteria (i) and stylobate (ii), column (2) with shaft (iii) and capital of trachelium (iv) echinus (v) and abacus (vi), entablature of architrave (3), frieze (4) and cornice (5) with guttae (vii), regula (viii), taenia (ix), triglyph (x), metope (xi), mutule (xii), corona (xiii), and pediment (6) with tympanum (xiv), raking cornice (xv), sima (xvi) and acroterium (xvii); (b) conjectural restoration of primitive timber structure (after Dinsmoor);

3.11b

in the handling of the heavy new material.

The column and the architrave are obviously the post and beam. Between them, the main capital motifs (echinus and abacus, recalling Cretan and Mycenaean forms) express the need to cushion the impact of load on support, to protect the post from splitting. The incised rings at the top of the shaft (trachelion) retain the impression of binding for further reinforcement. The joists carried by the beams had exposed ends cut across the grain in timber which needed protection: this was evidently provided by attaching terracotta tiles moulded to marry grooves cut into the timber: hence the triglyphs that distinguish the frieze of the Doric Order. The pegs that held the timbers together reappear in stone below the triglyphs as guttae. The joists carried the inclined rafters of a pitched roof. The acroteria covered the ends of the ridge beam but were often repeated at corners; antefixes covered the joints between the tiles; lions' heads framed drainage spouts. The ends of the rafters (mutules) and the fascia bordering the lowest row of tiles (corona) are visible in the over-hanging eaves (cornice) all round hipped roofs: below the gable ends of pitched roofs (pediments) they are repeated against logic for symmetry. The voids between the joists (metopes) and within the pediment (tympanum) were filled with relief sculpture relating self-contained episodes of mythology relevant to the dedicatee. Ornament is again disciplined by structure, as at Mycenae.

Columns were sometimes monolithic but were usually composed of drums turned on a lathe and joined by wood or metal dowels. The shafts were fluted in situ, usually with twenty grooves recalling the impressions of a curved adze in the dressing of tree-trunks. The top of the shaft and the capital were usually of a single block but the junction was bevelled and the trachelion grooves were incised with increasing emphasis for clear definition. The shaft was tapered from bottom to top in reverse of Cretan practice. This was decreased gradually and, in conformity with the widening of the upper diameter, the slope of the echinus was reduced progressively to effect a tauter relationship between load and support.

As architrave and beam were doubtless of the same width in timber, they could be superimposed in the same plane over the centres of the corner columns where they returned across the ends. After the introduction of heavy roof tiles, the architrave needed to be stouter than the beams resting on it, especially over intercolumniations, and if the outer faces of beam and architrave were to be kept in the same plane, the beam had obviously to be displaced from the centre of the corner columns. To allow for the equal spacing of the beams and mutules along the sides, the width of the metopes was adjusted and the space between the last two columns of each side (i.e. the intercolumniation next to each corner) was diminished.

Because of its colour and ease of handling, terracotta continued to play an important part in the decoration of the temple long after the transition from timber to masonry in structure. Well before the end of the 6th century BCE, it had generally been supplanted by stone carving in various degrees of relief and paint. Metopes were always in partial relief but pedimental sculpture appears in the round from this time. The main cornice fascia, the architrave and the column were always left uncoloured but the rhythm of the frieze was enhanced by contrasting dark blue triglyphs, regulae and mutules with the red inherited from terracotta for the plain surface of the metopes and this was reflected on the underside of the cornice. Carved parts of guttae or capital were clarified in contrasting colours, and figures were often equipped with gilt bronze.

The Order derives from the relationship of the column to the human ideal but the equation was no more than qualitative so long as bulk was exaggerated for strength in the design of the column. Increasing efficiency in the use of stone approached the canonical proportions of the mature male athlete towards the middle of the 5th century. Well before that, however, anthropomorphic abstraction could cede to literal manifestation in images of load-bearing man (atlante) supplementing the column – but that was rare.**3.12**

›3.12 ACRAGAS (AGRIGENTO), SICILY, TEMPLE OF OLYMPIAN ZEUS: early 5th-century remains of atlante.

In the evolution of the Doric Order after the transition from structural timber to stone, elements irrelevant to the new material became decorative. This may seem illogical but, given a need for decorative relief (denied early in the 20th century CE), surely it is more logical to find it in terms derived from building than in nature at large – to remember structure in ornament, to use ornament to articulate structural principles. That is architectonic decoration and it was to be characteristic of high Classicism throughout the western tradition. In detail, at least, it was less rigorous in the Ionic style.**3.13–3.16**

The Ionic Order

As in their sculpture, the Ionians tempered rationalism with sensibility – even sensuality – in the evolution of their Order of architecture. Everything in the Doric Order may be explained in terms of structure but this is not the case with the Ionic Order: dentils in the frieze represent joists and the volutes acquired by the bracket capital towards the middle of the 6th century play the same cushioning role as the Doric echinus, but such considerations do not fully explain the forms of either element.

If the proportions of the Ionic column were lighter than those of the Doric, representing the ideal maiden who may stand for the column as the caryatid, the load carried by the column was lighter too and richer in decorative mouldings. The three-tiered architrave often carries the dentils directly over an egg-and-dart ovolo but an interpolated frieze of stylized floral motifs or a continuous figurative narrative may mask architectural logic after the example of the reliefs on the dadoes and parapets of Mesopotamia. Continuous bands of the palmette and rosette first appear in the sima as the setting for the lion-head drainage spouts: the double curve of the cyma recta here was developed from the Egyptian cavetto by curving the bottom inwards. Contrary to Doric practice, moreover, the Ionic column retains a base: the torus is its most common motif but superimposed astragal and scotia mouldings may also be included.

The Ionic capital derives from the bracket of the timber structural system but – most clearly contrary to Doric – its most characteristic feature is its embellishment. The source of inspiration is controversial: some see ram horns in it, others more plausibly relate it to the curled tendrils of a vine, the fronds of the Mesopotamian palmette or the petals of the Egyptian lotus. It was anticipated by the so-called Aeolic capital, which cer-

›**3.13** DELPHI, SIPHNIAN TREASURY, C. 530 BCE: (a) caryatid, (b) section of frieze (Delphi, Archaeological Museum).

This small structure, entirely of marble but conforming to the megaron prototype with cella and an inset twin-columned porch (distyle in antis), has the earliest-known Ionic entablature incorporating a frieze embellished with figures in high relief over the plain architrave.

3.14a   3.14b   3.14c

›3.14 AEOLIC CAPITALS: (a, b) recovered from early 6th century BCE sites at Larissa and Neandra (Istanbul, Archaeological Museum); (c) from Selinunte, c. 550 BCE.

The rising volutes characteristic of the Aeolic capital (but not the Ionic) clearly recall the lotus motif of Egypt. The related Mesopotamian palmette is inserted between the volutes. The torus with leaf pattern was a base moulding in Assyria.

›3.15 EARLY IONIC CAPITALS AND CORNICES: (a) from the Temple of Apollo at Naucratis, c. 566 BCE; (b) fragment from Locri, c. 480 BCE; (c) water-spout frieze from Ortygia, Temple of Athena, late-6th century BCE; (d) lion-spout cornice, Colonia, Calabria, c. 425 BCE.

›3.16 THE IONIC ORDER (from the mid-4th-century BCE Temple of Athena Polias, Priene, after Wiegand and Schrader) with (1) column of base with plinth (i), scotias (ii), spira (iii) and torus (iv), shaft and capital with egg-and-dart moulding (v) and volutes (vi); (2) entablature of architrave (vii), frieze of dentils (viii), and cornice of corona (ix) and sima (x).

The form of base shown here was usual in Ionia but an alternative, developed in Athens, had a single scotia separating two torus mouldings, the lower one broader than the upper. Unlike the Ionians too, the Athenians preferred narrative friezes, sometimes in addition to dentils, and their architraves sometimes had only two fascias.

tainly derived from these sources, appreciating the decorative value of stylized plant life and growth in the way that people mesmerized by fertility had always done. But Aeolians and Ionians may have drawn on these sources independently: the earliest-known capital with spiral volutes connected horizontally over an egg-and-dart ovolo was found at the Milesian trading colony of Naucratis in Egypt.

The main problem raised by the capital was how to treat the corners: if the outer face was parallel to the architrave of the front, as decorum dictated, it would obviously present its butt-end to the side elevation. So long as the length of the original bracket was emulated, two capitals were crossed with one another at right angles on the corners but with Classical contraction adjacent volutes of two perpendicular faces were bent forward to project together at the corners.

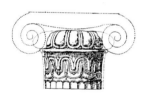

3.15a   3.15b

3.15d

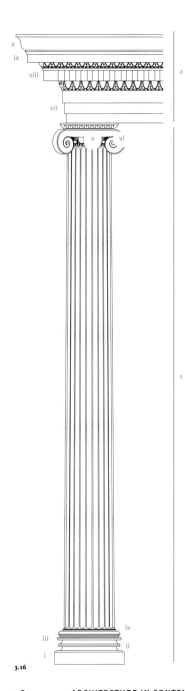

3.15c

IONIC INCEPTION

The rulers of Ionia loved display. Emulating the magnificence of the hypostyle halls of Egypt, they commissioned colossal temples with two colonnades all round (dipteral) aligned with sumptuous open-air altar platforms. The fabulously wealthy King Croesus of Lydia led with the transformation of the Heraeion at Samos and the Artemesion at Ephesos c. 560 BCE. **3.17**

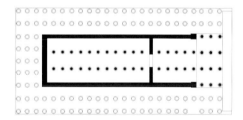

3.18 @ 1: 2000

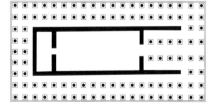

3.19a @ 1: 2000

3.16

Archaic Ephesos

The Artemesion was described by several Antique commentators including Vitruvius – the Roman engineer who dedicated his treatise on architecture to Octavian Caesar in 27 BCE – and the encyclopaedist Pliny the Elder who compiled his *Historia Naturalis* around 75 CE. The ancient sources attribute the work to Theodoros of Samos and Chersiphom of Knossos who was succeeded by his son Metagenes.

Facing west in accordance with the primitive temple of Artemis, the building had a deep porch, a cella containing the original shrine and a shallow opisthodomos. It stood on a stylobate of two steps, c. 56 by 110 metres. This was possibly smaller than the contemporary Heraeion of Samos, but the peristyle there was smaller because a wider gap was left between the edge of the platform and the bases of the columns.

The west front was octastyle, the intercolumniations increased in width from the sides to the centre (where one slab spanned 8.6 metres) and the columns in thickness. The east end had nine columns, the central one obviating the great span of the front and closing the axis beyond the blind wall of the opisthodomos. Each side had twenty-one columns, those framing the end bays set further apart than the rest to give a sense of lightness to the whole vast structure. Responding to the fifty-five

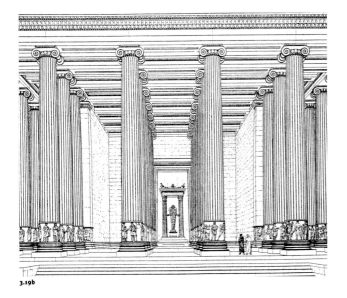

3.19b

›3.17 DELPHI, NAXIAN VOTIVE COLUMN, c. 570 BCE (Delphi, Archaeological Museum).

›3.18 SAMOS, HERAEION: reconstructed plan as developed from c. 560 BCE (but never completed).

Soon after its construction, the original elongated cella was given a protective verandah (pteron): the addition – the earliest of its type so far identified – originally took the overall dimensions to 9.5 by 36.9 metres; its later widening to 11.7 metres produced 3.2:1 as the ratio of length to width. To leave a clear space in which the image of the deity was not obscured, the central supports were replaced with parallel rows of posts tied to those of the pteron: this produces six-post (hexastyle) porticoes. The temple faced an uncovered altar, like the king's megaron at Tiryns, and beyond that the rising sun – as was to be the norm.

The work for Croesus was attributed in ancient sources to Theodoros and Rhoikos of Samos. The pteron was set back from the edge of a double-stepped stylobate. It was entirely surrounded by a double colonnade (dipteral) augmented front and back by a third, inner, row of columns and there was a double row in the cella to support the roof. There were probably twenty-one columns to each outer side of the pteron, nine or ten to the back and eight to the east front where the intercolumniations were graded from the wide centre (c. 8.62 metres) to the narrower side ones (c. 6.1 metres). It is estimated that the pteron was 97.5 by 49 metres (c. 300 by 150 Ionic feet).

3.19c

›**3.19 EPHESOS, ARTEMESION (TEMPLE OF ARTEMIS)**, c. 560 BCE, destroyed by fire in 356: (a) plan, (b) restored perspective after 356, (c) detail of capital.

columns of the outer peristyle were forty-seven inner ones and there was a third row of four before the pronaos. Further, four pairs of columns in the pronaos suggest the division of the cella into nave and aisles for the support of the roof though, as this may have been inhibited by the preservation of the original shrine within, the cella was possibly left unroofed (hypethral).

The proportions of the original columns were reputedly 1:8. This presumably meant those of the sides and back, which were 1.6 metres at base, rather than those in the centre of the front which progressed to 1.9 metres. Their bases established the norm of a square plinth and three superimposed pairs of astragals separated by scotias and surmounted by a torus; the lowest drum was sometimes carved with figures in low relief. The densely fluted shafts, some necked with an anthemion valance, raised the capital to a height equal to some eight diameters after 560 BCE. The capital was elongated like a bracket and its volute spiral, masked by a rosette or entwined with an astragal, was concave in profile rather than convex as was usual by the middle of the 5th century. The triple architrave had three zones, which was to be normal in Ionia. The dentils rested on a huge egg-and-dart ovolo. There is no trace of a narrative frieze, but the sima parapet had figures in low relief alternating with lion-head spouts.

The largest temples of their age, the Heraeion at Samos was further developed in the last quarter of the 6th century but never completed.[3.18] The Artemesion at Ephesos, destroyed by fire in 356, was rebuilt on the same plan to the wonder of the ancient world. Both encompassed the evolution of the Ionic Order from the Archaic to the Classical and, though little of the original Samian contribution survives, its form of capital can hardly have been unrelated to the work of contemporary Ephesians and Naxians.[3.19, 3.20]

›3.20 PAESTUM (POSEIDONIA): view from the Archaic Temple of Hera I (basilica, c. 550 BCE) through the Classical Temple of Hera II (Poseidon, 460 BCE) to the late-Archaic Temple of Athena (Demeter, 520 BCE).

›3.21 OLYMPIA, TEMPLE OF HERA, founded late-8th century BCE, rebuilt early 6th century BCE: (a) view of remains, (b) plan.

On a stylobate 18.75 by 50 metres (1:2.66), there were six by sixteen columns. In 173 CE the Roman commentator Pausanias recorded that one of the original timber posts remained in the opisthodomos; the rest were stone. The surviving ones, a few of which are monolithic, differ considerably in width, in diminution from base to top and in outward-swelling profile (entasis): the timber posts are estimated to have been c. 0.98 by 5.22 metres (lower diameter to height); the later stone columns ranged from c. 1 metre to 1.28 metres by c. 5.22 metres producing ratios of 1:5.22 and 1:4.08.

Except at the corners, where the intercolumniations were narrowed because the triglyphs were displaced to the edges, the columns of each front were slightly further apart than those along the sides since the central ones were aligned with those in antis in the porches, giving the entrance a sense of greater openness.

2 DORIC FROM ARCHAIC TO CLASSICAL

The stone temples of the Dorian mainland, in contrast to the early Ionic exercises, were modest in scale, simple in plan and increasingly strict in regularity with the evolution of the conventions essential to the concept of order. Some had only porticoes, like the sanctuary treasuries that recall the primitive form, but most of the main Archaic Doric temples were surrounded by a peristyle with six columns on the ends (hexastyle) and fifteen or more along the sides. The cella within, usually divided into nave and aisles by two rows of internal columns, was preceded by a porch and backed by a matching opisthodomos, each with two columns between the projecting walls (distyle in antis).**3.6**

Virtually all significant early Archaic works in mainland Greece were rebuilt after the middle of the 6th century BCE, apart from the Temple of Hera at Olympia. Reputedly originally dedicated to Zeus, this shrine was

3.21a

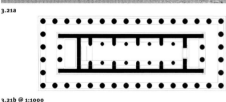

3.21b @ 1:1000

so venerable that the replacement of its timber structure by stone seems to have been done in a piecemeal manner, as the timber rotted over the course of generations: varied in proportion and age, the remaining columns are the most significant representatives of early Archaic form. The structure clearly developed from a walled enclosure to one protected by a pteron and inside the columns displaced from the centre were attached alternately to short spur walls at the sides. In ruins in its beautiful glade, it is easy to see the temple as a sacred grove – with posts for trees – and there the origin of the garden lies.**3.21**

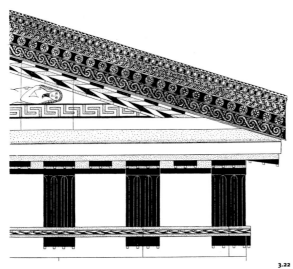

WESTERN COLONIES

Doric works in the west were less rigorously logical than their mainland contemporaries. Indeed, they were often heterodox in form and emulated the Ionians in scale and embellishment. The Temple of Artemis at Corfu is the pre-eminent example.**3.22** With eight columns to its ends, it seems to have set a standard of opulence challenged by the colonies further west, all far richer and more ostentatious than the cities of the homeland and always more interested in experiment than convention. This is demonstrated by Temples C at Selinunte,**3.23** Apollo at Siracusa,**3.23** Zeus at Cyrene in Libya,**3.24** Olympian Zeus at Agrigento in Sicily,**3.26** or Hera I and Athena at Paestum in southern Italy.**3.20, 3.27, 3.28**

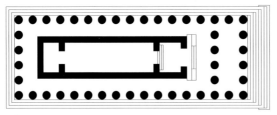

3.23a @ 1:1000

3.22

›3.22 CORFU, TEMPLE OF ARTEMIS, c. 580 BCE: restoration of west pediment and entablature.

Especially noteworthy is the appearance of the so-called Greek-key pattern with the Minoan rosette and spiral wave. The latter is clearly the origin of the so-called Vitruvian wave.

On a stylobate 23.5 by 49 metres, there were eight by seventeen columns. Though little is left on the site, it seems that the walls of the cella and the two rows of columns dividing it into nave and aisles were aligned with the four central columns of the front, giving a pteron the width of two intercolumniations.

3.23b

›3.23 SELINOS (SELINUNTE), SICILY, TEMPLE C, c. 550 BCE: (a) plan, (b) metope of Perseus slaying the Gorgon.

On a stylobate 23.9 by 63.7 metres – a ratio of 1:2.66 – there were six by seventeen columns, c. 1.98 by 8.6 metres, giving proportions of 1:4.78 to 1:4.53. The sides ones were more closely spaced than the end ones for the last significant time in Sicily. Following Ionic examples, the porch had columns prostyle rather than in antis. Though terminated opposite the fifth columns of the sides, the interior walls were aligned with the second intercolumniations: freeing the width of the cella from dependence on the front colonnade meant its dimensions could be determined by the timbers available to cover it without internal supports.

›3.24 SIRACUSA, TEMPLE OF APOLLO, c. 560 BCE: (a) column from south-east corner, (b) model showing unorthodox hipped roof at west end (Istanbul, Miniaturk).

›3.25 (PAGES 394–395) CYRENE (LIBYA), TEMPLE OF ZEUS, dated by Dinsmoor to no later than c. 540 BCE, less plausibly later by others.

The limestone temple was many times restored, renovated, rebuilt (most lately after riots in 211 CE) but over the original plan and with Archaic elements or elements Archaic in style: on a stylobate 30.5 by 68 metres, the eight by seventeen columns are 1.9 by 8.9 metres with the weighty capitals (2.7 metres wide) and entablature (4.2 metres high) expected of the mid-6th century. The interior was remodelled in the imperial Roman era.

3.24a

3.24b

3.26a

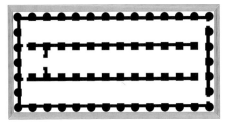

3.26b @ approximately 1:2000

›3.26 ACRAGAS (AGRIGENTO), SICILY, TEM-
PLE OF OLYMPIAN ZEUS, early 5th century BCE:
(a) model, (b) plan.

This gargantuan work – at nearly 53 by 110 metres the largest of Doric temples – was furthered in celebration of victory over the Carthaginians in 480 but may well have been conceived before the end of the 6th century to eclipse the contemporary Temple of Apollo at Selinos.

The colossal scale dictated the psuedo-peripteral plan: seven by fourteen widely spaced half-columns, nearly 4 metres in diameter and perhaps 20 metres high, were built of ashlar masonry and embedded in external walls. As the intercolumniations could not be bridged by single blocks of stone, the atlante are most plausibly seen as providing intermediate support for the ashlar masonry of the entablature and accommodated in recessions to the upper walls. The stringcourse supporting these atlante included an Ionic ovolo moulding and, like Ionic but contrary to Doric practice, the Order was given a base. Responding to the columns, pilasters relieved the inner faces of the peripheral walls and square piers punctuated the screen walls of the cella. The latter was nearly 14 metres wide and the problem of roofing it may have remained unresolved.

In the colonies new temples were often built on new sites near the old ones – as at Paestum. Including the most complete of all Archaic Doric remains, the range there offers a particularly instructive comparison. The Temple of Hera I (c. 550) was prophetic in its pteron of nine by eighteen columns but its great width could not be roofed without the primitive central row of supports blocking the main axis.**3.27** The Temple of Athena (c. 520) to the north represents the degree to which the colonists were advanced in planning while still Archaic in their unconventional attitudes to the Order: Doric and Ionic were mixed.**3.28** Almost complete beside its predecessor, the second Temple of Hera (or Poseidon; c. 460) acknowledges the apogee of Doric recently attained at Olympia.**3.20 (centre), 3.36c**

3.27a

›3.27 PAESTEUM, TEMPLE OF HERA I: (a) general view, (b) plan, (c) interior from west.

On a stylobate 24.5 by 54.3 metres (1:2.21), the nine by eighteen external and seven internal columns are 1.4 by 6.4 metres (1:4.47).

As in several Sicilian works, the columns on the ends are actually set closer together than those on the sides except for the end bays of the latter, next to the corners. The alignment of the pronaos with the third column of the flanking colonnades, giving a wide pteron, is in line with contemporary practice at Selinos and the Ionic scale suggests a familiarity with the Artemesion at Corfu – though the logic of the model's octastyle plan (eight by seventeen columns) apparently eluded the Italian colonists, who were generally more backward even than the Sicilians at this stage.

Exaggerated entasis and diminution in the upper diameter of the columns were countered by the exceptionally broad, flat echinus. The underside of the latter was chased with ornament instead of annulets and the deep necking beneath it was incised with leaves.

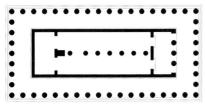

3.27b @ 1:1000

3.27c

3.28a

Continual rethinking of the relationship of the parts to one another and to the whole, and even the shape of the whole, is clearly apparent across the generations spanned by the temples at Paestum. As at the Olympian Heraeion, the proportions at first are much stockier, tougher, and the capital is broader and flatter, representing the idea of cushioning in a literal way. Some seventy years later all the elements have been brought into a tauter relationship.

REFINEMENT OF PROPORTIONS

While refining the proportions of the human form and its abstraction for the Order, the Greeks were also refining the order of the plan. The great length of buildings like the Heraeion at Samos had been modified and the ratio of end to side adjusted at Olympia. However, the irrational relationship of 6:15 was sustained as the norm in major later-Archaic works such as the temples of Apollo at Corinth c. 540, and Delphi c. 525 – the form incorporating a room beyond the cella (adytum) in addition to porch and opisthodomos.**3.29, 3.30** Archaic terracotta had ceded to stone – or marble – carved in partial relief in the metopes,

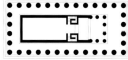

3.28b @ 1:1000

>**3.28 PAESTUM, TEMPLE OF ATHENA,** c. 520 BCE: (a) view from the south-east, (b) plan.

On a stylobate 14.53 by 32.87 metres (a ratio of 1:2.26) there are six by thirteen columns of 1.27 by 6.12 metres (1:4.84). There was a prostyle portico but neither opisthodomos nor adytum. As in Hera I, there is considerable decorative elaboration to the Doric capitals, especially the introduction of a florid neck and lower band to the echinus, and the remains of the pronaos Order have Ionic characteristics. Without corona and shorn of mutules, the cornice was reduced to an Ionic egg-and-dart ovolo and a similar moulding replaces the regulae and guttae below the Doric frieze. The end metopes of each side were left wider than the others by the failure to adjust the spacing of the corner columns to accord with the displacement of the outer triglyphs from their centres. Coffered eaves were carried all round the temple in place of the usual Doric cornice of mutules, and bent up over the ends to form the pediments.

›3.29 CORINTH, TEMPLE OF APOLLO, c. 540 BCE: (a) plan, (b) view.

Six by fifteen columns stood on a stylobate 21.5 by 53.9 metres (a ratio of 1:2.5). The front columns were 1.74 by 7.24 metres (1:4.15) and the distance between their centres was 4.03 metres – hence the ratio of axial spacing to base diameter was 1:2.31 and to height was 1.80:1. The diameters of the columns and the spacings between them were reduced on the sides and the spacing further reduced on the corners, as in the Heraeion at Olympia. In response to the columns of the pronaos and opisthodomos, the flanking walls extended from the cella terminate in shallow returns (ante). The echinus, restrained in its bulge, is in tauter relationship to the column than hitherto and there is no entasis.

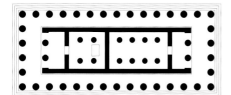

3.29a @ 1:1000

3.29b

in three full dimensions in the pediments, and the visual impact of the temple was immeasurably enhanced.

To counter optical illusion and enhance vitality, strict rectangularity and regularity were avoided in the main elements. As at Olympia and Paestum, columns were tapered from bottom to top and their sides were given a gentle bulge (entasis) to avoid the appearance of splaying and waisting, though this is less exaggerated in later-Archaic works on the mainland. A subtle upward curvature was introduced to the stylobate and naturally reflected in the entablature. First apparent in the Temple of Apollo at Corinth, this doubtless facilitated drainage but it was seen to deny the illusion of sagging in parallel horizontals separated by repeated verticals. Further, the narrowing of the intercolumniations at each corner was originally devised to sustain regularity of rhythm in the frieze when the end triglyphs were moved outwards from their proper place

3.30a

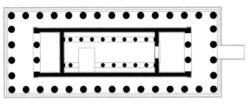

3.30b @ 1:1000

›3.30 DELPHI, TEMPLE OF APOLLO, built in place of several predecessors in the last quarter of the 6th century BCE, destroyed by earthquake in 373 and rebuilt (with modified Order) after 366: (a) elevation, (b) plan, (c, d) views of remains and of external altar from below.

The six by fifteen columns stood on a stylobate 21.7 by 58.2 metres (a ratio of 1:2.68). The structure was largely of limestone but the east end was executed in marble at the expense of the Athenian reformer Kleisthenes after 513 to woo those in attendance on the oracle.

The splendid polygonal masonry incorporated in the temple's podium survives from the late-Archaic campaign of aggrandisement initiated c. 548 BCE.

over the centre of the column. However, it was also recognized that this countered the illusion that slender verticals seen against a void – like the corner columns against the sky – are further apart than those seen against a solid – like the columns against the cella walls.

3.30c

3.30d

›3.31 AEGINA, TEMPLE OF APHAEA, C. 500 BCE:
(a) cutaway axonometric, (b) plan.

Of stuccoed limestone with marble pediment sculpture, it replaced a work which was distyle in antis like the early 6th-century temples of Delphi and Athens. There the opisthodomos was omitted but here the sequence of spaces was conventional except for an off-centre door between the opisthodomos and the cella.

On a stylobate of 13.8 by 28.8 metres (a ratio of 1:2.1) the six by twelve columns are c. 1 by 5.26 metres (1:5.32 except for the slightly thicker corner ones). The axial spacing is 2.26 metres – hence in the ratio of 2.01:1 and 1:2.65 to column height and base diameter respectively – on the front and slightly narrower on the sides. Given the base to height ratio of 1:5.3, internal columns high enough to carry the ceiling of the cella would have taken up most of the floor so two Orders were superimposed. Supporting the roof and dividing the cella into nave and aisles, these Orders tapered in line with one another. Galleries were inserted over the aisles on the intermediate architrave.

Abandoning the Archaic practice of making all the columns of each end thicker than those of the sides, the architect here thickened only the corner columns to counter their apparent attrition when seen against the void and to enhance the sense of stability. The impression that the façades splayed out at the top, given by the heavy entablature bearing down upon a regular series of relatively slender verticals, was obviated by the inward inclination of the side columns.

The precinct preserves rare remains of a late-Archaic propylaea. With twin back-to-back porches (both distyle in antis), it clearly originates in the Mycenaean form of bit-hilani without flanking towers – like the entrance to the Temple of Hatti and Arinna at Boghazkoy.

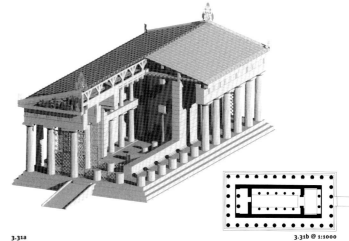

3.31a

3.31b @ 1:1000

TRUTH VERSUS APPEARANCE

Despite the recognition that reason had sometimes to cede to sensation, at the end of the 6th century irrational ratios were rejected for the 1:2 ideal appreciable in pure geometry. In the Temple of Aphaea built on the island of Aegina c. 500 BCE, two squares define the base for a pteron of six by twelve columns.**3.31**

On its realization at Aegina, the ideal seems to have been found wanting. The eye can actually register only up to eight elements at once. So the eye could read the six end columns as a unit but not the greater number of side columns – the corner column, common to both ranges, assimilated itself to the end, leaving the side apparently short of a unit. Having spent centuries questing after the ideal and finding it in proportion and rational geometry, the Greeks were now confronted by a discrepancy between what reason dictated and what seemed right to the eye. They had to make the extraordinary psychological leap of denying Truth for the sake of appearances. To cope with this problem of optical illusion, they wilfully reverted to the irrational: the next generation of temples had one more column to each side than twice the number on the ends – usually six by thirteen.

3.32a   3.32b

THE IDEAL AND VITALITY

By the beginning of the 5th century BCE, the Dorians had also arrived at the set of proportions for the human figure which was to be considered canonical – a standard approximating the ideal. In the 'Strangford Apollo' the relationship of the various parts of the body to one another and to the whole has been idealized.**3.32a** So perfect is it in its symmetry, representing timeless truth rather than transitory appearance, that it inspires no feelings: it is inert. The divine ideal abstracted from man denied the gods something manifest in man: vitality. How was this extra dimension of life to be represented within a perfect form?

Vitality implied movement and movement by its very nature would upset the ideal balance between the parts drawn from coherent proportions and rational organization in terms of symmetry. Mastering perspective and

3.33

›3.32 CANONICAL PROPORTION: (a) kouros (the 'Strangford Apollo'), marble, c. 500 BCE – contemporary with the three-dimensional pediment sculpture that distinguishes the Aegina temple (London, British Museum); (b) kouros attributed to Kritios, c. 485 BCE (Athens, Acropolis Museum)

Stepping forward slightly, the later figure abandons symmetry in the hips and, in compensation for the declination of the right, the head is slightly turned in that direction – the line of advance.

Polykleitos is generally considered to have been a contemporary of Phidias, and the Doryphoros was probably produced after 450 BCE. The original is lost but the comparison of surviving copies and fragments suggests that this one in Naples, recovered from Pompeii and therefore before 79 CE, is among the most accurate.

Galen (the 2nd-century CE medical writer) quotes Chrysippus (a 3rd-century BCE Stoic) as maintaining that 'beauty consists in the symmetry not of the elements but of the numbers ... of finger to finger and of all these to hand and wrist, and of those to forearm, of forearm to arm and of all to all, as it is written in Polykleitos's *Canon*'.

abandoning the convention of the characteristic view with the foreshortening of limbs in the representation of transitory states, probably first in Ionia, Hellenic painters and sculptors found divine stasis not in motionlessness but in equilibrium. An early step in this direction was taken c. 485 by the boy attributed to Kritios.**3.32b** The culminating achievement in the mainland was the Doryphoros of Polykleitos, c. 450: in a cycle of movements preparatory to throwing a spear, his limbs have been caught in a moment of assymmetrical balance.**3.33**

Polykleitos wrote his *Canon* to transmit the ideal proportions of his athletes and the formula for achieving their celebrated equipoise. Most of the text and the original statue are lost, but ancient commentators described the figure as 'foresquare' and it is clear from Roman copies that it matched the weight of the mature Doric Order. As to the formula, the copies reveal that it requires the balancing out of the forces across the body: the leg bearing the weight of the body is counterbalanced on the other side by the active arm; the other arm and the opposite leg are in relaxation. Tension and relaxation, the straight and the bent, are counterposed across the body. The key is in plotting the centre of gravity, as distinct from the given centre of a symmetrical form: as the essential element is irrational, success depends on intricate adjustments inspired by the genius of the artist and the keen eye of the observer.

Stemming from the study of foreshortening in perspective, Polykleitos's formula for balanced asymmetry was to be enduringly influential on sculpture and architecture. His synthesis of weight and suppleness was anticipated in the Order of the Temple of Zeus at Olympia c. 470, as his asymmetry is approached in the greatest of the superb sculptures there.**3.4, 3.34**

3.34a

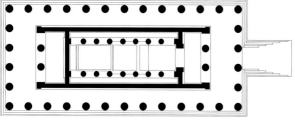

3.34c @ 1:1000

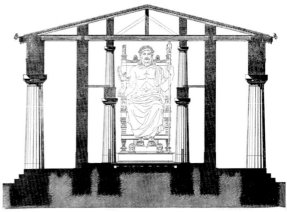

3.34b

›3.34 OLYMPIA, TEMPLE OF ZEUS, c. 470 BCE: (a, b) reconstructed elevation and section (from Olympia II, 1892), (c) plan, (d, e) model (Paris, Louvre).

On a stylobate 27.7 by 64.1 metres (a ratio of 1:2.32) the six by thirteen columns were 2.26 by 10.44 metres (1:4.64) on the front and slightly thinner on the sides where they were all inclined inwards to counter apparent splaying, as at Aegina. The axial spacing on the front was 5.25, giving a ratio of 1:2 to column height and 2.32:1 to base diameter – and minutely narrower on the sides.

Doric at its apogee: the Temple of Zeus at Olympia

Among the largest of Doric temples in mainland Greece, this seminal work was designed by Libon of Elis after the precedent set c. 490 in the first Temple of Poseidon on Cape Sounion for one more column to each side than twice the number on the ends – six by thirteen columns had also appeared in the Archaic temples of Athena at Delphi, Paestum and at Assos (a rare Doric temple in Asia Minor). However, whereas hitherto the dimensions of the cella were established first, leaving those of the peristyle dependent, here the procedure was reversed and the essential measurements throughout the building were derived from the common denominator of the intercolumniation, any variation from which was calculated to counter optical illusion.

In Doric feet: the height of the columns was 32, the intercolumniations 16, the width of the abacus and the spacing of the triglyphs 8, the spacing of the mutules and lion-head spouts 4, etc. While the main parts were thus in the ratio of 1:2, the irrational ratio of 6:13 between the columns on

3.34d

the fronts and sides took account of perspective foreshortening. The curvature of all the main lines countered optical illusion with vitality. At 1:4.7 the proportions of the column are hardly those of the athlete, but certainly match his combination of strength and virility in spirit.

The structure was of the local coarse limestone covered with marble plaster coloured in accordance with convention. The sculpture was in Parian marble. The splendid groups in the two pediments (the contest for the Peloponnesos between the Achaean invader Pelops and the incumbent Oenomaos, on the east, and the battle of Lapiths and Centaurs, representing the triumph of the Hellenes over barbarism, on the west) were more carefully calculated to fit their triangular fields than ever before. Masterly too was the concentration of the high-relief sculptures, representing the twelve labours of Hercules, in the square fields of the frieze metopes over the back and front porticoes within the peristyle. The metopes of the latter bore shields. Phidias's stupendous cryselephantine statue of Olympian Zeus, inserted some years after the completion of the building between the columns that divided nave from aisles and supported an interpolated gallery in the cella, drew maximum dramatic impact from overfilling its space.

3.34e

3·35a

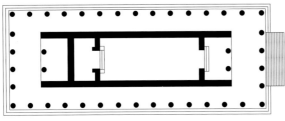

3.35b @ 1:1000

3·35c

Unfortunately, the great temple at Olympia was destroyed in an earthquake but the near-contemporary temples of Hera at Selinos and Paestum are substantially intact.**3·35, 3·36** The colonists of the latter had done extremely well in the Olympic Games of 468 BCE and they thanked their patron deity with a temple inspired by the great Olympian work. Yet it is conservatively long, like the

›3.35 SELINOS, TEMPLE OF HERA, C. 460 BCE: (a) view from the south-west, (b) plan, (c) metope of Artemis and the slaying of Adonis.

On a stylobate 25.3 by 67.7 metres (1:2.67), the six by fifteen columns are 2.26 by 10.13 metres (1:4.48). The axial spacing is 4.7 metres – hence the ratios are 2.15:1 and 1:2.08 to column height and base diameter respectively. Variation at the corners was insignificant.

3.36a

›3.36 PAESTUM, TEMPLE OF HERA II ('POSEIDON'), c. 460 BCE: (a) exterior, (b) plan, (c, pages 408–409) interior.

On a stylobate 24.26 by 60 metres (1:2.47), the six by fourteen columns are 2.11 by 8.88 metres, but slightly narrower on the sides) giving a ratio of 1:4.20 on the front. The axial spacing is 4.47 metres on the front (1:1.99 and 2.12:1 to column height and base diameter) and slightly wider on the sides except where, following Sicilian precedents, the penultimate bays were narrowed in conformity with the bays either side of each corner.

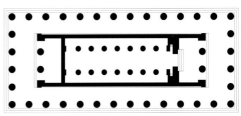

3.36b @ 1:1000

slightly older foundation at Selinos, and the proportions of the Order are conservatively stocky. Following mainland practice after the Temple of Aphaea at Aegina, the interior was divided and the roof joists supported by twin colonnades of two superimposed, consistently tapered Doric Orders; the lower Order has architrave but no frieze and there were no galleries. The internal staircase serves the roof.

3.37a

3.37b

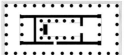

3.37c @ 1:1000

›3.37 ATHENS, HEPHAESTEION (TEMPLE OF
ATHENA AND HEPHAESTOS OR THESEION),
c. 449 BCE: (a, b) views from the Agora, east, and from
the precinct, south, (c) plan.

On a stylobate 13.7 by 31.77 metres (1:2.32), the six
by thirteen columns are c. 1 by 5.70 metres (1:5.61).
The axial spacing is 2.59 metres – hence in the ratio of
2.21:1 and 1:2.54 to column height and base diameter.
The plan is conventional except for the return of the
internal colonnade around the west end of the cella
with a single column on the main axis behind the cult
images, and the careful alignment of the pronaos ante
with the third column of the sides. The external frieze
is regular too, but only the metopes of the front and
the first two intercolumniations before the pronaos
were embellished with relief sculpture. However, the
Doric columns of the pronaos and opisthodomos carry
Ionic friezes with continuous narratives in high-relief –
the eastern one extending across to the peristyle, further to emphasize the space before the pronaos – and
like those of the pteron they are exceptionally slender.
This is critical as the entablature is relatively higher
than normal.

Apart from adjusting the proportions to counter perspective foreshortening, which reflected a major preoccupation of contemporary artists, over-refinement may be sensed in the unknown architect's incorporation of all the optical-illusion controls developed by his predecessors to enhance the sense of strength and vitality. These include contracting the corner bays and thickening the corner columns, inclination of vertical lines and the curvature of verticals and horizontals in particular. Moreover, this was the first Doric temple to be built entirely of Pentalic marble.

›3.38 SOUNION, TEMPLE OF POSEIDON, c. 450 BCE.

The architect of the Athenian Hephaesteion is credited with the similar, slightly later Temple of Poseidon at Sounion: also primarily viewed from below, its columns are even more slender (1:5.78).

If not the second Heraeion at Paestum, then the Hephaesteion in Athens provides our best image of a Doric temple and if not the temple of Zeus at Olympia, it is this work which took the Doric Order to its apogee, though it may be seen as over-refined. Begun in 449 BCE, just before the Parthenon, it follows the Olympian example in plan except inside the cella. However, to counter foreshortening when viewed from the main vantage point in the Agora below, its proportions of 1:5.61 are nearly Polykleitan.**3·37** The near-contemporary Temple of Poseidon at Sounion went further.**3·38** This posed an inescapable problem for the future development of the Doric Order: was further slenderness compatible with its nature? The architects of the Parthenon thought not.

3.38

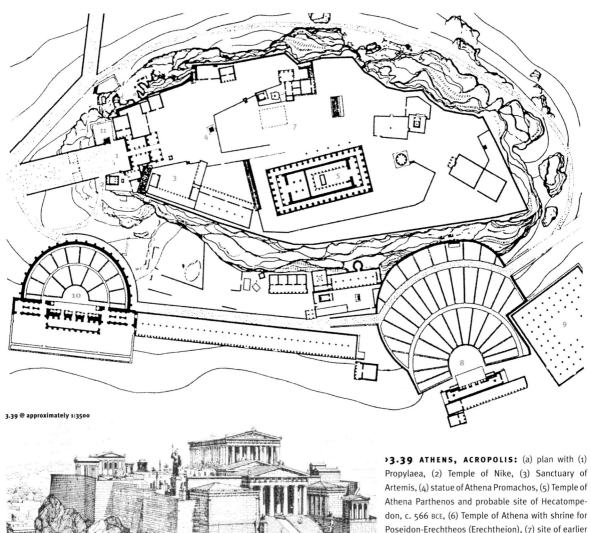

3.39 @ approximately 1:3500

3.39b

›3.39 ATHENS, ACROPOLIS: (a) plan with (1) Propylaea, (2) Temple of Nike, (3) Sanctuary of Artemis, (4) statue of Athena Promachos, (5) Temple of Athena Parthenos and probable site of Hecatompedon, c. 566 BCE, (6) Temple of Athena with shrine for Poseidon-Erechtheos (Erechtheion), (7) site of earlier Erechtheion, (8) Theatre of Dionysos and (9) odeon, (10) Roman odeon, (11) so-called pedestal of Agrippa (in fact, erected by Eumenes II of Pergamon in 178 BCE to support votive sculpture); (b) reconstruction of site in the early 5th century with the Temple of Athena Polias (so-called Hundred-Foot Temple or Hecatompedon); (c, d) post-Periklean model from north and south (Athens, Department of Archaeology and London, British Museum).

3.39c

3 PERIKLEAN APOGEE

Athens reached the height of its power and prosperity under Perikles (c. 495-429 BCE), and he proclaimed it in mid-century by inaugurating the transformation of the Acropolis after its devastation by the Persians a generation earlier. The dominant work was a great new temple (the Parthenon) dedicated to the city's patron deity, Athena. However, the task also involved the complete rebuilding of the gate-house (the Propylaea) and the temple complex known as the Erechtheion, as well as the founding of several entirely new works and the restoration of surviving fragments.**3.39**

At least three great architects were employed on the Periklean Acropolis: Iktinos, Kallikrates and Mnesikles. However, the supreme success of the Parthenon – one of the most admired buildings of all time – is due to the collaboration of Phidias – one of the greatest sculptors of all

3.39d

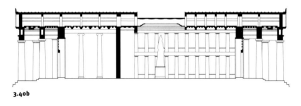

›3.40 ATHENS, ACROPOLIS, PARTHENON, 447–432 BCE: (a, pages 414–415) view from west-south-west; (b, c) section and plan; (d) detail of south-west corner showing outer pteron, opisthodomos and Ionic frieze; (e, f) reconstruction of east front and diagram of colonnade exaggerating the devices designed to control optical illusion, (g, pages 366–367) detail of Phidias's frieze.

3.40b

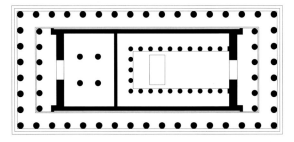

3.40c @ 1:1000

On a stylobate of 30.9 by 69.5 metres (a ratio of 1:2.25 or 4:9), the eight by seventeen columns were 1.9 metres by 10.44 metres, giving proportions of 1:5.48. The axial spacing was 4.29 metres except for the corner bays, which were more than usually contracted, apparently in response to the greater width of the façade. The ratio of base diameter to interaxial width and of the width of the pteron to the total height of the Order was 1:2.25 or 4:9.

time. If the apogee of the male Order was achieved by Libon for Zeus at Olympia,**3·34** Kalikrates, Iktinos and Phidias eclipsed it for the patroness of Athens: incorporating Ionic elements, their work is eclectic and it is no accident that the Orders were crossed in Athens where Achaeans intermingled with Aegeans on their way to the islands and Ionia.**3·40**

The Parthenon

The platform and much of the material prepared for a project begun c. 488 BCE and destroyed by the Persians in 480 were reused but the new work was shorter and wider. Of eight by seventeen columns, the peristyle preserved the proportions established at Olympia. Octastyle, unprecedented in mainland Doric buildings, was common in Ionia: in the Parthenon the extra width accommodated the great chryselephantine statue of the deity more commodiously than in Libon's building.**3·34b** Both pronaos and opisthodomos were reduced to shallow porticoes but had the greater width of six columns standing free of the contracted ante (prostyle hexastyle).

The Panathenaic procession, held in Athens every four years to endow

3.40d

417   ›ARCHITECTURE IN CONTEXT »THE CLASSICAL WORLD

the cult statue of Athena with a new robe, is followed from pronaos to opisthodomos around the cella walls in the flowing movement of Phidias's frieze; that sublime narrative work is essentially Ionic, in contrast to the episodic zoning of the traditional Doric metopes of the external pteron.**3.40g** As Phidias lightened the proportions of his predecessors in the figures of his frieze – approximating those of Polykleitos's *Canon* and generating the flowing movement from the formula for balanced asymmetry – so too Iktinos lightened the proportions of his pteron and introduced subtle variations in the dimensions of the parts to obviate stiffness. The result was no less Doric than the Polykleitan ideal but in one special case, deep inside, the Ionic Order prevailed.

In addition to porch and opisthodomos, antechamber and cella, a secure room was needed for the treasury – the 'parthenon' that gave its name to the building. In the cella there was room for the usual superimposition of columns to provide intermediate support for the roof – and the system returned parallel to the west wall to form an ambulatory behind Phidias's image of the goddess. In the restricted space of the treasury this would have looked cluttered and a single Doric Order rising from the ground would have taken up most of the floor space – even in Iktinos's lightened mode. The naturally slender Ionic provided the solution.

The main structural elements – columns, architraves and coronas – which were stuccoed in white marble plaster over stone in most Doric temples, were here the natural colour of the marble. Secondary – or originally protective – elements, such as the incisions at the top of the columns, triglyphs, regulae and mutules, were blue. The guttae were white and the horizontal tenia and via mouldings below and above the frieze were red and gold. The sculpture was the natural colour of the marble – except for gilt-bronze detail – but the Panathenaic frieze, at least, had a blue background. In contrast to its low relief, the metopes were in exceptionally high relief: they represented the battles of gods and giants on the east front, of Athenians and Amazons on the west, of Lapiths and Centaurs on the south side, and of Greeks and Trojans on the north. The pediment figures, even as fragments, rank among the supreme masterpieces of sculpture in the round. The eastern pediment was dedicated to

3.40e

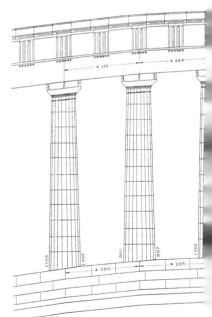

3.40f

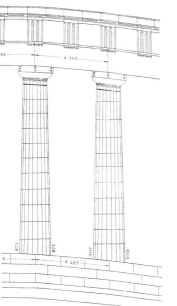

the birth of Athena; the western one contained the contest of Athena and Poseidon for Attica.

No other building has had its strength and vitality enhanced at greater cost through the subtle combination of curves and inclination of horizontals and verticals. Yet all the optical controls employed by Iktinos were invented by his predecessors:

1 end bays had been contracted to cope with the displacement of the triglyphs since the early Archaic period – as in the Heraeion at Olympia.**3.21** This also lent the appearance of greater strength at the corners and obviated the apparent attrition of columns seen against the light of the sky rather than against the mass of the cella walls. Corner-bay contraction here was double the norm and the metopes of the peristyle were graded in increasing width from the sides to the centre;

2 following the abandonment of the Archaic practice of making all the columns of the ends thicker than those of the sides, attrition was countered and strength enhanced by thickening the corner columns – as in the Temple of Aphaea at Aegina.**3.31** The corner columns of the Parthenon were augmented by one-fortieth of the standard diameter. In the Hephaesteion it is one-fiftieth, as recommended by Vitruvius;**3.37**

3 the sense of attrition had been counteracted from the earliest Archaic period by curving columns outwards (*entasis*). Often exaggerated until late in the 6th century BCE, the refinement of this device marked the development of the Doric Order. The Parthenon's entasis expanded to 1.75 centimetres over the straight line drawn from column top to base. Expansion was just over 5 centimetres in the Archaic Temple of Hera I at Paestum;**3.27**

4 the upward curvature of horizontals in the later-Archaic period was perhaps first adopted to shed water – as in the Temple of Apollo at Corinth – but it was also seen to counteract a sense of sagging and to enhance apparent vitality. The curvature of the Parthenon's stylobate produces a rise of 6 centimetres on the ends and 11 centimetres on the sides;

5 the consistent inclination of vertical lines obviated the sense of splaying at the top for greater apparent stability – as first encountered in the Temple of Aphaea at Aegina, though there, as in the Temple of Zeus at Olympia, only the side columns were inclined. In the Parthenon the pteron inclines inwards by 6 centimetres.

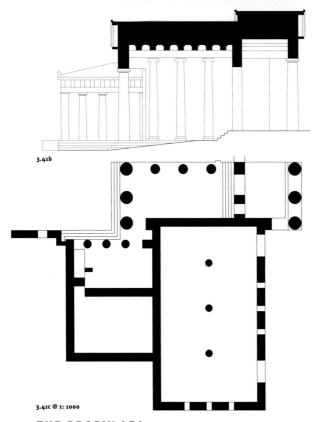

3.41b

3.41c @ 1: 1000

437–432 BCE: (a, pages 420–421) view from south-west, (b, c) section and half plan (as north but unreal-ized south), (d) view of central passage and Ionic Order.

Probably designed by Mnesikles, the Propylaea replaced a structure demolished in 437 BCE but remained incomplete after the outbreak of the Pelo-ponnesian War. The double portico of the Mycenaean type, facing west and east, was separated by a wall with three main doors and two posterns. The sacred way rose 1.75 metres along its axis. Though the six Doric columns before each front had the same diame-ters (1.56 metres), at nearly 8.8 metres high, the west-ern ones – seen from below – were just under a third of a metre taller than the eastern ones. Their respective proportions are 1:5.65 and 5.47. The central intercol-umniation was wider than that of the sides, obviously to facilitate passage up the ramp which cut through the stylobate. The inner portico was shallow enough to be spanned in marble without intermediate sup-port, but at more than twice the depth to shelter wait-ing visitors, the outer one needed internal supports. The two rows of three Ionic columns (with proportions nearing 1:10) introduced here carried a marble ceiling which, spanning 5.5 metres over the aisles, remained a wonder even to Pausanias more than five hundred years later.

Halls planned to flank the eastern portico were never erected. Pendant wings were planned to project westward, facing each other across the sacred way, but only the northern one was completed (as a picture gallery). The southern one, stopped short by the sanc-tuary of Artemis to its south-east, was left open to the west as an entrance to the Nike precinct. The portico's south wall ended opposite the outermost column of the temple's north side, beyond which was an isolated pier to effect symmetry with the north wing.

THE PROPYLAEA

Through the concessions he made to the Ionic, Iktinos demonstrated that the days of pure Doric were over: the flexible Ionic admitted of development, the rigid Doric did not. And in the Propylaea the architect looked to Ionic for the solution to a problem unresolvable in Doric terms. The outer and inner porticoes are on different levels and the way rises through a waiting area between them. As the ceiling was to be consistent in level throughout, the columns supporting it in the intermediate zone obviously had to be taller than those of either portico and, if they were Doric, they would have to be thicker. To avoid that discrepancy and the narrowing of the passageway, the architect introduced the flexible Ionic.**3.41**

3.41d

3.42

Conceived by Kallikrates on a larger scale in 449,
the Temple of Nike was erected from 427 to reduced
plans – 5.4 by 8.2 metres at its base – accommodating
it to the smaller site left by the construction of the
Propylaea. The pronaos was dispensed with in favour
of a shallow portico (prostyle tetrastyle) and the cella
was diminished to a virtual square beyond screens
between piers in antis. A matching portico was applied
before the blind west wall. The proportions of the
Order (1:7.82) were unusually stocky for Ionic. The
Attic form of base achieved its exquisite canonical
form, with a single scotia separated by two torus
mouldings, the lower one broader than the upper.

›3.43 ATHENS, ACROPOLIS, ERECHTHEION,
420–405 BCE: (a, b) elevation and plan, (c) view from
the south-east, (d) detail of architrave mouldings
(London, British Museum).

Superseding a synthetic Doric-Ionic work probably
dedicated to Athena Polias c. 530 and destroyed by
the Persians, the present complex was built from 420
to 405 on a split-level site to the north of its predecessor. The architect had to accommodate the olive tree
and well (erechtheis) produced respectively by Athena
and Poseidon in their contest: he also had to shelter
trident marks left by Poseidon and house the venerable olive-wood statue of Athena Polias saved from the
Persians.

Athena Polias was given a rectangular cella behind
the eastern portico (prostyle hexastyle). The lower
level to the west was subdivided for the cult of Posei-
don-Erechtheis by screens that did not reach the full
height of the space. This area was entered from the
west, through the compound of Athena's tree. To provide height for the door, the western colonnade was
raised over a substantial basement. Evidently displaced further east than originally planned at the
insistence of those responsible for Athena's tree, the
six columns of this front were attached in whole or part
to a screen wall with three windows (possibly later).

Both the caryatid portico to the south and the
prostyle tetrastyle northern portico sheltering the
marks of Poseidon's trident overlapped the main block
to the west – the northern one very awkwardly.

The Erechtheion was built of Pentalic marble, inset

THE TEMPLE OF NIKE AND THE
ERECHTHEION

The Periklean transformation of the Acropolis continued
in the 430s with the small Temple of Nike, on a promontory west of the Propylaea, and the Erechtheion, both
probably due to Kallikrates. The former is an orthodox
prostyle tetrastyle building.**3.42** The Erechtheion is extraordinary: diversified in its plan to incorporate several sites
sacred to Athena and Poseidon in their legendary contest
for Athens, it was built on various levels that would have
been extremely difficult to handle given the restriction of
the Doric proportional system.**3.43**

with black stone behind the friezes. The height of the columns varied, with proportions ranging from 1:9 to 1:9.5. The door from the northern portico and the capitals throughout were exceptionally rich, with compound spiral volutes intertwined with a bronze fillet and an anthemion decoration. The architrave had the traditional three fascias and a sculpted frieze, but dentils were omitted from the cornice except on the southern portico. With their clothes falling in flute-like folds over the weight-bearing leg, the caryatids are the supreme masterpieces of the genre.

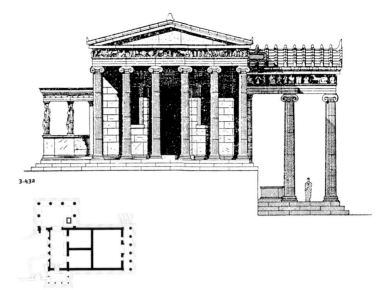
3.43a

3.43d

3.43b @ 1: 1000

3.43c

THE SANCTUARY OF DIONYSOS

The Acropolis complex was completed with the sanctuary of Dionysos at the foot of its south-eastern slope. This included a great theatre. Apart from the temple, the theatre was the most important Hellenic building type: also with a religious role to play, as drama furthered the cult of the gods, it originated to provide for choral dances associated with the mysteries of Dionysos to which Thespis introduced an actor at Athens c. 534 BCE.**3·44**

The Theatre

The original dancing place (orchestra) was a circle of stamped earth. A raked timber structure must soon have been provided for the viewing place (theatron) but the collapse of such a structure in or near the Athenian Agora some time during the 70th Olympiad (500–496), prompted the development of the cult on the southern slopes of the Acropolis where nature provided the base for permanent tiered seating and a splendid view beyond the orchestral circle over the adjacent sanctuary of Dionysos. The proliferation of parts for actors after the age of Perikles prompted the development of facilities for them in a building erected beyond the orchestra. As this blocked the view, painted scenery was hung on it behind a low stage.

When the theatre was first established on the southern slope of the Acropolis early in the 5th century BCE, the natural rock seating was supplemented in timber. The front banks of seats had been regularized in masonry before the end of the century. In the mid-4th century the theatre was enlarged to cover some 5600 square metres and to accommodate ten thousand people (the ideal number of citizens). The semi-circle of the auditorium extended in two parallel banks, forming a U about the orchestra.

The timber structure provided for the actors appeared early in the second half of the 5th century BCE. This building was rebuilt about the turn of the century as a hall attached to the back of a colonnade bordering the sanctuary. The new work had projecting wings (parascenium) framing a timber stage (proscenium), which was removed when not required. This temporary arrangement seems to have lasted until c. 150 BCE.

As the theatre originally served the Dionysiac mysteries, which offered a promise of beatitude to the initiates, theatrical masks played a significant part in funerary rites, especially apparently in the colonies of the Aeolian Islands.

3.44a

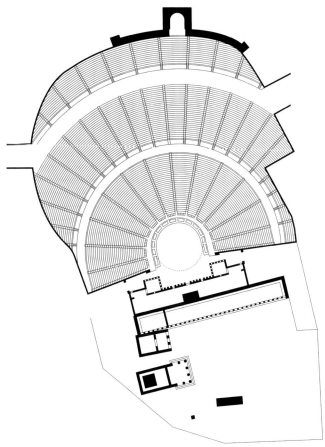

3.44b @ 1:1500

    A music hall (odeion) built to the east of the theatre was square with seats on three sides and a timber roof supported on nine rows of nine columns. The type was established for the shrine built for the mysteries of Demeter at Eleusis. The original building there seems to have had three rows of seven seats; seven rows of seven were projected in mid-century, but this was reduced in execution to six rows with a central lantern. The mysteries of Demeter and Dionysos were presumably not dissimilar, at least in their procedures.

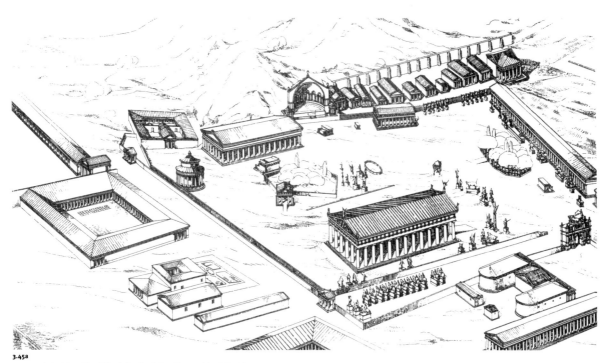

3.45a

4 PLANNING AND
TECHNOLOGY

Before considering the disposition of the great works on the Acropolis, we must return to the venerable sanctuary of Zeus at Olympia. There is no formal order in the relationship between the different elements in the irregular space enclosed by a wall and centred on a sacred grove there. Even the two main buildings, the temples of Hera and Zeus, are slightly out of alignment with one another though both were orientated east–west for cult purposes, and the little treasuries are not aligned in a neat row. Except in the much later works to the south and west, the discretion of each building is scrupulously respected apparently in a process of ad-hoc growth – though an appreciable sense of balance between the forms was doubtless effected through the intervention of planting,

›3.45 OLYMPIA, SANCTUARY OF ZEUS: (a) drawing of the site, (b) plan with (1) Heraeion (Temple of Hera), (2) Temple of Zeus, (3) central altar of Zeus (there were sixty-nine other altars and shrines on the site), (4) Metroum (late-Classical building dedicated to the mother of the gods), (5) treasuries (mostly consisting of simple rectangular cellas with porticoes distyle in antis), (6) Philippeion, erected as a dynastic shrine by Philip II and Alexander the Great – there were many other monuments to past victors and donors, usually columns or pedestals supporting statues or trophies, (7) colonnades (stoas) protecting promenades and stalls selling everything from 'devotional requisites' to food and drink, (8) state dining halls (prytaneia), (9) main entrance to the sacred enclosure (given the form of a triumphal arch in the Roman imperial period, but originally probably a double portico as at Samos and Aegina incorporating stoas for the shel-

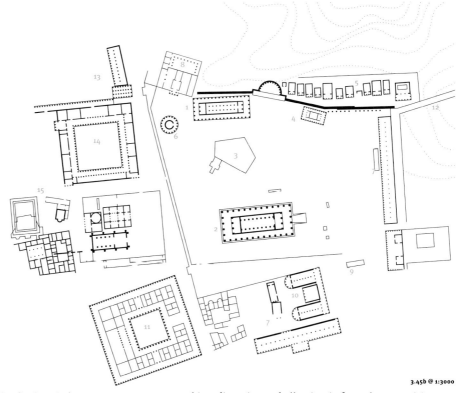

3.45b @ 1:3000

ter of pilgrims), (10) council chamber (bouleuterion) for the authorities charged with maintaining the site and organizing the Games (consisting of two Archaic apsidal megarons with central colonnades with a connecting colonnade and court added in the 4th century BCE), (11) leonidaeum (a hostel for pilgrims or attendants at the Games), (12) the oldest Hellenic stadium for races (built into embankments in the absence of a natural hill to support the seats on either side of the 183-metre track), (13) gymnasium for athletics (traditionally open, but framed with porticoes and given a monumental gate in late-Classical times), (14) palaestra for wrestling (always enclosed, but in late-Classical times given a Doric peristyle before separate spaces for different age groups), (15) baths, with a cold-water washroom and separate cubicles associated with the palaestra.

masking disparity and allowing informal compositions to coalesce.**3.45**

The discretion implicit in the sanctity of individual sites determined informal relationships on the Athenian Acropolis too but here the informality was not ad hoc: the main elements were rebuilt with concerted effort in the Classical era of Perikles. From the restoration of the complex, it is certainly clear that when the Greeks related buildings to one another they did it visually – in accordance with Ionic sensitivity. An informal balance was achieved by adjusting the size, shape and weight of one mass *vis-à-vis* the other elements on the site about a centre of gravity – just as in the formula of Polykleitos.**3.46**

The Athenian Acropolis

Informed by the reconstructed model, some imagination will reveal that in the characteristic view from the hill to the south-west the large simple mass of the Parthenon, with its extended horizontals and contracted verticals, was complemented by the disposition of the smaller, more complex masses of the Erechtheion and Propylaea, to either side of the centre of gravity established in the west front of Athena's great temple.

The Acropolis model and plan illustrate another crucial aspect of Greek site organization: the significance of sightlines. Framed by the inner portico's central intercolumniation, the visitor in the Propylaea would have seen the cult statue of Athena just to the left of centre.**3·46b** Its base is perpendicular to the line of sight but not parallel with the wall behind it and the deflection points to the corners of that wall. A straight line drawn from our visitor's viewpoint to the right-hand corner may be extended to the central intercolumniation of the Parthenon's portico. A straight line similarly drawn in the other direction will arrive at the central intercolumniation of the Erechtheion's main portico: so sightlines from the threshold plot the most important points on the site. This informal way of relating elements in space respects their integrity as mirror-image symmetry would not have done.

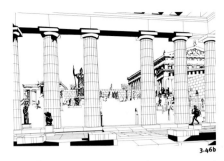
3·46b

›**3·46 ATHENS, ACROPOLIS:** (a, pages 430–431) view from the south-west, (b) view from Propylaea.

›**3·47 SEGESTA, SICILY:** (a) temple (of Athena?); (b) theatre, both late-5th century BCE.

Begun while the city was allied to Athens after 426, the temple was left incomplete (with six by fourteen unfluted columns and no interior structure) after the defeat of Athens by Syracuse in 413 BCE and the subsequent intervention of the Carthaginians. The theatre well represents the stage of development reached in Athens a generation earlier.

Sensitivity to the nature of the site was the Classical norm and this is nowhere better illustrated than at Segesta in Sicily.**3·47** Consummate in its discretion, the temple complements rather than compromises a beautiful place. The same is true of the theatre: the simple semi-circular rings of seats are accommodated by a natural curve in the hillside, and over the low stage beyond the orchestra the audience could view the action taking place against the backdrop of a spectacular view, itself part of the unfolding drama lit by the changing light of the sun. An imposed rationalism, the pure geometry of a mind that sees in it the key to understanding the order of creation, complements the beauty of this world, imperfect though that was thought to be as a reflection of the design of the gods.

3.47a

3.47b

3.48a

3.48b

›3.48 ATHENS: (a, b) Stoa of Attalos: exterior and interior (as rebuilt by the American School); (c) plan of ancient town and agora with (1) Hephaesteion, (2) new bouleuterion (like its predecessor, this late-5th-century BCE building was square with one side walled off to form an entrance lobby and seats for seven hundred around the other three sides, each c. 23 metres long, (3) Poikile ('painted') Stoa, (4) Basileios ('royal') Stoa, (5) Zeus-Eleutherios Stoa, late-5th century BCE, (6) tholos, c. 470 BCE, the official dining hall of the Athenian senate (this was a walled rotunda 18.3 metres in diameter with a conical roof supported by six internal columns), (7) site of original theatre, (8) Theatre of Dionysos, (9) odeon.

Though dating from the mid-2nd century BCE, this example of a stoa follows the form evolved at Athens, Olympia and other early Hellenic sites during the 5th century though a second storey may not then have been usual. Open to the front through a Doric colonnade and walled to the back, the space was divided into two aisles by a central row of Ionic columns supporting the ridge of the pitched roof. The form was adapted for the arsenal and boat sheds at Piraeus and for similar storage purposes elsewhere.

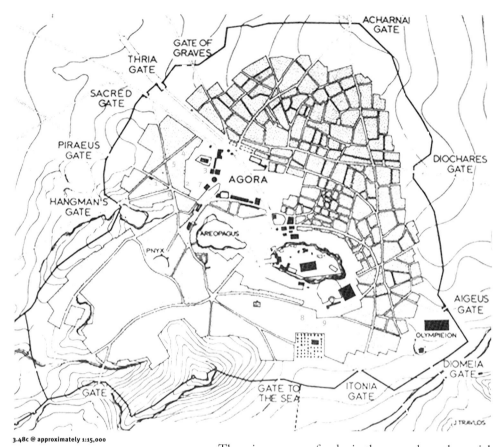

ACHARNAI
GATE

GATE OF
GRAVES

THRIA
GATE

SACRED
GATE

DIOCHARES
GATE

PIRAEUS
GATE

AGORA

HANGMAN'S
GATE

AREOPAGUS

AIGEUS
GATE

PNYX

OLYMPIEION

DIOMEIA
GATE

GATE

GATE TO
THE SEA

ITONIA
GATE

J.TRAVLOS

3.48c @ approximately 1:15,000

There is no sense of order in the areas about the social and commercial centre of ancient Athens – the Agora. These followed the traditional growth pattern of towns before the intervention of planners, where feet tended to pick the easy way through the site contours in making the paths that became streets. Later planners begun to impose regular lines and to relate buildings to one another in accordance with clear geometrical patterns with the insertion of stoas. Usually Doric with an internal Ionic colonnade supporting the ridge of the roof, these were extended porticoes for promenading and informal gatherings, often subdivided along the back into shops.**3.48**

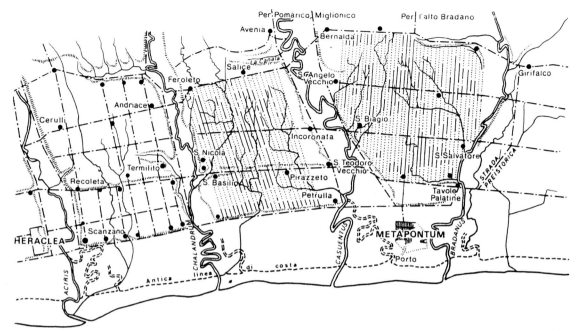

THE DEVELOPMENT OF FORMALITY

While the cities of Hellas generally grew organically, formality was brought to bear on rebuilding after devastation by war or earthquake and, especially, in the laying-out of new towns in the colonies. Precedents were provided by the Babylonians and Egyptians: the great chronicler Herodotus knew about the regular division of the land in Egypt and believed the Greeks learned the principles of land surveying from the Egyptians. In Magna Graecia a regular grid appears in the late-7th century BCE not only in urban areas but also in the countryside – as at Metapontum.**3.49** Grids with broad arteries were also adopted for Selinos, Akragas, Paestum, Naples and many other settlements in Magna Graecia. However, the most celebrated exercise in Hellenic town planning was the rebuilding of Ionian Miletos in the generation following its destruction by the Persians in 494 BCE.**3.50**

›**3.49 METAPONTUM, SOUTHERN ITALY:** plan showing the regular division of land in town and country, late-7th century BCE.

Surveys and sample excavation have revealed two phases of land division: with orthogonal tracks in the mid-6th century BCE, then with a similar grid of drainage ditches less than a century later.

›**3.50 MILETOS, IONIA,** the city as rebuilt in the second quarter of the 5th century BCE (a) plan with (1) south agora, the main civic space, originally with stoas to the north, south and west sides and finally enclosed with the eastern stoa in the late-Classical period, (2) bouleterion, built under Antiochus IV (175–164 BCE) beyond an open court, surrounded by Doric colonnades and containing an altar, the chamber itself, with its theatrical arrangement of seats, was covered by a truss roof supported by the walls and four Ionic columns, (3) north agora, enclosed and extended to the west with stoas forming subsidiary squares in the late-Classical period, (4) Roman theatre, (b) site view to north from theatre.

In the northern sector, where redevelopment

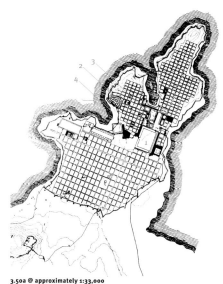

3.50a @ approximately 1:33,000

3.50b

began, the blocks of c. 23.8 by 29.3 metres were defined by streets c. 3.7 metres wide, except for one lateral artery running west from the central complex of public buildings. The southern sector was divided by two main arteries running north–south and east–west. These were c. 7.6 metres wide, the other streets were c. 4.3 metres wide and the blocks were 35.7 by 42.1 metres .

Miletos

Recalling Ionian precedents for orthogonal planning – like the early 7th-century rebuilding of Smyrna – a grid of nearly square blocks was imposed on the rugged promontory to either side of the harbour. Much of the city has gone and the centuries have eroded the site, but the arrogance of man asserting himself over nature is still apparent here. The plan is associated with the name of Hippodamos, a local physician concerned with healthy circulation of air, but is far more rigid than his known work elsewhere: he is credited by Aristotle with the ordered rebuilding of Piraeus (towards the middle of the 5th century BCE), and ancient sources also associate him with the founding of the colony of Thurii in southern Italy (444 BCE). However, there is no evidence that he produced the exceptionally repetitive scheme for his native town.

The Miletan project was important not only because of its imposition of the grid to organize the domestic quarters, but also for its engagement of the contours of the site to define different aspects of the city's life and different classes of housing. In the low ground beyond the harbour, towards the centre, public space and civic buildings separate the residential quarters from the commercial districts. The agoras, if more regular than before, were not axially aligned: the formal relationship between buildings was the concern of later ages.

3.51 @ 1:10,000

HOUSING

Regularization was more supple at Olynthos, where a new suburb was laid out c. 430 BCE. The grid of differentiated streets defines rectangular blocks containing ten square domestic plots.**3.51** In accordance with timeless tradition in the lands to the east of the Mediterranean where civilization developed, the houses turned largely blind fronts to the public domain and were orientated to the enclosed court that provided the main living space. Entrance was invariably off-centre so that the main part of the court could not be seen from the street. There was usually a portico on the northern side, facing south before the main room (oecus), which contained the hearth, as in the ancient megaron.**1.85–1.87** There was usually also a separate dining room (andron) for the master of the house and his friends. All these features were present in Athenian houses built several generations earlier on more typically irregular sites.**3.52**

›3.51 OLYNTHOS: plan with suburban extension c. 425 BCE.

The main axes ran north–south, secondary streets east–west and the blocks were divided by alleys – also running east–west – into the two rows of plots c. 17 metres square on which the south-facing courtyard houses were built.

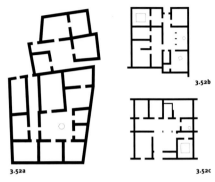

3.52b

3.52a
3.52c

›3.52 GREEK HOUSE PLANS, 5th century BCE (approximately 1:1000): (a) Athens; (b, c) Olynthos.

From the early Archaic period, the typical house had a court entered from a corner with rooms to three sides. In Athens spacious houses were rare, except in the suburbs, but two storeys were not uncommon.

The off-centre entrance to each house in Olynthos was from the north or south, according to the situation of its plot in the block. In the former case (top right) the main suite of rooms separated the court from the street but was breached by a corridor; in the latter only a vestibule screened the entrance. Sometimes the northern portico was extended all around the court as a peristyle. Lit from two sides on a corner, the andron was surrounded by couches for the diners raised above a central trough from which scraps could be flushed out into the adjacent street.

›**3.53** PAESTUM, EAST GATE IN THE WALLS OF
THE GREEK COLONY, 5th century BCE: inner face.
  The Greek colonists of southern Italy seem to have
been less prejudiced against the arch than their metropolitan contemporaries. The gate of Velia, another
Greek colony to the south of Paestum, may date from
the late-6th century.

3·53

BUILDING TECHNOLOGY

The Greeks were concerned with refining their trabeated
system, not with technological innovation. Supported by
terraced ground, even their theatres required no
advanced building technology. Rejecting irregularity
towards the end of the Archaic period, they developed
masonry of great precision in wall as well as column.
Large polygonal blocks, like those of the Apollonian
temple podium at Delphi,**3·30** subsisted in fortification
for their greater cohesiveness but otherwise rectangular
blocks were laid in regular courses of the same or varied
size. Concealed surfaces were often roughly cut to reduce
weight, and outer faces were sometimes left coarse (rusticated) for greater apparent strength. Stability depended
on dead weight but in the most important buildings the
blocks were secured to one another with metal dowels
and clamps rather than mortar until late in the Classical
age.

  The Hellenes knew of the arch but they were predisposed towards the aesthetics of trabeation and generally
bridged openings with a lintel or corbels. However, applying Oriental arcuate building technology to the construction of arched gates in their city walls from at least as early
as the early 5th century BCE, the colonists of Magna Graecia left a major legacy to the Etruscans and Romans.**3·53**
It was not until the mid-4th century that the true arcuate
vault appears in Greece, and then only in the subterranean
tombs of Macedonian kings. Arches, corbelled and true,
were not uncommon in defence works and utilities (such
as drains) throughout the Greek world by then but had to
wait another two centuries for public display in a place of
civic dignity.

›3.54 THE DEATH OF SOCRATES (Jacques-Louis David, 1787, New York, Metropolitan Museum of Art).

5 POLIS IN CRISIS

The houses of Olynthos and the temple at Segesta bring us to the period in which Hellas was destroying itself in the Peloponnesian War (431–404 BCE). The conflict between a league of Dorians led by the Spartans and the largely Ionian one led by the Athenians placed in opposition those very traits that had fused to take Hellenic culture to its summit – Doric virility and strength, but rigidity; Ionic grace and vitality, but capriciousness – and destroyed the institution upon which that unique achievement depended: the polis. The very existence of leagues was inimical to it in principle. The complexity of their conflict and its causes, the complexity of warfare itself, promoted the professional specialist and, therefore, the individual, whereas the polis required all its citizens to be good, if essentially amateur, 'all-rounders'. All were left exhausted and the confidence of all but the Spartans in their institutions was undermined.

The Spartans triumphed, briefly, partly through the

invincibility of their army but more through Persian aid and the folly of the Athenians in squandering their sea power on extraneous adventures – most lamentably in Sicily. Persia was the real victor, as the price for the Great King's intervention was Ionia. Elsewhere Spartan 'protection', exercised through the imposition of oligarchies on the defeated democracies, soon excited reaction.

A renewal of war ended in 387 BCE with the mediation of Artaxerxes III as the guarantor of autonomy among the constituents of Hellas. Thebes challenged Sparta in leadership and astonished everyone by actually defeating the Spartan army in battle in 371. But Thebes was not cap-able of sustained dominance and the rude northern kingdom of Macedon was the ultimate beneficiary with the accession of the wily Philip II in 359: he imposed his own peace with garrisons. On his early death, his extraordinary son Alexander not only sustained Macedonian dominance in Hellas but led the Hellenes to over-run the empire of the Persians which, by then, extended over most of the world known to them.

PLATONIC RATIONALISM

Contemptuous of the disastrous factional amateurism of Athenian democracy, the great philosopher Plato sought the ideal alternative in the name of his master Socrates (470–399 BCE) – who had himself perished at the hands of Athenian democrats.**3.54** The vast scope of his teaching in his academy, established in Athens early in the 380s, goes way beyond our concern but his rationalism is of fundamental importance to all aspects of Classical culture, not least architecture.

In the disillusioned Athens of the period following the severe reverses of the Peloponnesian War, the sceptical teachers known as Sophists challenged the old puritan values in a spirit of pragmatic humanism, Protagoras in particular denying that there were absolute standards and objective truths with the contention that 'man is the measure of all things, of things that are that they are, and of things that are not that they are not'. Precisely because man is the arbiter, in practice in society the majority must prevail with the customs and conventions accepted by it.

Didactic in purpose, predisposed to belief in the absolute Good, Plato pits his master against the Sophists on ground that is at once rationalist and mystical. If he acquired his ethical bias from Socrates, it was from the greatest of the pre-Socratic philosophers, Parmenides and Herakleitos respectively, that he extracted the positive and negative ideas that all being was eternal, homogeneous and logically unsusceptible to change, and that there is nothing stable in the sensible world. The combination led back to Pythagoras and Orphic mysticism.

To Plato, the philosopher is a lover of the vision of Truth: it is difficult entirely to disassociate the vision from the mystical or the love from the ecstasy of the mysteries. Apprehension of Truth alone is knowledge and that is to be gained not from experience but through deductive reasoning from self-evident axioms like mathematics: it is not empirical (*a posteriori*) but rational (*a priori*). Knowledge is of universals, the ultimate realities that Plato identifies as Ideas or Forms made by God. Reason will lead the soul to their vision. Sense perception, on the other hand, informs only opinion for it is attuned to the particulars of this ever-changing, contradictory world – beautiful things, for example, may also be ugly, as distinct from Beauty itself, which is immutable. Moreover, if this physical world was perverted by 'irrational necessity', Plato held it as self-evident that Reality, as opposed to appearance, was completely good. Thus if the ideal was intellectual, like the Pythagorean Good it was also mystical: knowledge was the revelation of the divine.

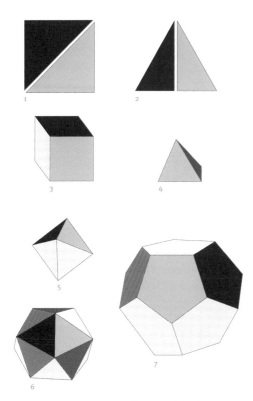

›3.55 PLATONIC SOLIDS: (1) square divided on its diagonal into isosceles triangles, (2) equilateral triangle divided into scalene triangles, (3) cube, (4) tetrahedron, (5) octahedron, (6) icosahedron, (7) dodecahedron.

In pursuit of perfection, Soul builds by introducing mathematical form and harmony to the conditions of chaos, first defining the four basic elements and relating them in constant proportions. Contrary to appearances, these are the four regular solids constituted from the most elementary of plane figures, the triangle: the tetrahedron (fire), octahedron (air) and icosahedron (water) generated from the scalene halves of the equilateral triangle, and the cube (earth) generated from the isosceles halves of the square. Though not similarly generated from triangles, the dodecahedron is added to represent the universe, which is otherwise defined as spherical because 'like is fairer than unlike and only a sphere is alike in all aspects'.

Qualified in the Pythagorean terms of number, Plato's theory of Forms provided the basis for his explanation of the cosmos. Returning to mythology in arguing against chance, Plato postulates the rational and therefore comprehensible purpose of a creator: Soul. Like elemental Mind, Soul is also like – but not called – Zeus. He presides over a hierarchy of powers but is (unfortunately) not omnipotent as Craftsman. His reason is not sovereign over the irrational force of physical necessity since the material he has to use (evidently pre-existent) will not be consistent in all its properties with the faithful reproduction of his Model. That is the world of Being, the true world of Forms, the Good; the product is the world of Becoming, our imperfect world.**3·55**

The concept of a supersensory world of eternal ideals, inherently discounting the material world of appearances, was to be perennially attractive in the West. Yet Plato's attempt to deal with the idea of the universal with his theory of Forms was incompletely resolved – especially for material things and negatives – failing to address the problem of relating Reality's timelessness to its creation. His pupil, Aristotle, rejected it.

ARISTOTELIAN EMPIRICISM
Aristotle (who was tutor to Alexander of Macedon without clear effect) agreed that philosophers must seek objective truth in the knowledge of immaterial and unchanging universals but he promoted argument from verifiable premises as well as from abstract hypotheses like those of mathematics – inductive as well as deduct-ive reasoning. Totally detached from the experience of this world, the first principles on which Plato's deduction depends are articles of faith to which he could not subscribe. And he found in Plato's conception no convincing explanation of the concrete individual things of our experience which he

saw as the primary realities. To Aristotle, universals were not transcendent but imminent in the general characteristics of the particular things we perceive. Hence it was to this changeable world that he looked for the unchangeable objects of true knowledge – not beyond it.

Plato, of course, looked for unchangeable Reality elsewhere precisely because he could not identify it in a world of apparent change. In abandoning that position, Aristotle had to account for unchangeable Reality and the reality of change. He distinguished form, matter and substance, potentiality and actuality: substance is matter defined by a particular form; form is potential in raw matter, actual in substance moulded by evolution. By definition specific substances lose their identity in change but, beyond them, Aristotle saw evolution progressing to ever-greater actuality: its objective is the perfect form and unchangeable actuality of God.

Though the philosophy of his predecessors was mainly rationalist, Aristotle's empiricism was hardly revolutionary. He sought a balance between the rational and the empirical: in his ethics it is as a mean between extremes that he defines virtue. Experience had naturally governed some lines of earlier Greek enquiry, notably medicine, and it is difficult to imagine that the Greek artist framed the anthropomorphic ideal of the gods without reference to himself and the people about him – seeking a mean between extreme examples, as we have seen.

If the rationalist concept of the mean guided the development of Classical art to its apogee towards the middle of the 5th century BCE, empiricism accompanied by loss of faith in old reason produced a very different art in the first half of the 4th century. Just when the Dorians triumphed in war, the Ionians triumphed in art: in both sculpture and architecture, the Doric canon succumbed to Phidias's introduction of Ionic lightness and grace.

>**3.56** AGRIGENTO, 'TEMPLE OF CONCORD',
from early in the last quarter of the 5th century BCE:
view from the east.

On a stylobate 16.9 metres by 39.4 metres (1:2.32)
there are six by thirteen columns 1.4 metres by 6.7
metres (1:4.61) throughout. The two bays on either
side of each corner were contracted – as in the similar
but slightly older Temple of Hera Likinia nearby on the
same ridge. The cella was aisleless: its walls remained
intact to cornice level when the building was converted
to a church.

ECLECTICISM AND THE ADVENT
OF CORINTHIAN

The old pre-Iktian Doric proportions were sustained
abroad, as the temple of Concord at Akragas in Sicily
demonstrates,**3.56** but the impact of the Athenian masters
was inescapable in the homeland. The next important work
after the Parthenon was the Temple of Apollo at Bassae in
the Peloponnesos, sometimes attributed to Iktinos. The
columns of its Doric pteron approach the proportions of
those of the Parthenon and the architect furthered the
eclecticism of the great Athenian work.**3.57**

3.57a

The Temple of Apollo Epikourios at Bassae

Pausanias attributes the temple to Iktinos and ascribes the dedication to gratitude for relief from the plague. The outstanding novelty of the design is the magnificent high-relief frieze within the cella supported by the attached Order of Ionic columns and the single column, centre-west, with a capital inaugurating the development of the Corinthian Order. This contrasts with the Archaic proportions of the plan, which may be explained by the wish of the remote provincial patrons to acknowledge the precedent of the great Temple of Apollo at Delphi.[3.30] The Order was modern in its proportions and the steep slope of the echinus, but the patrons seem also to

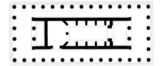

3.57b @ 1:1000

3.57c

3.57d

›3.57 BASSAE, TEMPLE OF APOLLO EPIKOU-RIOS, last quarter of the 5th century BCE: (a) view; (b) plan, (c) reconstructed view of the interior, (d) detail of cella frieze with Hercules confronting an Amazon, (e) proto-Corinthian capital (engraving of the fragment found during excavations of 1812 but lost).

On a stylobate 14.5 by 38.2 metres (a ratio of 1:2.64) were six by fifteen columns 1.17 to 1.12 by 5.96 metres, giving proportions of 1:5.13 on the front and 1:5.31 on the sides. The axial spacing was 2.71 metres on the front – a ratio of 2.34:1 and 1:2.19 to base diameter and column height respectively – and slightly narrower on the sides.

3.57e

have had their Archaic way in the three incised rings at the top of the column. The provincial builders, moreover, were apparently not called upon to cope with sophisticated optical-illusion controls such as the curvature of stylobate and entablature, though the columns have slight entasis.

The internal Order is peculiar, not only in the introduction of the Corinthian capital but also in the form of the Ionic, with volutes to all three exposed sides and bell-shaped bases. No special provision seems to have been made for lighting the battles between Greeks and Amazons and Lapiths and Centaurs in the frieze.

Not of high-quality marble, the frieze seems sometimes rough in execution. The artists may have been working from a master's drawings rather than life models – and recall many traditional motifs perfected by Phidias, most notably the so-called 'heroic diagonal' assumed by Hercules and his Amazon opponent here. But the original artistic intention was to describe the staccato violence of battle: the frieze was designed to be read as a continuous entity but each slab is devoted to a discrete episode and juxtaposed to the ones on either side with wilfully disturbing changes of rhythm. Thus, though there is a proto-Baroque theatricality of movement in individual parts, the whole might be termed Mannerist for its virtuoso synthesis of the episodic Dorian mode with the narrative Ionian, naturally defying the harmonious, fluid Ionic convention that reached its apogee in the Parthenon frieze and, at times, naturalistically portraying violence with unmodulated brutality in defiance of the Classical ideal.

3.58a   3.58b

3.59

PRAXITELES AND LYSIPPOS

Developments in sculpture took a similar course. Compare Praxiteles – perhaps the most significant sculptor in the generation after Phidias – with Polykleitos.**3.58a, 3.33** Dating from c. 390 BCE, Praxiteles's image of a languid youth contemplating a lizard on a tree is identified as Apollo – but clearly it has a distinctly female lightness, grace and elegance. So lacking is it in virility, in fact, that it can no longer support itself but leans on the tree trunk – in contrast to the discretion of Polykleitos's original bronze. The emasculation also reflects Ionic sensuality: Praxiteles's marble now has the softness of flesh rather than the hardness of muscle, and the softness of the modelling is enhanced by the modulation of the light.

Praxiteles abandoned the fixed frontal viewpoint of his predecessors and composed in the round: this statue belongs to our space. Interest in human space and human traits informed Praxiteles's achievement. His was an essentially realistic response to the emotional and physical realities of this world, the representation of figures less

›**3.58** PRAXITELES: (a) Apollo Sauroktonos ('lizard-slayer'); (b) the Knidian Aphrodite (Roman copies of mid-4th century BCE originals).

›**3.59** DRAPED MALE FIGURE, artist unknown, early 4th century BCE? (Marsala, Archaeological Museum).

This sculpture, discovered off the Sicilian island of Motya, has been called a charioteer and dated to the 5th century BCE by some scholars. However, in the exposition of form through clothing the artist's pursuit of the ideal has clearly taken a turn in the direction found enticing by sensualists from the next century onwards.

›3.60 ATHLETE IDENTIFIED AS AGIAS OF PHARSALOS (from a Delphic monument dedicated c. 335 BCE by King Daochos II of Pharsalos, associated with a contemporary bronze signed by Lysippos): (Delphi, Archaeological Museum).

Sculptor to Alexander the Great, Lysippos reputedly claimed to have been schooled by Polykleitos – specifically the Doryphoros – and nature. His fame rests on his having revised the Polykleitan 'foursquare' ideal against his own conception of nature producing a taller, more slender body with smaller head. More naturalistic than its high-Classical 5th-century inspiration, especially in its expressively deep-set eyes, the result was still ideal not least in its refined modification of Polykleitos's conception of balanced asymmetry.

as abstract ideals than as human. His late-Classical successors were to further the refinement of the Polykleitan canon and the evocation of human feeling, ultimately producing a naturalistic and expressive ideal without effeminacy – though not without sensuality.**3.58b** The evocation of personality followed naturally.**3.59, 3.60** Beyond that, the ultimate Hellenistic achievement was intense realism in the representation of emotion.

Against the background of the Peloponnesian Wars, interest in the real, the human, the sensual, the emotional may be traced to the collapse of the old austere ideals that devalued the realities of this world in the certainty of order in creation as a whole. Most significantly, the internal space of the temple was now to be seen as a context for man.

INTERNAL EMBELLISHMENT AND AMBIGUITY

Before Bassae, the Doric temple had been primarily an object of external formal perfection. It was not a congregational building: the priests performed rites within; the public participated in worship outside. Addressing the structural problem of supporting the cella roof, Bassae's architect took a revolutionary interest in the embellishment of interior space – serving god but engaging man.

Two superb little round buildings from early in the 4th century BCE (the type is called 'tholos') continue this line of development, producing an increasing visual richness at the expense of strength and self-reliance. The older one, in the sanctuary of Athena at Delphi, is Doric outside but has an inner ring of proto-Corinthian columns attached to the cella wall.**3.61** The tholos in the compound of Asklepios at Epidauros is also Doric outside but inside a ring of freestanding Corinthian columns achieves the same height on a much narrower base.**3.62**

3.61a

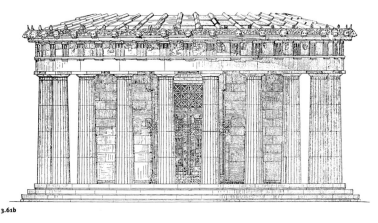

3.61b

›**3.61 DELPHI, THOLOS IN THE SANCTUARY OF ATHENA PRONAEA,** early 4th century BCE: (a) view of the ruins from the north, (b) reconstructed elevation.

Attributed to Theodoros of Phokaea, who wrote a treatise on it, the marble rotunda – 13.5 metres in diameter – consisted of a circular cella surrounded by a ring of twenty Doric columns outside and nine attached Corinthian half-columns on a raised ledge inside (the door occupied the place of the tenth). The Doric Order probably matched that of the Temple of Apollo Epikourios at Bassae, unlike the modern reconstruction which is almost certainly anachronistically elongated at 1:8.46.

The remains of an Archaic precedent for this type of

circular building were discovered in the main precinct at Delphi. Of limestone, this had an outer ring of thirteen Doric columns, to which the twenty metopes and their defining triglyphs in the frieze were evidently entirely unrelated.

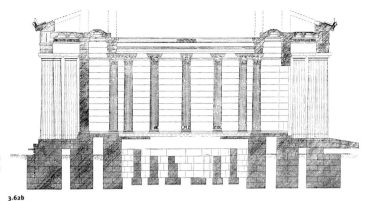

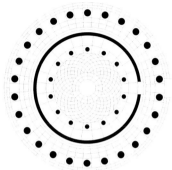

3.62a @ 1:500

**›3.62 EPIDAUROS, THOLOS IN THE SANCTU-
ARY OF ASKLEPIOS,** c. 360 BCE: (a, b) plan and section, (c) detail of surviving fragments of external and internal Orders (Epidauros Museum).

Attributed to Polykleitos the Younger by Pausanias, this was built of tufa without and marble within. On a stylobate 21.3 metres in diameter, the circular cella was ringed by twenty-six Doric columns outside and fourteen freestanding Corinthian columns inside. The Macedonians produced a variant on the theme for their dynastic shrine at Olympia, the Philippeion – it is not known how, or whether, it was roofed.

3.62b

3.62c

3.63

The column had been the main agent of support before Bassae; now it was reduced to the decorative role of articulating the forces implicit in the exercise. Fostering ambiguity between appearances and reality, this development had achieved maturity by the middle of the 4th century BCE in the temples of Zeus at Nemea and Athena Alea at Tegea.**3.63, 3.64** In both, the proportions of the external Doric Order approximated the Ionic: virility ceded to effeminacy. In both, the Corinthian interior approached maturity: structural logic ceded to ornament.**3.65**

At Nemea the internal colonnade was freestanding, as at Epidauros. At Tegea it was attached, as at Delphi, but

›**3.63** NEMEA, TEMPLE OF ZEUS, C. 340 BCE: the ruins from the south.

On a stylobate 20 by 42.6 metres (a ratio of 1:2.12) the six by twelve Doric columns were 1.63 by 10.36 metres, giving proportions of 1:6.35. The axial spacing was 3.75 metres on the front – a ratio of 2.29:1 and 1:2.76 to base diameter and column height respectively – and minutely narrower on the sides. Typical of late-Classical practice in dispensing with an opisthodomos, the plan retained a sunken adytum, which was screened from the cella, as at the Temple of Apollo Epikourios at Bassae. Most unusually, the Corinthian Order was surmounted by the Ionic.

›**3.64** TEGEA, TEMPLE OF ATHENA ALEA, c. 350 BCE (built in place of an Archaic work destroyed by fire in 394): (a) section, (b) plan.

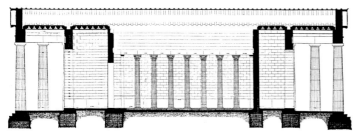

3.64a

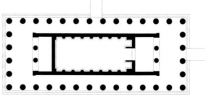

3.64b @ 1:1000

On a stylobate 19.2 by 47.5 metres (a ratio of 1:2.48) were six by fourtenn columns 1.55 by 9.47 metres, giving proportions of 1:6.11. The axial spacing was 3.61 metres on the front – a ratio of 2.33:1 and 1:2.62 to base diameter and column height respectively – and minutely narrower on the sides.

The building is attributed to the sculptor Skopas, and seems to have been commissioned to rival the nearby Temple of Apollo Epikourios at Bassae. It was typical of its time in its slender Doric proportions and combination of Orders, but not in its retention of an opisthodomos, or the extension of its sides to fourteen columns to contain the opisthodomos and accommodate a door to the cella in the centre of the northern side.

›**3.65** DEVELOPMENT OF THE CORINTHIAN CAPITAL.

on a much more significant scale than there, it marks the abrogation of the logic on which Classical lucidity was based. The very ambiguity of the situation in which column and wall were confused with one another, charging the space they enclosed with tension, elicited an emotional response against the appeal of reason.

The development of the Corinthian capital

At the Temple of Apollo Epikourios at Bassae,[3.57e] the designer – identified as Kallimachos of Corinth by Vitruvius – returned to the Egyptian lotus motif of the proto-Ionic,[3.14] combined it with the Mesopotamian palmette, and added two rows of twenty small acanthus leaves in alternation above the concave recessions and raised edges of the flutes of the column.

(1) Delphi, tholos in the sanctuary of Athena Pronaea: restoration from excavated fragments of the proto-Corinthian capitals attached to the interior of the rotunda. This permutation recalls the Order of the Temple of Apollo Epikourios at Bassae, except that the central tendrils are united with the corner ones in an 'S' scroll.

(2) Epidauros, tholos in the sanctuary of Asklepios: engraving of a model capital buried at the time of construction and recovered intact. In essence, the architect Polykleitos the Younger achieved the canonical form of the Corinthian capital here. No longer alternating in two small bands, the acanthus leaves rise to more than half the height of the bell and the tendrils spring up from behind them; there are flowers in the centre of each side.

(3) Tegea, Temple of Athena Alea: engraved restoration from excavated remains of the capitals of the half-columns attached to the cella walls. The form is related in general to the Epidaurian model, with generous acanthus foliage, but the proportions are squatter, the spiral tendrils supporting the corners of the abacus are sheathed with partially open leaves (caulicoli), and there is another leaf instead of the central spirals.

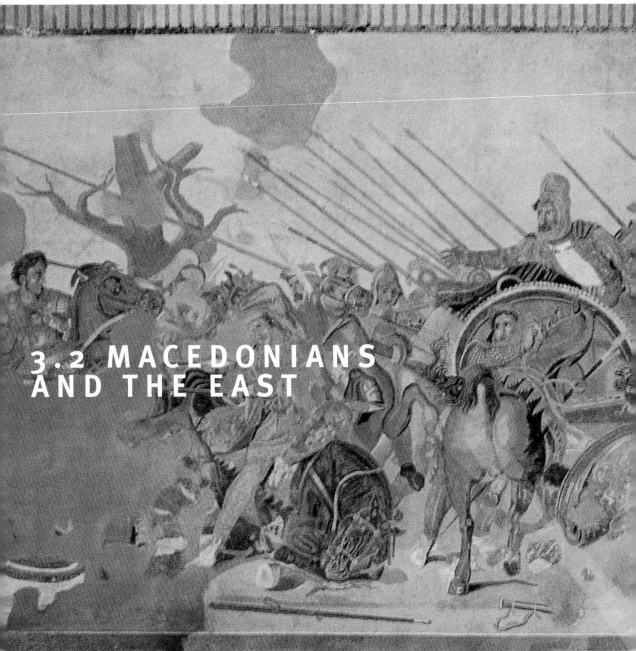

3.2 MACEDONIANS AND THE EAST

INTRODUCTION

In one of the most astonishing careers of conquest in history, Alexander of Macedon (356–323 BCE) swept through the vast Achaemenid empire bent on realizing the long-cherished Greek dream of revenge on the heirs of Darius I. Hardly twenty-three years old, he defeated the last of the 'Great Kings', Darius III, at Issus in northern Syria in 333 and, two years later, finally dispatched him at Gaugamela on the Tigris, near the ancient Assyrian capital of Nineveh.**3.66**

After ascending the Achaemenid throne and consolidating his conquest as far as the Indus, Alexander died unexpectedly in 323. His conquests were divided between his Macedonian generals. Some squabbled over Macedonia and the protection of Hellas. The pragmatic Ptolemy Soter took Egypt, which he knew to be readily defendable, and assumed the mantle of pharaoh in 306. Alexander's governor of Babylon, Seleucos Nikator, took Syria and tried to hold sway over all the territories that had been incorporated into the main body of the empire, from the borders of India to the edge of Anatolia.

The Achaemenids had held the diversified peoples of west Asia together most effectively with their great army and firm grasp of administration – under supreme Ahura Mazda and the special protection of all-seeing Mithra, god of light, defender of right, enemy of evil (sec pages 207–208). But by the mid-4th century BCE their authority amounted to little more than nominal hegemony over virtually independent monarchs – such as Maussollos of Karia. Though Alexander settled colonies of veteran soldiers throughout his conquests, Seleucid control was even less effective beyond Syria, Palestine and eastern Turkey – despite the un-Hellenic assumption of the religious aura that traditionally clothed kingship in much of the area – and the Achaemenid heartland was soon claimed by the Parthians.

Parthia first appears in inscriptions of the Achaemenid king Darius I (521–486) as a province of his Persian empire roughly equivalent to modern Khurasan. Like neighbouring Bactria, it was assigned to a Greek satrap in the new Seleucid regime and like his Bactrian neighbour the satrap of Parthia took advantage of Seleucid preoccupations in the west to declare independence about the middle of the 3rd century BCE. For most of the Seleucid era the area had been prey to incursions by great horsemen of Scythian extraction, prominent among whom, at least at the time of Parthian independence, were the Pani. One of their leaders, a chief called Arsaces, presented himself as the deliverer of his kinsmen from the Greeks and seized Parthia from the rebel satrap. Claiming descent from the Achaemenids and reviving their fire-centred cult, which the Greeks called Zoroastrian, his Arsacid dynasty was to last nearly five hundred years.

DIVINE MONARCHY

The complex problems of Alexander's successors are beyond our immediate interest, but the devices of their theologians certainly do concern us. In the world of the Greeks poised to conquer the Persians, the pantheon of Homer and Hesiod honoured throughout the Classical age of the Hellenic polis had been discredited by the catastrophe of the Peloponnesian War. State honour sustained a public role for the Olympians but in private people looked elsewhere for solutions to ethical problems. The aspiring dynast was naturally committed to seeing man in the image of the gods, but, turned about by sophists like Protagoras ('Man is the measure of all things'), gods in man's image had little to offer the growing body of intellectuals committed to scientific enquiry. Anthropomorphic mysticism was confronted by anthropocentric rationalism. Yet, as Hellenistic monarchs could not fail to

>**3.66** THE BATTLE OF ISSOS: Alexander (left) confronts Darius III (centre right), mosaic pavement from the House of the Faun, Pompeii (Naples, Archaeological Museum).

3.67a

>**3.67** MUTABLE DIVINITY: (a) Serapis (Roman bust, c. 100 CE; Rome, Vatican Museum); (b) Isis (Graeco-Roman bust, 2nd century CE; Aghios Nikolaos, Crete, Archaeological Museum).

The god bears a grain measure (modius) on his head as a symbol of his Osirid powers of fertility. The goddess bears the queen's head-dress, including the sun disc of her father and the cow horns of Hathor.

3.67b

see, increasing numbers of increasingly individualistic Hellenes at large were turning from the emotional void left by Zeus and his family – let alone Protagorean pragmatism – to fate and foreign mystery cults promising personal salvation.

Attempts had been made to endow Zeus with a sense of purpose as World Mind and with morality as Lord of Oaths. He was now to be assimilated to a variety of oriental creator-gods. In Egypt, most significantly, Ptolemaic theologians furthered the native syncretic tradition by identifying the Olympian father with Amon-Re and his brother Hades with Osiris – as whom Egyptian kings were always immortal (see page 54). Promoting a new royal cult, the new regime gave the Graeco-Egyptian deity a new anthropomorphic identity and associated the centre of his worship with the greatest library of antiquity in the new capital, Alexandria.

By the time of Ptolemy I (effective ruler of Egypt as satrap 323–306, king 306–285), Osiris was specially prominent in Lower Egypt in the circle of Ptah, the old creator-god of Memphis, centred on the compound at Saqqarah where the progenitive Apis bulls were kept in regulated succession, embalmed and entombed. There – it is thought, not without controversy – the soul of Osiris was believed to live through the unbroken Apid line and the mummified animal was identified with him in worship as Osor-Hapi. Ptolemy's theologians translated Osor-Hapi/Hades into Sarapis for their new Alexandrine cult. Ptolemy's sculptors presented Sarapis with a distinct fraternal resemblance to Zeus and the Romans were to identify Sarapis as Serapis with Jupiter.**3.67a**

As Osiris – son of the sun-god Re, the vegetation god triumphant over death – Sarapis promised salvation and naturally claimed the power of healing which the Greeks ascribed to the sun-god Apollo – son of Zeus. Just as naturally he claimed Osiris's wife and sister, Isis.**3.67b** Healer of the healing, her cult was pre-eminent in Egypt by the end of the Dynastic period and embraced that of Hathor, goddess of motherhood. Embarking with Sarapis on a new career, she in turn naturally claimed the attributes of the sister of Zeus and Hades, Demeter – heiress of the Great Mother – and with them her mysteries. After all, plants live again with her brother-husband whose reconstitution and resurrection were due to her enchanted powers.

As mother of Horus through whom divinity came to earth in pharaoh, Isis was mother of salvation. Mystic and pantheistic, indeed monotheistic in tendency, her cult was pregnant with promise for the future – here and in the life hereafter. Meanwhile, if Ptolemy became Osiris/Sarapis in the afterlife, his queen became Isis: the great Sarapeum disappeared with ancient Alexandria but it is no mere accident that the best-preserved Antique buildings in Egypt are Archaicizing Ptolemaic temples of Horus and Isis with royal birth houses.**3.68, 1.15, 1.16**

The cult of the ruler was endemic in most of the world east of Hellas and even in Hellas itself the post-Homeric tradition honoured men of exceptional achievement as comparable to the gods. What more natural in an anthropocentric state than that the king should claim such honours? Alexander seems to have become megalomaniac enough actually to believe in his own divinity. In Asia, as in Egypt, few of his successors went as far but, vulnerable as usurpers, they did legitimize themselves with divine pedigrees (including blood relationship to Alexander in the case of Ptolemy). Vicars of god in life, their tangible omnipotence – earned in victory and moral responsibility – promised more than their assumed ancestors had realized but not until they joined the line in death do they seem actually to have been worshipped.

›**3.68 HARPOCRATES:** Ptolemaic bronze (Alexandria, Greco-Roman Museum).

A Greek identification of 'Horus the Child' originally depicted as an infant with a finger in his mouth but the god here is the quintessential Hellenistic icon of youthful royalty. Son of Isis and Osiris, avenger of his father, by the end of the New Kingdom he was central to the rebirth or resurrection aspect of the fertility cult and manifest in the sun rising through the first two hours of the day. He was thus of obvious relevance to the new king – Phaoronic and Ptolemaic.

TRANSFORMATION OF THE HELLENIC IDEAL

The term 'Hellenistic' has been coined for the hybrid art forged from the cross-fertilization of Hellenic and Asian ideals under Alexander and his heirs. The cultural consequences of the triumph of the Macedonians over the Achaemenids were profound, of course, yet the influence of oriental attitudes on Ionia had been formative and the importation of Greek ideals into Asia goes back at least to Cyrus the Great.

The appeal to emotion rather than reason through the manipulation of form and scale and the promotion of oriental splendour was a major motive behind the evolution of art in the generation – and more - before Alexander's conquest of Persia. It ultimately promoted the style of sensational theatricality later to be identified as Baroque. First, however, late-Classical masters proved themselves adept at anticipating what was to be called Mannerism: virtuosity of invention in ornament and the wilful flouting of convention – hence expectation. Thus they intermixed the elements of the Orders and, above all, wilfully confused the roles of column and wall by denying the independent virility of the former and reducing it to a mere agent articulating the forces implicit in the latter. Mannerism was to prove perennially popular at royal courts and Baroque well served the superstate.

Long before the accession of Alexander, even before Dorian logic and lucidity were being flouted at Tegea, a new dimension of lavishness celebrated the self-inflicted ruin of the polis. This had always been to the taste of the more sensual Ionians.**3.69** Now it was manifest in the elevation of the Persian emperor's servants in Ionia, such as Maussollos, Satrap of Karia.**3.70** Beyond the central importance that man had always had in Hellenic culture, men thus asserted their own importance as autocrats in a

›**3.69 (PAGES 460–461) SARDIS, TEMPLE OF ARTEMIS-KYBELE,** begun c. 360 BCE (in place of its predecessor, destroyed in 497), but left unfinished.

On a stylobate 45.7 by 99 metres (a ratio of 1:2.17) was an outer pteron of eight by twenty columns, on average 1.9 by 17.73 metres, giving proportions of 1:9.31. Within the pteron, both pronaos and opisthodomos were given prostyle tetrastyle porticoes. The cella floor was raised above the level of the pronaos. The opisthodomos opened into a vestibule, beyond which was an adytum.

The largest columns erected in their time, those of the outer pteron had plinths and bases of scotia and torus mouldings conforming to the Ionian norm but with varied embellishment to the torus. Most of them were never fluted. Two each of the pronaos and opisthodomos columns were smaller than the rest since they stood on square pedestals which were apparently meant to be sculpted in emulation of the embellishment to the lower drums of the columns at the Artemiseion in Ephesos. The capitals were embellished with acanthus scrolls or the Mesopotamian palmette in concession to Persian taste (as Dinsmoor plausibly speculates).

way that the Hellenes had rejected before emerging from their Heroic period. Their gods were conceived in ideal human terms, of course, even to scale: they might occasionally be represented as overwhelming in size – like Zeus at Olympia or Athena on the Athenian Acropolis – but the assertion of the superiority of an individual man over other men had not been a theme of Hellenic art. Colossal building was uncommon too, except occasionally in the colonies and in Asia Minor where oriental magnificence had always been an inspiration. With the eclipse of the polis – and the emasculation of the Doric Order – the Dorian had had its day and the Hellenistic age of the Macedonian was to issue from the cross-fertilization of the Ionian and the Persian.

TOMBS AND MONUMENTS

The Greeks had traditionally honoured their dead – especially if victorious at the games or in the field of battle – with stelae representing them in the niches of necropolae.**3.71** As the 5th century BCE progressed towards the apogee of Classicism, this was often to be framed by a miniature temple front consisting simply of a pair of columns or pilasters supporting a pediment (known subsequently as an aedicule after the Latin *aedicula*, 'little house'). Symptomatic of the cult and magnification of personality in the Ionian world of the 4th century BCE was the emulation of foreigners – Persians rather than Egyptian initially – in the conception of the tomb as a monumental structure on a substantial base. The type achieved its apotheosis for Maussollos of Karia at Halikarnassos. Its ascent may be traced in Xanthos, capital of neighbouring Lykia, the southern Anatolian state that lost its independence to the Persians in 545 BCE.

Like many other peoples, the Lykians first carved tombs in the shape of their houses either in the rock-face of cliffs

›**3.70 MAUSSOLLOS OF HALIKARNASSOS,** Satrap of Karia, statue from his mausoleum, after 353 BCE (London, British Museum).

Identification is conjectural and not without controversy: in favour is the expressively individualized portraiture not shared by the other dynastic heads recovered from the site – though these represent only a fraction of the original corpus. Attribution is also controversial: Skopas is known to have worked on the monument and his was perhaps the most-celebrated talent of the time – especially for expressive naturalism – but this statue was found in a position related to the north front of the mausoleum where Bryaxis is reputed to have been in control.

›**3.71 ATHENIAN FUNERAL STELE,** late-5th century BCE (London, British Museum).

3.71

3.72a

›3.72 LYKIAN FUNERARY MONUMENTS: (a) house type on pillar (early 4th century BCE, Xanthos); (b) rock-cut tombs in the form of a house and of temples distyle in antis (early 4th century BCE, Telmessos); (c) temple type named for the maidens in the simulated Ionic pteron (Istanbul, National Archaeological Museum); (d) temple derivative named for the Erotes which act as caryatids in place of pteron columns (Side, Archaeological Museum).

3.72c

3.72d

3.72b

or freestanding on rectangular pillars. Probably after the example of the Tomb of Cyrus the Great at Pasagardae, the pillar gave way to the stepped podium and, in deference to the Greeks on the other hand, the sarcophagus shed the image of the house in favour of the temple. Rock-cut examples at Xanthos are echoed elsewhere and miniature freestanding temples abound.**3.72**

3·73

The rock-cut precedent set by the Achaemenid tombs at Persepolis can hardly be without significance for the works at Telmessos.

›3.73 XANTHOS, LYKIA, SO-CALLED NEREID MONUMENT, c. 410 BCE: view of reconstruction (London, British Museum).

The small temple on its podium was a development of the traditional Lykian reproduction of a portable timber coffin as a sarcophagus with a gabled lid raised from the ground on a high rectangular base. In addition to statues of Nereids between the columns there were four friezes – two on the podium, another around the cella and the fourth on the architrave.

The first major manifestation of the impact abroad of the standard of the Ionic style established on the Athenian Acropolis under Perikles, the miniature temple's Order has capitals and entablature recalling respectively those of the Erechtheion's north porch and the porch of the caryatids, and the coffered ceiling is modelled on that of the Propylaea.

Xanthos also set the precedent – as far as the accidents of survival testify – for the substitution of a complete temple for the traditional house-type sarcophagus on a substantial podium around 400 BCE. Doubtless dedicated to a ruler, this is known as the Nereid Monument because of the seaborne female figures in flowing drapery that occupied the intercolumniations.**3·73**

The type proved readily exportable, reduced in scale to the sarcophagus.**3·74, 3·72d** However, its apotheosis was achieved in the middle of the 4th century BCE for Maussollos of Halikarnassos. Built to assert the pretensions of the former Satrap of Karia, its reconstruction is controversial but to the temple on its elevated podium was certainly added the most potent image of royal immortality, the pyramid.**3·75**

›3.74 THE 'ALEXANDER SARCOPHAGUS', late-4th century BCE, from the royal necropolis of Sidon (Istanbul Archaeological Museum).

The reliefs, executed by a follower of Lysippus, portray hunting and warfare, specifically the Battle of Issos. The work – which does not always give the upper hand to the Macedonians – was probably executed for the Persian nobleman Abdalonymus who was confirmed as Satrap of Sidon by Alexander after his defeat of Darius III in 333.

›3.75 HALIKARNASSOS, THE TOMB OF MAUSSOLLOS ('Mausoleion'), 353 BCE: model (Istanbul, Miniaturk).

The Tomb of Maussollos

Attributed by followers of Vitruvius to Pytheos of Priene, in association with Skopas and others, the building's reconstruction on the basis of Antique descriptions (by Vitruvius and Pliny) is still controversial. Pliny divides the elevation into four parts: podium, peristyle, pyramid and crowning statue group with a four-horse chariot (quadriga). He gives the perimeter as 440 Ionic feet (129.3 metres), the total height as 140 Ionic feet (41.1 metres), the height of the pteron of thirty-six columns as 37.5 Ionic feet (11 metres) and the height of the pyramid of twenty-four steps as equal to that of the element below it – leaving the remaining 65 Ionic feet (19.1 metres) to be divided between the podium and the quadriga group (if the element below the pyramid is taken to be the pteron alone). Modern excavation has defined the base as 32 by 26 metres.

As Dinsmoor reveals, the main problems of reconstruction arise with the distribution of the columns, the definition of the relative height of column and entablature, the disposition of the friezes, fragments of which were recovered from the site, and the dimensions of the base of the pyramid in relation to (and possible support by) either the pteron or the cella.

However it is reconstructed, the Mausoleion represents the final per-mutation of the Lykian tomb. With its temple-like structure on a high podium, the Nereid Monument represents the penultimate phase late in the 5th century BCE. It was perfection of the formula by Pythios and his collaborators that earned the Mausoleion its reputation and Maussollos the association of his name with the monumental tomb forever.

›**3.76 KNIDOS, SO-CALLED LION TOMB,** mid-4th century BCE: reconstruction.

›**3.77 SAMOTHRACE, ARSINOEION:** after 270 BCE: reconstruction.

The Arsinoeion at Samothrace represents an inverted variant on the Halikarnasson theme: a cylin-der some 20 metres in diameter, it had a raised inter-nal Corinthian colonnade attached to external Doric piers. Emulating the Phillippeion at Olympia, the building commemorates Queen Arsinoe of Egypt, wife and sister of Ptolemy II, patroness of the Phrygian Cabiri deities of Samothrace venerated by sailors: she was associated with the cult after her deification as a manifestation of Isis on her death in 270.

›**3.78 VERGINA, TOMB OF PHILIP II OF MACEDON,** C. 340 BCE.

›**3.79 ATHENS, CHORAGIC MONUMENT OF LYSIKRATES,** 334 BCE.

Among many types of commemorative or votive monument erected in or on the way to sacred sites, trophies won in choragic contests in the theatre were usually set up on a pedestal in the sanctuary of

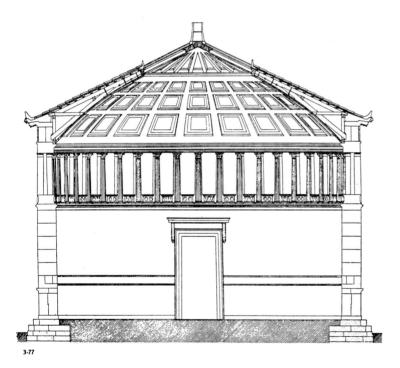

3·77

Dionysos or the street leading to it. Superseding simple podia, in the 4th century BCE several of them took the form of miniature tholoi, most notably the one erected by Lysikrates to display the trophy he won in the contest of 334. Set on a square podium of limestone and circular stepped stylobate of blue marble, the rotunda of white marble is ringed by six Corinthian columns engaged to the cylindrical core. The capitals seem overwrought, the acanthus leaves rising out of rushes, with tendrils not growing naturally from them but improbably joined into a heart-shaped form semi-detached from them. For the first time in an external context, the Order is given a full entablature with both sculpted frieze and dentils.

3.78

3.79

Many rulers copied the Mausoleion at various scales. Perhaps the best surviving example, with a pyramid above its Corinthian colonnade, is the 'Lion Tomb' of Knidos but the lost Philippeion of Olympia and Arsinoeum of Samothrace (c. 270) were influential inverted variants on the theme.**3.76, 3.77** Otherwise, various tomb types remained popular in the Hellenistic period, including the tumulus and the catacomb: among the latter those of Alexandria include examples from the 2nd century modelled on the domestic peristyle; the most important examples of the former include the temple-fronted, vaulted burial chambers of 4th-century Macedonian rulers.**3.78**

In the superhuman size of Maussollos's statue, as in the conception of his tomb as a whole, the celebration of irresponsible mastery was characteristic of a civilization whose faith in man, his polis and its gods had ceded to the realities of this world. And in the most eminent of old polities, Athens, even a chorus master is honoured in a manner comparable in form if not scale: a tholos on a substantial podium, the monument to Lysikrates – victor of a choral contest in 334 – is a variant of the formula adapted to the Nereid Monument at Xanthos. Applying Corinthian columns to the exterior of his tholos, moreover, the architect took the final step in exposing the structural pretensions of the Order as facile in that context.**3.79**

3.80a

IONIC APOTHEOSIS

Viewed from Sardis, the former capital of Lydia from
which the Persians ruled Ionia again after 387 BCE when
the Great King imposed his peace on the exhausted Hellenes, new prosperity recalled the age of Kroesos in lavish
building – not least in the rebuilding of the Artemiseion
at Sardis itself. Palaces and civic amenities received more
attention than in the golden age of the polis but so vast
were the temples founded in Ionia at the time that most
of them were beyond completion even after centuries of
effort. Conservative in planning, if sometimes free with
the conventions of the Orders, they emulated the Temple
of Artemis at Ephesos, which was itself being rebuilt c.
330 BCE following a fire in 356.**3.80**

Apart from Samos and Ephesos – and Sardis – Didyma
and Magnesia are the outstanding Ionian sites. Characteristically, the only comparable undertaking in mainland
Greece is Athenian: the Temple of Zeus below the Acrop-

3.80b

3.80c

›3.80 EPHESOS, TEMPLE OF ARTEMIS: (a)
model (Istanbul, Miniaturk); (b, c) capital and base
from c. 330.

Built of marble but now a mere platform supporting
one column and rubble, the new temple had a higher

platform than the old (51.4 by 111.5 metres) but evidently a similar plan – though perhaps without the third row of columns east. Rising to 60 Ionic feet (17.65 metres), the columns were reputedly higher than their predecessors, with uniform diameters of 1.84 metres (producing the proportion of 9.6:1) and all had twenty-four flutes. Bases were of the usual Ionian type with scotias and a torus, and they were set on plinths. After the rebuilding, there were still thirty-six sculpted base drums, some square, some round. The earlier expansiveness of volute was reduced in the mid-4th-century capitals to accord with a near-square abacus. The architects are recorded as Paionius of Ephesos and Demetrios, 'the slave of the temple'.

>**3.81** DIDYMA, TEMPLE OF APOLLO, begun c. 313 BCE: (a) reconstructed perspective view, (b, pages 470–471) exterior of ruins, (c) pteron bases, (d) interior of ruins, (e) plan, (f) detail of cella pilaster capital.

On a stylobate of 51.1 by 109.3 metres, ten by twenty-one columns of 2 metres at base and 19.7 metres high (giving a ratio of 1:9.7) were set 5.3 metres apart.

olis to the south-east. As at Ephesos and Samos, little remains above the foundations of the Temple of Artemis Leukophryene at Magnesia, under construction c. 150 BCE, but the ruins of the Temple of Apollo at Didyma, begun in 313 BCE, are truly spectacular.**3.81**

The Temple of Apollo at Didyma

Built to the plans of Paionius of Ephesos and Daphnis of Miletos in replacement of an Archaic temple destroyed by Darius I in 494 BCE, work dragged on for several hundred years, but was left incomplete. It was excelled in superficial area by the Artemiseion at Ephesos but by few other Greek temples. Like the Artemiseion, it was dipteral but the outer pteron was unique in having ten by twenty-one columns. An antechamber was inserted between the generous pronaos and elongated cella and the opisthodomos was omitted.

The columns are not known to have been exceeded in height or slenderness by any other significant Hellenic work. The bases were

3.81a

exceptionally varied, most conforming to the Asian norm with scotias and torus, but several on the front had circular or polygonal blocks. Several capitals (possibly executed under the Attalids of Pergamon in the first half of the 2nd century BCE, or even later under the Romans) had busts of gods or animals entwined by the volutes. Medusa heads emerged from the acanthus foliage of the frieze inserted (also probably by the Attalids) in the entablature below the bold dentils. The pediments were never executed.

With double porticoes of ten columns (dipteral decastyle), the vast structure at Didyma remained unroofed – indeed, it contained a grove of trees. At base level some 4 metres below the antechamber and screened from it by piers with attached Corinthian columns, this was reached from the north-east by a grand flight of steps on axis with a small prostyle hexastyle Ionic shrine housing the Archaic statue of Apollo salvaged from the original temple. The inner walls, conceived on a scale unprecedented except in the aberrant Temple of Zeus at Acragas,[3.26] are relieved with pilasters whose uncanonical capitals were linked by a continuous frieze. Derived from the ante that had terminated portico walls from early Archaic times, the buttress-like pilaster was to be the standard form adopted to limit the ambiguity implicit in confronting an Order with a wall.

3.81d

3.81c

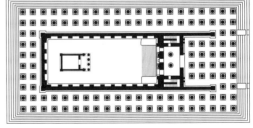

3.81e @1:2000

3.81f

There were, of course, many smaller temples commissioned in the late-Classical era in Asia Minor and beyond in the Hellenistic world: it is rare that more than the foundations and a few columns remain. One of the most significant is the Temple of Athena Polias at Priene dedicated by Alexander in 334 BCE. Its architect, Pytheos, who served Maussollos at Halikarnassos, did more than anyone other than his Ephesian contemporary Paionius to establish a canon for the Ionic Order: an account of the Mausoleion, which he wrote in collaboration with his principal colleagues there, is now lost but his treatise on the Priene temple survives in fragments quoted by Vitruvius.**3.82**

The west front of Pytheos's temple was completed – or rebuilt – by Hermogenes of Priene just before the middle of the 2nd century BCE. Hermogenes codified the rules for Pytheos's Order and based his own system of ideal proportions on density, relating the diameter and height of the column to the width of the intercol-umniation in five gradations – the wider the spacing of the columns, the lighter the entablature in weight and proportions. Hermogenes's principal work was the Artemeseion at

›3.82 PRIENE, TEMPLE OF ATHENA POLIAS, c. 340 BCE: view of remains.

On a base 19.5 by 37 metres (a ratio of 1:1.9), there were six by eleven columns of 1.3 by 11.4 metres, giving proportions of 1:8.84. The rectangle defined by the columns' centres was 60 by 120 Ionic feet (17.6 by 35.2 metres). The rectangle defined by the walls enclosing the cella, elongated pronaos and truncated opistho-domos was 40 by 100 Ionic feet (11.75 by 29.38 metres). Above square plinths, the bases of the columns – 6 Ionic feet (1.76 metres) square and 6 apart, giving interaxial spacing of 12 Ionic feet (3.5 metres) – had a torus over superimposed scotias as usual in Ionia. The volutes of the capitals were joined by the traditional downward-curving line, but the columns at the inner corners had contracted whole volutes. As usual in Ionia, there were heavy dentils but no frieze.

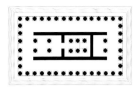

3.83a @ 1:2000

›**3.83** **MAGNESIA ON THE MAEANDER,
TEMPLE OF ARTEMIS LEUCOPHRYENE**, C. 150
BCE: (a) plan, (b) restored elevation.

On a stylobate 41 by 67 metres, eight by fifteen
columns were 1.4 metres in diameter at their base but
of unknown height. Except in the wider central intercolumniation of each end, the relationship between
the diameter of the columns at base and their interaxial spacing was in a ratio between 1:3 and 1:4,
approximating the proportions of 1:3.25 (that is
Hermogenes' preferred eustyle mean between the
heavier systyle and lighter diastyle in his range of five
systems). The height of the columns is estimated to
have been 9.5 times their diameters at base, which
Vitruvius quotes Hermogenes as recommending for
eustyle.

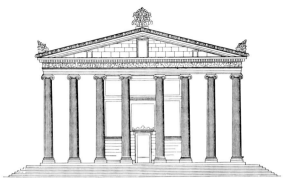

3.83b

Magnesia, which seems to precede the definition of his
theories.**3.83**

Vitruvius drew heavily on Hermogenes too, transmit-
ting his system to posterity, and quotes him as the source
for the statement that 'sacred buildings ought not to be
constructed of the Doric Order because faults and incon-
gruities were caused by the laws of its symmetry'. Doric
was certainly still used for temples in the Hellenistic
period but it was rare. The problems of Doric rigidity
apart, rich free-flowing ornament naturally complemented great scale in the Ionian world.

Still richer and more elegant than its Ionic parent, and
unproblematical at corners, the Corinthian Order was to
become the most popular with Hellenistic patrons. In
Egypt the Ptolemies usually sustained the ancient Egyptian tradition except in domestic buildings and their imitation in tombs.**1.15,1.16** For Macedonians seeking to supplant
the late lavish Achaemenids, however, the richest of the
Classical Orders was indispensable: Seleukos Nikator first
promoted it to the exterior of a temple for Zeus Olbius at
Diocaesarea in Cilicia early in the 3rd century BCE.

The apotheosis of the Corinthian Order came with
Antiochos IV's commission of c. 175 for the completion of
the great Athenian Olympeion. The largest temple in the
Greek mainland, it was founded in the late-Archaic period

3.84a

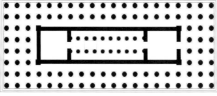

3.84b @ 1:2000

›3.84 ATHENS, TEMPLE OF ZEUS OLYMPIOS, 2nd century BCE and later: (a) view from the south, (b) plan, (c) Corinthian capital.

Founded by the heirs of Peisistratos c. 520 BCE, re-begun under Antiochos IV in 174 to the design of Cossutius (a Roman citizen probably of Greek origin), this huge work was completed and dedicated under Hadrian in 132 CE. On a stylobate 41.11 by 107.9 metres (a ratio of 1:2.62), were eight by twenty columns 1.93 by 16.9 metres, giving proportions of 1:8.81, in the outer pteron, and six by eighteen columns in the inner pteron. The pronaos was walled (with no columns in antis) and balanced to the east of the cella by an ady-

in Doric but not far advanced when work was interrupted by the Persians. Its Hellenistic style marks the full maturity of the Order first encountered at Bassae some two hundred and fifty years earlier.**3.84**

tum in place of an opisthodomos. According to Vitruvius, the cella was unroofed, and it is probable that the columns originally designed to support a roof were those taken to Rome by Sulla in 86 BCE to be incorporated in the rehabilitation of the Temple of Jupiter Capitolinus.

Cossutius's design for the Corinthian capitals marks the full maturity of the type, with the proportions of those in the tholos in the sanctuary of Asklepios in Epidauros (c. 360 BCE) combined with the caulicolus introduced at the Temple of Athena Alea at Tegea (c. 350 BCE). Here, spiral fronds curved to the sides and the centre, as at Epidauros, and each pair sprang from a single caulicolus out of higher acanthus leaves than at Tegea.

3.84c

3.85a

6 LATE-CLASSICAL PLANNING AND DEFENCE

In the time-honoured way of the colonizer, the imposition
of a grid to discipline the rebuilding of devastated cities or
the development of new sites was common in the Hellenistic period. After the particular approach credited to
Hippodamos, zones were defined by major arteries and a
grid of secondary streets formed the blocks of the residential quarters. Refounded on a new site below a high
acropolis in the middle of the 4th century BCE, Priene is
the outstanding example extensively preserved.**3.85**

The public buildings were still not axially aligned
within the grid but, as at Priene and even in the originally organic context of Athens, the framing of ever-
more-extensive agoras with grand stoas was a regular
feature of Hellenistic towns. Colonnades were gradually

>**3.85 PRIENE:** (a) site view from west, (b) site plan with the acropolis, top, and the palaestra, bottom; (c) monumental arch, c. 150 BCE; (d) detail plan of central area with (1) Temple of Athena Polias, (2) theatre, (3) ecclesiasterion, (4) agora, with its regular perimeter of stoas at the intersection of the two main streets, and a secondary east–west artery diverted behind the southern stoa, (5) monumental arch.

The grid of streets (east–west) and stepped alleys (north–south) formed blocks of 120 by 160 Ionic feet (35.4 by 47.2 metres), which enforced regularity across, and largely against, the contours. The line of the perimeter defences, by contrast, followed nature as far as possible.

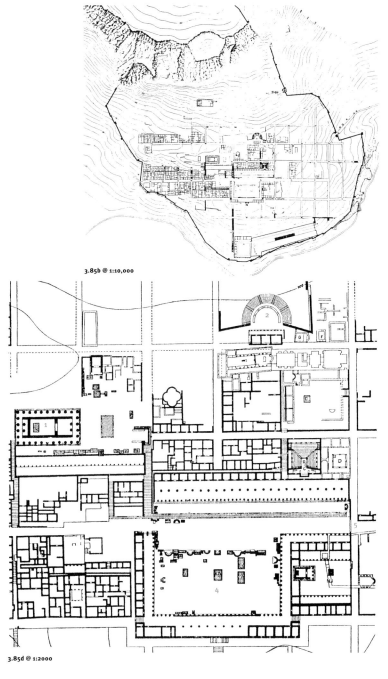

3.85b @ 1:10,000

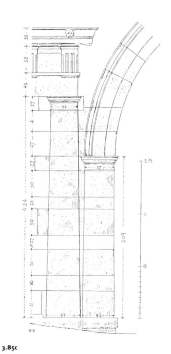

3.85c

3.85d @ 1:2000

3.86a

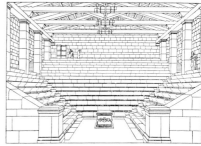

x3.86b

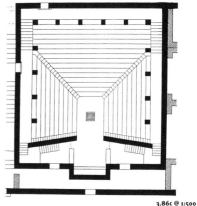

3.86c @ 1:500

extended along the main arteries of the many new towns built or rebuilt to regular plans by Alexander and his Seleucid successors as bases for Hellenization throughout their domains. Sometimes of two storeys and usually backed by shops or other public facilities, they protected the pedestrian and, providing a context for civic process, formed the most consistently magnificent streets the world had ever seen. Spanning the eastern entrance to the agora at Priene was a freestanding semi-circular Ionic architrave buttressed by the adjacent stoa walls: extracted from its natural context in defence walls, here perhaps for the first time in Greek architecture, the monumental arch would provide the Romans with their major motif of triumph.

The central role in Priene's grid is taken by the seat of the town's governing body, the discreet block of the Ecclesiasterion. Like the late-5th-century bouleterion (council chamber) of Athens, this had seats arranged on three sides of an altar before the speaker's platform. A prominent arch in the wall behind this platform was apparently original. The reconstruction of the roof over the main space with a triangular truss is conjectural.**3.86**

›3.86 PRIENE, ECCLESIASTERION (HOUSE OF ASSEMBLY): (a) view from the north, (b) reconstructed interior, (c) plan.

Within a rectangle 18.3 by 20.1 metres,some seven hundred seats were arranged on three sides of an altar before the speaker's platform. The seating was supported by the sloping ground. Entrance to the lower gallery, behind the speaker's platform, was from the level of the agora; entrance to the upper gallery was from the street below the temple platform.

›3.87 PRIENE, THEATRE, c. 300 BCE and later: view from the north-east.

In conformity with the example of the Theatre of Dionysos at Athens – extended in the mid-4th century BCE and given a temporary stage soon after – the theatre at Priene marks the maturity of the type. Permanent timber stages seem first to have appeared at provincial centres possibly late in the 4th century. The earliest stone ones were several generations later. The

3.87

stage was usually raised on a Doric colonnade representing a palace – 2.7 metres high at Priene – and
backed by a gallery (episcenia) that could be screened
with scenery or used for interior sets. Classical plays
with limited action were probably performed in the
orchestra against the background of the colonnade,
while the raised stage was designed to cater for complex modern plays. The city fathers would have sat in
the semi-circle of chairs in the front row.

›**3.88 EPIDAUROS, THEATRE,** attributed by Pausanias to Polykleitos the Younger and therefore sometimes dated to the mid-4th century BCE, but probably
built at the beginning of the 3rd century: (a) overview,
(b) plan.

From the pure circle of the orchestra, 20.4 metres in
diameter, the auditorium's semi-circular banks of seats
fan out on a radius of 59 metres asserted by the stairways. There is a gangway at base level, serving the spe-

THE THEATRE

Retaining the traditional semi-circular banked seating on
a curved sloping site,**3.44ᵇ** Priene's theatre is one of the earliest known to have had a stage building (skene). This was
the starting point for the development of the stage as we
know it, with the backdrop for scenery rather than a view
of the natural environment.**3.87** Classical plays with limited action were probably performed in the orchestra
(originally the dancing place), against the background of
the colonnade, while the raised stage was most plausibly
designed to cater for complex modern plays. The most perfect surviving example of this type of theatre, developed
to accommodate the wide range of individual characters
introduced when tragedy was supplemented by comedy, is
the contemporary theatre at Epidauros.**3.88**

3.88a

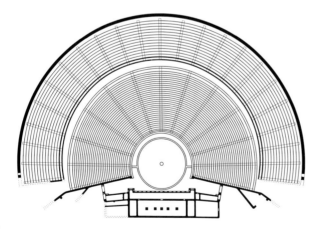

3.88b @ 1:1500

cial inner ring of seats for dignitaries, and another somewhat more than half-way up. Double the size of Priene's theatre, the seating capacity was twelve thousand. As at Priene, the only departure from true concentricity was the slight splaying of the segments of seating beyond the base diameter of the auditorium's semi-circle to limit the degree to which they turn back upon the stage.

The original stage building seems to have contained a hall – 19.5 by 6.1 metres – with parascenia framing a narrow timber stage before it. The fully developed stage seems to have been raised on fourteen piers with attached Ionic half-columns 2.4 metres high. Access to the raised stage was provided by ramps on each side. Sometimes the permanent stage cut into the orchestra, but here, as at Priene, it was built far enough back to preserve a pure circle.

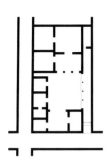

3.89a @ 1:1000

›3.89 HELLENIC HOUSING, 3RD CENTURY BCE: (a) Priene, plan; (b) Delos, plan; (c) Kos, domestic court with megaron and impluvium.

The blocks in the more affluent quarters at Priene were divided into plots of 60 by 80 Ionic feet (17.6 by 23.5 metres), elongated north–south. The entrance, always to the side and opening into a colonnaded passage, was from the north or south, according to the position of the plot in the block. In the 2nd century BCE several houses at Priene, including this one, were renovated with a complete peristyle surrounding the court as in the more lavish houses of Delos. There was usually a sunken trough (impluvium) in the centre of the peristyle and a rainwater cistern below fed from the roof through a pipe in one of the columns. Covered drainage channels led out to the extensive network of street drains.

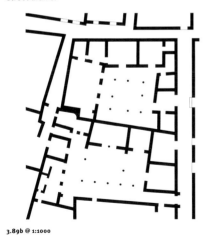

3.89b @ 1:1000

3.89c

HOUSING

Priene also provides important examples of 3rd-century BCE houses. The reconstruction of one excavated just to the west of the main temple – presumably a zone for the affluent – shows the entrance opening into a side passage that flanks the central court, preserving its privacy from the view of the street. As at Tiryns, the courtyard is roughly square with the patron's megaron dominating the main block to the north and smaller rooms for the rest of the family and service on the other sides.

Most late-Classical houses were built to similar plans, though not necessarily with a clearly differentiated megaron. Light and air were drawn from the court as the outer walls were largely blind except where they were relieved by the occasional shop. Thus, though often regular, the streets of the domestic quarters were little more than corridors for communication and drainage – as they had always been.**3.89, 3.90**

3.90

<figure>
›**3.90 DELOS:** overview with 2nd-century BCE residential district in the foreground.
</figure>

3.91

DEFENCE

Thick high walls punctuated occasionally with towers providing cover for the recessed wall face are as old as the town they were required to defend.**1.99c** And, naturally, they immediately provoked the development of means to overcome or undermine them in siege warfare: scaling towers on the one hand, battering rams, sapping and mining on the other.**3.91** An elevated site on a bed of rock – an acropolis in Greece, as at Mycenae**1.84** – was the most natural defence against all known techniques. Irregularity of plan was dictated by the contours of the site and was exploited to proved maximum embarrassment to a would-be invader by forcing him repeatedly to expose his unshielded right flank at sharp angled turns in the line of approach through narrow, barred, canyon-like corridors – as at Tiryns.**1.87**

For a millennium after the heroic age of Tiryns and Mycenae, Greek fortifications advanced little in form and incorporated mud-brick as well as stone since few of the city states that had emerged by the early 5th century BCE could afford the resources for the sophisticated siege

›**3.91 SIEGE-WARFARE DEVICES:** ram, catapult and tower.

warfare which might have stimulated development – hence their vulnerability to the Persians.

The intervention of the Persians actually discouraged walling in much of Greece – as it was rarely proof against the enemy and usually served to secure his conquests – and advance had to wait till prompted by the sieges of the Peloponnesian Wars. The most notable product was the system linking Athens and its port at Piraeus with a walled corridor nearly 6.5 kilometres long, but that was destroyed in the Spartan triumph. The most notable survivor is the key element in the system first devised to protect Syracuse from Athenian aggression.**3.92**

The Syracusan castle of Eurialos

Begun under the tyrant Dionysos I (405–367 BCE) on an eminence that can hardly be described as an acropolis, the castle of Eurialos projects from

3.90a

3.92b

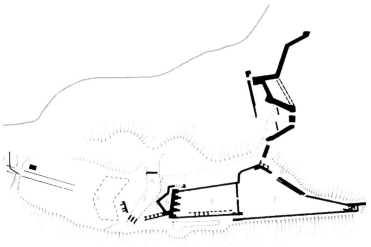

3.92c @ 1:4000

›3.92 SYRACUSE, CASTLE OF EURIALOS, 4th century BCE and later: (a) trench between outworks, (b) northern gate, (c) plan with (1–3) outer, middle and inner ditches, (4) access to subterranean galleries, (5) five-towered keep, (6) inner ward, (7) outer ward, (8) northern gate at junction of outer defences, (d, pages 488–487) view from over inner ward to five-towered keep.

Begun under the tyrant Dionysos I (405–367), the first of several campaigns of work included the three ditches excavated from the elevated rocky ridge. Amplification of the inner wards followed under Agathokles (317–289).

the town walls along a rocky salient like a dart to protect the landward approach to Syracuse. The system had innumerable precedents and successors on seaside sites; indeed, the integration of a high citadel with a ring of walls is ubiquitous and well represented at landlocked Priene where there are substantial surviving sections serrated in the ancient Trojan manner.[1.85]

In an exceptionally well-developed demonstration of defence in depth, the first of several campaigns of work at Syracuse divided the rocky salient into walled wards for massed troop encampment, protected by three ditches backed by salient ramparts. These were joined to the perimeter walls with rectangular towers and were dominated by a massive five-part inner tower from which the defenders could cover the line of approach to the first ditch, not only with archery but above all with weapons capable of throwing large missiles.

The inner wards were amplified under the usurper Agathokles (317–289). A campaign of work on renovating and strengthening the walls was begun late in the 3rd century by Archimedes, who also applied his knowledge of torsion to the development of a more efficient catapult for the city's defenders. This last phase was not far enough advanced to prevent the city falling to the Romans in 212 BCE.

Most Greek urban defences, like most of the walls of Syracuse, have disappeared with the settlement they were built to protect or under its later development – for which they usually provided invaluable quarries. Assos, on the southern coast of the Troad in north-west Turkey, is an outstanding exception: its high acropolis, overlooking sea and land, retains the most complete ramparts of the ancient Greek world and much of the city wall, largely 4th century bce but incorporating some Archaic work, survives too. Of great significance, in addition to the relatively regular sequence of the traditional rectangular flanking towers and splendid twin-towered gates, is the projection of semi-circular bastions in the most exposed positions: circular structures are inherently more coherent than rectangular ones, hence more difficult to undermine, their curved surfaces deflect shot and the circular plane of their platforms provided for easier manoeuvrability of large ballistic weapons.**3.93** The round tower would play a major role in defence for as long as man ringed himself in stone.

›3.93 ASSOS, FORTIFICATIONS: late-4th century BCE and later.

Round towers capable of mounting significant ballistic weapons were generally raised higher than the walls to provide the defenders with greater range than their ground-based opponents. The upper level might be a roofed chamber (casemate) for the protection of the machine and its operators against missiles and weather.

3.94a

PERGAMON

Occupied by Alexander, Karia was absorbed into the Seleucid empire with most of Asia Minor – not without the opposition of the Ptolemies. In the late-260s BCE the north-western province of Pergamon asserted its independence under its elderly governor's energetic nephew, Attalos. Having repulsed an invasion of Celtish tribes ('Gauls') and defeated the Seleucids in league with them, Attalos went on to take Karia and proclaim himself king over most of Ionia. His dynasty dominated the area until the last of them bequeathed his kingdom to the Romans in 133.

The Attalids exploited the natural contours of a splendid site in developing their seat at Pergamon. The acropolis was crowned by a series of terraces containing the major public and cult buildings – among the most magnificent in the whole of Antiquity and certainly a textbook example of Greek planning. The terraces fan out as they ascend the curved hill around the theatre, whose pivotal orchestra draws the composition together.

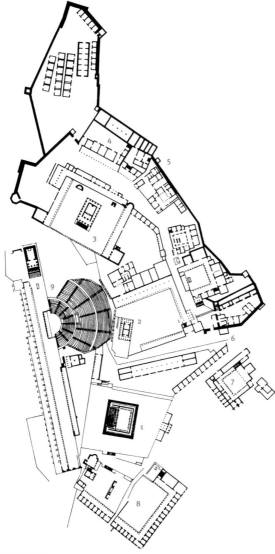

›3.94 PERGAMON, ACROPOLIS, developed under Attalos I and Eumenes II (whose reigns spanned from 241 to 159 BCE): (a) view from Asklepion, (b) plan with (1) lower terrace with Great Altar of Zeus, (2) middle terrace with Temple of Athena Polias and its precinct, (3) upper terrace with the Temple of Trajan on the site of the main Attalid palace, (4) barracks, (5) grand peristyle houses for principal members of the royal entourage, (6) citadel gate, (7) Heroum, the palatial shrine of the deified kings, (8) agora, (9) theatre and sanctuary of Dionysos, (c) model; (d, e) Altar of Zeus, model and view of the north wing (Berlin, Pergamon Museum).

The residential quarters were ranged down the southern slope of the hill towards the main agora and sanctuary of Demeter. Further settlement was associated with a sanctuary of Asklepios on the plain below.

The way the terraces are related to one another is no less significant and the middle one, at least, was carried on arcades of a monumentality unprecedented in Greek architecture.**3.94**

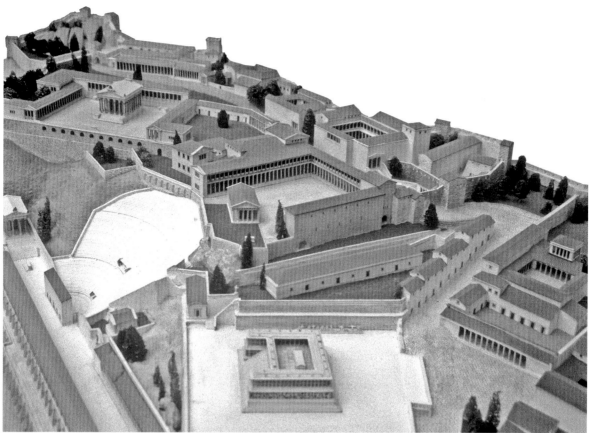

3.94c

The Great Altar of Zeus, Pergamon

Commissioned by Eumenes II (197–159 BCE) to commemorate Attalid victory over the Gauls, this work on the lower terrace of the Pergamene acropolis took the most ancient of Hellenic building types to its apotheosis. The traditional Hellenic altar was a narrow pedestal equal in width to the temple associated with it. Here, the Great Altar (ascribed, not without debate, to Zeus) stood in its own precinct on a podium 36.4 by 34.2 metres and 5.3 metres high, approached from the west and walled to the north, east and south. An Ionic colonnade to the outside of the wall and piers with attached Ionic columns to the inside both continued across the west front.

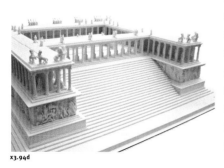

x3.94d

3.94e

A frieze in low relief, depicting the Pergamene foundation myth, embellished the inside of the wall. The great frieze (2.3 metres high) representing the dynastic struggle against the Gauls as the battle of gods and giants in high relief, ran all around the podium, except where the broad flight of steps ascended to the altar terrace. As the altar podium is out of alignment with the compound wall, the view through the columns of the propylaeum is aimed not at the centre of this great frieze, but just to the left of the right-hand corner. The narrative begins and culminates here.

Like the sculptor of Bassae, the master who conceived the Pergamene frieze – it was doubtless executed by many different hands – was indebted to Phidias and his mentors for the form of individual bodies in conflict (the 'heroic diagonal' most dramatically). However, his purpose of celebrating dynastic triumph is served not with the harmony and restraint of the Parthenon ideal, nor with the Mannerism of Bassae, but with overwhelming floridity, theatricality and dynamism, propelling the narrative around the perimeter of the building and up the stairs where its world surges into reality.

Much in the conception of the Pergamene altar frieze – the physical and emotional dynamism, the theatricality above all – is characteristic of the style later to be called Baroque. The celebrated sculpture group of Laokoon and his sons succumbing to pythons is as florid and theatrical as the Pergamene frieze: executed for a Roman patron mid-1st century CE, but possibly based on a two-figure Pergamene group excluding the boy off the base to the right. The father and the other boy, who shares his base, are fused in the movement of their agony – but here the dynamic is one of torsion within the writhing serpents. Until the Attalid period, Greek architecture tended to reflect developments in sculpture but the stasis of Classical Greek building was not to cede to Baroque movement until the Romans learned to mould form and space in brick and concrete. Pergamon's greatest sculpture may be called proto-Baroque, but there is much that is Mannerist in Attalid architecture.**3.95**

›**3.95 PERGAMENE SCHOOL, LAOKOON GROUP:** attributed by Pliny to the Rhodian sculptors Hagasadros, Polydoros and Athenodoros (Rome, Vatican Museum).

3.96a

3.96b

MIXED ORDERS

Dating from c. 250 BCE, the Temple of Athena Polias at
Pergamon was Doric. Even with Ionic proportions, this
was exceptional among Hellenistic temples: it was usual
for utilitarian works like stoas. Like the Attalid stoa of the
Athenian agora,**3.50** the two-storey stoas that framed the
Pergamene temple precinct and its portal were Doric
below and Ionic above. The superimposition of the Ionic
over the weightier Doric was to be canonical for multi-

›**3.96 PERGAMON, PRECINCT OF ATHENA:**
(a) restored entrance (Berlin, Pergamon Museum),
(b) stoa elevation with mixed Doric and Ionic Orders.

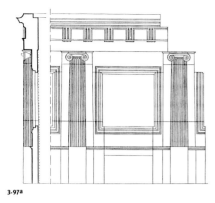

3.97a

›3.97 PTOLEMAIS (CYRENAICA): (a) palatial basement of mixed style, c. 270 BCE; (b, c) hybrid capitals enriched with the grapes of Bacchus and the head of Jove.

3.97b

3.97c

›3.98 MILETOS, BOULEUTERION (COUNCIL CHAMBER), c. 170 BCE: (a) section, (b) reconstructed perspective

3.98a

3.98b

storey buildings but the Ionic Order of the Pergamene example had a Doric frieze.**3.96**

Highly uncanonical – daring in its breach of conventional expectation – a hybrid style was certainly not atypical of the Hellenistic era. For instance, the palace at Ptolemais in Cyrenaica had an external Order of engaged Ionic columns with a Doric frieze, the council chamber at Miletos had Doric pilasters with freestanding Ionic columns inside, Doric half-columns outside.**3.97, 3.98** That building was commissioned by Antiochos IV of Syria (175–164 BCE), the patron of the Athenian Olympeion whose mature Corinthian was to be the style of the future – especially in Hellenistic Rome.

3.3 REPUBLICAN ROME
AND ITS MENTORS

3.99a

INTRODUCTION: LEGEND, ARMS AND MORES

According to tradition, Rome was founded in 753 BCE. History is less precise. Moulded by severe authority at first,**3·99** the base for imperial expansion began as a rude settlement straddling seven hills by the Tiber in central-Italian Latium: a thousand years later, two hundred years before her fall, Rome was the greatest city the world had ever seen, the capital of its richest empire. And for most of the subsequent centuries her empire and her architecture were emulated by all who would be grand.

Though Minoan traders reached southern Italy, they seem to have made no impression on the primitive indigenous pastoralists who have left little more than traces of conical huts. Aryan tribes must have been infiltrating at much the same time, in the last quarter of the 2nd millennium BCE: their Apennine settlements, including Rome, were distinguished by large rectilinear houses and many of them were stoutly fortified by the end of the millennium. Their culture was transformed, perhaps by a final wave of invaders, with the introduction of iron and with iron they were to extend their sway over much of Italy – both as soldiers and as farmers. Their new hill villages, founded as centres for mining and improved farming, included major ones on the Palatine and neighbouring hills: the urban complex of Rome began when these were united in the 7th century BCE about the low central plain that was to be their common forum.

GREEKS AND ETRUSCANS

Well before the unification of Rome, two energetic new peoples had entered the scene. Attracted by fertile plains and plentiful supplies of minerals – and preceded by Phoenicians with ideas from the Near East – Archaic Greek colonists brought a virile culture, already relatively high. They reached as far north as Cumae, just over 200 kilometres south of Rome. To the north of Rome on the other hand, between the Tiber and the Arno, there were the Etruscans: ancient tradition identifies them as immigrants from Asia Minor, Lydia in particular, but lack of recognizable linguistic links with the peoples there has suggested to some ancient and modern scholars that they were indigenous. If so, they were clearly impressed by their Aryan invaders and adopted their culture a century in advance of their neighbours.

The Etruscans maintained independent city-states, inspired by the Hellenic polis, for five hundred years. Their constitutions varied and they squabbled over territory and trade but they formed a loose confederation which controlled all Italy from the Po to Campania for more than a hundred years from the late-7th century BCE. Latium was ruled by kings deriving from Tarquinii in Etruria: the Etruscans seem to have had a formative influence on the religion, constitution and fabric of the rude towns that were to be Rome.

On the expulsion of the seventh and last Etruscan king of Rome, Tarquinius Superbus, the Romans established a republic in 509, the year in which the great temple to Jupiter Capitolinus was dedicated. Capua, the confederation's capital from the end of the 7th century BCE, was lost to Samnites about 423 and with it went Campania. The Gauls began harassing the Etruscans from the north in the 5th century, took the Po valley around 400 and, raiding Etruria itself, went on to sack Rome in 386 BCE.

›3.99 ROME: (a) model of the city c. 300 BCE viewed to the north (Rome, Museum of Roman Civilization); (b) the Capitoline Wolf (5th century BCE with Rome's legendary founders, Romulus and Remus, added by A. Pollaiulolo in the 15th century CE; Rome, Capitoline Museum).

According to the legend, Romulus and Remus were the twin sons of Mars by the Vestal Rhea Silvia, daughter of King Numitor of Alba. Their mother's uncle, who had usurped the Alban throne, cast them adrift in the River Tiber but, grounded in marshes below the hill later called Palatine, they were discovered and suckled by a she-wolf and then adopted by shepherds. They grew to lead a band of shepherd vigilantes based on the Palatine, restored their grandfather to his throne and founded Rome on the site of their salvation. Challenged by neighbouring tribal chiefs, Remus was killed but Romulus compacted with his most formidable neighbour, the king of the Sabines, and on the latter's death was sole master of a considerable domain.

Of the site's seven hills, the Aventine rises to the south-west (bottom left here); to its north-east, beyond the site of the Circus Maximus, is the Palatine; to the north-north-west of that is the Capitoline, dominating the Forum Boarium by the bend in the river (towards the top left here) and the Forum Romanum (centre); beyond this the Quirinal, Viminal and Esquiline range from north to east (top right here); and the Caelian rises towards the south-east (bottom right).

The Etruscans defended their towns by supplementing the natural escarpments of their elevated sites with great ashlar walls. The Romans learned to do the same – though the Servian Wall, which unified the defences of the settlements on the seven hills, was of stone-faced earthworks. This was consolidated largely after the settlements' primitive individual defences, which reinforced cliffs with terraced walls and crossed flatter ground with dykes and ditches, had been overcome by the Gauls in the first quarter of the 4th century.

The Greeks of Campania recognized the strength and ceremonial value of the voussoir arch in defensive works at least as early as the 5th century BCE at Velia and Paestum, as we have seen.**3.53** In the earliest Etruscan arches the voussoirs did not match the courses, but they were being cut to fit by the 4th century BCE, when the earliest-known Roman examples appear.

ABSORPTION OF ETRURIA AND DESTRUCTION OF CARTHAGE

Pressing up from the south, the Romans took their first major Etrurian prize in 396 BCE. The Etruscans presented protracted resistance and timeless walls,**3.100** but by the end of the 4th century BCE, the Gauls having been subdued and Latium dominated in the process, Rome had won supremacy over most members of the confederation and was in direct contact with the Greeks in the south. By the middle of the next century, Rome had extended a system of alliances across Samnite Campania to all Magna Graecia.

On this basis Rome was able to challenge Carthage, the main power in the western Mediterranean which, implanted by Phoenician maritime adventurers in north Africa, extended to Sicily, Sardinia, Corsica and Spain. After the loss of the three great islands in the 240s and epic retaliation in which African and Spanish forces were led by Hannibal to the very gates of Rome, the Carthaginians were beaten in 202 and Spain annexed. Finally, attempting resurgence, Carthage itself was destroyed in 146 BCE and Rome annexed North Africa. The Romans were then free to turn their attention to the east.

RIGOUR AND RELIGION

In his 'Oath of the Horatii',**3.101** the late-18th-century French painter David shows the sons of Horace swearing on their swords not to return from war unless victorious, to live only to honour their father and to serve the state. Promoting the revival of moral rigour in its own time, it admirably represents the austere discipline of the early Romans in their essentially religious dedication to a superior purpose.

Ulterior purpose, the motive force behind all existence

– comparable with fate – was deified as Numen in central Italy. As farmer and soldier knowing that man could not hope to deflect the inexorable from its predetermined course, the Roman sought to co-operate with it – like his Etruscan mentor. Beyond practical experience, that depended on the ability of special diviners (augers) to determine Numen's purpose through the interpretation of omens (auspices) discernible in certain natural phenomena – in particular the conformation of sacred birds in flight over sanctified ground reflecting the ritual quartering of the sky and the configuration of the similarly quartered entrails of sacrificial animals.

The formulas for augury and the design of its precinct passed to the Romans from the Etruscans. So too did the anthropomorphic conception of Numen's named manifestations (*numina*) as deities, which the Etruscans derived from the Greeks. Jupiter, the power of the sky (Zeus), was first but he was soon joined by Juno, the Mother (Hera), and Minerva, Wisdom (Athena), as father in a family triad.

POLITICAL DISCIPLINE

Highly authoritarian beliefs matched a highly authoritarian society. It was dominated by the father who had the power of life and death over the members of his family. He was responsible for propitiating Numen and was thus a priest. In Rome's first polity, the king was high priest but the fathers formed colleges to assist him in regulating religious practice in general, in taking the auspices and in tending particular manifestations of Numen.

The king was appointed by a council of senior patriarchs (the Senate) on the approbation of the people. After the rejection of the autocratic pretensions of the Tarquins in 509 BCE, the Senate and people appointed two consuls to share the power of the king (*imperium*). They were replaced each year but could be superseded by a sole dictator for a strictly limited period in times of crisis.

As the Senate met regularly, unlike the council of the people, and the consuls were checked by each other, the senior patriarchs and their families (*patricians*) dominated. To counter this, the majority of the populace (*plebians*), who manned the army and increased as trade grew with empire, first won the right for their council to appoint protectors (*tribunes*), then under certain circumstances to pass statutory resolutions (*plebiscites*), and finally to promote a plebian to one consulship each year.

Further extension of popular rule was checked by the protracted wars with Carthage: these, of course, promoted the power of the executive and the strength of the Senate into which all ex-magistrates were automatically enrolled – increasing its representativeness and authority. However, the popular cause was furthered by the non-patrician general Marius – at least through the limiting of patrician constraint on the freedom of election, at most through basing personal power on the acclamation of the regular troops in standing armies.

›3.102 GODDESS WITH CHILD, recovered from the precinct of the Capitoline Temple, Rome, and attributed to Vulcan of Veii who is known to have worked there towards the end of the 6th century BCE for Tarquinius Superbus, the last Etruscan king of Rome. The deity may be seen as intermdiary between Egyptian Isis and Roman Fortuna.

7 ETRUSCAN LEGACY

Submission to authority was central to Roman Republican mores and the severe discipline of structure characterizes early Roman building. Like the ashlar walls and voussoir arches of Perugia,**3.100** this was the legacy of the Etruscans, who may have brought their skills to Italy from Anatolia but probably derived the arch from the Greeks in Campania. Adept themselves at supplementing the natural defences of hill and river with walls built against Gauls and Etruscans, pre-eminent at engineering indeed, the pragmatic Romans long left art to the Etruscans**3.102** – and to the Campanian Greeks from whom the Etrus-cans themselves had derived the simple, robust order with which they disciplined their native tradition. Moreover, if the Romans depended on imported architects, their conception of both temple and house responded to the beliefs they shared with the Etruscans.

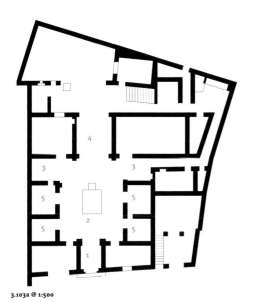

3.103a @ 1:500

>**3.103** THE EARLY ITALIC HOUSE: (a) Pompeii, 'Surgeon's House' c. 300 BCE, plan with (1) entrance hall (vestibulum), (2) atrium (with impluvium inserted later), (3) transept wings (alae), (4) principal room (tablinum) used as master bedroom, (5) bedrooms (cubiculae); (b) Etruscan funeray urn, c. 300 BCE, reproducing in miniature a gabled house with arched entrance (Florence, Archaeological Museum).

3.103b

HOUSES AND TOMBS

From the early 6th century BCE most urban Etruscans lived in rectangular houses in ordered towns. Looking back at the Etruscan record after several centuries of affluence, Vitruvius lists seven house types but actually these reduce to two: rectangular rooms aligned along a single axis, like the megaron, or arranged around a relatively expansive nuclear space (atrium) with the principal room (tablinum) occupying most of the side opposite the entrance. The former is common among the remains of early Etruscan settlements; the latter has so far been found first in the Samnite south from the beginning of the 3rd century.**3.103** This atrium type was later extended with a colonnaded court (peristyle), borrowed from the Greeks, to provide a more private nuclear space beyond the tablinum. Wattle-and-daub remained common in the 6th century but was then superseded by mud-brick.

Houses were reproduced in miniature as terracotta models for holding ashes from about 400 BCE, and to full scale as rock-cut tombs in town-like necropolises from the 7th century.**3.103, 3.104** Within the primitive tumulus, the earlier tombs follow the form of the megaron, with an inclined access passage instead of the porch: at first this type often had a pitched roof expressed as a gable on the entrance front and reflected in the ceiling of the main hall but rectilinear forms dominated later.**3.105** The more lavish late tombs have an increasingly large central space corresponding to the atrium, with a main room like the tablinum on axis with the entrance and several smaller chambers to the sides: the most elaborate scheme incorporates the furniture, equipment and images of the deceased. Subsidiary space may be simulated in fresco, enlivened with domestic scenes, and the roof may be decorated with geometric patterns or imitation structure supporting a central opening (compluvium).**3.106**

3.104a

3.104b

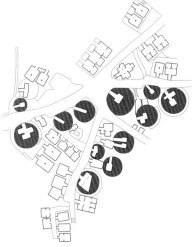

3.104c @ 1:2000

›3.104 CERVETERI (CAERE), BANDITACCIA CEMETERY, 7th–3rd century BCE: (a, b) views showing tumuli and streets of imitation houses; (c) part plan showing tumuli and excavated square and megaron tombs; (d) single pitched-roof chamber of Tomba della Capanna ('hut') type (late-7th century BCE); (e) succession of chambers with slightly pitched roofs of Tomba della Casetta ('little house') type (6th century BCE); (f) main chamber of Tomba della Cornice type with flat 'beamed' roof over cornice and doors to subsidiary rooms (6th century BCE); (g) main chamber of Tomba dei Relievi (late-4th century BCE), early atrium type.

The chamber of the Tomba dei Relievi, excavated from tufa below ground level and without the tumulus usual at the site, has thirteen double burial niches in the walls and some thirty compartments on the floor. The paired rectangular piers supporting the slightly pitched roof have Aeolic motifs in their capitals – elsewhere Ionic or Corinthian Orders are approximated. The low-relief stuccowork represents arms, tools and domestic utensils as hanging on the walls. Each niche has a pair of tufa-cut beds and cushions. To the base of the parapet below the main one, on axis with the entrance, is a low bench with a pair of sculpted sandals. To its left is a chest with folded clothing.

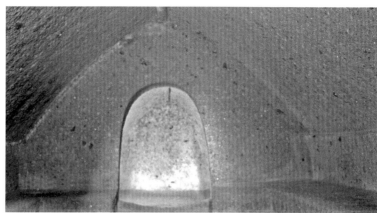

3.104d

3.104e

3.104f

3.104g

3.105

›3.105 CERVETERI, **6**TH CENTURY BCE SAR-
COPHAGUS: of the most sumptuous Etruscan type,
with husband and wife reclining on a bed (Paris,
Louvre).

›3.106 TARQUINIA, ATRIUM TOMB TYPE:
(a) Tomba dei Gattopardi (early 5th century BCE);
(b) Tomba di Mercareccia (3rd century BCE).

The compluviate roof is sometimes supported by four columns and may slope down or up from the sides to the centre (impluviate and displuviate respectively). These alternatives account for sub-types listed by Vitruvius.

3.106a

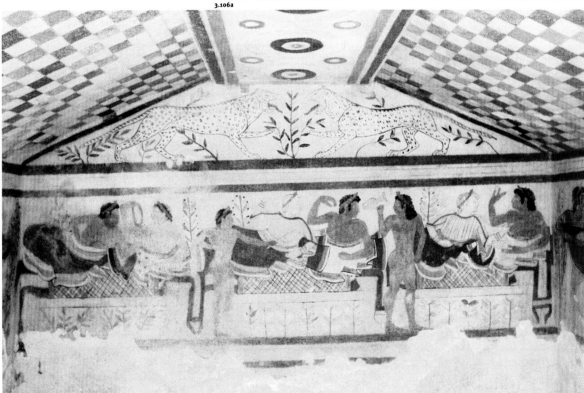

3.106b

3.107b

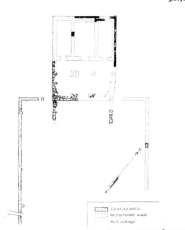

3.107c @ 1:1000

TEMPLES

The religion of the Etruscans seems first to have focused on rites of augury performed in a ritually squared, sanctified enclosure (templum). The addition of a monumental building followed contact with the Greeks. This was a megaron in essence but, unlike the Greek temple, it stood on a podium with a single flight of steps to the front and addressed the sanctified ground before it – as the tablinum addressed the atrium in the house – with a single portico that clearly provided a stage for the performance of the augurs under the auspices of the deity in the cella.**3.107** The pronaos columns were occasionally continued along the sides of the cella, but not the back, and the portico always stood free in clear distinction from the rest, as in the great Roman Capitoline Temple with its triad of cellas dedicated to Jupiter, Juno and Minerva.**3.108** Thus service to the authority of Numen is acknowledged in the authority of the axis and in the hierarchical disposition of the elements along it from the entrance to the cult image standing before the blind back wall of the cella.

›3.107 ORVIETO, BELVEDERE TEMPLE, 5th century BCE: (a) view of the remains from the southwest, (b, c) elevation and plan.

Typically, a square precinct (temenos) with free-standing altars was entered at the centre of its southern side, opposite the steps and portico of the shrine building (contrary to the Greek norm of east–west orientation, recommended by Vitruvius).

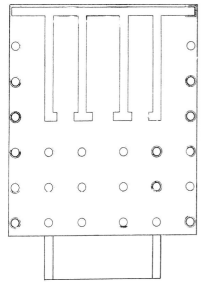

›3.108 ROME, TEMPLE OF JUPITER CAPITOL-INUS: plan of Etruscan foundation attributed to Tarquinius Priscus (616–579), completed under Tarquinius Superbus (535–509), dedicated in 509 BCE.

Originally of timber, brick and stucco on a stone base 62.25 by 53.3 metres, the temple burned down in 83 BCE and was rebuilt to the old plan in marble with columns taken from the Athenian Temple of Olympian Zeus. It was rededicated in 69 BCE.

›3.109 COSA, CAPITOLIUM: reconstructed portico detail showing decorative terracotta revetment.

Typically, the rafters continued beyond the architrave to provide the eaves, and the joists projected to the front, supporting a subsidiary roof below the pediment. The design of much of the detail derived from Archaic Greek practice, though the Italians were more capricious in the conception of fabulous form.

›3.110 SOVANA, SO-CALLED TOMBA IDEL-BRANDA, 2nd century BCE.

Imitating a hexastyle temple with a triple cella and three columns returning on each side (like the Roman Temple of Jupiter Capitolinus but without the deep portico), this late-Etruscan, Hellenized rock-cut work incorporates a burial chamber below its podium.

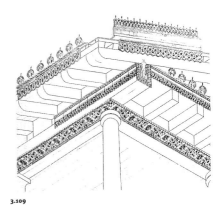

3.109

3.110

The typical Etruscan column is an unfluted version of Doric with a simple torus base derived from Ionic. The typical Etruscan portico has four columns, widely spaced. Thus architraves were made of timber long after masonry was introduced for columns in the 6th century, and the timber structure of the roof permitted wide eaves for the protection of the mud-brick and timber walls of the cella. The exposed timber, in turn, was protected by richly moulded terracotta revetment.**3.109** The podium was built of stone from early in the 7th century BCE, soon after the introduction of the rock-cut tomb.**3.110**

FROM TEMPLE PRECINCT TO URBAN ORDER

The regular geometry and axial alignment of the elements of the Etruscan temple complex provided a nucleus of urban order. In the early hill villages the norm naturally was organic growth defined by the lines of defence and governed by the contours of the site. Formality, preserved in the necropolis, appears in new settlements founded on the plains after expansion into Campania brought the Etruscans into contact with the Greek colonies of the south. As we have seen, there is evidence for orthogonal planning – indeed for the rectangulation of urban and rural land – in Magna Graecia from at least as early as the mid-6th century BCE and the Etruscans must have been impressed with its efficiency in the laying out of colonies. The earliest traces of an Etruscan town grid are at Marzabotto near Bologna.**3.111**

The Romans of the late Republic believed they had learned land-surveying from the Etruscans. There is no evidence that the Etruscans had developed it before their contacts with the Greeks. Herodotus thought the Greeks had derived it from Egypt where its institution by the pharaoh made it a sacred science – but the Greeks probably adopted it pragmatically. In Etruria, though obviously practical and somewhat irregular, it shadows the ritual quartering of the sky in principle. In Etruria and Rome, as in Egypt, the forging of temple complexes from interdependent parts aligned axially – providing a nucleus of order even in the unplanned town – contrasts with the discretion preserved for their entities by both Dorians and Ionians.

The foundation of Rome, of course, long pre-dated town planning. Even after it was sacked by the Gauls in 386, the city was rebuilt with its primitive irregularity following the contours of the site.**3.99** The low-lying land

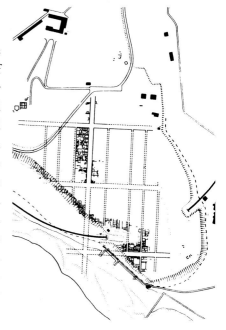

3.111 @ 1:10,000

›3.111 MARZABOTTO, founded in the late-6th century BCE and destroyed by the Gauls in the early 4th century BCE: plan.

The town was strictly orientated by surveyors – flat stones at major intersections have been identified as the base for the groma (the principal implement of the ancient surveyor, consisting of a horizontal cross on a vertical staff for sighting the grid lines). The rectangular blocks, defined by three main east–west arteries and one running north–south, varied in width but were consistent in length. Etruscan cemeteries laid out on a grid, seeming to reproduce the houses and streets of a town, precede Marzabotto by at least a generation.

between the hills was liable to flood and fire became an even worse hazard as people crammed in from all over the expanding empire. However, regularity was the hallmark of the fortified colonies of Roman citizens established to control the expanding network of the Republic's dependencies all over Italy. With the extension of Rome's power beyond Italy, the pattern was repeated all around the Mediterranean – especially in the west where the town was the novel vehicle of civilization. Surprisingly enough, it was at the outset of this process, in conflict with Epirus c. 275 BCE, that the Roman army learned the advantage of formal organization in its camps. These often developed into towns and the camp engineer would usually have assumed overall responsibility for the planning of new settlements.

The authoritarian approach to planning for an authoritarian religion marked the organization of the base for the expansion of the authority of the Roman state but it also extends a much more rigorous division of the countryside than anything produced by Greeks or Etruscans. As in the temple complex, the axis rules; as with the temple precinct, the square is ideal and the ideal unit was the square of 2400 Roman feet, equalling one hundred smallholdings (hence centuratio), orientated to the cardinal points.

Theoretically, centuriation of territory was independent of town planning, but the convergence of similarly orientated grids was inevitable. Certainly the main lines of external communication often continued through gates at the cardinal points as the main town arteries – the lateral decumanus, the longitudinal cardo – to the quarters of authority at their intersection in the centre. Of course, practice was generally determined by the condition of sites chosen for their defensive potential or their administrative or commercial advantages. The norm is

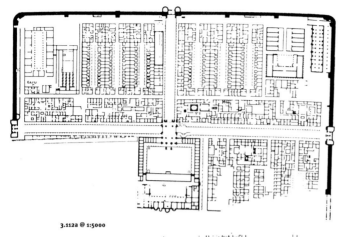

3.112a @ 1:5000

›3.112 LAMBAESIS AND TIMGAD, late-1st century CE: (a, b) plans.

The camp of the Third Augustan Legion, established c. 80 CE to protect the frontiers of the provinces of Africa and Numidia (in modern Algeria), was typical in facilitating the efficient deployment of the garrisons along the two main axes and a complete circuit of streets within the walls. The grid of lanes regimented the disposition of houses or tents in the quarters.

The colonial town laid out in 100 CE by military engineers from Lambaesis for veterans of the Third Legion had outgrown the original square settlement within a century and expanded along the external arteries.

3.112b @ 1:5000

well represented by the towns on the plains of northern Italy along the via Aemilia. Nowhere did military and civil order conform more closely than in the town of Timgad and the camp of Lambaesis from which it was founded at the close of the 1st century CE but it had long been approximated.**3.112, 3.113**

›3.113 **ARLES:** model (Arles, Archaeological Museum).

A Greek settlement on the site was refounded c. 50 BCE by Julius Caesar as a colony for veterans.

8 HELLENIZATION AND ENGINEERING

During its early centuries of struggle for survival and dominance in Italy, the rude town on the Tiber had acquired a veneer of Greek civilization through the Etruscans and from direct contact with the colonies of Campania. In the last quarter of the last millennium BCE, after Magna Graecia had been absorbed and the Hellenistic world was being conquered, Rome itself was conquered by Hellenism – overwhelmed, indeed, by the flood of trophies taken from Hellas and the Hellenistic kingdoms of Asia.

The Romans took liberally from the Greeks: from our point of view the most significant acquisition was the Greek concept of architectural order manifest in the Orders both as structual members and as agents of mural articulation, liberated from load-bearing responsibilities. Beyond enforced stability, however, the Romans also gave liberally – not least in the patronage of building. They restored or extended venerable monuments and were soon to endow Hellas with new ones, not all of which were conceived to assert alien authority though – not without irony – their most celebrated Athenian survivor asserts the alien wall as the prime element of form.**3.114**

EASTERN CONQUEST

Rome first clashed with a major Hellenistic power when it turned on Macedonia to punish its king for his support of Carthage: this was effected in 197 BCE and the Greek states exchanged Macedonian for Roman protection. After renewed trouble, the Macedonian kingdom was destroyed in 167 and annexed in 148, the Greek protectorates being incorporated into the province in 146.

At about the same time, the Seleucids lost most of Mesopotamia to the Parthians. The remaining Seleucid territory in Anatolia was under pressure from Pergamon in the west and Pontus to the north. Pergamon passed to Rome on the death of Attalos III in 133. The challenge of the Pontine king, Mithridates, who fomented rebellion in many Greek cities, was first met by the great Roman general Sulla in Greece in 85 and defeated finally by Pompey twenty years later. Pompey dispatched the last Seleucid in 64 and made the rump of his empire into the province of Syria. Ptolemaic Egypt followed just over thirty years later, at the end of the Republic.

Though austere in her own beliefs, Rome was tolerant of other traditions provided they were not perceived to be a threat to the state. The Hellenic conception of order in design was not difficult to reconcile with native Roman ways. However, the city-state constitution could not cope with absorbing divine kingdoms and empires – themselves decadent – and its society could not comprehend the material wealth and exotic attitudes of Asia and

Egypt. With them came a taste for luxury and a self-indulgent sensualism inimical to the puritan ethic at the base of the Roman tradition of authority – the authority of right and duty, of the father and of the polity, for which self-sacrifice was the supreme virtue.

The Greek Stoics provided a philosophical basis for submission to the laws of nature, which conservative Romans readily equated with Numen. However, many in the populace – its ranks swollen by immigrants to Rome – now sought their own salvation in the afterlife promised by eastern mystery cults such as those of Osiris/Serapis and Isis – who was particularly important to the Romans in identification with Fortuna.**3.115** And here on earth credit was accorded to the victor personally rather than to Jupiter or the genius of Rome. Hellenization lent grace to Rome's fabric, but corrupted its republic.

REPUBLIC IN CRISIS

Until the middle of the 2nd century, Rome was generally reluctant to extend direct rule over defeated territories, unless they were uncivilized, preferring instead to leave them to govern themselves as allies or protectorates. However, the extinction of the kingdom of Macedonia led to the development of a provincial system of fundamental significance. Apart from its effect on moral authority, annexation in the east changed the basis of power in practice. Provinces were governed by magistrates acting on behalf of the consuls (proconsuls): unlike consuls, however, proconsuls were not paired, their terms were often extended by popular demand and the greatest of them ruled in place of divine monarchs. Allied to the command of triumphant armies – professional standing armies rather than citizens' forces since the reforms of Marius at the end of the 2nd century – and fabulous booty, this was the basis for extraordinary power.

›3.115 FORTUNA: late-1st-century marble (Rome, Vatican Museums).

The female force of destiny, perhaps comprehensible as the inspiration of Numen, was of Etruscan origin – or at least adoption. Empire endowed her with pantheistic significance but the constituents of Ptolemaic Isis became central to her own constitution. The object of particular devotion by women in hope of fertility, she was the focus of hope in general. Her attributes were the cornucopia (as the bountiful), the rudder (as the controller of destiny) and the wheel (as the turner of fortune).

Venality was not long in corrupting the Senate. With decadent government in Rome, loyalty to the state ceded to loyalty to the bountiful commander whose personal ambition was readily confused with reform. With perpetual crisis the normal officers of state were often superseded, most notably by Sulla and his aides. Of the latter, the most prominent were Pompey, who played a leading role in the suppression of the anti-patrician Marian revolt in the late-80s before settling Spain in the 70s, and Crassus, who had put down the revolt led by Spartacus in the late-70s. These were to be eclipsed by the aspiring patrician Julius Caesar, who had clashed with Sulla.

Pompey's star was ascendant in the 60s, propelled by his singular success against the pirates who threatened Rome's Mediterranean lifelines, his triumph over Mithridates of Pontus and his annexation of Syria and Palestine in 64 and 63. The wary Senate was diffident towards him, however, and baulked at ratifying his eastern settlement. After complex manoeuvres, Crassus and Caesar variously saw advantage in collaborating with him to beat the opposition in 60 and they constituted an uneasy triumvirate to sustain their extraordinary coercive power.

With Caesar in Gaul (France), Crassus and Pompey shared the consulate in 55 and were thereafter assigned Syria and Spain respectively. While Pompey remained in the capital, its master as controller of the corn supply, and Caesar was advancing to triumph north of the Alps, Crassus led Rome to the extreme humiliation of the loss of his life, his legions and their standards to the Parthians at Carrhae in 53.

The two remaining triumvirs inevitably fell out when Caesar was on the point of returning from his conquests with immense power: Pompey tried to counter by championing the Senate but Caesar descended on Rome and unleashed civil war in 49. Pompey departed for the east but Caesar first went to Spain to secure his adversary's forces there and then turned to defeat Pompey himself in Thessaly before pursuing him to his death in Egypt in 48.

Caesar had been declared dictator in 49. Seemingly bent on transforming his position into monarchy, he was assassinated in 44 BCE by a faction of Senators who claimed commitment to the cause of Republican orthodoxy. Chaos followed. From the fray the most unlikely contender, Caesar's young nephew and adopted son, Octavian, emerged dominant over the favourite, Caesar's erstwhile lieutenant Mark Antony, who lost himself to indolence with Cleopatra in newly conquered Egypt.

EARLY HELLENISTIC ROMAN BUILDING

The Hellenization of Rome was nowhere more prominently displayed than in the rebuilding of the great Capitoline Temple after 83 to the old plan but with the columns pillaged by Sulla from Cossutius's Athenian Temple of Zeus Olympios.**3.84** Below was the Forum, the nuclear market and meeting place from which the wayward pattern of streets took its departure. As Hellenization advanced with the complexity of urban society and the development of structural technology, it was surrounded by a magnificent series of buildings for the offices of state and varied specialized purposes, in addition to temples, but it was never to be reformed on strictly regular lines.

Little survives from the earliest phases of the Forum. However, the combination of primitive form and Hellenistic Order is well represented by the small Ionic temple on the Forum Boarium beside the Tiber.**3.116** At Tivoli, moreover, the Corinthian tholos of Vesta – the goddess personifying the Numen of the hearth fire – takes the elemental form of the conical hut to heights excelled only in the spectacular theatral temple at Palestrina.**3.117, 3.118**

>3.116 ROME, TEMPLE OF FORTUNA VIRILIS, Forum Boarium, built early 1st century BCE of tufa and travetine probably on an Etruscan base.

>3.117 TIVOLI, TEMPLE OF VESTA: first half of 1st century BCE.

The form may be indigenous, but the influence of the Greek tholos in disciplining it is inescapable. The adoption of a stylobate in place of a podium is obviously a response to the circular form. The cella is an early example of concrete construction.

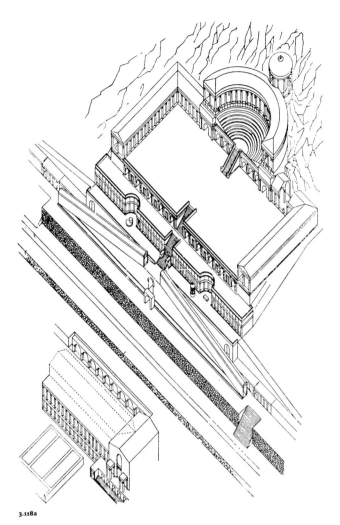

3.118a

The Temple of Fortuna Primigenia at Palestrina

Though Roman liturgy – like Greek – included ritual dancing, there seems to have been no drama until the 3rd century BCE. Thereafter it played a significant enough part for theatres to be incorporated in the design of sacred compounds, most spectacularly at Palestrina. As in several other late-Republican sanctuaries, the authority of the axis is reinforced by a succession of forms revealed progressively, but here the richness of their variety is unprecedented: the columned hall at the lowest level, the diag-

›**3.118 PALESTRINA (PRAENESTE), TEMPLE OF FORTUNA PRIMIGENIA,** late-2nd or early 1st century BCE: (a) reconstructed axonometric, (b) model.

The earliest-known precedent for the incorporation of a theatral element in the design of a sanctuary is provided by the so-called Temple of Juno at Gabii (late-3rd or early 2nd century BCE). There, however, the cavea stepped back from the outer edge of the terrace before a rectangular temple, as in the sanctuary of Hercules Victor at Tivoli.

›**3.119 (PAGES 524–525) SBEITLA (SUFE-TULA), FORUM AND TRIPLE CAPITOL COMPLEX:** late-1st century CE.

3.118b

onal ramps, the orthogonal stairs that cut through the superimposed terraces, the barrel-vaulted hemicycles, the colonnaded precinct, the semicircular theatral element with its enclosing colonnade and the circular temple at the top. Recalling Pergamon, the terraces – 100 metres wide – are carried on monumental arcades which remain as witnesses to former magnificence.

Other late-Republican terraced sanctuaries are those of Jupiter Anxur at Terracina (c. 80) and Hercules Victor at Tivoli (c. 70). Unlike the latter, where strength is naked, the arcades at Palestrina were concealed behind colonnades or embellished with an applied Order, as at Tivoli. The barrel vaults of the hemicycles in the intermediate terrace are among the earliest surviving examples of coffering: the progressive thinning of the membrane achieved by pouring the concrete on formwork overlaid with timber plates diminishing in size and bent to the profile of its centring. Though distorted by the curvature, the resulting grid pattern was doubtless inspired by a traditional timber structure of joists and beams.

THE HELLENIZED ROMAN TOWN
AND PUBLIC BUILDING TYPES

As its formal arrangement demonstrates, the forum of a Roman town had a dual origin: it was a meeting and market place but it was also a ceremonial space, axial in its planning, derived from the temple precinct. In the assertion of Rome's authority, the capitol dominating the forum in the centre of the colonial town reproduced the Capitoline temple's triad of cellas for Jupiter, Juno and Minerva. Sometimes each had a separate building.**3.119**

One of the earliest representatives of the colonial type, the forum of Pompeii stands at the head of a distinguished line of urban spaces dominated by a temple and flanked by stoa-like colonnades before shops and civic buildings. Authority is here as everywhere in the Roman conception of planning but the Hellenization of style was advanced at Pompeii in both public and private buildings.

Apart from the temple, the palace and (later) the nymphaeum and the triumphal arch, the main Roman public-building types – the basilica, the council and guild hall, the market building, the thermal bath house and palaestra, the theatre and amphitheatre – all appear in monumental form first in Campania where the Hellenic and Italic traditions met. The ruins of Pompeii include substantial remains of each of them.**3.120**

Pompeii

Buried and substantially preserved by the eruption of Vesuvius in 79 CE, Pompeii is related to the Campanian Greek settlements from which the Etruscans derived urban order. The central nucleus (shaded in the plan), where the forum and main public buildings were developed, was laid out on a low hill in the 6th century BCE. The quarters to the north and east were developed probably after the Etruscans were defeated by the Greeks at Cumae in 474 BCE, possibly after their loss of Capua to the Samnites in 423: a grid was applied in a rudimentary way – perhaps by

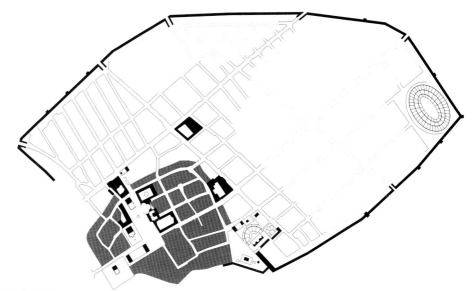

3.120a @ 1: 10,000

natives, perhaps by Etruscans – in the last quarter of the 6th century and expanded with much more assurance in the 5th century BCE. After Rome had suppressed the revolt of its Italic allies in the so-called Social War, a veterans' colony was established at Pompeii in 80 BCE and the eastern quarter was further extended to accommodate the amphitheatre with its adjoining gladiatorial palaestra. The regularity of the rectangular blocks increased as the town grew – where existing roads allowed.

Clearly representing the synthesis of temple compound and market place, the forum at the heart of the old town was strictly reformed – Hellenized – in the second half of the 2nd century BCE. The original tufa colonnades were in the process of reconstruction in travertine when the city was severely damaged by earthquake in 62 CE and the work remained incomplete when Vesuvius erupted in 79. The Temple of Jupiter to the north, rebuilt in Hellenistic form with the forum and adapted for the triad of the Roman Temple of Jupiter Capitolinus after the establishment of the Roman colony in 80 BCE, was severely damaged in the earthquake and was still being restored in 79. The Temple of Apollo was built earlier and escaped serious damage. The basilica and the three halls associated with the Curia, built as an adjunct to the new

3.120a @ approximately 1:3000

›3.120 POMPEII: (a) plan showing phases of development; (b, c) model of forum quarter from south-west (Naples, Archaeological Museum) and mature plan of central area with (1) forum, (2) capitolium, (3) Temple of Apollo, (4) Temple of Venus; (5) basilica, (6) Curia (senate house) and magistrates' halls, (7) voting hall, (8) Eummachia's building, dedicated to Concordia Augusta and used as the clothiers' hall, (9) Temple of Vespasian, (10) Treasury and Sacrarium of the Lares (shrine of the city's tutelary deities), (11) fish or meat market, (12) theatre complex with (i) open theatre, (ii) closed odeon, (iii) palaestra, (13) Temple of Hercules with so-called Triangular Forum, (14) Temple of Isis (Roman Fortuna), (15) Temple of Zeus Melilchlos, (16–18) Stabian, Central and Forum Baths, (19–21) houses of the Faun, Pansa and the Vettii.

3.120b

forum in the second half of the 2nd century, also suffered heavily in the earthquake and were still being restored in 79.

The Temple of Isis, the larger theatre (with uncovered seating for five thousand on earthworks) and the Stabian Baths were probably built in the last quarter of the 2nd century BCE, though the baths were extended after 80 BCE and the theatre was modernized under Augustus for popular spectacles (with improved access and an integrated stage building). All were badly damaged in the earthquake, and it is testimony to the popularity of mystery cults that the Temple of Isis was one of the few buildings completely renovated between 62 and 79 CE. The smaller theatre (a concert hall of concrete with seating for one thousand under a timber roof) and the Forum Baths date from the early years of the colony: damaged in 62, they were in use again by 79. The buildings on the east side of the forum date from the imperial period, the Temple of Vespasian and the Sacrarium of the Lares, like the Central Baths further east, from after the earthquake.

Rebuilt after the earthquake of 62 CE on the lines of a pre-colonial shrine, the cloistered precinct appropriate to a mystery cult contained the small freestanding prostyle temple of the goddess herself, the shrine of her son Horus/Harpocrates aligned with it in the centre of the eastern colonnade, an external altar and, in the south-eastern corner, a chapel with stairs to a reservoir of water from the Nile. Behind the western colonnade were rooms for the ceremonies associated with initiation to the mysteries.

In the Vitruvian hierarchy of building types the temple naturally takes precedence. Pompeii had several dedicated to members of the Graeco-Roman pantheon, including the orthodox prostyle-hexastyle Capitolium dominating the forum from the north and the Temple of Apollo to the west.**3.120b2,3** The Temple of Isis was the most popular of several shrines to the exotic eastern mystery cults that seduced many from the old austere mores after Rome's conquest of the Hellenistic east.**3.120b14, 3.121**

Of the secular types, the basilica is first and the one to the south-west of the Pompeiian forum is the earliest-known representative of a long-lived type, the first in which internal space took precedence over external form. Greek in name but unknown in Hellas before the advent of the Romans, despite its affinity to the peristyle, the inverted peripteral form was devised for public assembly and adapted for the administration of justice: a central nave, framed by colonnades on one or two levels, flanked

›3.122 POMPEII, BASILICA, c. 120 BCE: interior view of ruins.

With superimposed Orders, the type of hall represented by the basilica at Pompeii was defined by Vitruvius as Egyptian as distinct from a Corinthian hall which has only one Order rising either from the ground or from a podium (Book VI, 3).

by aisles for communication, was dominated from the end opposite the door by a recessed dais elevating the seat of the presiding authority. At Pompeii the dais projects into the western cross-aisle from the rear wall.**3.120b5, 3.122** Subsequently it was the norm to raise the dais in a semicircular apse projecting beyond the main volume, after the pattern of the Pompeiian curia.**3.120b6** Variations on the theme served other civic and commercial purposes.

The peristyle also produced the market building and palaestra. The Campanian addition to the former was an easily sluiced central rotunda for the dressing of meat or fish.**3.120b11** Itself borrowed from the Greeks as the

exercise ground for sport, the palaestra was an invariable adjunct to the types of building for recreation and entertainment.

The Romans promoted both sport and drama as media of religious devotion at first, like the Greeks, later as increasingly popular entertainment. The forms of theatre for both were borrowed from the Greeks. Development of the type depended on the exploitation of the arch to support the cavea where there was no conveniently curved hill but earthworks remained fundamental well into the last century BCE, as in the Circus Maximus in Rome. As in Hellas, earth and rock were supplemented first by timber and paint, then by stone. The theatral temple at Palestrina is the supreme example of the development of a precipitous site with varied masonry structures on a series of terraces.**3.118**

›3.123 (PAGES 532–533) POMPEII, AMPHITHEATRE: C. 80 BCE.

The amphitheatre's seating for twelve thousand rests on earthern embankments – 135 by 107 metres – retained by concrete arcades. There is no system of internal spaces or communication. Officials reached their seats in the lowest row through tunnels at ground level; the public gained access up external staircases, doubled on the western side. Rome had no comparable facility until half a century later.

›3.124 POMPEII, BATHING COMPLEXES: (a–c) Stabian Baths (end of 2nd century BCE): palaestra, frigidarium, and plan with (1) palaestra, (2) swimming pool (natatio), (3) changing room (apodyterium), (4) cold room (frigidarium), (5) warm room (tepidarium), (6) hot room (calidarium), (7) latrine; (d, e) Forum Baths, calidarium, view to southern end with hot-water plunge bath, and tepidarium, detail of vault with stucco decoration (renovated).

3.124a

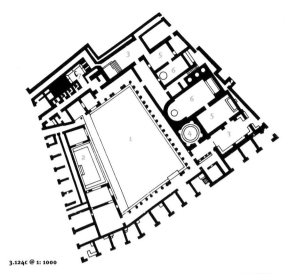

3.124c @ 1: 1000

3.124b

Recalling the age-old association of sport and theatre with religion, the Samnites had built their theatre in the vicinity of Pompeii's oldest shrines (to Hercules and Zeus) and incorporated two palaestrae in the complex – the larger southern one primarily for athletics, the smaller northern one for wrestling. In the era of the Roman colony, in addition to the large semi-circular theatre of c. 120,**3.120b12** the elliptical amphitheatre first appears as an arena for large-scale exhibitions of combat between men and beasts: the project incorporated a vast palaestra and a swimming pool.**3.120a, 3.124**

The Greeks bathed in cubicles with simple troughs but the salutary volcanic springs of Campania prompted the elaboration of the exercise in temperature-controlled complexes: naturally enough, bathing for health and hygiene was combined with sport and social intercourse. Monumental formality was to supervene in imperial Rome but in late-Samnite Campania the arrangement was essentially pragmatic: behind shops and beyond the palaestra, dressing and massage rooms adjoined a sequence of cold, warm and hot halls ranged side-by-side. Pompeii's baths are all like this.**3.120b16–18, 3.124**

The Stabian Baths are the earliest and the complex incorporates the earliest substantially surviving domical vaults.**3.124b** When they were first built, braziers heated air and water as required in the halls themselves, but soon after 80 BCE they were converted to the more efficient, cleaner hypocaust system: subterranean boilers produced hot air and steam for circulation through ducts in the concrete floors and walls as in the new Forum Baths. And as there the concrete was lavishly masked: the floors with marble or mosaics, the walls with frescoes or stucco, the vaults with painting and stucco in which human and animal motifs were supported by stylized flora.**3.124d, e**

3.124d

3.124e

DECORATION AND THE HOUSE

As a macrocosm, the town finds its reflection in the microcosm of the house. Like the Greek one, the Roman town house (domus) normally had a blind front to the insalubrious street or was set back behind shops.**3.125** Exceptionally, some of the most sumptuous houses had upper storeys with windows or even colonnades overlooking the street. The introverted form submits to the

authority of the axis, no less than the planned town, and the forum as breathing and congregational space clearly had its domestic counterparts in atrium and peristyle.

As we have seen, the Italic atrium is generally associated with the Etruscans, though first discovered in Campania. The peristyle, borrowed from the Greeks for

3.126b

3.125b

›**3.125 HERCULANEUM:** (a, pages 538–539) view of the ruins showing atrium houses (centre) and the street elevations of houses in the background; (b) house exterior. Herculaneum suffered the same fate as Pompeii in 79 CE.

›**3.126 POMPEII, HOUSE OF THE VETTII:** (a) plan with with (1) entrance porch (vestibulum) or passage (prothyrum), (2) atrium with impluvium, (3) main reception room (tablinum) with side passage (fauces), (4) dining room (triclinium) usually, (5) bedrooms (cubicula), (6) peristyle, (7) main private living/dining room (oecus), kitchen, (b, c) atrium and peristyle.

Several of Pompeii's most spectacular houses – including those of Pansa and the Faun – date back to the mid-2nd century BCE, the House of the Vettii to nearly a century later. Obviously there were important changes in the course of the relatively long lives of the earlier ones, at least: in particular, the second atrium

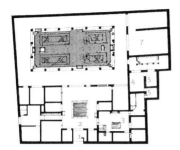

3.126a @ 1:1000

in the House of the Faun seems to have been the nucleus of a separate house and its incorporation marks the introduction of columns around the impluvium, the trough sunk into the floor below the compluvium. Absent from Etruscan house-tombs, the impluvium – the norm in later Campania – seems to have come from the Hellenistic east with the peristyle.

the ordering of the old walled garden, was increasingly important in the centuries of pervasive Hellenism. Attracting the private rooms, including a summer dining room (oecus, also of Greek derivation), it was to eclipse the atrium as population growth reduced the space available to house-builders, but by the end of the Republic the two were ideally aligned on axis through the tablinum, as in the Pompeiian House of Pansa.[3.120b20] Property extension led to variation, as in the Houses of the Faun and the Vettii,[3.120b19,21, 3.126] but from the 1st century extension was often effected illusionistically in paint. Most walls were painted, sometimes above marble dadoes, and most floors were paved in marble or mosaic.[3.129, 3.66]

3.126c

Foreign to the Greeks, axial planning was so pervasive with the Romans that they even took it with them to the country, despite their appreciation of nature and the relatively relaxed context of life that encouraged a measure of extroversion there. There were two main types of country house (villa): the estate house with considerable accommodation, and the relaxed retreat, often near town or by the sea. Primarily for recreation or entertainment rather than extended residence, the latter were the most sumptuous in internal spatial variety yet sensitive to the natural qualities of their sites.

The seaside villa usually had a variety of facilities – living rooms, reception rooms, baths, terraces, etc. – devolved along the shore with more or less formality.**3.127** In countryside and suburb it was common to build on platforms raising the rooms to enjoy the view. By the end of the 1st century the most lavish villas had several terraced platforms, aligned or freely disposed in accordance with the contours of the site. Symmetrically planned on an arcaded basement outside Pompeii, the so-called Villa of the Mysteries – named after a fresco cycle in one of the principal rooms supposedly dedicated to Dionysiac rites – is an outstanding example of the platform type.**3.128**

Various permutations of style have been distinguished in the painted decoration of the houses at Pompeii and elsewhere in the Hellenized Roman Republic. The first, current around 200–80 BCE and reflecting Hellenistic fashion, imitated polychrome marble revetment in dividing wall surfaces into a dado and panels with moulded frames, frieze and/or cornice: it was tectonic if not yet architectonic, though pilaster panels were occasionally included. Then, for less than half a century after Pompeii became a colony in 80 BCE, the fully architectonic Second Style denied the wall and feigned

›3.127 SEASIDE VILLA: fresco from Stabiae (1st century CE).

3.128 @ 1:500

›3.128 POMPEII, VILLA OF THE MYSTERIES, 2nd-century BCE foundation, extended and redecorated over the following two generations: plan with (1) arcaded podium with cryptoporticoes, (2) entrance, (3) internal garden court with later peristyle, (4) atrium, (5) tablinum, (6) external portico.

The plan around a court seems to have included porticoes on three sides of the main block from the outset. A peristyle was added on the north-easterly fourth side, reducing the original court to an atrium – in reverse of the usual sequence of development (as Vitruvius, Book VI. 5) requires. A semi-circular extension was later projected into the garden on the main axis, beyond the south-west porticoes.

3.129a   3.129b

3.129c

›3.129 POMPEIIAN-STYLE DECORATION:
(a) late-First Style tectonic scheme with theatrical insertion, 1st century BCE (Palermo, Archaeological Museum); (b, c) theatrical illusionism in frescoes of the Second Style from Pompeiian house (Naples, National Museum) and from the House of Augustus on the Roman Palatine; (d) a late-First Style tectonic scheme with figures subsequently overlaid (Pompeii, Villa of the Mysteries).

increasingly complex extensions of space scenographically, as in the theatre. Ultimately these framed illusory views of garden or countryside, often as the setting for figures in mythological episodes. The figures were sometimes brought forward and enlarged, eclipsing their context like players on a stage, as in the Villa of the Mysteries.**3.129** Thereafter, theatricality reigned.

3.129d

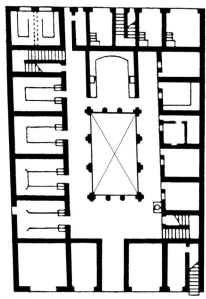

3.130 @ 1:500

›**3.130 TYPICAL ROMAN TENEMENT BLOCK (INSULA):** (a) plan, (b) reconstruction.

Anticipated by the multi-storey house, the insula became the major urban building type with the improvement of brick and concrete building technology. Between three and five storeys were common. Raised from the street by shops but relatively easily accessible and usually taller than the levels above, the first floor was considered the best location. The courtyards varied in extent in accordance with the general affluence of the proprietors, but in all types were usually surrounded by arcaded galleries of communication with staircases in the corners. Left unsheathed in an essentially extroverted and utilitarian genre, the brick exteriors depended on the relationship between window and plane wall. Glass was introduced to the more luxurious blocks before the middle of the 2nd century BCE. Flexible, the form was adaptable to many purposes from offices to warehouses – like its multi-storey metal and glass successor in the 20th century.

3.130b

MASS HOUSING

With the growth both of the town and of the urban economy in the 1st century CE, the pattern of housing had to change. The rich resorted to their villas. For those of the expanding middle class who could afford a house, the type with a grand atrium as well as a peristyle was old-fashioned by the time Pompeii was destroyed. The atrium had been reduced to little more than a vestibule and the peristyle dominated, often with more than one storey of accommodation around it. Given crowded conditions and advanced building technology, on the other hand, the less-affluent majority lived in multi-storey tenements (insulae).**3.130**

Recorded as early as the late-3rd century BCE, insulae were still seen as a Roman phenomenon by Vitruvius two hundred years later, but blocks of apartments were also to be developed on a grand scale in Ostia, Rome's port, and elsewhere in the imperial period. Built around courtyards of varied dimensions, they usually had single-level apartments superimposed on three or more storeys and lit by windows overlooking the street. The ground-floor street frontages were invariably occupied by shops.**3.131**

Insulae were notoriously prey to squatters who erected shanties on their roofs in inflammable materials. Before the end of the last century BCE planning reforms limited the height of buildings in Rome to 21 metres and imposed fire regulations, but impact on the existing fabric was inevitably limited and much of the city was destroyed in the famous fire of 64 CE. Thereafter the authorities again attempted to regulate rebuilding: widening and straightening streets, lining them with colonnades, enforcing the earlier height restrictions, increasing the distance between buildings, ensuring their structural integrity and limiting the use of inflammable materials. But the problems of enforcement remained insuperable.

ENGINEERING AND BUILDING TECHNOLOGY

The advance of building technology under the Romans, like their planning, related directly to the discipline of their military life and the authority of their administration: to move vast armies required great organizational skill, not only in regimenting people but also in developing transportation and service facilities. The authority of Roman road and aqueduct had been inescapable since 312 BCE when the magistrate Appius Claudius built the Aqua and via Appia. The former was the first of fourteen great channels for the city's water supply. The latter connected Rome to Capua and the conquered cities of Campania. Pressed on, the way was paved to the towns of Magna Graecia and the ports of embarkation for conquest overseas. As the legions advanced so too did the roads, deviating as little as possible from the authoritarian line – even in the undulating islands of Britain.

Roads and aqueducts had to cross chasms of various size, naturally, and that needed arches. Discipline is again implied by submission to the authority of structure, of

3.131a

3.131b

›**3.131 SHOPS:** (a) at Ostia, early 2nd century CE; (b) reconstruction (Rome, Museum of Roman Civilization).

›3.132 AUTUN, PORTE SAINT-ANDRE, c. 15 BCE.

Twin carriageways, upper gallery and flanking towers were ubiquitous features of the grander Roman city gates from late in the Republican period until towards the end of the empire: here the missing towers were rectangular with semi-circular projections to the outside.

›3.133 THE GREAT ROMAN AQUEDUCT: (a, pages 548–549) Nimes, Pont du Gard, c. 19 BCE (260 metres long and 49 metres high); (b, pages 550–551) Segovia, c. 50 CE (823 metres long and 92 metres high).

engineering serving the expansion of the authority of the state. Nowhere is this better illustrated than by the great structure built from 19 BCE over the River Gard to Nimes in the south of France. Except perhaps in the greatest of city gates, nowhere is there more splendid testimony to the perseverance of Roman ashlar masonry – and to the beauty of functional design.**3.132, 3.133**

3.132

The Pont du Gard, Nimes

Built entirely of stone, the triple-storey bridge – carrying a road at first level and the slab-covered water channel at the top – is 269 metres long and 49 metres high. Its superimposed arcades represent the apotheosis of a tradition of utilitarian public works dating back to the Pons Aemilius (142 BCE), the overground Aqua Marcia (144 BCE), and beyond.

Often using pipes, occasionally pumps, the essentially practical Romans kept their aqueducts just above or below ground level wherever possible. This one great structure over the Gard enabled them to do this for virtually all the rest of the 50 kilometres between the springs of Uzès and Nimes.

Other utilitarian arcuate structures included market halls and warehouses for storing foodstuffs, and sewers. As much of Rome's grain was imported from at least as early as the 5th century BCE, granaries were needed: the earliest large-scale warehouse is thought to be the Porticus Aemilia by the Tiber below the Aventine of the early 2nd century BCE. Rome had sewers in Etruscan times: the main one – the Cloaca Maxima – descends from the 6th century BCE and was vaulted around 100 BCE.

MATERIALS

Hellenization notwithstanding, the Romans of the Republican era rarely built with costly materials – even for temples. As we noted at the outset, the Romans learned from the Etruscans to build their major public works with finely dressed blocks of stone whose dead weight held them together. By the 3rd century BCE they had developed a hard-setting mortar made of volcanic sand (pozzolana), lime and water that freed them from reliance on the dead weight of massive blocks. Well before the middle of the 2nd century BCE they were mixing this mortar with light rubble to make a primitive concrete, and forming walls by laying it between courses of brick or stones that could be set in increasingly intricate and regular patterns because all the strength lay in the bond.**3.134a** By c. 100 temple walls were occasionally of tufa but generally of concrete sheathed in tufa or travertine and plastered and painted. Orders were usually of travertine – the imported marble columns of the Capitoline temple were, of course, exceptional.

The lightness and malleability of concrete not only made construction easier and cheaper but, poured over a temporary timber mould (centring) for arch and vault, it prompted radical advance in the conception of form.**3.134b** The principle of the arch was simply extended

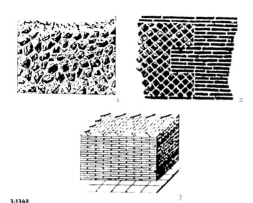

3.134a

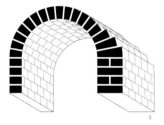

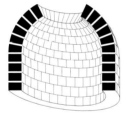

3.134b

to form the semi-circular barrel or tunnel vault and then turned on its centre to form the semi-spherical domical vault. As we have seen, the Stabian Baths in Pompeii had both types of vault before the end of the 2nd century BCE. New standards of concrete construction and spatial diversity had been set by the Forum Baths soon after 80 BCE and later developments depended on moulded concrete to distinguish the varied stages of the bathing process.

The development of the architecture of space, which took its departure from buildings such as the Stabian Baths, is a distinct issue of fundamental importance to the whole tradition of architecture. On the other hand, following the Hellenistic lead with no less significance for the future, the Romans also realized the full implications of the column's abstraction from its structural role and its application to the wall as an articulating agent. These developments coincided with the reformation of the empire by Julius Caesar's heir, his nephew Octavian.

›3.134 MATERIALS AND TECHNOLOGY:
(a) revetment of *opus caementum* (mortared rubble): (1) *opus incertum* (irregular patchwork), (2) *opus reticulatum* (chequerboard), (3) *opus testaceum* (brick); (b) vaulting: (1) tunnel or barrel, (2) domical; (c) construction of a bridge on timber centring.

The main trend in masonry was towards greater regularity, though polygonal work subsisted with squared ashlar due to the abundant cheap limestone quarried north of Rome that split irregularly. Tufa and travertine quarried in Latium cut readily into rectangular blocks and were used either in solid blocks or more often in sheets as revetment for the concrete walls of temples and other prestigious buildings.

3.134c

3.4 AUGUSTAN ROME AND ITS EMPIRE

3.135a

3.135b

INTRODUCTION: FROM CAESAR TO CONSTANTINE

Octavian, having defeated Antony and Cleopatra and the decadent East in 31 BCE, surrendered to a purged Senate. which accorded him the title of Augustus. Elevated to lead the college of priests (as *Pontifex Maximus*), he promoted a return to old values and could ultimately claim to have restored the Republic. He also launched a programme of physical and moral regeneration.**3.135**

AUGUSTUS

From 27 BCE until his death in 14 CE, Augustus was re-endowed annually with the disposal of the consulship (which gave him prime authority) and with the tribunitian power (which gave him the popular role). His most effective endowment, however, was a general proconsular imperium which ran to supreme command of the armed forces. Called *Princeps* (first citizen), in principle he left the Senate to decide whether his extraordinary accumulation of powers would survive him. In fact, however, he set the precedent for nominating his heir from his family and his adopted family name, Caesar, came to be associated with the position forever after.

It would be difficult to overestimate the importance of

Apotheosis – elevation to the realm of the gods (most potently on the wings of an eagle) – has never been more graphically conveyed than in the Antonine relief of the emperor and his wife escorted by eagles as they are born heavenwards over Rome and the Tiber by eagle-winged Aion, spirit of eternity.

3.135c

Augustus in ensuring the survival of the Roman Empire for some four centuries – fourteen until the fall of its eastern successor – and of Classical civilization indefinitely. He reformed the army, stationing divisions in permanent camps around the frontiers, and developed a professional civil service, drawn mainly from the middle class. But the effectiveness of the Augustan system depended on the character of the *Princeps* and without a generally accepted formula the succession was insecure, to the cost of both dynasty and empire.

3.136a

IMPERIAL SUCCESSION

Augustus adopted his successor – his stepson, the much-maligned Tiberius (14–37) – as he himself had been adopted by his uncle, Julius Caesar. Adoption was obviously calculated to save the succession from falling hostage to the fortune (or ill-fortune) of birth but it certainly did not prevent inter-family rivalry from favouring the inadequate. Many good men had been eliminated before the succession of Caligula (37–41) and the spoilt Nero (54–68). In between, the army set an ominous precedent in promoting Claudius – though he proved to be well-advised. After the assassination of Nero, military might triumphed with the authoritarian Vespasian (69–79), who had no time for the fiction of a restored republic.

Having instituted a hereditary monarchy in his Flavian line, Vespasian was succeeded by his sons Titus and Domitian. The latter's autocratic style provoked his murder (in 91) and the ultimate legatee was another great soldier, Trajan (98–117), who was no less a monarch. After Trajan, adoption, birth and the army – even the Senate – all produced emperors, and for more than a century most of them were at least creditable and several were outstanding, notably Hadrian, Antoninus Pius, Marcus Aurelius, and Septimius Severus. Under them, with security and sound administration sustained by the professional army and civil service, agriculture, industry and trade flourished, promoting a higher standard of living for more people than ever before, regardless of race or creed.

EXPANSION AND DECLINE

Augustus advised against extending the empire beyond the Rhine, the Danube and the Syrian desert. Early in the 2nd century Trajan decisively ignored this both in Europe and the east. Celebrated in the spiral frieze of the commemorative column that once dominated his forum,**3.136a** his success was limited, especially in the struggle with Persia, and his successors were subjected to the incessant strain of fighting on widely dispersed fronts. This was especially taxing after c. 225 when the exhausted Parthians were replaced in the east by the virile Sassan-ians. Their leader, Ardashir Sassan of Fars, claimed descent from the Achaemenids as the Parthian Arsaces had done half a millennium earlier and founded a dynasty that was to rule for some four hundred years to the discomfort of Rome and its successors: the new era was initiated by the humiliating defeat and capture of the emperor Valerian by Ardashir's son, Sharpur I, in 259.**3.136b**

3.136b

The very security and prosperity within the empire promoted provincial independence. Many provinces had drawn civilization from Rome and grew strong and wealthy in provisioning the imperial regime. Many had been wealthy and powerful kingdoms before Rome: wealthy and powerful again, they rediscovered their own identities in an age when complacency towards them on the one hand, distraction by remote frontier problems on the other, were sapping the vitality of the capital. And in the army the Italian contingent was far outweighed by soldiers from the provinces – even from the barbarian tribes it existed to combat.

›3.136 ROMAN EXPANSION AND REVERSE: (a) Rome, Forum of Trajan, commemorative column with spiral reliefs representing the campaign that extended Roman rule beyond the Danube into what is now Romania; (b) Naqsh-i-Rustam, the humiliation of Valerian by Sharpur I (Sassanian relief) – the astonishing event was widely proclaimed by the Sassanians but the point is made most forcefully below the tomb of Darius I where, of course, it would be seen to revive the glory of the great Achaemenids from whom the Sassanians claimed descent.

3.137a

›**3.137 ROME, LATE SETTLEMENTS:** (a) the walls of Aurelian with the Porta Ostiensis and the Mausoleum of Cestius; (b) Diocletian's Tetrarchs (twin 4th-century Egyptian sculpture groups applied to the outer corner of the treasury in the south side of St Mark's basilica, Venice).

Emperor Aurelian (270–75) acted on the urgent need to defend the capital from the barbarian tribes who had recently reached as far south as the Po. His walls, finished five years after his assassination, were 19 kilometres in circuit, up to 4 metres thick and nearly 8 metres high, with a continuous wall walk, square towers at regular intervals (100 Roman feet – 19.6 metres) and eighteen double or single gates between twin round towers. Brick-sheathed concrete was used throughout except for the stone-built gates. Later emperors were responsible for strengthening and heightening exercises. The tomb pyramid of Cestius (left) is dated to c. 12 BCE.

With the decentralization of power explicit in the institution of the Tetrachy, Rome was supplemented by

By the middle of the 3rd century the empire was on the point of extinction: the cost of constant conflict with the Germanic 'barbarians' in the north-west and the Parthians in the east had undermined it politically and economically. The effort promoted the numerous commanders of increasingly barbarized legions whose rivalries rent the empire within: the succession was at their bidding and they made emperors whose paramount concern was to keep them satisfied. Miraculously the corrupt system promoted two great generals to supreme power and timely reform.

Aurelian (270–75) began the reconstruction of the imperial defences and reversed military misfortune with a reformed army.**3.137a** Assassinated before he could consolidate a new order, he had restored an authority which provided his aide, the Dalmatian Diocletian, with the basis for radical reform. Elevated by the army within a decade of Aurelian's death, this extraordinary ruler (284–305) realized that the empire was beyond the control of one man, divided it and appointed the Pannonian soldier Maximinianus as his associate in 286.

Diocletian was *Dominus* (lord), rather than *Princeps*, but he shared the title *Augustus* with his associate and, to ease the succession no less than the burden of far-flung rule, each had an assistant *Caesar*. Under these four co-rulers (the Tetrarchy), the empire was divided into four prefectures, the old provinces were replaced by twelve dioceses and these were subdivided into new provinces.**3.137b** The civil and military powers of the proconsuls who had governed the old provinces were also split, the former between the 'vicars' and 'counts' of the new dioceses and provinces, the latter between generals supporting them but responsible to the *Dominus*: no viceroy was to have both. Individuality and free enterprise were curtailed. Rome was no longer the unique capital and the republican system 'restored' by Augustus – but retired by the authoritarian Flavians – was officially dead.

Cocooned in a court developing along oriental lines, despite the Tetrarchy the elderly emperor remained preeminent as Dominus in his great camp-palace at Split. In 305, however, illness prompted him to resign power in concert with Maximian to the 'Caesars' Galerius and Constantius. The latter died the following year and, despite the appointment of two new caesars, his son Constantine was proclaimed emperor by his victorious army in Britain. Maximianus's son Maxentius challenged this and secured Italy but was finally dispatched by Constantine in October 312, at the Milvian Bridge on the northern approach to Rome. The consequences were to be as profound as any in the history of Europe and the Mediteranean littoral.

3.137b

new capitals – Trier, Milan, Salonika, Split and Antioch were among the most important – and the Roman Palatine, formerly the only official residence of the emperor, was widely emulated. Built outside existing settlements or within distinct compounds, most of these works have left scant remains: among them, familiar is the proximity of a circus in which emperor and people met but new is the emphasis on fortification and the incorporation of an imperial tomb – as at Split, the exceptional survivor of the type.

3.138a

3.138b

THE CULT OF THE EMPEROR

Restoring confidence in Rome, Augustus re-established the basis for a revival of the old religion and its mores. A key element in his policy was state-sponsorship of Virgil and the revival of epic literature in his account of the foundation of Rome by the Trojan refugee Aeneas, which acknowledged the shared history of the Roman and the Greek but asserted the triumph of the Latin genius in glorifying the destiny of Rome. Tolerance of other beliefs was sustained but foreign cults were rigorously excluded from the sacred boundaries of the metropolis.

Yet the traditional devotion to the genius of Rome acquired an eastern aspect in its identification with Caesar – the so-called cult of the emperor. The genius of Rome was embodied in a long line of venerable men, personifications of its fundamental values. As heirs to Aeneas, they might be seen as superhuman in the light of Homeric mythology but the idea of man becoming god – of his apotheosis – was one of the exotic eastern imports that appalled puritanical Republicans.

In the place of the Hellenistic king, however, Romans did achieve apotheosis: in the east, recently renewed tradition attributed divinity – at least of inspiration – to the ruler who sustained his mandate in furthering prosperity and security. In the newly settled west, on the other hand, civilization, prosperity and security were due to Rome. Thus meaning different things in different places, the cult of Rome and Augustus was generally maintained as the affirmation of dedication to the imperial ideal.

Temples were dedicated to Rome and Augustus after the death of the *Princeps* and many of his successors were similarly honoured – as indeed was his uncle. But the building type specifically designed to celebrate the apotheosis of imperial power was the triumphal arch. Proclaiming the glory of the ruler, the gate in the urban limits was ideally

3.138c

›3.138 CEREMONIAL GATE AND TRIUMPHAL

(a) Rimini, Arch of Augustus (27 BCE); (b) Susa, Arch of Augustus (9 BCE); (c) Rome, Porta Maggiore (built by Emperor Claudius c. 50 and incorporated in the walls of Emperor Aurelian c. 275); (d–f) Forum Romanum, view through the Arch of Titus (c. 80) to the Arch of Septimius Severus (c. 200) and details of the triumph and apotheosis of Titus embellishing the arch.

The ceremonial gate in Rimini's wall was built to mark the end of the restored via Flaminia (with its twin standing in the northern outskirts of Rome). The unresolved relationship between the arch, the Order, the pediment and the putative attic (which was to develop into a standard element of the triumphal arch) marks the work as preceding the promotion of Hellenic logic and precision in the mature Augustan age.

The deletion of the pediment in the revision of the formula for the Arch of Augustus at Susa effectively solved the major problem, though the relationship between the Order and the arch required further thought: with only one column set well beyond a flat section of wall to each side of the arch, the entablature was over-extended and the two elements merely coexist.

The standard solution to the design problem addressed but not fully resolved at Susa was to support the arch with distinct piers and double the columns to frame them. The motif emerges as a series of aedicules in the special context of the twin-arched Porta Maggiore in Rome. This carried the Aqua Claudia and the Aqua Anio Novis across via Labicana and via Praenestina at the eastern entrance to the city.

The imperial norm is first represented in the reconstruction of the Forum of Julius Caesar, in the later Arch of Titus and in the dominant triple-arched type in which a pair of minor openings penetrates the piers.

extracted from that context to mark the Sacred Way of triumph to the Temple of Jupiter Capitolinus in cities all over the empire, as in Rome. With the apotheosis of the ruler on eastern lines, it assumed the Hellenized form of the ancient Mesopotamian twin-towered palace portal where divinity appeared before man through the agency of the king.[1.52] The Roman commemorative arch goes back at least to the triumph of Scipio Africanus in the Carthaginian wars but the Classical form appears with Augustus, if not Julius Caesar.[3.138]

3.138e

3.138f

3.138d

3.139

9 AUGUSTAN ROME AND VITRUVIUS

The moral regeneration of the Augustan age was supported by regeneration of the arts – not least architecture. Inspired by the grand plans of his uncle and aided by his great minister, Agrippa, Augustus was certainly vigorous in his determination to renovate the fabric as well as the polity of Rome – and conquest provided a seemingly inexhaustible fund. Utilitarian public works were certainly not neglected but in his testament, *Res Gestae*, he claimed to have found the capital a city of brick and left it a city of marble. This was effected by opening the quarries at Carrara. The new material called for neo-Hellenic standards of detail and craftsmanship – indeed, the importation of craftsmen from Greece – which gave the era a Classicizing image despite the wide diversity of its buildings.

Agrippa's major effort was concentrated on developing the area around the Campus Martius, to the west of the Capitoline, with forums, porticoes, baths, a basilica and the Pantheon: much of his work was destroyed by fire in 80 CE. Apart from the extraordinary Ara Pacis (Altar of Peace) on the Campus to the north of Agrippa's baths, Augustus's major effort was concentrated on the programme of renovation and extension initiated by his uncle around the Forum Romanum.**3.139–3.142**

>**3.139 ROME, FORUM OF JULIUS CAESAR WITH TEMPLE OF VENUS GENETRIX:** reconstruction.

>**3.140 IMPERIAL ROME:** (a) model of central area and (b, pages 566–567) plan with (1) Capitoline with the Temple of Jupiter Capitolinus (the Temple of Jupiter Optimus Maximus, Juno and Minerva, the cult centre of the city's patron deities) and site of the ancient citadel (Arx) to the north-east; (2) Forum Romanum with (i) Regia (the Etruscan royal megaron), (ii) Temple of Vesta (with sacred hearth, symbol of the city's life) and neighbouring House of the Vestal Virgins, (iii) Temple of Castor and Pollux, (iv) Temple of Divus Julius with Arch of Augustus beside it, (v) Temple of Antoninus and Faustina, (vi) Basilica Aemilia, (vii) Basilica Julia, (viii) Curia (senate house) by the place of public assembly (comitium), (ix) Rostrum (for address to public assembly), (x) Arch of Septimius Severus, (xi) Temple of Saturn, (xii) Temples of Concord and Vespasian, (xiii) Tabularium (state archives); (3) imperial forums: (xiv) Julium and Temple of Venus Genetrix, (xv) Augusteum and Temple of Mars Ultor, (xvi) Transitorium and Temple of Minerva, (xvii) Trajan with, from north-west to south-east, Temple of Divus Traianus and its precinct, column, Basilica Ulpia, and outer court and equestrian statue flanked by semi-circular market buildings; (4) Forum Boarium with (xviii) Temple of Fortuna Virilis; (5) Theatre of Marcellus by the Tiber bridge; (6) Circus Maximus; (7) Palatine with (xix) House of Livia (Augustus's wife) and other early Julio-Claudian palaces, (xx) Flavian Palace, state apartments with basilica, aula regia and lararium to the north-east of the central peristyles, triclinium to the south-west and private apartments and garden on lower level to the south-east; (8) via Sacra with (xxi) Arch of Constantine, (xxii) Basilica of Constantine, (xxiii) Hadrian's Temple of Venus and Rome and Arch of Titus; (9) site of Nero's Golden House (Domus Aurea), redeveloped for the Colosseum and the Baths of Titus and Trajan; (10) Campus Martius quarter with Agrippa's Saepta and Baths (rebuilt by Nero, Domition, and Antoninus (xxiv), Pantheon (xxv) and Augustus's Ara Pacis (xxvi).

3.140a

Central Rome

The Forum Romanum was originally an unpaved market place flanked by
shops (tabernae), narrowing towards the via Sacra to the south-east and
rising with the slope of the Capitoline to the north-west. Public assemblies

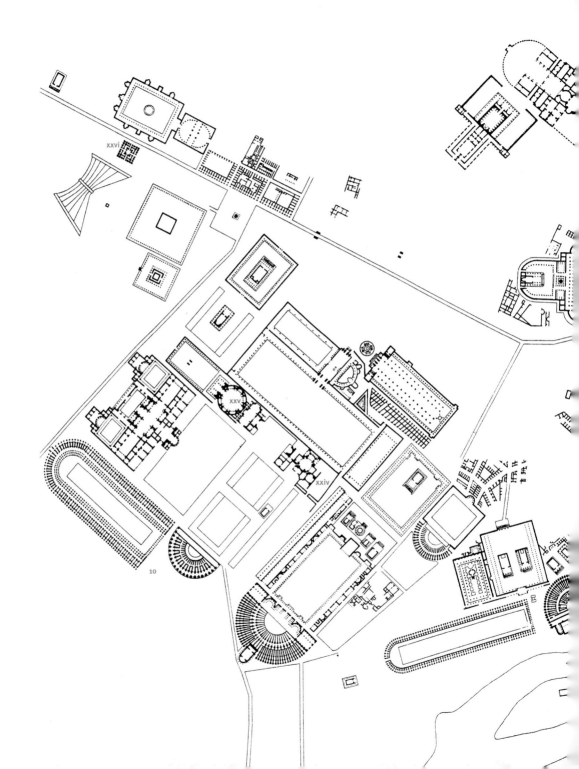

xxvi

xxv

xxiv

10

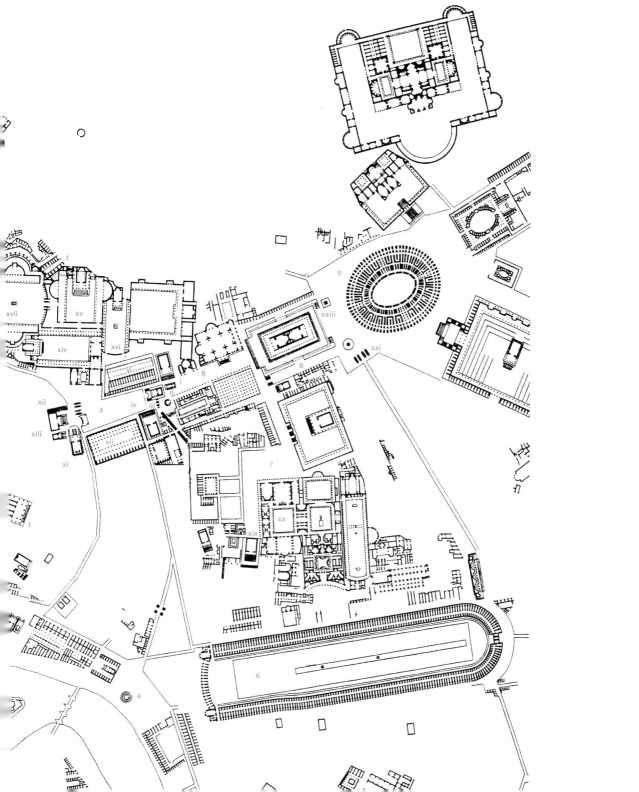

were held in front of the Curia. By the end of the Republic the only signifi-cant Etruscan survival (apart from the foundations of temples) was the Regia below the Palatine. Hellenization transformed the other public buildings, lending order to their environment, but the organic growth pattern was never entirely erased. The old tabernae (cubicles with living rooms above) to the north were destroyed by fire in 210 BCE and by 179 they had been replaced by the Basilica Aemilia behind a shopping stoa. This complex was rebuilt after 55 BCE by Julius Caesar, who also rebuilt the neighbouring Curia c. 45. Both were rebuilt again by Augustus after a fire in 14 BCE. Beside the Temple of Castor and Pollux – founded in the early 5th century BCE, rebuilt in 117 and again from 7 BCE – the shops along the southern side (out of alignment with those on the north) were replaced by a stoa in 169 and this in turn gave way to the Basilica Julia, which was built by Caesar after 54 and rebuilt with concrete vaults (rather than the usual timber ceiling) by Augustus after a fire c. 12 BCE. Regularization at the western end was inhibited by the slopes of the Capitoline hill with the Temple of Saturn (reputedly from the early 5th century but rebuilt c. 30 BCE) to the south and the public assembly ground at the base of the northern spur supporting the Arx. The asymmetrical composition was effectively closed in 78 BCE by Sulla's construction of the Tabularium and Caesar's relocation of the Rostrum in conjunction with his work on the curia. The eastern end was closed in 29 BCE by the Temple of the Divus Julius, which masked the irregular Etruscan distribution of the Regia (restored in 36 BCE), and the Temple of Vesta.

To the south side of the Temple of Divus Julius, the Arch of Augustus – attached c. 19 BCE to commemorate victory over the Parthians – eclipsed the Fornix Fabianus (built in 121 to commemorate victory over barbarians and rebuilt in 57 BCE), which provided the precedent for it – and, presumably, for the arches of the Forum of Julius Caesar. Augustus completed that great work – planned after its patron's victory over Pompey in 48 BCE and dedicated to Venus Genetrix as the source of the Julian line – which itself completes the process of Hellenization advanced in the forum at Pompeii. In emulation, the *Princeps* then began the ultimately extensive sequence of imperial forums to the east of the Forum Romanum, by importing Athenians to create his own Forum and Temple of Mars Ultor.

3.141a

3.141b

›**3.141 IMPERIAL ORDERS:** (a) Corinthian capital and entablature from the Temple of Jupiter Stator; (b) Corinthian capital from the Temple of Mars Ultor which dominated the Forum of Augustus; (c) Corinthian capital from the Pantheon (attributed to Agrippa but possibly Hadrianic); (d) Composite capital and entablature from the Arch of Titus.

Whereas the Corinthian Order retained the Ionic form of cornice, sometimes supplemented by consoles above the zone of the dentils (as in a and b), the Composite (of Ionic and Corinthian capital elements) always included such consoles.

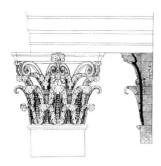

3.141c

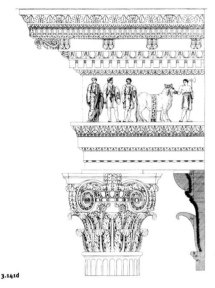

3.141d

Slightly expanding the formula promoted by Caesar, but bringing the temple further forward between concave exedrae, the Augustan forum marks the apogee of the regime's Classicizing tendency at the end of the last century BCE. The surviving fragments of the Forum and the contemporary Ara Pacis of the Campus Martius (Field of Mars) indicate that, along with a somewhat pedantic Hellenic historicism reproduced in new opulence, the Athenian craftsmen imported by Augustus brought with them a vital Hellenistic taste for the uncanonical in proportions and decoration. The caryatids of the surrounding colonnades represent the historicism; the 'Pegasus' capitals represent uncanonical vitality. Deriving respectively from the Erechtheion on the Athenian Acropolis and buildings like the Temple of Apollo at Didyma, both recall the inner propylaea donated to the sanctuary of Demeter at Eleusis by the Roman Appius Claudius Pulcher c. 50 BCE.

The later imperial forums are overshadowed by the great complex laid out for Emperor Trajan by Apollodorus of Damascus and dedicated in 113 CE. Developing the formula bequeathed by Augustus, the architect provided a rich sequence of spaces. The temple precinct to the north-west was preceded by a colonnaded court flanked by semi-circular market buildings with more than one hundred and fifty shops in addition to a great hall of six groin-vaulted bays – 28 by 9.8 metres – further up the terraced slopes of the Quirinal hill. Between this and the precinct was a transverse basilica (the Basilica Ulpia with its double aisles and two apses). The outer court was centred on an equestrian statue of the emperor and the inner precinct was preceded by a monumental column, 38 metres high, supporting another statue of the emperor and embellished with a spiral relief of his conquest of Dacia.

On the Palatine – the traditional residence of the Pontifex Maximus, who had inherited the religious functions of the Tarquin kings – Augustus and his wife Livia were accommodated in relative, and much flaunted, modesty. His successors augmented this, but it was not until the reign of Domitian (81–96) that a truly imperial palace eclipsed all earlier work – even the seats of Hellenistic monarchs, from which its builders drew their inspiration though developing their own conception of space.

3.142a

Though a considerable amount survived to inspire the Italian Renaissance of the 15th century,**3.143** little of all this remains now. Indeed, the most complete representatives of a varied age, apart from the Ara Pacis in Rome,**3.142** are the Arches of Augustus at Rimini and Susa,**3.138a,b** the Temple of Augustus and Livia at Vienne,**3.145** and the so-called Maison Carrée at Nimes.**3.144**

3.142b

›3.142 ROME, ARA PACIS AUGUSTAE: (a, b) detail of frieze and reconstruction.

Dedicated in 9 BCE to the peace imposed by Augustus, this unique work consisted of a square enclosure protecting a square platform and altar. Made entirely of marble, the enclosure's principal embellishment was a frieze of unsurpassed quality representing the procession held in July, 13 BCE connected with the foundation.

›3.143 ROME, PORTICO OF GAIUS AND LUCIUS, late-1st century BCE (drawing by Giuliano da Sangallo, late-15th century).

This Doric portico has been identified with the one sheltering the shops in front of the Basilica Aemilia. If the identification is correct, the trabeated system imposed on the walls would have contrasted with the arcades of the Basilica Julia on the other side of the forum.

3.143

3.144

> **3.144 NIMES, THE SO-CALLED MAISON CARRÉE,** 1st decade CE.

This temple, the finest surviving work of the period, was officially dedicated to Caius and Lucius Caesar as the heirs to the *Princeps*. The pseudo-peripteral form conforms to the Italic norm, but the precision of the workmanship and the details of the Order follow the example of the Temple of Mars Ultor and the acanthus-scroll frieze that of the Ara Pacis.

> **3.145 VIENNE, TEMPLE OF AUGUSTUS AND LIVIA,** early 1st century CE.

The age of Augustus sustained the orthodox Republican tradition of the hexastyle temple with peristyle extending only partially along the sides, but articulated the last side bays and the rear with pilasters.

3.145

VITRUVIUS

The theoretical basis for Augustan architecture was provided by Vitruvius Pollio, the only ancient architectural theorist whose text has descended to us intact. He developed in an age of political and architectural adventure. The concrete dome would not have been new to him but the articulation of multi-storey buildings with superimposed Orders was a recent development which greatly impressed him. A military engineer in the service of Julius Caesar, his only building specifically discussed in his treatise is the basilica at the Julian colony of Fano (Book V. 1). He was widely travelled and knew the great sites of Greece and Asia Minor. He was also widely read and quotes numerous Greek writers among his sources. For all the rationalism derived from them, however, he reveals an engineer's pragmatism in urging common-sense respect for the circumstances of site and programme. He compiled the work in the decade or so after Caesar's assassination, when political chaos stifled practice, and dedicated it about 27 BCE to the new *Princeps* who promised great opportunities to architects.**3.146**

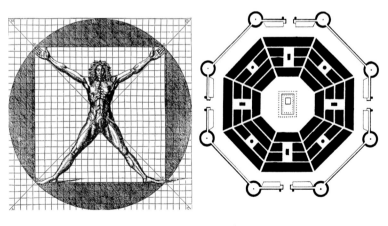

›3.146 THE VITRUVIAN IDEAL MAN AND IDEAL TOWN.

Vitruvius's original illustrations were not reproduced in the copies of his work that survived the collapse of Classical Antiquity. New ones, many controversial, were provided in the editions that appeared following the renaissance of humanist studies and Classical architecture in 15th-century Italy. Forcing conformity between idea and image, Cesare Cesariano's strident figure of the Vitruvian man (Como, 1521) has some advantage over more celebrated versions in the clarity – if unsubtlety – with which the grid determines the proportions of the symmetry described by square and circle.

For his ideal town, Vitruvius specifically recommends a circular perimeter to avoid salient angles that might shelter enemies. The towers punctuating the perimeter wall may be circular or polygonal. Most of his editors produce a polygonal plan for the whole. The positioning of gates off-axis with the streets radiating from the central forum follows from Vitruvius's determination to shut out the winds. The approach accords with the time-honoured defensive device of turning entrance through right-angles.

De architectura

The first seven of Vitruvius's ten books deal with architecture, building and decoration and the last three with mechanics and engineering. After differentiating public building from private, religious from secular and describing the ideal town, Book I defines the basic principles and concerns of architecture: order, propriety and economy; strength, utility and beauty. Having traced the origins of architecture to the cave and the hut woven like a nest or won from the living tree, Book II surveys sophisticated building materials and methods. Opening the account of building types with temples, Book III defines order.

Order in composition begins with symmetry which, for Vitruvius, is correspondence between the parts and the whole drawn not merely from consistent distribution but from the consistent proportioning of their dimensions in accordance with a common module (a basic unit selected as standard). The supreme exemplar is the ideal man proportioned on a grid and described by square and circle – the key to the Hellenic identification of microcosm and macrocosm, man and universe, as we have seen. By implication, rational geometry is the essence of complete coherence in planning – as in the ideal town.

Writing 'On symmetry in temples and the human body', Vitruvius defines the essence of order as proportion: 'a correspondence among the measures of an entire work, and of the whole to a certain part selected as standard.... Without symmetry and proportion there can be no principles in the design of any temple; that is, if there is no precise relation between its members, as in the case of those of a well-shaped man'. After defining the ideal ratios between the parts of the human body ('the length of the foot is one-sixth of the height ...', etc.), he notes that 'if a man is placed flat on his back, with his hands and feet extended, and a pair of compasses centred at his navel, the fingers and toes of his two hands and feet will touch the circumference of a circle described therefrom. And just as the human body yields a circular outline, so too a square figure may be found from it.... Therefore, since nature has designed the human body so that its members are duly proportioned to the frame as a whole, it appears that the ancients had good reason for their rule that in perfect buildings the different mem-

bers must be in exact symmetrical relations to the whole general scheme'
(Book III. 1).

Pursuing the analogy between architectural order and the human body, Vitruvius introduces the Orders and asserts that there are two: male and female. These are the Doric and Ionic respectively, the Corinthian being an an elaboration of the Ionic, the Tuscan a primitive translation of the Doric which merits comparatively little attention. Propriety governs their application in accordance with the virility of the dedicatee, the status of the patron and, in multi-storey civil works, with the need for apparent strength at the base, lightness and grace above. Beyond that, tracing the details of both systems to timber construction, he promotes an architectonic approach to decoration.

In accounting for the origin of the Orders, Vitruvius relates that the Dorians, 'wishing to set up columns [for a temple to Apollo] ... and being in search of some way by which they could render them fit to bear a load and also of a satisfactory beauty of appearance ... measured the imprint of a man's foot and compared this with his height. On finding that, in a man, the foot was one-sixth of the height, they applied the same principle to the column and reared it, shaft and capital, to a height six times its thickness at its base. Thus the Doric column, as used in buildings, began to exhibit the proportions, strength and beauty of the body of a man.... When they desired to construct a temple to Diana in a new style of beauty, they translated these footprints into terms characteristic of the slenderness of a woman ...' (Book IV. 1). The Doric Order attained the proportions of 1:6 long after its maturity, but that does not invalidate the anthropomorphic thesis.

3.147a

10 FORM AND IMPERIAL STYLE

It was in the context of the multi-storey buildings of their engineers, the theatres or amphitheatres and stadia carried on superimposed arcades in particular, that Vitruvius's followers perfected their architectonic approach to ornament through the application of the Order to the wall as a metaphor for load and support – their synthesis of the native and Hellenistic traditions.

THE THEATRE AND ITS ARTICULATION

Mastery of the arch had achieved superimposed galleries of stone to provide support for, and access to, the cavea on flat sites. The strictly semi-circular structure was closed beyond a relatively deep stage by a scenae frons in the form of a permanent palace façade integrated with and rising to the height of the cavea. The first such theatre was begun in Rome in 55 BCE by Pompey.**3.147** Its descendants have proved the most durable of Roman legacies.**3.148–3.152**

Articulation with superimposed Orders stamped a coherent framework of proportions on a multi-storey building while differentiating each level in accordance with the prescriptions of Vitruvius – the male canon for strength and virility at the base, the female for lightness and grace above. This was most prominently displayed from c. 78 BCE in the two storeys of the tabularium that overlooked the Roman Forum from the west. However, the Theatre of Marcellus is the earliest work surviving in substantial part in which Doric and Ionic Orders are superimposed on tiered arcades – there was almost certainly a Corinthian one applied to the tall parapet at the top too. The Colosseum is the supreme example: three tiers of arcades are framed by Doric, Ionic and Corinthian Orders of half columns and the parapet, blind except for windows in every second bay, has Corinthian pilasters.**3.150** Subsequently the Composite Ionic-Corinthian Order was introduced to enhance the lightness and grace at the top of multi-storey buildings but it was certainly not to be confined to fourth storeys, as the Arch of Titus elegantly demonstrates.**3.138d**

›3.147 ROME, THEATRE OF MARCELLUS, completed c. 10 BCE: (a) view, (b) detail of Order, (c) model.

Incorporated into a medieval fort and then into a Renaissance palace, the cavea is well preserved in part, but the scenae frons has disappeared. There were three tiers of seats accommodating about eleven thousand people – the lower two of stone, the top one of timber. The seating was carried by arches ascending in height on the radii. Ramps were inserted between radiating walls at regular intervals and the external galleries, arcaded within the Orders around the circumference and radially vaulted, provided both buttressing and access to them.

3.147b

3.147c

The Roman theatre and amphitheatre

It is known that there were elaborate temporary theatres in Rome in the first half of the 1st century BCE – the fantasy theatres that feature prominently in the Third Style of Pompeiian wall-painting presumably reflect them – but there were no permanent buildings for public entertainment there until Pompey built his stone theatre in 55 BCE. Preceded by the large theatre of Pompeii – among many others in Magna Graecia – it was modelled on the Hellenistic theatre at Mitylene, but with the semi-circle

3.149a

closed by the diagonal scenae frons. As at Palestrina,**3.118** a peristyle ran round the cavea at the top with a circular tempietto in the centre, recalling the sacred origin of drama and mollifying puritan objection to the erection of monumental theatres. With timber seating terraced over superimposed ambulatory arcades and divided into sectors by radiating staircases – as at Arles – the type had clearly established itself in stone by the time of Augustus.

Conforming to precedent, most recently stated for Pompey in 55 BCE, the theatre named after Augustus's protégé Marcellus was planned under Caesar but not completed until towards the end of the penultimate decade BCE. The strictly semi-circular structure was closed beyond a relatively deep stage by a scenae frons in the form of a permanent palace façade integrated with and rising to the height of the cavea. A derivative type, crossed with the Greek type of the bouleterion, is the roofed auditorium for concerts and lectures called odeon: apart from the one at Pompeii, dating from the early years of the colony, the most prominent example is the one built by Agrippa c. 15 BCE on the south-west of the Acropolis at Athens.**3.44**

3.149b

3.149c

›ARCHITECTURE IN CONTEXT »THE CLASSICAL WORLD

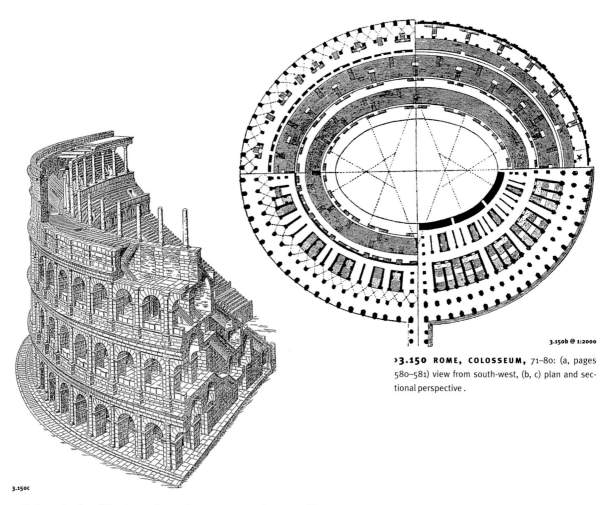

3.150b @ 1:2000

›3.150 ROME, COLOSSEUM, 71–80: (a, pages 580–581) view from south-west, (b, c) plan and sectional perspective .

3.150c

Built on the site of Nero's notorious palace to accommodate some fifty thousand spectators, the Colosseum is 188 by 156 metres. Unprecedented in scale if not in form, travertine outside, tufa inside and with concrete limited to the foundations and the upper walls and tunnel vaults, the awesome structure was hardly novel towards the end of the 1st century CE. The cavea of the Theatre of Marcellus anticipated it in most of its essentials and the elliptical form had long been established at Pompeii though the latest precedents in Rome were temporary structures of Caligula and Nero.

›3.151 EL DJEM (TUNISIA), AMPHITHEATRE, late-2nd century CE: view of tiered arcades which once supported seating in this, the fourth largest work of its kind in the Roman world.

The tiered arcades with their applied Orders doubled as access and buttressing for the cavea with barrel vaults following the circumference all round, unlike those of the Theatre of Marcellus where each bay had its own vault following the radial lines. The radial staircases (rather than ramps) divided the cavea into distinct sections, with banks of seats separated by gangways. The seating was of marble up to the top of the third level, with timber above, where the parapet provided a relatively insubstantial retaining wall – possibly backed by a colonnade. The corbelled blocks on the outer face of the parapet supported the poles from which the vast awning (velarium) was suspended over the seating.

›3.152 ORANGE, before 100 CE: detail of back-stage wall.

3.152

3.153a

›3.153 VARIATIONS ON THE THEATRICAL SCE-
NAE FRONS: (a–d) Sabratha (late 2nd century); general view, and scenae frons, details of stage-front
embellishment; (e, f) Lepcis Magna (early 1st century
CE, refurbished with extensive work on the scenae frons
late in the 2nd century), plan and interior view.

SCENOGRAPHY

If the Roman theatre had achieved definitive form by the
end of the 1st millennium BCE, the process of elaborating
the scenae frons was endless: it provided the ideal context
for an appeal to emotion through the manipulation of
form.**3.153** Free from the logic of structure, the Orders were
applied to the development of a fantastic scenography in
variations on the theme of the palace façade. The composition was developed from the flat plane of the floor as at
Aspendos, like many earlier works following the formula
of the Theatre of Marcellus in Rome. The wall itself had
been moulded into a curve well before the end of the 1st
century, as in the imprecisely dated theatre at Orange.

3.153b

3.153e

3.153c

3.153d

Ultimately, as at Lepcis Magna and Sabratha in Libya, the wall is masked by a screen in which the superimposed Orders articulate three semi-segmental exedrae – the central one slightly deeper than the others.**3.152, 3.153**

The style recurs in many public buildings, notably ceremonial portals and the reservoir fountains (nymphaea) which, as the source of water for most, played a major part

3.154c

›3.154 THE COLONNADED STREET AND JUNCTION ARCH: (a, pages 588–589) Apamea, main north–south artery; (b, c) Palmyra, overview from south-west (pages 590–591), detail of the wedge-like portal building masking the oblique angled junction between two sections of the main artery; (d, e) Lepcis Magna, Arch of Septimius Severus at the first rectangular arterial crossing.

Deriving from the extension of the Hellenistic stoa, the street with continuous colonnades imposed on the fronts of its individual buildings seems to have originated in Syrian towns like Apamea in the 1st century. It had reached east to Palmyra by the end of that century and west to the Aegean coast of Asia Minor shortly afterwards. The Apamaea street is exceptional in its dimensions: 2 kilometres long, it is 22.5 metres wide between the colonnades and its portico walls were 40m apart.

in the scenography of the colonnaded street. And the colonnaded street of the Roman town at its apogee has never been exceeded in magnificence.**3.154, 3.155**

The colonnaded street is certainly the most ubiquitous manifestation of Roman scenographic planning. Beyond it, the temple complex provided splendid opportunities for arranging rich vistas through varied spaces. The imperial forums, particularly that of Trajan, set a standard rarely surpassed but little of the principal colonnaded spaces –

3.154d

3.154e

3.155a

›3.155 SCENOGRAPHIC BUILDING: (a) Jerash, fountain, c. 190; (b) Miletos, West Market Gate c. 160; (c) Rome, Septizodium, dedicated by Septimius Severus in 203 probably as the façade of a fountain (model, Museum of Roman Civilization).

At least from the era of Trajan the fantasy palace façade of the theatrical scenae frons had been realized in urban monuments, nymphaea in particular, perhaps first in Asia Minor but in Syria and beyond well before the end of the 2nd century: structures elaborated in terms of superimposed Orders, but rarely fronting buildings of any spatial complexity, they were designed to close urban vistas, frame squares or simply mask undignified intrusions.

3.155b

3.155c

3.156a

3.156b

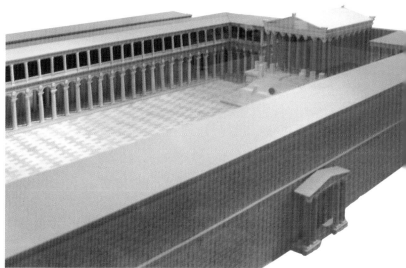

›3.156 LEPCIS MAGNA: (a) market complex (late-1st century BCE, restored at the latest under Septimius Severus); (b–e) Severan forum complex, c. 200, street to east of basilica, detail of arcade, model, and plan with (1) dynastic temple, (2) colonnaded/arcaded precinct (c. 60 by 100 metres), (3) basilica, (4) colonnaded street; (f–h) basilica, model, detail of Corinthian pier beside the apse and interior.

3.156c

3.156d

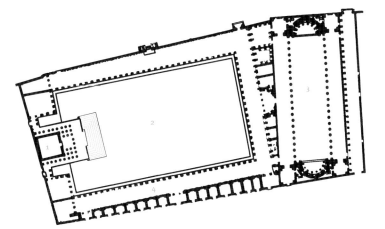

3.156e @ 1:2000

roofed or unroofed – survive.**3.156, 3.140iii** In emulation, eastern builders were particularly spectacular. The remains of the cloistered temenos of the unorthodox hybrid temple of Bel at Palmyra, with its hexastyle propylaea, provide substantial testimony to this.**3.157** Nowhere, however, was the potential more spectacularly realized than in the sanctuary of Jupiter at Baalbek.**3.158**

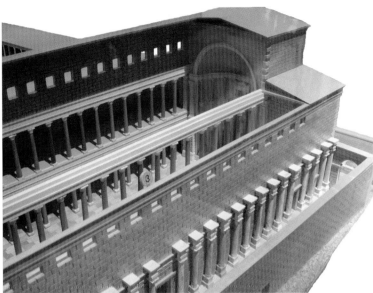

3.156f

3.156g

3.156h

3.157a

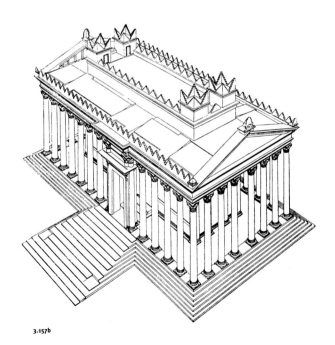

3.157b

3.157c

›3.157 PALMYRA, TEMPLE OF BEL: (a) view within temenos to main shrine, (b) axonometric reconstruction, (c) detail of ceiling in southern sanctuary of main shrine (dedicated 32 CE).

Dominating the prosperous trading city sited on an oasis in the middle of the Syrian desert, the octastyle Temple of Bel had fifteen columns on its eastern side but only fourteen on its western side, where the elaborately framed entrance unconventionally intruded off centre. A sanctuary was raised on steps and roofed at each end of the cella. Staircases in three of the four corner towers communicated with the terraced roof. Here the hybrid nature of the exercise, remote from the models of metropolitan Classicism, is at its clearest: though there were pediments at each end, merlons fringed the east and west sides of the higher walls of the cella.

By the middle of the 2nd century CE the temenos had been enclosed by colonnades, the taller western range incorporating propylaea.

3.158a

Baalbek

Long a cult centre of Ba'al and his offspring Tammuz (the local vegetation/regeneration deity), who were associated respectively with Zeus and Dionysos by Hellenistic theologians, the site was preferred by the Roman governors of Syria as a focal point of imperial devotion to Jupiter and Bacchus – themselves the Roman equivalents to Zeus and Dionysos. Jupiter's huge temple, founded about the time of the first emperor's death, was substantially complete by the middle of the 1st century CE. The richly articulated shrine to Bacchus followed a century later. By the middle of the 3rd century the former had a grand temenos flanked by colonnades with

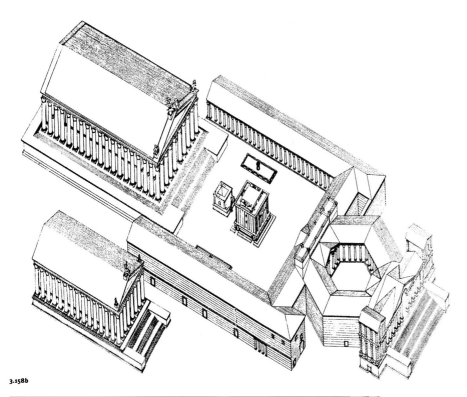

3.158b

x3.158c

>**3.158** **BAALBEK, SANCTUARY OF JUPITER HELIOPOLITANUS:** (a) remains of Temple of Jupiter, (b) restored axonometric projection of sacred precinct with Temple of Jupiter (top) and Temple of Bacchus, (c) detail of temenos with curved and rectangular exedrae and scallop-shell niches, (d, e) plan and detail of interior of Temple of Bacchus.

The enormous temple to the great Capitoline god – 48 by 88 metres with ten by nineteen unfluted columns rising to nearly 20 metres – was built on an imposing podium over earlier shrines. It was initially Augustan in style, at least in detail.

Outside the compound, to the south, the Temple of Bacchus was finished by c. 150 CE. With eight by fifteen columns, it was 35 by 66 metres. The cella walls, complex in plane and exceptionally rich in articulation, enclosed a raised and canopied sanctuary at the western end derived from the tradition of enthroning the image of the deity in a canopied aedicule.

alternating rectangular and semi-circular exedrae and preceded by an exceptional hexagonal forecourt and triumphal propylaeum. The curving of its entablature up with an arch, penetrating the pediment of a temple front between towers, recalls the twin-towered portal of the ancient Mesopotamian palace – the place of epiphany of god (or his representative) among men.[3.158, 3.152]

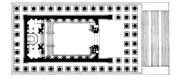

3.158c @1:2000

3.158e

The form of portico with arch penetrating pediment is called fastigium. It symbolizes the canopy of heaven which first achieved apotheosis on the ziggurat of Ur-Nammu at Ur.[1.49] Adapted to the tent of appearance, it became the ciborium or baldachino, the domical canopy ubiquitously carried over thrones and altars which prompted the arching of the entablature over the central bay and was typically echoed in the great niche above palace portals. As we shall see, it was to play a major role in the villa of Emperor Hadrian at Tivoli. And taken to decorative extreme, it appears in many variations on the theme of the palace in the frescoes of Pompeii. It first appears on the Arch of Tiberius at Orange at the beginning of the imperial era.

MANNERISM

Imperial Romans far exceeded Hellenistic builders in the prolixity with which they embellished temple interiors. But their interests went beyond mere opulence: they early learned to use the Orders against the expectations induced by the convention of the metaphor, to defy rather than to elucidate structure, and anticipated the virtuoso Mannerism of the Italian 16th century. Even as early as the reign of Tiberius, the interpenetration of the pediment in the fastigium motif on the Arch of Tiberius at Orange wilfully contradicts the logical articulation of the Arch of Augustus at Susa.[3.159, 3.138b]

Breaking the pediment and the interpenetration of

3.159

>**3.159 ORANGE, ARCH OF TIBERIUS,** C. 21 CE: oblique view from the south-west.

The earliest-known work of its type to incorporate three arches as part of the original design, it is precociously lavish in sculptural relief as well as in the uncanonical interpenetration of arch and Order. A consequence of arching the entablature up into the pediment was the removal of the arch from its natural context in the wall altogether, recalling the arch at the eastern end of the agora at Priene. Anticipating the fastigium of complexes like the one at Baalbek, this was a major imperial motif by the time of Emperor Hadrian (117–138).

>**3.160 MANNERIST SYNCOPATION:** (a) Ephesos, Library of Celsus, c. 120 CE, court front; (b) Sardis, baths, 2nd century CE, view from gymnasium.

The alternation of segmental and triangular pediments was a popular means of enlivening composition from late-Hellenistic times. Projecting the upper ones over the recessions in the lower Order, contrary to expectation, was a 2nd-century development.

The introduction of pedestals below the bases of the columns permitted an augmentation of height without exaggerated attenuation of the proportions of the Order.

one structural form with another were to become clichés of Mannerism. Another major motive was the denial of the normal relationship between solid and void in the syncopation of the rhythm of projection and recession between storeys: the outstanding Antique examples, the Library of Celsus at Ephesos or the baths of Sardis, may be contrasted with the West Market Gate at Miletos.**3.160, 3.155b**

The wayward dislocation of load and support was anticipated in the Porta dei Borsari at Verona. There too, as at

3.160a

3.160b

3.161a

>3.161 VERONA: (a) Porta dei Borsari, late-1st century CE: outer face of the city gate; (b) amphitheatre, late 1st century CE, detail of perimeter.

This work is comparable with the Colosseum in structure if not in size. At 152 by 123 metres, it held up to twenty-eight thousand people and the Orders of pilasters framed only two arcades, the third level of arches rising above the uppermost seats.

The rustication of the Order was anticipated by several Roman works of Emperor Claudius (41–54), most notably the double archway carrying his new aqueducts over converging streets, now known as the Porta Maggiore, and the podium of the Claudianum (Temple of the deified Claudius).

3.161b

Apamaea and elsewhere in the east, the spiral fluting of columns twists the conventional expression of the primitive means of dressing stone cylinders into a torsion contrary to their nature.**3.161a** Furthermore, on the exterior of the amphitheatre at Verona the convention of articulation in terms of the familiar metaphor so clearly elucidated at the Roman Colosseum, that the Order is the active agent, the wall passive, is mocked by the projection of the rusticated masonry to embrace – rather devour – the pilasters.**3.161b, 3.150**

›3.162 ROCOCO DECORATION: (a) Qanawat, so-
called basilica, second half of 3rd century CE, portal;
(b, c) Pompeii, House of Loreius Tiburtinus: wall paintings in the Third and Fourth Styles of decoration.

3.162a

ROCOCO

Mocked for their pretensions as articulating agents,
twisted and displaced, the Orders and the Classical repertory of ornament associated with them ultimately succumb
to stylized nature, as in the portal of the basilica at Qanawat
where the pilasters are overwhelmed by a rampant
vine.**3.162a** That takes us ahead, to the period when the
empire itself was succumbing to forces beyond its control.
Before the opening of the new millennium, however, the
Third Style of Pompeiian decoration showed the way – to
the disgust of Vitruvius. Formerly realistic, the architecture was then treated with increasing fantasy as a foliage-
entwined filigree scenae frons about landscapes or

3.162b

3.162c

3.163c

mythologies pictured in panels.**3.162b** In the Fourth Style, developed just before the catastrophe of 79 CE, the framework overcomes all substance or, as occasionally in the Second Style, the mythologies are played out against the architecture like a theatrical entertainment.**3.162c**

The rampant-vine motif, popular in all forms of decoration, is manifestly anti-architectonic. Structure is overwhelmed by decoration as it would be again in the Rococo and art nouveau styles of the early 18th and 20th centuries. These were propagated by reformers who, like their Roman predecessors, renounced the tired tradition initiated by the Achaeans and sought the rebirth of vitality in the realm of the Earth Mother.**3.163**

›**3.163 ROMAN MOSAICS FROM THE IMPER-IAL PERIOD:** (a, b) in the so-called Arabesque or Grotesque style from which the Rococo was later to be elaborated (Tunis, National Museum); (c, d) depicting fish and a ship at sea off a villa (Ptolemais and Tripoli, Archaeological Museums).

3.163a

3.163b

3.163d

3.164

›3.164 NAQSH-I-RUSTAM, ZOROASTRIAN
FIRE ALTAR: possibly 3rd century CE.

›3.165 ASSUR, PARTHIAN PALACE, early 1st
century CE?: (a) plan, (b) restored elevation (after
reconstruction in Berlin, Pergamon Museum).

With its irregular geometry, approximating a central square, this is the earliest-known example of the four-iwan plan – apart perhaps from the one at Nisa. If the general approach to planning in terms of a warren of rooms about a nuclear court is traditionally Mesopotamian, like the dominant arch, the eclecticism of the Parthians is marked not only by the Roman dressing but also by the inclusion of a columned hall descended through the Achaemenids from the Urartians – and, ultimately of course, from the tent. The bands of geometric patterning incised in the gypsum plaster which covered the façade is both Classical and native Parthian, the latter perhaps reproducing the motifs woven into fabric.

As we have seen, the reproduction of the multi-storey palace façade as the scenae frons of the typical Roman theatre, reflected here, did not much precede the reign of Augustus. Of course, this building and the theatrical scenae frons may derive from a common palatial type now best represented by the Library of Celsus at Ephesos or the baths at Sardis.

PARTHIAN POSTSCRIPT

The Parthians were to sap Roman strength in the east but borrow much from the architecture of their enemies – not least its scenography. However, if eastern Syria was prolix in its mannerisms, it must be said that debasement of the Hellenistic tradition through misunderstanding of its styles as agents of order – rather than merely decorative detail – is characteristic of the attempted emulation of the Romans in the fastness of far-off Parthia. As their Zoroastrian fire altars were naturally hypethral, though perhaps sheltered by a tower, their architectural legacy – such as it is – is essentially secular.**3.164**

The first capital of the Arsacids was at Nisa in Turkmenistan, their last was Ctesiphon which faced the old Seleucid capital, Seleucia, over the Tigris near modern Baghdad. However, as their monarchy was modelled on that of the Seleucids and centralization was not strong, there were many important regional centres: some of great antiquity like Assur, the old Assyrian capital, some relatively new and prolific former Greek colonies and some still younger ones like Hatra, the seat of Arab desert kings.

Leaving the tents of their nomadic past for exposure to the influence of the Hellenized west, in addition to older Persian and Mesopotamian traditions of monumentality,

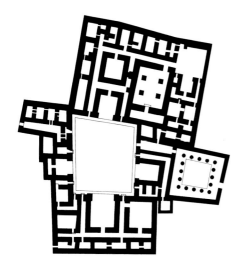

3.165b

›3.166 (PAGES 610–611) HATRA: general view of remains.

Situated between the Tigris and the Euphrates, Hatra's prosperity depended on control of one of the few oases in the northern Mesopotamian desert crossed by the east–west trade route. It was occupied by Arabs in the 1st century BCE and was the seat of a monarchy from c. 156 to 241. Culturally, at least, it was dependent on both the Romans and the Parthians though the Romans failed to take it and it remained largely independent of the Parthians. It fell to Shapur I and was then abandoned.

the Parthians and their vassals in these centres evolved a hybrid culture. The most characteristic feature of their architecture is the iwan, derived through the great arched portals of the Assyrians and Babylonians at least as early as Mari. An early example has been recovered from the ruins at Nisa. A later one at Assur has four iwans set into perpendicular façades reminiscent of the Roman theatrical scenae frons with uncanonical Orders.[3.165] Beyond its echo at more-nearly canonical Hatra, this provided the basis for the glorious achievements of Persian architecture in the service of Islam over a millennium later.[3.166]

11 MASS AND IMPERIAL SPACE

After his death in 14 CE, Augustus was interred in a mighty mausoleum on the banks of the Tiber near the northern entrance to Rome. Like the perennial pyramid,**3.167** it was a monument of geometrical purity, and with its superimposed cylinders forming tree-planted terraces its descent from the age-old tumulus is a tangible reminder of the antiquarian aspect of Augustan reform.**3.168a** Solid mass was to cede to vaulted space as building technology advanced with concrete but the former was revived on an unparalled scale by Emperor Hadrian**3.168c** just as the domed rotunda achieved its apogee in the Pantheon a century and more after the death of Augustus.

›3.167 ROME, TOMB OF AUGUSTUS (28–23 BCE), model.

The first emperor's tomb took the ancient Etruscan tradition of the walled tumulus to unprecedented proportions. Over a drum of travertine-sheathed concrete – 88 metres in diameter and centred on the tomb chamber – the tree-covered tumulus rises to a second drum with a tiered roof supporting a colossal bronze statue of the emperor. Many other imperial burials took place here in the 1st century CE.

›3.168 ROME, TOMB OF HADRIAN (begun c. 134, unfinished on the emperor's death in 138): (a) as reconstructed by Gismondi in his great model, Rome, Museum of Roman Civilization; (b) Castel Sant'Angelo (as engraved by G.-B. Piranesi); (c) Emperor Hadrian, marble, 2nd century CE (Rome, Vatican Museum).

Hadrian's elaboration of the formula incorporated a podium – 84 metres square and 10 metres high – below the drum, which was 64 metres in diameter and contained burial chambers for the emperor and his successors. Both these elements were sheathed in marble. As an alternative to the tempietto shown rising from the tree-planted tumulus here, some restorations postulate another, smaller podium and drum. A colossal statue of Hadrian or a quadriga group crowned the whole. The tomb was used until the death of Caracalla in 217. Stripped of its lavish ornament, the building was converted into a fortress (Castel Sant' Angelo) by the early medieval popes.

3.168a

3.168c

3.168b

CONCRETE SPACE

The realization of the potential of concrete for the moulding of space with varied vaulting dawns with the Augustan age, the context having been provided by the engineers of the late-Republic in utilitarian and thermal buildings. Concrete is by nature a malleable material which coalesces into a homogeneous membrane, unlike masonry. Relatively light, its weight may be reduced in a vault by varying the density of its aggregate – substituting pumice for stone in particular – as well as by attenuation and coffering. This was facilitated by the introduction of slower-drying mortar, so that each layer fused readily with the next, and the continuation of strictly horizontal bedding to the top instead of setting the aggregate in radial courses to form the perimeter of a dome – as in works like the Stabian Baths at Pompeii.**3.124b** The final realization of the logic of concrete structure liberated building from the limitations of traditional masonry and planning from the strictures of the rectangle. Thereafter spatial variety was to be the principal characteristic of imperial architecture.

In the baths of Pompeii, domical and tunnel vaults carried on heavy walls distinguish separate spaces. The tunnel vault was perhaps to achieve its apotheosis on the Palatine before the end of the 1st century CE. Well before that, the crossing of tunnel vaults had produced the groin over a square bay defined by four arches: within a sequence of such bays the forces entrained by the lateral thrust of the arches are counterposed, permitting the reduction of the mass of supporting masonry to relatively slender piers and the penetration of light from all four sides.**3.169**

Probably from the time of Nero – if not Titus – the spectacular spatial diversity of the great imperial thermae depends on the disposition of all three types of vault: indeed, their central halls led to the apotheosis of the groin vault in the last great space of imperial Rome, the Basil-

›**3.169 GROIN VAULT.**

ica of Maxentius. Meanwhile, the apotheosis of the dome – and of space as the prime concern of architects – served Hadrian's great circular temple to all the gods. Hadrian built much in the orthodox tradition and often to heroic proportions, most notably the colossal peripteral decastyle Temple of Venus and Rome beween the Forum Romanum and the Colosseum, but in size at least there was no precedent for the great rotunda of his Pantheon – though it was perhaps inspired by the type of Greek shrine represented by the Phillipeion at Olympia if not the Arsinoeion at Samothrace.**3.170, 3.77**

3.170a

The Pantheon

Central to the new district laid out by Agrippa in the peninsula formed by the bend in the River Tiber to the west of the Capitoline, the original Pantheon was dedicated early in Augustus's principate, destroyed with most of its patron's other monuments in the great fire of 80 CE, rebuilt by Domitian, evidently in its original rectangular form, and destroyed again in 110. Hadrian's work, begun c. 118 and completed a decade later, was essentially new. The inscription on the frieze of the pedimented portico, crediting it to Agrippa, has led most to conclude that this element was reused, especially as it is so ill-related to the great rotunda which forms the body of the building. Scientific analysis does not support this view, however, and it is now generally thought that the inscription was replaced in due honour to the original founder.

Built mainly of concrete, Hadrian's work consists of a cylindrical drum, with exedrae accommodating the principal deities separated by piers

›**3.170 ROME, PANTHEON,** c. 118: (a) interior (G.-B. Piranesi), (b) exterior with portico, (c) detail of structure, (d) interior detail, (e) plan.

The drum, 43.2 metres in diameter, is based on a concrete ring 4.5 metres deep and in its final form more than twice as wide. The superstructure diminishes in thickness from just over 6 metres in the drum to just over 1.5 metres at the rim of the oculus (though masonry sheathing was needed to perfect the hemispherical profile of the dome, masking the junction of

3.170d
the true intrados with the heightened drum). The grading of the aggregate from basalt at the base to pumice at the top, together with the coffering, are crucial in further lightening the load.

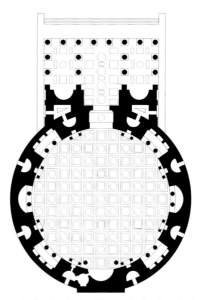

3.170e @ 1:1000

with aedicules, and a hemispherical dome. As the drum is half the height of its diameter, the dome rises to a height equal to the diameter, conceptually to encapsulate the sphere of heaven embracing all the gods. The weight of the dome, lightened in substance, structure and form, is transmitted directly to the ground through the drum. The exedrae 'excavated' from the perimeter mass enhance its monumentality by revealing its depth but still further lighten the load on the foundations. Moreover, within the plastic mass of concrete above the exedrae, relieving arches of brick deflect the pressure of the dome to the intermediate piers containing the aedicules. The two registers of the drum had a revetment of vari-coloured marble. Red and grey Egyptian granite columns, nearly 12 metres high, screened the exedrae, countering the entrance axis and deflecting the eye into the once-stuccoed dome. The exterior, masked by the colonnaded forecourt, was divided into three registers but was otherwise plain – except, of course, for the stone portico which once carried sculpture groups.

The Pantheon has rarely been equalled for size and durability: it has survived virtually intact to inspire architects for nearly two thousand years. Among its earliest followers, on a relatively small scale, is the Temple of Asclepius and the crypt of its neighbouring rotunda at Pergamon.**3.171** We shall encounter much more important examples in the greatest of the Roman thermae. Beyond these, however, the challenge for the future was to raise the hemispherical form over a rectangular volume rather than a cylinder.

›**3.171 PERGAMON, SANCTUARY OF ASCLEPIUS**, mid-2nd century: brick-vaulted rotunda crypt.

The Pantheon was often to be emulated, perhaps first on a relatively small scale in the Temple of Asklepios and the crypt of its neighbouring rotunda at Pergamon. The lack of suitable ingredients for concrete in the eastern provinces inhibited the development of an architecture of space on the metropolitan model. Materials were ultimately to be imported, but at first brick was pressed into service, as at Pergamon. The form of the large rotunda was new, but the tradition of the grand brick vault goes back to ancient Mesopotamia.

Religious architecture is generally conservative. Secular building, with its much more diversified requirements, naturally took the lead in the diversification of space. Augustus's residence on the Palatine was modest. Tiberius built on a grander scale there and, after a long line of Campanian examples, set a standard of secluded integration with nature in a sumptuous retreat on the island of Capri:**3.172** the former was superseded – and largely obliterated – by the third Flavian emperor, Domitian; the Capri villa surpassed by the last of the Giulio-Claudians, Nero – but in the centre of Rome, scandalously, not by the seaside.

Whatever their shortcomings as rulers, both Nero and Domitian rank among the greatest patrons of architecture.

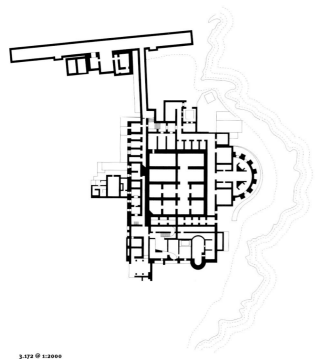

3.172 @ 1:2000

Both were responsible for extensive rebuilding after devastating fires, Nero notoriously expropriating a considerable amount of the wasted area for his own purposes but Domitian following the lines originally developed by Agrippa in the area around the Pantheon, at least. Apart from markets and sporting facilities, Nero provided a magnificent and much-needed thermal complex to supplement the Baths of Agrippa. Domitian built temples and a new forum beside that of Augustus and followed Nero with a new stadium on the Campus Martius. Both left indelible imprints on the history of architecture with their palaces.

Domitian's stadium and forum were conservative, marking the end of development in the old tradition of limited internal space and elaborated external form, but his palace was to have rooms of unprecedented scale. There was spectacular variety of moulded space too, but nothing in Domitian's private apartments exceeded the complexity of the principal reception room of Nero's Domus Aurea.**3.173, 3.174**

>3.172 CAPRI, VILLA JOVIS, c. 25–35: plan.

Capri was originally developed by Augustus. The Villa Jovis, the retreat of Emperor Tiberius, was built on terraces over the eastern cliffs high above the sea and comprised four wings relatively informally related to one another on different levels around a rectangular court built over a water reservoir. The largest and lowest wing, to the south, contained the entrance and baths. Rooms for attendants were stacked on three storeys to the west.

The imperial apartments were isolated from the rest of the complex in the east and north wings: the main state room projected out over the cliff to the east, embracing the view of the sea; the emperor's personal accommodation occupied the highest ground to the north, with views from a loggia over the Bay of Naples and a ramp leading down to an elongated terrace facing in the same direction and centred on the dining room.

Domus Aurea

Before the fire of 64 Nero had built a palace (Domus Transitoria) on family land between the Esquiline and the Palatine, deflecting the line of the via Sacra. Swept away in the clearance after the fire, what little remained to be incorporated in the foundations of the Temple of Venus and Rome indicates considerable spatial variety – in particular a rotunda in a cross with groin-vaulted arms. After the fire the land to the east of the Domus Transitoria was sequestered and added to Nero's estate to provide the setting for his new palatial villa, the Domus Aurea built c. 65 by the architects Severus and Celer.

At the end of the via Sacra, by the site of the Domus Transitoria, the three wings of a colonnaded propylaeum framed a colossal statue of the emperor, beyond which the palace itself addressed an artificial lake through a great recession in its main façade. This stamped it as a grand

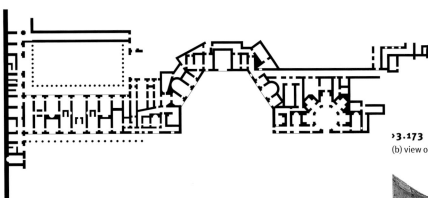

>3.173 ROME, DOMUS AUREA, c. 65: (a) plan, (b) view of main reception room.

variation on the form of the seaside villa.3.127 Incongruous in the principal urban residence of the head of state – and its expansive park, won from the sequestered land – this certainly made it no more acceptable.

The main reception room, addressing the park, consists of an octagon surrounded by an ambulatory with rectangular spaces opening from its five inner sides. The octagon has a canopy vault springing from the imposts of an arcade surrounding the ambulatory and the subsidiary spaces are alternately barrel- and groin-vaulted. A central oculus admitted a strong shaft of light to the main chamber, the lunettes formed by the arches rising above the latter's canopy admitted moderate and relatively uniform light to the ambulatory which was borrowed as a dim glow by the inner chambers: space was moulded not only by virtuoso concrete work but also by light. The enigma of this room has fascinated its visitors ever since it was rediscovered early in the 16th century: solid but void; centrifugal in form but centripetal in effect; dazzling engineering but incompletely resolved geometry (the awkward little triangles between the subsidiary spaces have not escaped censure); sophisticated yet unprecedented. Buried under later building and detritus, it was one of the 'grottoes' in which Raphael and his circle discovered the Antique mode of decoration.

After Nero's assassination the artificial lake gave way to the Colosseum, the palace itself disappeared under the platform of the Baths of Titus and the propylaeum under that of the Temple of Venus and Rome.

3.173b

3.174a

Domus Augustana

The official imperial residence on the Palatine was built by the architect Rabirius over the first ten years of the reign of the third Flavian emperor, Domitian, and extended eastwards over terraces beyond the stadium-shaped garden by Septimius Severus (193–211). Officially known as the Domus Augustana (but popularly called Palatium and therefore giving its name to the genre of great palaces descended from it), it eclipsed the earlier imperial residences on the site. That was now divided between public ceremonial to the west, with ready access from the Forum below, and private retreat to the east. The disparate characters of the two parts were uncompromisingly manifest in their distribution and massing: the

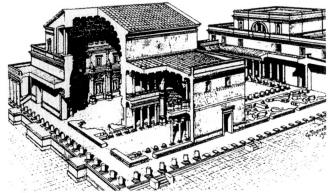

3.174b

imperious hall of audience, basilica and chapel addressed the state banquetting room over the colonnaded entrance court; the intricate rooms of the main private apartments look south from two levels over a garden court.

The palace of Tiberius, which itself had eclipsed that of Augustus to the west of a saddle in the hill, was adapted to give grand access from the forum below. The new work, sited to the east of the saddle, was designed to provide for public ceremonial as well as private retreat. The state rooms were built partly on terraces over the falling ground towards the west, where they communicated with the Domus Tiberiana and were also served by the road running up through the declivity. The private apartments were secured to the east, where they communicated with the imperial box overlooking the Circus Maximus.

The public entrance to the palace from the forum opened into a vestibule unprecedented in its dimensions – 33 by 24.5 metres – as a covered space, except by the greatest of Rabirius's works on the Palatine above. Beyond this was a guardroom and the ramp which tacked back and forth up to the Domus Tiberiana. Over the declivity and its road, the entrance to the ceremonial quarters was a domed pavilion in the centre of a range of varied spaces fronting the central peristyle but also from an outer portico which bent around the northern corner. To the north of the peristyle were the great audience hall (29 metres wide), the neighbouring aisled basilica, the imperial seat of justice (14.5 metres wide) and the much smaller chapel. Io the south was the state banqueting room (29 metres wide).

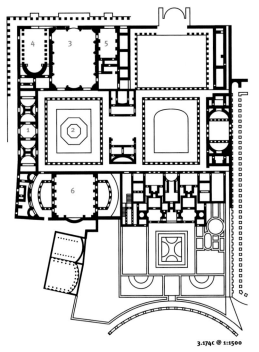

3.174c @ 1:1500

›**3.174 ROME, DOMUS AUGUSTANA,** inaugurated in 92: (a) model, (b) reconstructed perspective of the state rooms, (c) plan with entrance (1), central peristyle (2), the hall of audience (3, aula regia), basilica (4), and chapel (5, lararium), the state banqueting room (6, triclinium), (d) axonometric section and plan of the rooms facing the garden court, (e) view of remains of main residential block addressing the garden court.

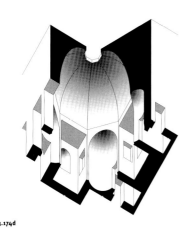

3.174d

3.174e

Entered from the south in the centre of a concave portico flanking the Circus Maximus, the private wing was arranged on two floors beside the stadium-shaped garden (incomplete on Domitian's death) and around a garden court. The upper level communicated with the ceremonial block through a second peristyle to the north-east, close to the centre of the complex. Between court and peristyle, the main range of the private apartments had an axis of loggias and halls between two similar suites overlooking the garden court and backed by loggias facing the peristyle.

The nature of the vaulting over the ceremonial rooms – indeed, whether there were vaults over the larger ones – is open to question. Unbuttressed but colonnaded towards the central peristyle and the twin fountain courts, the banqueting room must have had a flat ceiling. It is usually accepted that the lararium could easily have been vaulted and that the colonnaded basilica had a flat ceiling and a semi-dome over the apse where the emperor sat. However, there is less readiness to agree that these lateral structures could have buttressed a great barrel vault over the audience hall: the supposition is supported by the ambitious-ness of Domitian and Rabirius, no less than by evidence of strain in the partition walls, despite their great mass. The piers dividing the latter internally into bays were framed by colossal marble columns echoing those on either side of the niche for the imperial throne which termin-ated the main longitudinal axis.

3.175a

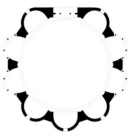

3.175b @ 1:1000

›3.175 ROME, SO-CALLED TEMPLE OF MIN-
ERVA MEDICA, early 4th century: (a) detail of original structure, (b) plan, (c) model.

The apse opposite the colonnaded entrance was
slightly deeper than the others but the opening of the
lateral pairs to the exterior through colonnades is
enigmatic. The concrete forming the dome was laid in
courses separated horizontally by tiles and vertically
by brick ribs. In similar structures it has been observed
that the lack of a developed relationship between the
ribs and the piers between the arches below denies
the former the primary structural role of distributing
the load of the vault. Indeed, the ribs seem to have
risen with the vault rather than as a preconceived
structural frame; like the tiles, their purpose seems to
have been to localize settlement as the concrete dried.
Several of the ribs here survived long after the concrete fell, leaving an impression of structural virility
not lost on later builders.

Heavy barrel vaults would have admitted light only at the ends, of
course. Naturally, the infusion of space with light depends on the lightening of structure in response to the lightening of load – especially its
distribution to isolated points – and Rabirius could manage that too:
excavation in the lower level of the Domus Augustana's private apartments has revealed an octagonal room surrounded by alternating rectangular and semi-circular spaces with a dazzling array of canopy, barrel and
semi-domical vaults. The apsidal recessions imply the principle of the
squinch (an arch thrown across the corners of a square space to support
the rim of a dome) which was to be widely employed in the development
of spatial architecture.

In all essentials, Rabirius's Palatine garden rooms anticipate the Pantheon on a tiny scale and later variations are
numerous: among the most celebrated is the relatively
simple, late-imperial decagonal pavilion in Rome's Licin-
ian Gardens known as the Temple of Minerva Medica but
possibly a tomb.**3.175** On the other hand, the great hall of
Trajan's Quirinal market complex still provides a measure
of what Rabirius might have achieved in vaulting with the
groin rather than the tunnel – assuming that he attempted
any vaulting on the imperial scale of the Domus Augustana's throne rooms.**3.176**

3.175c

›3.176 ROME, TRAJAN'S MARKET: (a) reconstructed axonometric, (b) interior of main market hall, (c) street.

Beyond the magnificent colonnaded precinct of the forum with which (in 113) he completed the imperial series begun by Augustus to the north-east of the Forum Romanum,**3.140.xvii** Trajan commissioned a complex of shops and offices on the terraced lower slopes of the Quirinal hill. Served by streets at three levels, the shops were of the traditional tunnel-vaulted single-cell type built of concrete faced with bricks with travetine details. These remains project perhaps the clearest image of the ancient urban fabric's unceremonial norm though the base-level hemicycle – with its segmental and triangular pediments, some of them halved – responded to the ample grandeur of the forum's exedrae. Towering above the latter was the three-storey six-bay market hall, in which the superimposed shops face one another across the groin-vaulted mall (28 by 9.8 metres). Similar, no doubt, to the lost main hall of Trajan's Baths, this is the earliest surviving example of such a structure on such a scale.

3.176a

3.176c

3.176b

3.177

THE APOTHEOSIS OF THE VILLA

It is no accident that the most daring example of Roman
vaulting known to us occurred in a villa-like palace. In contrast to the extreme formality of distribution about atrium
and peristyle typical of the greatest town houses in the
early imperial period, the villa was informal, rich in spatial variety, extroverted in aspect and sensitive to the natural qualities of its site. Furthering the Campanian
tradition built on by Tiberius and Domitian – if not Nero
– the younger Pliny provided detailed descriptions of his
several country and seaside villas, now lost: spatial variety
was the key with the principal rooms projecting from the
main mass to embrace garden or view and loggias – covered verandah-like spaces, screened to the outside only by
columns – effecting the transition from interior to exterior. The greatest representative of the type is Hadrian's
Villa at Tivoli.**3.177–3.179**

>**3.177** THE SEASIDE VILLA OF PLINY THE
YOUNGER, c. 61–112: model (Oxford, Ashmolean
Museum).

Pliny describes two villas, one in the Tuscan
Appenines, the other by the sea near Ostia: though
somewhat detailed, the accounts have lent themselves to varied interpretation.

3.178a

Hadrian's Villa at Tivoli

In extending a vast array of buildings over a considerable tract of country-side Hadrian was probably emulating Domitian, who augmented several existing villas with much new work in the great estate he amassed between Albano, Castel Gandolfo and the via Appia. In incorporating facilities for sport, study and entertainment – gymnasia, libraries, theatres, galleries – Domitian himself was following the lead set by the magnates of the late Republic. In accordance with a well-established conceit, the titles given to several of the major elements of Hadrian's complex refer to famous places elsewhere: for instance, 'Canopus' recalls the sanctuary of Canopus outside Alexandria; 'Poikile' the painted stoa of the Stoic philosophers at Athens.

Laid out on the scale of a town, its stunning variety of buildings included fora and baths as well as reception and living rooms. Except for the Great Baths, which had the largest of groin vaults, the patron's prime interest was not in the grandeur of covered space but in intimacy. Curve and counter-curve are woven into the most intricate of forms, a few daringly vaulted, many open to the sky, some introverted, others extroverted in aspect but all related to one another informally in accordance with the contours of the site – recalling the sensitivity of the Greeks for whom Hadrian had a particular affinity.

Immediately beyond the entrance court, the so-called Triclinium was the ceremonial space where the emperor received the acclamation due to his semi-divine nature. The place of epiphany, it descended from the royal vestibules of the Hellenistic east, themselves descended from the tent of appearance of campaigning monarchs from time immemorial. The *heb-sed* festival tent of the Egyptian pharaoh, expanded to a monumental scale for the great hall of Thutmosis III at Karnak, is the most potent witness to this tradition. The twin-towered bit-hilani of the Hittites and their heirs, the columned halls of the Urartians and Achaemenids, are related permutations. The Ptolemies, Hellenistic rulers of Egypt, mod-

›3.178 TIVOLI, HADRIAN'S VILLA, c. 125–37: (a, b) model, (c) plan with (1) entrance and 'Poikile', (2) Triclinium, (3) stadium, (4) Small Baths, (5) Great Baths, (6) 'Canopus'; (7) private apartments, (8) Piazza d'Oro, (9) 'Teatro Marittimo' retreat, (10) academy, (11) 'Roccabruna' belvedere; (d, pages 630–631) view over Canopus.

3.178b

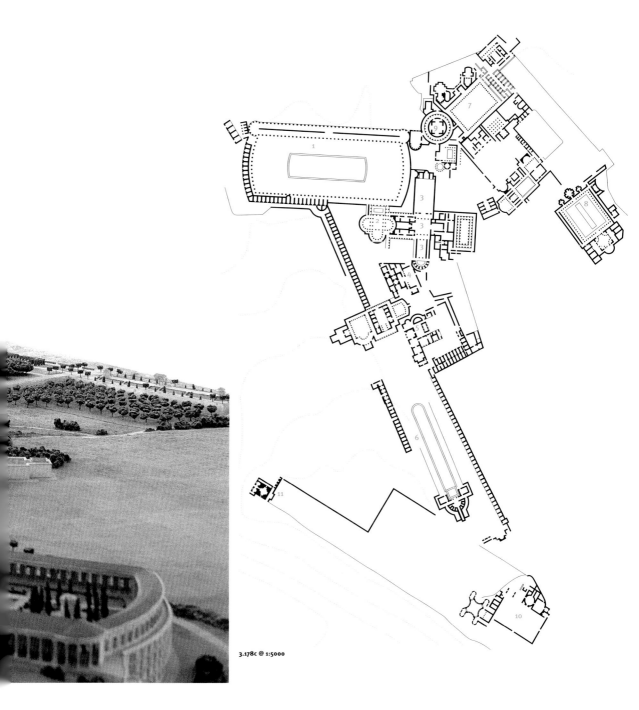

3.178c @ 1:5000

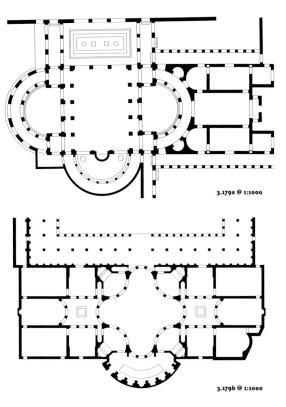

>3.179 TIVOLI, HADRIAN'S VILLA: (a) Triclinium, plan; (b, c) Piazza d'Oro complex, plan and entrance pavilion; (d) Small Baths, elongated 'octagonal' room vaulted over the undulating perimeter; (e, f) 'Teatro Marittimo' overview into the moated fountain court and plan; (g) Great Baths.

3.179a @ 1:1000

3.179b @ 1:1000

elled themselves on the pharaohs, as we have seen, and the contemporary Seleucids on the Achaemenids. Ptolemaic or Seleucid, the prototype for Hadrian's vestibule has disappeared, but it is doubtless recorded in the Roman fastigium, a portico whose canopy-like image we have encountered on the Tiberian arch at Orange and the propylaeum at Baalbek.[3.159, 3.158]

Deep within the complex, the 'Teatro Marittimo' was an exceptionally intricate and intimate retreat, and the 'Piazza d'Oro' provided for the appearance of the superhuman monarch among the most select of men. The domical entrance pavilion is another manifestation of the tradition of palace vestibules inherited by the Seleucids from their predecessors in Syria and Mesopotamia. It was more immediately inspired by the main

3.179e

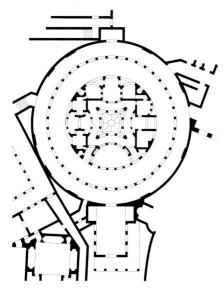

3.179f @ 1:1000

entrance to the Domus Augustana and the garden rooms of the private apartments there, with their alternately rectangular and semi-circular exedrae, though its external mass follows the form of the interior space – unlike the work of the earlier architect. Resembling an umbrella, the dome springs from the imposts of the arches over the recessions, without a rim – let alone a drum. The squinch is anticipated, as in the Flavian prototypes.

The complex at the head of the peristyle enshrined the ultimate scene of imperial epiphany, the throne room. Given Hadrian's antiquarian interests, particularly his quotations from Ptolemaic Egypt, the precedent was doubtless another lost Hellenistic one. Considerable speculation persists over whether the undulating colonnades, alternately concave and convex in forming a partially double-skinned quatralobe, could have carried a vault like that of the octagonal room of the Small Baths. If so, the transformation of the tent of appearance in accordance with the symbolism of heaven could hardly have been more clearly articulated.

3.1798

›3.180 NIMES, SO-CALLED TEMPLE OF
DIANA: actually a thermal hall, c. 130 CE.

THERMAE

Roman experiments with the diversification of space cul-
minate in the great thermae built all over the empire, by
successive emperors vying for prestige – and expanding
vault types and mortared-rubble construction techniques
crucial for the future development of architecture in east
and west alike. Unlike the Pompeiian baths, the imperial
baths of the 2nd and 3rd centuries were distinguished by

the development of an axial approach to planning ultimately in tune with the natural line of progression in the bathing process from cool to hot and back again. From the entrance and changing rooms, many would go first for a plunge in the pool of the cold zone (frigidarium), then on through a tepid chamber to the hot zone (calidarium), best placed on the southern side. Alternatively one could go straight from the changing rooms through the tepid zone to the hot rooms and then, perhaps, back through the tepid zone for a swim in the pool.**3.179, 3.180**

A strong axis of symmetry was probably first established by Nero in the Campus Martius complex restored or rebuilt several times, notably by Domitian after the fire of 80 and by Alexander Severus c. 227.**3.140.10** If entrance there was from the north (as the scanty 16th-century records imply without clearly distinguishing the original work), the axis opened by it and terminating in the calidarium projecting from the southern façade would have directed the bathing process from cold to hot and back again. Be that as it may, a strong axis but no logical progression is apparent in the Baths of Titus (c. 80 CE, as recorded by Palladio in the 16th century): the entrance seems to have been through or beside the hot zone in the south, forcing the user to proceed in the opposite sense to the bathing process.

In the next great complex of which there are significant traces, the Baths of Trajan (built by Apollodorus of Damascus and dedicated in 109), plan and process are developed in harmony: the entrance is from the north, the hot zone to the south beyond the great groin-vaulted central hall or concourse which fulfilled a social function as a meeting place while providing a tepid zone of transition.**3.181** The type culminated in the Baths of Caracalla (c. 216) and those built by Diocletian some eighty years later.**3.182–3.184**

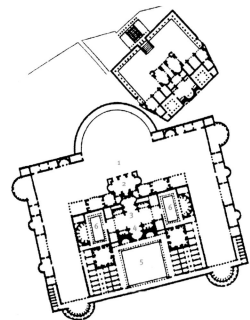

3.181a @ 1:5000

3.182b

The apogee of the imperial thermae

After the troubled generation following the death of Marcus Aurelius in 180, Septimius Severus and his successors addressed the urgent need to repair many existing buildings and provide Rome's ever-expanding population with new bath houses. By far the greatest of these were the Baths of Caracalla, the second ruler of the line. Unlike the earlier imperial

›**3.182** ROME, BATHS OF TITUS AND TRAJAN: (a) plan with (1) entrances from the north, (2) swimming pool (natatio), (3) central hall with troughs of cold water (frigidarium), (4) vestibule with troughs of tepid water (tepidarium), (5) hot-water room (calidarium), (6) palaestra, (b) model viewed from the north with the smaller complex of Titus top.

›**3.183** ROME, BATHS OF CARACALLA: (a, b) model and plan with (1) entrances from the north, (2) swimming pool, (3) central hall with troughs of cold water), (4) vestibule with troughs of tepid water, (5) hot-water room, (6) palaestrae, (c) detail of polygonal chamber with domical vault and pendentives.

›**3.184** THE PENDENTIVE: recipe.

Take a grapefruit, cut it in half, set it aside. Take a melon, cut it in half, slice off the top of one half to the diameter of the grapefruit. Slice vertically to form a square. Place the grapefruit on the residue of the melon, which represents the pendentives.

In the construction of a dome over a polygonal space, naturally the dome rests on the centres of the straight sides which will be pierced with arches if the space is integrated with its context. One solution to the problem of supporting the dome over the corners is to throw extra arches across them (squinches) – as in the garden rooms of the Domus Augustana or the entrance pavilion to the Piazza d'Oro of Hadrian's Villa. Another is to proceed as though building two domes, the lower one springing from the imposts of the arches defining the space. The lower dome will be obliterated

3.183a

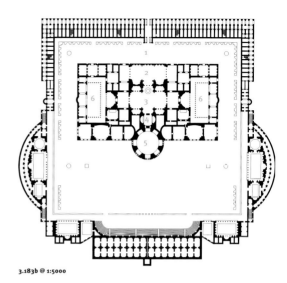

3.183b @ 1:5000

3.183c

in the main by those arches and the upper dome. Remaining between these elements, where they diverge, are four spherical triangles – fragments of the larger, lower dome. These are the pendentives.

Of course the upper dome (the 'orange') may be omitted: then the pendentives and the vault will derive from a single hemispherical membrane (the 'melon'), generally known as a pendentive dome or sail vault.

The pendentive was known to the Romans at least by the middle of the 2nd century: the best-preserved examples include several sail-vaulted chambers in the West Baths at Gerasa (c. 170). The development seems to have passed by the builders of the later Minerva Medica.

thermae, except the Great Baths of Hadrian's Villa, Caracalla's complex survives in substantial part – some of the walls of the main block of 214 by 110 metres still rise to their full height, though most of the vaulting has gone. The model was obviously the Baths of Trajan but the vast compound was expanded to provide water storage as well as fields for athletics bordered by libraries, meeting and reception rooms.

Paired changing rooms, presumably for men and women, to either side of the northern entrance lead sideways to the outdoor swimming pool or forward through the three-bay central hall with dependent cold-water troughs and a vestibule with tepid ones, to the hot-water room and adjoining steam chambers in the south. The opening of a lateral axis through the hall provides for exercise in palestrae in addition to bathing.

The calidarium recalls the Pantheon – their diameters were 35 metres and 42.5 metres respectively – but the later work was taller and lit by arched windows in the drum. Only on this side of the main block did the regular repetition of colonnaded openings around the great rotunda and to either side of it lend significant relief to the massive brick-lined concrete walls. Shops masked the entrance front framing the compound to the north, the curved side of the stadium was flanked by a huge reservoir on the southern side and halls with oval vestibules were accommodated in semi-circular recessions off-centre on the other two sides.

3.185a

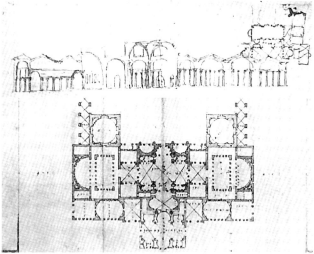

3.185b

Among the subsidiary elements there is at least one example of a domical vault over a polygonal space: with great importance for the future,
semi-spherical triangular elements called pendentives bridge the gap
between the circular and angular surfaces.[3.185] As these members def-
elected the load of the vault to corner piers, arched windows could be
opened between them like the lunettes between the great groins of the
central halls, high above the surrounding chambers.

The vaulting of Caracalla's hall has gone but the core of Diocletian's
complex survives complete with some of its original colossal Egyptian
granite columns: it was converted into the church of S. Maria degli Angeli
in the 16th century. The scheme followed the general lines of distribution
set down by Caracalla's architect but is less supple in plan and more
restrained in its spatial variety than its predecessor. The main block (240
by 144 metres) was still larger. Instead of a domed rotunda at the culmination of the progression along the main axis, the calidarium echoes the
three-bay central hall on a smaller scale, with apses in the centre of each
side. The vista along the lateral axis was enhanced by inserting colonnaded screens between the palaestrae and the grid of inner chambers. Circular forms come to the fore as exedrae in the outer perimeter, but the
symmetry with which the elements are disposed is somewhat mechanical,
especially on the eastern and western sides.

Organized around the simple principle of choice presented by two lines of development, the mature imperial thermal complex included spaces aligned on the main and subsidiary axes which were varied in shape and vaulting to great scenographic effect. Little of this impressed itself on the exterior in these grand concrete complexes but on the smaller, less formal, scale of the exceptional Hunting Baths at Lepcis Magna, mass matched space.**3.186**

›3.185 ROME, BATHS OF DIOCLETIAN, c. 298: (a) the central hall (S. Maria degli Angeli), (b) section and plan (with Baths of Agrippa after restoration by Domitian), sketched by Palladio.

›3.186 LEPCIS MAGNA, HUNTING BATHS, c. 200: (a) interior, (b) exterior.

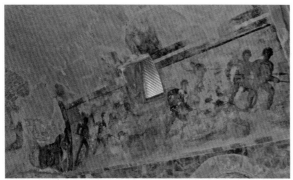

3.186a

3.186b

›3.187 ROME, VIA LATINA, TOMB OF THE
ANICII, 2nd century. The ephemeral architecture of
the lunettes feigns the articulation of walls as in the
Tomb of the Caetennii.

DECORATION

With diversity of space went exuberance of decoration,
with adventurousness fantasy. As concrete freed form
from the constraints imposed by traditional materials,
naturally it freed the decorative imagination from the
constraints of traditional logic. In the dramatic light of
plastic space, the articulation of the forces implicit in
masonry mass was seen to be irrelevant. Furthered by the
natural propensity towards convolution – and the countering of expectation – the process goes back to the origins of the Fourth Pompeiian Style and fashion was
doubtless led by the lost precedents for the octagonal
room in the Domus Aurea.

On vaults stucco remained the most popular material,

at least for smaller-scale works**3.187** it relieved large-scale coffering with large-scale motifs but it was mainly moulded with great delicacy into the frames of painted panels, carved into figures – divine, human, animal or ambivalent – and spun into webs of stylized foliage and ephemeral architecture – as in the Third Pompeiian Style. Often bizarre in detail, this type of decoration was first rediscovered by the artists of the Italian Renaissance in cavernous, subterranean remains (and called *grottesche* after the Italian for cave).

The vaults of the Pompeiian baths were stuccoed,**3.124** but plaster does not lend itself to humid environments or intricate detail for vaults on the scale of those in the imperial thermae. Mosaic was more suitable there: in marble on floors, marble and glass on walls, glass on vaults.**3.163** With the proliferation of glass tesserae, structure was dissolved: as engineering became more daring, physical reality was denied. The implications were to be profound.

At the beginning of the imperial period marble was still rare in Italy, even for revetment. However, the imitation of polychrome panelling in fresco was characteristic of the First Style of Pompeiian ornament, reflecting Hellenistic taste in the eastern provinces of the empire, as we have seen. Under Augustus, when marble began to replace travertine in the structure and decoration of the more important buildings, outside and in, it either articu-lated – even provided – structure or was laid in geometric patterns of contrasting colours. As the 1st century progressed and the logic of concrete superseded that of masonry, the Carrara quarries were developed and marble became more common: free-flowing atectonic motifs ramped in intricate marble inlay or mosaic over floors as well as the wall surfaces of intimate spaces, but architecture long held its own in marble – or granite – and plaster in grander ones.

›3.188 ROME, VATICAN CEMETERY, TOMB OF THE CAETENNII, 2nd century.

Continuing the Etruscan tradition of interment of the cremated in urns, the Romans built freestanding tombs within which the recession housing the main patron's urn was distinguished by an aedicule as Hellenization advanced. By the middle of the 2nd century aedicules had proliferated in a decorative band broken only by a great arched niche to distinguish the main one – often above an arcaded podium in which the elongated cavities accommodated full burials.

The motif of half pediment – to each side here – appeared in late-Pompeii, but features most prominently on the hemicyclical façade of Trajan's market building.

By the end of the 2nd century inhumation had replaced cremation in Rome. Richly carved sarcophagi resulted, and rich fresco or mosaic embellished the plane surfaces of tomb walls around the elongated cavities designed to accommodate coffins.

BAROQUE MASS

The exteriors of brick and concrete buildings like the Roman thermae rarely revealed the complexities within: even the Pantheon's third external register denies the inner nature of the dome and its relationship to the drum. Individual complexities, like the main room of Nero's Domus Aurea or the garden rooms of Domitian's Domus Augustana, were encapsulated within walls – often at the cost of producing dead space. The domed octagon at the entrance to the Piazza d'Oro of Hadrian's Villa marks a significant departure towards matching space and volumes in standing free with all its spatial complexity expressed openly in the mass.**3.179c** The hunting baths at Lectis Magna are a splendid example of this applied on a larger scale.

3.189

The traditional drum and podium are articulated as a cylindrical tempietto over a cube with concave façades: the latter represents the typical aediculed burial chamber, as in the Vatican Tomb of the Caetennii, turned inside out – the niche distinguishing the main aedicule in counterplay with the tempietto.

›3.190 BAALBEK, TEMPLE OF VENUS, c. 200, reconstruction.

Seven-sided, this latter-day tholos had a column supporting the scalloped entablature at each angle except the one spanned by the entrance portico.

Beyond the functionalist aesthetic, however, the moulding of space had its counterpart in the moulding of mass into dynamic forms, not necessarily expressing the nature of the interior. The game was admirably played by the designers of tombs, who were particularly liberal in the development of the old formula of drum and podium with cross-reference to the eastern tomb tower, the Etruscan urn niche and the Hellenistic aedicule. At Capua, for example, the concave curve of the podium counters the convex curve of the tempietto tower to dramatic effect.**3.189, 3.190**

>**3.191 BOSRA,** c. 200, reconstructed: cavea and scenae frons.

An Arab settlement subject to the Nabataens from the mid-2nd century BCE and annexed with much of the Nabataean domain by Trajan in 106, Bosra was the capital of the Province of Arabia.

If the outside of their theatres provided the main context for the perfection of the architectonic approach to decoration, the scenae frons behind the stage inside provided the opportunity for mannerist display but it was still more the ideal place to appeal to the emotions through the development of a dramatic sense of movement. Proto-Baroque, there is something of this in the undulating screens of Lepcis Magna and Sabratha but the most substantial surviving example, at Bosra, well illustrates the introduction of graded concave curves to amplify the orchestration of a crescendo in the centre of multiple colonnades.**3.191**

3.192b

3.192 PETRA: (a, pages 648–649) general view with 'palace tomb' (left); (b, c) 'Treasury', exterior and interior; (d) 'el-Deir' Mausoleum, 2nd century.

Petra was the capital of the Nabataeans, whose kingdom was extinguished by Trajan in 106. Its wealth, based on controlling the trade routes between Syria and Arabia, is most tangibly recalled by the tombs carved into the red sandstone cliffs – though whether the most elaborate ones were excavated before the city's annexation is controversial. Unrelated in exterior and interior form, they range from the representation of the tower type common in the east, with or without a veneer of Classical ornament, to the free superimposition of Classical building types reproduced in three dimensions. Here the rich mix includes the temple, the tempietto (and ciborium), the triumphal arch and the aedicular burial chamber turned inside out – complete with half-pendentives.

Variations on the same theme are represented by the major monuments of the necropolis at Petra, where the full upper storey has its pediment broken in deference to the iconographically significant tempietto – rather than merely in indulgence of the mannerist whim to deny structural logic. Dramatic effect is restrained by the orthodoxy of the base Order at the so-called Treasury but concave undulation generates the emotive vitality with which the central bay and its pavilion burst forth, contrary to the nature of stone, at the later 'Monastery'. To heighten the sense of movement and the excitement of the climax there, moreover, a progression was developed in the weight of the Order from sides to centre. But the game was not confined to the world of the dead.**3.192**

3.192c

3.192d

SASSANIAN DIGRESSION

The influence of Roman domical space was far-reaching, not least initially to the Sassanians – the empire's most formidable eastern enemies. The builders of Ardashir's line reiterated the Parthian scenae-frons-framed iwan for the palaces of their capitals, first at Firozabad in the progenitor's Fars homeland, later in the hunting lodge at nearby Sarvistan, finally in the imperial capital Ctesiphon near modern Baghdad. Behind the iwan behind the scenae frons, moreover, Roman influence extended to domed chambers decorated in stucco. These were usually cubical in main volume, unlike the grandest Roman ones, and the transition from square to circle was effected with arches thrown across the four corners (squinches) rather than the pendentives of the lesser chambers of the Baths of Caracalla and its progeny. And the domed cube entered the service of Zoroastrianism, revived by the Parthians after the Greek interregnum, as the form of the Fire Temple.**3.193–3.195**

›3.193 FIROZABAD, PALACE, mid-3rd century: (a) plan; (b) court viewed towards the north-west with the northern iwan on the right; (c) central reception room.

The main façade, facing north, was dominated by the great central iwan (now largely fallen) in which the king could have sat in public audience. Flanked by paired halls for guards and attendants, it led to three great domed rooms well suited to more exclusive reception and private audience. Beyond these was a court flanked by the royal apartments with iwans to the north and south. The traditional tripartite division of the oriental palace has rarely been clearer.

Some of the plaster which presumably once covered the whole building survives in the domed halls. The eclecticism of the Sassanians' Achaemenid ances-

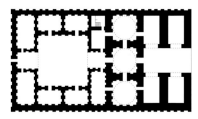

3.193a @ 1:2000

3.193b

3.193c

tors is revived in the decorative detail: mouldings remotely Classical in their derivation, distant echoes of the Roman 'grotesque' style, joined to Egyptian coved architraves. Roman precedents for placing a dome over a square space were ready to hand: in the baths at Gerasa, for example.

›3.194 SARVISTAN, SASSANIAN HUNTING LODGE, mid-4th century: (a) view from the north-west, (b) detail of dome with oculus and squinches in the main hall.

In the countryside north-east of Firozabad, this smaller building – 34 by 42.5 metres – is generally dated to the middle of the reign of Shapur II (309–79). The main domed hall, preceded by an iwan to the north, was flanked by a court to the east. Both were surrounded by barrel-vaulted halls, the larger ones to the north and south with shallow aisles defined by truncated columns – as in a basilica. The subsidiary domed space in the north-west corner (to the right here) may have been a fire temple: certainly the typical Iranian fire temple is a freestanding domed cube open to all four sides.

›3.195 CTESIPHON, SASSANIAN PALACE, mid-6th century.

Generally attributed to Chosroes I (531–79), who revived the flagging fortunes of the long-lived dynasty, the palace is orientated with the central iwan facing north – as usual with the Sassanians. The blind façade to either side of the huge elliptical vault – 24 by 49 metres rising to 36 metres – screened parallel rows of magazines. No great domed chamber survives.

3.194a

3.194b

3.195

3.196a

PALACE AND BASILICA IN THE AGE OF DIOCLETIAN

Anticipating the dislocation of the centre of power from Rome and the impending decline of the great city which had lent its name to the greatest empire the world had ever seen, Diocletian retreated to the Dalmatian coast and cocooned himself in a court developing along oriental lines in a great camp palace on a beautiful site overlooking the Adriatic.[3.196]

Palace of Diocletian, Split

In its rectangular compound wall – 180 by 212 metres – with a gallery overlooking the Adriatic to the south above a water gate, gates flanked by octagonal towers to the north, west and east, and square towers at the corners and towards the middle of each inland section, the complex was like a great camp. Soldiers and servants seem to have been lodged in the cells backing on to the walls to each side of the twin-towered land gates. Each of these contained square vestibules, presumably always domed, the main one to the north (sometimes called the Golden Gate) providing the emperor with a place of appearance before the world at large. The entrance pavilion to Hadrian's Piazza d'Oro is of the type, while contemporary descriptions suggest that the immediate precedent for both palace and vestibule was provided by the Roman proconsular palace at Antioch, now vanished, and that this in turn followed a venerable near-eastern tradition descending through the seat of the Hellenistic Seleucids in the same city.

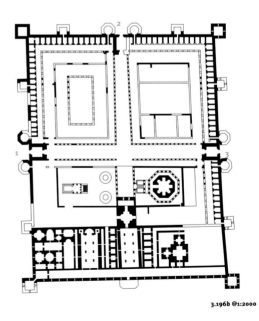

3.196b @1:2000

3.196d

›**3.196** **SPLIT, PALACE OF DIOCLETIAN,** c. 300: (a) model, (b) plan with land gates east, west and north (1–3), southern water postern (4), peristyle (5), Temple of Jupiter? (6), mausoleum (7), fastigium vestibule before entrance hall (8), aula regia (9), triclinium? (10), baths? (11), private apartments (12), (c) view along peristyle to the fastigium of the main residence, (d) interior of octagonal mausoleum with original superimposed Corinthian Orders in the context of later Christian embellishment.

The colonnaded cardo and decumanus crossed in the centre, to the south of accommodation for the household and guests and to the north of the Temple of Jupiter and mausoleum, which were themselves to the north of the main palace buildings. On the central axis, continuing the route from the north which passes between the temple and mausoleum, a portico (fastigium) preceded a domed vestibule, the imperial place of appearance or epiphany. Beyond that an atrium provides the nucleus of the private apartments, with various reception basilicas balancing one another on either side.

Enshrining the remains of the deified emperor, the mausoleum belongs to the centralized type of building known as a heroum. Diocletian's was octagonal, with alternating rectangular and semi-circular exedrae separated by a ring of columns below a domical vault – like a miniature Pantheon. It provided an immediate precedent for imperial builders of Christian monuments. The arched fastigium portico recalls the form favoured by Hadrian and the long line of divine rulers who preceded and followed him.[3.155] Columns and arches are freely combined in many parts of Diocletian's building, not least to form the gallery overlooking the sea.

3.196c

3.197b

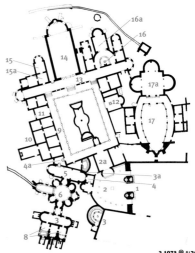

3.197a @ 1:2000

›3.197 PIAZZA ARMERINA (SICILY), SO-
CALLED 'VILLA IMPERIALE' (2nd–4th centuries
CE, repaired after an earthquake of c. 365): (a) plan
with (1) triple arch entrance, (2, 2a) atrium and
vestibule, (3, 3a) latrines, (4, 4a) entrances to the
thermal complex, (5) exercise gallery named after its
circus mosaic, (6) frigidarium, (7) tepidarium, (8) cal-
darium, (9) peristyle, (10) servants quarters, offices
and guestrooms?, (11) salon with the 'Small Hunt'
mosaic, (12) family dining room (?) with Orpheus

In spectacular contrast, the lavish contemporary villa at Piazza Armerina in Sicily represents the ultimate fruition of the organic tradition most expansively rampant at Tivoli – though the layout in whole and in main part is curiously, presumably wilfully, irregular rather than informal. Dating is far from uncontroversial but the weight of recent archaeological evidence suggests that the definitive complex was developed over extensive 2nd-century foundations largely from c. 310, possibly for Diocletian's colleague Maximian. A single-storey structure of mortared rubble, stone faced, revetted or paved in rich marble and embellished with fresco, its remains are celebrated above all for the luxuriant mosaics which distinguished – indeed, identified – its many varied spaces.

Accepting the archaeological evidence for an early 4th-century date and detecting images of Tetrarchs in the Hunt Mosaic, speculation has favoured Emperor Maximian or his son Maxentius as the patron of Piazza Armerina – though neither is known to have had particular Sicilian connections or the inclination to build retirement homes. There is, in fact, no evidence for the association of any emperor with the site but Sicily was perennially popular with Italian patricians and there was no shortage of native magnates.

Imperial in opulence, the Armerina work is certainly the

3.197c

mosaic, (13) apsidal corridor with the 'Great Hunt' mosaic, (14) reception hall known as the basilica, (15) private apartments with Ulysses and Polyphemus mosaic in 15a, (16) private apartments with Neraid mosaic in main salon 16a, (17, 17a) court and triapsidal triclinium with Hercules mosaics, (b) Africa from the southern apse of the great corridor where the decoration proclaims the span of the empire, (c) Tetrarchal figure called Maximian by those who wish to identify the villa as imperial, (d) Ulysses and Polyphemus, (e) detail of the fall of the giants from the series of Herculean subjects from the triclinium.

Comparison with late-imperial work elsewhere in the central zone of the Mediterranean indicates that the mosaics were executed by masters from the Province of Africa – now Tunisia – which is exceptionally rich in the tradition, as we have seen: one guiding hand – even the dominance of one particular workshop – is neither apparent nor likely in an exercise of this extent and complexity. The stylistic consistency of these mosaics – in the main – seems to contradict the impression conveyed by the irregularities in distribution that there were several distinct phases of development. However, in the most obviously disparate elements – the bathing complex to the west and the tri-apsidal hall and its precinct to the south – the mosaics are notably inferior and superior respectively to the work elsewhere in the complex: these areas most probably resulted from revisions of the initial conception while work was in progress.

3.197d

3.197e

outstanding example of its type and age so far revealed to us but it was not unique. Contemporary – or late-4th century – villas, comparable in complexity and in the quality of their embellishment, remain incompletely excavated elsewhere in Sicily, notably at Marina di Patti. And tantalizing remains of similar opulence have been partially uncovered in Italy, notably at Desanzano by Lake Garda, at several sites in France, most notably Montmaur in the south-west, in Iberia, in Germany and even in Britain: consistent is a succession of courts aligned on axis in the context of much stricter regularity than appealed to the patron of Piazza Armerina, and the hemicycle proved enduringly popular for the distinction of main spaces **3.197**

The complex at Split – if not the villa at Piazza Armerina – was the last great imperial palace before Constantine finally re-established the capital at Byzantium. First having established his position in Rome, however, Constantine completed the last great space of imperial Rome, the basilica whose ruins dominate the via Sacra as it leads into the Forum. Nearby, he commemorated his achievements with a triumphal arch of the traditional type, reusing earlier imperial sculpture. He completed works on a grand

›3.198 TRIER, PORTA NIGRA: aula regia of imperial Palace: (a) exterior, (b) restored interior.

Trier was the base of Constantius Chlorus, Diocletian's deputy in the west from 293. The gate, taking the early imperial formula represented at Autun to its apogee, may have been built after the catastrophic barbarian raids of 276, but the unfinished state is shared with other buildings begun by Constantine in Trier. The palace replaced the headquarters destroyed in 275 but was completed under Constantine.

Built of brick and roofed in timber, the aula regia – 29 by 58 metres – was one of the largest spaces in the colonies. To the south of the hall was a narthex; to the north a generous apse. The severe exterior was plastered and relieved only by timber galleries below the windows; the interior once had a revetment of marble. The windows of the apse are lower and smaller than those of the hall, but the eye, expecting consistency, sees the extension as greater than its physical reality. Illusionism of this kind is unmatched by the accidents of survival in Rome.

3.198a

3.198b

>3.199 ROME: (a) Arch of Constantine; (b, c) Basilica of Constantine, reconstruction and remains.

Begun by Maxentius (306–12) and completed by Constantine in 312, the vast basilica's three great groin-vaulted bays rose above barrel-vaulted side bays to admit light to the core, fusing its interrelated spaces into a whole much greater than their sum. The central hall – 80 by 25 metres and 35 metres high – was originally to be entered from the east opposite an apse to the west, but Constantine's architect opened the central barrel-vaulted bay of the south side to a porch opposite a new apse in the north.

scale north of the Alps too – where the barbarians were menacing. The Porta Nigra at Trier and the great hall of the palace in the same northern capital are the outstanding examples: the latter has been largely reconstructed.**3.198** Of the stupendous Roman basilica, the groin-vaulted central hall has gone, but three huge tunnel vaults survive to the north: even in this ruined state its impact was to prove inescapable.**3.199**

Colossal scale, scenographic alignment of varied spaces, theatrical movement in mass, complexity of planning, dra-

3.199a

3.199b

matic lighting, illusionism, rich materials – all of which we
have seen variously in Roman imperial building from
Nero's Golden House to Hadrian's Villa, from the Pantheon to the great thermae and basilicas – were to be the
main techniques of the Roman Baroque fifteen hundred
years later. Meanwhile the arcades and vaults of the baths
and basilicas dominating Rome and its colonial towns
were of prime inspiration to the builders of the 'Middle
Ages': in the east they favoured domes; in the west
Romanesque architects emulated the barrel vaults but also
transmitted to their Gothic followers an understanding of
the principle of the counter-opposition of forces, so splendidly demonstrated by the groin-vaulted central bays of
the Baths of Diocletian and the great basilica built by his
successors on the via Sacra.

3.199c

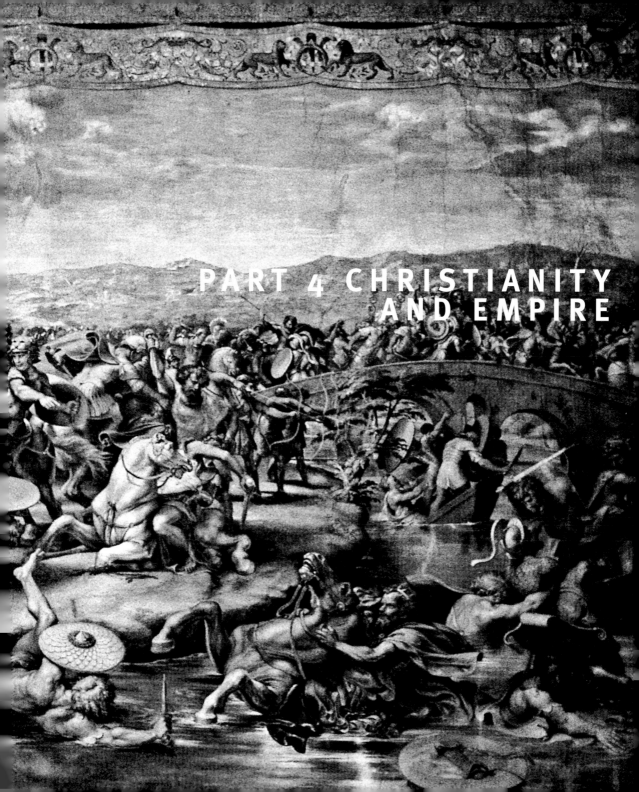

PART 4 CHRISTIANITY
AND EMPIRE

4.1 ROME AND NEW ROMES

INTRODUCTION: CONSTANTINE AND THE DOMINION OF CHRIST

Constantine's victory over Maxentius in October 312 at the Milvian Bridge on the northern approach to Rome marked the beginning of a new era – but it took the new emperor more than a decade to eliminate the last heirs of the Tetrarchy (see page 560). Diocletian's complex system of power sharing had been destroyed in truth to the dictatorship which produced it.

The lasting legacy of the old *Dominus* was to assert naked absolutism, clothed in the splendour of eastern monarchy, over the fiction of the constitutional 'principate' instituted by Augustus to mollify the Senate: that had been challenged abortively by the Flavians but generally sustained in theory thereafter. Believing that essential general reform could be effected only by dictat, like his mentor, Constantine completed the process after the failure of the tetrarchal system: Diocletian had adopted trusted aids to share and ultimately to inherit power; recalling the Flavians, Constantine substituted the principle of hereditary succession in his own family line – the *Gens Flavia* – and fostered a new official aristocracy to serve his dictatorial purpose in eclipse of the old disputative senatorial class.

Diocletian bequeathed an administration concerned primarily with taxation to pay for the army, the bureaucracy and the court. Constantine completed the separation of the military and civil powers, confirming the absolute independence of the *vicarii* in charge of provincial administration from the *duce* in military command and appointing *comites* from the official class to oversee matters, backed by an army of spies. He reformed the legal system, introducing a measure of Christian mercy in the treatment of those in bondage. He reformed the currency and tax system to encourage enterprise and achieved economic revival but he granted immunity to his new grandees and increased the burden on the rest of society to pay for his capital works.

Like Diocletian, he recognized that the centre of imperial gravity had shifted to the east of Rome and he established a second Roman capital in the ancient Greek city of Byzantium, renamed Constantinople in 330. As Rome was inextricably associated with the veneration of the Augustus and the Capitoline triad, the move was also prompted by his most astonishing achievement: the establishment of a new religion. Acknowledging that his Milvian victory had been won under the banner of Christ, the divine Augustus, embodying the genius of Rome, transformed himself into the vicar of a subversive cult.**4.1**

CHRISTIANITY IN CONTEXT

Rome was tolerant of foreign religions if they were not seen to be subversive or immoral. In practice they were licensed under the Law of Association if their adherents were prepared to pay homage to the state gods, particularly to Rome and Augustus, and that was seen as an affirmation of political rather than religious faith. In any case, most pagan cults were concerned with propitiation rites designed to ensure the good will of the gods towards man's achievement of his own will and they were readily assimilable – indeed, the tendency was enshrined in the Pantheon.

Mystery cults had long been popular in Rome: individualistic and promising spiritual salvation, they provided the emotional satisfaction wanting in, but not necessarily incompatible with, the state cults. Those of Isis and Serapis were the most important by the time of the destruction of Pompeii in 79 CE and their temples proliferated long after.**4.3** But there were many others, Hellenic and oriental in origin. By the time of Dioclet-

›4.1 (PAGES 662–663) CONSTANTINE AT THE MILVIAN BRIDGE: VICTORY (frescoes by Raphael and his circle, Rome, Vatican Palace).

›4.2 FIRE IN THE BORGO (frescoes by Raphael and his circle, Rome, Vatican Palace).

›4.3 BERGAMA (PERGAMUM), TEMPLE OF SERAPIS, c. 130: (a) general view, (b) south court.

Beyond an extensive cloistered precinct, which bridges the River Selinus, the main hall of the temple was flanked by two smaller colonnaded courts which formed the precincts for a pair of rotundas. The structure was generally of brick clad in marble. A water trough ran down the centre of the main hall's marble pavement to a high podium on which the cult statue stood. This was not directly lit, and a space below the podium penetrated the base of the statue, presumably so that the congregation could be addressed through the god's image.

The stoas of the square side courts were supported by Atlantes and Caryatids in the Ancient Egyptian mode, the male images to one side, the female not exclusively to the other. The paired pools they framed are taken as representing the Nile. It is the Egyptian imagery which has identified the building as a Serapeum (not without dissent). It was converted into the basilican Church of S. John in the early Byzantine period.

4.3a

4.3b

ian those surrounding Mithras and Christ were particularly prominent.

The prestige of Mithras, the Iranian god of light, protector of the righteous and hence lord of oaths and guardian of warriors, grew with the de-Romanization of the army. His cult had been exported to their conquests by the Achaemenids and to the west from Anatolia (see pages 207–208). Transformed in the process, it came to polyglot Rome with a veneer of Greek anthropomorphic imagery and a veil of mystery borrowed from the initiation rites of Demeter and Bacchus: sacrificer of the sacred bull, incarnation of primordial existence from whose death came life on earth, Mithras promised eternal life to the initiated – men who had undergone ordeals and performed arcane

4.4a

4.4b

rites, including sacrificial meals, qualifying them for service as the disciplined champions of the Good. Obviously appealing to soldiers – and the ethos of Rome – the faith expanded rapidly among the legions and reached its apogee, if not with the initiation of Commodus (180–193), then by association with the state cult of Sol Invictus (invincible sun) instituted by Aurelian in 274.**4.4**

The followers of Christ were very different – though they too saw themselves as militants and underwent initiation rites qualifying them for service as the champions of the Good. Central to Christ's mystery was his triumph over death, promising rebirth and eternal life to those champions too, and much in it was not only paralleled in Mithraism but also prefigured in the mysteries of Osiris/Serapis and Isis. Mithras, Isis and Serapis – like Rome and Augustus – were prepared to tolerate other gods (see pages 456–458). The followers of Christ were not. Those other religions admitted of pantheism: Christianity sprang from the resolutely monotheistic tradition of Judaism.

The monotheism of Christ's Jewish ancestors takes primacy for many over all the faiths of Antiquity but it has left no tangible architectural trace beyond the platform of

›4.5 TRIUMPH OF TITUS: relief from the arch dedicated to the emperor in Rome, showing the procession of the spoils of war against the Jews.

its one great building – the Temple of Solomon in Jerusalem, which was finally destroyed by the Romans because of the intransigence of the Chosen People. They had been released from Babylonian captivity by the Persians, regrouped and dedicated themselves to sustaining the Covenant – the agreement of Moses on Mount Sinai to worship God only and obey his commandments in return for his protection – in beleaguered isolation while awaiting the triumph of their saviour, the Messiah.

Frustrated under the Seleucids, Hebrew anticipation increased in fervour after the Romans annexed Judea with Syria in 63 BCE. Ruled through client kings and accorded the privilege of worshipping their god exclusively, their rebelliousness ultimately provoked reprisal and dispersal under Titus in 73 CE.**4·5** Both the privilege and the dispersal favoured the spread of Christianity.

Christianity embraces the mystery of Jesus of Nazareth, a humble descendant of the house of David, king of Israel, who began his mission in the second decade of the reign of Tiberius – the third of the era that now bears his name. He is recorded to have avowed that his mission was to fulfil the word of the prophets, reinstate sacred law and lead man – fallen from grace through his essential freedom of will – back to God.

Though apparently careful to distance himself from politics, even to respect Roman authority, Jesus was hailed by his followers as the Messiah come at last – the Chosen One (*Christos* in Greek): Son of God. But through the mystery of his birth of the Virgin Mary, he was also seen as the son of man leading a human life on earth: his Father had prepared his human body for sacrifice as a scapegoat in expiation of sin and promised renewed Grace to those with faith in his divine immortality. He was crucified for blasphemy at the instigation of the Jewish hierarchy.**4·6**

After his suffering and death – his Passion – he was seen by his devotees to have risen and ascended into heaven to join his Father pending his return for the final judgement of man. It was the moral imperative to pass this judgement that distinguished Christianity so sharply from paganism – if not from other mystery religions.

According to the accounts of his mission – the Gospels, written by four of his twelve original disciples – it was the Apostle Peter who first recognized Jesus as Christ and Jesus charged him with the construction of his church. He opened initiation into that church to all through the sacrament of baptism (the cleansing of the soul symbolized by the immersion of the body in water). He sealed the brotherhood of all who would be saved through him in the eucharist (his sharing of his sacrificed body and blood through the elevated bread and wine consecrated for the purpose at his last supper).**4·7**

Denounced by the Jewish establishment, however, the church was in fact built abroad – in the world the Jews called 'gentile' – though, of course, all twelve Apostles were Jews, joined in the mission by other Jews – most notably Saul of Tarsus who espoused the cause with fervour as Paul and took Christianity to the world at large. And in the world of Rome, Christianity, as uncompromising in its commitment to the One True God as the Judaism from which it sprang, was bound to clash with imperial paganism. Moreover, though far from unique in their faith in a divine king sacrificed as scapegoat and resurrected as saviour, even in their veneration of a virgin mother – Osiris and Isis will be recalled in particular and, indeed, such parallels doubtless assisted in the popularization of the new faith – Christians set themselves apart with their mysterious rites of initiation and brotherhood and were bound to attract suspicion.

Popular revulsion against a secret society supposedly

›**4.6 ROME, S. SABINA:** entrance portal panel with the earliest-known representation of the Crucifixion (mid-5th century).

dedicated to such abominations as eating human flesh and drinking blood provoked spasmodic persecution. Persistently refusing to honour Rome and Augustus, it provided the authorities with ideal scapegoats: as in the pogrom under Nero following the great fire of 64. Christ had been a scapegoat too and his sect thrived on martyrdom.

By the end of the 1st century the new faith was widespread, especially among the poor whose cause was dear to Christ. A rudimentary organization was emerging: volunteer chief administrators in urban districts or rural villages (*episkopoi* = bishops), backed by a council of elders (*presbyters*), were assisted by stewards (*diakonoi* = deacons) primarily in the organization of worship and the maintenance of property, the burial of the dead and charity.

RETREAT

Christianity developed in the context of Roman urban life and, during their persecution, Christians worshipped in the discretion of their homes or were literally forced underground. Beyond that, after the example of Christ himself and his predecessor, S. John the Baptist, the most devout retreated to the wilderness for refuge: Sinai was particularly popular with ascetics because of its remoteness and its venerable association with Moses. Wherever the wilderness, caves provided rudimentary shelter as they had done for earliest humanity – and for the earliest evangelists in hiding or exile. At the extreme, of course, even

4.8a

the comfort offered by the cave was rejected: to pointed effect by the most notorious, with celebrated perseverance by the prime monk.**4.8, 4.9**

S. Anthony Abbot, who began his inspiring retreat to hermitage in the wilderness c. 270, came to be seen as the pioneer of Christian monachism in devising a regime for the disciples settled around him. Within a century his emulators were attracting followers so consistently that the isolated hermitage was eclipsed by the collection of cells loosely associated with one another for communal services (lavra). The ordering of the first such community, in Egypt, is attributed to S. Pachomius who died c. 346. Not much later the cells were being linked in a compound dominated by a church, a refectory and other communal facilities (coenobium). Thus the monastery was formed – though it was to be long before a standard formula for its architectural organization had been devised. Below Sinai, S. Catherine's originally founded in 337 by Emperor Constantine's mother, S. Helena, was one of the first to produce – organically – the embryo of order.**4.66c**

4.8b

4.9

›4.8 UNCOMFORTABLE RETREAT: (a) Mount Sinai, (b) S. Anthony tempted in the wilderness (H. Bosch, Madrid, Prado); (c) S. Simeon Stylites on his column (etching, G. Moreau).

The Syrian ascetic S. Simeon (390–495) is reputed to have spent the last forty years of his life thus supported up to 15 metres above ground – hardly without courting notoriety.

S. Anthony, (born in Egypt c. 250) withdrew to the wilderness near Fayum and later to a mountain in Sinai where he was tempted by the devil with material comforts and then with desire, fear and finally pride in his resistance: in the absence of anything so graphic from the early Middle Ages, Bosch's late-Medieval invocation of the terrors of rough solitude can hardly be bettered.

›4.9 CAVE CHURCH OF S. JOHN ON PATMOS.

S. John the Divine – identified with the Apostle not without dispute – was banished to Patmos in 95 by Domition and received his Revelation there.

Monasticism had reached Syria early in the 4th century and soon spread throughout Mesopotamia. It was taken to the Greek communities in Asia Minor c. 340 and regulated for Greek conditions by S. Basil (329–79). Also about 340, it was taken to Rome by S. Athanasius and had penetrated Europe before the century was out.

FROM PROSCRIPTION TO PRESCRIPTION

By the end of the 2nd century, Christians, many now rich and influential, were in a majority in some provinces of the east – notably those of Asia Minor – and numbered up to fifty thousand in Rome. Before the middle of the 3rd century there were converts in the highest echelons of public service and even the imperial court. Authority was now an institutional hierarchy doubling that of the imperial administration: the base was parochial, the priest responsible to a bishop in each town or rural district and the bishop to an archbishop in each province. And the definition of canonical dogma was advanced by men of outstanding intellect – the first Fathers of the Church.

Towards the middle of the 3rd century general measures were taken against a perceived threat to the state from an expanding, well-organized force which refused army service in principle, fervently sought the second coming of its Messiah and looked for the destruction of all except the faithful – including, implicitly, the Roman Empire. Christian assembly was proscribed and church property seized, sacrifice to the imperial gods was made mandatory for all citizens and the punishment of those refusing to comply was especially harsh for officials admitting Christian sympathies. Christianity thrived nonetheless.

Galerius – who built the last Antique Classical rotunda of the Pantheon type – took the final steps in concert with Diocletian in 303: Christians were deprived of Roman citizenship and with it the right to hold office and the full protection of the law; priests were to be imprisoned and forced to sacrifice; churches were to be destroyed wholesale.[4.10] Yet citizenship meant little more than tax liability to many while the church offered communion of a very different kind: while the magistrate represented oppression, the bishop promised salvation.

Eight years after the unleashing of the great persecution Galerius issued the Edict of Toleration: the persistence of great numbers in the Christian faith was admitted, the measures against them were withdrawn and they were required to pray for public welfare. Most remarkably, only two years later Constantine's Edict of Milan granted Christianity official status: Christ, his aid at the Milvian bridge the year before, had charged the new emperor with his mission to reform the empire.[4.1]

Though baptized only on his deathbed in 337, Constantine dubbed himself the 'Thirteenth Apostle' and thus the divine Augustus became the vice-regent for Christ. Denying the competence of the state to interfere in matters of conscience, indeed sustaining Rome's old tradition

4.10a

4.10b

›4.10 THESSALONIKI: (a) imperial rotunda (c. 300), converted to the church of H. Georgios (late-4th century); (b) Galerius sacrificing to the imperial gods (Arch of Galerius, early 4th century).

Traditionally identified as the mausoleum of Galerius but, associated with the palace which was the co-emperor's principal eastern seat, the rotunda (24 metres in diameter) may have been the throne room rather than a tomb.

of religious tolerance, he and his immediate successors tolerated paganism but fostered a catholic church in the belief that Christian unity was the key to imperial unity: Christian symbols replaced pagan ones on the imperial coinage from the mid-320s.

The religion spread rapidly around the Mediterranean littoral: reputedly, it was taken into Gaul by S. Denis in the reign of Emperor Decius (249-51) and to Iberia by no less a figure than Christ's brother, S. James the Great. His shrine in north-west Spain was to be a major centre of pilgrimage and the cross-currents of pilgrimage both west and east to the numerous sites associated with the Apostles between Rome and the Holy Land of Christ himself, vitalized the catholic cause. After Julian the Apostate's quixotic attempt to restore the old gods in 361, Theodosius I finally withdrew tolerance in 378 – but now paganism was proscribed and the temples expropriated.

AUTHORITY

As tribes became nations in the west, fragmenting the Roman polity, and their chiefs were converted to Christianity, the church found itself the sole instrument of supranational significance. The early hierarchy of government within the church recognized the prime importance of Rome, Constantinople and Alexandria but acknowledged no single supreme authority – despite Christ's charge to S. Peter and the prestige of the 'eternal city' as the see of the Apostolic succession. However, recognition of the need for strong central government in the church preceded the abdication of the last Western emperor, Romulus Augustulus, and the primacy of Rome was asserted by Pope Leo I (440–460). Even the Vandals, Visigoths and Ostrogoths were prepared to concede this but it was more than a century until Gregory I (590–604) formally assumed the care of all the churches.

In the west, centralization through the consolidation of papal power proceeded over another five hundred years, at least, to its culmination in face of a revival of the emperor's title. In the east, the survival of the emperor as constituted authority had the opposite effect of inhibiting centralization of power in the church. As the Thirteenth Apostle and chairman of the supreme ecclesiastical synod, the emperor appointed the Patriarch of Constantinople and the heads of the several national churches of the imperial domain and was ready to see them as largely autonomous. And the number of these churches increased as the Slavic tribes, who had penetrated eastern Europe in the wake of the hordes which sapped Rome, were converted to Christianity by missionaries from the east.

DOCTRINE AND DEBATE

With no scripture from Christ, but four different accounts of his life, the early Christian movement was plagued by doctrinal difference. The most notable was provoked by the contention of the early 4th-century Alexandrian presbyter Arius that, as God the Father is uniquely self-existent and immutable, Christ could not be divine.

Official recognition and the imperial will to reinforce political unity with a church catholic in practice – as the faith was catholic in principle – promoted the definition of canonical dogma from the Gospels and the epistles of the Apostles to the early churches. For this purpose Constantine, asserting his authority in religious affairs as *Pontifex Maximus*, convened the first general church council in his palace at Nicaea in 325. It defined the concept of the Trinity – central to the faith in God the Father, Son and Holy Ghost – in terms of God one in substance but three in persons and hence determined the Creed to be affirmed by all the faithful.

The Nicene orthodoxy was not to go unchallenged, despite attempts at compromise issuing from Constantinople. As the emperor failed to appreciate, Arianism did not admit of compromise on its fundamental tenet: it was adopted by most of the barbarians within the empire perhaps because it represented opposition to the establishment. Responding to this and other virulent 'heresies' in the quest for a canon of belief, the official church acquired intellectual standing to rival the pagan philosophers through the contributions of great theologians. Not the least of these were writing before the end of the 4th century: Jerome, who undertook the task of producing a canonical Latin text of the Bible in the 380s; Ambrose, who defended the eternity of Christ's godhead against the Arian heresy that he was created by, and therefore must be inferior to, the Father.**4.11**

NEOPLATONISM AND THE LIGHT OF GOD

Tracing concordance between Gospel and post-Socratic philosophy was an enduring concern of Christian thinkers – in both the past millennia. Naturally the earlier Church Fathers addressed themselves to the last phase of Hellenistic philosophy, known as Neoplatonism. They found themselves irreconcilably opposed on the defining Christological dogma of divine incarnation and resurrection but not on the objective of salvation, not on the ethics of purification, enlightenment and unification, not necessarily on the efficacy of abstruse asceticism – though, typically, Neoplatonists were humanistically non-self-mortifying – and not on mysticism.

Neoplatonists were sceptical of empirical knowledge, denying supremacy to the rational mind, and committed to belief in a universal human consciousness beyond the Hellenic. Their 3rd-century Alexandrine masters re-

espoused Platonic metaphysics yet drew inspiration from all the religions known to the Graeco-Roman world in the belief that man's ultimate satisfaction, the reunion of his soul with the Supreme One – in which everything has its purpose like Plato's Good – depends on revelation.

The prime source was Plotinus (c. 205–70): the highest plane of existence accessible to human comprehension is the perfect image projected by the One; that image in turn is reflected in 'Soul' – or 'Life' – collective and individual; 'Soul', by nature celestial, may descend to contamination in the world of sensual materialism – to false diversity from 'Truth' – but may reascend to the salvation of its proper nature in contemplation of the One through the practice of a hierarchy of virtues (in ascending order 'civil', 'purifying' and 'divine'). Above and beyond the sensible, ultimate bliss is the ecstacy of absorption in the revealed light of the

Supreme Being but eschewing in first principle a worshipful godhead as saviour comprehensible to ordinary mortals.

In Alexandria the late-Classical tendency was towards the theocentric coalescence of the main schools of Platonic, Aristotelian and Stoic philosophy. Fundamental here indeed is the Platonic distinction between the sensible and intelligible world – and the ultimate principle of being, Truth. It will be recalled that, to Plato, the philosopher is a lover of the vision of Truth reflected in the universal realities (Ideas or Forms) of the cosmos, that the apprehension of Truth alone is knowledge and that such knowledge is gained not from experience of this world but through deductive reasoning from incontrovertible axioms (like those of mathematics). However, as we have noted, it is difficult to disassociate Plato's vision of Truth from the mystical or his love of that vision from the ecstacy of the mystics – the rationalism notwithstanding.

Many of Plotinus's followers, in particular, denounced the duplicity of Christian theologians in promoting belief in Christ's divine incarnation and resurrection, and seemed to espouse pantheism in their championship of a wide range of theologies and philosophies current in the late-Roman world. After the triumph of Christianity most Neoplatonic schools were closed by a Church virulent in its extirpation of polytheism. But the school of Athens (which revived the study of Aristotle as well as Plato in the 5th century) survived to transmit a dualist legacy, rationalist and idealist, to the medieval world and to Christianity an extra dimension of mysticism.

The conversion to Christianity of the mystical Neoplatonic conception of soul's descent from and reascent to the Ultimate Source is credited to 'Dionysius the pseudo-Areopagite', a luminary anachronistically – but most prestigiously – identifed with a convert of S. Paul elevated to responsibility for the first church of Athens: the corpus is known to have been cited no earlier than 533 at the Council of Constantinople and its Neoplatonic core obviates a date before the 4th century. Dionysius's Ultimate Source – the Good – is, of course, God the universal and immanent Trinity, who radiates the vital essence as Grace and directs its stream through His agents. Ranged in descending triads (seraphim, cherubim and thrones; dominions, virtues and powers; principalities, archangels and angels), they conduct the purifying illumination of Grace to raise man towards God. Couched in terms of divine effulgence, radiation and illumination, this was the theology of Grace as Light manifest to man both spiritually and physically.

LITURGY

If the emperor was concerned to codify dogma, his vision of a catholic empire clearly also saw the need for standardized liturgy. The form of the mass as it had evolved over the previous three centuries was established as canonical. Culminating in the holy meal of the Eucharist, it had always admitted communal preliminary prayers with the baptized and the catechumens preparing for baptism but required the withdrawal of the latter before the presentation of the Eucharistic host under the presidency of the bishop. In the 3rd century, the separation of the clergy and the laity was promoted and the administration of the host to the latter was restricted. The relegation of the laity was accompanied by decreasing emphasis on the humility of Christ, increasing emphasis on the grandeur of his representatives and on the solemnity of ecclesiastical ritual.

As we have noted, well before Constantine accorded Christianity official status, it had evolved an hierarchical structure of authority in parallel to the imperial administration: this, of course, was greatly reinforced when the officers of the Church were accorded like rank and privileges to their secular counterparts. The ritual then acquired a quasi-imperial aura: the bishop, robed in splendour and accompanied by his presbyters in vestments modelled on those of the emperor's retinue, progressed to his enthronment like an imperial magistrate in the high sanctuary of an elevated building which emulated the magnificence of the imperial palace. For the bishop was the representative of the Lord, as the magistrate was the representative of the emperor and, above all, as the emperor was Christ's vicar on earth, Christ was emperor in heaven.**4.12**

›**4.12 THE EMPEROR JUSTINIAN** with ministers and (to his left) his ecclesiastical suite led by Archbishop Maximian of Ravenna (c. 545, Ravenna, S. Vitale).

ICON AND ICONOCLASM

Christian purists had long opposed anthropomorphism as contravening the second commandment of God to Moses on Mount Sinai ('Thou shalt not make to thyself any graven image, nor the likeness of anything that is in heaven above …') and at first Christ was represented only through symbols such as the cross or the lamb of the good shepherd's protection and sacrifice.**4.13** On the contrary, it was contended that as God had assumed human

4.13a

form in Christ, he should be so represented. Beyond pragmatism, the Neoplatonic school of Christian thought maintained that, as image and subject were similar not in substance but in essence, through the contemplation of that which could be seen, the mind might rise to comprehend that which could not be seen. From the idea that the seen suggests the unseen, it was a short step to the belief that the seen contains the unseen. But to avoid the next step, reversion to the idea that the physical appearance was identical to the unseen essence, a strictly two-dimensional canon was established for iconic representation.

4.13b

›4.13 CHRISTIAN SYMBOLS: (a) cross; (b) sacrificial lamb (apse mosaic and 6th century sarcophagus, Ravenna, S. Apollinare in Classe).

Growth in popular veneration of icons was dramatic after the 5th century, when the earliest-known image of the Crucifixion appeared.[4.6] Fearing that the process had led to idolatry despite the strict conventions governing iconic imagery, Pope Leo III (717–41) issued a decree proscribing it in 730. Wholesale destruction of images throughout the Byzantine world resulted. The proscription was lifted by the Council of Nicaea in 787 but Iconoclasm persisted until 843.

Essentially anti-Classical – non-humanist – the theology underlying the Christian canon of iconography rejected the celebration of this world which is merely a base prelude to the glory to come, a glory that is not susceptible to reason but attainable only through faith, faith in the operation of a transcendental power incarnate as Christ. Moreover, denying that God's work can be comprehended through worldly experience, that the divine could be deduced from the observation of physical phenomena and represented by the idealization of humanity, it deposed the mind of man from its central position in humanism – though the Neoplatonists sustained a rationalism that was to cause Christian scholars much debate.

Masterpieces of high-Classical art – the Parthenon frieze and the best of its followers, the Battle of Issos and its rare mosaic peers,[3.40g, 3.66, 3.129] the most accomplished frescoes from Pompeii and their like – are instructively to be compared with the archetypical Byzantine Christian image, pre- and post-Iconoclasm.

Phidias offered his followers a supreme statement of the will to idealize and to represent that ideal realistically in space: his relief is shallow but the figures and horses appear to stand naturally one in front of the other. The Pompeiian artists who reproduced the Greek image of Issos may not have been as great but they realized a similar objective under the even tighter constraint of working in only two dimensions. In both cases the fore-shortening of form depends upon the rational analysis of the principles of perspective in the perceived diminution of objects in space.**4.14**

The Christian artist may not construct images of corporeality or tangible space for his figures – let alone the cross – to stand on. They must be like cardboard cut-outs superimposed against a flat background in which the reality of perspective is ignored as irrelevant. The Christian artist is concerned with the supernatural, with God as man not man as god, and with a heavenly hierarchy. By definition his icons are timeless ideograms abstracted from physical, let alone personal, reality: their spiritual significance eclipses that reality.

The Classical artist conveys an ideal of physical beauty worthy of the gods. The Christian artist conveys the spiritual ideals of God's sacrificial mystery, suffering, compassion, devotion – and of motherhood. Yet hybrids – hieratic but corporeal – had long been produced, especially in the eastern reaches of the Romanized world, and a measure of Classical anthropomorphism survived Christian abstraction, especially in the service of the secular facet of the imperial ideal.**4.15**

Meanwhile, it was established that the order of the Orderer of creation could be reflected in the pure geometry of the church – the image of His heavenly mansion. According to early Christian cosmologists – notably the mid-6th-century merchant-monk Cosmos of Alexandria, known as Indicopleustes for his extensive travels – the main constituents were a rectangular plane, in the centre of which was earth surrounded by ocean, covered by a domical vault sustaining heaven. The realization of a similar ideal order in the geometry of the church was an eastern achievement after the 6th century, as we shall see.

4.14a

4.14b

4.14c

›4.14 CLASSICAL ARTS RECALLED:
(a) Orpheus, Eurydice and Hermes (early imperial Roman copy from a villa at Torre del Greco of a post-Phidian Greek funerary relief of c. 400 BCE); (b) birds drinking from a bronze bowl, mid-1st-century CE Pompeiian mosaic related to the work of the 2nd-century BCE Pergamene painter Sosos; (c) Perseus and Andromeda, Flavian-era fresco from the Pompeiian House of the Dioscuri after a Greek original attributed to the late-Classical Athenian master Nikias (Naples, National Archaeological Museum).

›4.15 EARLY CHRISTIAN ICONIC ART:
(a) image, possibly of the Palmyran sun-god with the aureole and palm which would subsequently become the attributes of the Christian martyr (Palmyran limestone sculpture, 1st century BCE, Damascus, Syrian National Museum); (b) mid-8th-century fresco of the Crucifixion from the Chapel of SS. Syriacus and Julitta in S. Maria Antica, Rome); (c) Coptic cross with palm-like oriole, 6th century (Alexandria, Greco-Roman Museum); (d) 9th-century iconic relief panel (Thessaloniki, Museum of Byzantine Culture); (e) Classicizing ivory panel of the Forty Martyrs of Sebasteia (Byzantine, 10th century; Berlin, National Museum).

4.15a

4.15c

4.15d

4.15b

4.15e

CHRISTIAN BUILDING TYPES: THE ROMAN INHERITANCE

The principal object of Christian architecture was, of course, the church. However, as Christians entered the fold through baptism and often left it through martyrdom, special buildings were required to provide for the one and to commemorate the other.

The origin of the church was in the house – as we have seen, Christianity developed in the context of Roman urban life and during their persecution Christians worshipped in the discretion of their homes. In any case, the requirements of their primitive liturgy were little more than domestic: apart from communal prayer on Sunday, it centred on the Eucharistic meal and both could be accommodated in the triclinium which usually occupied the upper floor of all but the meanest urban houses; a withdrawing room was needed for converts who could share in the prayers but not in the ritual breaking of the bread before baptism; and baptism could be administered at the well in the service court. **4.16, 4.17**

As the body of the faithful grew so, naturally, did its needs: when the house proved inadequate to accommo-

4.17a

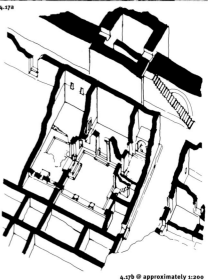

4.17b @ approximately 1:200

›4.16 QIRQBIZE, 5th century. The entrance in the centre is distinguished by a symbolic cross.

›**4.17 DURA-EUROPOS,** dated from graffiti to 23: (a) remains of a typical courtyard complex, (b) isometric view.

At Dura-Europos the patron's room is beyond the court on the east–west entrance axis (in the place of a Roman tabularium). A bench-bordered andron (triclinium or divan) in the south range was adapted for congregational worship c. 245 when the andron was extended into the neighbouring room, the tabularium was converted into the sanctuary (or, possibly, the separate congregational space for catechumens) and the adjacent room in the north range was equipped as a baptistery.

date baptism, teaching, preaching, prayer, the celebration of the Eucharist, the administration of charity, storage, etc. in a series of connected rooms – a redundant thermal complex with its water supply to halls and chambers of varied size and shape must have seemed particularly suitable for adaptation as a communal meeting centre. Be this as it may, in addition to partitioning the catechumens from the baptized in the main meeting hall, it was the practice by the mid-3rd century to erect a balustrade between the laity and the clergy attending the altar – the sacrificial table inherited from the primitive dining room. The sanctuary beyond the rail would be the presbytery when it accommodated a bishop and his entourage.

Beyond service to the living there was the need to accommodate the dead in ground unpolluted by pagan rites and to provided facilities for obsequies and memorial services involving a banquet. Christians, looking for the bodily resurrection of the dead and therefore rejecting the Roman proletarian norm of cremation, were interred – sometimes in subterranean catacombs for economy of land use. Though prejudiced against pagan burial grounds, the more affluent Christian did not disdain the form of rectangular tomb building familiar to pagans of similar means, providing for funeral banquets either in the tomb chamber or its vestibule. The poor majority, interred in the ground, were sent off in simple trabeated porticoes bounding the smaller sites or – apparently not much earlier than 300 – in communal banqueting halls at the larger cemeteries.

Funerary banquet halls were probably the first large-scale buildings initiated by Christians. On a smaller scale there were memorials marking a holy figure's grave or place of martyrdom. The halls were doubtless utilitarian structures but the martyria borrowed the idea, form and style of the pagan heroum – the focus of hero-worship, as the name implies. The Christians, of course, denied apotheosis to pagan heroes and emperors but endowed their holy figures with the aura of divinity in canonization: the appropriation of the pagan form as the context for the commemoration of their heroes must have had the added advantage of despoiling the false for the true.

Focused on the monument or grave of the incumbent, the heroum was ideally centralized, generated as a circle (or regular polygon) from a single centre. At its simplest it was a hypaethral precinct with a canopied niche. It was commonly a cubicle, domed like the empyraean, sometimes open like a baldachino to all four arcaded sides or with exedrae to three sides and a porticoed entrance (triconch). At its grandest it was a tholos like the Philippeion at Olympia or Diocletian's mausoleum at Split.**3.45, 3.196**

Nothing of significant monumentality survives from the earliest Christian cemeteries, though martyria with altars over the grave proliferated in the mid-3rd and early 4th-century reigns of persecution, and vaulted cubes with exedrae to three sides or short cross arms to all four appear c. 300. The oldest-known martyrium, associated with the grave of S. Peter, is a 2nd-century roofless precinct with niche and aedicule in the Vatican necropolis below the great basilica dedicated to the Prince of the Apostles.

Symbolism may have encouraged the Christians to build martyria in an Antique form but when they were able to build churches openly they rejected the temple as a model for both symbolic and pragmatic reasons. The beliefs enshrined in the temple were, of course, anathema but it was also rejected because the form was non-congregational.

Christianity was a proselytizing religion in need of large congregational spaces in which the Gospel could be preached and the mystery of the Eucharist revealed – though sermons were not common until the 6th century.

The Roman meeting hall – the basilica – with its typical nave for seating and aisles for access, provided just such a space but the Christians also favoured it for its symbolic significance. Certainly not invariably, but most usually, the basilica was an elongated hall of judgement in which the magistrate – vice-emperor – dominated the assembly from his throne on the dais in an apse at the end.**3.198** Appropriating the form for adaptation to its various requirements, Christianity in its triumph substituted the infallible judgement of God for the fallible judgement of man – the bishop, as Christ's vicar, for the magistrate as the representative of secular power.**4.18**

After elevating the church into an imperial institution, moreover, the emperor prescribed for its congregation a building type of the highest dignity and materials of the greatest richness. On its superior plane like the throne room of the palace, this could hardly be other than a magisterial basilica: 'basilica', indeed, derives from the Greek for 'place of the king' and the divinity of the ruler had long endowed it with sanctity. Its raised apse, dominated by the bishop's throne and sometimes screened by the fastigium of imperial dignity, elevated a monumental altar covered by a baldachino like the imperial throne. Palace imagery thus pervaded the Christian conception of the church as both a building apart, the institution of God's elect and, beyond all, the door to God's heavenly mansion.

The triumphal arch has been seen as the Classical descendant of the twin-towered gate of ancient Mesopotamia.**1.51, 1.52** Both were places of epiphany, of the appearance of god among men, the triumphal arch commemorating the progress of state hero or emperor from mortality to immortality: apotheosis. As such, its symbolism is of obvious relevance to a faith centred on the concept of resurrection and, indeed, the form was

›**4.18 ROME, S. AGNESE,** 625: apse and throne.

adopted for the portal of the church. It was certainly also remembered for the palace of the Christian emperor – or his representative, the exarch.**4.19, 4.20**

A hierarchical institution, the church required clear distinction between its building types: baptistery from congregational church, both from the cemetery hall and martyrium to which pilgrims now flocked in need of special facilities. The basilican church headed the hierarchy and within it were distinct spaces, hierarchically ordered. Primacy, of course, went to the sanctuary where the mass was performed from the place of lay congregation, but distinct provision also had to be made for male and female worshippers, for catechumens and their baptism, for the veneration of holy relics or images and for the procession of clergy and pilgrims. Yet, given the wide diversity of local

›4.19 CONSTANTINOPLE: reconstructed (a) plan and (b) elevation of the principal ceremonial entrance (Chalka) of Constantine's palace, 332.

The Chalka was originally built between towers in the ramparts of the citadel: early chroniclers record a pendentive dome at the intersection of tunnel vaults, the side ones extending the volume beyond the square. Above the outer arch was a sculpted image of Christ (traditionally, but controversially, dated to the reign of Constantine).

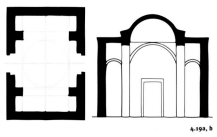

4.19a, b

›4.20 RAVENNA: A BYZANTINE IMPERIAL PALACE, mosaic in S. Apollinare Nuovo, dedicated 490.

The mosaic has usually been identified as the residence of the Ostrogothic king Theodoric. References have not surprisingly been detected in it both to the Palace of Diocletian at Split and to the imperial palace at Constantinople. The twin-towered portal (right), symbol of royal power from time immemorial, could derive from either the Golden Gate or the Chalka of Constantinople. The fastigium, flanked by the colonnades of a peristyle, clearly recalls the entrance to the imperial reception suite at Split – though the colonnades there are at right angles to it. The galleried upper storey, not present in the peristyle at Split, was known to Constantine's builders.

conditions and traditions in the far-flung territories of the late empire, no precise correlation may be imposed on form and function in early Christian architecture.

With its distinct nave and aisles, its elevated apse at the culmination of its longitudinal axis, the basilica was adapted to most Christian requirements. Typically, but not invariably, aisles were multiplied and a transept introduced before the apse to provide – with clearly relevant symbolism – distinct assembly space in the side arms and special sanctuary at the crossing. The altar might be in the sanctuary, or in the crossing at the head of the nave. The sanctuary might be distinguished by a change of level or a screen or both. Women might or might not have a separate enclosure. Catechumens might be relegated to an aisle or to a separate room. Baptism might fill a transept arm but not with convenience: it was originally administered by the total immersion in water of the body whose soul was thus symbolically cleansed and the space devised for it was naturally focused on that central event.**4.21**

›4.21 RAVENNA, ARIAN BAPTISTERY, c. 500:
vault mosaic showing the baptism of Christ.

›4.22 TRANSLATION OF RELICS TO A CHURCH UNDER CONSTRUCTION in the presence of emperor and patriarch (5th/6th-century ivory panel, Trier Cathedral Treasury).

The context has been identified as Constantinople from the Chalka portal with its image of Christ (to the left). The basilica would thus be H. Sofia. The Roman arcaded building with spectators behind is doubtless the Hippodrome but it may also prefigure the church interior. The emperor is likely to be Constantine's successor Constantius, under whom the basilica was completed, but has also been seen as Theodosius II, under whom the building was repaired and embellished after a fire c. 404 and to whose reign the panel is sometimes dated.

1 CONSTANTINIAN BUILDING

Effecting the transition from the essentially domestic tradition of Christianity's clandestine youth to a public – indeed imperial – one, Constantine founded the preeminent basilicas of the ascendant faith. Equally, the centralized form of the burial rotunda recommended itself not only for the mausoleums or martyria built to commemorate the propagators and defenders of the faith but also for the baptisteries dedicated to its expansion.**4.22**

The emperor called for the most dignified of architectural forms for the church, as we have seen, and for the richest materials. There were gold or silver vessels and jewelled fabrics, semi-precious stone or richly veined marble for colonnades and revetment. In practice the latter, usually pillaged from the pagan past with scant care for consistency, were confined to interiors and the grandest façades. In both halves of the empire, the structure even of the major early Christian churches was usually of mortared rubble with brick revetment and roofing was invariably of timber until brick vaults – tunnel, groin and domical – became common in the Byzantine east in the 6th century.

THE BASILICA

The major seats of imperial power were all endowed by Constantine with basilicas. From the variety of basilican forms produced over nearly half a millennium his architects chose the longitudinal plan with colonnaded aisles for communication to each side of a wider, higher nave terminating in a raised apse and lit through windows in its upper walls (clerestory) below a timber roof. From the house they extracted the atrium and expanded it into a galleried forecourt whose inner range provided a sheltered entrance hall (narthex).

Foremost in time and significance among the basilicas of Rome were the cathedral of Rome, S. Giovanni Laterano, and S. Pietro in Vaticano. The former was associated with a baptistery beside and a palace donated by the emperor soon after his triumph in 312. The latter was built over the grave of S. Peter to whom Christ had entrusted the keys of his church.**4·23**

Pre-eminent Christian basilicas: S. Giovanni Laterano, S. Pietro in Vaticano

In 313 Constantine designated the Lateran imperial palace as the residence of the bishop of Rome: *ex-voto* for victory, the cathedral – the Basilica Constantiniana – was founded on the adjacent site of the guard barracks probably in the same year. The initial conception took a long time to be realized and, though respected in early 10th- and 14th-century refection, most of it has been eclipsed by later work, especially that of the 17th and 19th centuries. However, earlier images and the plan provide the basis for reconstruction. The great nave, terminating in a generous apse beyond a chancel at its western end, was flanked by doubled aisles, the outer ranges lower than the inner and leading to slightly projecting chambers at their western ends (the overall dimensions were 95 metres long and 55 metres wide). The columns screening the aisles internally supported arches but the main nave colonnades may have carried an architrave – though their last observers record arcades. The interior

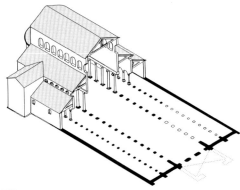

4.23a @ 1:2000

4.23b

>4.23 ROME: (a, b) S. Giovanni in Laterano (begun
c. 313), axonometric and part plan and record of
interior; (c, d) S. Pietro in Vaticano (begun c. 320,
largely complete in structure by 330), record of interior
(frescoes by F. Gagliardi, c. 1650, in S. Martino ai
Monte) and plan (with the early 5th century mausoleum
projected for the emperor Honorius attached to the
south transept).

decoration was lavish: in addition to multi-coloured marbles and mosaics,
there were gilded roof timbers and silver altars.

Unlike S. Giovanni in Laterano, S. Pietro in Vaticano was designed as a
cemetery church intended for obsequial rites rather than for the regular
celebration of mass before a permanent congregation – though it was
capable of accommodating up to two thousand of the many pilgrims
drawn to it. Preceded by a cloistered atrium, the main building had a
broad central nave – essentially a covered burial ground – screened by
colonnades from twin aisles to each side and terminating in an apse
beyond the Apostolic shrine to the west (the overall dimensions were 119
metres long and 64 metres wide). As the tradition was yet to be firmly
established that Christian churches were built so that the priest at the
altar faced the rising sun of the holy Levant (hence the word 'orientation'), entry from the east was through an atrium with a cleansing fountain in the form of an Antique pine cone.

Work on the Vatican basilica started at the west end, where the 2nd-
century monument reputedly marking the Apostle's burial place was
embraced by a lower cross-arm inserted between nave and apse. This
was the first important transept in Christian architecture, needed to
accommodate the crowds aspiring to worship at the Apostle's tomb and
to act as chancel during commemorative services. Separating sanctuary
from nave, this transept admirably served the official church's hierarchical purpose and was generally to be retained throughout the history of
Christian architecture – at least in the west. In the 7th century the floor of

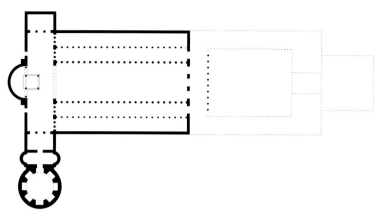

4.23d

4.23c @ 1:2000

the sanctuary was raised over the Apostle's tomb crypt and an ambulatory passage was developed around it at ground level in the curve of the apse: that too was prophetic of the later pilgrimage church norm.

The characteristic Christian basilican profile of high nave flanked by low aisles is clearly recorded in the early 16th century by Raphael in rich chromaticism which was not characteristic of the façades of Constantine's period – as in the great buildings of the imperial past, decorative splendour was internal. Placed impressively close together, the columns screening aisles from nave were pillaged from earlier buildings and varied widely in stone texture and colour. The capitals were oddly assorted Corinthian and Composite of different heights. Above the projecting entablature, also formed of marbles pillaged from pagan buildings, the clerestory was frescoed in the 5th century with scenes from the Old Testament but mosaics enriched the chancel arch and apse. Over the tomb a ciborium was carried on spiral columns. Still preserved in the great 16th-century building which replaced Constantine's work, these are associated with the Temple of Solomon in Jerusalem and their form is consequently known as Solomonic.

At a site associated with a martyr, the Roman cemetery pilgrimage church represents a variant of the Petrine type with naves, accommodating obsequies and burial, flanked by aisles which continue around the apse to form an ambu-

latory: S. Lorenzo fuori le Mura and S. Sebastiano, with many mausolea attached to the walls, are outstanding examples.**4.24** There were grand new halls also for the veneration of relics: most notable among the latter was the basilica of S. Croce in Gerusalemme built beside her Roman palace by the emperor's mother, Helena, to enshrine the fragments of the True Cross which she believed she had recovered from the Holy Land.

At the old northern capital, Trier, where he had been based before his triumph, Constantine commissioned a double basilican cathedral associated with the palace – one begun as early as 315, the other ten years later.**4.25**

At Constantinople, the imperial architects probably adapted the basilica for the episcopal church of H. Eirene and the form was amplified for the palatine church of H. Sofia – begun under Constantine and furthered by his heir. However, both these great works were destroyed in the Nika riots of 532, along with much else, and our knowledge of them as eastern prototypes – indeed of the development of church architecture in the capital between the reigns of Constantine and Justinian – is sadly limited.**4.22**

BAPTISTERY AND SHRINE

The early Christian martyrium derived from the Roman tomb type, well represented on the via Latina. This was often rectangular, but dedication to a single significant martyr obviously prompted centralization. Baptism too

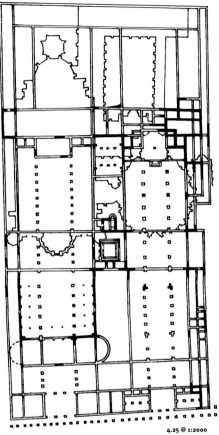

4.25 @ 1:2000

›4.25 TRIER, CATHEDRAL: plan of Constantinian double foundation, c. 315 and 325.

The arrangement was anticipated on a much smaller scale at Aquileia at the outset of the reign. The sanctuaries in both complexes were rectangular rather than apsidal, but the linking element differed: at Aquileia there was a minor transverse aisled hall in the western sector of the broad intermediate space, probably for catechumens; at Trier, where a section within the western entrance of each hall seems to have been screened for catechumens, there were small vestibules at each end of the much narrower gap, a central square baptistery and a broad atrium.

had a single dominant focal point in usual practice, recommending a centralized form. Beside the Lateran basilica Constantine's architects seem to have initiated the octagonal plan. On a grander scale, the mausoleum of the emperor's daughter Constantia, built beside the covered cemetery of S. Agnes, is the most complete surviving example of the early Christian centralized shrine.**4.26**

4.26b

4.26a

›4.26 SEMINAL ROMAN CENTRALIZED WORKS: (a, b) baptistery of S. Giovanni in Laterano, exterior and interior (the Constantinian work dates from c. 330 but the present arrangement of superimposed Orders descends from the remodelling carried out c. 430 under Pope Sixtus III); (c) S. Costanza, c. 330–50, interior.

Seminal centralized Christian building

Appropriating and converting the typical late-imperial heroum – the theatre of apotheosis most prominently represented by the mausoleum of Diocletian – Constantine's architects found particular significance in the octagonal form: it is focused on the centre where cleansing immersion presaged eternal life in Christ and the number of its sides – the number of the day of His Passion on which Christ rose from the dead – symbolizes regeneration. Only parts of the Lateran structure have survived refurbishment but the idea of a colonnade screening an ambulatory from the font was probably original – it is merely an adaptation to centralized form of the standard procedure for screening nave from aisles in a basilica.

The earliest Christian mausoleum known to have been attached to a basilica – and thus converting the ancient type of the heroum to Christianity – was built beside the narthex of SS. Pietro e Marcellino to a circular plan with alternating rectangular and semi-circular niches: probably originally destined for the emperor, it was assigned to his mother, S. Helena. The mausoleum of the emperor's daughter – now the church of S. Costanza – was given a barrel-vaulted ambulatory screened with arches springing from the columns in place of the canonical entablature. The focal point in the centre was the obvious site for the tomb (as for a font) and the axis of entry, naturally established at no one point on the uniform circumference, had arbitrarily to be extended for the altar. Now, in fact, an altar occupies the centre and the sarcophagus is sheltered by a recession in the ambulatory opposite the entrance.

4.26c

HYBRIDS

Though the basilican church was to dominate throughout the empire for centuries and the centralized form of circle or octagon was to be repeated endlessly for baptisteries and martyria or tombs, the first imperial Christian builders were experimental and certainly did not confine themselves to standard types. In several seminal works – now known largely from descriptions – they developed and combined centralized and longitudinal forms, open and closed, as the Roman builders of complexes ranging from villas to thermae had done for centuries.

In Constantinople, the Church of the Holy Apostles, built by Constantine as the imperial mausoleum and widely influential, was cruciform with a central dome sheltering the emperor's sarcophagus and statues of the twelve Apostles – with whom he was to be venerated on equal terms. The rotunda followed the Antique precedent of the tholos heroum, like the tomb of Galerius at Thessaloniki and, indeed, the tombs in Rome assigned to Constantine's mother and daughter; the addition of the arms obviously converted the pagan form to Christianity. It initiated a series of freestanding Christian heroa, including the cruciform shrine of S. Byblas at Kaoussié near Antioch.**4.27**

In the centre of imperial Antioch, the palatine chapel known as the Golden Octagon had semi-circular exedrae to the eight sides and an ambulatory over which a second level of colonnades provided a gallery. The double-shell structure, formed by superimposing a gallery over an encircling ambulatory, was novel in the ecclesiastical context – but precedents may be found in Hadrian's Villa at Tivoli. Galleries were not new: the form is implicit in the upper colonnade of the typical Greek temple interior and reappears in works like the Pompeiian basilica.**3.122**

Constantine's architects, who had probably provided

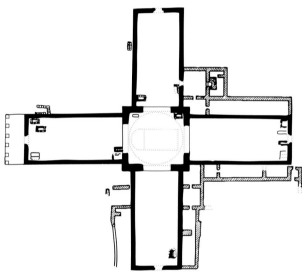

4.27 @ 1:1000

›4.27 ANTIOCH, KAOUSSIÉ, MARTYRIUM OF S. BYBLAS, 379: plan.

The altar and the grave of the local saint, Bishop of Antioch, were in the central square, presumably covered by a timber pyramidal roof. The lower arms were aisleless. With the addition of a baptistery and sacristy, the complex served as a church. Except for these additions, the scheme clearly followed the model of the Apostoleion, though there is some doubt about the latter's initial conception: in his exhaustive studies of Byzantium and its architecture, C. Mango maintains that Constantine built the rotunda for his mausoleum and that his son Constantius (337–61) added the cruciform structure for relics he acquired in 356.

galleries over the doubled aisles of H. Sofia in Constantinople, also adopted them in the complex enshrining the place of Christ's crucifixion and the Holy Sepulchre in Jerusalem. Like the Church of the Nativity at Bethlehem, this great work combined the basilica with the martyrium but they were no longer fused, the latter appropriating the centralized form of the late-imperial mausoleum as the context for indubitable apotheosis.**4.28**

›4.28 JERUSALEM, CHURCH OF THE HOLY SEPULCHRE ON GOLGOTHA (c. 326–36): (a, b) 'Edicule' enshrining Christ's tomb, model (5th century?; Narbonne, Museum of Art and History), (c) early 17th-century sectional perspective of the Anastasis (engraved by Callot), (d) plan, (e) model.

4.28a, b

The Church of the Holy Sepulchre

According to his chroniclers, Constantine ordered a church more beautiful than any other to be built on the site of Christ's Passion. Here, the tomb traditionally identified as the one from which Christ rose from the dead seems to have been cut from its cliff, and the ground to the east levelled around and beyond the rock of Calvary – the site of the Crucifixion – which was also cut to shape.

Little of Constantine's work survives later rebuilding – especially by the Crusaders in the 12th century – but according to Constantine's historian, Eusebius, both the sacred places were embraced by a cloistered precinct: a tempietto of twelve columns, the Anastasis, was erected as a ciborium for the tomb (as for S. Costanza in Rome); a double-aisled basilica was built over the eastern half of the site, butting on to the ancient street giving access to it. The basilica had galleries over the aisles perhaps for the first time in a major Christian building, and its atrium was

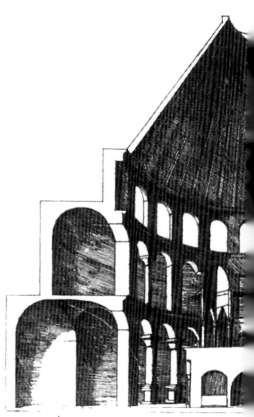

4.28c

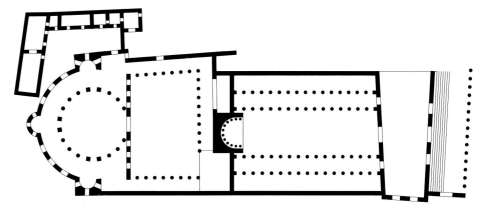

4.28d @ 1:1000

entered through a propylaeum. If the original rotunda had galleries over its ambulatory, as later records indicate, it must be seen as double-skinned like the Golden Octagon of Antioch – though neither ambulatory nor gallery continued across the entrance.

According to one interpretation of Eusebius, the semi-circle of the basilica's apse was continued round the ends of the flanking sacristies to form the rotunda. However, the excavated remains include a colonnaded court separating apse and rotunda, the latter ringed internally by columns grouped in four triads between paired piers.

The Church of the Nativity at Bethlehem (c. 333 but also rebuilt or renovated several times) had a cloistered atrium, a double-aisled basilica and an octagonal shrine sheltering the cave in which Christ is believed to have been born: basilica and octagon were fused.

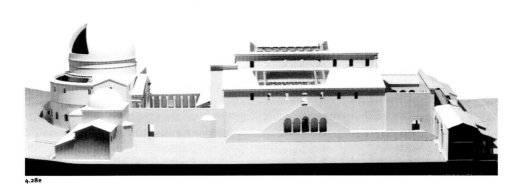

4.28e

2 DIVISION AND LATE-IMPERIAL ROME

Constantine bestowed a great deal of imperial patronage on traditional public works and Christianizing the ancient imperial seat. However, his principal residence was Constantinople from 330 – when it was dedicated to the Blessed Virgin. His successors moved their bases frequently as defence, in particular, required but Rome and Constantinople were the pivots until the fomer was eclipsed by Milan in the mid-4th century. Thereafter Constantinople was the centre of the world for a thousand years.

After repelling the Goths in central Europe and suppressing rebellion from the heir of his last co-ruler in 335, Constantine delegated responsibility for quarters of the empire to his three oldest sons and nephew as *Caesars* but remained *Augustus* alone until his death two years later while preparing to defend the eastern frontier against the Sassanians. The new 'Augustus' was the oldest brother, Constantine, who had been named 'Caesar' soon after his birth in 317. His attempt to rule as *primus inter-pares* with the next in line, Constans and Constantius, ended in his death in contention with the former in 340. Constans then asserted his imperium over all the west. Constantius had inherited the east but won the west too when his brother died in 350. He in turn died in 361, after endless conflict with the Sassanians, and the reunited empire passed to his younger brother, Julian, who had already been acclaimed in the west.

After Constantine – under successors constantly fighting Sassanians, Goths and one another – the state waxed at the expense of its citizens. Many were taxed out of land and industry: their assets passed to the imperial authorities or great magnates and they became serfs tied to the land of others. This too derived from Constantine's completion of his predecessor's work: the hereditary principle was extended to social purpose – professional, industrial, commercial and agricultural.

With state ownership of the means of production, distribution and supply, went state organization of labour into the caste system from which the guilds of medieval Europe emerged. As improvement of the individual lot was taxed at a still higher rate there was little incentive. The initiative which underlay the prosperity of an old empire was crushed by its successor superstate and stagnation set in. With stagnation came corruption – not for the last time.

THE ETERNAL CITY ECLIPSED

Imperial unity was based on a common language, coinage and law, an international army and long-established patterns of trade. A primarily non-Roman army was inherrently unreliable and economic development, not least as a result of Constantine's reforms, laid the foundations for provincial self-sufficiency. With their old urban civilization and prominent merchant class, Egypt and Syria were

4.30a

4.30b

›4.30 CONSTANTINOPLE (ISTANBUL), defensive land wall constructed between 408 and 413 at the beginning of the reign of Theodosius II (408–450): (a) western range (restored) and (b) Golden Gate.

The ramparts straddling the isthmus of the capital's peninsula site provide the earliest significant surviving example of a double ring of walls within a moat for defence in depth – though the principle was known to the ancient Indians among others. The outer range, punctuated by ninety-six rectangular and semi-circular towers with embrasures facing to front and sides, was 7 kilometres in extent, 9 metres high and 5 metres thick. The inner range (55 metres from the scarp beyond the moat) had more massive rectangular and octagonal towers, over twice the height of the outer ones. The materials were rubble bound with concrete, reinforced with courses of brick and faced with brick relieved by bands of limestone. A similar system deployed towards the middle of the century at Thessa-

4.31

loniki incorporated triangular, rather than octagonal,
bastions – anticipating the key element of Europe's
most sophisticated star-shaped fortifications by a
thousand years.

›**4.31 EPHESOS,** the marble street of the emperor
Arcadius.

  One of the last of its kind, this splendid artery linked
the theatre with the harbour: 600 metres long and
11 metres wide, it was flanked by shops and lined with
mosaic-paved pedestrian colonnades, 5 metres deep.
At the half-way stage, statues of the four Evangelists
on Corinthian columns were erected by Emperor Justinian in the mid-6th century.

difficult to contain. In the less-developed west, on the
other hand, long prey to unsettling barbarian forces, the
old aristocracy entrenched itself and consolidated its
estates as power bases independent of – even hostile to –
the crumbling imperial regime.

  Reversing Diocletian's religious policy, Theodosius I
revived Diocletian's state policy: in 393 he divided the succession between his two sons, Rome and the western
provinces passing to Honorius, Constantinople and the
eastern provinces to Arcadius.**4.29** Neither proved to be
competent. Arcadius (395–408) defended Constantinople
and sustained urban development elsewhere in the traditional imperial manner,**4.30, 4.31** but Honorius (393–423)

lost Rome. From the middle of the 4th cent-ury the pressure of barbarian hordes on the old hub had led to the removal of the imperial seat to northern provincial centres, first Milan, then Ravenna where Honorius went in 402 for greater security from the marauding Visigoths. Under his sister, the regent Galla Placidia, her son Valentinian III (425–55) and their ephemeral successors, Ravenna remained the capital until the end of the Western Empire.

The Visigoths sacked Rome in 410, then moved on through Gaul, taking Provence and Aquitaine, to occupy Spain. And the eternal city was sacked again in 455 by the Vandals, who had taken North Africa. Meanwhile, Burgundian tribes had settled in the Rhone valley, northern Gaul was falling to the Franks, southern Germany to the Thuringians and Bavarians, the Saxons were spreading from eastern Germany to Britain and Slavic tribes were harrying the east. In 476, finally, the last Western emperor, Romulus Augustulus, abdicated under pressure from the Germanic tribal leader Odoacer, who had established himself at Ravenna as king of Italy.

Nominally under the suzerainty of the Eastern emperor Zeno, but with the support of the Roman Senate, Odoacer controlled most of northern Italy, at least, until confronted by the Ostrogoths under Theodoric. Questing for land in the Balkans and raiding well into Asia Minor, they were deflected from Constantinople by Zeno's endowment of their chief with the Italian kingship in 488. Theodoric led his forces to the promised land in 490, rapidly occupied the north, reached an accord with the Romans and eliminated Odoacer early in 493. Soon after he married one of his daughters to the Visigothic king and, when the latter lost his life and Aquitaine to the Franks in 507, he took the son of the marriage into his care and assumed responsibility for all the Goths.

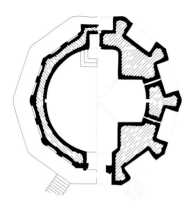

4.32a @ approximately 1:330

›4.32 RAVENNA, TOMB OF THEODORIC, 526:
(a) plan of both main levels, (b) exterior from entrance.

Rather than one of the Roman chamber tomb types Christianized as martyria, Theodoric's pretensions recommended the revival of the Augustan and Hadrianic ideal of a drum on a podium – though the scale betrays the extent to which reality constrained ambition. The podium has a cruciform interior but is a decagon with powerful semi-circular voussoir arches to each exterior side. The upper storey is also decagonal, though circular inside, and seems originally to have been encircled by an arcaded gallery. The extraordinary monolithic domical roof adds a recollection of the age-old tumulus.

4.32b

Ruling from Ravenna in imperial style, embracing the Arian creed like most barbarian Christian converts but dedicated to religious tolerance, Theodoric sustained peace between Goths and Romans and maintained relative stability in much of the peninsula north of Naples – and much of Dalmatia – until his interment in 526 in his quasi-imperial tomb.**4.32** His dominions were divided between his grandsons, the Visigoth securing Iberia.

Irritated by encroaching Slavs in the Balkans, but not faced with the most aggressive of the Sassanians, the heirs of Arcadius in the east fared better than their western cousins. However, the east was rent with doctrinal differences over the nature of Christ – whether he was wholly divine or part-human. In brief, the Egyptian church of Alexandria maintained that the human and the divine were united indistiguishably in Him (monophysitism). Antioch maintained that they coexisted separately (dyophysitism). In 451 Constantinople and Rome reached accord embracing two natures, perfect and perfectly distinct. Egypt and part of Syria rejected this and their monophysitism bolstered separatism based on the prosperity of their individual economies.

BUILDING UNDER
CONSTANTINE'S SUCCESSORS

Constantine inaugurated an age long focused on ecclesi-astical work – first in Rome then, as the court moved, in Milan and Ravenna. After the foundations had been laid under him, experimental structures erected and their influ-ence exported to sacred sites as far afield as Bethlehem, there was a period in which the main types – the congre-gational basilica, the baptistery and the martyrium – were clarified, forms consolidated, details regulated. Neverthe-less, the persistence of regional traditions in building and divergent developments in ritual ensured variety of style, structure and the distribution of supplementary elements within each type – of species within the genus.

The principal genus was the aisled and apsed basilica, now regularly orientated so that the apse with the altar projected towards the eastern dawn of Christ's salvation. As the Roman basilica was varied in form, so too the shape of its early Christian successor – east or west – was dic-tated by many considerations which took precedence over respect for a remote metropolitan model. Liturgical developments and regional traditions promoted variety: standard elements proliferated and new ones were added to the standard formula. There was usually a narthex but not necessarily a transept or an atrium and, in the case of cathedrals, a throne in the apse, side chapels and a distinct baptistery.

Species may be distinguished by the inclusion of towers, galleries over aisles, galleries continuing around or across transepts, a special space for the preparation of the Eucharist in a transept or in one of a pair of rooms flanking the apse, the position of the altar and the shape of the apse – semi-circular, semi-polygonal or even trilobed with the altar in the centre, the bishop's throne on axis in the central recession, the host to his right and other liturgical requirements to his left. The eastern apse might be extended and screened with columns and/or parapet walls to form a distinct enclosure (bema) and approached along a raised pathway (solea) – as at the Lateran.

The baptistery was typically a detached octagon but there are circular, square and rectangular examples, outside and inside the church. There was distinct provision for the veneration of martyrs, too, typically in a freestanding centralized structure – like the baptistery – but often within the church. We shall encounter all these species and others in a progression around the Mediterranean littoral.

ROMAN STANDARDS

Prototypes – for the west, at least – were set in the many new basilicas built in place of primitive domestic – or thermal – churches and to commemorate early Christians associated with the defence of the faith in the imperial capital. Of the latter, outstanding examples are the patriarchal basilicas of S. Paolo fuori le Mura and S. Maria Maggiore as begun in the 380s and 430s respectively. With the two senior patriarchal basilicas of S. Giovanni in Laterano and

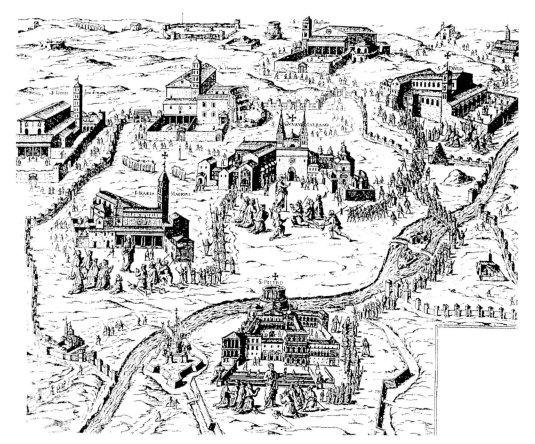

S. Pietro in Vaticano – whose double-aisled plan was followed for S. Paolo – these take primacy among the 'Seven Churches of Rome', the major destinations of pilgrimage. The others, founded under Constantine and later rebuilt or augmented, are S. Sebastiano, S. Lorenzo fuori le Mura and S. Croce in Gerusalemme. **4.33, 4.34**

The standard late-4th-century Roman basilica may well be represented by S. Clemente: it was rebuilt in the 11th century with the reuse of original elements and intent to revive early Christian style. **4.35** The early 5th-century Aventine church of S. Sabina, intact and stripped of later accretions, represents the maturity of the Roman type in

›4.33 ROME: THE SEVEN MAJOR PILGRIMAGE CHURCHES (late-16th-century engraving): S. Giovanni in Laterano (centre), S. Pietro in Vaticano (bottom), then (clockwise) S. Maria Maggiore (founded by Pope Liberius at the command of an apparition of the Virgin in 352, and given much of its present form by Sixtus III from 432), S. Lorenzo fuori le Mura (founded c. 330 to enshrine the martyr's grave in the main cemetery of early Christian Rome, rebuilt by Sixtus III from 432 and extended under Pelagius II c. 579), S. Croce in Gerusalemme (a hall in the Sessorian palace converted to enshrine the True Cross which Constantine's mother, S. Helena, had recovered from the Holy Land), S. Sebastiano (c. 330, originally dedicated to SS. Peter and Paul at the site of their temporay burial and later of S. Sebastian's burial), S. Paolo fuori le Mura (a Constantinian shrine at the reputed site of the Apostle's original grave, rebuilt from 386 by Theodosius the Great to accommodate the Apostle in a way comparable with that of S. Peter and again after the catastrophic fire of 1823).

›4.34 ROME, S. PAOLO FUORI LE MURA: (a, b) record of remains before and after the fire of 1823 and restored interior, (c, pages 712–713) interior.

The largest of Rome's basilicas after S. Pietro, the nave was 97 metres long and 24 metres wide. S. Paolo fuori le Mura was given the distinction of the patriarchal double-aisled plan with continuous transept, the latter embracing the tomb as at S. Pietro but higher and more fully integrated with the main volume than its model. Carefully matched columns and newly carved capitals carried arches suppressed in the rebuilding.

4.34a

4.34b

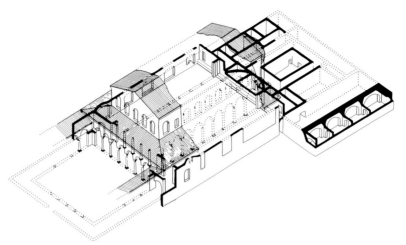

4.35a

its proportions: greater length and height relative to width in the nave, greater height to width in the clerestory windows and the aisle arcades.**4.36**

A nave terminating in a semi-circular apse and flanked by colonnaded and/or arcaded aisles is lit through stained-glass or alabaster windows in the high clerestory which carries the timber truss roof. A chancel, usually bounded by a parapet and sometimes raised, extends from the apse to form the sanctuary. Usually within it, to left and right respectively, there were pulpits for reading the Gospel and Epistle but sermons were not yet common Roman practice. S. Clemente had a narthex and atrium but this was not invariable. Entrance façades may have been plastered but the brick skin of the concrete mass is usually unconcealed throughout – as it was in imperial basilicas and thermae. In contrast, interiors were rich in substance and colour with marble for the architectural detail and mosaic or fresco revetment according to the resources of the patron.

S. Sabina's superbly matched Corinthian columns were spoils from an Antique building – as was usual under Con-

›4.35 ROME, S. CLEMENTE, c. 380, rebuilt after 1084: (a) isometric reconstruction, (b) apse mosaic (early 12th century in an Archaizing style).

4.36a

›4.36 ROME, S. SABINA, c. 422: (a) interior from west, (b) exterior from south-east.

The twenty-four splendid fluted Corinthian columns may have come from the 2nd-century Aventine Temple of Juno. The chancel parapet, with provision for ambo and pulpit, has been reconstructed from fragments of the original work.

4.36b

stantine and his immediate successors – but the early 5th century saw the fabrication of new elements for specific new projects, often of the splendid marble from the imperial quarries on the island of Prokonnesos in the Sea of Marmara. With this went a self-conscious – if selective – revival of Classical order and the consolidation of form in planning. The uncanonical association of column and arch, as in S. Costanza, persists over the decades separating S. Paolo fuori le Mura from S. Sabina – despite the unusual regularity of the latter's colonnade – but Classical order is fully restored at S. Maria Maggiore and S. Lorenzo fuori le Mura.**4.37, 4.38**

Inspired by imperial Roman secular architecture, the attempt to expand the centralized form to provide for a parish congregation in S. Stephano Rotonda (before the

›4.37 ROME, S. LORENZO FUORI LE MURA: (a) entrance front, (b) interior showing ambo and pulpit.

The rebuilt nave of S. Lorenzo (from 432) is marked by canonical regularity. Set into the terraced site of the cemetery, the inner church was rebuilt from 579 with galleries over the aisles providing upper-level access to relieve the pressure of pilgrims on the main floor. Galleries, familiar to Constantine's architects in the east, had not hitherto been common in Rome.

4.37a

4.37b

4.38a

›4.38 ROME, S. MARIA MAGGIORE: (a) interior, (b) plan.

Single-aisled and originally without transept or atrium, thus resembling the standard non-patriarchal type of S. Sabina, the conception of S. Maria Maggiore (from 432) responded to the regularizing incentive of a Classical revival under Pope Sixtus III inspired specifically by the Basilica of Trajan. The narthex was added – or replaced – in the 12th century and a transept opened within the original volume before a new, polygonal apse in the late 13th century. Some of the mosaic panels above the near-canonical Ionic Order are original but the ciborium and ceiling are later.

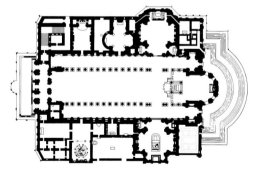

4.38b @ 1:2000

middle of the 5th century) was apparently deemed unsuccessful – at least in the west. Yet on lesser occasions the
martyrium became the church – as at S. Gereon in
Cologne where the earliest ovoid work (late-4th century,
reworked) was derived from the decagonal Roman Minerva Medica. And freestanding centralized buildings,
derived from such Antique models or more routinely
cross-shaped with equal arms and a groin vault over the
central square, dominated for martyria and mausolea in
the orbit of Rome and beyond.**4.39**

›4.39 ROME, S. STEFANO ROTONDO, first half
of the 5th century: interior.

Not unrelated to Constantine's Anastasis rotunda
and S. Constanza, but assumed rather to have been
inspired by an imperial villa or garden pavilion – the
precise precedent is lost – this work is a rare exercise
in combining circle and cross. Probably built to
enshrine a relic of the earliest of early Christian martyrs
– apparently never installed – the main cylindrical
space is ringed by an Ionic colonnade forming an ambulatory which, ceding nothing in its regularity to the
colonnaded aisles of S. Maria Maggiore, opens on to
segmental courtyards between rectangular chapels

4.39b

disposed as the arms of a cross. The tall clerestory is part of the original conception but not the present vault, and the original arrangement of the courts beyond the ambultory, recorded in the 15th century, has been lost.

MILAN

S. Maria Maggiore was the last great basilica of 5th-century Rome: thereafter even papal patronage declined with the city's fortunes and its population. Its main rival, Milan, had emerged as a significant centre of monumental church building even before the emperor moved there in the mid-4th century. The cathedral was laid down c. 350 on the double-aisled lines of the Roman patriarchal basilicas but with transepts subdivided by colonnaded screens aligned with the aisle arcades from which they were divided by spur walls. As at the Lateran, the sanctuary projected well into the nave. As at the Lateran, too, there was a detached octagonal baptistery with square and semi-circular niches, which was probably begun before the cathedral was finished under S. Ambrose, bishop of Milan from 374 to 397.**4.40a**

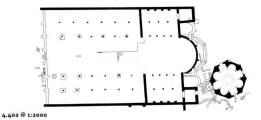

4.40a @ 1:2000

S. Ambrose was a particularly vigorous patron. He commisioned the temporary imperial capital's Church of the Apostles with a Latin-cross variation on the plan of its namesake in Constantinople for the interment of relics of SS. Andrew, Thomas and John the Evangelist.**4.40b** He begun S. Simpliciano, also built on a cruciform plan but with an exceptionally grand nave four times the length of the transept arms.**4.40c** And the huge basilica of S. Ambrogio, conceived by the great bishop as his burial place about five years after the construction of S. Clem-ente had begun in Rome, is witness to the rapid exportation and amplification of the standard type with the shift in the

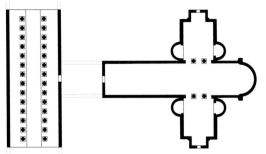

›**4.40** MILANESE BASILICAS: (a) the cathedral (c. 350, later S. Tecla), plan; (b–d) Church of the Apostles (c. 382, partially rebuilt in the 11th century as S. Nazaro), plan, interior of nave and crossing; (e, f) S. Simpliciano, interior and exterior of crossing.

4.40b @ 1:2000

4.40c

4.40d

centre of political gavity to the north – or would be had it not been entirely replaced in the 11th century. It was often emulated – in plan if not in scale, and with inevitable variations. Of these, perhaps the most important was the shape of the martyrium invariably attached to an aisle: the one at S. Ambrogio – for the Milanese S. Victor – was roughly square; others were cruciform.

4.40e

4.40f

There were many variations on polygonal freestanding types – not least the reliquary Church of the Mother of God built to the order of Emperor Zeno on Mount Garizim in Palestine. Most prestigiously, centralized forms derived from the place of the emperor's appearance in Roman palaces were adopted for palatine chapels, as at Antioch.**3.178, 3.197** The double-skin quatralobe, recalling the throne room of the Piazza d'Oro complex in the villa of Emperor Hadrian at Tivoli, was preferred in many parts of the empire, from northern Italy to Syria and later Armenia. The grandest example, the Milanese church now dedicated to S. Lorenzo, had galleries and was preceded by a triumphal entrance screen.**4.41**

4.41a

›ARCHITECTURE IN CONTEXT »CHRISTIANITY AND EMPIRE

4.41c

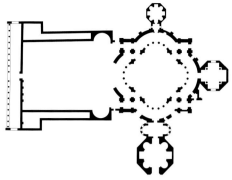

4.41b @ 1:2000

›**4.41 MILAN, S. LORENZO,** c. 380: (a) exterior from original entrance, (b) plan, (c–e) chapel of S. Aquilino with late-4th-century mosaic and sarcophagus.

Milan, S. Lorenzo

This major landmark, originally a palatine chapel, rose beyond an atrium incorporating imperial Roman colonnades. Entrance to the atrium was distinguished by a fastigium which descends through the Palace of Diocletian at least from the motif applied to the Arch of Tiberius at Orange. Apparently inspired by the octagonal palatine chapel of Antioch – at least as a double-skinned, centralized structure providing a continuous ambulatory and upper gallery – the building is, however, basically square and the projection of exedrae from the sides recalls the triclinium of Hadrian's Villa – though there were only three in that place of imperial epiphany. The identification of secular power with the divine could hardly be clearer. Variations on the form distinguish several 6th-century Syrian churches.

4.41d

The original conception of the square space surrounded by two-storeyed semi-domed exedrae was respected in the rebuilding carried out towards the end of the 16th century under the direction of Martino Bassi – though the present piers replaced columns. Bassi preserved the towers of the original which possibly buttressed a central groin vault. This was crowned by a fifth square tower in place of the present dome and its octagonal drum.

The domed octagon attached to the south, dedicated to S. Aquilino, was probably originally intended as an imperial mausoleum and retains a sarcophagus attributed to Galla Placidia. It recalls the form of the entrance pavilion to Hadrian's Piazza d'Oro and, beyond that, the garden rooms of the Domus Augustana on the Roman Palatine. The main volume was preceded by a narthex with an apse at each end – as in the slightly later complex now incorporated in S. Gereon at Cologne.

4.41e

In the second half of the 5th century octagonal baptisteries were built beside standard basilicas at several
sites in northern Italy and southern France – notably
Aquileia and Novara, Frejus, Marseilles and Aix-en-
Provence. Often expanding into niches, as at Novara,
the main volume was sometimes set in a rectangular
room, as at Aquileia c. 450.

RAVENNA

Honorius retreated from Milan to Ravenna early in the
first decade of the 5th century. Just before that, the city's
Orthodox community had laid down its double-aisled
basilican cathedral (destroyed in 1733) and octagonal
baptistery after the Lateran example adopted by the
Milanese. Unvaulted in its primitive form, the baptistery
was given a masonry dome and stunning mosaic revetment
by the incumbent bishop c. 450, when the city was still
bathed in the afterglow of imperial splendour.[4.42, 4.43]
After the advent of the Ostrogoths in the 470s, the Arian
community of their followers confronted their Orthodox
rivals with a standard basilican cathedral and octagonal
baptistery, the latter embellished with equally resplendent,
if simpler, mosaics depicting saints attending the baptism
of Christ.[4.21]

Meanwhile, c. 425, Honorius's sister Galla Placidia had
founded the first of Ravenna's imperial churches – now
known as S. Croce. Inspired by the Church of the Apostles in Milan, it was cruciform with unequal arms. Like the
martyria which proliferated in the Milanese orbit after S.
Ambrose, cruciform too was the tomb attached to its
extended narthex for the patroness's itinerant brother,

›4.43 RAVENNA, ORTHODOX BAPISTERY, c. 450: (a) exterior, (b) vault, (c)interior.

4.43b

4.43a

4.43c

4.44a

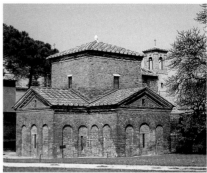
4.44b

4.44c @ 1:250

whose departure from Rome lost him the mausoleum projected at S. Pietro in Vaticano.**4.23c** Rome's last imperial
tomb was a rotunda but, after the example of its Ravenna
substitute, cross-shaped martyria were not uncommon in
northern Italy and the form was to become extremely
important in the churches of the east.

Ravenna's basilica of S. Giovanni Evangelista, built by
Galla Placidia about the same time as S. Croce, reverted
to the S. Sabina formula but with narthex and polygonal
apse after the Greek style.**4.44** The Ostrogothic Arian
cathedral (later the Orthodox Santo Spirito) was a standard basilica – at least in so far as the elements incorporated
in the 16th century rebuilding testify. However, the
Graeco-Italian hybrid was amplified on a grand scale for
S. Apollinare Nuovo, built by Theodoric as his palatine
church, and S. Apollinare in Classe, begun under the late-
Arian Ostrogoths c. 535.**4.45, 4.46** In addition to the polygonal form of apse, the capitals in the aisle arcades of both
works follow the contemporary Constantinopolitan
model rather than the late great Roman Classical example, large windows in the outer walls ensure more even
lighting. In both works the proportions of whole and parts
are more ample, less aspiring, than in Roman churches like

›4.44 RAVENNA, WORKS ATTRIBUTED TO GALLA PLACIDIA: (a–c) S. Croce and imperial tomb, from c. 425, interior and exterior of tomb, plan; (d, e) S. Giovanni Evangelista, c. 425, exterior from the east, interior from the west.

The Christian symbolism of the tiny tomb's Latin-cross plan was promoted by the need to accommodate the emperor together with, but in hierarchical distinction from, his sister and brother-in-law: the imperial remains were interred at the culmination of the main axis beyond the altar at the crossing, those of Galla Placidia and her husband in the flanking transept arms.

S. Giovanni Evangelista was altered c. 600, when the aisle arcades were raised and the clerestory reformed, and rebuilt after severe damage in World War II: the original outer walls and columns survive but the narthex disappeared when the nave was lengthened in the 7th century.

4.44d

4.44e

›4.45 RAVENNA, S. APOLLINARE NUOVO, c. 490: interior.

S. Apollinare Nuovo, originally dedicated to the Saviour, passed from the Arians to the Orthodox under Bishop Angellus (556–69) and was rededicated to S. Martin. The definitive dedication followed the installation of the saint's relics in the 9th century .

The gorgeous mosaics of saints processing along each side of the nave have the broad sweep of continuous narrative rather than the episodic incident of typical Roman compartmented embellishment.

S. Sabina.**4.36** The influence of basilican Ravenna was pervasive on both sides of the northern Adriatic.

The 9th-century Benedictine abbey church at Pomposa, north of Ravenna, conforms to type and Torcello cathedral in the Venetian lagoon stands out among the most celebrated examples of medieval rebuilding over venerable standard basilican foundations. And the persistence of the late-4th-century standard basilican type in Italy into the second Christian millennium is well

4.46a

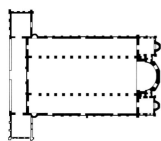

4.46c @ 1:2000

›4.46 CLASSE (THE PORT OF RAVENNA),
S. APOLLINARE IN CLASSE, founded c. 535,
consecrated in 549: (a) exterior, (b) interior from west,
(c) plan.

The crypt was installed and the chancel raised in
the 9th century but otherwise the original work largely
survives.

4.46b

demonstrated by the rebuilding of many Roman basilicas in the 8th and 12th centuries, not least S. Clemente, S. Maria in Trastevere and S. Maria in Cosmedin – to which we shall return in context. **4.47, 4.48**

›4.47 GRADO, S. MARIA DELLA GRAZIA, c. 500: interior.

Of the Ravenna type, the basilica's aisles are separated by arcades incorporating five ill-matched columns to each side; behind the colonnaded screen the apse retains its semi-circular bench and bishop's throne. The basilica is overawed, and was probably superseded by, the adjacent cathedral to which it is linked by a baptistery. Twice the size of S. Maria, the cathedral was founded in 568 as the seat of the patriarch of Nova Aquileia which was eclipsed by Venice in the 11th century.

4.48a

›4.48 POMPOSA, BENEDICTINE ABBEY CHURCH, possibly founded in the 8th century but still under construction later: (a) exterior of narthex, (b) interior from west.

The ample, open narthex of Pomposa is notable for the inset Byzantine relief panels on its external walls. The basilican hall, without transept and unvaulted, preserves much of its original pavement but the fresco cycles date from the 14th century.

4.48b

4.49a

3 EARLY IMPERIAL BYZANTIUM AND DIVERSITY

Many though its permutations were, the basilican genus was the norm for the congregational church, large and small, throughout western Christendom – Italy and the western provinces of the empire, including those of North Africa – until the early 7th century when the reconquest of northern Italy by the Byzantines was having significant architectural effect. It remained the norm in the east until the triumph of Islam in the second half of the 7th century.**4.49ª** Between the two great halves of empire, Dalmatia emerged as a distinctly eclectic enclave open to the influence of east and west – if predominantly the latter. On the other hand, the Greek-speaking Aegean region, centred on Constantinople, emerged as distinct from both the Latin west and the linguistically diversified east with the triumph of Justinian in the mid-6th century.

4.49b

The screening of apse and transept arms clearly distinguish the central crossing, where the high altar was sometimes located, in furtherance of liturgical purpose as it developed in the 5th century – especially in the east. In the west the clergy were accommodated in the apse and the preceding sanctuary bay or the crossing if the altar had been brought forward of the apse; the congregation remained in the nave. In the east the laity were restricted to the aisles, narthex and atrium as the clergy claimed the nave as well as the sanctuary in the early 5th century: the

4.49c

>**4.49 THE BASILICA ABROAD,** c. 500: (a) Ptolemais, mosaic pavement; (b) Maktar, Tunisia; (c) M'shabbak, Syria.

latter for the celebration of the Eucharist, the manifestation of the flesh of God, the former for readings from the scripture and preaching, the manifestation of the word of God. The aisle colonnades were curtained, the nave raised and the altar projected into it with a chancel (bema) closed to the sight of the laity by a screen hung with icons but linked by a causeway (solea) to a pulpit (ambo) addressing the narthex. To relieve the pressure on congregational space, the aisles were sometimes doubled, surmounted with galleries and/or extended across the end of the nave to double the narthex (exonarthex).

THE ORBIT OF CONSTANTINOPLE

The pre-Justinian standard in the new capital is obscure as the great Constantinian models and most of the many other works carried out under lavish court patronage in the first two centuries of the new capital's eminence were destroyed in the Nika riots of 532. Fragments of the propylaeum of H. Sofia, rebuilt after a fire in 404, give an inkling of stylistic development beyond the orbit of Rome in the first century of official Christian building: in particular, departure from the late-Classical norm for the Corinthian capital (with centralized disposition of naturalistic acanthus leaves) in favour of the syncopated repetition of sharply abstracted foliage.

Subsequent development of plan and form may be deduced from the only substantial mid-5th-century remains, those of the monastery church of H. Ioannes Studios. The scheme included porticoed atrium, three-bay narthex, broad nave, paired aisles with superimposed trabeated Orders, the upper one for galleries after the style of an Ancient Greeek temple but generously lit, raised bema, solea and ambo, apse with faceted exterior and semi-circular interior ringed by tiered seats for the clergy.**4.50, 4.22**

Evidence is limited too in Constantinople's immediate

4.50a

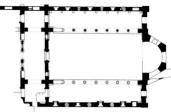

4.50c @ 1:1000

REMAINS: (a–c) H. Ioannes Studios (founded c. 450), interior of shell, detail of Order, plan; (d, e) cornice and capital from the narthex colonnade of H. Sofia (c. 404).

H. Ioannes's colonnaded atrium led to the colonnaded narthex and the colonnaded nave flanked by a pair of well-lit aisles: a permutation of the Composite Order, related to the early 5th century work on the propylaea of the Constantinian H. Sofia, supported an Ionic Order framing galleries over the aisles; the apse is polygonal outside, semi-circular within and was ringed by tiered seating (synthronon); the sanctuary floor is distinguished by a slight rise in level and projection from the apse into the nave.

4.50d

4.50b

4.50e

sphere of influence – extended by trade around the Aegean, around the Black Sea and into the Balkans – due to much rebuilding and much destruction by Islam, but enough remains to demonstrate that the diversification of species in the basilican genus is marked by the mid-5th century: galleries, tripartite transepts, trefoil sanctuaries are not uncommon. There are quatrefoil churches too, usually palatine chapels, and multi-lobed, cruciform or circular martyria with ambulatories.

c. 500: (a) exterior, (b) interior.

Inside, the central domed space rises above the arms of the cross: between the latter to all four corners are square subsidiary spaces covered with pendentive domes. The dating has been made on the basis of decorative style.

4.51a

4.51b

THE AEGEAN LITTORAL

Little survives in Greece from the 4th century, but 5th-century examples reveal influence from places as far apart as Milan and Constantinople – not surprisingly in a maritime country linked by trade to both the east and the west since time immemorial and incorporated in the See of Milan after the imperial court settled there in the mid-4th century. In accord with the ubiquitous norm, but varied in scale, the Greek basilica – and its Balkan derivative – usually has an atrium and a narthex with side chambers, triple entrance to a nave flanked by arcaded aisles and a semicircular apse: as in Constantinople, the latter has tiered seating and there is a bema.

Materials are commonly mortared rubble with brick revetment, timber for roofing and masonry for the semi-domical vault over the apse – as throughout the Aegean littoral. The small church of Ossios David in Thessaloniki of c. 490 was domed in masonry: in a putative experiment with centralization, the dome was carried on pendentives over the central square bay of a Greek cross in a square enclosure.**4.51**

A prestigious precedent for Ossios David may, of course, be found in the imperial mausoleum built at Ravenna by Galla Placidia.**4.44** And distant sources may also be found for the principal urban variations on the standard basilican formula: western is the tendency to project the transept arms beyond the perimeter wall; eastern is the elevation of galleries over the aisles and their continuation across the west end to form an esonarthex. The latter is well illustrated in the Church of the Acheiropoietos in Thessaloniki, c. 450. In the same city c. 490 the builders of H. Demetrios combined all these features in new maturity with the doubling of the aisles and the screening of the transepts to distinguish the central bay of the crossing.**4.52**

4.52a

4.52b

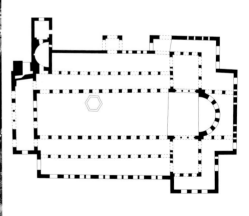

4.52c @ 1:1000

›ARCHITECTURE IN CONTEXT »CHRISTIANITY AND EMPIRE

›4.52 THESSALONIKI: (a–b) Church of the Acheiropoietos, c. 460: interior from west, overview from east; (c–h), H. Demetrios, c. 470, rebuilt early in the 7th century and after a fire in 1917: plan, narthex detail view from south aisle to north transept showing capitals, exterior from west, (pages 738–739) nave from west to apse, with (inset) original inner-aisle arcade detail.

Thessaloniki's 5th-century apogee

The Church of the Acheiropoietos originally had both outer and inner (exo- and eso-) narthexes, the latter communicating through corner chambers with the aisles to form a semi-ambulatory about the nave to the north, west and south: a triple portal (tribelon) provides the western entrance from the esonarthex; low parapets enclose all but the end bays of the side arcades. The raising of galleries over the aisles follows the earlier Constantinopolitan example of H. Ioannes Studios but at both levels the columns carry arches rather than entablatures – as in Constantine's Anastasis rotunda in Jerusalem and, possibly, his major works in his new capital. The interior revetement was of marble, on the walls, mosaic on the curved surfaces of the apse and arcades: the capitals are related to those of H. Ioannes Studios – and, ultimately, the early 5th-century narthex of H. Sofia in Constantinople.

At H. Demetrios, too, the narthex and outer aisles are linked through corner chambers and the galleries over the inner aisles continue over the narthex: transept and narthex rise above the outer aisles to the height of the inner galleries for the clerestory lighting of the latter and the nave. Piers punctuate the nave colonnades to produce a rhythm of 4:5:4 bays, over which the columns carry arches on both levels. The line of the nave

4.52d

4.52e

4.52f

colonnade is continued by a smaller Order, screening the chancel from the transept arms in assertion of its distinction and a larger one beyond the apse to screen the central section of a rectilinear ambulatory. In addition to capitals of the early 5th-century Constantinopolitan type, there are 'wind-blown' and zoomorphic examples. Some of the original marble revetment survived for reuse after a devastating fire in 1917.

On the other side of the Aegean, the early 5th-century basilican cathedral at Ephesos, like many lesser basilicas in Ionia, was hardly less eclectic than its mainland Greek contemporaries. The plan was generic but there were no aisle galleries; the circular apse was flanked by rectangular rooms behind a straight wall, like several 5th-century works futher east, and the northern atrium colonnade served a freestanding, niched octagonal baptistery of the type built about the same time beside the Milanese cathedral.

ASIA MINOR

Remains are sparse on most of the Anatolian plateau beyond Cappadocia, somewhat richer in Armenia, richer still in the south coastal hinterland. Walls are of stone-faced rubble, rather than rubble and brick as in the Aegean area, and, as wood was not plentiful, stone is the normal material even for vaulting – tunnel vaulting extending along naves and aisles at late-6th-century sites like Binbirkilise and Armenian Ereruk.

The aisled basilica remained standard, sometimes with the projecting transept apparent in Milan and in Thessaloniki, but foreign to Constantinople and Ionia except in apostolic shrines. The influence of Constantine's Apostoleon is also apparant. A rigorously centralized variant – the octagonal junction of orthogonal and diagonal crosses within a square – enshrined the supposed tomb of the Apostle Philip at Hierapolis (Pamukkale). More directly

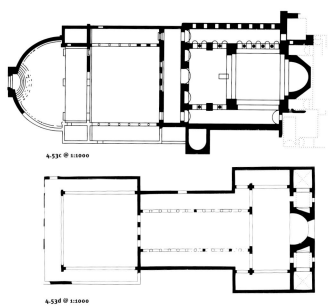

4.53c @ 1:1000

›4.53 ANATOLIAN VARIANTS, late-5th– early 6th century: (a, b) Alahan Manastir, plan and interior; (c) Meriamlik, 'domed basilica', plan; (d) Perge, Basilica A, plan; (e) Tomarza, Panaghia, plan.

Identification of Meriamlik as a domed basilica is not uncontroversial: the aisles were galleried and tunnel-vaulted in stone but the two compartments of the nave may have had differentiated timber roofs.

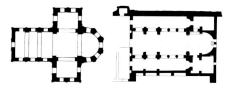

4.53e @ 1:500   4.53a @ 1:500

4.53b

4.53d @ 1:1000

related to the model, the tomb shrine of S. John at Ephesos had basilican arms of unequal length and width.

The cruciform plan, with enhanced emphasis on a crossing roofed in wood or vaulted in stone and buttressed by tunnel-vaulted arms obviating aisles, had made its appearance in Cappadocia c. 500: at Tomarza the incorporation of a dome over the crossing of the Panaghia was prophetic. Elsewhere in Asia Minor and Armenia variations from the norm included horseshoe-shaped arches, apses with polygonal external revetment or flanked by rectangular chambers within a rectangular block: both features are represented in Basilica A at Perge, though the former is lost to the latter. At Meriamlik the chambers flanking the apse of the huge S. Thecla basilica have small apses of their own and the narthex opened to both aisles and nave through a tribelon. **4.53a,b**

Meriamlik is most celebrated, however, for the late-5th-century remains of the earliest domed basilica so far recognized. The monastery church of Alahan Manastir is a more sophisticated plan variant produced slightly later, incorporating a Greek cross. There the timber roof was carried on transverse arches slightly incurved at base: the origin of this 'horseshoe' form, which was to have a great history, is obscure but – if not a pragmatic development from the familiar form of the scallop-shell niche – it may be an architectural abstraction from the radiant aureola associated with the divine and, especially, with the saintly victor over the worldly.**4.53, 4.15a**

SYRIA

The square bays terminating the aisles of Anatolian churches, like that at Alahan Manastir, were raised over the surrounding roofs as towers and sometimes twin towers flanked the front. Paired towers flanking the portal are first known in late-5th-century Syria, where the bit-hilani palace portal and the propylaea of temples had long sustained the ancient Mesopotamian tradition of the twin-towered gate as the place of epiphany.**1.151, 1.152** Pagan too is the repertory of types, basilican and centralized, and the stock of parish and monastic churches is rich, especially in rural Syria where depopulation after the Muslim conquest has meant a higher degree of preservation than in most other areas of early Christendom.

Though the quatrefoil was popular for special palatine or episcopal occasions, the overwhelming majority of works in Syria – as in Palestine – is as usual basilican. There is some distinction between north and south but in the main the type reflects the basic Aegean standard – with atrium, narthex, nave and twin aisles, occasionally galleries, and semi-circular apse with polygonal exterior. Transepts were rare but characteristic was a distinct D-shaped platform for the clergy in the centre of the nave, a freestanding bema curving in sympathy with the apse. Nave arcades may have columns or piers in regular

›4.54 SYRIAN VARIANTS: (a–c) Qalb Lozeh (c. 450), parish church, exterior from the east showing towers and apse, plan, interior; (d, e) R'safah, S. Sergius, interior and plan.

At Qalb Lozeh the clerestory bays are defined by colonettes on brackets and the exterior of the apse was articulated with superimposed attached Orders. At R'safah the division of the nave in accordance with paired aisle bays is asserted by embracing arches and slender pilasters supporting a minor Order in the clerestory. At both sites the sanctuary is flanked by rectangular – or square – chambers, as was common in Syria from the early 5th century.

4.54a

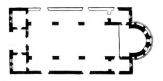

4.54b @ 1:1000

4.54c

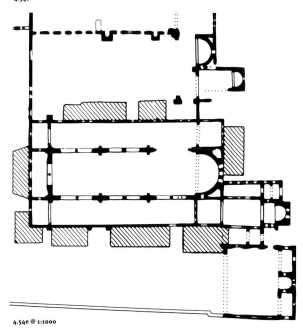

4.54e @ 1:1000

repetition or a richer rhythm may be generated by alternating columns and piers. Stunted towers over rectangular chambers might flank the apse as well as the front portal and there may be a secondary entrances from the side – also in accordance with Syria's pagan tradition.**4.54**

Material is often stone throughout, even for vaults, as timber was rarely available. This prompts heavy walls pierced by small windows and the substitution of piers for columns. Ornament is minimal, except for portals, but highly characteristic is the rustic – at first crude, later crisply delineated and virile but essentially un-Hellenic – elaboration of the Corinthian Order, particularly in transforming the sedate Classical acanthus motif into a wind-blown thicket. Syria's was an austere architecture of boldly articulated mass, rather than light and elegant space, which achieved its most monumental expression c. 500.

4.54d

The masterpiece among the ecclesiastical remains of Syria is undoubtedly the monastery and shrine of S. Simeon at Qal'at-Sim'an. Basilica and cruciform martyrium were combined to enshrine the column of S. Simeon, as in S. John's complex at Ephesos, and the scale ceded little to the imperial Apostoleon prototype.**4.55**

S. Simeon Stylites

The triumphal entrance to the south narthex accorded with the Levantine tradition of endowing the precincts of temples with propylaea: the motif was doubly appropriate as the patron was Emperor Zeno (474–91). Unlike Constantine's Apostoleon, with its square crossing, Zeno's combination of basilica and martyrium for S. Simeon has a central octagon. Originally roofed with timber, if it was roofed at all over the saint's column

4.55a

>**4.55 QAL'AT-SIM'AN, MONASTERY CHURCH OF S. SIMEON STYLITES,** c. 480: (a) baptistery interior, (b) plan, (c, d) southern entrance and detail of 'windswept' Order, (e) crossing with base of the Stylite's column, (f, pages 746–747) general view of complex.

4.55e

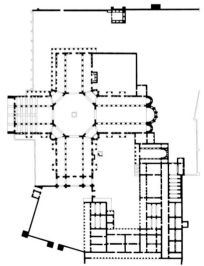

4.55b @ 1:2000

4.55d

rising from its centre, it is joined by four aisled basilicas to form a cross of 90 metres on the east–west axis, 80 metres north–south. There were narthexes to the west and south. Apses, with superimposed external Orders, terminate nave and aisles to the east. As elsewhere in Syria, detail was anti-Classical: the acanthus of the Corinthian capital, in particular, was windswept into asymmetry then intricately chiselled and undercut into a stylized filigree of foliage. Yet, despite this and architraves rising unbroken from the horizontal to curve over arches, in monumentality and even Classicism, this great church eclipsed all its contemporaries.

The baptistery, detached from the main complex, is an octagon with niches in the canted sides enclosed in a rectangular ambulatory: the form is familiar in the Aegean region but not in contemporary Syria where a square chamber usually adjoins an aisle of the basilica.

4.55e

EGYPT AND NORTH AFRICA

The architecture of Coptic Christian Egypt had its provincial idiosyncracies but the province's prime importance attracted significant imperial patronage. The dominant pattern of maritime links through Alexandria with the heart of the empire promoted the development of the Aegean, indeed metropolitan, styles there.

At Hermopolis, north of Cairo, the cathedral (c. 435) was colonnaded and galleried in the Greek manner and the system ran right round the transepts: apsidal, these formed a triconch with the sanctuary.**4.56a** In the church of the White Monastery at Deir al-Abaid near Sohag in Upper Egypt, c. 450, the sanctuary itself is trilobed: the exercise is imperial in its monumentality but there is no precise metroplitan precedent for the form which may have been North African.**4.56b** Nowhere in Egypt was the imperial style more pervasive than in the basilica of S. Minas at Abu Minas, west of Alexandria, executed under the patronage of Emperor Zeno (474–91): the basilica was

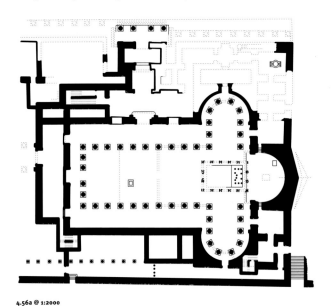

4.56c @ 1:1000

4.56a @ 1:2000

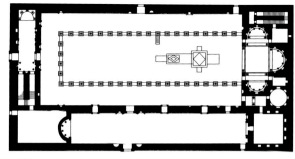

4.56b @ 1:2000

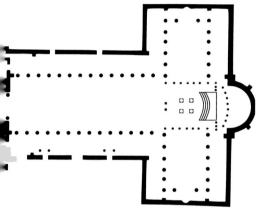

›4.56 EGYPTIAN VARIANTS, c. 440– 50: (a) Hermopolis, cathedral, plan; (b) Deir al-Abaid, White Monastery church, plan; (c) Abu Minas, Egypt, S. Minas, plan.

probably indebted to Constantine's work in the new capital and much of the detail derived from there; the shrine of the dedicatee – in place of the atrium, east of an octagonal baptistery – was a tetraconch and beyond it the narthex was biapsidal.**4·57c**

The Classicism of Zeno's reign spread from Alexandria west into Cyrenaica. By the beginning of the 5th century it had reached Tebessa, near the border of modern Tunisia and Algeria. Apsidal proliferation is rather more prevalent in these rich central provinces of North Africa than elsewhere.**4·57b** At Khirbat bou Hadef in Algeria the sanctuary is trilobed. At Tebessa, near the border of modern Tunisia and Algeria, the major shrine in the south range of the monastery church – a notably elaborate complex with colonnaded propylaeum and peristylar atrium – is a trilobe martyrium which predates the church.**4·57a**

The trilobe was not uncommon in the pagan and early Christian funerary architecture of the rich central provinces of North Africa. The form may have been exported from there to southern Italy though it is present in the cemeteries of Rome c. 300, as we have noted: the earliest-known apsidal example terminating a basilican nave is in the church built c. 400 for S. Felix at Nola in the Campania north of Naples, a region which was rather more closely linked to Tripolitania than to Rome until the late-5th century. On the other hand, the idea of incorporating the trilobe into the design of the basilica may have come from Egypt – from sites like Hermopolis – with the metropolitan style.

Church building – generally of stone for the structure and timber for the roof – was prolific in North Africa: the late-4th-century Roman standard basilica was widespread but the elements proliferated too – of the church and of the communal complex of which it was an integral part. There were those with twin churches or forechurches – Constan-

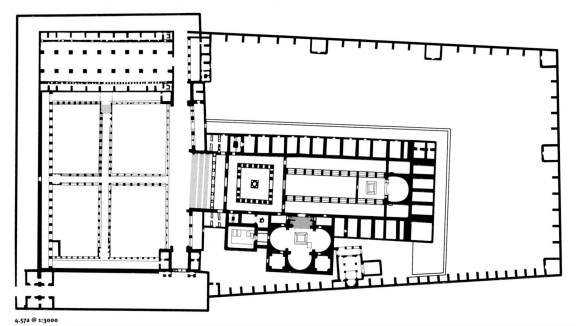

4.57a @ 1:3000

4.57b

tinian features perhaps retained by a conservative clergy for the separate devotions of the orthodox and heterodox. For no determined reason, at the extreme there were eight aisles in the great early 5th-century basilicas of Demous al-Karita, Carthage, and Tipaza, Algeria. The latter was not uncommon in incorporating a counter-apse: usually at the western end, this was invariably a martyrium or burial shrine and similar exedrae enshrining relics of lesser significance often projected from outer aisles as well. Arcading often continued across the sanctuary apse and the altar was displaced into the nave.

BAPTISTERY

Throughout the east, the typical baptistery was square or octagonal, freestanding or connected with the church whose community it served to increase. Despite the virile regional tradition of centralized or semi-centralized planning, however, in Africa the baptistery was usually a small rectangular room at the end of an aisle within the main structure. Its distinguishing feature was invariably an elaborately tiled sunken trough with steps descending in a cruciform pattern from all four sides.**4.57d**

4.57d

4.58a

4 BEYOND THE PALE: ETHIOPIA

The Axumite empire embraced Christianity at the height of its power in the early 4th century (see pages 183–191): instead of the sun disk and crescent moon of the pagan past, the imperial coinage bears Christian symbols from 341. The king at the time was Ezana. Uniquely in a region soon to be overwhelmed by the forces of Islam, Ezana's successors sustained the faith throughout the extended history of their monarchy and the church developed in isolation from the rest of Christendom at least until the arrival of Portuguese prelates in the 16th century.**4.58a** In isolation here, consequently, a contracted coverage of the main phases of that development will take us way beyond the temporal limits of this volume – extended as they are.

›4.58 THE ETHIOPIAN CHURCH, SAINTS AND
SCHOLARS: (a) a scribe in his cell; (b) the eight com-
panions of Abba Aregawi, reputedly from Syria.

4.58b

THE CHURCH IN AXUM

King Ezana, who is traditionally associated with his
brother Saizana as Abreha we Atsbeha, was reputedly converted by Syrian missionaries known as Fromentius and
Aedissius. Fromentius was consecrated as the empire's first
bishop by the patriarch of Alexandria and known as Abba
Salama: for him the king founded the five-aisled basilica
of Tsion Maryam at the centre of his seat. Doubtless by
imperial decree, lesser centres were endowed with tripartite basilicas.

Though its progenitors were Syrian, the Ethiopian
church could hardly avoid Coptic tutelage, not least perhaps in Monophysitism: as Fromentius was consecrated in
Alexandria, most of his successors were nominally
subject to the Alexandrian patriarch until modern times.
Like the Alexandrians, the Axumites rejected the anti-
Monophysite dictat issued by the Council of Chalcedon
in 451. Yet, as it developed in the obscurity of isolation
despite pilgrimage down the Nile and on to Jerusalem,
Ethiopian Christianity was uniquely influenced by ancient

Jewish practice, specifically in rites centred on the veneration of the Ark of the Covenant or, rather, the tablets (tabot) on which the Covenant was inscribed. Ezana is supposed to have built his palatine cathedral to enshrine the Ark of the Covenant but the tradition is supported by no contemporary evidence. Moreover, at least a millennium was to elapse before the claim to Solomonic legitimacy for the Ethiopian royal line was elaborated in Ge'ez – the Ethiopian orthodox liturgical language derived from the vernacular – and churches were centred on a generous tabot sanctum penetrable only by select priests.

At least a century after Abreha we Atsbeha the faith – which doubtless had its vicissitudes – was boosted by the arrival of nine Monophysite monks under a leader known as Abba Aregawi: reputedly from Syria, they were probably at the head of a band of refugees from various sees in which the orthodox establishment considered them heretical.**4.58b** They implanted – or reinforced – their doctrine and introduced monasticism to Axumite practice: they were responsible for many foundations, including the monastery of Debre Damo whose main basilican church is usually considered to be the prime early Christian survivor of several waves of desecration in the old Axumite domain.

In so far as the accidents of survival testify, the plan imported by Abba Aregawi for his foundation on Debre Damo is elementary basilican: beyond the outer and inner narthex the nave terminates in a square apse between the pastophories at the head of the twin aisles but there is no special provision for a tabot replica. The arcaded internal elevation, particularly the representation of the sanctuary proscenium as a triumphal arch, is of the same inspiriation as the plan – not foreign to Syria or Coptic Egypt or most other centres of early Christianity. The standard

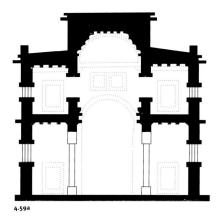

4.59a

›4.59 DEBRE DAMO: (a) section, (b) vertical perspective reconstructed (the foundation is traditionally attributed to Aregawi and the structure to the reign of Gabra Masqal in the late-6th century at the earliest: it was renovated in 1948 under D. Mathews who dated most of the surviving substance to the 11th century).

The perimter is rectangular with recessed central bays to each side, in the Axumite manner. Between massive stone quoins, the material is undressed stone in a framework of timber. The entrance from the west is through a portico inset in the recessed central bay: it is divided in two by a square pier in antis. Similar piers divide nave from aisles and support a blind clerestory, with typical Axumite detail in timber, which in turn supports the flat coffered ceiling.

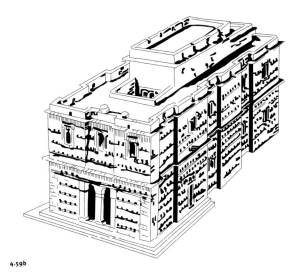

4.59b

repertory of Classical mouldings – cyma, cavetto and torus – are supplemented by the Greek cross and floral motifs are stylized in the manner familiar throughout eastern Christendom. Bracket capitals, sometimes with a cushion profile, are ubiquitous.**4·59**

The major stylistic traits are specifically Axumite: the projections and recessions of the wall; the alternating courses of stone and timber framed by stone quoins which would originally have been rendered with plaster; the rectangular and cylindrical protrusions of the wooden crossbeams joined to the internal and external architraves and horizontal timber courses to brace the rubble structure; the trabeated frames of doors and windows, not least in the blind clerestory supporting a coffered ceiling; and the stepped podium which, elsewhere, doubtless derived from the pagan temple. All these features – except, of course, the coffered ceilings and the spaces they covered – are represented in stone on the stelae which constitute the major legacy of the old imperial capital (see page 191): by extrapolation, the Debre Damo church is taken to perpetuate the structural and spatial reality.

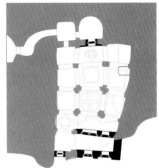

›**4.60 AGULA, BASILICAN REMAIN**s (engraving published by R. Acton, *The Abyssinian Expedition and the Life and Reign of King Theodore*, 1868).

THE LATE-AXUMITE CHURCH

The depredation of Axum and its provincial centres followed an extended period of decline beginning c. 550 after King Kaleb, in response to an appeal from the Byzantine emperor Justin, took his empire to its greatest extent with the conquest of Yemen to protect the Christians there. The scale of the imperial building programme was legendary: Kaleb probably rebuilt Maryam Zion in Axum and the major churches in provincial cities, Adulis, Agula and Matara in particular. He is most celebrated for founding a great basilica in Sana'a with three aisles and a vaulted transept. The cost of all this must have been exhausting: gold coins were still minted in the late-6th century but the next generation of issues were solely in copper.**4.60**

Decline accelerated in the late-6th century when hostile Sassanian dominance in Arabia severed Ethiopia's traditional trade routes to the ultimate benefit of the Arabs. Architectural activity seems, in consequence, to have been decentralized. The capital was reputedly relocated to a lost site in the south-east. Certainly the rough terrain of Tigrai, with its characteristic amba (flat-topped protrusions of rock left isolated by erosion), was the church's main scene of excavation and construction – particularly in the east, on the edge of the great Rift Valley where the

4.61a @ 1:500

4.61b

4.61c

›**4.61 TIGRAIAN CHURCHES OF THE LATE-AXUMITE PERIOD** (all traditionally dated to the reign of Abreha we Atsbeha, but up to a millennium later in their definitive forms): (a–c) Debre Maryam Korkot (probably 13th century), plan and sections of monolithic excavation with structural façade; (d–f) Abreha we Atsbeha (definitve form c. 1000), plan of excavated church with sanctuary flanked by sacristy and tomb chamber and later structural portico, details of entrance and crossing; (g) Zarema Giyorgis, cutaway axonometric.

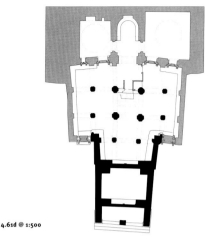

4.61d @ 1:500

4.61e

4.61f

line of internal trade descended from the agricultural areas of the old imperial northern highland heartland to the vital salt-producing Danakil depression further east.

The Debre Damo type recurs widely in Axum's Tigraian hinterland where many churches were at least partially cut from the cliffs and isolated pillars of rock in the second half of the millennium of Ethiopian Christianity, when such wealth as there was accrued to the church. Though many foundations in the area are attributed to Abreha we Atsbeha, Abba Salema or one of the nine 5th-century evangelists, the dating of their definitive form is elusive. An early example is Medhane Alem Adi Kasho which may be dated to the 10th century. The basilica expanded thereafter, notably in the Gherlata and Tembien areas: Debre Maryan Korkot may be taken as representative. **4.61a–c**

In the 11th and 12th centuries the type was supplemented by a variant of the contemporary Byzantine quincunx based on a cross inscribed in a square and distinguished, in part at least, by barrel-vaulting: Abreha we Atsbeha, Wukro Chircos and Mikael Imba mark stages in the evolution of the type from the 10th to the 12th centuries. These churches, all embellished with a similar geometric design woven about multiple crosses, were funerary: the large chapel to the south of the sanctuary in the richly decorated Abreha we Atsbeha is reputedly the last resting place of its twin royal namesakes and it is not impossible that relics were removed from the capital to the comparative safety of the remoter cliffs of Tigrai in the centuries of Axum's protracted decline. **4.61d–f**

Freestanding, the splendid Zarema Giyorgis – near Atsbi in the far east of the Tigrai region – is a truncated basilica with cruciform extensions into porches, north, south, and (ultimately) west. Like the nearby cave church of Debre Mikael Salem, also a truncated basilica with cru-

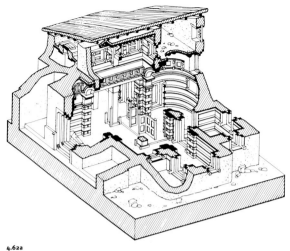

4.62a

>**4.62** YEMREHANNA KRISTOS, MONASTERY
CHURCH: (a) entrance front, (b–d) details of interior
arcading and vaulting.

ciform extension, the structure is Axumite in its white-washed layers of stone and wood and even in the use of small metal clamps to secure the masonry: the rectangular ends of timber bracing members are revealed in the

Set within a large cave, the monastery provided lodging for the king in a primitive palace adjacent to the more magnificent – if small-scale – church: the namesake and probably founder of the monastery was the third king of the Zagwe line, who acceded c. 1087. Built of granite in courses separated by timber in the striated

4.62b

4.62c

4.62d

4.62e

Axum manner, the church is lit through Axumite grilled windows and relieved in the usual Axumite way with the square and circular ends of bracing timbers. The timber ceiling within the truncated pitch of the roof is elaborately coffered over flying trusses.

frames of doors and windows but the idiosyncratic cylindrical ones are absent.

Similar in its Axumite structure and semi-cruciform basilican plan is the church of Yemrehanna Kristos, built within a cave near the first seat of post-Axumite power well to the south at Lalibela.**4.62**

4.63a

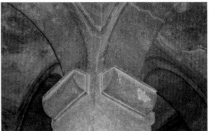

4.63b

4.63c

LALIBELA

Axum, its cathedral and most of the early Christian work of its heartland were destroyed by forces traditionally assigned to the Falasha queen Yodit, revolting against Christian oppression following Axumite expansion southward into Jewish territory: the emperor fled from the catastrophe south to Showa. Tradition dates Yodit's death to the end of the 9th century but an appeal from an Ethiopian king for Nubian help against a rampant queen places it a century later. After her – or whoever she stands for as the Jewish resistance leader – the situation is more than usually obscure. By the mid-12th century power had moved south to the Lasta area – the heartland of Yodit's forces – with a new ruler who had taken the name Zagwe. The capital was established at Roha, later renamed in honour of its most prominent benefactor, the late-12th-century king Lalibela, who sought to make it a new Jerusalem.**4.63**

›**4.63** LALIBELA, EXCAVATED CHURCHES: (a) Bet Golgotha, memorial relief on the east wall; (b–e) Bet Medhane Alem, detail of arcading, cross-axial interior, exterior, plan; (f–h) Bet Maryam, exterior with western portal, interior details; (i) Bet Gabriel, entrance; (j) Bet Emanuel, exterior; (k–n) Bet Giyorgis (Greek-cross monolith) site and details interior, exterior and fenestration.

4.63d

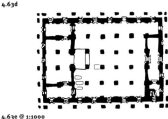

4.63e @ 1:1000

At 33.5 by 23.5 by 11 metres, Medhane Alem is the largest rock-cut church anywhere in the world and there is ample room for circumambulation between it and the roughly vertical sides of its precinct.

The apogee of Ethiopian excavation

Widespread in Ethiopia after Axum, the art of excavating churches from rock was taken to its apogee at – and reputedly by – Lalibela. There are twelve wholly or partially excavated works at the site, one in isolation, the rest in two main groups. Stepped podiums are still the norm and the projecting ends of bracing members are still represented in the Axumite style in the context of foreign arcading and barrel vaults carried on the cushion capitals of massive square piers. However, each of the twelve works is individual in plan and elevation.

The most substantial example is the five-aisled basilican Bet Medhane Alem: monolithic except for some of the repaired piers which make it peripteral – with un-Hellenic irregularity – it reputedly reproduced the cathedral of Tsion Marayam at Axum. Regularity does not extend to the

4.63f

4.63g

4.63h

top: the 'roof' and the 'entablature' of its peristyle conform to the slope of the escarpment. Inside, four rows of massive rectangular piers divide the doubled aisles from the tunnel-vaulted nave. There is a minor entrance in the northern colonnade but the main entrance is through the west front.

Adjacent in the north-western group, in the second precinct with subsidiary shrines cut from its perimeter, the monolithic Bet Masqal is a smaller three-aisled basilica in a rectangle, extending to a cross to form porches on the north, south and west sides. The nave arcade supports a blind clerestory of the Axumite Debre Damo type. The coffered ceilings of the aisle bays and the arcading are lavishly embellished in low relief picked out in paint, some of which may date to the original campaign of excavation. The mass of rock bounding the precinct to the west accommodates Bet Debre Sina and its inner funerary chapel, Bet Golgotha, still on the north-east–south-west axis, with life-sized reliefs of saints to its entrance wall. The latter reputedly enshrines the tomb of Lalibela.

The first work in the second group, to the south-east of the main one, is Bet Gabriel: distinguished by its arcaded façade but not by its plain interior, it is one of the site's earliest excavations and may originally have been conceived as a residence for a royal refugee from Axum. The group's principal work, the royal family chapel, is Bet Emanuel. Another tripartite

4.63i

4.63j

basilica, its heavily rusticated exterior is replete with the full repertory of Axumite forms: recessed bays between pier pilasters, regularly recessed courses presumably representing the inset timber of trad-itional Axumite structure, window and door frames with rectangular blocks projecting from each corner and a mezzanine of arcaded windows with Axumite imposts.

Isolated to the south is the site's most celebrated exercise, Bet Giyor-gis. It is most memorably excavated to the depth of two storeys (15 metres) on a Greek-cross plan with Greek-cross embellishment to the ceilings of the internal compartments produced by this plan form.

4.63k

4.63l

4.63m

4.63n

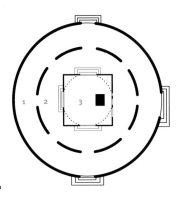

4.64a

4.64b

4.64c

GONDAR AND TANA

The last king of the Zagwe line was supplanted – voluntarily or violently according to the source – c. 1270 by a pretender to Solomonic legitimacy from Showa, the resort of the last Axumite emperor: soon after the legend of the descent of the Axumite kings from Solomon and the Sabean Makeda through Menelik first appears fully articulated in the *Kebre Negre* – a chronicle of kings written in the vernacular Ge'ez language which certainly promoted the cause of the successful claimant. For at least a century the centre of power moved with itinerant kings as they pushed out from Showa, consolidated their hold on the Zagwe heartland of Lasta, encircled Lake Tana and pressed on towards Tigrai, but ultimately the capital was settled on Gondar to the north of Tana.

Debre Berhan Selassie, the principal surviving church at Gondar, is rectangular except for the apsidal east end, and the greatest king of the Gondar line (Facilidas, 1632-67) rebuilt the Axumite cathedral on its original rectangular stylobate.**4.65** However, the vast majority of churches in the Gondar era and area are circular with square sanctuaries, like Debre Sina Maryam at Gorgora. The foundations are usually venerable and the circular form is as old as the local vernacular but as the materials are also those of the vernacular tradition – timber, thatch

›4.64 THE TANA VERNACULAR AND THE CIRCULAR CHURCH: (a) typical plan with (1) ambulatory (qene malet), (2) lay worship space and western sector theatre of the emanation of grace (enda ta-ammer), (3) tabot sanctuary (maqdas); (b–f) Gorgora, Debre Sina Maryam (founded 14th century, renovated and decorated in the early 17th century and later), exterior, ambulatory detail, tabot sanctuary entrance and details of guardian saints George and Michael; (g–l) Dek Island, Narga Selassie (founded c. 1745), exterior from inside and outside protected compound, and interior sanctuary, quadripartite tabot portal, iconic fresco of the patron as the venerable Solomonic king.

4.64d

4.64e

4.64f

4.64g

4.64h

4.64j

4.64i

4.64k

and rubble – little of external substance predates the 17th century.

To support the broad overhang of the conical roof, an ambulatory of trabeated timber or, later, arcaded masonry rings the cylinder of the cella. That and the Axumite details in the fenestration and door surrounds lend the exercise its most obvious architecural distinction

(consecrated 1694, substantially renovated 1818): (a)
nave to sanctuary portals; (b) detail of cherubic ceiling.

The replacement of Ezana's Axumite cathedral in the
17th century, under the influence of Portuguese missionaries and their European architectural background, conforms to the type represented by the Debre
Berhan Selassie: the basilican nave precedes a sanctum which is almost as large. However, as only one living dedicatee could withstand exposure to the product
of God's direct intervention, the sanctum at Axum
enshrines a replica of the tabot like all other churches
built after the resurgence of the Solomonic dynasty.
The original tabot is believed to be housed in a special
separate shrine to the cathedral's north.

4.65a

4.65b

but rational geometry is thoroughgoing in the plan:
within the circles of ambulatory and cella cylinder, the
sanctuary enshrining the tabot is invariably a cube with a
cylindrical attic providing intermediate support for the
conical roof. In the residual quadrants of internal space
there is little room for a congregation: only the elect of
the laity enters during services, the rest attend in the
ambulatory or the precinct beyond it. To most observers,
however, the chief distinction of the exercise is not spatial or even formal but iconographical: all the surfaces of
the sanctuary are covered with holy images and their
impact is, of course, immeasurably enhanced by their
tight confinement.[4.64]

Perhaps the new plan type is to be explained simply by
the prevalence of the vernacular over the imported with
distance in time and place from the old, discredited centre of early Christianity in Ethiopia. Yet it hardly seems
coincidental that the symbolism of the New Testament is
supplanted in church planning by that of the Old Testament – the cross as the body of the church by the tabot and
its central Solomonic sanctuary – in the land once assigned
to the Jews at precisely the time that the assertion of the
doctrine of Solomonic succession was central to imperial ideology.

4.64l

4.2 JUSTINIAN AND THE APOTHEOSIS OF BYZANTIUM

REVIVAL IN THE EAST

Initiated by Constantine, furthered by Theodosius, the Byzantine achievement was brought to its culmination by Justinian (527–65). There would be other great emperors in the millennium left to new Rome but none could fairly claim to have eclipsed Justinian – in conquest, consolidation or construction.**4.66**

At the outset of the reign, disaster attended administrative and economic reforms at the centre promoted by imperial ministers who were seen as oppressive: in 532 the factions into which Constantinople's population was divided for competition in the Hippodrome, but which acquired a distinct political complexion from their identification with specific classes, found themselves exceptionally at one in insurrection (the Nika riots). In the face of the destruction of much of the capital, the emperor was on the verge of flight but his remarkable empress, Theodora, stiffened his resolve. He survived and continued the reforms.

Ultimately the supreme autocrat, Justinian was dedicated to unity, political and religious, in all the lands once ruled by Roman emperors. That meant repelling the barbarians from Italy but also from all their conquests along the Mediterranean littoral to Spain which, in turn, meant securing the eastern frontier on the Euphrates in accord with the Sassanians to free troops from engagement there. It meant a powerful army and stout garrisons in an endless string of frontier forts – and fortified monasteries. It meant efficient administration and the codification of the whole corpus of Roman law since Hadrian. It meant stamping out heresy and promoting conformity of creed in east and west. It required blinding glory for the autocrat and, as autocrats have always found, that was best reflected from great buildings – in the capital rebuilt after the Nika riots and in the main provincial centres of power.

4.66a

4.66b

4.66c

And all this was advertized by the court chronicler, Procopius, upon whom we still depend for much of our information on this extraordinary era in the history of empire and architecture.**4.67**

>4.66 JUSTINIAN FORTIFICATION: (a, b) R'safah, overview and portal; (c) S. Catherine's Monastery, Sinai.

4.67a

Constantinople

Byzantium was founded in the 7th century BCE as a Dorian colony. Much developed in the early 3rd century CE under Emperor Septimius Severus, it was chosen by Constantine as his new Christian capital, divorced from the ancient centre of state paganism, because of its strategic position in relationship to the rich provinces of the eastern parts of the empire, its relative remoteness from barbarian threat, its harbour and its defensible narrow isthmus.

4.67b

Little survives from Constantine's period, indeed virtually nothing of secular importance remains from the so-called Byzantine period at all with the important exceptions of the magnificent walls, the foundations of an early 5th-century palatial complex near the imperial centre – in which the relationship of the main circular or hexagonal rooms to an open exedra recalls the representational core of Nero's Domus Aurea – and the spectacular forest of columns rising from the underground water cisterns (now known as Yerebatan Saray). One of the main squares of the modern city is formed by the perimeter of the Hippodrome – the main arena for public entertainment in the new capital, which was originally built by Septimius Severus c. 200, renovated by Constantine in the 330s and enlarged in the 380s by Theodosius I who then embellished it with the Egyptian obelisk rising from its commemorative base.**4.29**

4.67c

The intimate connection of church and Byzantine state was asserted from the outset in the proximity of palace and cathedral. Justinian's H. Sofia survives, converted to Islam. The palace, which stretched from the

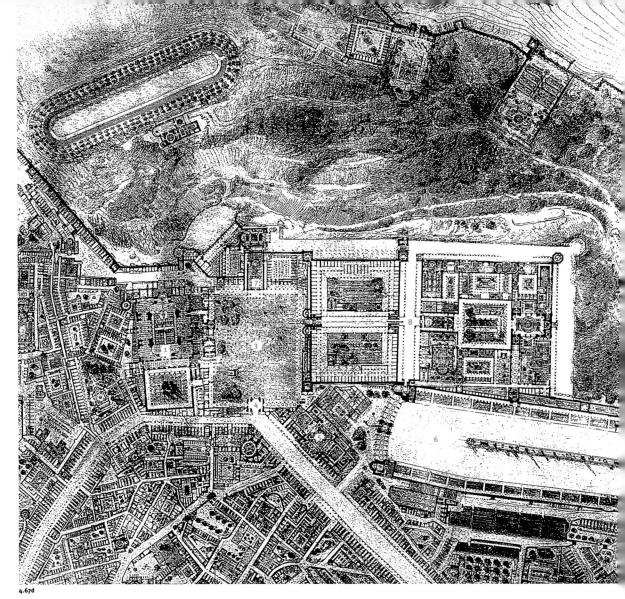

4.67d

cathedral and Hippodrome to the south-east quadrant of the peninsula's coast, has disappeared under the 17th-century Blue Mosque of Sultan Ahmed and myriad less-distinguished buildings. Its many terraced courts and pavilions were often extended, renovated and rebuilt – invariably in sumptuous marble and mosaic. Here the 6th-century complex is imagina-

>4.67 CONSTANTINOPLE: (a) Yerebatan Saray; (b, c) fragments of mosaics from palace hall; (d) plan of central area as rebuilt under Justinian from 532 (according to a reconstruction of 1906 based primarily on documentary evidence) with H. Sofia (1) and H. Eirene (2) the Augustaeum (the main public forum, 3),

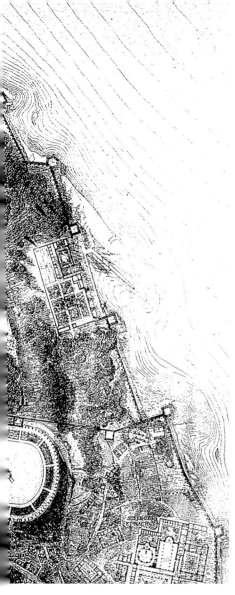

the Milion (4), the Baths of Zeuxippus (5), the Hippodrome (6), the Senate (7), the Imperial Palace entered
ceremonially through the Chalke (8) and culminating in
the Chrysotriclinos throne room (9), H. Sergius and
Bacchus (10).

tively reconstructed along the formal lines of the Domus Augustana on the
Roman Palatine and its Tetrarchal emulators.[3.174] However, Byzantine
records viewed in the light of archaeology suggest that it was rather more
informal in its grouping of varied elements – more like the imperial villas
at Tivoli or Piazza Armerina.

The palace compound was completely walled only by the time of Justinian II (685–95, 705–11) – contrary to pre-Tetrarchal precedent – but
close connection was sustained between the emperor's apartments and
his box overlooking the circus – traditionally the main scene of the ruler's
contact with the people. As was also common by the time of Constantine,
public baths (of Zeuxippos) adjoined the main entrance at the head of a
processional avenue, south-east of H. Sofia. Called the Milion, the bal-
dachino-like ceremonial tetrapylon through which the emperor entered
or left the imperial quarters of his capital incorporated a fastigium. At the
other end of the avenue was the Chalke (the 'House of Bronze', because
of its doors).

Descriptions of court ritual and Procopius's history of Justinian's reign
make it clear that the Chalke was the first of many domed vestibules to
successive parts of the palace, each a canopy-like pavilion for the
epiphany ritual of an emperor who, as vicar of Christ, equal to the Apostles, retained a measure of the religious significance of his pagan predecessors. The Chalke sustained a long tradition embracing the entrance
pavilion of Hadrian's Piazza d'Oro at Tivoli – if not the trilobed triclinium
there – and the vestibule of the Palace of Diocletian at Split.[3.178, 3.196]
Doubtless domed from the outset, according to Procopius it was rebuilt
by Justinian as a cruciform hall, the main axis running north–south, with
a central dome and vaulted arms. Contemporary references suggest that
there was a chapel on an upper level and a place of appearance between
towers. As in Hadrian's Villa, the scene of ultimate epiphany was the
throne room preceded by a peristylar court. The conjunction of court and
hall is common to all major palatial complexes – the Palatine model,
Hadrian's Tivoli, Diocletian's Split and at the villa at Piazza Armerina in
Sicily. The audience hall on the Palatine, as at Split, was basilican; the
Constantinopolitan one is here restored as a quatralobe, as at Tivoli,
though it may have been trilobed like the triclinium at Armerina.

The uniform legal code was perhaps Justinian's most enduring achievement but his attempts at doctrinal compromise failed to unite Christendom in one canonical creed. Exhaustion after his long campaigning and the incompetence of his successor soon lost many of his conquests. However, the reform process was revived under Maurice (582–602): the provincial administration was reorganized into exarchies divided into duchies and, in so far as the accidents of survival testify, the exarchs – like earlier governors – were housed in buildings of venerable symbolic significance.**4.68, 6.69**

Maurice and his heirs fell to the mutiny of their unpaid soldiers. The ensuing strife was terminated by Heraclius (610–41) who paid the soldiers by settling them on lands confiscated from dissident nobles: they formed *themes* identified with their regiments and these became units of local administration which, like Maurice's duchies, marked the political map for centuries.

Heraclius went on to military victory throughout the empire, not least against Persia after the assassination of the Sassanian Chosroes II in 628. But he had no more success than his predecessors in solving the problem of doctrinal difference. After his passing, disaffected Egypt and Syria were ready prey to the Islamic Arab forces unleashed following the death of the Prophet Muhammad in 632. Mesopotamia was lost before the decade was out. Alexandria fell in 642 and the whole of North Africa was soon to follow. Constantinople itself was besieged twice between 670 and 720.

The reduced empire was prey to stultifying bureaucracy, expanded with conquest but not contracted in defeat, and the rapid advance of Islam totally disrupted the long-established pattern of commercial life. Towns declined. Agriculture was again dominant but to the benefit largely of great landowners adroit at avoiding the

›4.68 RAVENNA, PALACE, 7th century: façade.

With its superimposed arches between massive bays, the façade of the building attributed by some to the Exarch of Ravenna – associated with the site of the earlier palace of Theodoric – probably echoes the form of Constantinople's Chalke. Blind at the top, open below, the side bays recall the piers of the triumphal arch, which itself has been recognized as a formal derivative from the ancient Mesopotamian twin-towered portal of epiphany.

›4.69 APOLLONIA, PALACE REMAINS, 6th
century.

The main secular complex at Apollonia (Marsa Susa,
Libya), was doubtless built – or rebuilt to a grander
design – after Justinian's reassertion of control over
North Africa. Little of external significance survives but
the major internal spaces are well represented: on a relatively modest scale, naturally, these follow the imperial example of a sequence of vestibules, flanked by
apartments, culminating in a peristylar court before the
seat of power in its basilica.

imperial tax collector. The economy severely hit, the
empire was undermined by religious conflict – of which
the most virulent was provoked by iconoclasm. Exacer-
bated by ethnic difference, this ultimately proved disastrous in the face of vigorous external pressure.

Most of Italy, lost to the Lombards in the century after
their advent in 598, had disintegrated into independent
duchies by the mid-8th century: only the south and Sicily
remained to the empire west of the Adriatic. Venice, one
of several island settlements of refugees from the barbarians in the lagoon at the head of the Adriatic, had been
incorporated into the empire under Justinian and ruled by
a duke nominated by the emperor: it asserted its independence in the 10th century. On the strength of trade it was
building an empire along the shores of the Adriatic by the
end of the 11th century and won from Constantinople special trading privileges.

The Slavs, who emerged as an agricultural nation in
the Transcarpathian land between the Vistula and the
Dniester towards the end of the last millennium BCE,
began to infiltrate the Balkans in the 4th century: their
impact over the following three centuries undermined
the urban economy even in Greece. The Bulgars, warlike
nomadic herdsmen related to the Huns, swept across the
steppes to the Volga in the 4th century and settled there:
pressed on by new hordes from the east, they crossed into
the Balkans in 679 and had emerged to prominence in
the land now named for them by the early 9th century.
Like the Slavs, they were converted to Christianity by
missionaries from Thessaloniki and were thus bound
into the Byzantine world. They arrogated the imperial
title (*czar*) to their leaders and set their sights on Constantinople.

JUSTINIAN SPLENDOUR: BASILICA AND DOME

Ironically, the greatest monument to Justinian's imperial ambition, the palatine church of H. Sofia built on the ruins of Constantine's original basilica after the catastrophic Nika riots of 532, is the most palpable witness to the failure of his unifying mission.**4.70** It was devised to assert the splendour of God's vicar on earth as universal sovereign but, a radical departure from the basilican norm, it was also to serve the purposes of eastern liturgy which were now quite foreign to those of the west.

›**4.70 JUSTINIAN CONSTANTINOPLE:** general view with H. Sofia left and H. Eirene left background.

The longitudinal basilican form was not entirely rejected by Justinian's architects. The most important example, perhaps, is the replacement c. 560 of Constantine's Nativity Church in Bethlehem. However, as the plan culminated in the quasi-centralized trefoil composition of apsed transept and sanctuary, the exercise might be seen as a Greek cross lost to a Latin extension. As we have seen, various expedients were adopted to adapt the basilica for the accommodation of the laity on the periphery. However, rather than the pragmatic modification of the obsolete Latin form, a specifically Greek solution was required. The centralized form of the Greek cross – with equal projections to all four sides, unlike the Latin form – was the key to the evolution from the basilica of a church type specifically designed to cater for eastern ritual: it transformed the nave bay before the sanctuary which, partitioned from the transepts for the use of the clergy and the exclusion of the laity, had hitherto approximated a square.

Though the domed basilica and Greek cross, with pendentives, were anticipated before the end of the 5th century from Greece to Cappadocia – and doubtless beyond where stone vaulting was common – the credit for effecting this solution on the imperial scale is fairly due to the architects of Justinian: they were Greek, but the solution was essentially Roman – as were the ambitions of their patron: the event marks one of architectural history's clear turning points.

CROSS AND DOME

The most direct Justinian expression of the domed cross type was in the rebuilding of the Chalke Gate to the imperial palace in 532. No less direct, but to much enlarged scale, were the rebuilding of the Church of the Holy Apostles in Constantinople, begun in 536, and its variant, the church of H. Ioannis at Ephesos, begun a decade later. On a

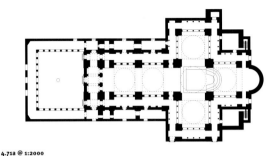

4.71a @ 1:2000

Greek-cross plan, the former – obliterated by the great mosque of the 15th-century Ottoman conquerors – is known from contemporary descriptions to have had five domes, one over each arm and the crossing. On a Latin-cross plan reflecting the original, the Ephesos church had a dome over a second, contracted, nave bay in addition to the five of the crossing.**4·71**

A powerful variant of the Greek-cross ideal, anticipated in the second half of the 5th century at Cilician Meriamlik and Alahan Manastir,**4·53a,c** was developed c. 536 in the rebuilding of Constantinople's episcopal church of H. Eirene. There is some doubt about the initial conception – as about the Constantinian original – and there has been much rebuilding, but analysis of the existing structure credits Justinian's patronage with a novel domed basilica: the central ranges of the aisles, arcaded below a tunnel-vaulted gallery, doubled as the arms of a transept and the crossing was domed.**4·72** There is no certain metropolitan precedent for H. Eirene but one may have been provided by the church of H. Polyeuktos built c. 524 by Princess Anica Juliana next to her palace in Constantinople: only fragments survive.**4·73**

The greatest exercise involving the interpolation of a domed cross into a longitudinal envelope was conducted by the engineer-architects Anthemios of Tralles and Isodoros of Miletos for the stupendous church of H.

›4.71 EPHESOS, CHURCH OF H. IOANNIS, founded 450, rebuilt under Justinian between c. 540 and 565: (a) 6th-century plan; (b) partially recon-structed remains.

Justinian's architects here extended the centralizing formula adopted in the rebuilding of the Apostoleion: a standard aisled basilica was transformed into a complex of six domes, one each over the sanctuary, crossing and transept arms, two slightly elliptical ones over the nave. Pendentives effected the transition from square to circle and the lunettes over the galleries of the nave bays were walled and doubtless pierced with slender windows.

›4.72 CONSTANTINOPLE, H. EIRENE, begun shortly after 532 in place of the Constantinian basilica destroyed in the Nika riots, reconstructed in the mid-8th century: (a, b) plan and section, (c) exterior, (d) interior.

Analysis of the materials and their use demon-strates that much of the basilican substructure and the domed crossing is original though extensively repaired after a fire in 564. The present domes over the nave date from the rebuilding: whether the original concep-tion included both these domes and the tunnel vaults flanking them to all four sides is a subject of some speculation but the weight of opinion favours first a domed crossing preceded by a barrel-vaulted nave and the insertion after 564, at least, of the second domed bay in the nave. The dome may originally have rested

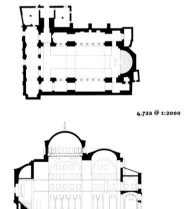

4.72a @ 1:2000

4.72b

4.72d

on heavy side walls with small windows but at some time before the 8th century (most probably in the later 6th century) trabeated galleries were introduced above the aisles (their ends survive embedded in later masonry): it is hard to imagine how the dome was then buttressed unless there were lateral as well as longitudinal tunnel vaults above the roofs of the galleries.

4.72c

4·73a

4·73b

4·73c

›**4.73** CONSTANTINOPLE, H. POLYEUKTOS, c. 534: (a) piers (removed to Venice c. 1204 and erected beside the basilica of S. Marco); (b, c) fragment of arch and capital (Istanbul, Archaeological Museum).

The foundation remains imply a vaulted centralized element with six semi-circular exedrae within a rectangle but the reconstruction of the main space remains highly conjectural. The motifs liberally extended over the surviving architectural fragments are considerably distant from Classical standard: there are bizarre geometrical patterns and lush palmettes but the acanthus is still detected among stylized vegetation of an Iranian type and vines ramp up shafts in the essentially antiarchitectonic – 'Rococo' – late-Classical Syrian manner.

Sofia.**4·76** First, however, Justinian commissioned H. Sergius and Bacchus in Constantinople, c. 527, and assumed responsibility for completing S. Vitale in Ravenna, which had been founded in 526 under the late Ostrogoths.**4·74, 4·75, 4.12**

The influence of works like the so-called Temple of

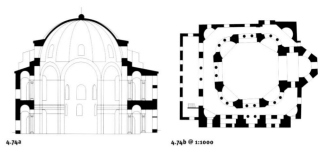

›**4.74** CONSTANTINOPLE, H. SERGIUS AND
BACCHUS, begun before 527: (a) section, (b) plan,
(c) interior.

Begun by Justinian as a chapel associated with the
palace he occupied as heir to the throne, H. Sergius and
Bacchus was completed c. 535. It was interposed on an
awkward site between the palace and the new basilica
of SS. Peter and Paul, communicating with each
through galleries at both levels. Hence the conception
and slightly irregular execution: a domed octagon
encapsulated in a near-square with space between the
two for the galleries of communication.

The principal masses are built somewhat irregularly
of brick with bands of stone for reinforcement. The six-
teen-sided dome, built of brick laid on edge in mortar,
rises through a clerestory straight from all eight arches
of the octagon but is folded like an umbrella to meet
the corners. Instead of concrete, thin long brick had
been used for vaulting in Asia Minor from the 3rd century at least and this lighter load permitted bolder
skeletal structures.

4.74a   4.74b @ 1:1000

4.74c

4.75a

>**4.75** RAVENNA, S. VITALE, c. 530–45: (a) exterior from south, (b) plan, (c) section, (d) interior from south-west, (e) apse mosaic of Empress Theodora and her suite.

4.75b @ 1:1000

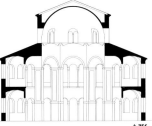

4.75c

4.75d

Commissioned by Bishop Ecclesius (521–32) and probably begun just before his death, S. Vitale was not completed much before the death of Bishop Victor (538–45). The atrium precedes an oddly tangential narthex, separated from the main body of the building by wedge-shaped vestibules, neither of which opens the main axis. Beyond, octagon is inscribed in octagon, unlike the scheme evolved for H. Sergius and Bacchus, but as circle was ringed by circular ambulatory for S. Costanza.**4.26c** There is a gallery level, as in H. Sergius and Bacchus, but here all eight arches supporting the central dome frame semi-circular exedrae except to the east, where the ambulatory is interrupted by a square chancel before the sanctuary apse. Regularity of rhythm has been preferred to alternation and the proportions have been corrected to the advantage of the verticals. The relatively open site allowed more windows to admit much more light.

Lavish embellishment was confined to the interior: as in the tradition of imperial Rome, at least after Hadrian, the exterior mass responds to the interior volume with a frank functionalism, impressive in its austerity – though the dome, made of hollow tubular tiles in the Italian manner, is hidden from outside by a timber roof. Frescoes from the 18th century mask the octagonal umbrella vault and the squinches used in combination with pairs of minute pendentives to support it. However, the pavement, columns and associated revetment of imported marble remain from the original campaign of work on the interior. Begun in 546, this also included the rare and important pre-Iconoclastic mosaics which embellish the chancel: iconic images of Christ and angels flanked by S. Vitalis and Bishop Ecclesius; Emperor Justinian and Empress Theodora with their attendants.

4.75e

Minerva Medica in Rome may well be seen in the design of the central octagon of H. Sergius and Bacchus but precedents for its encapsulation in a rectangle are harder to find. The so-called Golden Octagon built by Constantine as a palatine chapel in Antioch – lost but described by contemporaries – was an octagon, domed possibly from the outset, with exedrae enveloped by a colonnaded ambulatory and galleries. Elsewhere double-skinned quatralobes are not uncommon: S. Lorenzo in Milan is perhaps the grandest. Similar forms are to be found in the Balkans, Anatolia and Armenia and were popular in Syria. Behind all these, of course, is the simple idea of ringing a centralized space with a columned ambulatory – as in S. Costanza.**4.26c**

Unlike H. Eirene, both H. Sergius and Bacchus and S. Vitale are essentially rationalist compositions and both demonstrate the appeal and limitation of rationalism in church architecture. The central space is octagonal with eight great arches supporting the dome. Alternately straight and semi-circular colonnades support the upper gallery and screen ambulatory from nave at both levels – except to the east where an apsidal projection provides the sanctuary opposite the entrance. As all the sides are equal, the location of the entrance can only be determined pragmatically – on the line of access – or by convention – on the axis of prayer facing east. The main focus of prayer, the altar, should be below the dome in the geometrical centre but if the clergy are to be separated from the laity, pragmatism likewise dictates the projection of a sanctuary out opposite the entrance. Yet, as we know, eastern liturgy assigned the nave to the clergy and therefore provided a rival focal point to the altar hidden behind the iconostasis.

On unique terms of reference, the solution to the problem of focus was found in the synthetic hybrid: H. Sofia may be seen as an axial, biapsidal, aisled basilica but also as a Greek cross in which the central square is domed and the western and eastern arms are rounded off to form hemicycles. The main volume of H. Eirene is an obvious relation, except for the hemicycles: twice the size, H. Sofia's central dome has almost three-quarters the diameter of the Roman Pantheon. Eschewing the constraining support of cylindrical walls, however, it floats over its pendentives. The apotheosis of Roman spatial architecture, the antithesis to the Antique temple and the stamping of form with the order of the gods as originally devined by the Greeks, this is the conception of space as the prelude to heaven. **4.76, 4.70**

Hagia Sofia

The main basilica of Constantine's capital, seat of the patriarch and palatine chapel, was dedicated only in 360 and rebuilt after a fire in 404. After it was destroyed in the Nika riots of 532, Justinian immediately decided to rebuild it on an unprecedented scale: his architects oversaw the achievement in five years and the church was consecrated on 27 December 537. The principal church of eastern Christendom, it was converted to a mosque immediately after the fall of Constantinople to the Ottomans on 29 May 1453.

Inscribed in a rectangle about 70 by 75 metres are a square – 100 Byzantine feet or just over 32 metres per side – and two semi-circles flanked by twin series of smaller squares and rectangles. An extrusion of the H. Sergius and Bacchus scheme, the plan thus resembles a basilica with atrium and narthex but with square nave, two apses and subdivided aisles. Some 55 metres high, four arches carry the huge dome with the aid of the most monumental pendentives ever conceived. Though contemporary, H. Eirene may well have offered the opportunity to test the system on a smaller scale. The technique had been well tried in lesser contexts earlier elsewhere, as we have seen, but not in H. Sergius and Bacchus where the oblique angles of the octagon are continued as groins in the dome: adapting the pier-borne pendentive to the monumental scale of H. Sofia, Anthemius and Isadorus avoided the awkward groins but kept the ribs as real or apparent reinforcing agents.

The central arches spring from four great piers buttressed to the north and south by great masses of masonry which impose the major divisions between the groin-vaulted aisle chambers. Not to the degree intended, perhaps, east–west buttressing is provided by the semi-domed hemicy-

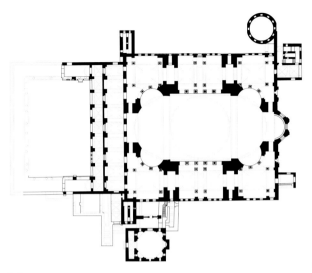

4.76a @ 1:2000

cles which form the two huge apses. Semi-circular exedrae punctuate their perimeters, as in H. Sergius and Bacchus and S. Vitale, leaving piers to frame the west entrance from the atrium and the apsidal sanctuary in the east.

Many different coloured marbles were brought from the furthest reaches of the empire and beyond for the columns of the nave arcades and exedrae, entablatures, the revetment of the walls, and the pavement: green Thessalian marble was used for the nave columns, red porphyry (possibly recycled) for the lower storey of the exedrae, and white Proconnesian marble for the shafts of the columns of aisles and galleries. Smaller in the upper levels, the columns were increased in number and set closer together than those below, perhaps in modification of the original design. Bronze bands protect the main shafts from splitting and capitals incorporate impost blocks now that columns regularly support arches.

The vaults and domes were originally covered in non-figurative mosaics, now mainly lost or obscured. The windows were glazed in various colours, grading the quality of light from the sombre aisles to the relatively bright nave, but the original effect is difficult to recapture since the blinding of many openings to reinforce the structure. The focus has been lost with the original, sumptuously furnished sanctuary and the

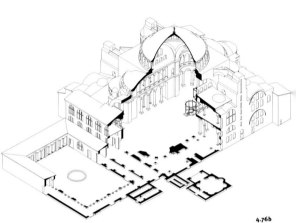

4.76b

›4.76 CONSTANTINOPLE, H. SOFIA (CHURCH OF THE HOLY WISDOM), begun 532: (a) plan of main volume, (b) axonometric reconstruction of original building, (c) model from north (Istanbul, Miniarturk), (d, pages 790–791) general view from south, (e, f) interior and dome, (g, h) narthex and Empress's Gallery, (i) detail of upper exedra gallery, (j, k) mosaics of Christ flanked by Emperor Constantine IX and Empress Zoe (mid-11th century) and with S. John (c. 1260), south gallery, (l) detail of marble revetment above the south narthex door, (m, pages 770–771) mosaic above the south narthex door showing the emperors Justinian (left) and Constantine (right) presenting models of Haghia Sophia and the city, respectively, to Mary.

deflection of the main axis to establish the direction of Mecca for the orientation of Muslim prayer.

The order of repeated squares and circles and the regular sequence of
three, five and seven elements is certainly apparent, but here too the
original impact is masked by later interventions – not least the huge Muslim discs inscribed with the names of God. However, many of the subsidiary spaces are residual, and viewed through their screening columns
even the pure geometry of the main spaces was always denied.

As at H. Sergius and Bacchus, the detail of capitals and impost blocks
is extremely refined. The tendency to reduce the Corinthian acanthus to a
decorative gauze, anticipated in the windswept capitals of Qalat-Siman
and furthered in 5th-century Constantinople, is now complete. No longer
recognizably Corinthian at all, the undercut filigree of stylized foliage car-

4.76c

4.76f

4.76g

ried by the lower columns undulates through curve and counter-curve while the upper ones still bear residual Ionic volutes below filigree impost blocks.

Behind the sumptuous skin, the novelty of Justinian's achievement – a huge canopy dome floating high over a cubical space – depended on the use of brick as much as on the exploitation of the pendentive principle. The eight great piers are built of stone; the walls are of brick reinforced with courses of limestone; an incredibly thin, hence light, layer of brick set in thick mortar forms the vaults. This too was anticipated at H. Sergius and Bacchus. New, however, and of seminal importance, are the

4.76h

4.76j

4.76i

flying buttresses which transmit the thrust of the arcades to piers reinforcing the wall of the outer narthex, facing the missing atrium.

For all their celebrated command of physics, the architects did not
anticipate the buttressing requirements of the relatively shallow dome:
the piers and arches supporting it soon began to splay outwards and,
shaken by earthquake, the dome fell through in 558. The arches and piers
were strengthened and the expanse of void reduced within the great
lunettes to the north and south as enhanced support for the steeper
ribbed dome completed in 563. Support for this was augmented in the 9th
century with more flying buttresses but it collapsed partially in 989 and
again in 1346. These remedial measures explain in part the extraordinary

4.76k

pragmatic approach to the exterior – the organic build-up of forms in response to structural necessity, rather than aesthetic principle, which seems so overwhelmingly impressive to the post-Functionalist eye.

Procopius and other contemporaries liken the dome of the nave in a centralized church to the vault of heaven: its supporting arches mark the cardinal directions of space, its piers and pavement the mountains and plains of earth. In the unique case of H. Sofia the patriarch and clergy, whose hierarchy reflects that of the angels, represent heaven and in their ceremonial evoke the spiritual world of the resurrected Christ. The performance took place in the theatre of the nave; the people witnessed it from the aisles. It required two entrances, the Lesser and the Greater. In the former the patriarch and clergy were joined by the emperor and his entourage, the earthly equivalent of the heavenly hierarchy: the emperor

4.761

entourage, the earthly equivalent of the heavenly hierarchy: the emperor progressed through the nave to the imperial tribune over the south aisle; representing the presence of Christ among his faithful, the clergy progressed with the Gospel through the nave along the solea to the bema which occupied the whole of the great eastern apse; they re-emerged to read the scriptures to the lay congregation in the ancilliary spaces. For the Greater Entrance, representing Christ's Passion, the clergy and patriarch would re-emerge from the bema, progress down the nave to receive the elements of the Eucharist brought from their tabernacle and, joined by the emperor alone, return along the solea to the bema.

It remains unclear where the Gospel and the species of the Eucharist were kept before being revealed to the congregation in the entrance ceremonies: early practice in the Aegean littoral, at least, was for both to be kept in a room at the junction of the north aisle and narthex where the faithful deposited offerings from which the species might be drawn. This arrangement, never universal, had ceded to twin rooms linked to the sanctuary at the eastern ends of the aisles in most of Byzantium by the 8th century but apparently later in Constantinople than elsewhere.

The rooms to either side of the eastern apse of H. Sofia were entrance vestibules but there remains considerable space within the exedrae, linked to the sanctuary apse: this was used for robing the emperor (south) and clergy (north) and could ultimately have doubled for the storage of the Gospel and species. If it is unclear where these were kept in the greatest of all Orthodox cathedrals, the route of their procession is also unclear: one way or the other it could hardly have avoided one aisle, at least, and as revelation was the principal motive of the entrances it would have been pointless to do so: certainly in the vast aisles of H. Sofia there was plenty of room for both the procession and the people.

At the culmination of the entrance ceremonials, the emperor and patriarch emerged from the bema into the nave to exchange a kiss of peace under the dome. The emperor was stationed there to receive communion from the patriarch after the sacred celebration of the central mystery of the faith had taken place in the strict seclusion of the bema. Together in this unique church, at once cathedral and palatine chapel, emperor and patriarch represented the dual nature of Christ. And the Christian empire was dependent on their conjunction, effected in the great ceremony of the imperial mass for which the bi-apsidal space was devised and made manifest under the heavenly dome in the centre.

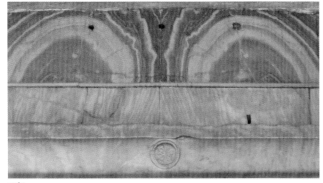

4.76m

‣**4.77 CAIRO, CHURCH OF THE VIRGIN** (called 'Suspended' due to its site on Roman bastions), founded 7th century, rebuilt 11th century and renovated 19th century: interior.

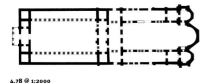

4.78 @ 1:2000

‣**4.78 ABOBA PLISKA (BULGARIA), BASILICA,** dated from the regularity of distribution and masonry to the 9th century against some contention that it is earlier: plan.

5 CONSOLIDATION AND STANDARDIZATION IN THE EAST

The daring experiments and innovative achievements of Justinian's architects were metropolitan. The basilica long subsisted in the provincial east – especially in outlandish places commited to the vernacular and in heretical areas hostile to central regulation, but also in the oldest centres.**4.77** On the other hand the eclectic combination of traditional and novel forms was promoted by the reassertion of empire over much of the known world. Eclecticism is apparent in the 6th-century Balkans, for example, but the basilica was dominant then and again from the 9th century at least until the end of the 11th century. The czars of Bulgaria converted to Christianity in the late-9th century – three generations after the advent of their tribes to Byzantine lands – and sought to surround themselves with an imperial aura recalled from works as diverse as Diocletian's mausoleum at Split and the Balkan churches of the great age of Justinian though, in fact, these did not represent the major achievement of that age.**4.78**

FROM DOMED BASILICA TO QUINCUNX

Under Justinian, the great imperialist, plans may have been sent from the capital to the most important provincial centres: finished architectural members were certainly exported from the imperial Proconnesian quarries. But the realization of the ideal at its most lucid with the increasingly rigorous co-ordination of square and circle, aspiring to the perfect geometry of the City of God, may be traced only from the 8th century throughout the contracted Byzantine world and on into the lands occupied by the Slav inheritors of Byzantine civilization.

Destruction, the decline of the town and reconstruction have left little to show for the two centuries after Justinian. In the rump of the empire little reveals innovation. In the lost lands of the Levant and North Africa church building did not cease altogether but the limited remains of limited activity reveal nothing innovative there.

Much effort went into renovation, especially at the holy sites of Palestine, but various domed forms made their appearance in new work and reconstruction as far south as Jerusalem when Byzantium reconquered much of Syria in the 10th century. Like the east-Syrian fortress church of Qasr Ibn Wardan, built at the end of Justinian's reign, the new churches were sometimes domed basilican variants of the H. Eirene type – debased, of course, with distance from the centre and the elapse of time.**4.79, 4.80**

The more significant survival is of the cross-in-square or quincunx type: the cross is of the Greek kind with equal arms, the northern and southern ones displacing aisles, the western and eastern ones perhaps joining additional narthex and sanctuary space, and to all four corners of the central square, the residual square spaces are also domed. Too little survives for the evolution of the type to be traced comprehensively. Its remote origin was in the cruciform,

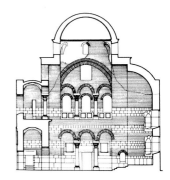

4.79a

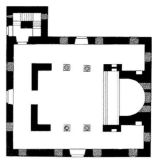

4.79b @ 1:500

›4.79 QASR IBN WARDAN, 6th century: (a) section, (b) plan.

The church appears to be a palatine chapel in a desert fortress dated through an inscription of 564 found among the ruins of the palace.

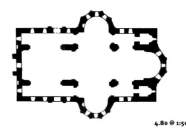

4.80 @ 1:500

›4.80 T'ALINN, ARMENIA, mid-7th century: plan.

Tunnel-vaulted and domed, the earlier Armenian church is distinguished by polygonal apses to transept arms and sanctuary, the latter flanked by apsidal chambers within rectangular walls: in general disposition and structure it has several related compatriots.

usually groin-vaulted, mausoleum which derived from the Antique heroum, as we have seen. More immediately, it is to be found approximated in the domed basilica with a cross of near equal arms developed in the plan, like H. Eirene or even H. Sofia. Square in square, it is also implicit in the double-skin building, like H. Sergius and Bacchus and its antecedents.

The centuries after Justinian recalled the double-skin type, usually of quatralobe in square, sometimes for martyria, sometimes for palatine chapels – but such complexity was increasingly rare as the ambiguity it was calculated to elicit fell from favour. Instead, the cross-in-rectangle of the H. Eirene type, with gallery arcades screening the north and south aisles, was corrected with strict rationality to make it immediately apparent that space flows from the central square into the equal cross arms and around piers or columns into the corner squares.

Though implicit in Justinian's major metropolitan churches, the essential square geometry of the quincunx may derive from work in the secular field even going back to the Parthians through the palaces, if not the fire temples, of the Sassanians: one of the more immediately relevant works which may be related to that tradition is the audience hall at R'safah attributed to Justinian (c. 560). However, the square geometry was certainly prompted by developments in the eastern liturgy in concert with the evolution of the basilican plan.

Chambers occasionally appeared at the ends of the aisles to either side of the sanctuary at least since the 5th century – perhaps first under towers in Syria.**4·54** Over the next two centuries these pastophories were given apses which assimilated them to the sanctuary in a screened tripartite composition and it became canonical to keep the Gospel in the southern diaconicon and the Eucharistic specie in the northern prothesis. There was direct communication between the sanctuary and the side chambers via the screened eastern arm of the cross, but the tripartite composition had decided effect on the ceremony of displaying the Gospel and the Eucharistic specie in the lesser and greater entrances: as revelation was the point, these must now have passed down both aisles perhaps even as far as the narthex for entry to the nave on axis with the bema – though there must often have been little room for both the procession and the people.

The accidents of survival have left the Koimesis (Dormition) at Nicaea (Iznik) and H. Sofia in Thessaloniki – generally dated to the early and mid-8th century respectively – as major landmarks on the way to the evolution of the canonical ecclesiastical quincunx. Both have a dominant central domed space and subordinate square corner chambers, domed in the earlier example, but the geometry is still disturbed by the non-alignment of the pastopheries and the residual galleried aisles which communicate through the western corners with the narthex to form an ambulatory.**4.81, 4.82**

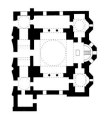

4.81 a and b @ 1:1000

›4.81 NICAEA (IZNIK), KOIMESIS, c. 700: (a) plan, (b) section.

Destroyed in 1920, the Nicaean Koimesis had four subsidiary spaces in the corners of the cross, those to the east forming pastophories out of alignment with their western counterparts. Twin piers – perhaps supporting galleries – screen the transept arms from the aisles. Dating to the beginning of the 8th century is based on the ratio of bricks to mortar, favouring the latter in a 7th-century manner, and fragments of pre-Iconoclastic mosaic superceded by post-Iconoclastic work.

›4.82 THESSALONIKI, H. SOFIA, late-8th century, restored: (a) exterior, (b) detail of windswept capital, (c) plan and part axonometric, (d) central dome with Ascension mosaic (late 9th century), (e) nave and chancel.

4.82a

4.82e

4.82d

The dating is based on the association of the monogram of Emperor Constantine VI (780–96) with an inscription relating to the foundation incorporated in the mosaic embellishment of the apse.

The western arm is slightly longer than the others and the domed pastophories are stepped in from the perimeter, out of alignment with the cross-vaulted chambers to either side of the triple-domed narthex. Rather than a triple arcade to each side arm, as at Nicaea, here two arcaded bays with single columns are separated by central piers and the motif is repeated in contracted form within the western piers.

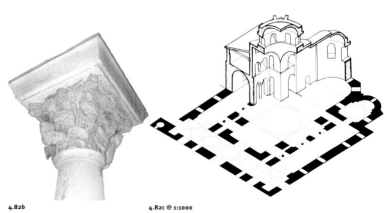

4.82b

4.82c @ 1:1000

4.83a @ 1:1000   4.83b @ 1:1000   4.83c @ 1:1000

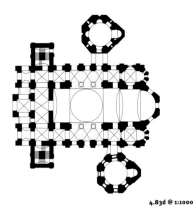

4.83d @ 1:1000

›**4.83 VARIANTS OF THE DOMED-CROSS PLAN:** (a, b) Vagharshapat (Armenia), the churches of S. Gayane (c. 630) and S. Hrip'simé (c. 618); (c) Ankara, H. Kliment (early 9th century); (d) Dere Agzi church (c. 800 or later).

A nearer approximation to regularity, still not strictly square, and a beautiful variant with curves in all directions, appear earlier than at Nicaea in substantial ashlar at Vagharshapat in Armenia: support of the masonry dome on squinches suggests knowledge of the Sassanians, probably through R'safah, which may explain the precocity in the purification of the metropolitan form. Be that as it may, these Armenian permutations of an ultimately imperial type were sustained for centuries and other approximations are known elsewhere, often with an extra sanctuary bay balancing the narthex, sometimes with a canopy vault completing the arc of the pendentives but usually with a dome and drum.**4.83**

Given the accidents of survival in a hostile area, it is possible that the earliest fully developed quincunx may be found among the churches hewn from the limestone cliffs of Cappadocia and Apulia perhaps as early as the late-8th century. The very prolixity there may well be taken as an indication of the scale of the losses elsewhere: in addition to the quincunx, the Greek cross, the domed octagon, the trefoil and the quatrefoil proliferate singly or combined in Cappadocia and similar forms may still be traced in Byzantine Europe, especially in reliquary chapels.**4.84**

The canonical regularity of the quincunx, prompted by the structural efficiency of bilateral symmetry in the disposition of the tunnel-vaulted bays supporting the dome, seems not to have been achieved in Constantinople until some time in the 9th century – but evidence is sparse. The form is found earlier in the west.

4.84a

›4.84 THE EXCAVATED QUINCUNX: (a) Goreme
(Cappadocia), Elmali Kilise, view towards the sanctuary; (b) Vaste (Apulia), crypt of S. Stefano: interior of
one of the cave chapels.

Activity at Goreme continued for many centuries and
though this example probably dates from the 11th century there are precise precedents for it among the
works datable from their non-figurative frescoes to
before the end of the Iconoclastic period. The proliferation of cave churches in Apulia began with the influx of
monks seeking refuge in that remote area from the
strictures of the iconoclastic Emperor Leo III (717–41).

4.84b

EPILOGUE: THE LAST HALF MILLENNIUM OF BYZANTIUM

4.85

INTRODUCTION

The Bulgars, pursuing their imperial ambitions, besieged Constantinople three times between 814 and 924. Like the Arabs, they were repelled each time and, astonishingly, Byzantium revived, restored its defences, renovated its palaces, renewed its arts: the occasion was the assertion of a new dynasty – the Macedonian – with Basil I (867–86) and the restoration of ecclesiastical peace with the abrogation of Iconoclasm in 843. The resurgence of commerce inside and outside the rump of the empire, following the establishment of viable Muslim polities, was the condition: the venerable capital lay on the east–west and north–south crossroads of trade, pilgrimage, diplomacy and thought.**4.85**

Revenge on both Arabs and Bulgars was decisive at the hands of Emperor Basil II whose long reign (976– 1025) was one of the most successful in the annals of Byzantium. About the millennial year he succeeded in driving the Arabs – their power fragmented – from Asia Minor: they were never to return. In 1014 he crushed the Bulgars with such ferocity that their czar, Samuel, died of shock at the revelation and the Bulgarian empire died with him. Thereafter, Basil was able to reassert himself throughout the Balkans, the Levant, Palestine and even into northern Mesopotamia. His gains were lost by a succession of weak emperors but such was Byzantine prestige that most of the world long recognized Constantinople as the imperial centre and its ruler as the only legitimate claimant to the Roman succession. That, of course, had always been maintained by the Byzantine emperor himself and it is no coincidence that the Classicizing tendency in Byzantine art was never stronger than when Byzantine power was at a low ebb.**4.15**

Asia Minor was open to the Selcuk Turks on their annihilation of Emperor Romanus IV and his army at

Manzikert in eastern Anatolia in 1071. Southern Italy was lost to the Normans too. Yet cultural prestige and the skilful diplomacy of the new Comnene dynasty – based on readiness to compromise with the barbarians in the Balkans if they acknowledged the emperor and Christianity – sustained Constantinople into another century of revived activity. Turning the threat posed by the forces of the west's first crusade, Alexius I Comnenus (1081–1118) secured a promise to return any cities won from the Turks and thus regained most of Asia Minor. Though denied Syria, Alexius and his successors expanded the empire throughout Asia Minor and the Balkans.

The Serbs had begun reasserting themselves in the late 1160s and the Bulgars founded their second empire immediately after the death of the able Manuel Comnenus twenty years later. Then the dynasty lost all to palace intrigue inflaming enmity between Byzantines and Latins. The fourth crusade was deflected to Constantinople in 1204 by its Venetians carriers at the behest of a claimant to the imperial throne but the expedition ended in the sack of the city, Latin occupation and fragmentation of the rump of the empire.

The successor states included Trebizond, Epirus and the so-called Empire of Nicaea, whose rulers were effective enough to secure western Asia Minor and elevate their capital into the major eastern Christian cultural centre of the mid-13th century. In 1261 the regent of the boy king, Michael Paleologus, took Constantinople from the enfeebled Latins, dispatched his royal ward and sparked the final efflorescence of Christian Byzantium – not unaffected by the infiltration of western ideas. The empire now consisted only of Greece, Thrace, Macedonia and western Asia Minor. The European territories were open prey to the Serbs and Bulgars and by the middle of the 14th century the

›4.85 (PAGES 806–807) EASTERN IMPERIAL PRESTIGE AND PROSPERITY: The Virgin and Christ child with Emperor John II Comnenus and Empress Eirene (H. Sofia, upper south gallery panel, c. 1118): the conjunction of temporal and spiritual authority in the Vicar of Christ is clearly asserted here – in contrast to the marked duality in the west.

4.86a

4.86b

›4.86 NORTHERN ANATOLIA, SUMILA MONASTERY, 1360: (a, b) model and detail (Istanbul, Miniaturk).

›4.87 THE FALL OF CONSTANTINOPLE (from *Voyage d'outre mer*, Bertrandon de la Broquière, c. 1470; Paris, Bibliothèque Nationale).

emperor retained only the hinterland of Constantinople, Thessaloniki – the alternative capital – and the Peleponnesian Morea: Thrace had been lost to the Bulgars under Czar Ivan Alexander (1331–71), Epirus and Macedonia to the Serbs under their great kings Milutin (1282–1321) and Dusan (1331–55).

Nemesis came with the Osmanli Turks, who had been settled near Nicaea by the Selcuks. They asserted their independence on the latter's retreat, began to expand at the expense of the Nicaeans in 1288 and had taken most of western Asia Minor within half a century: naturally many Christians took refuge in monasteries.**4.86** Civil war in Paleologue Byzantium invited them to cross into Europe: they secured Thrace, moved the capital to Adrianople and encircled Constantinople. The Christian capital seemed doomed by 1390 but reprieve attended the unwonted defeat of the Ottomans (as the Osmanlis are usually called) in the east. The Ottomans had recovered by the second decade of the new century. The emperor, John VIII Paleologus, journeyed west in quest for help in the late 1430s: no help was forthcoming and Sultan Mehmet II (1451–81) finally achieved his dynasty's goal: Constantinople fell to him on 29 May 1453 and the millennial Christian empire was extinguished in the east.**4.87**

4.88

›4.88 PATMOS, MONASTERY CHURCH OF H. IOANNIS: interior of quincunx with iconostasis.

›4.89 CONSTANTINOPLE, EARLY CENTRAL-IZED CHURCHES OF THE MACEDONIAN DYNASTY: (a–d) Myrelaion (Bodrum Camii, 920), reconstructed perspective section (after Kraut-heimer), plan, exterior and interior; (e, f) Constantine Libs (Fenari Isa Camii, 907), plan, interior of crossing.

Raised on a brick and stone terrace enclosing a lower church, like the Nea, the brick-built quincunx of each of these small but tall works has a galleried narthex with niched end bays, niched pastophories and polygonal apses – five in the earlier work. In each case the central square on both levels may originally have been defined by columns – the lower ones carry-ing groin-vaults, the upper ones supporting penden-tives, drum and dome – but there are now piers in the Myrelaion and in the Libs church bracing arches were inserted after earthquake damage. The corner bays are groin-vaulted; so too are the cross arms of the Myre-

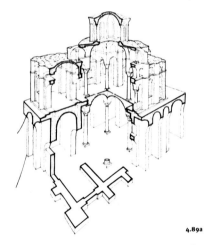

4.89a

4.89b @ 1:500

THE PREVALENCE OF THE QUINCUNX

By the opening of the Macedonian era in Byzantium a centralized space crowned by a dome was widely seen as the ideal theatre for the performance of mass in accord-ance with the liturgy as it had developed from Justinian's day: the mystery of the Eucharist was celebrated in a cur-tained enclosure from which the priests emerged into the naos to minister to the laity crowded into the ancillary spaces. Promoting the pure geometry of the Greek cross, eastern procedure also prompted the development of the iconostasis. The accidents of survival have left no clear trace of the stages of the latter's elevation from a parapet beyond which the sanctuary vault was visible to a wall of

4.89c

laion, but they are tunnel-vaulted in the Libs church. The latter's dome (c. 4 metres in diameter) is a simple saucer, the former's (c. 3 metres) is ribbed and scalloped: often identified as 'umbrella' or 'pumpkin', that form (approximated in H. Sergius and Bacchus) is thought to have been familiar in the capital by the time of the Nea and its near-contempory church of S. Mary Pharos – there were doubtless many other examples. The drum of the Myrelaion's central dome is relieved with triangular piers and semi-cylindrical buttresses provide exceptionally strong articulation below.

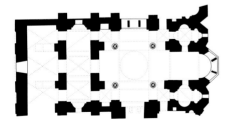

4.89e @ 1:500

4.89d

many-tiered holy images: well before the advent of the Comnenes there was often more than one range below the image of the enthroned Christ flanked by the Virgin and S. John the Baptist (the *Deesis*) and, like the quincunx, this was to remain characteristic of the eastern church throughout its history.**4.88**

As far as imprecise contemporary descriptions testify, the true quincunx appeared in Constantinople with the New Church (Nea) of Basil I c. 880: it has disappeared and the earliest datable examples of the type belong to the next century.**4.89** By the dawn of the new millennium it was dominant and the basilica obsolete – except for occa-

4.89f

sional rebuilding – in the remaining domains of the empire, in southern Serbia but not generally in the barbarian kingdoms of the Balkans. Long familiar in the furthest reaches of Asia Minor, it was still in the process of evolution in the excavations of Cappadocia.

Excavated, the Cappadocian legacy is unique in being almost entirely spatial: less elevated than their structural counterparts, freedom from the normal constraints of statics allows domes even over cross-arms.**4.84** In the European rump of the empire, much varied effect was won from expressing the hierarchy of internal volumes in the mass. Moreover the design of otherwise sparsely embellished exteriors was enlivened by the patterning of the masonry: the combination of stone and brick, particularly the 'cloisonné' method of framing stone blocks with brick strips, patterned brickwork, brick and thick-laid mortar and mortar masking alternately recessed brick courses to enhance its thickness. Dating of the many middle-Byzantine churches, problematical in the usual absence of foundation inscriptions, is assisted by an established chronology of formal variations and changes in masonry techniques.

In Thessaloniki, the major centre of architectural activity in northern Greece – revivified by the Macedonian ascendancy – little of major significance survives from the middle-Byzantine period other than the splendid brick quincunx church of the Panagia Chalkeon. Developments in the capital were clearly observed but there are new – or enhanced – elements as well: most notably the ancillary chapels, the parekklesion, in the end bays of the esonarthex and the towers over them. Hardly less significant is the replacement of the bema curtain with a parapet on which icons could be hung. The brickwork is richer in plane and patterning than work in the capital and that was to be characteristic of Greece.**4.90**

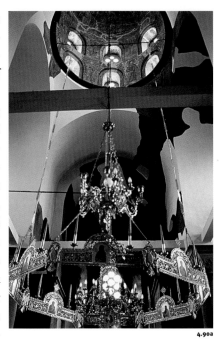

4.90a

›4.90 THESSALONIKI, PANAGIA CHALKEON, 1028: (a) interior, (b) exterior from the south-west.

The façade is articulated with colossal engaged columns, like those to all sides of the capital's Myrelaion, but the integrity of the internal wall plane is preferred to the concave recessions which enliven the metropolitan work. On the other hand, greater variety of geometry complements simpler brickwork on the exterior and windows are set deeper than those of the capital in more expansive triple recessions. There are no domes over the corner bays of the quincunx but, like those of the esonarthex, the dome of the crossing has a higher drum than the Constantinopolitan norm: it has an unbroken cornice, like many in the capital, but the eaves of the precociously assertive front pair undulate over the arched windows and niches in the manner to be familiar in Greece.

4.90b

As Thessaloniki was the administrative centre for church affairs in Thrace, Macedonia and beyond into the lands of the Bulgars – occasionally even the seat of the emperor – its style is widespread and mixed with elements drawn eclectically from other sources, not least the capital. More exotic influence often came with peripatetic abbots. Thus, for instance, the Katholicon in the Great Lavra of Mount Athos is an irregular quincunx with polygonal apses of the metropolitan type to the east but curved ones to the cross-arms, making it trilobed in the manner not unfamiliar to Asia Minor where the founder originated; the dome on high drum with undulating eaves is Thessalonikan. Further inland the cross-currents of influence occasionally produce minor masterpieces, rich spatially if poor in substance.**4·91** In the repertory of types persisting in Bulgaria – basilica, quatralobe, domed cross and quincunx – the commonest at the village level was the simple, rubble-built hall church.

In central and southern Greece the quincunx dominates as elsewhere but individuality of style derives from sharper geometry, limited planar variation and mixed masonry. Rigid as the nine-cell cross-in-square was in planning principle, in elevation it admitted variation. The dominant central dome might be borne on columns or piers or both – piers to the east, columns to the west. The cross-arms are invariably tunnel-vaulted but the corner bays might be domical, tunnel- or groin-vaulted. The expression of the triangular roof truss in gabled cross-arms is preferred to the reflection of the curvature of tunnel-vaulting and sometimes even the domes have low conical roofs. Drums are cylindrical or octagonal rather than multi-faceted and, aided by colonnettes, the frames of the slender windows push their semi-circular arcading up into the zone of the dome to more pronounced effect than in Thessaloniki – or, occasionally, the capital. The main walls are largely unrelieved by pilasters and blind arcading. Instead of brick courses varied in plane to accommodate enhanced bands of mortar – as in the capital – the most characteristic approach is to combine brick and stone, especially in the cloisonné manner, and to inset bands of serrated brickwork often in association with panels of script in low relief.**4·92**

The great majority of later Byzantine churches and even cathedrals were associated with monasteries and monastic communities, like parishes, were many and small. Conceived in an age of affluence in the order, monastic living

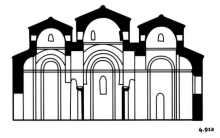

4.91a

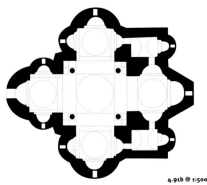

4.91b @ 1:500

›**4.91** PERISTERAI (NORTHERN GREECE), CHURCH, late-9th century: (a) section, (b) plan.

4.92a

›4.92 **ATHENS:** (a) Mikra Metropolis (Gorgoepikoos or H. Eleftherios, late-12th century), exterior; (b, c) Kapnikarea (c. 1060 with 13th-century porch, esonarthex and parekklesion), overview with narthex top and parekklesion right, detail of porch; (d–f) Apostoleion (c. 1000), exterior, interior, plan.

quarters might still be monumental but most houses had declined in numbers and size by the beginning of the new millennium. However, typical still was the double-walled enclosure providing for services and cellular accommodation behind galleries addressing a rectangular court – as at S. Catherine's on Mount Sinai: the church occupies the centre and other communal facilities, such as the refectory, are also freestanding.

4.92c

4.92b

4.92d

4.92e

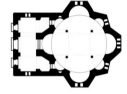

4.92f @ 1:500

Contraction was naturally reflected in the size of new churches planned compactly on the consolidated quincunx – at the extreme indeed, the contraction of the cross-arms left room only for the piers supporting the naos dome, obliterating the quincunx. However, expansion beyond galleries for the laity most commonly embraced the provision of an esonarthex and a parekklesion annexed to a side for supplementary rites or special masses for the dead: both might be domed over the central bay. Within, more space – real or implied – was achieved in various ingenious ways, especially in Greece. Exceptionally, cross-arms and corner bays of the Athenian Apostoleion were all embraced by a circle, concentric with the central dome, and an alternating series of large and small apses radiated from its circumference.**4.92f** The chancel may be extended before its

›**4.93 HYMETTOS, MONI ASTERIOU,** 11th century: overview.

apse and the pastophories are often trilobed. Occasionally triconches are formed with apses to the transept arms as well as the sanctuary – as in the church of the Great Lavra on Mount Athos.

More space could be achieved for the clergy by expanding the central dome to twice the width of the cross-arms and canting the corners over squinches to form an octagon, as in the Katholikons of Hosias Lukas and Daphni. A rare alternative is the erection of a domed sanctuary, larger than the crossing, beyond the eastern arm as in the Nea Moni on Chios.**4·93–4·95**

4.94b

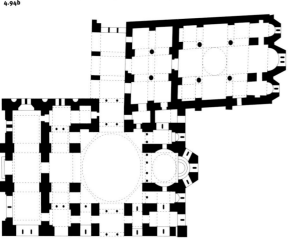

4.94a @ 1:500

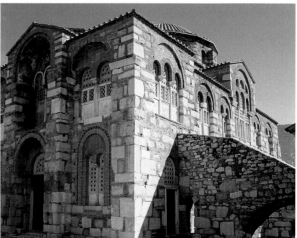

4.94d

4.94e

›**4.94** H. LUKAS, THEOTOKOS AND KATHO-
LIKON, mid-10th and early 11th centuries respectively: (a) plan of complex, (b) general view from east,
(c) Theotokos interior, (d–h) Katholikon entrance front,
narthex, vaults, narthex gallery, nave to sanctuary,
crypt.

These adjoining churches, tall and slim, well represent the simple quincunx plan of Greek cross in square
and its expansion with the interpolation of a domed
octagon wider than the arms of the cross. The earlier
Theotokos differs from the standard form only in the
degree to which the sanctuary and pastophories project beyond the main square body of the building. The
narthex and the upper corner bays of the Katholikon's
nave have galleries, and bridges at the same level are
carried across the transepts on arcades: the effect of
this partial doubling of elegant arcuate enclosure is, of

4.94f

4.94c

4·94g

4·94h

course, dramatic both spatially and in the subtle modulation of light. In both works the apses are polygonal, as was usual in Greece, rather than semi-circular. The mixture of brick and stone in the embellishment of the exterior is less regular than in standard Greek cloisonné work.

›4.95 CHIOS, NEA MONI KATHOLIKON, mid-11th century: (a) general view of monastic complex and its enclosure, (b) plan, (c) interior detail.

Founded by Emperor Constantine IX Monomachos and built by imperial workmen sent from Constantinople, this church presumably represents an otherwise lost metropolitan type. A double narthex, the outer one domed over all three bays, the inner one domed only over the central bay, leads to the grand square nave. There are no transepts, but the piers supporting four great arches on each side imply a Greek cross. Four smaller squinch-like arches link the main ones across

4.95a

the corners, transforming the square into an octagon at the base of the dome, though in fact the dome depends on pendentives. Contrary to usual Greek practice, but in accord with the metropolitan norm, the dome is segmental. The projecting sanctuary is flanked by square pastophories in the usual way.

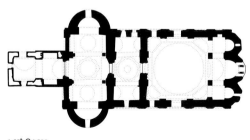

4.95b @ 1:500

4.95c

4.96a

THE ICONIC PANOPLY OF HEAVEN

Beyond the obvious analogy between the hierarchical triad of sanctuary, nave and ancilliary spaces and the head, body and limbs of Christ, to the Alexandrine *Topographia Christiana* and its followers, the church was domed like the heavens, rectangular at base like the earth, orientated away from western darkness towards Paradise and the salvation of sunrise. In accord with the pseudo-Areopagite's theology of light, its elements were emblazoned accordingly with a hierarchy of images descending from the light of the divine to the dark of man. The lightest, largest and highest is Christ ascending to heaven or presiding as the

4.96b

›4.96 DAPHNI, KOIMESIS MONASTIC CHURCH, c. 1080: (a) mosaic of the Pantokrator in the central dome, (b) exterior.

There are inner and outer narthexes and three apses. Four groin-vaulted bays form the arms of the cross. Canted between them over narrower groin-vaulted bays, the squinches which sustain support for the drum and dome are of similar diameter. That recalls the arrangement in the Katholikon at H. Lukas but here there are no galleries – no double skin. The main source of light is the ring of windows in the drum below the superb Pantokrator in the dome.

Outside, relative sobriety is apparent in the regular disposition of bricks to frame the stone blocks and dog-toothed bands to outline the brick voussoir arches of the windows.

›4.97 BYZANTINE MEDIA OF ICONOGRAPHIC DECORATION: (a) Ohrid, S. Kliment, c. 1295 frescoed crossing and sanctuary; (b) fresco in the sanctuary of H. Nikolaus Orfanos, Thessaloniki, 14th century and earlier, restored.

4.97a

final judge (*Pantocrator*), supported by the four archangels, in the centre of the dome.**4·96a** The Prophets and Apostles attend around the rim or in the drum. As transition from the celestial circle to the nave's terrestrial square is effected through the pendentives, there are the four Evangelists whose Gospels convey the transition from Christ's ministry on earth to his triumph in heaven. In the semidome of the sanctuary apse, the image of the Mother of God, intercessor for salvation, is of near equivalent effulgence to that of the Pantocrator: the vaults and walls of the chancel are dedicated to her life and subsequent divine advocacy. The lower vaults, lunettes and walls of the body of the church have scenes from the life and Passion of the Saviour. Worldly imagination may be licensed in the lowermost zones but the west wall is the statutory place for the Last Judgement. In the restricted space of the typical Byzantine church, as it was to evolve in purity of form and regularity of iconography over the first half of the second millennium, art overcame architecture as it had not done before in the orbit of the Hellenes.

There were two media for masking the physical fabric of the church with these images – for obliterating this world with the glory to come: mosaic or fresco according to the wealth of the foundation.**4·97** Assembled from myriad tiny pieces of glass backed by coloured enamel or goldleaf and laid in plaster inevitably at a slight angle to one another, mosaic is unrivalled in reflecting the flickering light of candles to produce a shimmering veil, dematerializing the enclosure – effecting its transfiguration into the empyraean. The vicissitudes of their patrons obviated the survival of few complete schemes even in the latest Byzantine era: the richest are naturally to be found in churches beyond the domain of Muslim conversion.

4.97b

4.98a

4.98c

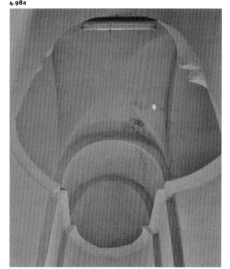

4.98b

4.98d

4.98e @ 1:1000

FROM CONTRACTION TO ORGANIC DEVELOPMENT

The church at Daphni has taken us to the threshold of the Comnene era, the Athenian Mikra Metropolis well into it and Ohrid's S. Kliment way beyond. Fusion of formerly distinct spatial elements or simplification through contraction are characteristic of the period spanned by these works in Greece. Similar simplification of plan is apparent in the later works at Goreme and elsewhere in Asia Minor. In the capital, on the whole, Comnene survivors are small but intricate, tightly restricted in plan but aspiring in elevation: presumably once rich in iconographic ornament, they mark a change in the metropolitan style from simplicity of surface and architectural detail to less-fluid stone carving, attenuation of verticals, greater complexity of brick patterning and multiplicity of articulating elements, such as pilasters and blind arcading, not always to the advantage of clear massing. Prominent examples include the Pantepoptes, H. Theodoroi, the Kyriotissa and the Pantokrator: to the last a gallery was appended to provide the imperial dynasty with a mausoleum.**4.98**

The quincunx provided distinct space for baptism but

4.98f

4.98g

>**4.98** CONSTANTINOPLE, THE COMNENE
CONTRIBUTION: (a–e) Pantepoptes (Eski Imaret
Camii, 1081), crossing to west, trilobed pastopherie,
exterior from south-east, detail of brickwork, plan; (f,
g) Pantokrator monastery churches (Zeyrek Camii,
1118), exterior from west and east; (h) Kyriotissa
(Kalenderhane Camii, mid-12th-century core incorporating earlier masonry), interior.

The early Macedonian formula was sustained under
the Comnenes in most essentials but there is some
contraction at the east end, as in Greece, and the central square is usually supported by piers rather than
columns. In contrast to the latter, the enclosing fabric is
lighter: there are triple arcades at the transept ends
and larger windows. On the other hand, there is less
interest in architectonic integrity: for example, the
internal cornice cedes to a decorative frieze and the
external one on the central drum may arch over its generous windows to undulate around the dome in the
manner familiar in Greece.

4.98h

in the last centuries of the dying empire it did not meet
the increasing requirements for the burial and veneration
of patrons and benefactors as well as deceased members
of the monastic community and saints. The order generated by the square geometry of the quincunx is no longer
an over-riding concern: organic growth – or at least
innovative accretion – and non-architectonic colouristic
articulation are the dominant characteristics of the
Paleologan achievement.

Parekklesia proliferated, sometimes in the form of the quincunx, often in galleries integrated with the main body of the church through arcades, at ground level, on the upper floor of the narthex, even on the roof. Narthexes were lengthened and joined to side galleries in a new permutation of the ambulatory, enveloping the main volume – old or new. Crypts were expanded into extensive lower churches. Elevation is generally enhanced: naves are taller, domes rise from taller drums and the tower, which began its career in the epiphany portals of Syria and became a major feature in the west, is a dominant belfry. The colouristic use of mixed materials, patterning the outside walls, particularly enhances arcading: often blind, this serves primarily decorative purposes rather than the articulation of structure; frequently asymmetrical, it responds in the main – if not in part – to the ad-hoc process of accretion common in the period. Inside, imagery is rampant, respecting structure in concept but not in physics.**4·97**

The sacking of Constantinople in 1204 deprived the Christian east of its major centre of architectural gravity: before the advent of the Paleologues the tendency towards spatial diversification was apparent in the capitals of the successor states into which the empire had fragmented after the Latin assault. Nicaea took precedence but in Epirus and Trebizond important regional styles emerged and there was considerable activity in the Balkans. The centre of gravity returned to Constantinople with the Paleologues in 1261: the first century of their epoch, marked by maturity c. 1310, is the richest in late-Byzantine remains in the capital, in Greece and, beyond, in the Balkans.

The quincunx remained the basic plan form: examples are found in all the successor states, often with regional variations. At Ohrid – which had passed from Byzantium to the Bulgars, back to Byzantium then to the Latins and

›**4.99** **TREBIZOND, H. SOFIA,** c. 1240: exterior from west.

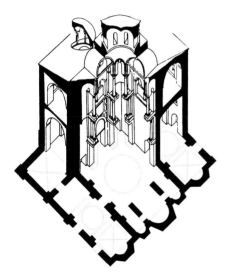

›**4.100** **ARTA, PARIGORITISSA,** c. 1285: isometric reconstruction.

The crossing is a domed octagon in contrast to the other examples at the site: these retain a more regular quincunx though the Kato Panagia is highly unorthodox in its tunnel-vaulted crossing. Like S. Kliment at Ohrid, the main volume here is sheathed in a U-shaped ambulatory.

the Epirots before falling again to the Bulgars – the late-13th century S. Kliment, as rich in its brickwork as Comnene Greece, is an outstanding example of the regular quincunx preserved within an ambulatory.**4.97a** On the other side of the Byzantine world, at Trebizond, regional variation is well represented by the extension of the north, south and western arms of mid-13th-century H. Sofia into arcaded porches.**4.99**

From Epiros to Bulgaria, where the vernacular sustained the hall church but centralized forms were favoured by court patrons, hybrid variations are numerous. For example, at or near the Epirene capital, Arta, several works built over the half century from c. 1240 combine a basilican nave with a centralized crossing.**4.100** The colouristic effect of patterned brickwork and cloisonné masonry inset with ceramic plaques, characteristic of these works at Arta, is found north through Thessaly to Ohrid, south through the Peloponnese to Mistra and in Constantinople.

An ambulatory runs through the corners and contracts the arms of the simple, small-scale H. Tryphon in Nicaea, built for Theodore II (1254–58) just before the reconquest of Constantinople by his son's Palaeologue regent. That precedent was soon followed in the capital by Empress Theodora – widow of the conqueror, who had become Michael VIII (1261–82) – for the doubling of the early 10th century quincunx monastery church of Constantine Libs to provide a dynastic mortuary vault after the example of the Comnene chapel in the Pantokrator complex. Subsequently a semi-ambulatory was formed by the conjunction of an exonarthex with a parekklesion added to the south as burial space was taken up within the south quincunx. In addition to their many new foundations, noble patrons similarly extended other monastic churches to the same end.**4.101**

In the Greek islands there are several variations on the

4.101a

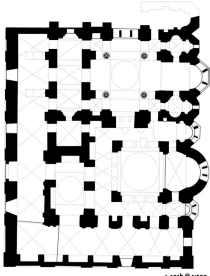

4.101b @ 1:500

domed octagon of Nea Moni and the Greek-cross octa
gon of Daphni is popular everywhere. An outstanding
example dominates the main complex at Mistra. Retaken
from the Latins in 1262, the despotate of the Morea was
given a virtually new capital by its Paleologue masters.
The earliest of the important works there is the basilican
cathedral of 1291, closely followed by the two churches of
the Brontocheion monastic complex: H. Theodoroi
(1290–96) is a Greek-cross octagon, without galleries;
the Aphentiko (1290–96) is a basilica in which the
arcaded nave is surmounted by a domed quincunx
formed by galleries. The latest generation of works at the
site lengthens the western arm of the quincunx in flirta-
tion with basilican form or, more radically, a basilican
lower church is surmounted by a distinct cruciform
upper one – as in the reworking of the cathedral after
1400 and in the new Pantanassa foundation. Cloisonné
masonry is characteristic here, as elsewhere in Greece
and beyond.**4.102**

Thessaloniki, recaptured in 1224, was not an active cen-

›**4.101 CONSTANTINOPLE, CONSTANTINE
LIBS COMPLEX** as extended with the funerary church
of S. John the Baptist in the later 13th century and with
the ambulatory of c. 1312: (a) H. Ioannis's exterior from
the south-east, (b) plan.

The 10th-century scale was retained in Theodora's
work – but the central square is defined by piers rather
than columns. Already gloomy in part, because of the
proximity of the original church, the funerary ambulatory became darker still – naturally and not inappropri-
ately – when the unfenestrated, burial-niched, outer
parekklesion was built. The richly patterned and
recessed red brickwork, with its relieving bands of
white stone, is markedly distinct from the 10th-century
work.

›**4.102 MISTRA:** (a) Brontocheion monastery, general view with the domed octagonal crossing of H.
Theodoroi (c. 1290) to the right and the five-domed
Hodegetria (c. 1310) in the background; (b–e) Pantanassa church (c. 1428), plan, section, exterior from
the east, interior from the west.

4.102a

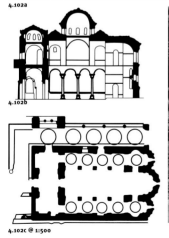

4.102b

4.102c @ 1:500

4.102d

4.101e

4.103a

tre of 13th-century building until the Paleologue era –
when it was the alternative capital. The major surviving
works are more regular than those of Constantinople, the
hierarchy of domed bays is expressed with increasing elevation and the exterior brickwork simulates the complex,
largely geometric, patterning of vernacular weaving. The
outstanding examples are H. Katherini and H. Apostoloi,

›4.103 PALEOLOGUE THESSALONIKI: (a) H.
Katherini (c. 1290), exterior; (b, c) H. Apostoloi (c. 1310),
exterior, plan; (d–f) Profitis Elias (c. 1360), exterior,
narthex and nave details.

The Panagia Chalkeion quincunx formula is revised
upwards (from nearly 1:4) within a niche-lined, U-
shaped ambulatory in the earlier work: the four corner
bays of the ambulatory have domes on low drums, off-
setting the tall central accent in clear expression of the
hierarchy of progressively aspirant space.

The elevated proportions are still more enhanced in
the Apostoloi church (1:5) and taller too are the drums
supporting the four corner domes of the ambulatory:
apparently not for burial, the latter has open arcades to
the south as well as the west where it is doubled by an
exonarthex. Segmental domes rise from undulating
cornices of the high drums over the corner bays of the
ambulatory as well as the central crossing.

4.103b

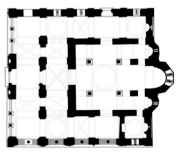

4.103c @ 1:500

4.103e

Profitis Elias acquires a trefoil form from the addition of lateral apses but the enlargement of the central square encroaches on the corner bays and domed cubes are attached to the exterior instead: apart from these and the enlarged central bay, there are domes on the ends of the narthex in the typical Thessalonikan manner.

4.103d

4.103f

from around the turn of the 14th century, and the later church of Profitis Elias. The aspiring proportions of the main volumes, rising above double-height envelopes, are more pronounced here than elsewhere in Greece – or the capital – but concern with massing does not inhibit the colouristic mixture of materials, particularly in horizontal courses of brick and stone, inlaid stone discs and panels, white stone and red brick voussoirs to the arcading – blind or true – and exuberant geometrical patterning in the brickwork.**4.103**

The influence of Thessaloniki was felt throughout Macedonia, where S. Sofia of Ohrid was given a two-storey exonarthex flanked by towers with octagonal drums. It penetrated well into both the Bulgar and Serb kingdoms.**4.104** It failed to eclipse the native preference for aisleless halls in Bulgaria, but domes were now inserted towards the centre and over the narthex, there were several variations on the longitudinal linking of contracted Greek-cross volumes and patterning in red and white masonry ran riot.

The Serbian king Milutin endowed Mount Athos with a monastery for his nationals and in the process his archi-

tects acquired familiarity with the latest style of Thessaly – if they did not in fact derive from Thessaloniki. They applied their skills to inserting domed crossings in older basilicas, to building new cruciform churches with central domes and contracted apsidal arms, and quincunxes with and without elongated western arms. Their outstanding masterpiece is the Gracanica church (c. 1320) with its relatively restrained cloisonné revetment, its extra domed bay for the sanctuary, its ambulatory terminating in domed pastophories and the superb hierarchy of domes rising from tiered semi-circles to heights surpassing even those of Thessaloniki.**4.105**

The colouristic use of materials was not always foreign to Constantinople – the Theodosian walls have bands of

›4.104 OHRID, H. SOFIA, c. 1315: view from the south-west showing galleried exonarthex.

In amplification of the Thessalonikan approach, a blind arcade is inserted between the two main tiers of open arcading. Simplicity is preferred to the undulating cornice line typical of the Paleologan works in Thessaloniki.

4.105a

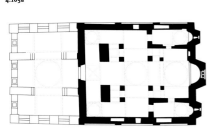

4.105b @ 1:500

›4.105 GRACANICA, CHURCH, c. 1320: (a) view from the south-east, (b) plan, (c) entrance front. The ratio of width to height exceeds 1:6.

4.105c

›ARCHITECTURE IN CONTEXT »CHRISTIANITY AND EMPIRE

stone relieving the brick**4.30** – but something even of
Bulgarian exuberance characterizes the last phase of
work there. That delighted in the supercharged low-
relief patterning in starkly contrasted red brick and white
stone but the motive and many of the motifs were essentially Thessalonikan. And Thessalonikan surface enrich-
ment is paralleled in the capital: whether the former
informed the latter, even via Bulgaria, or they both
derived from a common source – earlier Byzantine or
even late-Roman – is open to conjecture.**4.106** Not in
doubt, however, is the transmission to the capital of the
Thessalonikan form of two-storey narthex, open-
arcaded and crowned with domes at each end. However,
the full force of hierarchy in Thessalonikan massing is
spent before reaching Constantinople: rather than
enhancing the verticals over the horizontals, the capital's

>4.106 CONSTANTINOPLE, TEKFUR SARAY,
c. 1310.

The date of this palace pavilion astride the city's
land wall is obscure (estimates have ranged from the
mid-10th to the early 14th century): however, in both
the colouristic combination of red brick and white
stone and in specific motif, parallels have been drawn
between it and Bulgarian churches like H. Ioannes
Aleiturgitos at Nessebar of c. 1330. Related externally
to the multi-storey parekklesion, internally it consists
of two halls superimposed over a colonnaded and
groin-vaulted basement – like the keep of a Frankish
castle, 14th-century secular work at Mistra too, but
unlike any known element of the traditional Byzantine
imperial palace complex.

›**4.107** CONSTANTINOPLE: PAMMAKARISTOS
(Fetiyeh Camii), rebuilt c. 1300 by General Michael
Doukas Glaves Tarchaneiotes and enveloped c. 1310 by
his Paleologue widow: parekklesion exterior.

builders keep their proportions more firmly in balance
and never allow decoration to confuse tectonics.

We have seen the Constantine Libs complex doubled
by Empress Theodora to provide her dynasty with a mortuary chapel and later endowed with a southern gallery
conjoined with an exonarthex extended across the fronts
of both quincunxes: galleried, the latest addition has
domes on drum towers of the Thessalonikan type.**4.101**
This manner of extending older complexes was followed
by other noble patrons. One of the most prominent examples is the quincunx chapel added early in the 14th century
to the Pammakaristos monastery church, but most celebrated is the contemporary rebuilding and amplification
of the Church of the Saviour at Chora. In the latter, in particular, structure refuses mastery to ornament outside,
colourful though that is; inside, the overwhelming display
of fresco and mosaic is unrivalled in any of the surviving
churches of the Second Rome.**4.107, 4.108**

4.108c

4.108a

4.108d

4.108b

›4.108 CONSTANTINOPLE (CHORA), CHURCH OF THE SAVIOUR (Kariye Camii), 12th century; remodelled and enveloped c. 1310 by the great Paleologue statesman Theodore Metochites: (a) donor and Christ; (b) exterior from east; (c, d) narthex, detail of dome and interior; (e, f) parekklesion, detail of dome and apse.

4.108e

4.108f

GLOSSARY

ABACUS flat slab forming the top of a capital.

ACANTHUS plant, stylized images of whose leaves characterize Corinthian capitals.

ACLLAHUASI 'house of chosen women', type of Inca convent.

ACROPOLIS highest part or citadel of a city, usually the area containing the principal public buildings.

ACROTERIA plinths used to support statues, especially at the centre and ends of a pediment.

ADOBE a mud mixture used to form sun-dried bricks.

AEDICULE ornamental niche housing a sacred image, for example.

AGORA open space used, for example, as marketplace or assembly area.

AISLE side passage of a church or temple, running parallel to the nave and separated from it by columns or piers.

AMBA characteristic Tigraian terrain of flat-topped protrusions of rock resulting from erosion.

AMBULATORY semi-circular or polygonal arcade or walkway surrounding, for example, a sanctuary.

ANDRON dining room in a private house, reserved for the use of the master of the household.

ANNULET small flat ring around the shaft of a column.

ANTA pilaster at the end of the side wall of, for example, a temple, in a style different from the Order of the neighbouring columns.

ANTEFIXES blocks used as ornaments in, for example, the cornices of a building, especially to conceal the ends of tiles.

ANTHEMION ornament in, for example, a capital or cornice, usually in the form of honeysuckle flowers and leaves.

APADANA columned hypostyle hall usually square in plan, with portico on one or more sides.

APSE semi-circular domed or vaulted space, especially at one end of a basilica, hence **APSIDAL**, in the shape of an apse.

AQUEDUCT artificial channel or conduit carrying water.

ARCADE a series of arches supported by columns, sometimes paired and covered so as to form a walkway.

ARCHITRAVE one of the three principal elements of an entablature, positioned immediately above the capital of a column, and supporting the frieze and cornice.

ARCUATE shaped like an arch. Hence (of a building) **ARCUATED**, deploying arch structures (as opposed to trabeated).

ASHLAR masonry cut and placed so as to present a smooth finished surface (as opposed to, for example, Cyclopean or rubble construction).

ASTRAGAL small moulding with circular or semi-circular cross-section.

ATLANTE element in the shape of a male figure, used in place of a column.

ATRIUM inner court of a Roman house, usually unroofed at the middle, where the compluvium allowed rainwater to gather in the impluvium.

AULA REGIA public audience chamber in a royal or imperial court.

AXIS line used to establish geometry around which a building is designed. Hence **AXIAL PLAN**, showing relationship of building to fundamental (if abstract) two- or three-dimensional base-lines.

AYLLU basic political unit of pre-Inca and Inca life based on the extended family group.

BALDACHINO canopy raised on columns over an altar or tomb.

BALL-COURT I-shaped or sometimes oval structure, a long court in which violent ritual ball games were played. The court was bordered by ranges incorporating benches and surfaces off which the hard rubber ball could be played.

BAPTISTRY building, adjunct to a church, dedicated to baptism.

BASILICA temple or other public building, consisting principally of a colonnaded rectangular space with an apse at one end, generally enclosed by an ambulatory, or having a central nave and side aisles, and lit by a clerestory.

BASTION structure projecting from the angle of a defensive wall enabling enhanced vision and mobility for a garrison.

BATTERING reinforcement of walls and column bases by building sloping supporting structure.

BELVEDERE open-sided roofed structure, freestanding or situated on the roof of a building, placed so as to command a view.

BEMA sanctuary of a church, especially Byzantine.

BIT-HILANI columned portico, specifically of 1st millennium BCE Syria.

BOULEUTERION meeting hall for formal gatherings of senators/councillors, etc.

BRACKET CAPITAL load-bearing member projecting from a capital or forming a projecting capital, for instance an Ionic volute.

BUTTRESS support, usually stone, built against or adjacent to a wall to reinforce or take load.

CALIDARIUM hottest of the rooms in a Roman bath-house.

CALLANCA Inca administrative complex or assembly buildings.

CANCHA a four-sided walled Inca family compound. A group of rectangular buildings arranged around a central open space.

CAPITAL top part of a column, supporting the entablature, wider than the body of the shaft, usually formed and decorated more or less elaborately. The part of the column which, taken together with the entablature, forms the major defining element in the Greek Orders of architecture – Doric, Ionic and Corinthian.

CARDO road running north to south, later the main longitudinal road of a town or city.

CARYATID female figure used as a support in place of a column.

CATACOMB burial place, usually in the form of a passageway with recessed side-galleries for the disposition of cadavers.

CAULICOLI carved plant stalks supporting the volutes of a Corinthian capital.

CAVEA the seating within a theatre.

CAVETTO concave moulding with a quarter-circular cross-section.

CELLA the main body of a temple, usually containing a cult statue, not including the portico, etc.

CELT stone or metal tool shaped like a chisel or an axehead.

CENTRALIZED PLAN building design in which the structure is symmetrical in plan around the centre, allowing for reflection about both 90- and 180-degree axes.

CHAC MASKS stone mosaic masks with curved snouts used on façades and corners of Mayan buildings.

CHACMOOL a sculpted reclining figure holding a vessel or plate on its stomach, perhaps to receive offerings or sacrifices.

CHANCEL part of a church where the clergy and choir are ranged, separated by screen or railing from the main body of the building.

CHENES STYLE Mayan architectural style in which façades, often tripartite, are richly decorated with large stone masks around doorways. Half-human/half-animal figures are characteristic.

CIBORIUM canopy raised on columns so as to form a covering above an altar or tomb, for example.

CIUDADELA enclosure in the centre of a city with an interior space surrounded by four large platforms surmounted by pyramids.

CLERESTORY windowed upper level, providing light from above for a double-storey interior.

CLOISTER covered arcade, often running around the perimeter of an open courtyard.

COFFERING decoration of a ceiling or vault, for example, with sunken rectangular or other polygonal panels.

COLONNADE line of regularly spaced columns.

COLUMN vertical member, usually circular in cross-section, functionally structural or ornamental or both, comprising (usually) a base, shaft, and capital. Major defining element in the Greek Orders of architecture – Doric, Ionic and Corinthian.

COLUMN IN ANTIS column deployed in a portico projecting into a building as opposed to standing proud from the façade.

COMPLUVIUM rectangular opening above the centre of an atrium, allowing rainwater to collect in the impluvium.

CONSOLE support bracket, ornamental in form, with a curved outline.

CORBEL support bracket, usually stone, for a beam or other horizontal member. Hence **CORBELLED**, forming a stepped roof by deploying progressively overlapping corbels.

CORINTHIAN ORDER *see* Order, Corinthian.

CORNICE projecting moulding forming the top part of an entablature. More generally, a horizontal ornamental moulding projecting at the top of a wall or other structure.

CORONA projecting element in the upper part of a cornice, with a flat and usually plain vertical face, undercut with a concave soffit, thus preventing rainwater from running down the walls of a building.

COVE/COVING curved concave moulding forming or covering the junction between wall and ceiling.

CREPIDOMA steps forming the perimeter of a Greek temple's base.

CRYPT chamber disposed wholly or partly underground, often underneath the chancel of a church.

CYCLOPEAN masonry made up of massive irregular blocks of undressed stone.

CYMA RECTA wave-shaped moulding, usually forming all or part of a cornice, the upper part being convex and the lower concave.

CYMA REVERSA wave-shaped moulding, usually forming all or part of a cornice, the upper part being concave and the lower convex.

DADO the middle part, between base and cornice, of, for instance, a pedestal, or the lower part of a wall when treated as a continuous pedestal.

DAIS raised platform, usually at one end of an internal space.

DECUMANUS road running east to west, later the major latitudinal road of a town or city.

DENTILS small blocks deployed in horizontal lines, typically forming part of the Ionic and Corinthian cornices, less often forming part of the Doric.

DIPTERAL building, usually a temple, having a double row of columns on each side.

DISTYLE portico with two columns.

DISTYLE IN ANTIS inset portico having two columns set between two piers

DORIC ORDER *see* Order, Doric.

DROMOS entrance to a building in the form of a passage between, for example, colonnades.

ECHINUS quarter-round projection or moulding on cushion below the abacus of the capital of a (usually Doric) column.

EGG AND DART MOULDING decoration on an ovolo moulding, consisting of alternating shapes of eggs and arrow-heads.

ENTABLATURE that part of the façade of a temple, etc., which is immediately above the columns., and is generally composed of architrave, frieze and cornice. With the column, particularly its capital, forms the major defining element in the Greek Orders of architecture – Doric, Ionic and Corinthian.

ENTASIS slight bulge in a column, designed to overcome the optical illusion which would otherwise occur of a straight column being slightly concave, or waisted around the middle.

EUTHYNTERIA lower steps of a crepidoma, supporting the stylobate.

EXEDRA recess, usually apsidal, containing seats.

EXONARTHEX extension to the narthex of a church, formed by the aisles.

FASCIA plain horizontal band, usually forming part of an architrave.

FASTIGIUM pediment or other structure in the shape more or less of the gable end of a house, especially when dignifying the entrance to a temple precinct or palace, hence a place of epiphany.

FILIGREE decorative work formed of a mesh or by piercing material to give the impression of a mesh.

FILLET/FILET top part of cornice, or generally decorative moulding in the shape of a narrow raised band.

FLYING BUTTRESS an arch and more or less freestanding buttress which together take the load of a roof, for example.

FONT freestanding basin, usually of stone, sited in a church for use in the Christian baptism ritual.

FOOT unit of measurement.

    DORIC roughly equal to 0.33 metres (1.07 modern feet).

    IONIC roughly equal to 0.32 metres (1.05 modern feet).

FORUM central open space of a town, usually a marketplace surrounded by public buildings.

FRESCO method of painting done on plaster which is not yet dry, hence also the resultant artefact.

FRIEZE the middle part of an entablature, above the architrave and below the cornice. More generally, any horizontal strip decorated in relief.

FRIGIDARIUM coolest of the rooms in a Roman bath-house.

GALLERY upper storey projecting from the interior of a building, and overlooking the main interior space.

GEOGLYPH large-scale markings in the earth, sometimes figurative, sometimes baffling.

GLACIS slope or ramp in front of a defensive wall.

GROIN rib formed at the intersection of two vaults.

GUTTAE projections, more or less conical in form, carved beneath the triglyphs of a Doric entablature.

HANAN/HURIN the higher and lower parts of an Inca town, divided by the main plaza or plazas. Most of the structures of power and privilege would be found in the hanan half.

HEROUM shrine or memorial chapel dedicated to a demi-god or to the dead.

HEXASTYLE portico containing six columns.

HIPPED ROOF *see* roof, hipped.

HIPPODROME arena for horse-racing and, subsequently, for other sporting events.

HUACA Andean sacred place, or shrine, a place for veneration and ritual that could be marked by a compound or pyramid.

HYPETHRAL having no roof.

HYPOSTYLE HALL hall with a roof supported on numerous columns, more or less evenly spaced across its area.

ICONOSTASIS screen separating the nave from the sanctuary in a Byzantine church, latterly used for placing icons.

IMPLUVIUM rectangular tank in the middle of the atrium of a Roman house, especially for collecting rainwater.

IMPOST structural member – usually in the form of a moulding or block – at the top of a pillar, for example, on which an arch rests.

INCAHUASI (House of the Inca), palace.

INTRADOS curve defined by the lower surface of an arch.

IONIC ORDER *see* Order, Ionic.

IWAN vaulted hall or recess opening off a court.

JAMB side of a doorway or windowframe.

JOISTS horizontal timbers typically supporting a floor.

KORE female figure carved in stone, usually clothed and freestanding.

KOUROS male figure carved in stone, usually naked and freestanding.

LANTERN open structure, typically polygonal, admitting light and air, situated at the highest point of a building.

LARARIUM room in a Roman house used to contain images of the lares, the household gods.

LINTEL horizontal member over, for example, a window or doorway.

LOGGIA gallery open to the elements on one side.

LUNETTE semicircular window or recess, usually at the base of a dome or vault.

MACHICOLATION gallery or parapet projecting on corbels from the outside of defensive walls, with holes from which missiles might be dropped or thrown.

MAQDAS sanctuary in which the tabot is kept in an Ethiopian church.

MARTYRIUM shrine or chapel dedicated to Christian martyrs.

MASTABA Egyptian mudbrick structure built above tombs, predecessor of the pyramids.

MEGARON rectangular hall, especially Bronze Age Aegean or Cretan.

METOPE originally the space between the triglyphs in a Doric frieze, and subsequently the panel, often carved in relief, occupying that space.

METROUM temple dedicated to the mother of the gods.

MOSAIC decoration formed by embedding small coloured tiles (tesserae) in cement.

MUTULE projecting block above the triglyph of a Doric entablature.

NAOS main chamber of a temple, usually housing the cult statue.

NARTHEX chamber adjunct to the nave of a public building, usually a Christian church.

NATATIO swimming pool in a public bath-house.

NAVE central body of principal interior of, for example, a church.

NECROPOLIS cemetery, literally a community of the dead.

OBELISK tall monolith of more or less square cross-section, tapering towards the top and ending in an integral pyramid.

OCTASTYLE a portico with eight columns.

OCULUS circular window in a temple or church, for example.

ODEION/ODEON building for the performance of music, akin to a theatre.

OECUS/OIKOS principal room of a Greek private house. More generally, the actual and conceptual interior space within which family life, as opposed to public life, was conducted.

OPISTHODOMOS porch or room at rear of a temple.

ORCHESTRA semi-circular space in front of the stage of the theatre, where the chorus performed.

ORDER defining feature of Classical architecture, comprising a column – itself usually composed of base, shaft, and capital – together with its entablature.

CORINTHIAN an evolution from the Ionic Order, characterized by the replacement of the capital volutes with a more elaborate and deeper decorative arrangement. Later Corinthian columns evolved so as to be even taller relative to their base diameters than the Ionic. The entablature retained the comparatively light characteristics of the Ionic.

DORIC the oldest and most simply functional of the Greek Orders of architecture, characterized by a fluted and tapered column without a base, topped by a usually plain capital, surmounted by a relatively high entablature made up of architrave, frieze, and cornice.

IONIC slightly later and more elaborate order than the Doric, featuring fluted columns with bases and characteristically topped by a capital with scrolled volutes. The columns typically are taller relative to their base diameters than are the Doric, and are correspondingly less acutely tapered. The entablature is less tall than that of the Ionic, being originally composed of architrave and cornice only, though a frieze became usual later.

ORTHOSTATS stone slabs deployed on a vertical surface, for example, when used as wall-panelling.

OVOLO projecting convex moulding, either plain or with, for example, egg and dart decoration.

PALAESTRA public building for training in athletics, etc.

PALMETTE ornament exhibiting narrow divisions, reminiscent of a palm-leaf.

PARASCENIUM projecting wings extending from the scena to embrace the proscenium.

PASTOPHERIA in the Byzantine church, areas to the sides of the rear of the sanctuary, used by the priests for preparations for ritual.

PATIO outdoor space, usually paved.

PEDESTAL base supporting, for example, a column or statue.

PEDIMENT triangular area of wall, usually a gable, above the entablature, enclosed above by raking cornices.

PENDENTIVE curved concave triangular member used at the corners of a square or polygonal structure so as to enable reconciliation with a domed roof.

PERIPTERAL descriptive of a building whose main part is flanked by a single peristyle or row of columns.

PERISTYLE row of columns surrounding a building or courtyard, or the courtyard so colonnaded.

PIER supporting pillar for wall or roof, often of rectangular cross-section and/or formed from a composite mass of masonry columns.

PILASTER pier of rectangular cross-section, more or less integral with and only slightly projecting from the wall it supports.

PLAZA open urban space, often a centre of community life.

PLINTH rectangular base or base-support of, for example, a column or wall.

PODIUM continuous base or pedestal consisting of plinth, dado and cornice, to support a series of columns.

PORTA COELI 'gate of heaven'.

PORTICO entrance to a building, featuring a colonnade.

POST vertical element in, for example, a trabeated structure.

POSTERN small gateway or door, usually at the back of a building.

PRONAOS area in front of the principal room of a temple (the naos), typically having walls to the sides and columns to the fore.

PROPYLAEUM/PROPYLON gateway, especially to a temple enclosure.

PROSCENIUM stage on which the principal actors performed, in front of the scena and behind the orchestra.

PROSTYLE row of columns standing in front of a building, usually forming an open portico.

PRYTANEION/PRYTANEUM public hall for formal dining and entertaining of foreign emissaries and others.

PTEROMA/PTERON space between the walls and the colonnades of a temple.

PUUC Mayan architectural style characterized by carefully cut stone on which are plain at the base and richly decorated above.

PYLON monumental tower often associated with a temple gateway.

QUATRALOBE area composed of four interlocking circular segments.

QUINCUNX structure composed of an agglomeration of five elements, four being identical and disposed so as to form more or less a hollow square, its centre being filled by the fifth.

QUIPU coloured and knotted cords used by the Incas to record objects, numbers and other information.

RAKING CORNICE an inclined cornice, deployed above the tympanum of a pediment.

RAMPART defensive earthwork, usually surrounding a fortress or citadel, often with a stone parapet.

REGULA short band above the guttae on a Doric entablature.

RELIEF carving typically of figures, raised from a flat background usually by cutting away more (high relief) or less (low relief) of the material from which they are carved.

REVETMENT decorative reinforced facing for retaining wall, for example.

RIB raised band on a vault or ceiling.

ROOF
> **HIPPED** composed of pitched roof with inclined (as opposed to vertical) plane(s) at end(s).
>
> **PITCHED** composed generally of two inclined planes whose point of contact forms the ridge or highest line of the roof.

ROOF COMB ornamental construction on top of the roof of, for example, Mayan temples.

ROTUNDA circular room or building, usually with a domed roof.

SACRISTY room in a church for storing valuable ritual objects.

SANCTUARY the most sacred part of a church or temple, often where the altar is situated.

SARCOPHAGUS coffin or outer container for a coffin, usually of stone and decorated with carvings.

SCENAE FRONS the flat wall forming the back of the stage in a semi-circular Roman theatre.

SCOTIA concave moulding on the base of a column, often between two convex torus mouldings, thus providing an apparently deep channel between them.

SCREEN partition separating one part of an interior from another.

SCREEN WALL false (i.e. non-structural) wall to the front of a building, masking the façade proper.

SHAFT more or less cylindrical element of a column rising from the base to the capital.

SHINGLES thin pieces of wood used, overlapped like tiles, to form roof covering.

SIMA RECTA *see* cyma recta.

SIMA REVERSA *see* cyma reversa.

SOFFIT the underside of an architectural element in, for example, a cornice or architrave.

SPIRA concave moulding on the base of a column or other element.

SQUINCH arch placed across the corner of a square structure so as to form a polygon capable of being roofed with a dome.

STAFF-GOD Andean deity, fanged and with claws, and usually portrayed holding a staff in each hand.

STELE upright stone marker in shape of column or panel, usually with decorative carving and/or inscription.

STOA an extended portico or roofed structure with colonnade.

STRING COURSE projecting horizontal course of structural elements or moulding.

STUCCO plaster, especially used where decoration is to be applied.

STYLOBATE top step of a crepidoma, forming the base for a colonnade.

TABOT Ge'ez word referring to a replica – usually in alabaster, marble or wood and always protected by ornate coverings – of the Tablets of Law used in the practices of the Ethiopian Church.

TAENIA/TENIA fillet running along the top of a Doric architrave.

TALUD-TABLERO style characteristic of Teotihuacan, in which recessed rectangular panels, often decorated (tablero) project above sloping aprons (talud).

TAMPU roadside accommodation and store on the Inca road system, roughly a day's walk apart.

TEMPIETTO small temple.

TEPIDARIUM room of intermediate temperature in a Roman bathhouse (between the calidarium and the frigidarium).

TERRACOTTA baked clay used for construction or decoration of buildings or statues.

TESSERA small tile made of marble or glass, for example, used in conjunction with others to form mosaic.

TETRAPYLON four columns surmounted by a plinth, or monumental arch with intersecting passages, used to mark the junction of major roads in a Roman town or city.

TETRASTYLE portico with four columns.

THERMAE public baths, usually divided into frigidarium, tepidarium, and calidarium.

THOLOS dome, either freestanding or forming the centre of a circular building. Also a beehive-shaped Mycenaean tomb.

TORUS large moulding, typically at base of a column, of more or less semicircular cross-section.

TRABEATED structurally dependent on rectilinear post and beam supports.

TRACHELION grooved moulding at the neck of a Doric column, immediately below the echinus.

TRANSEPT that part of the interior of a large public or religious building which crosses the nave or principal interior space at right angles.

TRAVERTINE a light-coloured limestone.

TRICLINIUM dining-room or principal reception room in a Roman house.

TRIGLYPH block carved with vertical channels, used in a Doric frieze.

TUFA building stone of volcanic origin, usually grey.

TUMULUS ancient burial mound.

TYMPANUM triangular area of a pediment, enclosed by raking cornices above and entablature below; more generally, area, usually recessed, formed by a window- or door-lintel below and an arch above.

USNU a small elevated stone ceremonial platform used by the Incas as a throne.

VAULT structure forming an arched roof over a space.
    BARREL enclosing a more or less hemicylindrical space.
    CANOPY creating a roof for a niche or tomb.
    DOMICAL enclosing a more or less hemispherical space.
    GROIN enclosing a space composed of two intersecting more or less hemicylindrical shapes.

VERANDAH roofed colonnade attached to the side or the sides of a building.

VESTIBULE courtyard in front of the entrance to a Greek or Roman house; hallway to a building; space adjunct to a larger room.

VILLA a Roman country house or estate.

VOLUTE scroll or spiral ornamental and/or support member, characteristic of Ionic capitals.

VOUSSOIR wedge-shaped stone deployed in building an arch. Hence **VOUSSOIR ARCH**, where such stones are used.

WERE-JAGUAR a supernatural Olmec figure combining jaguar and human features.

ZIGGURAT building composed of a stepped series of concentric rectangles, the whole forming a truncated pyramidal structure.

FURTHER READING

This set of volumes, *Architecture in Context*, is based on a survey series of lectures covering the whole spectrum of architectural history developed over a quarter of a century at the Canterbury School of Architecture. It is therefore impossible, even if it were desirable, to enumerate all the books that I have consulted and, in one way or another, depended on, over that period. Beyond students of architecture, for whom this whole process was initiated, I hope that the present work will provide the general reader with a broad but also reasonably deep introduction to the way our environment has been moulded over the past five thousand years. With this in mind, rather than a bibliography, I hope it will be useful if I provide a rough guide to how I would go about developing a course in further reading, were I starting now.

First, for a broad overview in geographical context, I would consult the various historical atlases published by Facts on File. Second, I would consult the *Macmillan Dictionary of Architecture*, as much for the bibliographies attached to each section of each subject as for the individual articles – inevitably some are better than others as different authors naturally bring different standards of scholarship to bear on their products. Third, for greater depth and breadth, I would consult *The Pelican History of Art*, now published by Yale University Press; the quality in these works is in general much more even as each self-contained subject is usually given to one scholar of outstanding academic record. Again, the bibliographies appended to each volume will be an invaluable guide to even broader and deeper reading.

Fourth: specific histories of architecture. As any student of the subject knows, the inescapable primer is the work first published in 1896 by Sir Banister Fletcher as *A History of Architecture on the Comparative Method*: that was essentially a catalogue arranged roughly chronologically by area – starting with ancient Egypt and Mesopotamia – but as the method was gradually superseded more room was found in the later 20th-century editions for essential analysis. Beyond that, from my view in the 1970s the most useful general survey of architectural history was the multivolume series initiated by Electa in Milan, edited by Pier Luigi Nervi and published in English by Abrams (and later by others): it had its flaws, not least in the relationship of text to illustrations, and much was lost in translation from the authors' native languages into English. However, the range of scholars involved was impressive (notwithstanding some flagrant political bias) and, despite their age, some of the material not otherwise easily available is still essential reading – Mango on Byzantium, Hoag on Islam or Middleton and Watkins on the late-18th and 19th centuries, for example.

There are numerous one-volume histories of architecture – ranging from the mystical to the prosaic: it would be invidious to impose my choice of author – and, therefore, approach – but I do think the further reader will be stimulated by the consideration of both sides to the Pevsner–Watkin debate.

My own dependence on the contributors to the series cited in both paragraphs above will be apparent to even the most cursory reader, and I apologize that it is far too wide-ranging individually to acknowledge here.

Könemann and Taschen have both published lavishly illustrated multi-volume series that have perhaps been over-ambitious and therefore incomplete. Despite this, many readers will find them extremely valuable, often for their text, always for their magnificent illustrations.

THE ACHAEMENID EMPIRE, C. 650–330 BCE

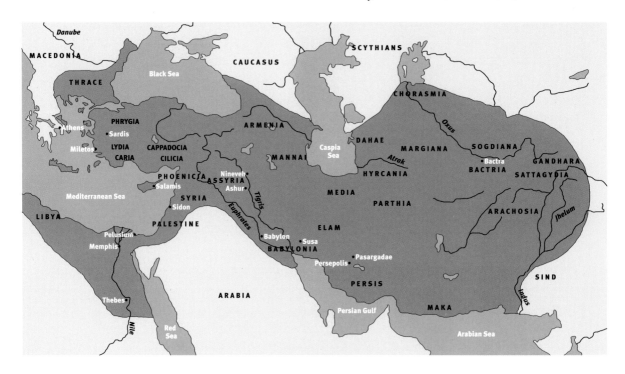

EGYPT, C. 2500 BCE

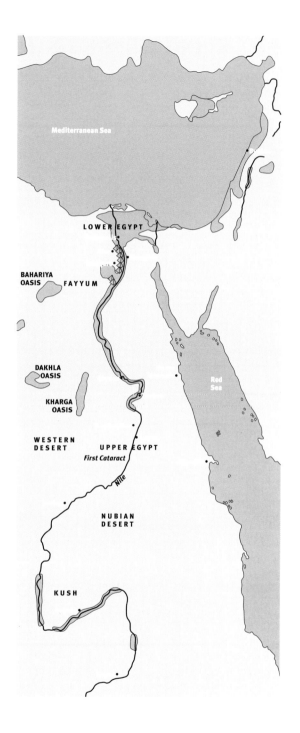

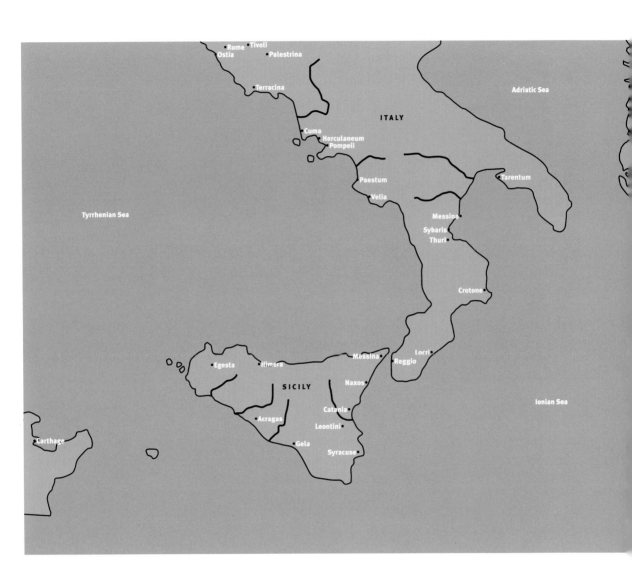

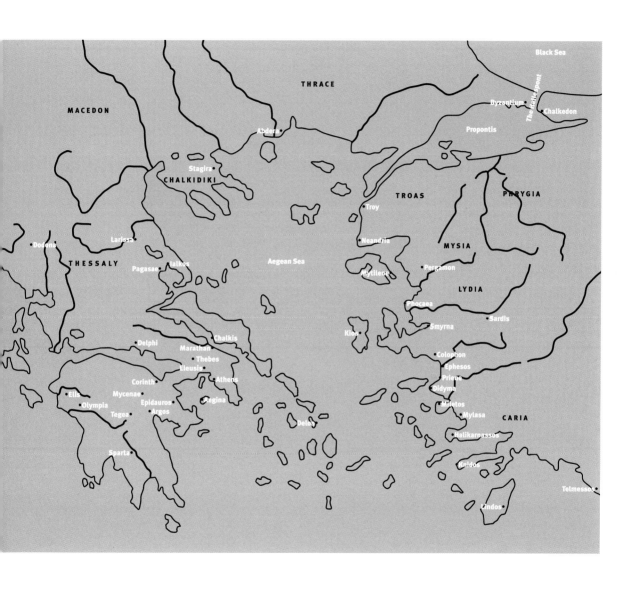

Black Sea

THRACE

MACEDON

Byzantium • • Chalkedon
The Hellespont

Propontis

Abdera •

Stagira •
CHALKIDIKI

TROAS

PHRYGIA

Troy •

Larissa •

Neandria •

MYSIA

Dodona •

Pergamon •

THESSALY

Iolkos

Pagasae •

Mytilene •

LYDIA

Aegean Sea

Phocaea •

Sardis •

Smyrna •

Chios •

Delphi •

Chalkis •

Marathon •

Thebes •

Colophon •

Eleusis •

Ephesos •

Athens •

Priene •

Corinth •

Didyma •

Mycenae •

Miletos •

Elis •

Aegina •

Mylasa •

Olympia •

Epidauros •

Argos •

CARIA

Tegea •

Delos •

Halikarnassos •

Sparta •

Knidos •

Telmessos •

Lindos •

THE ROMAN EMPIRE, C. 100 CE

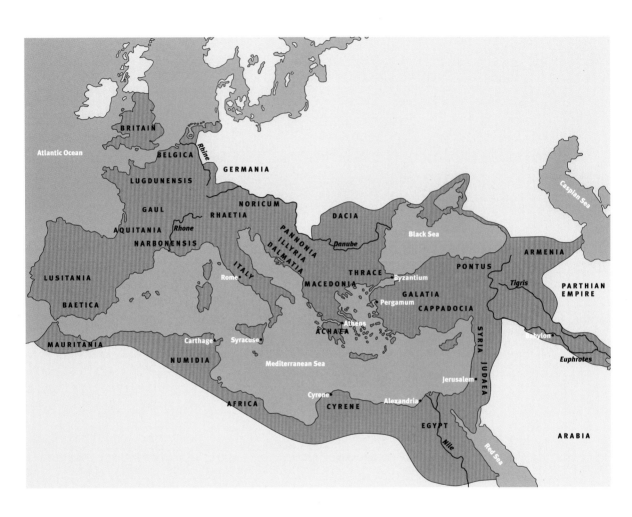

Atlantic Ocean

BRITAIN

BELGICA

Rhine

GERMANIA

LUGDUNENSIS

NORICUM

GAUL

RHAETIA

DACIA

Black Sea

Caspian Sea

AQUITANIA

Rhone

PANNONIA

Danube

ARMENIA

NARBONENSIS

ILLYRIA

DALMATIA

PONTUS

ITALY

THRACE

Tigris

PARTHIAN
EMPIRE

LUSITANIA

Rome

MACEDONIA

Byzantium

GALATIA

BAETICA

Pergamum

CAPPADOCIA

Babylon

MAURITANIA

Carthage

Syracuse

ACHAEA

Athens

SYRIA

Euphrates

NUMIDIA

Mediterranean Sea

JUDAEA

AFRICA

Cyrene

CYRENE

Alexandria

Jerusalem

ARABIA

EGYPT

Nile

Red Sea

THE CHRISTIAN WORLD, 700–1050

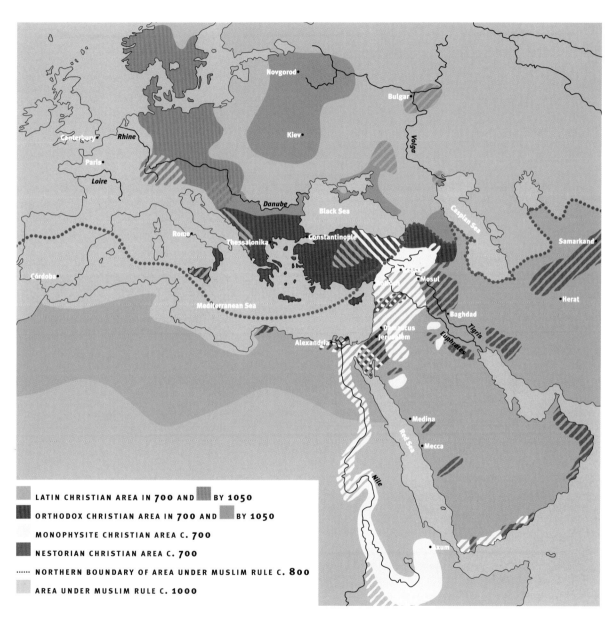

Novgorod

Bulgar

Kiev

Volga

Canterbury · Rhine

Paris ·

Loire

Danube

Black Sea

Caspian Sea

Rome ·

Thessalonika

Constantinople

Samarkand

Córdoba ·

Mosul

· Herat

Mediterranean Sea

Baghdad

Tigris

Damascus

Jerusalem

Euphrates

Alexandria ·

· Medina

Red Sea

· Mecca

Nile

·xum

LATIN CHRISTIAN AREA IN **700** AND ▮ BY **1050**

ORTHODOX CHRISTIAN AREA IN **700** AND ▮ BY **1050**

MONOPHYSITE CHRISTIAN AREA C. **700**

NESTORIAN CHRISTIAN AREA C. **700**

······ NORTHERN BOUNDARY OF AREA UNDER MUSLIM RULE C. **800**

AREA UNDER MUSLIM RULE C. **1000**

THE INCAS

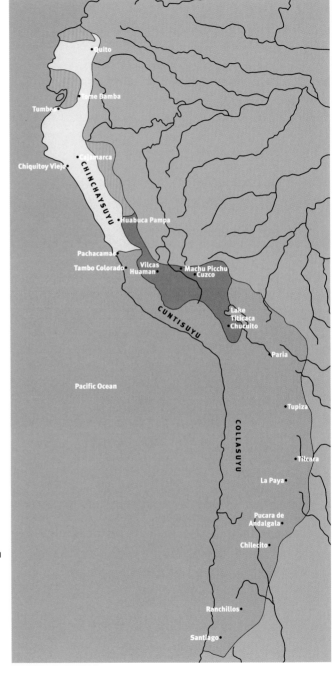

Quito

Tome Bamba

Tumbes

Cajamarca

Chiquitoy Viejo

CHINCHAYSUYU

Huabuca Pampa

Pachacama

Vilcas
Huaman

Machu Picchu
Cuzco

Tambo Colorado

CUNTISUYU

Lake
Titicaca
Chucuito

Paria

Pacific Ocean

Tupiza

COLLASUYU

Tilcara

La Paya

Pucara de
Andalgala

Chilecito

Ranchillos

Santiago

INCA EXPANSION

TO **1438**

1438–63, UNDER PACHACTUI

1473–71, UNDER PACHACTUI AND TUPAC YUPANQUI

1471–93, UNDER TUPAC YUPANQUI

1493–1525, UNDER HUAYNA CAPAC

THE AZTECS

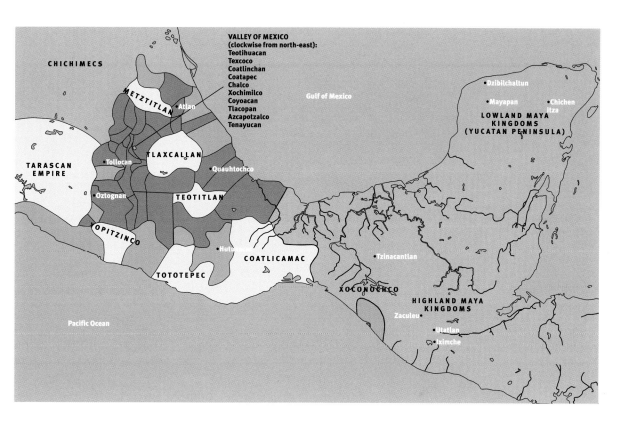

VALLEY OF MEXICO
(clockwise from north-east):
Teotihuacan
Texcoco
Coatlinchan
Coatapec
Chalco
Xochimilco
Coyoacan
Tlacopan
Azcapotzalco
Tenayucan

CHICHIMECS

Gulf of Mexico

Dzibilchaltun

Mayapan

Chichen
Itza

LOWLAND MAYA
KINGDOMS
(YUCATAN PENINSULA)

METZTITLAN

Atlan

TLAXCALLAN

Tollocan

Quauhtochco

TARASCAN
EMPIRE

Oztognan

TEOTITLAN

OPITZINCO

Hutusaca

COATLICAMAC

Tzinacantlan

TOTOTEPEC

XOCONOCHCO

HIGHLAND MAYA
KINGDOMS

Zaculeu

Pacific Ocean

Utatlan

Iximche

AZTEC EXPANSION

1438–81, UNDER ITZXOATL, MONTEZUMA I AND AXAYACTL

1486–1519, UNDER AHUITZOTL AND MONTEZUMA II

INDEPENDENT POLITY

INDEX

Assur-uballit I, king 169

Assurbanipal, king 168–9, *188*, 191, 202

Assurnasirpal II 188, 192; palace of (Kalhu) 193–5, *193*, *194*

Assyrians 169, 170, 171–2, 173, 188–91; and Babylon 191, 202; fall of 202; image of ruler *168–9*, *188–9*; seats of power 192–200

astragal 38

astrology, Sumerian 40

Atahualpa 344

Aten: temple of 132

Athanasius, S. 673

Athena (goddess) 370

Athens 374–5, 376, 415–27, 434, 435, 467, 478; Acropolis *412*, *413*, *413*, *414–15*, 424, 429, *430–1*, 432, *432*; Choragic Monument of Lysikrates *466–7*; Erechtheion 424, *424–5*, 432; Hephaesteion *410–11*, 411; houses 438; Kapnikarea *815*, *816*; Mikra Metropolis *814*, *815*, 825; Parthenon *366–7*, 413, *414–15*, 416–19, *416*, *417*, *418–19*, 432; and Peloponnesian War 440; plan of *434*, 435; and planning 435; Propylaea *420–1*, *421–2*, 422, 432; Sanctuary/Theatre of Dionysos 426–7, *426–7*, 480; sightlines and Acropolis 432, *432*; Stoa of Attalos *434*; Temple of Nike 424, *424*; Temple of Zeus 468–9, 475–6, *476–7*; Tower of the Winds *516*

atlante 396

atrium 505, 540, 541, 545, 693, 735

Attalids 491–2

Attalos 491

Attalos III 517

Attica 373, 381

audiencias 340

augury 502, 510

Augustus, Emperor 555–7, *556*, 561, 568–9, 612, 618, 665

Aurelian, Emperor 559, *559*, 668

Autun: Porte Saint-André *547*

Axayacatl 318

axial planning 92, *101*, 130, 158, 199, 542, 637

Axum 183, 185, 186, *186*, 756; Maryam Zion 756; Tomb of the False Door *186*

Axumites 185–7, 752–69

Azcapotzalco 318

Aznu *49*

Aztecs 220, 317–27; agriculture 320; causeways and aqueducts 322; conquest of city-states 318–19; and Incas 348–9; militancy of 319, 320; pyramids and temples 324–5, *324*, *326–7*; religion and gods 319–20, *321*; and Spaniards 322; stratification of society 321; structure of states 320–2; warrior kings 318; *see also* Tenochtitlan

Baalbek 599–601; sanctuary of Jupiter 595, 599, *599*, *600*, 601, 632; Temple of Venus 646

Babylon/Babylonians 38, 41, 97, 101, 169, 170, 171, 188, 189, 202–4, *203*, *204*; and Assyrians 191, 202; attack on by Cyrus 206; hanging gardens of 204; Ishtar Gate *32–3*, *34*, *34*, *203*, 204; Temple of Ninmah 204

Balkans 777, 799, 808, 812, 828

ball game/ball court 234, *235*, 251–2, *252–3*, 320

baptistery 708, *709*, 719, 724, *724–5*, 751, *751*; octagonal *724*, *724*, 740

Baroque 459, 495, 647, 660

Basil I, Emperor 807

Basil II, Emperor 807

basilica 526, 530–1, 708, *709*, 799; and Asia Minor 740–2; and Christian church 689, 691, 693–6, 699, 731; Constantinian building 692–6; domed cross 779–82; Greek 735; North Africa 749, 751; Roman 654–5; Syrian 742

Bassae 449, 495; Temple of Apollo Epikourios 445, 446–7, *446–7*, 450, 453

Bassi, Martino 723

baths 526, 535; Roman 635–42; *see also* thermae

battering *175*

Becan 292, *293*

Beidha (Jordan Valley) *10*

Beit Khallaf: mastaba at *64*

Beni Hasan (Egypt) 110

Bent Pyramid (Dashur) *72–3*, 80

Bethlehem: Church of the Nativity 700, 701, 779

bit-hilani *173*, 174–6, *174*, 178, 209, *372*, 742

Borsa: theatre 646, *647*

bricks: Cretan 153; Hellenic 439; mass production of standardized in Sumer 36; mud 27, 28, 29, 48, 505; sun-dried 11; used in Indus Valley 95

brickwork/patterning 812, 814, 836

bridges, Roman 547, *548–9*, 553

bronze 105, *307*, 344–5

Buhen: garrison tower at *105*

building materials: Cretan 153; Egyptian 28; Mesopotamia 28; Roman 552–3

building technology, Roman 546–52

Bulgaria 799, 807, 814, 829, 833; basilica 799

Bulgars 777, 807, 808, 809

bull leaping *148*, 150

bulls' heads 14, *14*

burials: Christian 687; Neolithic Europe 17; Olmec 233, 239; *see also* tombs

Byzantium *see* Constantinople

Caananites 38–9

Caesar, Julius 519–20, 557, 568

Cairo: Church of the Virgin 799

Caligula 557

Cambyses 207

Campanian Greeks 500, 504, 516, 526

Canaan 176, 177

capitals 210, 740, *782*, *803*; Achaemenid 211, *211*, 212; Aeloic 386, *386*; composite 568; Constantinople 734, *782*; Corinthian 447, *447*, 453, *453*, 467, 477, 568, 733; Doric 382, 383; Egyptian 28, 29, *29*, 110, 127; hybrid (Ionic and Doric) 497; Ionic 385–6, *386*, 389, *389*; Mayan 297

Cappadocia 804, *805*, 812

Capri: Villa Jovis 618, *619*

Capua 500; 'La Conocchia' mausoleum 646, *646*

Caracalla 638; Baths of (Rome) 637, 638–9, *638*, *639*, 640–1, 641

Caracol 245

Carchemish 173, 174, *174*, *190*, 191, 194

Carrhae 519

Carthage 501, 503

Carthaginians 396, 501

caryatids *425*

catacomb 467

Catal Huyuk (Anatolia) 13–15, *14*, 91, 146

cathedrals 709, 719

cave churches 805

caves 4, 6, 7, 8

cella 101

Cerveteri (Caere): Banditaccia Cemetery 506–7; sarcophagus 508

Chac masks 292, 297, 301, 304, 306, 315

Chalcedon Council (451) 753

Chaldaea/Chaldaeans 176, 189, 202

Chalke 775

chamber tombs 17

Chan Chan 340, 340–1, 355–6, 357

Chanca 342, 343

Chavin 226, 331, 332–3, 332, 333, 334

Chersiphom of Knossos 388

Chichen Itza 310, 311–16, 311–15, 316

Chichimeca 308

Chimu 339, 339–40, 348, 349

chinampa 244

Chios: Nea Moni Katholikon 817, 820–1

Chiripa 331, 332

Cholula 245, 310

Chosroes I 653

Chosroes II 776

Christianity 666–75; and authority 675–6; and Axumite empire 752–4, building types 686–91; see also churches; and Constantine 674–5; doctrine and debate 676–7; and Edict of Toleration 674; hierarchical structure of authority 673, 680–1; icon and iconoclasm 681–5, 685; liturgy 680–1, 686; and Neoplatonism 677–8; retreat of 671–3; spread of 671, 675; worship at home 686

Christians: persecution of 671, 674, 686

church(es) 686–701, 708–9; Asia Minor 740–2; Axumite 752–69; and basilica 689, 691, 693–6, 699, 731; Constantinian building 692–701; Constantinople 733–4; distinction between building types 690; domed basilica 778–98, 801; Egypt and North Africa 748–51; from contraction to organic development 825–39; Gondar and Tana 766–9; Greece 735–40; house as origin of 686–7; hybrid forms 699–701; Lalibela 760–3, 760–1; materials used 692; Milan 719–23; quincunx 757, 800–4, 810–21, 827, 828, 830; Ravenna 724–30; in Rome 709–18, 710, 711, 712–13; Syria 742–5; and triumphal arch 689–90

ciborium 89

Cilicians 191

citadels (Anatolia) 166–7

Claudius, Emperor 557, 604

clay tablets 37–8, 38

clerestory 14

cloisonné masonry 812, 814, 820, 829, 830

Coatlicue (goddess) 319, 321

coffering 523, 614, 644

Colhuacan 318

Collasuyu 343

Cologne: S. Gereon 718, 723

colossal heads: Olmec 233, 234, 235

Columbia 224

columns 100–1, 110; Achaemenid 211, 212, 216; Corinthian 449, 450, 451, 467, 715; Cretan 153, 156; Doric 382, 383, 384, 390, 392, 393, 394–5, 396, 397, 399–400, 399, 401, 401, 404, 422, 574; Egyptian 29, 29, 48, 82, 127, 128, 129; Etruscan 510–11; Hellenic 372, 419, 452, 469, 472, 474; Ionic 385, 387, 388–9, 388, 422, 422, 446–7; reed-bundle 50, 68; Roman 553

Commodus 668

Composite Ionic-Corinthian Order 576

concrete: and Romans 63, 552–3, 612, 614–15

Constans 703

Constantine, Emperor 560, 657, 659, 662–3, 665–6, 674–5, 676, 680, 692,702, 708

Constantinian building 692–701

Constantinople (Byzantium) 666, 690, 696, 702, 704–5, 705, 731, 733–4, 735, 771, 773–5, 774–5, 776, 807, 808–9; besieged by Bulgars and Arabs 807; church of H. Eirene 780, 780–1, 786, 787; church of H. Ioannes Studios 733, 734, 737; church of H. Polyeuktos 780, 782; church of H. Sergius and Bacchus 782, 783, 785, 785, 786; church of H. Sofia 733, 734, 773, 778, 778, 782, 786, 787–98, 788, 789, 790–1; Church of the Holy Apostles 699, 779–80; Church of the Saviour 837, 838–9; churches of the Macedonian dynasty 810–11; colouristic use of materials 836; Constantine Libs complex 810–11, 829, 830, 837; fall of to Ottomans 809, 809; Hippodrome 773; Kyriotissa 827; Myrelaion

church 810–11; palace 773–5; Pammakaristos monastery church 837, 837; Pantepoptes 825, 825; Pantokrator 825, 826; revival of 807, 808; Tekur Saray palace 836; Yerebatan Saray 773

Constantius 692, 703

corbel 29

corbel arch 297

corbel vaulting 285, 286, 287, 289, 299, 310, 350

Corfu: Temple of Artemis 392, 392

Corinth: Temple of Apollo 398, 399, 399, 419

Corinthian capitals 447, 447, 453, 453, 467, 477, 568, 733

Corinthian columns 449, 450, 451, 467, 715

Corinthian Order 475–6, 568, 574, 743

corn-god 238–9

cornices 29, 68, 386, 398, 734

corona 382, 383

Cosa: Capitolium 511

Cosmedin: S. Maria 730

cosmology, Egyptian 52–4

Crassus 519

Crete 17, 146–7, 164, 367; building materials 153; bull 148; burials 164; cataclysm 153, 156; houses 147; maritime power 147; Minos and the Bull 147–8; palaces 147; towns 147; see also Knossos

Croesus, King 202, 206, 376, 387

cross, domed 779–82

cruciform 720, 724, 741, 800

crypts 828

Ctesiphon 608, 652; palace at 653

Cuicuilco 244; pyramidal temple 240, 240–1

cuidadelas 340

cuneiform 38, 38

Cuntisuyu 343

Cuzco 342, 343, 347, 349, 352–3, 354, 354, 357, 358–9, 358; Coricancha complex 354, 354, 356, 356; Inca masonry at 352–3, 354, 354

cylinder seal, Sumer 35, 37, 39, 44

Cyprus 17

Cyrenaica 749

Cyrene (Libya): Temple of Zeus 393, 394–5

Cyrus the Great 206, 206–7, 376; camp-palace of (Pasargadae) 209, 209; tomb of (Pasargadae) 217, 217, 219, 463

Dalmatia 731

Daphni: Koimesis monastic church *822*, *823*, 825

Darius I 206, *207*, 208, 376, 456; palace of (Susa) 210, *210*, 216–17; rock-cut tombs of 217, *218–19*

Darius II 208, *209*

Darius III 209, 455

Dashur: Bent Pyramid *72–3*, 80; pyramids of Snofru *72*

David, Jacques-Louis: 'Oath of the Horatii' 501, *502*

Debra Damo 754–5, *755*; monastery of 186, 754

Debra Maryam Korkot *756–7*, 757

defence: Constantinople *704–5*; Etruscan *501*, 504; Hellenic 485–90; Roman 501

Deir el-Abaid: White Monastery at 748, *748*

Deir el-Bahri 102; mortuary and cult complex of Nebhepetre' Mentuhotep *106–7*, 107, 124; royal cult complex of Hatshepsut 113, 115–19, *115*, *116–17*, *118–19*

Deir el-Medineh 144, *144*

Delos 484–5; houses *483*

Delphi: sanctuary of Athena 449, *450–1*, 453; Siphnian Treasury *385*; temple of Apollo *371*, 398, *400*, 439

Demeter 371

dentils, Hellenic 385, 389

Didyma 468; Temple of Apollo 469, *469*, 470–1, 472, *472–3*

Diocletian 559–60, 674, 705; Baths of (Rome) *640–1*, 641, *642*; Palace of (Split) 654–5, *654*, *655*, 657

Dionysius 679–80

Dionysos (god) 370, 371

Dionysos I 486

divine monarchy, Hellenic 456–8

Djedefre 77

Djoser, king 56, *57*, 63; funerary complex (Saqqarah) 65–71, *66–7*, *70–1*, 110

dome 614, 645, 660

domed basilica 779–82, *780–1*, *783*, 800, 801

domed cube 652

domed octagon *783*, *784–5*, 785–6, *819*, 830

domed rotunda 612, 616–17

Domitian 569, 616, 618–19, 621, 627, 637

Dorians 367, 368, 390–412, 440; ideal and vitality 402–3; proportional system 398–400, 424, 445; religion and gods 368–9; temples 90, 404–11, 449; truth versus appearance 401; western colonies 392–8

Doric Order 381–4, *382*, 407, 411, 419, *450*, 462, 475, 496–7, 574 *see also* capitals, Doric; columns, Doric

drainage, Hellenic 483, *483*

drum 645, 646, *646*

duality: Mesoamerican 237, *238*, 246, 250–1

Dungar compound 187, *187*

Dur-Sharrukin (Khorsabad) 193, 195, *198*, 199

Dur-Untash-Naprisha *170*, *171*

Dura-Europos *686–7*

earth-mother 14–16, 40, 52, 367–8

Ebla (Tell Mardikh): palace of 86, *86*, 173

echinus 153, *399*

eclecticism 445, 799

Edfu: Temple of Horus 28–9, *29*, 34

Edict of Toleration 674

Edzna 293, *294–5*, 296, *296*, 297

Egypt/Egyptians 27, 50–85, 170, 191, 349, 457, 475, 707; and Achaemenids 207; agriculture 59, *60*; art *60*; Coptic Christian 748; cosmology 52–4; early settlements 51; gardens *142*, *143*; garrisons *105*; gods *50*, 52–4, *52*, 57, 106, 112–13, 457–8; grids and zoning 143–4; and Hebrews 176; hieroglyphs 56; and Hittites 164, 165; houses 40, 109–10, *142*, *143*, 144; industry and commerce *60*; land-surveying 512; and Macedonians 455; mastabas 63–5, *64*, 83–4; materials and structure 27, 28–9, 34; Middle Kingdom pharaohs and dynasties 102–5, 106; military expeditions 59; mummification 62; New Kingdom and empire 111–14; and obelisk 84, *85*; Old Kingdom succession 56–61; ornamentation and design 27, 34; palaces 140–3; Pharaonic 55–61; pharaonic continuum 62–3; pyramids 63–82, *108–9*; rivercraft and ships *60*, *61*, 105, 147; stone building and sculpture 56–7; technological developments 105; temples 79–80, 104, 106–10, 121, 124–9, 130–8; town planning 143–4, *144*; and trade 59, 183; villa *142*, *143*

El Djem (Tunisia): amphitheatre *583*

El Mirador 242

El Paraiso 331, 332

El Tajin 161, 245, *260*, 308; Pyramid of the Niches *274–5*

El-Lahun 109, *109*, 144, *144*; mortuary complex of Senwosret II *109*

El-Malqata: palace of Amenhotep III 140, *140*

Elam 86, 87, 94, 97, 170, 171, 191, 202

Elamites 44, 91, 92, 97, 169, 170, 191

empiricism, Aristotelian 443–4

Enki (god) 39–40, *39*, 41, 45

Enlil (god) 39–40, 45, 97

entasis 419

Ephesos 387, *388–9*, 705; cathedral at 740; church of H. Ioannis 780, *780*; Library of Celsus 602, *603*; marble street of emperor Arcadius 705; Temple of Artemis 387, *388–9*, *389*, 468, *468–9*, 469; tomb shrine of S. John 741

Epidauros 449; Sanctuary of Asklepios *451*, 453, *477*; theatre 481, *481*, *482*

Epirus 513, 808, *809*, 828

Eridu 41, 45, 87; temple 41, *41*

Esarhaddon 191

Eshnunna 92, 97, 98; palace and temple 92, *92*

Ethiopia 182–3, 752–69

Etruria 512

Etruscans 500; defence 504; houses 505; legacy of 504–15; planning 512; religion 510; temples 510–11, 512; tombs 505–9, *506–9*; urban order 512–14, 526

Eumenes II 493

Euphrates 11, *22–3*, 28, 35, 47

Europe, Neolithic 16–17

Eusebius 700, 701

Evans, Sir Arthur 149

excavation: Axumite 754–763, *754–765*; Egyptian *64*, 65, *69*; Malta 18–19, *18–19*

Ezana, King 752, 753, 754

Falashas 183

false doors 68, 69, 83, 84

fastigium 601, 723

Fertile Crescent 9–11, 12, 95, 172

fire altar 608, *608*

fire temples 652, 801

obelisks 84, 85, 126, *126*

obsidian 12, 230, 231, 244, 320

octagonal form: baptisteries 724, *724*, 740; and Christian building 697, 698

octastyle 416

odeon 578

Odoacer 706

Ohrid 828–9; S. Kliment *823*, 825, 829; S. Sofia 833, *834*

Ollantaytambo *358–9*, 359

Olmecs 226, 229–42, 307; centres 231–5; colossal heads 233, 234, *235*; emblems of elemental divinity 236–7, *236*; legacy of 239–48; religion 236–9; thrones 234, *235*; trade 231; and were-jaguar 237–8, *238*

Olympia: Sanctuary and Temple of Zeus 403, 404–6, *404–5*, 428, *428–9*; Temple of Hera 390–1, *390*, *391*, 428

Olympian gods 369–71

Olynthos 438, *438*, 440

opisthodomos 398, *399*, 401

optical illusion: and Dorians 399, 401, 404, 405, *411*; *see also* entasis

Orange: Arch of Tiberius 601, *602*, 632, 723; theatre *584*, 587

Orders, architectural *see* architectural Orders

Orpheus/Orphics 378

orthostats 19, 20, 194, 195, 200

Orvieto: Belvedere Temple *510*

Osiris (god) 52, *53*, 54, 56, 62, 72, 106, 457, 518, 670

Osmanli Turks 809

Ostia 545

Ostrogoths 675, 706, 724, 726, 782

Ottomans 809

Pacal, King 286, *288*

Pachacamac 334, 337

Pachacutec 343–4, 347, *361*

Paestum *390*, 398, 436; East Gate *439*; Temple of Athena 396, *398*; Temple of Hera I 396, *397*, 419; Temple of Hera II 406–7, *407*, *408–9*

Paionius of Ephesos 469

palaces: Achaean 158, *160*; Assyrian 193–200; Babylonian 204; Constantinople *836*; Cretan 147; Egyptian 140–3; Eshnunna 92, *92*;

Hellenic *372*; Inca 350; Knossos 149–52, *149–52*; Mayan 304–6; Olmec 233; Roman 526, 619–24, 654–5; Sassanian *652–3*; Teotihuacan *276*, 277; Uxmal 297

Palaeolithic period 6–7

palaestra 526, 531, 534, 535

Palenque 264, 268–9, *268–9*, 286–8, 293; decline 292; kings of 246, *246*; palace at 288, *289*, 290–1; temples 286, *287*, 288, *288*

Paleologues 828

Palestine 104, 111, 172, 721, 800

Palestrina 520, 534, 578; Temple of Fortuna Primigenia 522–3, *522*, *523*

Palmyra 590–1, *592*, 598, *599*; Temple of Bel 595, *598*, *599*

Pani 456

Parmenides 377, 442

Parthians 455, 456, 517, 558, 559, 608, *608–9*, 652, 801

Pasagardae: camp-palace of Cyrus 209, *209*; tomb of Cyrus the Great 217, *217*, 219, 463

Pashash 333

passage tombs *16–17*, 17

patio, Inca 357

Patmos: monastery church of H. Ioannis *810*

pediment 601, *602*, 650

Peisistratos 374

Peloponnesian War 440 1, 456, 486

pendentives *638–9*, 641, 824

Pepi I, king 59

Pepi II, king 59, 63, 102

Per-Wadjit (Buto) 51

Pergamon 491–5, 517; acropolis 491–2, *491*, *492*, *493*; Great Altar of Zeus 493–5, *493*, *494*; mixed Orders 496–7; Temple of Asclepius 618, *618*; Temple of Athena Polias 496; Temple of Serapis 667, *668*

Perge 741, *741*

Perikles 413, 429

Peristerai (Greece): church *814*

peristyle 505, 530, 531, 540, 541, 545, 578

Persepolis 210, 211–13; Great Palace 211–16, *212*, *214–15*; tombs at 219

Persians 204, 208, 416, 462, 468, 375-6, 441, *see also* Achaemenids

Peru 222–3, 223, 224

Perugia *501*, 504

Petra *648–9*, 650, *650*, *651*

Phidias 41, 416, 495, 683

Philae: Temple of Isis *30–1*

Philistines 172, 177

Phillip II 441

philosophy, Hellenic 376–7

Phoenicians 188–9, 367

Phrygians 191

Piazza Armerina (Sicily): villa at 656, *656*

pier 110, 270

Piquillacta *339*

Pisac 359, *360*

planning: Achaean 158; Etruscan 512; Hellenic 428–39, 478–80, 491–2; Roman 512–13, 526

plaster 644

Plato 378, 441–3, *444*, 679; theory of Forms 442–3, 679

platonic solids *443*

plaza 233–4, 265, 357, *361*

Pliny the Elder 388

Pliny the Younger 626

Plotinus 678, 679

polis 375, 376, 440

Polykleitos 403, 418, 429, 448; Doryphoros of *402*, 403

Pompeii 526–31, *527*, *528–9*; Amphitheatre *532–3*; Basilica 530, 531, *531*; decoration 542–3, *543*, *544*, 605–6, 644; development phases plan *528–9*; House of the Faun 541; House of Loreius Tiburtinus *606*; House of Pansa 541; House of the Vetii *540–1*, 541; Stabian baths *534–5*, 535, *536*, *537*, 553, 614, 644; 'Surgeon's House' *505*; Temple of Apollo 527, 530; Temple of Isis 529, 530, *530*; Temple of Jupiter 527; Villa of the Mysteries 542, *542*

Pompey 517, 519, *519*–20, 575

Pomposa 728; Benedictine abbey church *730*

portico 390, 422, 510, 655; bit-hilani *173*, 174–6, *174*, 178, 209, *372*, 742; columned 173–4, 209; Etruscan 510, 511, *511*

Poseidon 369

pottery 12, 37, 224

Praxiteles 448, 448–9, *448*

Priene 480; Ecclesiasterion 480, *480*; houses 483, *483*; plan 478, *479*; Temple of Athena Polias 473–4, *474*; theatre *480–1*, 481

triglyphs 399, 418

tripartite plan 91, *101*; Sumer 36, *36*, 41–2, 47, 91

triumphal arch *see* arch

Trojans 158

Troy (Hissarlik) 156, *158–9*, 162, 372

Tudhaliyas IV, king *165*

tufa 552, *553*

Tukulti-Ninurta I, king 170

Tukulti-Ninurta II, king 188

Tula 308, *308–9*, 310; fall of 317; Temple of Quetzalcoatl *308–9*

tumulus 63, *164*, 229, 467, 505, *507*, *612*

Tupac 344

Tutankhamun *114*, 119, 132; tomb of 121, *122*

tympanum *382*, 383

U-shaped terrace/plaza 330, 331, 332

Uaxactun 242; stepped pyramid at *242*

Ubaid houses (Sumer) 41, *41*

Ugarit (Ras Shamra) 165, 172; palace 173–4, *173*

Unis, king 59

Untash-Napirisha, king 169

Ur 47, 86, 87; sacred compound of 88–90; Sumerian successors and the palace 91–2; towns and houses 91; treasure of *46*; ziggurat of Ur-Nanna 88–9, 601

Ur-Nammu 87, *88*, 91, 94

Urartians 174–5, 191, 209

Uratu 191, 202

Uruk 36, 37, 41, 42, 48, 87, 94, 97, 169; Temple of Karaindash *170*, *171*; temples 42–4, *42–3*; vase *39*; White Temple 42–3, *42*

Utuhegal, king 87

Uxmal 293, 296–7, *298–301*, 299–301, 316; 'Governor's Palace' 301, *302–3*; 'Nunnery' 297, *299*, 301; 'Pyramid of the Magician' 97, *299*, *299*, 301

Vagharshapat (Armenia) 804, *804*

Valentinian III 706

Valerian 558

Valle of Oaxaca 239, 240, 241

Valley of the Kings *120*, *122–3*

Vandals 675, 706

Vaste (Apulia), Crypt of S. Stefano *805*

vaulting/vaults: Asia Minor 740; corbel 285, *286*, *287*, *289*, 299, 310, 350; Roman 553, *553*, *614*, *614–15*, 620, 623, *624*, *624*, *626*, 641, *643–4*, 659

Venice 777

verandah 372, *388*

Vergina: Tomb of Philip II of Macedon *467*

Verona: amphitheatre 604, *604*; Arco dei Borsari 602, 604; Porta dei Borsari *604*

Vespasian 557

Vesuvius, eruption of *526*, 527

Vienne: Temple of Augustus and Livia 570, *571*

Vilcashuaman *355*, 356

villa: Egyptian *142*, *143*; Roman 542, *542–3*, 545, *619*, *626–33*, 656, *656–7*

Viracocha (god) 329, 337, 347

Viracocha (Inca leader) 343, 347

Visigoths 675, 706, 707

Vitruvius *388*, 465, 474, 475, 505, 545, 572–4, 576; *De architectura* 573–4; ideal man and town *572*

voussoir arch *32–3*, 34, 48, *501*

walls *26*, 28; Constantinople *704*; Hellenic 485–6; Inca 351, *354*; Roman 552

wattle-and-daub 19, 50, 505

were-jaguar 237–8, *238*, 250

Winay Wayna 351

writing: development of in Sumer 37–9; in post-Classic Mesoamerica 308

Xanthos 462, 463, 464; Nereid Monument 464, *464*, 467

Xerxes I 208, 211, 376

Xipe Topec (god) 247, *248*

Xochicalco 245, 261, *261*; Platform of the Plumed Serpent 275

Yeha: temples of 183–4, *184*

Yemen 179, *180–1*, 182, *182*, 186

Yemrehanna Kristos: monastery church *758–9*, 759

Yodit, queen 760

yurt (ger) 7

Zagwe 760

Zapotecs 226, 240–1, 243–4, 247, 250

Zarathustra (Zoroaster) 208

Zarema Giyorgis 757–8, *757*

Zeno, Emperor 706, 744, 748, 749

Zeus 148, *368*, 369, 371, 377, 457

ziggurat 87, 88, 88–90, *96–7*

Zimri-lim, palace of (Mari) 97–100, *98–9*

Zincirli 173, 174, *174*

zoning 338, 478